JOHN LOCKE

EUROPEAN POLITICAL THOUGHT
Traditions and Endurance

Advisory Editor
J.P. Mayer

Editorial Board
Fernand Braudel
Maurice Cranston
Jack Lively
Harvey C. Mansfield, Jr.

See last pages of this volume
for a complete list of titles.

JOHN LOCKE

Maurice Cranston

ARNO PRESS
A New York Times Company
New York • 1979

Editorial Supervision: JOSEPH CELLINI

Reprint Edition 1979 by Arno Press Inc.

Copyright © 1957 by Maurice Cranston

Reprinted by permission of Macmillan Publishing Co., Inc. and
Longman Group Limited
Reprinted from a copy in the Newark Public Library

EUROPEAN POLITICAL THOUGHT: Traditions and Endurance
ISBN for complete set: 0-405-11670-5
See last pages of this volume for titles.

Editor's Note: On page xiii the editor wishes to note that the reader
should see now J.H. Franklin, *John Locke and the Theory of
Sovereignty, Mixed Monarchy and the Right of Resistance in the
Political Thought of the Revolution,* Cambridge University Press, 1978;
with an important bibliography.

Manufactured in the United States of America

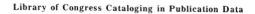

Library of Congress Cataloging in Publication Data

Cranston, Maurice William, 1920–
    John Locke.

    (European political thought)
    Reprint of the ed. published by Macmillan, New York,
under title: John Locke, a biography.
    Includes index.
    1. Locke, John, 1632–1704. 2. Philosophers—England
—Biography. I. Series.
B1296.C7 1979   192 [B]   78-67349
ISBN 0-405-11690-5

JOHN LOCKE

JOHN LOCKE, 1685
by Sylvanus Brownover

JOHN LOCKE

A Biography

MAURICE CRANSTON

THE MACMILLAN COMPANY
NEW YORK

THE MACMILLAN COMPANY
60 FIFTH AVENUE
NEW YORK II, N.Y.

*Printed in Great Britain by Richard Clay and Company, Ltd.
Bungay, Suffolk*

CONTENTS

ILLUSTRATIONS

John Locke, from an original portrait in plumbago on vellum, framed in a silver box. Signed and dated by Sylvanus Brownover, 1685 *frontispiece*

By permission of the owners, Messrs. Montague Marcussen.

INTRODUCTION

WHEN John Locke died in 1704 he left an escritoire filled with his personal papers to his young cousin Peter King, who began his career as the son of an Exeter grocer and rose to be Lord Chancellor of England. Until 1948 these manuscripts remained the closely guarded property of Lord Chancellor King and his descendants the Barons King, later Earls of Lovelace. In that year the present Lord Lovelace sold them to the Bodleian Library, Oxford, and the raw material for a full biography of Locke became at last accessible.

Several lives of Locke were written between 1704 and 1948, but the only biographer who saw the papers the philosopher left to his cousin was one of the Lords King who successively owned them, the seventh of the line. This nobleman was born in 1776, published the first edition of his biography of Locke in 1829, and died in 1833.

He is variously remembered. Though he spoke seldom in the House of Lords, he was an active pamphleteer on behalf of ecclesiastical and monetary reform. His ideas, appreciated later, were thought at the time to be unpractical as well as eccentric. Lord Brougham wrote well of him, but Lady Charlotte Bury described him as "a very dull man, neither ornamental nor agreeable". His eldest son, who became the first Earl of Lovelace, married Byron's daughter, one result of the union being that the King family owned for several generations many of the private papers of Byron as well as of Locke.

Lord King's biography of Locke is unfortunately not a good one. He transcribed with no great care or method the more legible of Locke's manuscripts and printed them in random sequence. It so happens that the more legible of Locke's papers are often also the less interesting. But no one was to know this at the time, for besides Lord King himself no person qualified to judge had seen the manuscripts. They were not seen even by Henry Richard Fox Bourne, who wrote the standard biography of Locke, published in 1876.

Fox Bourne was the biographer also of Cochrane and Mill and Philip Sydney, the historian of English Newspapers and of "The Romance of Trade", and the author of several books on race relations in Africa. He was versatile and industrious in a way that is less admired today than it used to be. He was also a Nonconformist, and a bitterness towards the Roman Catholic Church which he could not always moderate governed much that he wrote about religious questions in the seventeenth century. Fox Bourne was capable, for example, of saying, apropos of those aspects of Charles II's private life which so fascinate the Puritan mind, that the Catholic Church "was willing to commend his lusts as virtues".[1] However, in his indiscriminating antipathy to all things Popish, Fox Bourne was very like Locke.

His biography is an excellent one. He showed great enterprise in finding new material, and he examined all he found with the utmost care. His book is reliable, intelligent and systematic and, as far as was possible in the circumstances of the time, complete; and I do not claim with my biography to have displaced his. But Fox Bourne knew nothing of the papers owned by the then Lord Lovelace apart from what had been printed in Lord King's book.

The papers were seen after 1914 by Dr. Benjamin Rand of Harvard who later published a few of them in *The Correspondence of John Locke and Edward Clarke*. Dr. Rand's activities, which were devious enough, marked the beginning [2] of a new interest among scholars, collectors and dealers in what had come to be known as the "Lovelace Collection" of Locke manuscripts. The third Lord Lovelace was urged to sell it, but the claims of scholarship conflicted for a time with those of the antiquarian manuscript trade. The papers were, at one stage, consigned to an auctioneer for sale in small lots, then briskly recovered. Other negotiations were protracted. In the meantime, Mr. Jocelyn Gibb, who did much to preserve the collection intact, prepared a summary catalogue, and also published, in collaboration with Professor R. I. Aaron, *An Early Draft of Locke's Essay Concerning Human Understanding* from a notebook then in the Lovelace Collection, but later detached and separately sold in 1952 to Mr. Arthur Houghton, Jnr., of Queenstown, Maryland, U.S.A.

---

[1] F.B. I, p. 171.
[2] The Lovelace Collection was reported to the H.M.C. in 1919 but never examined in detail.

When war broke out in 1939 all the papers in the Lovelace Collection, still in the escritoire where Locke had put them, were in a wooden cottage in Sussex. During the Blitz they were housed in a furniture repository in Tunbridge Wells. A safer wartime refuge was provided in 1942 by the Bodleian Library, Oxford, where the authorities took the opportunity to have the whole collection examined by a philosophy scholar, Dr. Wolfgang von Leyden. As a result of his report, the Bodleian Library bought the Lovelace Collection after the war for £5,000.

The Lovelace Collection [1] contains nearly three thousand letters and about a thousand miscellaneous manuscripts. These latter include accounts, which, because Locke was always careful with money, are unusually detailed; library lists; notebooks containing entries on philosophy, politics, literature, science, theology, economics and colonial administration; several more elaborate manuscripts on the same subjects; recipes, inventories, certificates of various kinds, and ten volumes of Locke's journal. A further 166 letters written by Locke to Peter King were added to the collection in 1953.

Locke is an elusive subject for a biographer because he was an extremely secretive man. He modified a system of shorthand for the purposes of concealment; he employed all sorts of curious little cyphers; he cut signatures and other identifiable names from letters he preserved; at one time he used invisible ink.

I began writing this book in 1948, and because the Lovelace Collection is its principal source, it contains a large proportion of hitherto unpublished material. With Dr. von Leyden's help I have transcribed shorthand passages; I have modernised spelling and, with few exceptions, I have translated all quotations from classical or foreign languages into English; [2] otherwise I have printed the material as I have found it, allowing Locke and his contemporaries to speak as much as possible for themselves.

Apart from the Lovelace Collection my chief sources have been: the Shaftesbury Papers in the Public Record Office, London; the Remonstrants' Manuscripts in the University Library, Amsterdam;

---

[1] Dr. Wolfgang von Leyden describes the Lovelace Collection in the Introduction to his edition of Locke's *Essays on the Law of Nature* (Oxford, 1954) pp. 1–7, and in papers contributed to *Sophia* (Padua, Italy) January–March 1949, and to the *Philosophical Quarterly* (St. Andrews, Scotland) January 1952.

[2] The original language is specified in the footnote in every case.

and the Manuscripts Department of the British Museum. I have also drawn on papers in public and private collections both British and foreign.[1]

Certain perplexities beset every biographer.

Sir Harold Nicolson writes in the introduction to his biography of *King George the Fifth*:

> The habit possessed by eminent Englishmen and Scotsmen of frequently altering their own names is one that may trouble the reader, especially the foreign reader. Mr. A. of one chapter becomes Sir Charles A. in the next; three chapters further on he emerges as Viscount B.; and as we read further, he enters again, disguised as the Earl of C. I have dealt harshly with this problem, calling people by the names they possessed at the date of which I am writing.

Several of the men who figure in this book will be found changing their names in the manner Sir Harold describes. Anthony Ashley Cooper becomes Sir Anthony Ashley Cooper, then Lord Ashley and then the Earl of Shaftesbury; Charles Mordaunt becomes Lord Mordaunt, then Lord Monmouth, and finally the Earl of Peterborough. To add to the confusion another Monmouth—Charles II's natural son, the Duke of Monmouth—has also to appear in the story. However, I have decided to follow Sir Harold's example and refer to people by the names they had at the time of the events described.

A further and more complicated difficulty confronts the historian who writes of the period between 1582 and 1752 because two calendars were then employed. Most of the Western States of Continental Europe then used the Gregorian or New Style calendar; England conservatively and Protestantly (for the Gregorian calendar, though accurate, was Papal in origin) stuck to the Julian or Old Style calendar. As Locke corresponded on a considerable scale with continental friends, and spent several years in France and Holland, the disparity of dates according to the two systems of reckoning is bewildering to the student of his life and documents. To minimise the difficulty I have invented the following expedient: dates printed in Roman type are dates according to the Julian calendar (e.g. 21 January, 1681/2); dates printed in italic type are dates according to the Gregorian calendar (e.g. *11 January, 1682*).

---

[1] The American manuscripts I have seen only on film. A collection owned by the late J. Howard Whitehouse I have not seen at all, and have had to rely on the transcriptions of Dr. Rand.

In writing this book I have been greatly helped by many different people. I am indebted to Dr. Wolfgang von Leyden for allowing me to use his catalogue of the Lovelace Papers, and his key to Locke's shorthand; for several profitable conversations, and for his kindness in reading the manuscript of this book. I owe no less to Mr. Peter Laslett for the help he has given me at almost every stage in its preparation. I should like also to thank Miss J. M. Shaxby for the research and secretarial work she has done; Professor Gilbert Ryle and Mr. David Ogg for reading the manuscript; Mr. Anthony Powell, Mr. Daniel George and Dr. Kenneth Dewhurst for reading the proofs and, for the help they have given me or for their permission to use copyright material, the following: Mr. Philip Long, Dr. R. S. Peters, Dr. Bernard Samuels, Mr. Cyprian Blagden, Dr. Elisabeth Kluyt, Dr. Rosalie Colie, Mr. W. A. Sanford, the Right Hon. Lord Strachie, Miss Marjorie Strachey, Professor John Lough, Dr. R. W. Hunt, Mr. Sydney M. Edelstein, Mr. J. B. Whitmore, the Rev. Arthur Talbot, Mr. Stanley Pargellis, Mr. Jocelyn Gibb, Mr. Herbert D. Shields, Mr. W. Miller Higgs, Mr. Thomas G. Scott, Miss Carolyn E. Jakeman, Mr. L. M. Payne, Professor C. B. MacPherson, Dr. J. F. von Royen, Professor C. R. Sanders, Mr. Douglas Cleverdon, Mr. A. N. L. Munby, Mr. David Piper, Mr. Cecil Sprigge, Mr. W. G. Hiscock, Miss Mary Stanley-Smith, Dr. Clifford Dobell, F.R.S., Mrs. Jane Carpenter, Miss Elizabeth King, Mr. John Woodward, and the Delegates of the Clarendon Press.

ABBREVIATIONS

Aaron & Gibb	*An Early Draft of Locke's Essay* Together with Excerpts from his Journals. Ed. by R. I. Aaron & Jocelyn Gibb, Oxford, 1936.
Amsterdam	The University Library, Amsterdam.
Ath. Oxon	*Athenae Oxonienses* by Anthony à Wood. Ed. P. Bliss, 1813.
Aubrey	*Brief Lives and Other Selected Writings by John Aubrey.* Ed. with an Introduction and Notes by Anthony Powell. 1949.
B.L.	The Bodleian Library, Oxford.
B.M.	The British Museum, London.
Bonno	*Les Relations Intellectuelles de Locke avec la France* by Gabriel Bonno. Berkeley and Los Angeles, 1955.
Boyle	*The Works of the Honourable Robert Boyle.* Five Volumes. 1744.
Brown	*The First Earl of Shaftesbury* by Louise Fargo Brown. New York, 1933.
Christie	*A Life of Anthony Ashley Cooper, First Earl of Shaftesbury* (1621–1683) by W. D. Christie. Two Volumes. 1871.
Christophersen	*A Bibliographical Introduction to the Study of John Locke* by H. O. Christophersen, Oslo, 1930.
C.S.P.	Calendar of State Papers.
Éloge	*Éloge Historique de feu Mr. Locke par Mr. Jean Le Clerc* in *Oeuvres Diverses de Monsieur Jean Locke.* Rotterdam, 1710.
Essay	*An Essay Concerning Human Understanding* by John Locke. Two Volumes. Oxford, 1894.
F.B.	*The Life of John Locke* by H. R. Fox Bourne. Two Volumes. 1876.
H.M.C.	Historical Manuscripts Commission.
King	*The Life of John Locke with Extracts from his Correspondence, Journals and Commonplace Books* by Lord King. New Edition. Two Volumes. 1830.

L. and T.	*The Life and Times of Anthony à Wood, antiquary, of Oxford,* 1632–1695. Ed. Andrew Clark. Five Volumes. Oxford, 1891–1900.
Lough	*Locke's Travels in France,* 1675–1679, as related in his Journals, Correspondence and other Papers. Ed. with an introduction and notes by John Lough. Cambridge, 1953.
Mallet	*A History of the University of Oxford* by Charles Edward Mallet. Three Volumes. 1924.
Newberry	The Newberry Library, Chicago, 10, Illinois. (Esther Masham MSS.)
Ollion	*Lettres Inédites de John Locke et ses amis Nicolas Thoynard, Philippe van Limborch et Edward Clarke.* Ed. by Henry Ollion and J. J. de Boer. The Hague. 1912.
Original Letters	*Original Letters of Locke, Algernon Sydney, and Anthony Lord Shaftesbury.* Ed. by T. Forster. 1830.
Original Letters (Second Edn.)	*Original Letters of John Locke, Algernon Sydney and Lord Shaftesbury.* Ed. by T. Forster. 1847.
Pforzheimer	The Carl H. Pforzheimer Library, New York City.
P.M.L.	The Pierpont Morgan Library, New York City.
P.N.M.	*Patriarcha Non Monarcha or The Patriarch Unmonarch'd* [by James Tyrrell]. 1681.
P.R.O.	The Public Record Office, London.
Rand	*The Correspondence of John Locke and Edward Clarke.* Ed. by Benjamin Rand. London, 1927.
Several Pieces	*A Collection of Several Pieces of Mr. John Locke.* Never Before Printed or Not Extant in his Works. Printed by J. Bettenham for R. Franklin at the Sun in Fleet Street, 1720.
S.F.L.	*Some Familiar Letters Between Mr. Locke and Several of his Friends.* Printed for A. and J. Churchill at the Black Swan in Paternoster Row, 1708.
S. of A.	*Survey of the Antiquities of the City of Oxford* composed in 1661–6 by Anthony à Wood. Ed. A. Clark. Three Volumes. Oxford, 1889–1899.
W. von Leyden	*John Locke: Essays on the Law of Nature.* The Latin Text with a Translation, Introduction and Notes, Together with Transcript of Locke's Shorthand in his Journal for 1676. Ed. by W. von Leyden. Oxford, 1954.

NOTES

1. All references to entries in Locke's MS. journals are given with *dates* only, as both general readers and students are likely to find such referenc more convenient than references to folio numbers. Locke's journals the Bodleian Library are catalogued as follows:

November 1675–December 1676—MSS. Locke F 1	
1677	MSS. Locke F 2
1678	MSS. Locke F 3
1680	MSS. Locke F 4
1681	MSS. Locke F 5
1682	MSS. Locke F 6
1683	MSS. Locke F 7
1684–1685	MSS. Locke F 8
1686–1688	MSS. Locke F 9
1689–1704	MSS. Locke F 10

The journal for 1679, in the British Museum, is Add. MSS. 15642.

2. All printed books named are published in London unless otherwise stated.

3. Where manuscripts are in public collections and press marks can be specified printed sources are not stated.

Chapter One

THE SOMERSET CHILD

JOHN LOCKE was born at Wrington in Somerset on 29 August 1632. He was christened on the same day by the rector of that parish, Samuel Crook. A record of the baptism in Dr. Crook's hand can still be seen in the Wrington register; but in precisely what manner the office was performed it is difficult to conjecture. For Dr. Crook was both a wayward and a wilful servant of the Church of England, and it is certain only that he did *not* follow the rubric of the Prayer Book. He mistrusted the Prayer Book and may even have doubted the merits of infant baptism. Dr. Crook was a Puritan, and what he believed in was saving the souls of knowing adults. He had saved many since he had gone to Somerset in 1602, and his following in the county was strong. The people of Wrington were proud of their rector; and even his Bishop, who disliked and disapproved of Dr. Crook, would have admitted that he was, in his way, a great man.

Yet the Bishop would have done much to rid himself of Dr. Crook. William Piers, who was new to Bath and Wells, was on the side of Whitgift, Bancroft and Lancelot Andrewes, and therefore of his King, Charles I, in wishing to maintain the continuity of the English Church, the apostolic succession of her Bishops, the New Testament basis of her teaching and the ancient, tranquil pattern of her order. He was opposed to Puritans like Dr. Crook because they sought to overthrow the traditions of worship, faith and ritual in favour of the Calvinistic nostrum of sermons, personal conversion, ecclesiastical democracy and Old Testament taboo. Such people had been active in Somerset since Elizabethan times, and Dr. Piers found several of them among the beneficed clergy and considerably more among the curates. He did not trifle with them. The incumbents of Bathwick, Dunkerton and Bridgewater were disciplined; the unbeneficed preachers were, whenever possible, expelled the diocese. Only the Rector of Wrington proved more than the Bishop's match.

Dr. Crook was no fool. He was a Cambridge scholar, a some-time Fellow of both Pembroke and Emmanuel; and he had had thirty years to establish his hold in Somerset before Dr. Piers arrived. Dr. Crook lacked physical courage, as his parishioners discovered when the Civil War broke out and the rector nervously proclaimed that God was with the Parliament or the King according to which party had soldiers in Wrington; but he possessed great moral courage, which is to say that however much he may have been intimidated by the sword, he was never cowed by the pastoral staff. He resisted his diocesan with the utmost confidence, and his defiance went unpunished.

So the instructions of Dr. Piers would have made no difference to his procedure on that August afternoon in 1632, when the grandson of a local tanner was brought to him for baptism. There would have been no bowing at the name of Jesus, no making of the sign of the Cross, but it is reasonable to believe that Dr. Crook enlivened the occasion with a Bible sermon; he seldom preached fewer than three a day.

Wrington lies between Bristol and the Mendip Hills, a mile or two north of the main Bridgewater road. Today it is a place without character, a drab and colourless village, save only for the church, one of those elegant buildings in the Perpendicular style with which Somerset, of all English counties, is the most singularly blessed. Like the comparable, but not more handsome churches of Ilminster, Kingsbury, Cheddar, Dunster and Crewkerne, Wrington's was built from the profits of the wool trade, from money made in the towns, and sent back by Christian merchants to glorify God in the villages.

Industry had come early to Somerset. Through Bristol the county was close to the greatest source of all English wealth, the sea; while inland, the most important industry of England, wool, was also the most important industry of the county. The Mendips had been mined for lead since Roman times, and for coal since the thirteenth century. By 1632, however, the old medieval order which such churches as Wrington so nobly commemorate was already of the past; Somerset and Bristol merchants were no longer Catholics, most of them had come to be Puritans like Dr. Crook. The economic situation of the county was unsettled, and bred among some an urge to innovation and among others a yearning for the past. On the one hand there was dire poverty: butter had risen since the beginning of the seventeenth century to sixpence a pound and cheese to threepence, hungry people attacked the granaries, and 'many hanged themselves from want'.[1] On the other hand, there was increased wealth. The rising prices enriched the rack-renting landlords, the up-to-date farmers who could supply the towns with food, the big tradesmen and anyone else who could turn inflation to his own advantage.

This economic conflict reflected in a complicated way the religious conflict, and both were reflected in the nation's politics. High Churchmen against Puritans, enterprising capitalists against old-fashioned landowners, assertive politicians against an imperious king: each of these divisions in society presaged that great clash of principles, the Civil War; and as the country was divided, so too was Somerset, a county which, perhaps more than any other, was a microcosm of England. Civil War, when Locke was born, was still ten years in the future; but the forces which were sweeping Englishmen towards it were already in full tide. At the time of Charles II's Restoration, Locke himself recalled:[2] 'I no sooner perceived myself in the world but I found myself in a storm which has lasted almost hitherto'.

He was a child, on both sides, of the Puritan trading class. His grandfather, Nicholas Locke, was a clothier who had come to Somerset from Dorset and bought himself a house at Belluton, Pensford. Born in 1574, Nicholas Locke was the son of Edward Locke, churchwarden of Buckland Newton, Dorset, who was in turn the son of Sir William Locke, mercer to Henry VIII, alderman and, in 1548, sheriff of London. John Locke had the arms of that knight engraved on his seal.

Nicholas Locke married twice: first, at Pensford—technically in the parish of Publow, which forms part of the one little town—on 4 July 1603, to Frances Lansden, who bore him at least six children before she died in 1612; and for the second time in the same church on 18 November 1624, to a widow, Elizabeth Heale, who had been born, in 1597, Elizabeth Keene of Wrington.

One of the sons of Nicholas Locke by his first wife was named John. In July 1630, when he was twenty-four years of age, this son married Agnes Keene, a relation of his stepmother, and the daughter of Edmund Keene, tanner, of Wrington; the marriage

---

[1] *The Victoria History of the County of Somerset.* Ed. W. Page, 1911, II, p. 307.
[2] B.L. MSS. Locke, c. 28 f.2a.

was solemnised by Dr. Crook. John Locke the future philosopher was their first son.

Nicholas Locke had done well for himself in Somerset.[1] The old handicraft system gave way in his time to the 'putting-out' system, by which the clothier became a large entrepreneur and employer of labour. Such a clothier, as one historian [2] has written—

> had no resemblance to the medieval guildsman, who had himself been an apprentice—perhaps a journeyman—before becoming a master. The entrepreneur was a product of a new age, who might never have been engaged in . . . cloth-making, but who nevertheless might control all the stages through which the wool passed before it was ready for sale as cloth. He . . . bought up the wool, and distributed it among the cottagers, whose spinning-wheels turned it into yarn. The yarn was then collected and taken to weavers, who owned their own looms and wove it into cloth at piece rates.

By such methods certain Somerset clothiers gave employment to several hundred workers, and sometimes made considerable fortunes.

John Locke, the son of Nicholas, did not follow his father into this remunerative if speculative calling. He became a lawyer, and died a poorer man than he was born.[3] He did not even improve himself socially. A clothier was often fashionable as well as rich, as the satirist Willis observed: [4]

> Yea, I have lived to see the hour
> In which a clothier hath such power
> that lords are glad to buy him.

[1] Nicholas Locke's will is in the Bishop's Court at Wells. The philosopher, not yet sixteen when the will was signed on 25 August 1648, was one of the witnesses. His father and mother were among the beneficiaries, but there were too many others for anyone to receive much. The daughter Anne 'who married . . . contrary to mine and all her well-wishing friends' liking and consent' was left £300 on condition that her husband 'has no right or interest therein'. The son John was left tenements and grounds in the parish of Publow, and the grandson John (the philosopher) £5. Nicholas Locke made a characteristically Puritan bequest to the Church of St. Thomas, Pensford—ten shillings for the maintenance of the weekly Bible lecture.

[2] Godfrey Davies, *The Early Stuarts* (Oxford, 1937), pp. 286–87.

[3] He 'inherited from his father a much better estate than he left his son'. These words come from a letter written after the philosopher's death by his closest friend Lady Masham to his first biographer Jean le Clerc. Her letter is dated 12 January 1704/5 and (save for the last page, which is missing) preserved in the University Library at Amsterdam (Remonstrants' MSS. J. 57a). I shall make repeated references to it in the course of this book, but it must be remembered that Lady Masham is not a reliable authority on the events of Locke's earlier life, as she did not know him until he was middle-aged.   [4] *Time's Whirligig.*

Thus do the froth of all the earth,
A spawn sprung from a dunghill birth
now prince it in our land.

The philosopher's father, as an attorney and clerk to the Justices of the Peace in Somerset, would enjoy no greater distinction. Even a century later, as Mr. Somerset Maugham has written of another philosopher's father, the attorney's profession was 'held in small respect'.[1] Samuel Johnson once said of someone who had quitted the company that he 'didn't care to speak ill of any man behind his back, but he believed the gentleman was an *attorney*'.[2]

Locke's father was a small landowner as well as an attorney, but in taking a tanner's daughter for a wife he was not marrying beneath his class; many tanners were of the smaller gentry.

The philosopher himself was born in one of a group of humble thatched cottages at the gate of Wrington Church. The building is no longer there, but it stood until the age of the camera, and I have in my possession a photograph of it taken, to all appearances, in the 1880's. This shows how diminutive it was, with four tiny windows and a door leading directly to the cobbled street. Snobbish historians of Somerset, appalled by the thought of so great a man as Locke being born in so proletarian a dwelling, glamorised the place out of all recognition. Dugdale's *England and Wales* contains an engraving of a charming Tudor cottage, small but detached, with a garden in front, a pond and a background of luxuriant trees. A print in the *Gentleman's Magazine* for October 1829 is hardly less romantic, though Rutter, in his *Delineations of Somerset*,[3] described it as 'a small plain apartment, having few indications of former respectability'. An earlier writer, Collinson,[4] preferred to believe that 'the celebrated philosopher's mother, travelling in these parts, was here taken in labour and constrained to take up her residence'.[5]

The cottage was in fact no temporary refuge. It was Locke's maternal grandmother's home, the cottage where his mother had

---

[1] 'Edmund Burke', *The Cornhill* (London, No. 985, p. 34).
[2] Quoted by Maugham (*loc. cit.*).
[3] p. xxii.
[4] *History and Antiquities of Somerset* (Bath, 1791), I, p. 209.
[5] This is a variant on the story Lady Masham told Le Clerc (Amsterdam: Remonstrants' MSS. J. 57a) that Locke's mother was 'surprized' by labour pains on a journey 'and putting into a little house in a place called Broadwell Downs was there delivered': an entirely false story.

lived until her marriage. Standing in the very shadow of the parish church tower, and hard against the main north gate, it might well have served as a sexton's lodge. However humble, it was more conveniently placed than any other house in Wrington for access to services and 'lectures'. Agnes Locke had been bred on Dr. Crook's evangelism.

After her son's birth she did not stay long at Wrington. She returned to Belluton, the house which Nicholas Locke had bought at Pensford when he first came to Somerset from Dorset. The clothier had quit the place on his marriage to the widow Heale, who had a better house called Sutton Wick at Chew Magna, and his son John had taken over Belluton. This was the philosopher's home throughout his childhood and youth. It was not, like the house where Locke was born, mean; it was a pleasant Tudor farmhouse on a hill, commanding a magnificent view across the Mendip Hills towards Farmborough and Camerton and Midsomer Norton. The house has been entirely rebuilt since Locke's time, and only some parts of an adjacent cottage remain of the original buildings. I can trace no picture of Belluton as it was, but an inventory[1] among Locke's papers may help the reader to envisage it:

Parlour		
Two table-boards	13s. 4d.	
Six cushions	9s.	
Two carpets	5s.	
Two sideboards	2s.	
Six chairs	6s.	
Two cast-iron dogs and one back	£1. 0s. 0d.	

Hall		
One table-board and bench	5s.	
One settle	5s.	
Seven joined stools	12s.	
One iron back	13s.	
One pair of andirons	2s. 6d.	
Three chairs	5s.	
Two cupboards	8s.	
One rack	2s.	
One carpet	1s.	

Kitchen		
Three pairs of tongs, one fire shovel, one iron fork	6s.	

Kitchen		
Three pairs of hangels	2s.	
Two dripping pans	4s.	
Two frying pans	—	
Two pairs of pothooks	1s.	
Three spits	3s.	
One pair of cast dogs	5s.	
One pair of grills with a bar	5s. 6d.	
One beef fork	6d.	
One chopping knife	4d.	
One gridiron, one jack	2s.	
One smoothing iron	1s. 6d.	
Two brand irons	2s.	
One cleaver	6d.	
One sideboard	1s.	

Study		
Books	£5. 14s. 0d.	
One tableboard	2s. 6d.	
Two benches	1s. 0d.	
One stool	6d.	
One trunk	2s. 0d.	
One Clock	£2. 0s. 0d.	

[1] B.L. MSS. Locke, c. 25, f. 7.

Buttery

Nine barrels, one cheese rack, one silt, one sideboard, three shelves, one pair of butter scales £1. 0s. 0d.

Outward Chamber

One standing bedstead, with vallence and curtains, cord and matt; one Arras coverlet, one other coverlet, one pair of blankets, two bolsters, three pillows £6. 13s. 8d. In the same chamber is one chair, one coffer, two boxes, two trunks, one desk, one pair of andirons, one low stool, one pair of bellows, one iron back £2. 0s. 0d. Linen : two draper's tablecloths, one Holland tablecloth, seven dowlas tablecloths, two dozen of napkins, three bolster cases £6. 13s. 8d.

Inner Chamber

One standing bedstead, with cord matt vallence and curtains; one flock bed, two feather bolsters, two pillows, one pair of blankets, two white coverlets, one green rug £6. 13s. 8d. One press, one round table board, one desk, one coffer, one trunk £3.

Hall Chamber

Two flock beds, two feather bolsters, two pillows, three blankets, two coverlets, one truckle bedstead £2.

One hutch, one chair 10s.

One copper furnace at William Heal's £2.

Brass: four pots, two kettles, six brass pans, two skillets, one posnet, one warming pan, one mortar, two brass scales, two skimmers, one brass ladle, one copper furnace, three stills £8.

About forty pieces of pewter £2.

One silver tankard, six silver spoons, one gold ring, one watch £6.

Stable

Three hackney saddles 10s.
One pack saddle 2s.
One hutch 1s. 6d.
One iron bar for the door 3s. 4d.
About three loads of hay £2. 0s. 0d.
One more saddle 6s. 8d.
One yoking stand 6s. 8d.
One malt mill £1. 6s. 8d.

At the foot of the hill below Belluton is Pensford itself. Leland described it in 1540 as a 'pretty market town, occupied with clothing'. So it may have been a century later. Since then it has not improved. Mining has in the meantime successively increased and dwindled; and the place has acquired that nondescript appearance of other West of England towns where industry competes half-heartedly with agriculture. However, the countryside around is pretty, the River Chew flows, albeit often sluggishly, through the centre of the town, and there are orchards on the slopes behind the houses. Indeed, the landscape has been remarkably well preserved, and it is still possible to identify some of the holdings which the Locke family owned.

Close to Pensford were the houses of the philosopher's uncles and aunts. At Bishop Sutton lived Peter Locke, who had tried his hand at tanning and at brewing, and finally settled down as the owner, in a modest way, of land. Peter Locke was younger than his brother of Belluton, and lived for many years to look after his nephew's

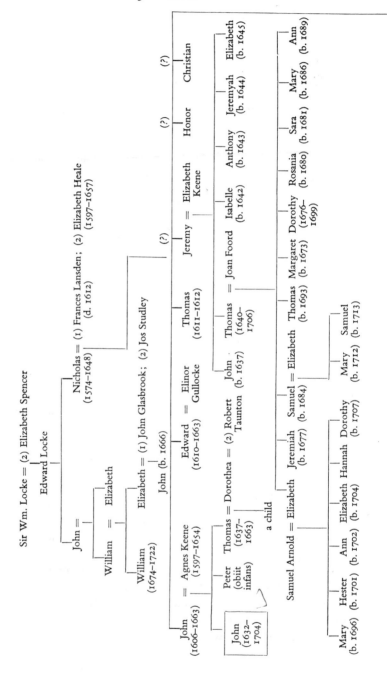

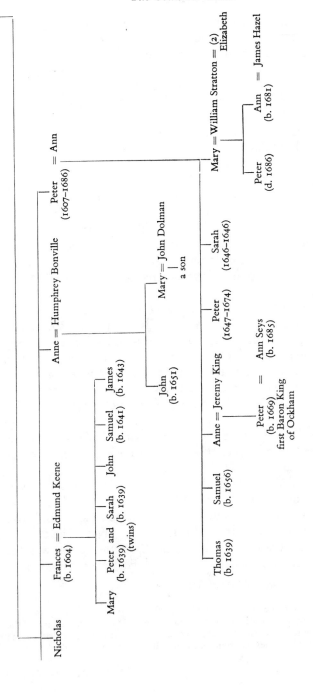

interests in Somerset, when the intellectual life summoned that nephew elsewhere. There was another uncle, an even younger one, named Edward Locke, who lived at Marcomb in Locke's infancy, but moved to Bristol when Locke was three, and made a fortune as a brewer. Lady Masham was given to understand 'that all the sons and daughters of Mr. Locke's grandfather were persons of very exemplary lives'.[1]

Both Peter and Edward Locke were more successful financially than their brother John. This is not to suggest that the lawyer was idle. His work as clerk to the Justices of the Peace was exacting, for the duties of magistrates had considerably increased since the beginning of the seventeenth century, and, as laymen, they inevitably leaned on the legal training of their clerk. In addition to their judicial functions, the magistrates were responsible for administering the Poor Law and such other measures as there were for social welfare; they even had the formidable task of regulating prices. And this was not all. After 1630 they were ordered to inquire into gifts for charitable uses, the training of youths in trades, the reform of prostitutes, the repair of highways and 'keeping watch and ward for the punishment of rogues and vagabonds'.[2] The magistrates also 'granted licences to and regulated tippling- and ale-houses, supervised the maintenance of highways, sea walls and bridges, dealt with the numerous cases of illegitimacy, overlooked the building of new cottages, ordered the maintenance of butts, and busied themselves in general with the most minute details of county administration'.[3]

In the first year of Locke's life King Charles I reissued, for the particular attention of Somerset, his father's *Book of Sports*. No one felt the blow as keenly as Dr. Crook.

The people of Wrington had their own particular game—fives. They played it in the churchyard, using the buttresses and the lower wall of the tower as their courts. They damaged the walls, broke windows and ran amuck among the new-dug graves. The damage distressed the churchwardens, but what upset the rector was the fact that the game was played on Sundays.[4] For generations Sunday

[1] Amsterdam: Remonstrants' MSS. J. 57a.
[2] *Victoria History*, II, p. 310.   [3] *Ibid.*, II, p. 312.
[4] Quite apart from the issue of Sunday games, Wrington churchyard fives remained a problem for centuries. Intermittent warfare between the players and the churchwardens continued until 1824, when cricket succeeded fives as the local game and the tomb of a Mr. James was built in the middle of the 'fives court'. Windows

had been regarded as the proper day for such recreations, the proper day, after morning service, for parish wakes, including ales and dancing as well as games like fives. In Wrington itself, Dr. Crook put a stop to these things, for no tenet of Puritan doctrine was considered more vital than that of keeping, in Hebraic fashion, the Sabbath 'holy'. Dr. Piers overruled, when he could, the Sabbatarian restrictions, and upheld the common people's right to innocent enjoyments on their one free day in the week.

But there were men of Dr. Crook's mind among the laity, and some of them went in a body to the Assizes and, claiming that the Sunday wakes were 'productive of much disorder and profanation',[1] asked the Judges to prohibit them. The Judges consented, and an order from the court was sent to every parish to be read on the last three Sundays in Lent. Dr. Piers was indignant. It was not only that he detested Sabbatarian innovations; he was also, and not unreasonably, incensed at the usurpation by the judiciary of ecclesiastical authority which belonged to him as Bishop of Bath and Wells. The decision of the Somerset Assizes was upheld by the Lord Chief Justice. This, in turn, outraged the new Archbishop of Canterbury, William Laud, whose feelings were precisely those of Dr. Piers, and Laud asserted his authority to have the order revoked.

The King himself supported Laud. His father's *Book of Sports* had been occasioned by an earlier attempt to enforce Mosaic Law on the English Sunday; and what James I sent to Lancashire in 1617, Charles I sent to Somerset in 1633. He ordered a declaration to be read in every church in the realm expressing his will that after divine service on a Sunday his

> good people be not disturbed, letted or discouraged from any lawful recreation, such as dancing, either men or women; archery for men, leaping, vaulting or any other such harmless recreation, nor from having of May-games, Whit-ales and Morris dances, and the setting up of maypoles and other sports therewith used. . . .[2]

The Sabbatarian crisis divided mortally not only Somerset, but England. Men who loved their Church and their traditions were

---

broken in Wrington Church by fives players between 1634 and 1660 cost the wardens £33 6s. 8d. Railings and traps to stop the game were erected without avail. In 1657, one of the Major-Generals then ruling England even accused the parish of setting up a *tennis court* in the churchyard (*Wrington Parish Manuscripts*).

[1] W. Phelps, *History of Somerset* (1836), I, p. 92.
[2] S. R. Gardiner, *The History of England from 1603 to 1640* (1886) VII, p. 321.

strengthened in their loyalty to their King and Bishops; the Puritans' hostility to both was hardened. The compulsory reading of the declaration brought war appreciably nearer. Truly could Locke assert that his birth in Somerset in 1632 had been into 'a storm'.

The family at Belluton remained small. Two other children were born, but only one of them, a second son, lived. The atmosphere of the household was austere. The father was a stern, unbending, taciturn man, not perhaps without a touch of sadism in his nature.[1]

After the philosopher's death, Lady Masham wrote: [2]

> . . . from Mr. Locke himself I have often heard of his father that he was a man of parts. Mr. Locke never mentioned him but with great respect and affection. . . . [His] father used a conduct towards him when young that he often spoke of afterwards with great approbation. It was that of being severe to him by keeping him in much awe and at a distance whilst he was a boy, but relaxing still by degrees of that severity as he grew to be a man, till he being become capable of it, he lived perfectly with him as a friend. And I remember on this occasion he has told me that his father after he was a man, solemnly asked his pardon for having struck him once in passion as a boy, his fault not being equal to that correction.

This testimony is supported by Locke's own words in the book on education which he wrote in his fifties: [3]

> For, methinks they mightily misplace the treatment due to their children, who are indulgent and familiar, when they are little, but severe to them, and keep them at a distance when they are grown up. For liberty and indulgence can do no good to *children*: their want of judgement makes them stand in need of restraint and discipline. . . .

Possibly his own father's 'restraint and discipline' seemed less agreeable to Locke as a boy than to Locke as a middle-aged bachelor.

Of his mother there is less to be learned. One interesting fact is that she was nearly ten years older than her husband. The lawyer was only twenty-six when his first son was born; his wife was

[1] A notebook belonging to the lawyer is preserved at the British Museum (Add. MSS. 28273). An entry headed 'Bastardie' specifies a method of dealing with that problem: namely that an unmarried mother be taken to a public place 'stripped from the middle upward' and whipped 'untill her bodie be bloodie—twice'. The problem of illegitimacy was one with which magistrates had to deal, and John Locke's position as magistrates' clerk would account for the appearance of this item in his notebook.

[2] Amsterdam: Remonstrants' MSS. J. 57a.

[3] *Some Thoughts Concerning Education*, 1693, p. 41.

thirty-five. Locke spoke of his mother in later life as 'a very pious woman and an affectionate mother',[1] but it seems that he never talked much about her. She died when he was twenty-two.

It is not unlikely that she was a beautiful woman. Her celebrated son was decidedly handsome, and one of his biographers saw a letter written in 1754, when she was eighty, by a Mrs. Frances Watkins, a granddaughter of Locke's mother's sister, saying 'My Aunt Keene was a most beautiful woman, as was the family.'[2]

The son who died in infancy was named Peter. Thomas was born at Belluton on 9 August 1637, when the eldest was not quite five.

Locke may sometimes have been lonely as a boy, but he grew up in a bookish home and there was much to absorb or amuse a child in the vicinity of Belluton. Among other things there were 'Druid' stones, Roman encampments and medieval mines. One such ancient relic Locke had occasion to remember in later life. Close to the little village of Stanton Drew, a mile or two from Belluton, the traveller can still visit, for a fee of threepence, an enormous circle of heavy stones, the remains of some prehistoric edifice, of precisely what nature archæologists have yet to determine. Locke went there often as a boy. And so, it happens, did his distinguished contemporary, John Aubrey,[3] who lived with his grandmother, Mrs. Whitson, at the manor house of Burnett, only three miles away from the Lockes in the direction of Bath. Years later, Locke and Aubrey met and talked about the stones at Stanton Drew, and exchanged letters on the subject.[4] They may even have met as boys.

Some distance south of Stanton Drew, but hidden by the contours of the landscape from Belluton, was a manor house to which Locke often went. Sutton Court was the seat of Edward Baber, one of the magistrates by whom his father was employed; its *châtelaine*, Elizabeth Baber, was a cousin by marriage of the Lockes, and her son, John Strachey, who was just two years younger than Locke, was one of his boyhood friends.

Sutton Court was built in the reign of Edward I, and despite Elizabethan, Jacobean and Victorian improvements, it has retained its character and beauty to the present day. It has a square tower with turret staircase, built on the plan of the Pele Towers, and a

[1] Amsterdam: Remonstrants' MSS. J. 57a.   [2] F. B. I, p. 4.
[3] Anthony Powell, *John Aubrey and His Friends* (1948), p. 31.
[4] Aubrey to Locke (B.L. Locke MSS. c. 3, f. 62); Locke to Aubrey (B.M. Egerton MSS, 2231, f. 202). I have printed these letters *in extenso* in *Notes and Queries* (Vol. 195, No. 26).

battlemented wall, which once surrounded and guarded the house, but which was later demolished on the south side to make way for a formal garden and to open a view across the Mendip Hills. The medieval hall, reduced in height by the Victorian improver, Wyatt, has lost its original minstrels' gallery, but the honey-coloured floor, the panelling and the fireplace and the windows are much as they were in John Strachey's time. His portrait beside that of his mother still hangs on the wall. Lord Strachie, the present occupant and owner, is a direct descendant.

Elizabeth Baber [1] owed her kinship with the Lockes to her first marriage—to Samuel Jepp, a cousin of the lawyer; John Strachey was the child of her second marriage; Edward Baber was her third and last husband. She was a woman of character, shrewd, resourceful, ambitious, and her wealth increased considerably with each new widowhood. Edward Baber was a mere lessee of Sutton Court, but after his death Elizabeth Baber contrived to buy it outright.

Edward Baber, who died when Locke was ten, had never, like his wife and stepson, much to do with the boy. Far more important to Locke in his youth was the interest of another leading magistrate and deputy lieutenant of the county, Alexander Popham. The Pophams were wealthy and celebrated men in both Somerset and Wiltshire. Alexander was a son of Sir Francis Popham and a grandson of Sir John Popham, Chief Justice of the King's Bench. It was Sir John who presided at the trial of Guy Fawkes and who originated transportation as a punishment for vagrancy, thus, in Aubrey's [2] words, setting afoot 'the Plantations, e.g. Virginia, which he stocked or planted out of the jails of England'. Sir John had two houses: one near Wellington in Somerset, the other, Littlecote, in Wiltshire, which Aubrey says he received for 'corruptly allowing a kinsman to escape the consequences of a most atrocious murder'. He was notoriously avaricious. His son, Sir Francis Popham, was as grasping as he, but a fool, and much of his money was squandered in useless litigation. Alexander, who was born in 1605, inherited his grandfather's prudence as well as his avarice. They were all Balliol men.

The elder Locke's connection with Alexander Popham was more

---

[1] She was born in 1605, the daughter of William Cross of Norton Fitzwarren, Somerset. She married: first, Samuel Jepp (died 1631), by whom she had two children, Samuel and Elizabeth; second, William Strachey (died 1635), by whom she had two children, John and Elizabeth (who died in infancy); third, Edward Baber (died 1642), by whom she had no children. She died in 1671.

[2] Aubrey, p. 186.

than that of clerk and magistrate: he served him also as his personal attorney, and could claim to be his friend.

The chief question which exercised the minds of Baber and Popham in their capacity as Justices of the Peace and which exercised still more the mind of their clerk in the earliest years of that clerk's son's life was Ship Money. The future philosopher was aged two when the first writ for this tax was issued by the King and eight on the appearance of the fourth and last. It mattered especially to Locke's father because it had to be collected by the magistrates, which meant that in practice it had to be collected locally by him.

The King's motive for reviving this Elizabethan tax was obvious to everyone with the slightest knowledge of current politics. Charles had chosen to rule since 1629 without summoning a parliament; conscious of the heavenly basis of his authority, confident of his own ability to wield that power for the good of all, he had dispensed with the guidance of the peers and representative commoners. The King, a man of prayer, did not miss their wisdom, but such was the inflation of prices that he did miss their money: and the law of the realm ordained that only Parliament could, except in an emergency, impose taxation. After trying various money-raising schemes with indifferent success, Charles decided that the situation of the country constituted an emergency (for pirates were raiding the shores and the navy was not strong enough to stop them) and that he would therefore be wholly within his rights in imposing a tax to pay for the national defence. His hope, which was barely, if at all, concealed, was never to summon Parliament again.

Charles wished Ship Money to be collected by Justices of the Peace because his previous dealings with tax-farmers had entailed prodigious waste; and the new arrangement proved, in some places, satisfactory. But many magistrates, and none more so than those of Somerset, were indignant—indignant not so much at the duty of collection but at the idea of Ship Money as such. For magistrates were usually men of what might be called the parliamentary class, men who had a particular interest in the summoning of a parliament because they were the kind of men to sit in one or to be represented by their like.

Ship Money *was* collected in Somerset. The notebook of Locke the lawyer, now in the British Museum,[1] contains his own calculation of the shipping belonging to Bristol and other English ports

[1] Add. MSS. 28273.

and of the contribution due from them by 1 March 1635/6. There follows a list of rateable persons in Publow, Pensford and the neighbouring parishes, together with the amount of Ship Money they had each to pay. The lawyer's own assessment is among them: it is for eight shillings and ninepence.

Yet only a fraction of the money the King could reasonably expect from a county as rich as Somerset reached him. Friends and loyal subjects he certainly had there: among the faithful Anglicans, the conservative gentry and the farmers in the West, many more among the poor; but the poor could not be taxed, and too many of the gentry and the rich commercial men were not loyal and evaded the tax. What was true of Somerset was true, in varying degrees, elsewhere. Then wars with the Scots made the King's need of money more desperate than ever.

At last in 1640 the King relented and Parliament met. Alexander Popham sat in the Commons as the member for Bath. A year later came the Grand Remonstrance, Parliament's terrible challenge to the King's authority and fitness to rule. Within a week of Locke's tenth birthday the Civil War began.

Alexander Popham became a colonel in the Parliamentary Army. Obliged like other such officers to raise his own troops, he made Locke's father a captain; and called together a company of horse. With other cavalry units, they did tolerably well at first. Parliamentary forces in Somerset engaged and defeated the Marquis of Hertford's troops, though it is not clear how great a share the Popham company had in the battle. Then, in June 1643, a Royalist army from Cornwall mustered with Prince Maurice and Lord Hertford at Chard, and by autumn all Somerset had been recovered for the King. Colonel Popham and Captain Locke, fighting under Waller, had been routed at Devizes in July. They achieved no glory in the field, but one less heroic exploit is recorded of them at Wells: [1]

> On Wednesday May 10, 1643, being Ascension, Mr. Alexander Popham's soldiers, he being a Colonel for the Parliament, after dinner rushed into church, broke down the windows, organs, fonts, seats in the choir, and the Bishop's seat, besides many other villainies.

After their defeat at Devizes, both the Colonel and the Captain decided to withdraw from the military life. When the Parliamentary

[1] Wells: Cathedral MSS.

Army was re-formed and went into action again—this time vic-
toriously—neither officer was in it. Colonel Popham had turned to
the pursuit of greater power at smaller risk through politics. Captain
Locke had taken on new civilian duties as county clerk for sewers.

Colonel Popham might well have felt that he had suffered enough.
His house at Wellington was burned down by the Royalists, a
disaster redeemed only by the prompt death of Sir Francis Popham,
which gave the Colonel possession of the other family house, Littlecote. Moving to Littlecote meant that Alexander Popham transferred his services as deputy lieutenant from Somerset to Wiltshire,
but he was still sufficiently near his Somerset possessions to retain
the services of his former captain as his attorney.

In the year 1647, when the Civil War was virtually won, Colonel
Popham found an occasion to render his attorney a small kindness
which had important consequences. Among the institutions
which the Long Parliament took under its control was Westminster
School. As Member of Parliament for Bath, Colonel Popham was
thus in a position to nominate boys for that distinguished foundation.
His attorney's elder son was fifteen years of age, not too old to be
a candidate. Colonel Popham put up his name and in the autumn of
1647 the boy was admitted to the school. Such was the decisive
beginning of a career from which all else flowed. The decay of
Locke's father's fortunes was attributed to the Civil War,[1] but if
there had been no Civil War, Alexander Popham would have had
no say in the running of Westminster School, and Locke would
never have gone there; if Locke had never gone there, he would not
have had the education which was the indispensable preliminary
to all that he achieved, and all that recommends his life to the
biographer.

[1] Thus attributed by Lady Masham who wrote of Locke's father: 'He was a captain
in the Parliamentary Army at the time of the Civil War in England, and by that
means a private sufferer in the public calamities: which probably was the sole
cause of his fortunes being impaired' (Amsterdam: Remonstrants' MSS. J. 57a).

Chapter Two

THE WESTMINSTER BOY

WESTMINSTER SCHOOL, when it was founded a century before Locke's time, had only forty pupils, all King's Scholars; but Elizabeth I granted a second charter to admit, besides the scholars, eighty other boys, who were variously known as *pensionarii*, *oppidani* and *peregrini*. By 1647, the year of Locke's arrival, this eighty had become two hundred.

The school had then a remarkable Master. Richard Busby was a right-wing Royalist, and it is some measure, if not of Puritan tolerance, of English inexpertness in the science of totalitarian government, that the Parliamentary Committee responsible for the school allowed him to remain in charge.

Richard Busby was a Lincolnshire man, aged forty-one. Himself a former King's Scholar at Westminster, he had become first a junior, then a senior Student of Christ Church. While an Oxford don he won great renown as an amateur actor. In the summer of 1636 a play, Cartwright's *Royal Slave*, was performed before Charles I and his Queen at Christ Church, and Busby played Cratander. His success was so conspicuous that he is said to have decided to take up a career on the stage.[1] It is hard to believe the report, for the actor in the seventeenth century was still a vagabond, and the profession did not draw its recruits from the high tables of Oxford colleges. In any case, it was as well that Richard Busby followed no such resolution, for the English theatres were soon to be closed for the duration of Puritan rule. He took holy orders; and providence rewarded him, for within a year he was appointed Master of Westminster School. His predecessor had described Archbishop Laud—at a time when the school was still under Church of England rule—as 'the little urchin' and 'the little meddling hocus pocus', and that was how the vacancy arose.

[1] 'So brilliant was his success on this occasion that he seriously thought at one time of adopting the stage as a profession', G. F. Russell Barker, *A Memoir of Richard Busby, D.D.*, 1895, p. 3.

Richard Busby remained at Westminster for the next fifty-seven years. He was a great teacher, and though he was free with the birch,[1] a popular one. Probably his theatrical gifts helped. His formula of hard working and hard living became the standard model for a classical education in England, and Gladstone could well claim that Dr. Busby was 'the founder of the Public School system'.[2]

The Master was fortunate in his pupils, who included a large proportion of the great men of later Stuart England. Steele said that 'Busby's genius for education had as great an effect upon the age he lived in as that of any ancient philosopher'.[3]

The Master made no secret of his political sympathies, and the atmosphere of the school was decidedly Royalist. Robert South,[4] who was at Westminster with Locke, later recalled, in his fervent Royalist way: 'For though, indeed, we had some of those fellows [i.e. Puritans] for our governors . . . thanks yet be to God they were never our teachers.' [5] Dr. Busby managed somehow to be true to his conscience without breaking the law. Called upon to subscribe to such Puritan declarations as the National Covenant, he simply reported sick; and his employers were content to accept the excuse.

For a boy like Locke, going to Westminster from a zealously Puritan home at an impressionable age, the political atmosphere of the school was both disturbing and compelling. It did not make him a conventional Royalist, despite the assertion of Robert South that 'the school [was] so untaintedly loyal [to the King] that I can truly and knowingly aver that in the very worst of times (in which it was my lot to be a member of it) we really were King's Scholars, as well as called so.' [5] But Westminster did purge Locke of the unquestioning Puritan faith in which he had grown up; and thus, however ironically, Dr. Busby, the great conservative pedagogue,

[1] His pupil Dryden once recalled how 'our Master Busby used to whip a boy so long, till he made him a confirmed blockhead' (*Works*, 1808, XVIII, 160).

[2] *Vide* L. E. Tanner, *Westminster School*, 1934, p. 16.

[3] *The Lover*, 27 April 1714.

[4] Robert South (1634–1716) went to Westminster a year before Locke and left a year earlier for Christ Church, Oxford. Privately ordained in 1658, he became chaplain to the Chancellor of Oxford University after the Restoration, a D.D. (1663), Canon of Christ Church (1670) and Chaplain-in-Ordinary to Charles II. He was a celebrated and witty preacher; late in life he was offered, but declined, the Deanery of Westminster and the See of Rochester.

[5] *Sermons*, 1823, III, p. 412.

must be given the credit for having first set Locke on the road to liberalism.

It was in Locke's second year at his public school that King Charles was beheaded nearby at Whitehall. The future philosopher did not witness that melancholy scene. Once again there is the testimony of Robert South: 'Upon that very day, that black and eternally infamous day of the King's murder, I myself heard and am now a witness, that the King was publicly prayed for in this school but an hour or two before his sacred head was struck off.' [1] The Master had kept the boys in school for this purpose.

It would be wrong to conclude that Dr. Busby used his position to engage in political propaganda. While his own beliefs were avowed, he taught his pupils to beware of persuasion, and never to accept without reflection the pretensions of men in power. Something of this is revealed by a conversation Dr. Busby had in later life with a former pupil, Philip Henry:

> 'Child,' the Doctor asked, 'what made thee a Nonconformist?'
> 'Truly, sir,' was the reply, 'you made me one; for you taught me those things which hindered me from conforming.' [2]

An account of daily life at Westminster School at the time can be read in a document written by an unnamed boy who was there under Busby a few years before Locke arrived : [3]

> [At] 5.15 a.m. called up by a monitor, and after Latin Prayers, wash.
> Between 6 and 8 repeat grammar—Lily for Latin, Camden for Greek [4]—fourteen or fifteen [boys] being selected and called out to stand in a semi-circle before the Master.
> Between 8 and 9 we had time for a beaver,[5] and recollection of selves and preparation of future exercises.
> Between 9 and 11 those exercises were read which had been enjoined us overnight (one day in prose; the next day in verse).
> At dinner and supper we read some portion of the Latin in a manuscript.

---

[1] *Sermons*, 1823, III, p. 412.
[2] Tanner *op. cit.* p. 16.
[3] P.R.O. State Papers, Charles I, col. clxxxi, 37.
[4] Lily's *Latin Grammar* and Camden's *Greek Grammar* were soon supplanted by Dr. Busby's own textbooks. The Master was also the author of an *Arabic Grammar*, and he wrote, but did not publish, a *Hebrew Grammar*. He insisted on pronouncing Latin as if it were English; and thus began another cherished tradition of the English Public Schools.
[5] Beverage; refreshment.

Between 1 and 3 the [classical] author chosen by the Master for the day was gone through by construeing and other grammatical ways.

Betwixt 3 and 4 a little respite.

Betwixt 4 and 5 we repeated a leaf or two out of some book of rhetorical figures and choice proverbs and sentences collected by the Master for that use . . .

After supper (in summer time) we were called to the Master's chamber and there instructed out of Hunter's *Cosmography*, and taught to describe and find out cities and counties in the maps.

The Scholars were governed by several monitors (Two for the Hall, as many for the Church, the School, the Fields, the Cloister). The captain of the school was one of these, and therefore called *monitor monitorum*. These monitors kept strictly to the speaking of Latin in their commands, and with all they permitted their complaints or accusations (as we called them) every Friday morning.

Locke was not, as previous biographers have stated, a King's Scholar when he entered Westminster in 1647.[1] He became one in 1650; and evidence of his election may be seen in the Westminster Abbey manuscripts.[2] He was admitted first as a *peregrinus*, lodging with a Mrs. Susan Bates. In the seventeenth century Westminster School could accommodate only King's Scholars as boarders. The buildings, which stood then, as they still stand, in the shadow of Westminster Abbey, were much smaller than they are today. All the general instruction was given in the one school hall, though sometimes several ushers would have charge of separate groups in different parts of the hall. The additional subjects were taught in the Master's study.

Locke's election as a King's Scholar in 1650 was his second decisive step to fame. The election was not of immediate financial importance, apart from the fact that a scholar was able to live in the school for nothing. Nor was the immediate distinction the most important part of it. What mattered was that this 'minor' election, as it was called, could lead to a 'major' election to a scholarship at Christ Church, Oxford, or Trinity College, Cambridge. The Westminster boy who went up to the university with such an award would have more than half his expenses paid, and enjoy the privileged status of a scholar.

The method of electing King's Scholars was known as the 'challenge'. Candidates started in school order, and the boy at the

---

[1] The same error is made in *The Record of Old Westminsters*, 1928, p. 586.

[2] Westminster Abbey Manuscripts, 43057.

bottom of the list challenged the boy above him to construe a particular classical author, to parse and give the rules of grammar and usage for any word he, the challenger, chose. If the boy who was challenged failed, the challenger took his place.

Evelyn, in his *Diary*,[1] records having witnessed such an election, and confesses that such exercises 'in Latin, Greek, Hebrew and Arabic in themes and extemporary verses, wonderfully astonished me in such youths . . . some of them not above twelve or thirteen years of age'. Locke, however, was nearly eighteen at the time of his 'minor' election.

In the list of 'minor' candidates for 1650,[2] numbers from one to twenty are marked against the names, presumably to show the order in which the candidates were placed at the close of the challenge. Henry Bagshawe[3] was first; Michael Gardiner,[4] second; Lawrence Wright,[5] third; William Godolphin,[6] fourth; Robert South, from whose reminiscences of Westminster School I have quoted, was sixth. John Locke was tenth.

An account-book Locke kept from the beginning of his third year at Westminster[7] shows that his income in the Michaelmas quarter of 1649 was £21 10s., and his expenditure £19. The next quarter he received £4 and paid out a little more; in the second quarter of 1650 he received £6 10s. and spent rather less. From the Michaelmas quarter of 1650, when he returned from the long vacation, until Lady Day 1651, he both received and disbursed £14. Until Christmas 1651, his quarterly income and expenditure remained approximately £3 5s.

---

[1] 13 May 1661.   [2] Westminster Abbey Manuscripts, 43057.

[3] Henry Bagshawe (1634–1709), who was sixteen, was also Captain of the school. He was elected to a Christ Church scholarship the next year. In later life he became a famous pulpit orator, but never achieved ecclesiastical preferment higher than a cathedral prebend.

[4] Michael Gardiner (b. 1633) was the son of a London vintner. He came head of the list of successful candidates for Trinity College, Cambridge, in 1652. He was called to the Bar from the Inner Temple in 1659.

[5] Lawrence Wright (b. 1633) was elected to Trinity College, Cambridge, in 1652, where he became Tutor in 1660. He enjoyed some success as a physician, taking the M.D. in 1666.

[6] Sir William Godolphin (1635–96) was one of Locke's closest friends at Westminster. He was elected to Christ Church in 1651. He was subsequently a D.C.L., F.R.S. and M.P. for Camelford (1665–8). He was Ambassador to Madrid (1671–8) whence he was recalled on suspicion of Popish sympathies, but he refused to return; he died a professed Catholic.   [7] B.L. MSS. Locke F. 11.

By the year 1651 Locke's younger brother, five years his junior, had joined him at Westminster,[1] and John Locke became responsible for Thomas's money as well as his own. Thus there appears among his accounts for 1652: 'Paid to Mrs. Jackson for a quarter ending on Lady Day for my brother £3.10.0.' Mrs. Jackson was the younger boy's landlady. Thomas never became, like his brother, a King's Scholar.

Locke's disbursements for his most costly quarter—Michaelmas 1649—are worth reproducing in greater detail for the light they throw on his schoolboy life:

	£	s.	d.
A pair of shoes		2	10
A looking glass			8
Abbot's *Geography*		1	6
A comb			6
Spent evening with Mrs. Susan [2]		1	0
For sending a letter			2
Pair of salts		6	0
Lucan's *Pharsalia* in English and Latin		3	6
A paper book			5
A general calendar			6
Buttons		3	0
Given to the maid			6
For mending my boots		1	0
A penknife for my brother			6
For mending my clothes			9
Cutting my hair			2
An Act for the School			6
Godwin's *Antiquities*		5	9
A trunk		3	6
Bandstrings		1	3
A purse			3
Candles			7
A box			4
A candlestick			5
A tinderbox and steel		1	0
For entrance [3]		10	0
For double commons		3	6

[1] Thomas Locke was accepted at Westminster on 15 May 1651, when Locke records having paid out 10s. for his admission fee. Agnes Locke evidently accompanied her younger son to London for the occasion, since her elder son records having 'delivered £1' to her on 26 May 1651.   [2] Mrs. Susan Bates.
[3] Presumably for entrance to the competition for King's Scholarships.

	£	s.	d.
A thread wind			4
For making two pairs of breeches		10	0
For *Homer*			10
For bringing the things		12	0
Given the woman for making the beds		1	0
For a bed	5	0	0
A knife for M. V. F. K.		1	3
A *Greek Grammar*		1	8
When I was not well		5	8
Comb-case and looking [glass]			8
For Four weeks' lodging and fire		18	0
To Dr. Busby	1	0	0
Washing		4	0

During the two last years at Westminster, Locke was paying Dr.
Busby a pound a quarter for extra tuition. His laundry cost six
shillings a quarter; paper and paper books half a crown a year;
candles about the same sum. He had his hair cut (for twopence,
threepence or fourpence) about twice a quarter, and bought several
presents, including a 'pair of gloves for Mr. Busby' at eight shillings;
a pair for his brother costing a shilling, a hat for his father at nineteen
shillings and sixpence and something for Mr. Vincent, the Under-
Master,[1] costing sixpence. He spent much on books[2] and other
miscellaneous payments were:

	£	s.	d.
Pies against the election		1	0
Sweeping the school		1	0
When I was sick (Lady Day 1650)		2	3
(Lady Day) 1651		2	6
A pair of bellows		1	6
A box to put my fine linen in			4
A lock and key and other things about the chamber		2	0
For washing my new gown		3	0
For mending my old gown			9
A sachel for my brother		1	0
Ointment for the itch			6

[1] Thomas Vincent, usher in 1634, afterwards Under-Master of Westminster School.
[2] In 1650 he bought *Livy's Works* (4s.), *Tully's Works* (8s.), Greek, *Roman and
Jewish Antiquities* (5s.), a *Lexicon and Grammar* (5s. 6d.), a Hebrew *Psalter* (1s.),
Epictetus (6d.), *Plautus* (6d.), *Lucan* (2s. 2d.), *Seneca* (2s. 2d.), an English *Bible*; in 1651
he bought an English Bible (3s. 3d.), Barclay's *Latin* (2s. 10d.), Homer's *Iliad* and
Odyssey (4s. each), Dr. Taylor's *Works* (7s.), Pliny's *Epistles* (1s.), Hebrew *Epistles*
(2s. 6d), a *Vergil* (2s. 8d.), *Horace, Juvenal and Caesar* (2s. 8d.) and *Minor Poets* (4s.).

Locke bought three pairs of shoes, at about three shillings each, during these two years, and had one pair mended once a quarter. He gave a quarterly tip of sixpence to the butler, and another of sixpence to 'the woman for making the beds'.

Another interesting item in his account represents a sum of five shillings spent on 'a pair of gloves for my —— Mary Lower'. The words 'for my —— Mary Lower' were scribbled over by Locke, but save for the middle word are nevertheless legible. Who, then, was Mary Lower and what was she to Locke in 1649? Possibly she was the sister of one of Locke's schoolfellows, Richard Lower,[1] second son of Humphrey Lower, of Tremeere, Bodmin, Cornwall; but this is no more than a guess.

During his first year at Westminster, Locke went home to Somerset for the long vacation, which lasted up to fifteen weeks.[2] When he became a King's Scholar, he had to spend his summers as a pensioner with the Under-Master, Thomas Vincent,[3] in the school's country house at Chiswick. Locke cannot have been entirely happy during his years at the school, for in later life he roundly condemned the sort of education he had received. He came to disapprove of *all* schools. Only once, in the case of an especially difficult boy, did Locke go so far as to recommend 'Westminster, or some other very severe school, where, if he were whipped soundly . . . he would perhaps be the more pliant and willing to learn at home afterwards'.[4]

What Locke experienced at school must have had a lot to do with his being afterwards so fervent a champion of the private tutor. In his *Thoughts Concerning Education* Locke asks: '. . . [is] it worth while to hazard your son's virtue for a little Latin and Greek?',[5] and adds:

He that considers how diametrically opposite the skill of living well and managing, as a man should do, his affairs in the world, is to that malpertness, tricking and violence learned among schoolboys, will think the faults of a more private education infinitely to be preferred to such improvements, and will take care to preserve his child's innocence and modesty at home . . .[5]

---

[1] Richard Lower (1632–91) was later one of Locke's medical teachers at Oxford. Matriculating at Christ Church in 1650, he was one of the first Students of the House to study chemistry. He helped Willis prepare his *Cerebri Anatome*; and taking his B.M. in 1665 he left Oxford to become, according to Wood, 'the most noted physician in Westminster and London' (*Ath. Oxon*, iv. 298).

[2] Westminster Abbey Manuscripts, 43190.

[3] B.L. Rawl. MSS. D. 216.

[4] Locke to Clarke, 26 February 1691/2 (Rand, p. 335).   [5] Second Edn. § 70.

In the spring of 1652, when he was nineteen, Locke became a candidate for what was known at Westminster as a 'major' election, the election for the places at Oxford and Cambridge. Such elections were different from the 'minor' elections. They were not simply tests of a candidate's intellectual abilities. There was admittedly a public ceremony at which orations were delivered in Latin, Greek, Arabic or Hebrew by the several candidates, but it was not the merits of a boy's performance on this occasion which really determined his success. Private negotiations before the ceremony were more important. However unjustly, influence played the greater part in a 'major' election.

Hence this was an occasion for Locke to measure the appreciation and the power of his friends, and for his father to do so too. Letters were written and representations made to several prominent persons, notably, as England was then under Cromwell's protection, to military officers.

At the time of the 'major' election in which he was a candidate Locke wrote what is probably the earliest letter in his hand still extant. It reads as follows: [1]

> Most dear and ever loving father,
> My humble duty remembered unto [you]. Yours by Mr. Wheeler I have received, and according to former order sent your letters [except] only those for Mr. Stapleton, which yet I have. That for Lieutenant-General Fleetwood [2] I sent to Captain Smyth, [3] who hath promised me to do his utmost. I doubt not much of the election with the help of some friends which I shall diligently labour for.
> Your letter to Mr. Busby I have delivered and he hath promised me to do what he can, which I cannot doubt of having so many assurances of his love. He hath made choice of my Oration before any of the rest to be perhaps spoken at the Election.
> Pray remember my humble duty and love to the rest of my friends. Thus, desiring your prayers, *sum*
> *Tuus obedientissimus filius,*
>
> John Locke
>
> Westminster, 4th May 1652.

[1] B.L. MSS. Locke, c. 24, f. 165.
[2] Charles Fleetwood was one of Cromwell's generals, and during his master's absence in Scotland in 1651, Commander-in-Chief of troops in England. In 1652 he married Cromwell's daughter Bridget, Ireton's widow, and was appointed Commander-in-Chief in Ireland. But he did not leave London for Ireland until September.
[3] Possibly a relation of Fleetwood's first wife, Frances Smith.

About the same time Locke drafted a Latin letter [1] to Alexander Popham. He addressed it 'O Patrone', in recognition presumably of that patronage which began, if not before, on his becoming a Westminster boy, and he went on to solicit the Colonel's help in securing a scholarship at Oxford. An eight-line Latin poem appended to the letter expressed Locke's longing to leave school, and compares his yearning to go to the University with that of Odysseus for his home.

On 11 May he wrote another letter to Belluton: [2]

Most dear and ever-loving father,

My humble duty remembered unto you. I have to my utmost done what lies in me for the preparation both of myself and friends for the Election. Captain Smyth I find most ready and willing to lay out himself for the accomplishment. Thereof neither is Mr. Busby anyway wanting, he having spoken to the electors on my behalf, and although my Latin oration be not spoken yet, he hath promised me that my Hebrew one, which I made since, I shall—which I would desire you to be silent of, for there has been something already spoken abroad more than has been for my good.

If I be not elected (but I have good hopes) pray send me word what I shall do, for we hear that there will be very few chosen.

Pray remember my humble duty to my mother, and love to the rest of my friends. Thus desiring your prayers, *sum*

Tuus obedientissimus filius

John Locke

His hopes were fulfilled. Before the end of May he was elected, last in a list of six candidates, to a scholarship at Christ Church. The others were (in this order): Nicholas Bowman, [3] Robert Osbaldeston, [4] James Carkesse, [5] Arthur Salway [6] and George Nourse. [7]

These boys may well have included Locke's closest friends at school and in his first few terms at Oxford, but only two

---

[1] B.L. MSS. Locke, c. 32, ff. 8–9 (it is endorsed '*Electio*').

[2] *Ibid.*, c. 24, f. 167.

[3] Second son of Nicholas Bowman of Westminster. Admitted to Gray's Inn, 1655.

[4] Son of Robert Osbaldeston, haberdasher, of London. Rector of St. James's, Duke Place, London (1661–4) and of Great Parndon, Essex (1662–80).

[5] Son of James Carkesse, Turkey merchant, of London. He became Headmaster of Magdalen College School (1663/4) and of Chelmsford School (1682).

[6] Son of Arthur Salway, rector of Severn Stoke, Worcestershire. He became Rector of Stanford-on-Teme, Worcestershire (1664–73).

[7] Son of Thomas Nourse, M.D., physician of Westminster.

contemporaries at Westminster were his friends in later years: John Mapletoft and Thomas Blomer.

Mapletoft, though not more than a year older than Locke, became a King's Scholar five years earlier, and left Westminster for Cambridge twelve months after Locke arrived. He was a High Church clergyman's son, having family connections with Little Gidding, but his own theological views became, like Locke's, latitudinarian. From Trinity College, where he was elected a Fellow in 1653, Mapletoft went to read law at Gray's Inn, and then became tutor to Lord Percy, son of the Earl of Northumberland. Later he turned to medicine, and became a distinguished Professor of Physic at Gresham's College.

Of Thomas Blomer Locke saw more at Westminster, since Blomer was younger than he and left Westminster a year later, being elected head of the list to Trinity, Cambridge, in 1653. Blomer was subsequently a tutor of his college, but left to become chaplain to the Earl of Northumberland when Mapletoft was in the same household as tutor to Lord Percy.

Two other boys whose names will recur in this biography were among Locke's schoolfellows at Westminster. One was destined to become next to Locke himself the greatest of them all: John Dryden.[1] The other was an undistinguished boy from a poor north-country home by name Joseph Williamson.[2] Williamson failed in the 'challenge' and had to go to Oxford as a bateller of Queen's, but he rose to be a great statesman, diplomatist and Civil Servant in later Stuart England.

---

[1] John Dryden (1631–1700), Poet Laureate, 1670–89, celebrated Cromwell in his poem in *Heroic Stanzas* (1658); Charles II in *Astraea Redux* (1660); the Anglican religion in *Religio Laici* (1682) and Roman Catholicism in *The Hind and the Panther* (1687), thus proving himself a true Hobbesian. A poem he wrote as a schoolboy, on the death of Lord Hastings, was published by Busby in *Lachrymae Musarum* (1649).

[2] Sir Joseph Williamson (1633–1701) became the first editor of the *London Gazette* (1666), M.P. for Thetford (1669), a Knight (1672), Secretary of State (1674–79), a Privy Councillor (1674), and President of the Royal Society (1677–80). Pepys called him 'a pretty knowing man and a scholar, but it may be that he thinks himself too much so'.

Chapter Three

THE OXFORD UNDERGRADUATE

LOCKE went up to Christ Church in the autumn of 1652. He had been elected at Whitsuntide, and matriculated on 27 November, according to the record in the Christ Church *Entry Book*, where he is described as a gentleman's son (*generosi filius*). He was twenty years old.

He had spent the long vacation at home in Pensford; and there survives from that summer a letter [1] he received from his friend James Heans, who was staying at Jersey in the Channel Islands:

> Noble heart. . . . A sheet of paper with the subscription of your hand raised my colour and gave me the happiness that attends the remembrance of a true friend. . . . Scatter my love (according to the ripeness and truth of it) towards Bristol and Horfield amongst our fast friends. . . .

One 'fast friend' accompanied Locke to Oxford: that redoubtable Colonel of Parliamentary horse, Presbyterian politician and one-time commoner of Balliol, Alexander Popham. The Colonel stayed in Oxford a few days while his *protégé* installed himself in rooms at Christ Church, and then left for London. Locke wrote [2] to tell him that after those first few days of enjoyment together, Oxford life had lost its lustre. However, he realised the advantages of a place of learning where he had 'worthies and most admired persons of former ages to converse with'.

In a later letter [3] Locke assured his patron that he hoped, as a result of his Oxford studies, to be of some use to the one who had placed him there.

'Sir,' he added, with a fine flourish, 'to say I am obliged to you is no more than to profess myself an Englishman. . . . The whole nation looks on you as a defender of its laws and liberties.'

---

[1] 14 September 1652 (B.L. MSS. Locke, c. 11, f. 180).
[2] *Ibid.*, c. 24, f. 289.   [3] *Ibid.*, c. 24, f. 223.

It was a kindly fancy and, however untrue, one cannot doubt it was well received. Locke was always a shrewd courtier.

The Oxford he entered in November 1652 was beginning to settle down after the confusions of the Civil War. The Puritan conquest of the British Isles was complete; Charles II had escaped to France; Parliament had passed an Act of Oblivion for all offences committed before the Battle of Worcester, and war against the Dutch was rekindling some spirit of national unity.

Oxford had been staunchly and generously Royalist in the Civil War. Money was found for the King in the University Chest, and every college surrendered practically all of its plate to his cause. From the autumn of 1642 until the spring of 1646, Oxford was the King's headquarters, Christ Church housing his Court, and Merton the Queen's Court. Then in the summer of 1646 Oxford had fallen to the Parliamentary Army. 'The University, its youth and treasure spent, its courts forsaken', was 'face to face with the authority whose power it had defied'.[1]

Many Puritans wished to abolish the universities, but Parliament decided instead to purge them. Samuel Fell, Vice-Chancellor of Oxford and Dean of Christ Church, was dismissed, together with the Heads of Magdalen, All Souls, St. John's, Brasenose and Trinity. All the Fellows, tutors, chaplains, undergraduates and even servants had to take an oath of submission to the new authority or go. Two-thirds of the dons went. At Christ Church, where thirty-five senior Students remained after seventy had resigned, first Edward Reynolds, a Presbyterian, then Cromwell's own chaplain, John Owen, became Dean. Other headships also went to Cromwell's relations and friends. For the rest, according to Anthony Wood,[2] places were filled 'from among the candidates who came trooping in from Cambridge, and by poor curates and schoolmasters from the country'.

There was need for reform at Oxford; not political reform, which the Puritans intended, but at any rate academic reform, which, it so happened, their purges and intrusions did in a measure promote, albeit not immediately and not, in Locke's time, at Christ Church. The education of an Oxford undergraduate was still medieval. He often matriculated when he was much younger than is now the rule, and remained several years longer. Locke was exceptional in going up at the age of twenty. John Freeston, who was born in

---

[1] Mallet II, p. 370. [2] *S. of A.* II, p. 634.

the same year as Locke, entered Wadham when he was fourteen. Being hardly more than boys, undergraduates were treated as boys, and their tutors were not unlike schoolmasters. Milton, who went to Cambridge in 1625, was whipped by his tutor and the experience was not unusual at either university.

The days were busy. Five o'clock was the undergraduates' hour for rising to attend morning chapel. Breakfast was at six. Four hours' work was done before dinner in Hall at noon. Two hours' work came after dinner, and supper was at seven. The three and a half years' preparation for the B.A. degree were mainly given to logic and metaphysics and the classical languages.

Conversation with tutors, or even between undergraduates in Hall, was always in Latin. Everything led up to the Disputation, in which, to qualify for a degree, a candidate had to maintain or attack a given thesis before an audience. This medieval institution had the place of the modern examination. Attendance at lectures was compulsory, and, after the B.A. degree, three more years' study was required for the M.A.[1]

William Laud, as Vice-Chancellor of the University, had in 1629 tightened the academic discipline, closed the taverns and brothels, and made the students' life a serious one; but the war and the King's occupation had undone most of his reforms. Oxford under the Commonwealth would never admit that its task was to go back to Laud, but the re-introduction of discipline was substantially this, except that in place of the rituals the great High Churchman wished to have observed, the Puritans ordered preaching. Oxford men of Locke's generation had to hear at least two sermons a day, and remember them. All undergraduates, and Bachelors of Arts as well, had to go every Sunday evening between six and nine o'clock to 'give an account to some person of known ability and piety (to be appointed by the Heads of Houses) of the sermons they had heard', and later they had also to pay nightly visits to their tutors 'to hear private prayers and to give an account of the time spent that day'.[2]

Locke's tutor at Christ Church was a man of twenty-six named Thomas Cole. He, too, had been at Westminster, but Dr. Busby's

---

[1] On 17 November 1652 (ten days before Locke's matriculation) Convocation introduced Declamations in place of lectures for B.A.s proceeding to the M.A. Previously, B.A.s had cut most of their lectures, and because the tutors had found themselves addressing the walls of empty rooms, such occasions became known as 'wall lectures' (C. M. Neale, *Oxford 1605–59*, B.L. MSS. Top. Oxon., c. 256, p. 323).

[2] *S. of A.* II, pp. 653–4.

teaching had not prevented his becoming a staunch Independent in religion. While he was said to have been 'of good learning and gentle spirit', he was not otherwise distinguished. .

The Dean, on the other hand, was an outstanding personality. Valiant in war—he had gone with Cromwell's troops into Ireland and Scotland to refresh their spirits with martial sermons—John Owen was gentle and tolerant in times of peace. Although the discipline he had to enforce in the House as Dean and in the University as Vice-Chancellor was strict, John Owen's justice was tempered equally with mercy and with sympathy for human frailty. He did not seek to root out Anglicans who practised their religion privately; and he showed no attachment to austerity for the sake of austerity. On the contrary, he was the leader of fashion in Oxford. Wood [1] alleges that Owen 'had as much powder in his hair that would discharge eight cannons'.

Wood disliked the Oxford Puritans; he called them [2] 'factious saucy, and some impudent and conceited . . . factious in college and delighting in petty plots. Scorning at anything that seemed formal, and laughing at a man in a cassock or canonical coat'. But even Wood admits that in Puritan Oxford there was academic 'disputing constantly and many good disputants then bred up, especially in philosophy'; disputing was indeed so vigorous that fighting broke out at the schools and even in the streets, 'to the great scandal of the gown'. Wood also reports that there was brisk sale of books, and that money was plentiful. The Puritans, he writes: [3]

used to love and encourage instrumental [4] music, but they did not care for vocal, because that was used in Church by the prelatical party. They would not go to ale-houses or taverns, but send for their liquors to their respective chambers and tipple it there. . . .

They were great enemies to May games and would never suffer anything thereof to be done in the University or city as Maypoles, Morrises, Whitsun ales, nay, scarce wakes. . . .

They would not suffer any common players to come into the University, nor scholars to act in private but what they did by stealth; yet at Act [5] times they would permit dancing the rope, drolls or monstrous sights to be seen.

They would not suffer any swearing or cursing, and if a scholar

---

[1] *L. and T.* I, p. 221.   [2] *Ibid.*, p. 296.   [3] *Ibid.*, pp. 298–301.
[4] John Owen, for example, played the flute.
[5] Public disputations at which the degree of M.A. was conferred were called Acts.

was found guilty of either, expulsion for the most part was his punishment.

Many also of them that were the sons of upstart gentlemen . . . were generally very proud, saucy, impudent, and seldom gave respect to any but the leading person. The inferior sort or juniors went very lavishly in their apparel; they always wore hats with riband, powdered hair, laced bands and tassel or snake bow band strings, half shirts and long cuffs: and no wonder seeing Dr. Owen, when Vice-Chancellor, had always his hair powdered . . . velvet jacket, his breeches set round at knee with ribbons pointed. . . .

Discipline was strict and severe . . . Acts were then well performed, as well in divinity as in philosophy. . . .

The university flourished in number, but few nobility, few gentry also. . . .

As Westminster in Locke's time was the most important English school, so Christ Church was the most important Oxford college. Planned in 1525 by Cardinal Wolsey to be a far bigger and better college than any which then existed, it had been revived by Henry VIII in 1532 as his own Royal Foundation. In Locke's undergraduate years, the buildings of Christ Church were unfinished. There was no Peckwater quadrangle or Library, nor was Wren's Tom Tower put over the gate-house until later in the century. Only the Cathedral, the Hall, the small quadrangles and three sides of the great quadrangle were then as they are today. A chapel to rival King's at Cambridge, which was Wolsey's plan for the north side of the quadrangle, never rose above its foundations.

The accounts [1] Locke kept during his first winter at Christ Church —he wrote them in the same book he had used at Westminster— reveal something of the details of his life at the House. On his arrival, he had, as was the rule, to buy the furniture from the man whose rooms he acquired. His predecessor was one Anthony Earbury, who had been up for two years, and was moving on, perhaps, to better rooms. Locke paid him ten shillings for his study, thirteen shillings for a bedstead, and fifteen shillings and sixpence for two tables; later he 'paid to Mr. Williams for curtains, chairs, etc., £4 10s. 6d.'

An item once entered during his first term, but later crossed out,

[1] B.L. MSS. Locke F. 11. After Easter 1654 Locke kept only haphazard accounts in this book, but the figures show some of the recurrent charges he met as an undergraduate, e.g., twenty shillings a quarter to Mr. Cole for 'pupillage', five shillings each a quarter to his bedmaker and laundress.

is eight shillings 'for entertaining our moderator', the moderator being an examiner. Other disbursements of Locke's first three months at Christ Church were:

	£	s.	d.
A pair of shoes		4	0
3 maps		3	0
Compounds for the headache			3
Perfume for my clothes			5
Paid Mr. Denniss for things received of him	2	17	0
For an antidote against infection of the small pox		1	0
For a pair of wash-leather gloves		3	0
For an hat		16	6
I paid my tutor for a quarter's pupillage	1	0	0
For matriculation		7	6
I paid to Mr. Warland	1	10	0
I left in my tutor's hands to pay the House	5	0	0
Journey		10	0

Like many another undergraduate, Locke was short of money during his first year. In the early summer of 1653 he was ill for a time; medicine cost him twenty-three shillings, and a journey into the country for a change of air, fifteen shillings.

It was in June 1653 that the Parliamentary Visitors instructed all college tutors to draw up lists of the undergraduates committed to their charge, and Heads to dismiss those who were not good Puritans. Although Locke survived the purge, that fact is no evidence of the state of his faith. Dr. Owen was not the man to expel his undergraduates to please the Parliamentary Visitors. He certified them all as being everything they should be.

In the following spring Locke paid a visit to Hampton Court. He preserved the letters of thanks [1] he drafted afterwards, but he cut off the name of the person to whom he addressed them and he tried to make the words 'Hampton Court' illegible. It is, however, still possible to discern both the 'Hampton Court' and the three last letters of the addressee's name, which are 'ine'. There are grounds for thinking that the name should read 'Martine'. Locke's accounts show that several sums reached him in his Oxford days 'from my cousin Gabriel Martine' and a woman with the same surname figures among his correspondents.

The two letters intended for Hampton Court were drafted on

---

[1] B.L. MSS. Locke, c. 24, ff. 3–5.

1 May 1654. They might be read as two drafts of a single letter to his hostess. Alternatively, it may be that the one, an obvious 'bread-and-butter' letter, was destined for his hostess, and the other for a younger woman in the same household. In the second letter there is a reference to an accompanying message in invisible ink.

In the body of this letter Locke wrote:[1] 'The same greatness of those favours I received from everyone, but especially from yourself, at my being with you . . . exacts a more than ordinary return of thanks.'

He offered his correspondent a gift, a book on heraldry: 'If any other shall please you better, you will vouchsafe to let me know it.'

It was in the postscript that Locke invited her 'to take out a leaf of clean paper inserted at the beginning of this book, and when you are alone warm it very hot by the fire. Beyond this I dare not trouble you. . . .'

Thus does Locke appear for the first time as a *mystificateur*. However inappropriately for a man who was to be remembered as the founder of the Age of Reason, Locke was both romantic in appearance and romantic in his ways. He seems to have taken a positively gothic pleasure in mystery for the sake of mystery.

The recipient of the message he wrote in May 1654 with invisible ink was possibly the same Mrs. Martine to whom he wrote fifteen months later a cheerful letter[2] about the birth of her first child:

> To my Cousin Martine.
> Madam,
> I have scarce so much charity left as to congratulate the late great blessing you received from heaven; and I give you no small proofs of a good nature and the power you have over me, to be able so to overcome those resentments your cruel silence might have wrought in me as to give you this testimony that I very much rejoice in your happiness, the relation whereof wanted nothing of being the welcomest news that ever I received, but that it came not from yourself, which was the only condition it wanted to make it perfect. Methinks the name of 'mother' hath wrought a change upon your disposition, and you begin with a more than ordinary forwardness to put on the providence of a careful parent. However it comes to pass that you are so much altered from that former freeness which appeared in all your actions, as that when you were possessed of the happiness of having a firstborn, a joy large enough to spread itself into more souls than yours, you could be

[1] B.L. MSS. Locke, c. 24, f. 5.   [2] 11 August 1655 (*ibid.*, f. 188).

so niggardly as not to afford him any part of it, who in spite of all your neglect is resolved to be

Madam,

Your most affectionate friend and faithful servant

John Locke

If you are resolved to save your ink and paper and not to write to me, yet pray spend a little of your breath for me in presenting my respects to your parents; as for your sisters,[1] I intend them particular remembrances.

In the same year—his twenty-second—Locke made his first appearance in print. After the English victory in the war against the Dutch, the Dean of Christ Church decided to publish an anthology of complimentary verses to Cromwell, to be written by members, junior and senior, of the University. The defeat of a foreign Power was a pleasure shared in some degree by Puritans and Royalists alike, and supporters of both parties contributed to Dr. Owen's garland. One of the contributors was Locke. Having already commemorated the victory by writing an ode to Colonel Popham,[2] Locke was encouraged to write two more pieces[3] in honour of the Lord Protector. The Latin one, as published by the Dean, opens with the lines:

> *Pax regit Augusti quem vicit Julius orbem:*
> *Ille sago factus clarior, ille toga.*
> *Hos sua Roma vocat magnos et numina credit,*
> *His quod fit mundi victor, et ille quies.*

The English poem is in rhyming couplets beginning:

> If Greece with so much mirth did entertain
> Her *Argo*, coming laden home again,
> With what loud mirth and triumph shall we greet
> The wish'd approaches of our welcome fleet,
> When of that prize our ships do us possess
> Whereof their fleece was but an emblem—Peace. . . .

---

[1] It is Locke's reference to parents and sisters, together with the absence of any reference to a husband, which prompts the suspicion that this Mrs. Martine was Gabriel Martine's daughter-in-law and not his wife.

[2] B.L. MSS. Locke, c. 32, f. 10.

[3] *Musarum Oxoniensium* 'ΕΛΑΙΟΦΟΡΙΑ (Oxford, 1654). Fox Bourne, having little else to print from Locke's youth, reproduces these two occasional poems *in extenso* (Vol. I, pp. 50–2).

In the autumn of 1654 Locke's mother was taken ill on a visit to her relations at Wrington. She was not well enough to return to Belluton, and on 4 October she died in the little cottage where her first son had been born. She was fifty-seven. Locke hurried to Somerset, but arrived in time only to attend her funeral.

He returned to Oxford to find an outbreak of small-pox there; 'a great spread of it', one historian says, 'but many recovered'.[1] Locke's father[2] wrote anxiously from Pensford saying: 'I have received nothing from you since your arrival there. I am greedy to be informed of your good health in these times of so much sickness.'

The long vacation of 1655 Locke spent once again at Pensford. Now that his mother was no longer alive, he was thrown entirely upon the company of his father. That the latter had some acquaintance with intellectual questions is evident from the few papers of his which are extant;[3] and Locke was presumably by this time at an age to be admitted to that friendship with his father which had been denied him in childhood; but it is fairly clear that Locke was bored at Belluton and wished he were back in Oxford. He wrote in September[4] to a friend at Hart Hall named Samuel Tilly[5] begging for a lively letter: 'If in friendship there be any sympathy you cannot but be sensible what I suffer in the absence from that place where you are.'

Tilly's reply (dated 11 September 1655[6]) brought Locke news of events in Oxford. Among other things he reported: 'Your reverend Dean, who came the last night from London, is (they say) that his honour may be proportionate to his person and merit, resolved on to continue Vice-Chancellor another year.'[7]

The following February Locke graduated as a Bachelor of Arts.

---

[1] C. M. Neale, *op. cit.*, p. 333.

[2] B.L. MSS. Locke, c. 14, f. 165.

[3] The notebook in the British Museum (Add. MSS. 28273) contains a short synoptic account of the nature and scope of philosophy (*vide* F.B., I, pp. 70–1, where it is reproduced in full).

[4] B.L. MSS. Locke, c. 24, f. 276.

[5] Samuel Tilly had gone to Oxford a little earlier than Locke. He matriculated at Wadham in March 1651, but moved to Hart Hall before he took his B.A. in 1654. Eventually he became a clergyman—his livings included the Somerset parish of East Lambrook—but at the time of his Oxford friendship with Locke he was reading for the degree of M.A.

[6] B.L. MSS. Locke, c. 20, f. 175.

[7] In the event John Owen remained Vice-Chancellor for two more years, i.e., until 1657, when Convocation was manifestly pleased to be rid of him. His successor was Conant, Rector of Exeter (Mallet, II, 395).

He was sufficiently happy at Oxford to look forward with pleasure to the three more years of residence required for his Master's degree, but his happiness there was not found in his work. Thomas Hobbes, an undergraduate at Magdalen Hall half a century earlier, had protested at the futility of the Aristotelian logic which was taught and the medieval disputations which were practised in the University. Locke reacted to the same training in the same way. According to Lady Masham: [1]

> Mr. [James] Tyrrell . . . tells me that he became acquainted with Mr. Locke in Oxford in the year 1658 and that *Mr. Locke was then looked upon as one of the most learned and ingenious young men in the college he was of* . . . But however justly Mr. Locke had at this time acquired the reputation of learning, I have often heard him say, in reference to his first years spent in the University, that he had so small satisfaction there from his studies (as finding very little light brought thereby to his understanding) that he became discontented with his manner of life, and wished his father had rather designed him for anything else than what he was destined to, apprehending that his no greater progress in knowledge proceeded from his not being fitted or capacitated to be a scholar. This discouragement (he said) kept him from being any very hard student, and put [him] upon seeking the company of pleasant and witty men, with whom [he] likewise took great delight in corresponding by letters . . .
>
> Whatever esteem was had of Mr. Locke for his learning when Mr. Tyrrell first knew him, I have understood from the same gentleman that [he] gained it not by disputation, a thing then much in vogue in the university, for he says that *Mr. Locke never loved the trade of disputing in public in the schools but was always wont to declaim against it as being rather invented for wrangling or ostentation than to discover truth.*

This James Tyrrell who was Lady Masham's informant was one of Locke's life-long friends. He was the son of Sir Timothy Tyrrell, baronet, of Oakley, near Oxford, and grandson of Archbishop Ussher. He seems to have inherited from his illustrious grandfather both a literary flair and an interest in the principles of statecraft. Tyrrell was the author of *Patriarcha non Monarcha* (1681), *Bibliotheca Politica* (1691), *A Brief Disquisition on the Laws of Nature* (1692), none of which caused much stir, and *A History of England*, which brought him fame in the last years of his life. He constantly urged Locke to concentrate on similar studies, and at least on one occasion

[1] Amsterdam: Remonstrants' MSS. J. 27a (Lady Masham's italics).

collaborated with him in writing a paper. But despite their enduring friendship, Locke regarded Tyrrell with a certain suspicion. However, there is no reason to doubt his word. Locke himself told Jean le Clerc [1] that he had been taught nothing at Oxford but the peripatetic philosophy and complained of its futility.

Yet even while he was still an undergraduate—even earlier, that is, than 1658—Locke discovered there was something in Oxford besides the peripatetic philosophy. Science had arrived, arrived under the auspices of John Wilkins, Cromwell's brother-in-law and intruded Warden of Wadham. Wilkins was a muscular man with no great liking for books, but with a passion for scientific experiments unmatched in any man since Bacon. It was Wilkins who first held weekly in Oxford 'an experimental philosophical club which began [in] 1649 and was the *incunabula* of the Royal Society'.[2]

In seventeenth century Oxford there was no such creature as a 'science don'. The only scholars who might have been scientists in their field were the medical men, but they were content to teach their subject as a branch of polite learning and philosophy. The curriculum for medical degrees was still made up of Aristotle and Galen, the aphorisms of Hippocrates and parts of the Canon of Avicenna, with, at best, a little botany and herbals added. A student who wanted the answer to a problem in, say, physiology would be referred to the classical texts. The authority for those texts was based on no one's known observations. It was taken for granted that the classical texts must be true because they were classical.

But already there were men who believed that the way to find out how the human body worked was to cut one open and see. All the then new knowledge which related to medicine, the discoveries of Vesalius, Harvey, Gilbert, Paracelsus and Helmont, had been derived from observation as well as from reading. Even in Oxford, where the reigning medical faculty was still tied to books, there were a few doctors who took up the empirical method, and such men were Warden Wilkins's most willing allies. They included the Warden of Merton, Jonathan Goddard, Cromwell's personal physician, who was content to be the general 'drudge' of the Oxford experimental club; [3] William Petty, Vice-Principal of Brasenose; Thomas Willis, author of *Cerebri Anatome* (with illustrations by Wren [4]), and Willis's

---

[1] *Éloge*, p. ix.   [2] Aubrey, p. 309.   [3] *Ibid.*, p. 234.
[4] Christopher Wren was born in 1632, the same year as Locke, but had already left Westminster School before his contemporary went there. Wren went up to

best pupil, Richard Lower. Lower made a number of important discoveries about the heart and he was the first man to effect a blood transfusion.[1] He was also Locke's friend; he had been his friend since they were boys at Westminster together. It was Lower who brought Locke to the study of medicine,[2] and introduced him to experimental philosophy.

When he looked back on the troubled history of his country, Locke saw two particularly potent sources of human error. One was unreflective adhesion to tradition: the fault especially of Royalists in political and social life and of philosophers in academic life; the other was 'enthusiasm' or the reliance on emotional conviction as a basis of truth, the fault especially of Puritans and dissenters. Reacting against both these attitudes, Locke embraced science gratefully: for here, instead of tradition, experience was the guide; and the constant appeal to reason precluded the dangers of 'enthusiasm'. Locke's links, as a mere Bachelor of Arts, with the leading *virtuosi* at Wadham College were slight, and although he did later become one of their number, he was never to achieve much as a practical scientist. What exercised his mind most fruitfully was not the experiments themselves as such but rather the principles on which those experiments were based. Locke's mission was to investigate the foundations of empirical knowledge; and already in the middle 1650's he was groping towards the problems

---

Wadham in 1649, and he became a Fellow of All Souls in 1653. He remained there, continuing his scientific studies until 1657, when, at the age of twenty-five, he succeeded another member of the Wadham circle as Professor of Astronomy at Gresham's College, London. He returned to Oxford as Savilian Professor of Geometry in 1661.

[1] H. M. Sinclair and A. T. H. Robb-Smith, *History of the Teaching of Anatomy in Oxford*, Oxford, 1950, p. 14.

[2] Lower is the acknowledged source of a large proportion of the entries in a medical notebook which Locke kept from 1652 onwards (B.L. MSS. Locke, c. 4). It is a vellum-covered book of 156 numbered pages. The date '52 is inside the front cover; and the first page has the words '*Farrago*. John Locke: Agnes Locke'. Among other things the book contains remedies for all kinds of illness and diseases; excerpts from medical textbooks, and a section in Latin headed 'L' (for 'Lower'?). A later medical notebook is also in the Lovelace collection (B.L. MSS. Locke, f. 19). Locke used it first at Pensford in 1659. Most of the entries are recipes for medicines, and many are in Latin. Again, the name of the person who contributed the recipe is appended. Dr. Ivie, the Lockes' family doctor in Somerset, appears together with the Oxford names.

which were to be the subject of his masterpiece, the *Essay Concerning Human Understanding*.

But if Locke at the age of twenty-four was already an empiricist in bud, he was certainly as yet no liberal. He might well have been; for in his own college at Oxford, in sermons delivered from the pulpit of Christ Church Cathedral, the Dean, John Owen, was almost daily propounding a political philosophy which strikes the modern reader as being in many ways 'Lockean'.[1] Owen was one of the first men to advocate toleration in a disinterested way. Though he once said that he never knew anyone 'contend earnestly for a toleration of dissenters who was not one himself',[2] Owen did so contend. He was of Cromwell's Independent sect, and had nothing to gain from the toleration of others. He based his case, in the approved Calvinist way, on the Bible, and he claimed that there was no authority in its pages for the belief, which Calvinists shared with Catholics and Anglicans, that heretics should be repressed. Owen maintained that all men should be free to think and worship as they pleased so long as their faith did not lead them to disturb peace and order. The duty of the Government, he said, was to maintain order and not to impose religion.

Locke gave serious thought to Owen's views, but he could not share them. Nearly all dissenters in the seventeenth century England, excluding Roman Catholics, were 'enthusiasts' of one sort or another, and Locke thought most of them too dangerous to be suffered. The measure of his intolerance of 'enthusiasm' may be judged from his comments on the trials of James Nayler and other dissident Quakers which he witnessed at Westminster Hall in 1656.

In a letter [3] he wrote from Westminster to his father in Pensford, Locke described how he had seen a Quaker's hat rudely knocked off his head, and he remarked, approving of the gesture, that it was 'dangerous for such mad folks' to keep their heads too hot. A little later Locke sent his father an eye-witness account of the judicial examination of the chief prisoner.

Nayler was a retired cavalry quartermaster with a facial resemblance to popular portraits of Christ. After working for some time as a roving evangelist for George Fox, he had proclaimed himself the

[1] *Vide* F.B., I, pp. 72–9 and *Occidente*, IX, 6, Turin, 1953: *Le origine dell'idea della tolleranza religiosa nel Locke*, by Ernesto de Marchi.
[2] William Orme: *Memoirs of the Life, Writings, and Religious Connections of John Owen, D.D.*, 1826, p. 43.
[3] 25 October 1656 (B.L. MSS. Locke, c. 24, f. 169–70).

Son of God. Many believed him, and he was led on a horse from
Exeter to Bristol by women shouting 'Holy, holy, holy!' and
'Hosanna'. The Western counties, having produced an impover-
ished proletariat sooner than other parts of England, were particularly fertile ground in the seventeenth century for both political
and religious agitators. At Bristol Nayler was arrested, and sent to
London for trial. His disciples followed him. Locke wrote the
following account of what he saw at Westminster Hall: [1]

> . . . I went to the room by the painted chamber, whither the committee
> ordered them to retire, where I found Nayler, one man more, and three
> or four women of the tribe, all with white gloves and the women's
> heads in white bags. Their carriage was strange to me. One of the
> women made a continued humming noise larger than the reach of an
> ordinary breath without [any] motion either of lips or breath that I
> who stood next [to] her could perceive. She ceasing, another sung
> 'Holy, Holy, Holy' with the addition of some other words; then the
> other, her song being done, gave some of their ordinary exhortation
> with their common mixture of judgement and threatening, and after
> a little pause they went over the same round without answering any
> questions which by the standers-by were proposed; and those which by
> the committee were urged, I observed they either not answered or did
> it with a great deal of subtlety besides the cover and cunning of their
> language, which others and I believe they themselves scarce understand.
> But I am weary of the Quakers. . . .[2]

Locke was weary just then of more than the Quakers. In a letter [3]
to a correspondent identified only as the 'prime statesman' of Pensford,[4] he described himself as a madman in a mad country (this
'great Bedlam England'), but as a stoic notwithstanding, a man,
warm in his affections to his friends, yet indifferent to the world.
He longed, he confessed, for a 'pilot' in life.

The weather that winter was unusually severe; and Locke protested to one friend that he was so cold in Oxford 'that I have
almost forgot what it is to be warm".[5] The spring brought warmer

---

[1] 15 November 1656 (B.L. MSS. Locke, c. 24, f. 171).
[2] After the trial Nayler was savagely punished for blasphemy and fraud.
[3] 8 November 1656 (*ibid.*, f. 14).
[4] Possibly Thomas Grenfield, rector of Combe St. Nicholas, Somerset, who was
writing about this time from Pensford. His letters to Locke (B.L. MSS. Locke, c. 10,
ff. 54–5) reveal a liveliness of mind which might easily have qualified for the modest
distinction of political pre-eminence in Pensford.
[5] 23 January 1656/7 (*ibid.*, f. 6).

weather but little good news. Oliver Cromwell was offered the title of King of England, but refused, and soon afterwards resigned the Chancellorship of Oxford University. His son who succeeded him as Chancellor dismissed John Owen from the post of Vice-Chancellor and appointed a Presbyterian bigot, Conant, in his place; and the result was a more rigid Puritan rule than anything the University had known before.

On 28 June 1658 Locke qualified as a Master of Arts and was duly elected a Senior Student of Christ Church. The rank was equivalent to that of a Fellow at any other college, but it was not permanent. Locke had yet to determine what career to follow. He found it difficult to do so. In September Oliver Cromwell died, and the condition of the nation thereafter became increasingly uncertain. Locke was only one of many Englishmen who lacked the confidence to plan for the future.

Letters which date from this period betray his uneasiness. Writing to his father in February 1658/9 [1] Locke declared that the whole of mankind was untrustworthy. In another letter [2] he confessed his complete despair of public affairs. He said he was neither frightened by the threats of danger and destruction which were made by one party nor persuaded by the promises of liberty and happiness the other side held out. In fact, he did not rely on anyone; but he added a pious declaration to the effect that he was fortified by a belief in God and in the life to come.

In 1659 a Parliamentary committee removed Owen from the Deanery of Christ Church, and re-installed the fanatical Reynolds; it happened that Locke spent longer than usual in Somerset that year, and when he got back to Oxford he wrote home to Pensford (presumably to his brother) [3] saying: 'We are all Quakers here and there is not a man but thinks he alone hath this light within and all besides stumble in the dark.'

In the same letter Locke wrote bitterly of 'fancy' as 'the great commander of the world' and of 'passion' being everywhere mistaken for reason. 'Truth', he could not help observing, entered people's minds, not by the strength and authority of its own evidence, but by handsome aspects and being composed to suit men's

[1] 6 February 1658/9 (B.L. MSS. Locke, c. 24, f. 172).

[2] 22 June 1659 (*ibid.*, f. 173).

[3] 20 October 1659 (*ibid.*, f. 182). The letter begins 'Dear Tom', and though subscribed 'your cordial friend J. L.' it was more likely than not addressed to Locke's brother Thomas.

affections. Man's knowledge was nothing but opinion moulded up between custom and interest: 'Since it is not agreed where and what reason is, let us content ourselves with the most beautiful and useful opinions.'

However, Locke had not lost his sense of humour. He wrote very cheerfully about the same time to Mrs. Sarah Edwards[1] of Westbury, on the occasion of the birth of her son:

> I am sorry you had not the clouts I promised you sooner, since I hear you had lately so much need of 'em. But who could guess that you would be so soon brought to bed with a youngster. . . . God give you joy on't; 'tis a chopping boy, God bless it, and though its looseness may sometimes offend the sheets, and it be troubled with the usual infirmity of children, yet age and whipping may mend that.

Locke's practical sense did not desert him either. His brother was now in his twenty-third year, and needed help to become established in a profession. Locke wrote[2] on his behalf to an old Westminster friend, William Godolphin, explaining that his brother was 'yet willing to become a votary for the law at a time when others forsake her', and asking Godolphin, who, though a Royalist agent, was a man of power, to take him under his wing. After some delay, Godolphin replied[3] in encouraging terms. Locke had no reason to suspect that his brother was soon to die.

Some time in 1659 Locke accepted an opportunity to set forth his opinions on the subject of toleration. He sent them to Henry Stubbe,[4] who had expressed views very similar to those of John Owen in a pamphlet entitled *An Essay in Defence of the Good Old Cause; or a Discourse Concerning the Rise and Extent of the Power of the Civil Magistrate in Reference to Spiritual Affairs.* Stubbe's pamphlet was both a history of toleration and a plea for its extension.

---

[1] B.L. MSS. Locke, c. 24, f. 39.

[2] *Ibid.*, f. 49. The draft is inscribed 'G. W.', which letters being reversed make 'W. G.', and thus afford the first clue to the identity of this correspondent.

[3] Writing to Locke on 7 July 1659 (*ibid.*, c. 10, f. 17) Godolphin said: 'I fear to tell you why I have delayed thus long the rendering you an account of the business you desired of me in your brother's behalf, which I desire you would not think to be for want of industry therein, but through my inconstant resolutions of seeing you. . . . On Monday . . . I hope, yet doubt of finding you; and then I shall supply the defects which great haste makes me guilty of at present'.

[4] *Ibid.*, c. 27, f. 12. The draft is inscribed 'S. H.' The reversal of these initials and certain internal evidence points to Henry Stubbe. Wood has a short biography of this remarkable writer. (*Ath. Oxon.* III, cols. 1067–83.)

The first paragraphs of Locke's letter were appreciative:

> The same messenger that carried my letter the last week to Bristol returned with your book, which I have read with very much satisfaction, and the only pauses I made in my hasty perusal were to reflect with admiration [on] the strength and vigour of your style . . . [the] many poignant passages of wit and sharp sallies, and that reason and plenty of matter wherewith every page is stuffed. . . .
>
> To this I must add that I am sorry you continued not your history of toleration down to these times and given us an account of Holland, France, Poland, etc., since nearest examples have the greatest influence, and we are most easily persuaded to tread in those fresh steps which time hath least defaced; and men will travel in that road which is most beaten, though carriers only be their guide. . . .
>
> If daily experience will demonstrate that men of different professions may quickly unite under the same government, and unanimously carry the same civil interest and hand in hand march to the same end of peace and mutual society though they have taken different ways towards heaven, you will add no small conviction to your cause and be very convincing to those to whom what you have already said hath left nothing to doubt but whether it be now practicable.

This, indeed, was the point. Locke himself thought that Stubbe's policy of toleration was *not* practicable. He went on to express the strongest disagreement with Stubbe's proposal to extend freedom to Catholics:

> The only scruple I have is how the liberty you grant the Papists can consist with the security of the nation (the end of government), since I cannot see how they can at the same time obey two different authorities carrying a contrary interest, especially when that which is destructive to ours is backed with an opinion of infallibility and holiness.

Locke's attitude to the question of toleration was still, in 1659, extremely cautious. He had some sympathy for Stubbe as he had for Owen, but he thought their ideals were dangerous. He was still afraid of anarchy.

The end of 1659 brought Monk to the centre of the national drama. The General had called his convention in Scotland, his army was preparing to march into England, and his mind was made up for the restoration of the Stuart King. There were threats of resistance to Monk, but the days of the Puritan republic were obviously numbered. Locke wrote to his father in December,[1] urging prudence. He said that he had thought of taking up arms himself, but he did not know on which side to fight. Moreover, he continued: 'Arms are the last and worst of refuges and in the great history of this shattered and giddy nation . . . wars have produced nothing but wars, and the sword cut out work [only] for the sword.'

He begged his father not to venture his rest, health and estate for ungrateful men on either side of the struggle; the present, he noticed sorrowfully, was 'a time when few men enjoy the privilege of being sober'. Wisdom lay, Locke thought, in keeping clear of politics, and doing nothing.

[1] B.L. MSS. Locke, c. 24, f. 175.

Chapter Four

SENTIMENTAL FRIENDSHIPS

THE traditional picture of Locke is of a man unaffected by the more tender emotions. The truth is quite otherwise.

A large number of the notes and drafts of letters which date from his early years at Oxford was designed to pay court to women. On none of these does the name of the intended recipient appear. Some are inscribed 'P. E.'; others 'E. A.' Some are headed 'Madam'; on a few the salutation 'Madam' is scrawled out and 'Sir' written over it.

The identity of 'P. E.' is one of the mysteries of Locke's biography, but there can be hardly any doubt about 'E. A.' First, in view of Locke's trick of reversing initials one must transpose 'E. A.' to 'A. E.'; secondly, a letter to Locke signed 'Anne Evelegh' reads sufficiently like a reply to one of Locke's drafts inscribed 'E. A.' to point to the conclusion that 'E. A.' was she.

Anne Evelegh was probably one of the daughters, but possibly a niece, of John Evelegh, who lived at Black Hall, St. Giles', Oxford. The present house of this name was erected in the seventeenth century, and there had been a farmhouse on the site since the Middle Ages.[1] Black Hall is mentioned several times in Locke's Oxford correspondence, together with gallant references to the ladies there. The Eveleghs were a Devon family. John Evelegh was a clergyman, and the son of a former Principal of Hart Hall, Oxford; he had at least one son and two daughters.

If 'E. A.' was Anne Evelegh, was not 'P. E.' Anne's sister? Had the initials appeared as 'E. P.', that hypothesis would be almost irresistible. But because Locke reversed initials, the 'P' and not the 'E' more probably represents the surname. There is yet another possibility: 'P. E.' may be another code sign for one and the same name. *Both* 'E. A.' and 'P. E.' may stand for 'Anne Evelegh', but I think this improbable.

[1] Herbert Hurst, *Oxford Topography*, Oxford, 1899, p. 113.

One thing which is suggested by the letters themselves is that Locke's courtship was not rewarded as he hoped. 'P. E.' welcomed love, but of a different sort from that which Locke offered her. She wanted a rarefied spiritual love. Locke was more ardent. He protested first with sadness and later with bitterness that her love was too cold.

In an early draft letter [1] Locke thanked his correspondent for a favour which choice and chance had waited to bestow on him. He said he was perfectly happy to be her friend, though originally made so by a lottery. The fact that his name had been written and worn by her raised him above the ambition of princes. In another draft [2] Locke thanked 'P. E.' for a letter in which she had called him invincible and unconquerable. He said it was the assurance of her friendship which enabled him to bear her railleries and challenges.

On another occasion Locke wrote [3] to her from the country, where his stay, he told her, had by no means civilised him, as she had thought it would. He referred to Black Hall as Elysium. Writing again from the same place, Locke thanked his friend for two letters full of beauty and perfection, which, he said, had rescued him from his melancholy state of mind and made him happy. He called Black Hall a Parnassus in which at least two Muses dwelt.[4] In another letter [5] he assured 'P. E.' that she was right in thinking he wished to come back to Oxford for the sake of people there; but he said she was wrong in putting her name after that of another person. However, he asked her to increase as much as she could that other person's friendship for him. This other person was named in the letter as 'Mr. T.' and Locke was a little jealous of him. He told 'P. E.' he could not believe that the new friendship between her and 'Mr. T.' would ruin their own friendship; but it looks as if he was afraid that it might.

'Mr. T.' was probably Gabriel Towerson, an exhibitioner of the Queen's College and a regular visitor at Black Hall.

A lovers' quarrel did disrupt the harmony between Locke and 'P. E.', but it was a short one. Soon afterwards Locke wrote thus to his 'Dearest Cousin': [6] 'All's well; the quarrel's ended and we are friends again, and I think it is very hard for us long to be enemies.'

[1] B.L. MSS. Locke, c. 24, f. 208.   [2] *Ibid.*, f. 209.
[3] *Ibid.*, f. 211.   [4] *Ibid.*, f. 210.
[5] *Ibid.*, f. 212.   [6] *Ibid.*, f. 220.

At the same time he said:

> I pray tell me too whether yours be true love or no (for our old philosophers say that love is a fire and a flame full of heat and warmth). If it be, certainly 'tis the coldest that ever was; for I dare say if one were covered all over with this sort of love, 'twould scarce make one warm.

In a draft[1] letter to an unnamed person Locke told his correspondent that it had been her privilege to captivate at a distance and to have taken a heart that supposed itself well fortified:

> You cannot loose again what you have once made yours. Absence (the great destroyer of others' love) that could not hinder, will not be able to impair mine; nor will time ever be able to blot out that bright idea I have of you in my heart.

A letter to 'P. E.', dated 4 June 1659,[2] was accompanied by a book—*Cléopâtre*, the French romance by La Calprenède which Richard Loveday had lately translated into English. This is interesting in view of a report by Joseph Spence in his *Anecdotes* [3] that Locke 'spent a good part of his first years at the University in reading romances'. Locke sent no comment on *Cléopâtre* in his letter to 'P. E.'; he said he would not allow his 'pen to expatiate' because his friend had made him realise 'I am not to procure any satisfaction at the expense of your time or patience.'

The same note of frustration recurs in a later draft: [4] 'It cannot with reason be thought that I should send . . . a love letter to a Platonic.'

However Locke had to confess that it was difficult for him *not* to speak in terms of extraordinary emotion:

> This (Madam) is not the least of those mischiefs you do me in robbing me of the use of my reason, which possibly would dictate other things . . . the retreat you have made from hence shall not be able to save you from my persecution, nor guard you from my revenge.

---

[1] B.L. MSS. Locke, c. 24, f. 13. [2] *Ibid.*, f. 8.
[3] Ed. S. W. Singer, 1820, p. 107. Locke's correspondence shows that Madeleine de Scudéry's *Le Grand Cyrus* and Francis Osborne's *Remedies of Love* were also read at Black Hall.
[4] B.L. MSS. Locke, c. 24, f. 11.

E

On one occasion,[1] Locke assured her, albeit without much conviction:

> . . . I think it not at all derogating from your merit and perfection that you have not a mind to engage in that passion which cost Cleopatra so many sighs and so many misfortunes; and that you content yourself with a love more refined (and, as it is called Platonic) and seated above those storms . . .

In another letter,[2] this time to an anonymous woman, he spoke of the power she had over him, and he thanked her for a letter which had given him a mixed feeling of hope, fear, joy, sorrow and envy. On a more mundane level, he mentioned contributions towards a dinner-party—salmon, cyder, wine, lobsters, birds and pastry—at which Mr. and Mrs. Pratt, William Uvedale, Gabriel Towerson and his correspondent's brother were to be guests. It is likely that this letter was intended for Anne Evelegh and conceivable that the Mrs. Pratt[3] who is mentioned in it was 'P. E.' One initial would at any rate be right, and it is quite possible that Mrs. Pratt was Anne Evelegh's sister: her very presence at such an intimate Black Hall festivity suggests some close connection with the household; but there is no other evidence for this hypothesis.

The following letter, written from Pensford on September 19[4] was almost certainly intended for Anne Evelegh:

> If the opinion which tells us that everyone has his tutelar angel be true, I am confident that you are mine, seeing that I find that under the protection of your company I am not only the happier but the better, too; and that those evils which assault me in other places dare not approach me while I am near you. 'Tis certain, had I not met you in the world, I had lost my journey into it, and my way in it . . .
>
> By these wanderings of my pen, I fear you will have reason to think that like one in darkness, I have only dreamt you a letter. But if it be a dream, 'tis too true, too troublesome, and [it] will become your goodness to send me day in your next letter and wake me out of it.

---

[1] B.L. MSS. Locke, c. 24, f. 12.

[2] *Ibid.*, f. 215.

[3] There is a reference to the Pratts in a letter to Locke from Gabriel Towerson dated 12 March 1660/1 (*ibid.*, c. 22, f. 5): 'All our friends at Mr. Pratt's are well and some of them have checked me for not writing to you before this'.

[4] *Ibid.*, c. 24, f. 9.

The letter was presumably a reply to the following, which Anne Evelegh wrote to Locke from Black Hall on August 30 1659:[1]

Worthy Sir,

You are not able to imagine with what content and satisfaction I read over your civil and most obliging letter, and to find myself not quite banished [from] your thoughts: nay, and to see I am mistress of the most accomplished person in the universe. I know not what your thoughts are, but I can with a great deal of justice complain that I am robbed of my servant, and your absence is a famine to me. Therefore had I the power of a mistress, I would command you back to Oxford that I might have the pleasure of your sweet society and pleasing company; for permit me to tell you without flattery or a compliment that my thoughts are wholly on you: and to see how a very fortune is to us all here: that on a sudden so much virtue as we all enjoyed in your presence was snatched from us in a moment! But why bewail I my own misfortune, since it is too great a happiness for me to enjoy. . . .

I could wish I had a Romantic pen that I might give you your due in expressing your perfections in a more quick and lively dress. I am sorry to hear that you rode out of your way, and repent with grief that I should be the cause of it, for I assure you that it was my prayers that you might have a happy journey. But I believe there is some mystery in it, in your saying the star of Oxford misled you. I could wish I knew that star which had so taken up your thoughts . . .

I am none of those wits which can speak and write high language when they please. No, you are better acquainted with my dull soul, which hath nothing of ingenuity. But I have a high esteem for you, which shall last eternally; but though you are no soldier, yet you can do more than an army of men, for whom you please you can conquer.

I am sorry to hear of the indisposition of your body. I wish we could prove good physicians, that we might send something that might be restorative.

Good Sir, excuse these rude lines of mine, but I have sent them to make you laugh and to serve for a diversion in the country. Thus with my father's and mother's and sister's respects unto you, who all honour you,

I remain, Your cordial friend,
Anne Evelegh

Another of Locke's rough drafts marked 'E. A.'[2] began: 'That my returns are not so quick as yours is not only owing to an impossibility of sending, but to that ecstasy your excellent letters put me into from which a week's time is but little to recover myself.'

[1] B.L. MSS. Locke, c. 8, f. 78.   [2] *Ibid.*, c. 24, f. 38.

Locke protested that he, as his mistress's servant, should not be clothed in garments which properly belonged to her, and he begged her not to disown all she had so long practised: 'Let us deal ingenuously, and not with compliments disguise truth, which will assure you that if you had a thousand servants and I as many mistresses our love cannot be more'.

In November 1659[1] Anne Evelegh wrote again to Locke in Somerset:

> Most accomplished Sir,
> Those generous expressions and marks of your friendship, which you have with so much zeal lavished away upon me, makes my dull genius at length produce this ill-shaped letter . . .
> You need not fear of any supplanting you, for it is not possible to find one in the universe of more merit than yourself, but I being conscious to myself of my own unworthiness, I may justly fear you are willing to be free from such a mistress. But stay, Sir, I will not part with my happiness at so cheap a rate as to give you your freedom to lose you for ever. For could I once claim that title of being sovereign, my ambition were at the highest pitch and my thought should be at rest and never think of aspiring no further . . .
>
> I am forced to view and review your letter over again, wherein I find such a grandeur of goodness and such sweet and obliging expressions which puts me in an ecstasy and makes me sigh that Somersetshire will outvy Oxford in engrossing so exquisite and so virtuous a soul all to themselves. . . .
> Your faithful friend
Anne Evelegh.
> My father and my mother remember their respects unto you.

This letter might be taken, on a superficial reading, for a reply to Locke's draft letter to 'P. E.' expressing his anxiety lest her new friendship with 'Mr. T.' should have ruined her friendship with him. But Anne Evelegh's second letter proves that the potential rival in her case is not 'Mr. T.', but Mr. Udall.

William Udall, or Uvedale, was a close friend of Gabriel Towerson ('Mr. T.'?); he, too, was of Queen's and often at Black Hall. Possibly while William Uvedale was Anne Evelegh's 'valentine', Gabriel Towerson stood in the same relationship to the other girl.

---

[1] 8 November 1659 (B.L. MSS. Locke, c. 8, f. 79).

For a second time in November 1659 [1] Anne Evelegh wrote to her 'most excellent Mr. Locke':

> You are not able to imagine with what joy I take a pen in hand to present these respects which my heart oweth you, and which you may justly challenge from me. The cause of my troubling you this time is that I have received out of Hampshire from my valentine with the enclosed, wherein he desires me to help make his apologies for his silence.
>
> I . . . am still in hopes that fortune will at last grow weary of persecuting me, and you will return to the comfort and satisfaction of all your friends. . . .

Anne Evelegh and 'P. E.' were not the only young women in whom Locke was interested at the time. During the summer of 1657, when Locke was in Oxford, his friend from Hart Hall, Samuel Tilly, then on a visit to his Somerset home, wrote to protest at Locke's habit of writing in riddles; and on 20 August [2] Tilly asked Locke to elucidate 'those mysterious passages towards the closure of your letter, which if they can but afford satisfaction proportionate to the hopes they have begotten, how acceptable their knowledge will be I must leave you to imagine'. Tilly's letter went on to refer elliptically, on Locke's own model, to a lady in whom he was interested. A week later Tilly wrote [3] to Locke at Oxford saying:

> I expect a comment and behold a text more difficult than the former. . . . [If you please], break through the mist of similes and metaphors so as I may clearly apprehend what return was made to your intended inquiries at those lodgings near Christ Church Westwards. Unless my nomenclature fail, you are mistaken in her name who was partly the subject of your last letter.

Whatever was west of Christ Church it was not St. Giles' and the cultivated ladies of Black Hall, and whatever the basis of Tilly's suspicions there is no mistaking the purport of a letter Locke received on another occasion from one Frank Atkins,[4] who was evidently a steward in a noblewoman's house in Somerset. It was addressed to Locke at Pensford:

> . . . My lady hath commanded me to do a little business for her at Chard upon Tuesday next, and though I am but badly horsed, yet if I may obtain thy company, I shall not want a caroach.[5] I did the more

---

[1] B.L. MSS. Locke, c. 8, f. 81.   [2] *Ibid.*, c. 20, f. 177.
[3] 4 September 1657 (*ibid.*, f. 178).   [4] *Ibid.*, c. 3, f. 55.
[5] A carriage.

greedily fasten on this command because it sorts luckily to my own desires. It may be Cupid may be one of the actors in a comical journey, and to that purpose I have sent already a footboy to my mistress to meet me on Tuesday or Wednesday night at Chard. She is one of thine own sect, and if she errs she doth it out of pure zeal and simplicity of soul. I cannot promise you she's handsome, but this, though I think she has the more scarlet in her cheeks of the two, yet you shall be her judge.

Cloris is just Agrippa-like, almost persuaded to go too; and if your consent be had, certainly there's little doubt to be made of this, notwithstanding the young horse and the cockes eye out, and I know not which eye be coldly and perfunctorily objected. If you dissent, then one sad word will be doom enough. But if otherwise, than I shall desire to meet you at the place near the coalpits, where we last parted when I came from Pensford, about four o'clock in the afternoon. Then we'll have a little love-duel, and Cloris his gravity shall dance a part. Meanwhile love and prosperity are wished thee from.

Thy entire friend
Frank Atkins

Here, at any rate, may be confirmation of something Locke once said to one of his Black Hall correspondents, namely that he found the girls of Somerset more 'warm-hearted' than those of Oxford. Frank Atkins was perhaps the proverbial 'bad companion' of Locke's youth. At all events he appears to have come to a bad end, or at least to have followed a Falstaffian career downhill. The only other letter [1] from him which still exists among Locke's papers was written on an April evening from the Horseshoe Tavern, Covent Garden, London. It was the sort of studiously polite letter which is written by a man who is drunk and knows it:

Sir,
... If you have the luck to receive this paper in such a place and temper as it is written in, I am confident we are agreed, and I may save the labour of further apology. But if it should chance to arrive at such an hour when your severer employments shall superciliate or furrow your then threatening b[r]ow, I hope you will but burn the innocent paper. ...

This so far as Locke was concerned seems to have been the last of Atkins. Locke was not by temperament a voluptuary. Nor did rivalry, whether real or sham, prevent his being on excellent terms

[1] B.L. MSS. Locke, c. 3, f. 59.

with William Uvedale and Gabriel Towerson. Thus, for example, did William Uvedale write to him from the country:[1]

> Lest you should think I have as bad a memory as Mr. Tilly and can forget my friends as soon as he, I have sent this to assure you of the contrary, and withal to tell you that I cannot but think myself very unfortunate in being thus long banished from Christ Church, I mean from you ... I dare not fold up my letter without enclosing in it a very low salutation to those ladies—shall I say goddesses?—at B. H. [i.e. Black Hall] and desiring you to convey it to them.

A draft[2] in Locke's hand inscribed 'U. W.' (*i.e.* 'W. U.') is clearly his reply to this message. Locke told his friend that he was sad in Oxford; even the spring did not cheer him; in fact the only consolation was the company at Black Hall: 'Whatever reason Mr. Tilly's silence may have given me to quarrel with him, I am yet perfectly reconciled with him as often as I consider it is to him that I owe the happiness of your acquaintance.'

In the manuscript the word 'friendship' is written above 'acquaintance', but the original substantive is not crossed out.

In the long vacation of 1659, when Locke was in Somerset, his father urged him to marry a widow of that county; the elder Locke had indeed already broached the subject in a letter[3] he sent his son on 21 May: 'Prepare to be here after the Act where a widow, young, childless, handsome, with £200 per annum and £1,000 in her purse may possibly occasion you to stay here.'

Nothing came of the father's project, but the son was detained in Pensford longer than his Oxford friends thought reasonable.

William Uvedale[4] protested to Locke: ... 'I know 'tis as impossible to recall you from Pensford yet as 'tis to raise a dead man from his grave, I mean unless Scribelia think fit to exercise her power and work miracles.'

Scribelia was one of the 'goddesses'.

Yet another name linked with Locke's at Oxford in the 1660's was that of Mrs. Parry. Gabriel Towerson, writing to Locke on 23 October 1660,[5] said: 'Mrs. Parry is as well as you can wish her, and so very much yours, that nothing but my sex and this secret address can authorise my subscribing myself your most affectionate

---

[1] B.L. MSS. Locke, c. 22, f. 173.   [2] *Ibid.*, c. 24, f. 280.
[3] *Ibid.*, c. 14, f. 167.   [4] *Ibid.*, c. 22, f. 175.
[5] *Ibid.*, c. 22, f. 1.

friend, etc'. Although no letter signed by the name of Parry survives, there is one written to Locke in 1662 [1] by a certain Ellen Price, who introduced herself as one who had often been the bearer of letters from Mrs. Parry to Locke. She informed him that Mrs. Parry had been entertaining a 'servant' named Bricknock who was very much in love with her, and that this Bricknock was very much admired by Mrs. Ringwell, with whom she, Ellen Price, lived. Locke was enjoined to reveal nothing of this to Mrs. Parry.

But who was Mrs. Parry? Locke's Oxford friends included an Irishman named John Parry, who had come to the University in 1651, and had been elected a Fellow of Jesus. His younger brother, Benjamin Parry, had become at the same time a Fellow of Corpus. John Parry resigned his Fellowship in 1660—presumably on his marriage—but although he was made a Prebendary of York and was given at least one Irish living, he continued to spend most of his time in Oxford until 1666, when he was appointed Dean of Christ Church, Dublin, and went to live in Ireland for the rest of his life.

Locke's Mrs. Parry was either John Parry's wife, or, as I think more probable, his sister. He had two sisters,[2] and there is evidence [3] (which I shall print in a later chapter) of a sentimental friendship between Locke and one of those sisters. 'Parry' once more recalls the initials 'P. E.'

[1] 21 October 1662 (B.L. MSS. Locke, c. 18, f. 7).
[2] *Vide ibid.*, c. 24, f. 221.
[3] *The Oxford Gazette.* 13 February 1665/6 (*ibid.*, c. 8, f. 62).

Chapter Five

EARLY POLITICS

'I STOOD in the Strand and beheld it', wrote Evelyn, 'and blessed God.'

To Locke also, as indeed to almost every Englishman, the return of Charles II to London and his father's throne was an occasion for rejoicing. Locke had put all the doubts of the past behind him; in 1660 he was a whole-hearted monarchist.

News of the events which preceded the Restoration reached him at Oxford from William Carr,[1] a Christ Church friend who had gone to Gray's Inn to read for the Bar and was for that reason in London during the early months of 1660. On 3 February, Carr wrote [2] to report:

> :.. Yesterday there was a very high mutiny among the common soldiers, diverse commanders being wounded and a lieutenant killed, but their mouths being stopped with money, they are for a time appeased. This day Monk came into London with his whole army—the best foot and the worst horse that ever was seen, and before every regiment there went two men playing on bagpipes. At this time there be several hundreds of Worcestershire men with Monk who declare for a free Parliament. . . .

At this point the letter broke off. For William Carr, too, had his less serious side; and pleasure importuned.

'Peg Brook', he explained, 'will let me write no longer.'

Hungry for news at a time when the destiny of England was in the balance, Locke wrote [3] back impatiently: 'Is there never an Order of Ladies about London whose business it is to excuse total silence as well as half letters?'

[1] William Carr was a man of Kent who matriculated at Christ Church in 1656 and was later a Fellow of All Souls. He had family links with Somerset and his sister Anne married Edward Popham, brother of Alexander Popham.
[2] B.L. MSS. Locke, c. 5, f. 9. (The letter is undated.)
[3] Ibid., c. 24, f. 27.

When Carr apologised once more for his silence, he drew from Locke another rebuke:[1]

> Your excuse is worse than your fault. . . . But what a true occasion would you give me of sorrow should this prove [to be] nothing but a Westminster disease, such as I have borne trouble with when I went to school there, which was then . . . according to the vulgar, called sloth!

In March Locke decided to go to London and see for himself what was happening. He did not stay long enough to witness the meeting of the Parliamentary Convention which issued the invitation to Charles to return, and he was not then well enough connected to know (though Alexander Popham could perhaps have told him) about the negotiations which prompted Monk to make that invitation unconditional. Locke was far away at Pensford on that day in May when the King was welcomed home.

The festive spirit of London was, however, reflected in a letter Locke had from a friend named Thomas Westron:[2]

> Dear John,
> I received your letter just as I came to town from Barnet, where I have scoured myself as a man should scour a gun. What I poured in at one end I squirted out at the other; but how clean I am, I know not, having yet cause to complain . . .

Such Falstaffian gusto may remind the reader of the letters of Frank Atkins. Indeed, Thomas Westron appears to have come to much the same end. His second and last surviving letter[3] to Locke begins:

> Honest John,
> . . . Would I had you here to see in what melancholy posture I now sit. Pity would persuade [you] to stay and be my comforter . . .

In the month of Charles's Restoration Locke's two friends and rivals at Black Hall, William Uvedale and Gabriel Towerson, were both elected Fellows of All Souls. Subsequently Uvedale inherited a fortune and retired to enjoy it; Towerson took orders and became, in time, an author. Towerson also encouraged Locke to write, and discussed the subjects of his earliest literary papers with him. Two of those subjects were Toleration and the Law of Nature.

[1] B.L. MSS. Locke, c. 24, f. 29. [2] *Ibid.*, c. 23, f. 73.
[3] 30 July 1660 (*ibid.*, f. 74).

Locke's early essays on the Law of Nature were not published until 1954, and his early essays on Toleration have yet to appear in print. They would, if they were published, astonish those who know Locke only for his mature views on Toleration and are familiar only with the story of his intellectual development put forward by previous biographers.

Both King [1] and Fox Bourne [2] realised that Locke had welcomed the Restoration; both published his comment [3] on it:

> I find that a general freedom is but a general bondage, that the popular asserters of public liberty are the greatest ingrossers of it too. . . . All the freedom I can wish my country or myself is to enjoy the protection of those laws which the prudence and providence of our ancestors established and the happy return of his Majesty has restored.

Nevertheless, in spite of the monarchist sentiments these words betray, Fox Bourne believed that Locke was a liberal in 1660 no less than in 1688. This notion 'that Locke had already arrived at conclusions in political science from which he never greatly swerved',[4] Fox Bourne derived from an essay entitled 'Reflections on the Roman Commonwealth' which is preserved among the Shaftesbury Papers in the Public Record Office. Fox Bourne thought Locke had written it in 1661. The views expressed in that document are assuredly liberal views; but Locke did not write it in 1661 or at any other time. The true author, whose identity was established as long ago as 1914, was Walter Moyle,[5] but the myth of Locke's perpetual liberalism survived this disclosure,[6] because no Locke scholar before Dr. von Leyden [7] realised its significance.

Locke first set forth his views on toleration in the form of a reply (which Fox Bourne never saw) to a pamphlet called *The Great Question Concerning Things Indifferent in Religious Worship*.[8] The pamphlet was unsigned, but both Locke and Towerson knew it had been written by a Student of Christ Church named Edward Bagshawe, junior. Already at the age of thirty-one, this Edward

---

[1] King, I, pp. 14–15. [2] F.B., I, pp. 154–5.
[3] B.L. MSS. Locke, c. 28 f. 2a and f. 2a *verso*.
[4] F.B., I, p. 147. [5] *Vide* his *Works* (1726), I.
[6] It was made by H. F. Russell Smith (*Harrington and His Oceana*, Cambridge, 1914, pp. 139, 143, 217, 218). [7] W. von Leyden, p. 22.
[8] Locke's own copy of this is preserved in the Bodleian Library (MSS. Locke, e. 5).

Bagshawe enjoyed a certain renown as a militant, if also an eccentric controversialist;[1] but *The Great Question* was not in the least bizarre. It was a reasonable presentation of the case for religious toleration, and its conclusions differed little from those of Owen and Stubbe. Bagshawe argued that the state (or 'civil magistrate') had a right to enforce whatever God commanded; but in matters where the commands of God were not specific, in matters 'indifferent', the civil magistrate should leave men alone to follow their own lights.

Locke, in his reply[2] to Bagshawe, maintained that the 'magistrate of every nation, what way so ever created, *must necessarily have an absolute and arbitrary power over all the indifferent actions of his people*'.[3] He wrote:

> I have chosen to draw a great part of my discourse from the supposition of the magistrate's power derived from, or conveyed to him by, the consent of the people, as a way [of argument] best suited to those patrons of liberty and most like to obviate their objections, the foundation of their plea being usually an opinion of their natural freedom, which they are apt to think too much entrenched upon by impositions in indifferent things. Not that I intend to meddle with that question whether the magistrate's crown drops down on his head immediately from heaven or be placed there by the hands of his subjects, it being sufficient to my purpose that the supreme magistrate of every nation, what way so ever created, must necessarily have an absolute and arbitrary power over all the indifferent actions of his people. . . . I think it will clearly follow that if he receive his commission immediately from God the people will have little reason thereupon to think it more confined than if he received it from them until they can produce the charter of their own liberty, or the limitation of the legislator's authority, from this same God that gave it. Otherwise no doubt, those indifferent things that God does not forbid or command, his vice-gerent may, having no other rule to direct his command than every person has for his own actions, viz., the law of God. And it will be granted that the people have but a poor pretence of liberty in indifferent things in a condition wherein they have no liberty at all, but by appointment of the great Sovereign of heaven and earth are born subjects to the will and pleasure of another.

---

[1] As a Christ Church undergraduate he had led a campaign for the abolition of academic dress, and was notoriously disrespectful to the then Vice-Chancellor. Later as Under-Master of Westminster School, he had quarrelled with Dr. Busby and afterwards sought public sympathy by printing an account of their dispute.

[2] B.L. MSS. Locke, e. 7, f. 35.   [3] My italics.

In the spring of 1661, Towerson [1] wrote to Locke:

> Mr. Bagshawe's book is so well liked . . . that it is probable it may
> pass a second impression; and you may perhaps do God and the Church
> a . . . seasonable service if you . . . print your answer to it.

Samuel Tilly [2] also pressed Locke to print the paper he had written
against an 'adversary'.

Thus urged by his friends, Locke prepared his treatise for publication, adding (probably in May 1661) a preface to explain that his
discourse had been written 'many months since' and not originally
for publication. He went on to say of its theme of freedom and
authority: [3]

> As for myself, there is no one can have a greater respect and venera-
> tion for authority than I. I no sooner perceived myself in the world but
> I found myself in a storm which has lasted almost hitherto, and there-
> fore cannot but entertain the approaches of a calm with the greatest
> joy and satisfaction; and this methinks obliges me both in duty and
> gratitude . . . to endeavour the continuance [of such a blessing] by
> disposing men's minds to obedience to that government which has
> brought with it the quiet and settlement which our own giddy folly
> had put beyond the reach not only of our contrivance but hopes.

Locke had once assured Towerson that 'my thoughts owe their
original to you'. *Some* of Locke's thoughts on the question of toleration, and possibly even more of his thoughts on the Law of Nature
may well have owed their original to Towerson, but rather more
of the thoughts Locke expressed in his answer to Bagshawe owed
their original to a source he did not acknowledge, namely Thomas
Hobbes's *Leviathan*. That anti-liberal masterpiece, published in-
opportunely in 1651, propounded the view that *any* government was
better than no government, and that men ought therefore, if only
on prudential grounds, to obey whoever ruled them. Hobbes held
that commonwealths or civil societies had been called into being
because men had found life in a state of nature intolerable. He
wrote in a celebrated passage:

> In such a condition there is no place for industry because the fruit
> thereof is uncertain, and consequently no culture of the earth, no

---

[1] B.L. MSS. Locke, c. 22, f. 5 (12 March 1660/1).
[2] *Ibid.*, c. 20, f. 179 (5 December 1661). A letter from James Allestry to Samuel
Tilly concerning the printing of a treatise and dated 14 May 1661, was also preserved
by Locke (*ibid.*, c. 3, f. 21).   [3] *Ibid.*, c. 28, f. 2a.

navigation nor use of commodities that may be imported by sea, no commodious building, no instruments of moving and removing such things as require much force, no knowledge of the face of the earth; no account of time, no arts, no letters, no society, and, which is worst of all, continual fear and danger of violent death, and the life of man solitary, poor, nasty, brutish and short.[1]

Locke in his answer to Bagshawe also described the horrors of the state of nature:

no peace, no security, no enjoyment, enmity with all men and safe possession of nothing, and those stinging swarms of misery which attend anarchy and rebellion.

It is not a good crib, but it is unmistakably cribbed.

Hobbes maintained that the creation of civil societies entailed the end of freedom, because men surrendered the liberty they enjoyed in a state of nature by the very fact of appointing a sovereign to rule them; and men could not both be ruled and free from rule. His argument reappeared in Locke's little treatise:

Every particular man must part with this right to his primitive liberty and entrust the magistrate with as full a power over all his actions as he himself has, it being otherwise impossible that any one should be subject to the commands of another who retains the free disposure of himself and is the master of an equal liberty.

Hobbes argued that insofar as sovereigns derived their power from the will of the people to be ruled, the particular edicts of sovereigns were the people's own edicts. Locke wrote:

. . . if the supreme authority be conferred on the magistrates by the consent of the people . . . then it is evident that they have resigned up their liberty of action into his disposure so that all his commands are but their own votes, and his edicts their own injunctions made by proxies.

Locke's borrowings from Hobbes were not confined to the treatise he wrote in answer to Bagshawe, but at no time in his life would Locke admit his debt to Hobbes. He even came to pretend he had never read Hobbes properly. Partly, perhaps, this pretence was the repudiation of a former master; it may also have been due to the fact that the word 'Hobbist' came to be a pejorative one

[1] *Leviathan*, chapter XIII.

in all but a very few quarters, and Locke was forever anxious to avoid a bad name.

Locke's second early essay on Toleration was written in Latin and entitled: '*An magistratus civilis possit res adiaphoras in divine cultus ritus asciscere, eosque populo imponere?*' Whereas the English treatise was written as a polemic, this Latin treatise dealt with the question in general terms of principle and contained no reference to Bagshawe's pamphlet. Here again Locke reproduced the Hobbesian argument, first, that the authority of a civil government depends on every subject surrendering his primitive liberty, and secondly that such an exchange of anarchic freedom for the tranquillity of settled order is a necessary condition for the existence of a political society. To this Locke added a religious argument, asserting that because God wills men to live in political societies, He wills them to surrender their primitive freedom and obey their political rulers.

A measure of liberty did indeed remain to the subject according to Locke's doctrine, but it was based, strange to relate (in view of Locke's supposed great hatred of Scholasticism) on a purely scholastic distinction between *obligatio materialis* and *obligatio formalis*. Whenever a magistrate ordered a man to do or not do what God already enjoined or forbade, then a man was *materially* as well as formally obliged to obey, because God as well as the magistrate commanded his obedience; but whenever a magistrate ordered a man to do or not do things 'indifferent' (that is to say, things not commanded or forbidden by God) a subject was only *formally* constrained. He would still have to *do* it, but he would not have to assent to doing it in his heart.

Locke drew a corresponding distinction between active obedience and passive obedience. A subject should always render active obedience to those commands of the magistrate which were also God's commands; to those commands of the magistrate which were not God's commands he need render only passive obedience. Even so, a subject should still *obey*, because a magistrate's authority was sanctioned by God, and whatever the magistrate commanded was for that reason always lawful.

For one reason or another, neither Locke's English treatise nor his Latin treatise on the civil magistrate was published. By the time his answer to Bagshawe was ready for the press, another reply had been published by George Morley, Bishop of Worcester (later of Winchester). What was more important, Bagshawe had been expelled from his Studentship of Christ Church, and expelled, according to Bagshawe's own account,[1] 'for no reason at all that I know of unless for the impartial and unbiassed discovery of my judgment about indifferent, or rather doubtful things in religious worship'. Far from having the success Towerson feared, Bagshawe's premature liberalism soon landed him in prison, and he died on bail from Newgate some few years later.

The second subject Locke and Towerson discussed in the early 1660's was *Lex Naturae* itself. On 5 November 1660[2] Towerson wrote to Locke, who was then at Pensford:

> The papers that have passed between us being now grown so voluminous . . . will you consider but those two things which I have now to propose to you. . . .
> (1) Whether (it being agreed upon between us that there is such a thing as a Law of Nature . . .) it were not much more for our advantage to proceed to our enquiry touching the Law of Nature. . . .
> (2) I would willingly know of you whether you think the being of the Law of Nature can be evinced from the force of conscience in those men who have no other divine law to square their actions by . . .

Locke set himself to answer Towerson's question in a series of manuscripts which are now preserved in the Lovelace Collection,[3] but as the edition of these essays prepared by Dr. Wolfgang von Leyden and published in 1954 includes a lucid and detailed commentary, I shall deal with them summarily. Towerson's thoughts on the subject may also be seen in print: they are set forth in the introduction to his *Explication of the Decalogue*, published in 1676.

The 'Law of Nature' is an expression seldom used in the twentieth century. It is too easily confused with the *laws* of nature which empirical scientists seek, and in itself it is a bewildering concept. The Law of Nature is 'the moral law which the Creator has made evident to and compelling upon every rational being'. It is a notion at least as old as Stoic philosophy. It had an important place in the theory, if not in the practice, of Roman jurisprudence. In medieval Christendom it was identified with the Law of God, and the Church

---

[1] White Kennet, *Register and Chronicle Ecclesiastical and Civil*, 1728, I, p. 603.

[2] B.L. MSS. Locke, c. 22, f. 3. (The letter is not dated '1660' but it is most unlikely that it was written in any other year.)

[3] *Ibid.*, e. 6; F. 30; F. 31.

assumed the duty of upholding it over the heads of temporal rulers. After the Renaissance the concept again figured prominently in the new theories of the State. But the crucial questions remained: Does the Law of Nature exist? Is it evident to every rational being? Is it compelling?

Locke confronted these questions, but he did not answer them satisfactorily. In the first Latin essay he put forward familiar rationalistic arguments in support of his belief that the Law of Nature exists. If (as Locke assumed) God exists and has made laws governing the workings of the universe, God must also have made rules relating to men's conduct. Such rules constituted the Law of Nature. Locke next considered whether men's knowledge of the Law of Nature was innate, traditional or sensory. Tradition, he decided, could not be an *original* source of knowledge. No less emphatically did Locke reject the suggestion that knowledge is innate. He was thus led to conclude that men's knowledge of the Law of Nature must be sensory or empirical. But he also claimed that it was *demonstrable*—demonstrable in the same way and with the same certainty as mathematics. And from the fact of its being in this sense necessary, Locke concluded that the Law of Nature was also compelling.

The curious thing about Locke's argument is that it offers more to defend the view that knowledge is derived from sensory experience than it does to prove the existence of a Law of Nature. As Dr. von Leyden has pointed out:[1]

[Locke] passes from the recognition that man is rational to the assumption that man's reason, on the basis of sense-experience, leads to the discovery of moral truths, nay, if properly employed, to the discovery of one and the same set of moral truths, i.e. natural law. From this he passes to the belief that the truths thus discovered are divine commands binding on all men, and hence to the assertion that the validity of such commands can be proved, and even shown to be necessary in the same way as a geometrical demonstration. The steps in his argument whereby he seeks to explain the existence, the disclosure, the binding force, and the validity of natural law are treated by him on one level, as if they were all concerned with one and the same meaning of rationality, and as if there were no difference in kind between a matter of fact, a way of knowledge, a dogma, and a logical truth.

[1] W. von Leyden, p. 59.

Dr. von Leyden suggests that Locke got himself into this muddle because he was really more interested in empiricism than in the Law of Nature. Some thirty years after he had written these essays, Locke was urged by James Tyrrell to look them out with a view to printing them. Locke had a fair copy made, but he decided not to publish. His decision is not surprising. He had by that time provided in the *Essay Concerning Human Understanding* a much *better* vindication of empiricism than he had had in the Latin essays and, furthermore, he had adumbrated in that *Essay* (notably in his section on *Words*) a critical technique which, once applied to the Law of Nature, would assuredly have shown his case to be untenable.

The literary background against which Locke wrote these papers has been explored by Dr. von Leyden,[1] who shows that Locke was most influenced in his writings on the Law of Nature by the Cambridge Platonist, Nathanael Culverwel,[2] and by two champions of rational Anglican conservatism Richard Hooker[3] and Robert Sanderson.[4] The latter Locke may have met in person. The author of, among other books, *De Obligatione Conscientiae*,[5] Sanderson collaborated in 1661 with James Tyrrell in editing a book written by Tyrrell's grandfather, James Ussher, Archbishop of Armagh, *The Power Communicated by God to the Prince and the Obedience Required of the Subject*. Ussher had written this book at the instigation of Charles I, and its contents fulfil the promise contained in the title. The Law of Nature, being the Law of God, was said by Ussher to justify the absolute authority of monarchs. Sanderson improved on this argument in a preface he contributed to Tyrrell's edition of Ussher's book, where he attacked the liberal notion (which was later to play so large a part in Locke's political philosophy) that governments derive their authority from the consent of the people, and maintained instead that the authority of a ruler is rooted in the Law of Nature and thus ultimately in God, so that obedience to civil rulers is perpetually binding.

Culverwel, on the other hand, had argued[6] that popular consent

---

[1] W. von Leyden, pp. 30 *et seq.*

[2] *Vide* especially his *Elegant and Learned Discourse of the Light of Nature.* (First Edn., 1654. Ed. J. Brown, 1852.)

[3] *Vide* his *Laws of Ecclesiastical Polity.*

[4] Locke also read Pufendorf's *Elementa Jurisprudentiae Universalis*, but the influence of this book on Locke was small compared with that of Pufendorf's later writings.

[5] Published in Latin and English versions in 1660.

[6] *Op. cit.*, chapters 8–10.

gave at any rate a secondary basis for the Law of Nature. Locke, though he followed Culverwel on other points, supported Sanderson in this matter, and, as Dr. von Leyden says, 'he rejected the view that the knowledge of natural law, let alone the binding force of it, can in any way be derived from the general consent of men'.[1]

Locke in 1660 and 1661 was thus a man of the Right, an extreme authoritarian. Within a few years his political views were to be radically changed.

[1] W. von Leyden, p. 42.

Chapter Six

THE OXFORD TUTOR

IN the year of the Restoration, John Locke the lawyer became seriously ill. His son wrote to him from Oxford[1] expressing his concern, but saying he was confident Dr. Meara[2] would find a cure. Such confidence, if it was genuine, is remarkable in view of Dr. Meara's reputation in the Oxford medical circles in which Locke moved. Edmund Meara (or Meary) was an Irishman with a doctor's degree from Rheims and a very successful practice in Bristol; he entered public controversy to deny the truth of Harvey's discovery of the circulation of the blood and of several other new discoveries in physiology. Locke's friend, Richard Lower,[3] called Meara a stupid ignoramus bent on obstructing scientific progress, as indeed he was.

It is hardly surprising that the patient at Pensford grew worse. Locke was summoned to his bedside just at the time when changes were taking place in Oxford as a result of the Restoration. At first the new régime made less difference to the University than many of its members had expected. The Anglican ritual and prayer-book were, of course, restored; surplices and organs came back into use; but there were no great changes of staff. The Puritan policy was not repeated. A Royalist Dean replaced Reynolds at Christ Church, and other headships changed, but fellows and scholars who had arrived as intruders were allowed to remain. Mallet writes:[4]

Of the Royalists who had suffered at the hands of the Parliament, comparatively few were in a position to return. Some had died. Some

---

[1] B.L. MSS. Locke, c. 24, f. 177.

[2] There are two prescriptions in Latin in Locke's handwriting, one inscribed 'Dr. Meara'. They are described as being 'for weakness and decays of the liver' and were probably intended for Locke's father in his last illness (*ibid.*, c. 29, ff. 3 and 4).

[3] Evidence that Locke and Lower were in touch with each other in 1660 is provided by a letter from George Percivall to Locke dated 19 December 1660 (*ibid.*, c. 17, f. 61). George Percivall, a Christ Church man, had gone to Dublin that year to study medicine. [4] Mallet, II, p. 414.

had married. Some had joined the Roman church or passed on to other callings. . . . There was no need, and there would have been no justification, for such sweeping changes as were made twelve years before. The University as a whole was perfectly ready to submit to the authority of the King.

So the friends who wrote to Locke from Oxford had little to report. 'Really', Towerson protested in October, 'the winter is a time of as little action in the University as it is in the campaign. . . .'

One event of personal importance to Locke did, however, happen in the University that winter. On Christmas Eve Christ Church elected him Lecturer in Greek. It was an event which marked the beginning of his career as a University teacher. Having returned to Oxford in time for the election, Locke wrote to Pensford on 20 December 1660:[1]

Most dear and ever-loving father,

I did not doubt that noise of a very dangerous sickness here[2] would reach you, but I am alarmed with a more dangerous disease from Pensford, and were I as secure of your health as (I thank God) I am of my own, I should not think myself in much danger; but I cannot be safe so long as I hear of your weakness and that increase of your malady upon you, which I beg that you would, by the timely application of remedies, endeavour to remove. Dr. Meara has more than once put a stop to its encroachment. The same skill, the same means, the same God to bless them, is left still. Do not, I beseech you, by that care you ought to have of yourself, by that tenderness I'm sure you have of us,[3] neglect your own and our safety, too; do not by too pressing a care for your children, endanger the only comfort they have left. . . .

Pray, sir, therefore make your life as lasting and comfortable as you can; let not any consideration of us cast you into the least despondency. If I have any reflections on, or desires of, free and competent subsistence, it is more in reference to another (whom you may guess[4]), to whom I am very obliged, than for myself. But no thoughts, how important soever, shall make me forget my duty, and a father is more than all other relations; and the greatest satisfaction I can propose to myself in this world is my hope that you may yet live to receive the return of some comfort for all the care and indulgence you have placed in

Sir,

Your most obedient son, J. L.

---

[1] B.L. MSS. Locke, c. 24, f. 179.
[2] There was a minor epidemic of small-pox in Oxford.
[3] i.e. of Locke and his brother Thomas.
[4] These words seem to suggest that Locke was contemplating marriage.

After Christmas, Locke went again to Pensford. Once at home he wrote[1] to another physician, Dr. Ivie, asking him to come and see his father, who was feverish and very weak. A month later, on 13 February 1660/1, the patient died at the age of fifty-four.

In his will, Locke's father left his elder son some land and a few cottages in the neighbourhood of Pensford. The estate brought Locke a fair income for the rest of his life. His uncle, Peter Locke of Bishop Sutton, acted for many years as his agent, collecting rents and managing the property. Locke was often agitated by some failure or delay in the receipt of his rents. He was not the most patient of landlords, and he had always a sharp eye on his money.

After his father's funeral, he returned to Oxford to take up his duties as a tutor. Christ Church was still the leading college in the University, and the new Dean was the outstanding personality among the Heads of Houses. John Fell was the son of the Samuel Fell who had been Dean in the time of Charles I. He was a conservative Royalist, imperious, high-handed, ambitious; but he worked wonders for his College. Mallet says:[2]

> He was determined that even the young bloods of the House should work. He would visit them in their rooms and examine them in their studies . . . As Vice-Chancellor he did his best to restore discipline and learning. He revised the rules for caps and hoods and gowns and sleeves . . . He revived the attendance at lectures and disputations. He would often be present at examinations. He would, if necessary, intervene to conduct an examination himself. He stopped the practice of coursing and the tumults which it led to. He disliked to see St. Mary's [Church] given up to business, and had no small share in the foundation of the [Sheldonian] Theatre. . . .

In Christ Church itself John Fell attended to the completion of the buildings. Money flowed in. Christ Church men were often rich, and subscriptions given for College plate the Dean spent on the fabric. Christopher Wren, who had turned from science to architecture and designed the Sheldonian Theatre, was called in to help. By July 1662, Wood[3] was able to report that the north side of the great quadrangle[4] was completed. Mallet writes:[5]

---

[1] B.L. MSS. Locke, c. 24, f. 58 (8 January 1660/1).
[2] Mallet, II, p. 427.   [3] *L. and T.*, I, p. 445.
[4] In 1680, if not earlier, Locke's rooms were in a smaller quadrangle: *vide* a list 'of Mr. Locke's things found in his study in Canterbury quadrangle, December 1680 and removed by Mr. Walls' (B.L. MSS. Locke, c. 25, f. 30).
[5] Mallet, II, p. 56.

Over Kill-Canon, the archway in the north-east corner [of the great quadrangle] Fell planned to make an observatory tower. Wolsey's parapet was replaced by an Italian balustrade, destined to give place again to battlements later. A broad terrace was raised on steps against the walls. A great stone basin was erected in the centre. Canon Gardiner, Doctor in Divinity, presented a fountain of water, running through a rock and globe and pouring out of the mouth of a serpent. The Chapter promised to maintain it for ever, and replaced it with a statue of Mercury before the century was out.

John Fell was also responsible for a new block beyond the cloisters towards Christ Church Meadow (since replaced by the present Ruskinian edifice) and for Wren's Gothic Tom Tower. The number of tutors at Christ Church was proportionate to the size and grandeur of the buildings, and Locke had never more than ten pupils at a time assigned to him.

A tutor's duties were not merely pedagogic; he stood *in loco parentis*; he would commonly have charge of his pupil's money and he would advise him in the conduct of his private life, though he had not, after 1660, to ensure the salvation of his soul.

Locke kept a record of his pupils' names, and the fees they paid him, in the same little account book [1] in which, as a schoolboy and undergraduate, he had kept note of his income and expenditure. In his first two years as a tutor, his pupils were the following:

Thomas Harborne, of Aylesbury, who was 17 when he matriculated at Christ Church; Henry Clayton (or Cleaton) of Shropshire, 18; Sir Charles Berkeley, K.B., 13; Thomas Goode, of Herefordshire, 17; John Pentlow, of Northamptonshire; John Pickering, of Cheshire, 15; Roland Townshend, of Worcestershire, 16; Aaron Rutland, of London, 16; Sir Hugh Cwen, of Cheshire, 15; Henry Searle, of Hampshire, 17; Robert Stenton, of Shropshire, 18; Robert Williamson, of Bristol, 18; George Wall,[2] of Gloucester, 17; John West, of Oxfordshire, 17; William Lake, of Bedfordshire, 16; Nicholas Philpott, of Hereford, 17; Morgan Godwyn, of Hereford; John Jones, of London, 18; John Alford, of Sussex, 17; William Duke, of Surrey, 18; Richard Vaughan, of Cornwall, 16; and Edward Pocock, of Oxford.

Some of these boys achieved in later life a modest distinction, but

[1] B.L. MSS. Locke, F. 11.
[2] Not to be confused with George Wall (or Walls) of Worcester, who matriculated on the same day as Wall of Gloucester, and who was later Locke's friend.

none became famous. Pentlow and Rutland died while still undergraduates. Seven of the others took holy orders and five became
lawyers. Pocock and Lake rose to be Canons of Salisbury; Williamson succeeded to the Somerset livings of Keynsham and Saltford;
Godwyn became vicar of Wendover, and Clayton rector of Stratton-
in-the-Dale, Shropshire. Goode, Owen and West went to the Inner
Temple, Searle to Lincoln's Inn; Townshend specialised in law at
All Souls; while Owen and Alford became M.P.s, the one for
Pembroke, the other for Midhurst.

All Locke's pupils were younger than he himself had been when
he matriculated, and his most exalted pupil was the youngest of them
all. Sir Charles Berkeley had been made a Knight of the Bath at the
age of twelve, and entered Christ Church in May 1662 at the age of
thirteen. He received the degree of M.A. after only four months'
residence; such privileges were then available to sons of noblemen,
and Sir Charles enjoyed his as the son and heir of the Earl of
Berkeley. He was happy under Locke at Christ Church, but after
fourteen months his father told Locke that he intended to transfer the
boy to Trinity College, Cambridge:[1]

> I fear you will be surprised (with the Dean) at my so sudden re-
> moving my son, which is wholly upon Dr. Pearson's score. I shall
> refer you to the Dean's letter, to whom I have writ at large. I return
> you my hearty thanks for your great care of my son. My removing
> him from you will not, I hope, be interpreted [as] any diminution of the
> extraordinary good opinion and value I have of your parts and piety
> and your excellent qualifications for the well governing [of] youth.

Lord Berkeley wrote on the same day to his son to remind him to
express his grateful thanks to his tutor and the Dean for their constant
care. The young knight needed no such reminder, and after his
enforced migration he continued to write to Locke from Cambridge.
He told his former tutor in one letter[2] how he had tried, but failed,
to persuade his father to let him return to Oxford:

> Here I am daily disputing with the Cantabrigians. Preferring Oxford
> before Cambridge, there is scarce one morning among ten but that
> there is a fog or a mist enough to choke the whole University, which
> [is what] I believe makes them so dull and stupid.

[1] 27 July 1662 (B.L. MSS. Locke, c. 3, f. 185).
[2] *Ibid.*, f. 189.

Locke kept letters from several of his pupils' fathers, but the parent with whom he was most closely connected was Pocock's father. The Professor of Hebrew and a Canon of Christ Church, Edward Pocock, senior, was the most distinguished orientalist in England, and despite his open avowal of royalist views during the Interregnum, his international renown had protected him: ousted from Christ Church by Cromwell's brother-in-law, French, he had had to move no further than Balliol. Locke, as an undergraduate, had attended Pocock's lectures and was probably influenced by his royalism; then on the Professor's return to Christ Church in 1660 he became his friend. Many years later Locke wrote of Edward Pocock: [1]

> The Christian world is a witness of his great learning . . . Nor could his devotion and piety lie hid and be unobserved in a college where his constant and regular assisting at the cathedral service . . . showed the temper and disposition of his mind. . . .
> He had often the silence of a learner where he had the knowledge of a master . . . Though he was a man of the greatest temperance in himself . . . yet he was of a liberal mind, and given to hospitality . . . He was always unaffectedly cheerful.

Among the younger tutors in Christ Church, Locke's closest friend in the earliest years of the Restoration was Nathaniel Hodges. [2] A man of humble origin, Hodges became a Student in 1657, and afterwards took orders. He was a proctor in 1666, and two years later he was chosen White's Professor of Moral Philosophy. In their Oxford days together, Nathaniel Hodges, James Tyrrell and Locke formed a fraternal company and knew each other by nicknames: Hodges was 'Lysis', Tyrrell 'Musidore', Locke 'Carmelin'.

Christ Church entertained royal visitors during Locke's first years as a tutor. In September 1662 Prince Christian, who was later King of Denmark, dined at the House, and Locke was called upon to deliver a Latin oration. [3] Exactly twelve months later the King and Queen of England were received, but although Locke had in the meantime [4] been elected Lecturer in Rhetoric, he seems to

---

[1] *Several Pieces*, pp. 332–43.

[2] Not to be confused with Nathaniel Hodges (1629–88), the physician, who was a Student of Christ Church from 1648 to 1654.

[3] B.L. MSS. Locke Notebook 20 *Principi Daniae Oxonium ex Itinere divertente*.

[4] On Christmas Eve, 1662. The duty of the Praelector Rhetoricus was not to give orations but to teach philosophy.

have made no similar speech to welcome the English royal family, who were honoured instead in verse by Thomas Ireland.[1]

After Charles and his Queen had left, Clarendon, the Chancellor of the University, remained to conduct a mild purge. Already the Act of Uniformity had caused several dons to resign for conscience sake; and the Chancellor, who was not an intolerant man, sped the departure of lingering Nonconformists as gently as he could. At just this time [2] the Dean and Sub-Dean of Christ Church, together with Canon Gardiner, signed a Latin testimonial to Locke's good character and conduct. It is not clear for what purpose this document was needed. It cannot have been required to exempt Locke from Clarendon's purge, for there could be no suspicions then of his conformity and loyalty. Possibly, but not probably, it was intended as a reference for the Bishop of Oxford; for in 1663 Locke was thinking of becoming a clergyman.

Such a step must have been urged upon him as the obvious course of action. The statutes of Christ Church laid it down that fifty-five of the senior studentships should be held by men in orders or reading for orders. Only five senior studentships could be held by others— two in medicine, two in law, and one in moral philosophy. There were clearly better prospects for Locke in Christ Church as a clergyman than as a layman. And yet he hesitated.

He was becoming increasingly preoccupied with science, and he had already half an eye on one of the medical studentships. Despite his duties as a college tutor he had found time to pursue his unofficial medical studies. He attended regularly the lectures [3] given in Christ Church by Richard Lower's master, the physiologist Thomas Willis; and his notebooks [4] show that he also received informal instruction in medicine from Willis's great friend, Ralph Bathurst. Despite the removal from Oxford of Wilkins and Goddard,[5] the

---

[1] Ireland's verses were not entirely tactful. Despite the presence of Lady Castlemaine in the royal party, the poet ventured to ask the King:

> 'What glory's that, that hovers by your side
> And gives you the embraces of a bride?'

[2] 3 October 1663 (*Ath. Oxon.*, I, p. lii).

[3] Locke's lecture notes are in one of his commonplace books in the Lovelace Collection (B.L. MSS. Locke, F. 19).

[4] *Vide* especially B.L. MSS. Locke e. 4.

[5] Wilkins had left Wadham in 1659 to become Master of Trinity College, Cambridge, from which place he was dismissed at the Restoration, as was Goddard from Merton.

Cromwellian pioneers of science, Willis and Bathurst, who were Royalists, had kept the 'experimental philosophy' alive in the University, Willis becoming Sedleian Professor of Natural Philosophy and Bathurst President of Trinity. But neither Willis nor Bathurst could be said to have succeeded Wilkins to the leadership of the Oxford *virtuosi*, and neither was Locke's chief scientific mentor. Those two distinctions belonged to Robert Boyle.

Boyle, a man of noble birth and considerable means, was not attached to any college, and it was his private house [1] in the High Street which became the laboratory and the meeting place of the experimentalists. Boyle made several discoveries in science. Aided by Robert Hooke, his paid assistant, he devised the air pump which made possible the formulation of 'Boyle's law', and again with Hooke's help he developed the barometer as a weather indicator. But Boyle's importance in the history of science far exceeds the importance of his discoveries in pneumatics and thermometry. He earned the title of the 'father of modern chemistry' both by his own achievements and by what he did to encourage the researches of other scientists in bringing them together, collecting information and providing the facilities for experiments.

Although Boyle had not Wilkins's aversion to books, he claimed to have 'purposely refrained' until 1657, when he was thirty, from reading Descartes 'or so much as Sir Francis Bacon *Novum Organum*, that I might not be prepossessed with any theory or principles till I had spent some time in trying what things themselves would incline me think'.[2]

Even so, Boyle's inductive method was essentially Baconian, and when he came, in the 1660's, to write about science, his theory was manifestly influenced by Descartes's 'mechanical philosophy', which reduced the happenings observed in the world to matter in motion.[3] The Cartesian philosophy became somewhat distorted as it passed through Boyle's mind, and this fact was of considerable importance to Locke's intellectual history. For Locke, as Boyle's pupil, absorbed

[1] It was close to University College on the site of the present Shelley Memorial.

[2] Boyle, I, p. 194.

[3] A. C. Crombie: *Oxford's Contribution to the Origins of Modern Science* (Oxford, 1954), p. 21: 'Descartes's "mechanical philosophy" . . . is the basis of Boyle's critique of the Aristotelians and the "Stagyrists" in the *Sceptical Chemist* and of the atomic theory of matter put forward in his *Origin of Forms and Qualities*, both published in Oxford during his residence here'.

much of the Boyleian conception of nature before he read Descartes and became interested in pure philosophy. Like Boyle, Locke brought no metaphysical preconceptions to the study of science; he tried, as Boyle had tried, to be a 'disciple of nature'.

When he was admitted to the charmed circle of Boyle's High Street rooms, Locke showed an early if not a lasting enthusiasm for experiments. In some of these he collaborated with Boyle's German *protégé* Peter Stahl. Wood in a well-known passage says that Locke behaved badly at Stahl's chemistry lectures: [1]

> This John Locke was a man of turbulent spirit, clamorous and never contented. The club wrote and took notes from the mouth of their master, who sat at the upper end of a table, but the said John Locke scorned to do it, so that while every man besides of the club were writing, he would be prating and troublesome.

In spite of this testimony (and Wood often wrote on hearsay) there is evidence of collaboration between Locke and Stahl in a letter [2] Dr. David Thomas, another Oxford *virtuoso*, wrote to Locke thirty years afterwards, saying:

> I have often designed to acquaint you that I have your cabinet in which are all those preparations I think you made with Stahl and what we with Dr. Blunt did together. I have only opened it as well as I could without a key, but have not tried the goodness of any one of them. You may now dispose of them as you think fit.

Locke became a close friend of Boyle's and remained his friend until Boyle's death in 1691.[3] Boyle was five years older than Locke, and he bore some physical resemblance to him. He had the same long face, large nose, full lips and soft, melancholy eyes. Like Locke, he was tall and thin; he suffered from the same poor health; and like Locke, he died a bachelor.[4] Because of—or in spite of—an education in Geneva, Boyle was an earnest Christian, and he encouraged the fashion among the Oxford *virtuosi* of combining

---

[1] *Ath. Oxon.*, I, p. lii.

[2] 11 December 1693 (B.L. MSS. Locke, c. 20, f. 121).

[3] Boyle made Locke one of the executors of his will.

[4] Aubrey said of Boyle: 'He is very tall (about six foot high) and straight, very temperate and virtuous and frugal. . . . He is charitable to ingenious men that are in want, and foreign chemists have had large proof of his bounty, for he will not spare for cost to get any rare secret. . . . He has not only a high renown in England, but abroad, and when foreigners come hither, tis one of their curiosities to make him a visit' (Aubrey, p. 124).

theological with scientific studies. Boyle knew his Bible well, and would have made an excellent clergyman.[1] Clarendon, indeed, urged him to become one and proposed if he did so to make him Provost of Eton.

Thus in 1663 both Locke and Boyle had considerable incentives for taking orders. Boyle—who was, after all, the richer and more influential man—made up his mind the sooner. He declined; he felt that having no vocation for the Ministry, he could do more for the furtherance of the Christian religion as a layman. Locke could not afford to consult his conscience in the same uncompromising way. He consulted John Strachey instead.

That friend from childhood days was now in a very comfortable position. Leaving Oxford—he was a Lincoln man—Strachey had at first become a Gray's Inn lawyer, a calling which had no great attraction for him and for which he showed no special aptitude. Unlike his pushful, shrewd and scheming mother, he was by nature indolent and sentimental. His earliest extant letter[2] to Locke— written when he was twenty-three—described the pangs of a lover's aching heart. His prospects were generally bleak. But when he was twenty-seven things providentially improved for Strachey. Samuel Jepp, his half-brother and his mother's favourite son, died. Elizabeth Baber, in her third and final widowhood, had bought the freehold of Sutton Court to present to Samuel Jepp. Because of his death she gave the house to John Strachey instead, and her generosity enabled that son to quit the Bar and set himself up as a prosperous country squire, a role for which his inclinations fitted him, and in which he must have looked—to judge from the fair, frank and bucolically moustached face depicted in his portrait[3]—at home. In December of 1662 he married the daughter of another Somerset landowner,[4] and his patrician dignity was complete.

Attributing, as a loyal friend would, the success of Strachey to Strachey's wisdom, and not to fortuitous circumstances, Locke regarded him as someone well qualified to give him counsel. And counsel Strachey gave: he said[5] Locke should certainly not take holy

[1] As it was, Boyle wrote a number of religious tracts.
[2] 23 January 1657/8 (B.L. MSS. Locke, c. 18, f. 188).
[3] At Sutton Court.
[4] His bride was Anne, nineteen-year-old daughter of George Hodges (C. R. Sanders: *The Virginia Magazine of History and Biography*, Richmond, Virginia, LIX, 3, pp. 275–96).
[5] 18 November 1663 (B.L. MSS. Locke, c. 18, f. 214).

orders, but should go abroad for a year or two instead. Locke remembered his advice, but shelved the decision.

His college duties at this time included lecturing and conducting disputations with Bachelors of Arts.[1] At least one subject, if not the only subject, of these disputations was (as Dr. von Leyden has shown [2]) the Law of Nature. Locke had his Latin essays on the subject copied by an amanuensis and revised them in his own hand for this pedagogic purpose. On Christmas Eve, 1663, he was elected at Christ Church to be Senior Censor, otherwise Censor of Moral Philosophy, a disciplinary office in which he served for twelve months and received a fee of £10 10s.[3]

When his term of office ended, Locke, according to the Christ Church tradition, 'died', and made his own 'funeral speech' in Latin at the ceremony of 'burying' the outgoing Censor. The speech [4] was made up partly of Baroque conceits on the desirability of death, partly of farewell greetings addressed in turn to the Dean and other dignitaries of the House. Locke compared life on earth to a prison, where there was no peace. Philosophy, he protested, offered no consolation; for her riches were nothing other than words—words, moreover, which served only to agitate an uneasy mind. Nor was there any consolation to be found in age, which merely destroyed a man's appearance. Wealth brought nothing but anxiety, nausea and surfeit: '*Ferre vitam tot calamitatibus onustam miserum est, miserius certe amare*'.

Turning to Dr. Fell, Locke compared his own brief life as Censor with the Dean's Jove-like immortality, and spoke of happiness as something 'only found here and under your rule'. He also paid tribute to the literary genius of Jasper Mayne, the Sub-Dean, who enjoyed some small reputation as a dramatist and poet. After greeting in turn the Prebendaries, the Masters, the Junior Censor [5] and the 'pall-bearers', Locke paid tributes to his pupils, the Bachelors of Arts, his 'fellow soldiers' ('or should I say my masters?') who had

[1] An undergraduate William Coker wrote to Locke on 31 January 1663/4 asking to be admitted to the disputations (B.L. Rawlinson MSS., D. 286, f. 6, Latin).

[2] W. von Leyden, p. 12.

[3] B.L. MSS. Locke Notebook, N. 27.

[4] B.L. MSS. Locke, F. 31, f. 120 *et seq.* W. von Leyden (pp. 218 *et seq.*) prints both the original Latin text and an English translation.

[5] Benjamin Woodroffe (1638–1711), who entered Christ Church from Westminster School in 1656, was Censor of Natural Philosophy during the year in which Locke was Censor of Moral Philosophy.

vanquished him in the philosophical arena. He suggested that their conduct had vindicated the very Law of Nature which they had attacked in their debates. He praised the industry and learning of the scholars, saying he had not needed, as Censor, to be a taskmaster; but he did remind the scholars of the importance of 'the hall where men learn to debate' as well as 'the temple where men learn to pray', of being a philosopher as well as a theologian.[1] Looking back on a year of office marred by only one disagreeable incident,[2] Locke assured his audience that he was glad to 'die'. His speech ended with the word: '*Morior*'.

At just the time when Locke was 'dying' in jest, his brother was dying in earnest. By the end of 1663 he was dead. Thus the philosopher alone survived of the little family of Belluton.

Thomas had, however, married, and he left both a widow, Dorothea, and a child. The only evidence for the existence of this child is the nuncupative will [3] of Thomas Locke (witnessed by Will Arundell and John Maggs), in which the testator divided his estate between his wife and child. It is extremely unlikely that this child lived much longer than its father. John Locke made no reference to a nephew or niece in any of his papers, and in later life he named a cousin as his heir.

In March 1664 [4] Locke bought the lease of a cottage and barn called Lighthouse in Pensford from his widowed sister-in-law, and in 1666 she re-married, her second husband being one Robert Taunton.

After relinquishing his censorial office, Locke sought no immediate academic promotion. He even put aside science for a time as well. He had decided to follow Strachey's advice and travel abroad. He found a diplomatic post for himself, and he actually went so far as

[1] These words are interesting in view of Locke's oft-quoted strictures *against* traditional disputations.

[2] W. von Leyden (p. 241) suggests that this may refer to an incident that took place during Locke's year of office when he was summoned before the Dean and Chapter 'to answer for the sconcing of one of the servants of the House' (*vide* also H. L. Thompson, *Christ Church*, Oxford, 1900, p. 101).

[3] Preserved at Exeter: Bishop's Court records. The will is dated 23 November 1663. It was proved on 4 February 1663/4.

[4] B.L. MSS. b. 5/2. Locke's father had bought a 99-year lease on this cottage in 1650.

to learn shorthand [1] in order to be the better qualified for diplomatic duties, though, as he later said, shorthand was something men generally might learn 'both for dispatch in what men write for their own memory and concealment of what they would not have lie open to every eye'.[2]

[1] The system he learned was that of Jeremiah Rich, but he added signs of his own devising. W. von Leyden (pp. 246 *et seq*) gives an interesting account of Locke's use of shorthand.

[2] *Some Thoughts Concerning Education*, Third Edition, § 161.

Chapter Seven

THE DIPLOMATIST

POSSIBLY it was William Godolphin[1] who arranged the post for Locke, or it may be that the King personally chose him for the mission. Charles must assuredly have made his acquaintance, if not on the occasion of the royal visit to Oxford in September 1663, then in September 1665, when the great plague of London brought the King's Court back to Christ Church for an even longer stay.

Locke left England in November 1665. His post was that of secretary to the diplomatic mission of Sir Walter Vane to Brandenburg. The embassy was of considerable importance to British policy because of the war against the Dutch. Charles had found an ally in the Bishop of Münster, and he hoped to find another one in the Elector of Brandenburg, or, at least, to ensure the neutrality of Brandenburg, which had a frontier with Holland.

Sir Walter Vane was the younger brother of the republican martyr, Sir Henry Vane, but his own Royalist record was impeccable. He had much to recommend him as a diplomatist, and although the mission failed, its failure was hardly his fault.

Sir Walter and Locke and a small staff reached Cleves, the seat of the Elector of Brandenburg, at the end of November.[2]

The Elector received the mission kindly. He told Sir Walter he would be delighted to remain neutral, or even to become an ally of England, if only he were adequately paid. With the situation as cut and dried as this, the embassy secretary had time to attend to other things beside diplomacy. It was Locke's first visit to the Continent,

---

[1] William Godolphin was by this time a powerful civil servant, right-hand man to Henry Bennett, first Lord Arlington, who was virtually Foreign Minister, and shared the highest government authority with Clarendon.

[2] The letters Locke wrote to the home Government in his own hand are preserved in the Public Record Office (German States, Series I, Nos. 128–55). A manuscript book in which Locke copied out his Government's replies is in the British Museum. (Add. MSS. 16272.)

and he found much to interest him. As soon as he was settled in
Cleves, he wrote to Robert Boyle:[1]

> We are here in a place very little considerable for anything but its
> antiquity, which to me seems neither to commend things nor opinions
> . . . The town is little, and not very strong or handsome, the buildings
> and streets irregular. . . .

He mentioned that the Calvinist, the Lutheran and the Roman
Catholic religions were all tolerated:

> They quietly permit one another to choose their way to heaven; and I
> cannot observe any quarrels or animosities amongst them on account of
> religion. This good correspondence is owing partly to the power of
> the magistrates, and partly to the prudence and good nature of the
> people, who, as I find by enquiry, entertain different opinions without
> any secret hatred or rancour.

Clearly Locke was already moving away from his Hobbesian
views of 1661.

While he was in Cleves, Locke wrote several letters to Strachey.[2]
In the first of them he sent an account[3] of the public entertainment the
Elector had given to welcome the English mission. Locke had not
enjoyed the occasion: 'Amidst a great deal of meat and company, I
had little to eat and less to say.'

He said he believed he would have slept out the meal but for the
wine; and he complained, in the proverbial British style, that 'the
meats were so disguised that they were more a mess than a meal . . .
What think you of a hen and a cabbage? Or a piece of powdered
beef covered over with preserved quinces? These are no miracles
here'.

He also told Strachey how he had been invited to dine at a
monastery 'with the Franciscan friars'. This had been a wretched
meal—pease pudding, fish, cheese and butter, accompanied by
conversation 'in bad Latin and worse pronunciation'. A day or two

---

[1] 12/22 December 1665 (Boyle, V, pp. 565–6).

[2] Strachey kept the letters Locke sent him from Cleves and returned them, at
Locke's request, to their author. They are now in the Lovelace Collection together
with Locke's original drafts of them, Locke's drafts being bound together with his
drafts of similar letters to William Godolphin. The letters printed by Lord King are
taken from the final copies, not from the drafts.

[3] 4 December 1665 (B.L. MSS. Locke, c. 24, f. 232).

afterwards Locke attended a service in the Lutheran Church, where, as he said:

> I found them all merrily singing with their hats on, so that by the posture they were in, and the fashion of the building, not altogether unlike a theatre, I was ready to fear I had mistook the place.

However, he admitted that the German congregation sang better than English congregations did. He also noticed that there were two sacred pictures in this Lutheran church, whereas the Calvinists had none.

'The Quakers', he added, 'agree with ours in other things as well as name, and take no notice of the Elector's prohibiting their meeting'.

Locke had at this time high hopes of the mission succeeding in its purpose. In a letter to William Godolphin drafted on *29 December*,[1] he suggested that the Elector could fairly easily be won round because his 'supporting coffers are not very full' and his debts 'increase daily rather than diminish', and also because of the Elector's 'fear of having his country (which lies scattered and very obnoxious to incursions) invaded by any of the Catholic Princes of Germany who should join with the Bishop [of Muenster] . . . (for I find that here generally is apprehended a war of religion)'.

On Christmas Day, Locke went to a Catholic church, and wrote afterwards [2] to tell Strachey about the crib he had seen there 'of the same size and make that our English puppets are, and might have deserved pence apiece'.

> This [he continued] was the show. The music to it was all vocal in the quire adjoining, but such as I [have] never heard. They had strong voices, but so ill tuned, so ill-managed that it was their misfortune, as well as ours, that they could be heard.

Locke liked the merchandise of Cleves no better than its religious institutions. He complained that it had taken him three days to find a pair of gloves, and that 'the next two days were spent in drawing them on'. He remarked on the small value of the Brandenburg currency: 'a horse load of turnips would be two horse loads of money'. A pair of shoes could not be made in less than six months. Indeed, he added, 'the first thing after they are married here is to

---

[1] B.L. MSS. Locke, c. 24, f. 251 v.
[2] *Ibid.*, f. 230 (undated).

bespeak the child's coat; and truly the bridegroom must be a bungler that gets not a child before the mantle be made'.

At a local monastery Locke witnessed a splendid medieval disputation, and confessed:[1]

> Our disputing in Oxford comes as short of it as the rhetoric of Carfax does that of Billingsgate. But it behoves the monks to cherish this art of wrangling in its declining age, which they first nursed and sent abroad to give it a troublesome, idle employment.

Locke's hopes of the mission succeeding soon faded. He told Strachey[2] that although the Elector had declared himself to be on neither side in the war between the English and the Dutch, he was in fact leaning towards Holland. Locke must also have realised by this time, although he would not repeat it to anyone as unofficial as Strachey, that the British Government was unwilling to pay the bribe the Elector wanted.

In a letter to Boyle[3] Locke had spoken of the dearth of learned society in Cleves:

> There is one Dr. Scardius, who, I am told, is not altogether a stranger to chemistry . . . The rest of their physicians go the old road. . . . This, I suppose, makes this town so ill-furnished with books of that kind, there being few here curious enough to enquire after chemistry or experimental learning.

Remembering Boyle's interest in alchemy, Locke also mentioned a Jesuit who had been in Hungary and visited a copper-mine, where he claimed there was a trough of water which made iron into copper.

Before the end of February, Sir Walter Vane and his party packed their bags to go. The English Government had declined to pay out money, and the Elector refused to make concessions on any other terms. On their way home through Antwerp, the English diplomatists heard that the Elector had been bought over by the Dutch and was sending them twelve thousand soldiers.[4]

During his absence abroad Locke was not forgotten by his women friends. He was particularly remembered by the one who variously

---

[1] B.L. MSS. Locke, c. 24, f. 231.
[2] *Ibid.*, f. 233.
[3] Boyle, V, p. 566.
[4] Locke to Strachey (B.L. MSS. Locke, c. 24, f. 235).

signed herself 'Elia', 'Scribelia' and 'Berelisa'. On 13 February 1665/6,[1] this lady compiled a short news-sheet which she entitled *The Oxford Gazette*, and which included the following items:

Merton Court.[2] The Queen's miscarriage possessed all with grief, but new hopes of a prince hereafter.

Christ Court.[3] In the absence of King and Canons, Mr. Hodges [4] will be chief there. He is to be Proctor by the absence of ——. 'Tis said he loses honours in travelling for it. Mr. Candish, commoner of Christ Church, is to marry the handsome Terill.

Oxford

Pocock,[5] the bookseller, came off with Honour from his last enterprise, he with a peaceful assault is now possessed of Mr. West's daughter, having stole her . . .

The fresh report now here is of a combat between Elia and Bereliza: 'tis believed for a German [6] that is expected shortly. Scribelia keeps her valour to disenchant you after your adventures.

Holland

'Tis supposed the States will not permit the prisoners stay in consideration of the little service they will do them. 'Tis wished the Germans would do the like and pack the English from them. Where would you be, A? [7]

Whitehall

The secretaries grumble damnably at the tedious dispatches of those beyond sea. They say they are too much taken up with writing to their mistresses; they neglect the greater affairs. But in zeal to the public, all such are to be called home. (You may be mistaken, so brought with the rest.)

Ireland

Mr. John Parry is in expectation of the deanery. 'Tis thought he will be persuaded to accept thereof. His sister then will cherish the German . . .

The Plague runs yet about London.

[1] B.L. MSS. Locke, c. 8, f. 62.
[2] The Queen's Court was temporarily established at Merton College.
[3] The King's Court was at Christ Church.
[4] Nathaniel Hodges (1634–1700).
[5] Samuel Pocock had a bookshop in the High Street which received University recognition in 1661. He had (1667) a wife named Eliza. Presumably this was 'Mr. West's daughter'.
[6] The German was clearly the returning diplomatist from Germany, Locke himself.
[7] 'A' for 'Atticus', the name by which Scribelia addressed Locke in several of her letters to him.

This little news-letter reopens the question of the identity of 'Scribelia' and of 'E. P.' I do not think the 'report of combat between Elia and Bereliza' can be taken as evidence of these being the names of two persons, either or both distinct from Scribelia. On several papers the handwriting suggests that Scribelia, Elia and Bereliza were one and the same person. Scribelia was the name she used most frequently.[1] The sentence promising that John Parry's sister 'will cherish the German' (i.e. Locke) might even be thought to suggest that John Parry's sister was herself the author of the newsletter. The report of John Parry's Irish expectations was certainly well founded. He was appointed Dean of Christ Church, Dublin, in April 1666.

Locke's work with Sir Walter Vane had impressed his employers favourably. As soon as he returned to London, he was invited to fill another post. 'I am now offered a fair opportunity of going into Spain with the Ambassador', he wrote[2] to Strachey. '. . . I am pulled both ways by diverse considerations and do yet waver: I intend to-morrow for Oxford and shall there take my resolution'.

The resolution he took was against going to Spain. He went to Somerset instead. Before he had left for Cleves, Locke had given power of attorney to his Uncle Peter, though, as he said, 'I think it best my tenants should not know I am out of England, for perhaps that may make them more slack to pay their rents.' Such forebodings proved well founded, and it was as an anxious landlord that Locke set off for Pensford in March 1665/6. Having no longer a house of his own in Somerset, he stayed at Sutton Court as the guest of Strachey. He assured his host in a letter[3] he wrote before he arrived that 'though I had my drink with the lusty Almans, yet my mirth and company I had only with you'.

While he was at Sutton Court, Locke received this message from 'Elia':[4]

When you parted from Bereliza you left her with her reason but [she] now intends to forfeit it to limit your time of stay from her.

[1] In a small calf-bound notebook belonging to Locke there is written 'Be mindful of yourself and what you owe Scribelia, Nov. the 12'. Another entry in the same (Scribelia's) hand reads: 'Do not suffer the —— to be unjust to Scribelia but persuade it to believe I value it with my life'. (B.L. MSS. Locke, F. 27.)

[2] 22 February 1665/6 (*ibid.*, c. 24, f. 235).

[3] 13 March 1665/6 (*ibid.*, f. 241).   [4] *Ibid.*, c. 8, f. 63.

She professes your journey to Germany did not create more fears than your now being near Bristol does, so that for her quiet and your own safety you are to return within that time she once mentioned to you . . .

'Tis now eleven o'clock, so that I must end and go and dress myself and prepare myself for a visit either from Mr. T.[1] or Scribelia and then you may guess what our discourse may be . . .

Another letter,[2] endorsed 'Sc. 66' (i.e. Scribelia, 1666), dated Shrove Tuesday and signed 'SBer', delivered this ultimatum:

. . . I must tell you from S[cribelia] that if you are the yet passionate Att[icus] and the real one you ever was, you will hide nothing from her. She must share in your concerns as she has share in your heart, and you must tell her all things . . . Heavens, my Best, shall I never see you? Shall I always lament your absence without any hope? . . .

In the postscript, Scribelia wrote: 'A father does not know of the correspondence, I think.'

Locke did go back to Oxford, but for reasons which were probably unconnected with this romantic heart-cry. Having once returned, he decided to stay there. He was offered yet another diplomatic post the same summer, that of secretary to the new ambassador to Sweden,[3] and again he refused. He had chosen medicine.

[1] Mr. Towerson?
[2] B.L. MSS. Locke, c. 8, f. 64.
[3] Charles Perrott to Locke, 21 August 1666 (*ibid.*, c. 17, f. 70).

Chapter Eight

THE PHYSICIAN

THE presence of the King and Queen at Oxford during the London plague had demoralised the University; even so staunch a Royalist as Wood complained of the 'very nasty and beastly ways'[1] of the courtiers, and their baneful influence persisted long after they had left.

For one thing, there was almost unprecedented drunkenness. Nearly four hundred taverns flourished in Oxford, and they were not the only sources of supply. The dons of Pembroke, St. John's, Balliol and All Souls set the pace for heavy drinking, and the Rector of Exeter was never sober after nightfall. Even at Christ Church, under the high-minded Dr. Fell, a clergyman, a bishop's son, was found dead of alcoholic poisoning, an empty brandy bottle in his hand.

With intemperance came 'easy manners, immorality, loose language, disrespect'; Wood writes also of the gross abuses in college elections and the depravity of chaplains. Wood was a prejudiced man, but he was not prejudiced against the Stuart Restoration, and Mallet says[2] one cannot doubt 'that in its main features the darkly coloured picture which he paints is true'.

Such was the Oxford to which Locke returned in 1666. His College urged him again to enter holy orders, for, however debauched the dons might be, it was still considered imperative for all except a small minority of them to be clergymen. But again Locke resisted and chose instead to concentrate on medical and other scientific studies.

On his visit to Somerset in 1666 he had been asked by Boyle to find out about the minerals in Mendip mines and to make observations of the temperature in the various pits. Boyle sent him the apparatus for the purpose, but the outcome was a fiasco. Locke wrote[3] afterwards to Boyle:

[1] Mallet, II, p. 421.   [2] *Ibid.*, p. 423.
[3] 5 May 1666 (F.B., I, pp. 125–7).

88

The sight of the engine [i.e. Boyle's apparatus] and my desire of going down into some of their gruffs [i.e. pits] gave them [the miners] terrible apprehensions, and I could not persuade them but that I had some design; so that I and a gentleman[1] that bore me company had a pleasant scene whilst their fear to be undermined by us made them disbelieve all we told them. . . .

Since I could not get down into their gruffs, I made it my business to inquire what I could concerning them. The workmen could give me very little account of anything but what profit made them seek after. They could apprehend no other mineral but lead ore, and believed the earth held nothing else worth seeking for. Besides they were not forward to be too communicative to one they thought they had reason to be afraid of. . . .

Locke added a few more general remarks about the character of the miners and their way of working, and also reported the results of some experiments made with the barometer at different levels of a 'pretty steep high hill', the experiment proving nothing beyond a fault in the apparatus.

The letter was manifestly of no scientific interest whatever, but Locke was naïve enough to say that if it 'should be thought fit to fill an empty space' in the *Philosophical Transactions* of the Royal Society, then 'I shall desire to have my name concealed'.

Boyle's reply was, not surprisingly, somewhat patronising in its tone. Although he said he looked on Locke as a *virtuoso*, he clearly regarded him as a very raw one. Boyle wrote:[2]

If your letter had found me at London, this return of it would have been brought you much earlier to Oxford. And though I am now in a place where a crowd of such persons whose quality or beauty requires a great deal of attendance, reduces me to make this letter short and hasty, yet I cannot but snatch time to return you my deserved thanks for some favour of yours, at some passages of which I could not but smile as well as you did, though I was troubled that so much curiosity and industry as you expressed, should by so gross a want of it in others be made so unsuccessful. But I hope this will not discourage you from embracing and seeking future opportunities to search into the nature of minerals, in order to which I wish I had time and conveniency to send you some sheets of articles of inquiries about mines[3] in general which I once drew up for the use of some friends and partly for my own.

[1] Probably John Strachey.
[2] June 1666 (B.L. MSS. Locke, c. 4, f. 150).
[3] There are several entries on the subject of *mines* in Locke's 'Goldsmiths Almanack' for 1667. (Mr. Sydney Edelstein's Collection, New York City.)

My absence from London kept me from receiving your account of the barometrical observations, till it was some days too late to make the use of it you allow. But I hope I may have another occasion to mention it pertinently as it deserves. The receipt I promised you is so plain and simple a thing, yet as I would not communicate to everybody a remedy of that approved efficiency, so I should fear that its seeming meanness would make you despise it, if the person 'tis now enclosed [1] to were not looked upon as a virtuoso, by

Sir, your very affectionate friend
and humble servant

Robert Boyle [2]

My humble service to Dr. Willis, Mr. Lower, Mr. Thomas and the rest of my friends at Oxford.

The 'Mr. Thomas' mentioned here was David Thomas, a Salisbury man who was a Fellow of New College and a general practitioner in the city of Oxford. In the year 1665 he was also one of the University proctors.

The earliest extant letter from Thomas to Locke was dated 9 July 1666,[3] but it was obviously written by a man who already knew his correspondent well. Among other matters Thomas mentioned vipers which he proposed to use for experimental purposes. In a second letter,[4] written ten days later, he promised some Hungarian mineral for Boyle, and complained that since Keffeler had died of the plague the previous year, there was no one to grind glass stopples.

Working in collaboration with David Thomas, Locke began to justify the name of a *virtuoso* in earnest. The two friends opened a small laboratory in Oxford, and sought the interest of other scientists in order to enlarge it. Locke told Boyle in February [5] that Thomas and he 'are now upon a new sort of chemistry; i.e., extracting money out of the scholars' pockets'.

In one of Locke's notebooks [6] there is a reckoning of his laboratory accounts with Thomas:

---

[1] The receipt is no longer with the letter.
[2] It is worth mentioning in connection with this letter that Locke's turn came to smile at Boyle's unsuccessful experiments with minerals—notably his life-long efforts to make gold; Boyle bequeathed his papers on the subject to Locke, and after Boyle's death, Locke (albeit with Newton's help) discovered Boyle's foolish mistakes.
[3] B.L. MSS. Locke, c. 20, f. 1.
[4] *Ibid.*, f. 3.
[5] 24 February 1666/7 (Boyle, V, p. 567).
[6] B.L. MSS. Locke, F. 12 (April 1667).

Mr. Thomas	£22 5s. 5d.
Mr. Blunt [1]	£5 15s. 11d.
J. L.	£4 13s. 5d. (besides £5 I had already paid to Mr. Thomas)

As Locke's papers contain no precise details of any experiments conducted, it may be that the laboratory was no more than a pharmacy. David Thomas, being himself a doctor, encouraged Locke to concentrate on such work, and it was not long before Locke became an outstanding physician. But he was never to achieve much in other fields of empirical science, and even in correspondence with Boyle, Locke is henceforth found discussing such subjects as drugs and herbals. In his letter to Boyle of 24 February,[2] he wrote:

> According to the directions you gave in your last letter to Mr. Thomas, I have endeavoured to provide paronychia, and I think I shall be able to procure pretty good store of it.

In another letter,[3] written a month later, Locke said:

> ... having from a passage in your writings taken the first notice of the time of gathering peony roots ... that it must be in April, when Sol is in Aries and at a plenilunium before the rising of the sun, I rode to a place where was pretty good plenty of male peony, and on the 14th instant, between ten and eleven in the morning, had some roots dug up, and am promised others to be dug up on the 30th instant before sun-rising. If there be any advantage in the time of gathering I owe the knowledge of it so much to you that I should be an unworthy reader of your writings if I should not return you my thanks and offer you some part of those roots. ...

Some time in the year 1667 Locke met, and began to collaborate with Thomas Sydenham, the greatest English physician, one indeed who was as distinguished in the fields of medical research and therapy as was Robert Boyle in the fields of chemistry and general science. The portrait of Sydenham by Mary Beale which hangs in the Royal College of Physicians shows a man of ample frame, a large sad face, and long hair parted in the middle; a typical Puritan in appearance.

---

[1] Probably Thomas Blount of B.N.C. (matriculated 1650), son of Colonel Thomas Blount, F.R.S.

[2] Boyle, V, p. 567.

[3] 24 March 1666/7 (*ibid.*, p. 568).

Sydenham was born into a Puritan family in 1624. His Oxford studies were interrupted by service with the Parliamentary army, but after eighteen months' training he took a Bachelor's degree in Medicine and became Fellow and Senior Bursar of All Souls. He left in 1655 to be married, and thereafter lived and worked in Westminster as a practising physician. Though Sydenham knew Boyle and the other Oxford *virtuosi*, he was never of their number nor wholly in sympathy with their aims. His post-graduate work was done at Montpellier, where his master was Charles Barbeyrac, the great French Protestant physician. It was from Barbeyrac that Sydenham learned the rudiments of that clinical method of medicine which he later developed and introduced into England. The new method did not recommend Sydenham to the conservative College of Physicians, which never elected him a Fellow and which was slow to grant him even a Licentiate. Nor did he ever receive the degree of Doctor of Medicine from Oxford; his M.D. was given him at Cambridge, *honoris causa*, when he was fifty-two.

Sydenham's approach to medicine was opposed alike to dogma tradition and authority. He explained: [1]

> I have been very careful to write nothing but what was the faithful product of observation. . . . I neither suffered myself to be deceived by idle speculations, nor have deceived others by obtruding anything upon them but downright matters of fact.

He summed up his method in these words: [2]

> The function of a physician [is the] industrious investigation of the history of diseases, and of the effect of remedies, as shown by the only true teacher, experience. . . .
> True practice consists in the observations of nature: these are finer than any speculations. Hence the medicine of nature is more refined than the medicine of philosophy.

A fragmentary manuscript [3] of Locke's entitled *De Arte Medica* shows how close his thinking was to that of Sydenham. Locke wrote:

> True knowledge grew first in the world by experience and rational observations; but proud man, not content with the knowledge he was

---

[1] B.M. Sloane MSS. 4376, f. 75.
[2] T. Sydenham, *Works*, 1848, II, p. 12 and p. 22.
[3] P.R.O. 30/24/472.

capable of, and which was useful to him, would needs penetrate into the hidden causes of things, lay down principles, and establish maxims to himself about the operations of nature, and thus vainly expect that nature, or in truth God, should proceed according to those laws which his maxims had prescribed to him.

Locke and Sydenham were very unlike each other as persons, but they had many ideas in common: if Sydenham was the teacher he was no scholar and he needed help to express himself in good Latin.[1]

In dedicating the third edition of his *Observationes Medicae* [2] to Mapletoft, Sydenham wrote:

> You know how thoroughly my method is approved of by an intimate and common friend of ours, and one who has closely and exhaustively examined the subject—I mean Mr. John Locke; a man whom, in the acuteness of his intellect, in the steadiness of his judgement, in the simplicity, that is, in the excellence of his manners, I confidently declare to have, amongst the men of our time, few equals and no superiors.

In the summer of 1666 Locke embarked on an even more important friendship than that with Thomas Sydenham. He met Anthony Ashley Cooper, first Baron Ashley. Two accounts of this meeting, differing in circumstantial detail, survive in manuscript, both written many years later: one by Lady Masham, who can have had no source of information besides Locke himself; the other by Ashley's grandson, the third Earl of Shaftesbury, who may have heard his grandfather's account of the meeting as well as Locke's.[3]

Lady Masham wrote:[4]

> In the year 1666 or 1667 the then Lord Ashley, afterwards Earl of Shaftesbury and Lord High Chancellor of England, went to Oxford

---

[1] The extent of Locke's collaboration with Sydenham, and the importance of Locke's own medical work, has been brought to light by Dr. Kenneth Dewhurst in various papers contributed to medical journals based on research in the Lovelace Collection.

[2] Published in London in 1676. The book is in Latin and like the second edition (1668) contains a Latin poem of fifty-four lines in honour of the author by 'J. Lock A.M. ex Aede Christ. Oxon'.

[3] Both accounts were given in letters to Jean le Clerc, in response to a request for biographical information about Locke, and both are preserved among the Remonstants' Manuscripts in the University Library, Amsterdam.

[4] Amsterdam: Remonstrants' MSS. J. 57a.

to visit his son, a young gentleman in the University, since Earl of Shaftesbury, and father of the present Earl of Shaftesbury, entirely beloved of his grandfather, though not twelve years old when he [i.e. the first Earl] died.

My Lord Ashley, designing to spend some days with his son at Oxford, had resolved at the same time to drink Astrop[1] medicinal waters there, and had accordingly written to Dr. Thomas, a physician in Oxford, to provide them against his coming. The Doctor, being obliged to go out of town,[2] could not do this himself, and requested of his friend Mr. Locke to take the care of getting the waters against my Lord's coming. Mr. Locke was no way wanting in this care, but so it fell out that through some fault or misfortune of the messenger employed by him to this purpose, my Lord came to town, and the waters were not ready for his drinking them the next day, as he had designed to do. Mr. Locke much vexed at such a disappointment, and to excuse from the blame of it Dr. Thomas, who had entrusted him herein, found himself obliged to wait upon my Lord Ashley (whom he had never before seen) to acquaint him how this had happened. My Lord, in his wonted manner, received him very civilly, accepted his excuses with great easiness; and when Mr. Locke would have taken leave of him, would needs have him stay sup with him, being much pleased (as it soon appeared) with his conversation. But if my Lord was pleased with the company of Mr. Locke, Mr. Locke was yet more so with that of my Lord Ashley; and he has often said that it perfectly charmed him. . . .

My Lord, when Mr. Locke took leave of him, engaged him to dine with him the next day, which he willingly promised: and the waters being then provided against the following day, and Mr. Locke having beforehand thought of drinking them himself, my Lord would have him drink them with him, so that he might have the more of his company. When my Lord went from Oxford he went to Sunning-hill[3] (where he drank the waters some time) and having (before he left Oxford) made Mr. Locke promise that he would come to him thither, Mr. Locke within a few days followed him. Soon after my Lord returning to London desired Mr. Locke that from that time he would look upon his house as his home; and that he would let him see him there in town so soon as he could.

---

[1] It was Richard Lower who discovered that the waters of Astrop had mineral properties of therapeutic value. Astrop, however, was remotely and unfashionably situated in the north of Oxfordshire, and in order that patients could enjoy the amenities inseparable from a spa, carriers were engaged to bring the waters to Oxford.

[2] Oxford.

[3] A watering-place near Windsor.

The third Earl of Shaftesbury's account [1] reads as follows:

> Mr. Locke came into my grandfather's family in the summer of the year 1666, recommended by his friend * Mr. Bennet of the town of Shaftesbury. The occasion of it was thus: my grandfather had been ill for a great while after a fall, by which his breast was so bruised that in time it came to an imposthumation within, and appeared by a swelling under his stomach. Mr. Locke was at that time a Student in Physic at Oxford, and my grandfather, taking a journey that way to drink the waters (having Mr. Bennet in the coach with him), he had this young physician presented to him, who though he had never practised physic, yet appeared to my grandfather to be such a genius that he valued him above all his other physicians, the great men in practice of those times.

A surviving letter from David Thomas to Locke shows that Lady Masham's story about the waters was correct. In this letter,[2] Thomas wrote:

> I must request one favour of you, which is to send me word by the next opportunity whether you can procure twelve bottles of water for my Lord Ashley to drink in Oxford [on] Sunday and Monday mornings. If you can possibly do it, you will very much oblige him and me.

On the other hand, Lady Masham was mistaken in thinking that Lord Ashley went to Oxford to see his son.[3] Both Lady Masham and the third Lord Shaftesbury were mistaken in thinking that Locke joined Lord Ashley in London almost immediately after his first meeting with him. It was not until the following Easter that Locke was asked to make Exeter House his home. Truly, Ashley's clerk [4] urged Locke to come to London in September 1666, but this was chiefly in order that Locke might use his medical skill to help the people who were victims of the plague and the Fire; but in December the same correspondent [5] told Locke that, although Lord Ashley would be pleased to see him in London, he could not entertain him at Exeter House while Lady Ashley was there.

At Oxford in the meantime Locke took steps to secure his position

---

* The [third Earl's] footnote reads: 'A gentleman of a sound Protestant family always in great friendship with ours. Both father and son were Members of Parliament for that Town and were stewards to my grandfather'.

[1] Amsterdam: Remonstrants' MSS. J. 20.

[2] B.L. MSS. Locke, c. 20, f. 1.

[3] Ashley may well have been accompanied by Bennet, but no known documents indicate that Bennet was already acquainted with Locke.

[4] E. Bedel to Locke (B.L. MSS. Locke, c. 3, f. 164).

[5] E. Bedel to Locke (*ibid.*, f. 166).

in the University, and the steps he took prove him to have been already a man of resource and influence.

Determined not to waste time on traditional medicine, Locke decided to make a bid for the degree of Doctor of Medicine without going to all the lectures required for the degree of Bachelor of Medicine. He did not appeal for this privilege to the faculty of medicine; he realised that they would never grant it. Instead he used particular, and perhaps political, influence with Clarendon, the Chancellor of the University. It is not certain who helped him in this instance. It was very probably Ashley himself. But whoever was behind it, the following letter to his subordinate officials of the University was written by Clarendon on 3 November 1666: [1]

Mr. Vice-Chancellor and Gentlemen,
I am very well assured that Mr. John Locke, a Master of Arts and Student of Christ Church, has employed his time in the study of physic to so good purpose that he is in all respects qualified for the degree of Doctor in that faculty, for which he has also full time; [2] but not having taken the degree of bachelor in physic, he has desired that he may be dispensed with to accumulate to that degree, which appears to me a very modest and reasonable request, he professing himself ready to perform the exercises for both degrees. I therefore give my consent that a dispensation to that purpose be propounded for him.

This communication was not well received by the medical faculty. Clarendon might be a distinguished statesman, but who was he to say that a man was 'in all respects qualified' for the degree of Doctor of Medicine? It was clear to the faculty that Locke wished to take the advanced exercises for a senior medical degree to avoid the trouble of attending lectures or doing other work required for a junior medical degree and, backward as the authorities were, they were quite fair and reasonable in thinking that advanced exercises alone were not sufficient evidence of the fitness of a man to practise as a physician. Clarendon's letter, coming as it did from the highest officer of the University, must have seemed no less than a command; but the medical faculty was jealous of its standards, and the letter was ignored.

Locke had more than one motive for seeking a medical degree. He wished, not unnaturally, to have academic recognition for its

---

[1] P.R.O. 30/24/47/8.
[2] That is to say, Locke had kept the number of terms required for the degree.

JOHN LOCKE'S BIRTHPLACE AT
WRINGTON, SOMERSET
above, in 1829, *below*, in 1885

JOHN LOCKE, 1672
by John Greenhill

own sake, but he also wanted the degree in order to secure a lay-man's place as a medical don at Christ Church. He was now quite resolved against taking holy orders. The unexpected failure of Clarendon's intervention did not cause that resolution to waver. If he could not be admitted a Doctor of Medicine, he would find another way of remaining at Christ Church as a layman. Again he sought outside help. This time he solicited a letter from a source that could not be ignored—namely, from the King himself. On 14 November, 1666, the following communication reached the Dean and Chapter:[1]

> Trusty and well-beloved, we greet you well.
> Whereas we are informed that John Locke, Master of Arts and Student of Christ Church in our university of Oxford, is of such stand-ing as by the custom of that college he is obliged to enter into holy orders or otherwise to leave his Student's place there; at his humble request that he may still have the further time to prosecute his studies without that obligation, we are graciously pleased to grant him our royal dispensation, and do accordingly hereby require you to suffer him, the said John Locke, to hold and enjoy his Student's place in Christ Church, together with all the rights, profits and emoluments thereunto belonging, without taking holy orders . . . and for so doing this shall be your warrant.

The letter was signed by the Secretary of State, Sir William Morrice, and as Morrice was Ashley's 'best friend',[2] it looks again as if Ashley must have had a hand in the matter.

The royal command was necessarily obeyed. Locke had no longer any need even to consider holy orders, and when John Parry, the new Dean of Christ Church, Dublin, wrote to him that Decem-ber,[3] suggesting that Locke should join him in Ireland and be ordained there, Locke did not hesitate to decline the invitation. He made these rough notes for his reply:[4]

> You cannot doubt but I have inclination enough to be in Dublin . . . it being the company of my friends (and how much you are so, your letter shows . . .) that makes any place desirable . . .
> But, Sir, . . . it is not enough for such places barely to be in orders, and I cannot think that preferment of that nature will be thrown upon a man that hath never given any proofs of himself nor never tried the pulpit . . .

---

[1] P.R.O. 30/24/47/22.   [2] Christie, II, p. 47.
[3] B.L. MSS. Locke, c. 16, f. 188.   [4] *Ibid.*, c. 24, f. 221.

H

Now that his academic position was secure, Locke could afford to have the same moral scruples as Boyle against entering the ministry without a proper sense of vocation. There is another point of interest in the letter to Parry. Locke said: 'If I am covetous of good fortune it is that one whom I love may share it with me.' At the end of the letter he sent his services 'to both your sisters'.

Once again the problem of identity arises. Who was 'the one I love', and was she one of Parry's sisters?

I have already mentioned the evidence[1] of a sentimental friendship between Locke and a Mrs. Parry. I have supposed this Mrs. Parry to be John Parry's sister rather than John Parry's wife—indeed, Locke is hardly likely to have written to John Parry about 'one I love' if that 'one' were John Parry's wife.

Was John Parry's sister Scribelia? The suspicion might have been prompted by the promise contained in the manuscript *Oxford Gazette* of February 1665/6,[2] that John Parry's sister will 'cherish the German' (i.e. Locke). There was also the letter from Scribelia to Locke endorsed '1666'[3] referring to a 'father's invitation' which Locke had refused. This invitation might well be the invitation from John Parry for Locke to come to Ireland, and although it is hardly credible that a sister should refer to her brother as 'a father',[4] mystification and false clues abound in Locke's amatory correspondence. It is clear from Locke's letter to Parry that Parry's sisters were with him in Ireland, so that if Scribelia were one of these sisters, her letters to Locke after the summer of 1666 would have been written from Dublin. Three of her letters date from that period, but only one[5] bears any address, and that is worded: 'direct yours to my Cousin R: as you did long ago to be left where I am at Angiere Street, Flanders'. 'Flanders' here is manifestly not a real place, but a code word. One idea I have is that 'Angiere Street' was Aungier Street, a prominent Dublin thoroughfare which runs into Stephen Street, where the Parrys[6] lived before they went to Oxford.

An alternative hypothesis is that Scribelia was Anne Evelegh's sister. The objection to this is that the Evelegh family moved to

---

[1] B.L. MSS. Locke, c. 18, f. 7.

[2] *Ibid.*, c. 8, f. 62.   [3] *Ibid.*, f. 64.

[4] There is also the sentence 'a father does not know of this correspondence, I think' in the letter from Scribelia dated 'Shrove Tuesday' by her and endorsed by Locke '1666' (*ibid.*, f. 64).   [5] *Ibid.*, f. 67.

[6] John Parry's father was Edward Parry, Bishop of Killaloe, who 'had a house in Stephen Street and probably occupied it until his death [in 1656]' (D.N.B.).

Ireland in 1661, when John Evelegh became Praecentor of Cloyne,[1] whereas Scribelia was still in Oxford in February 1665/6. Admittedly there is clear evidence linking Scribelia with Black Hall, but it is possible both that Scribelia was Anne Evelegh's cousin, rather than her sister and that Anne Evelegh's cousin was John Parry's sister.

If Scribelia was John Parry's sister then it is all the more probable that 'P. E.' was John Parry's sister, the 'P' of the reversed initials standing for Parry, and the 'E' standing for the name from which 'Elia', 'Bereliza' and 'Scribelia' are all doubtless derived: 'Elizabeth'.

In the winter of 1666/7 Locke ceased to act as a college tutor. Having been refused the status necessary to teach medicine, he was no longer willing to teach grammar and philosophy. His position at Christ Church, now assured by royal command, carried with it no obligation to teach, or even to stay in Oxford, and Locke did not wish to do so. He was probably a good tutor, nevertheless. A letter of farewell he wrote to one of his pupils suggests as much. It was addressed to John Alford and dated 12 June 1666: [2]

> 'Tis true you are now past masters and tutors, and it is now therefore that you ought to have the greater care of yourself, since those mistakes or miscarriages which heretofore would have been charged upon them, will now, if any, light wholly upon you, and you yourself must be accountable for all your actions . . .
>
> One may certainly with innocence use all the enjoyments of life; and I have always been of opinion that a virtuous life is best disposed to be the most pleasant. For certainly amidst the troubles and vanities of this world, there are but two things that bring a real satisfaction with them, that is virtue and knowledge. . . .
>
> Though riches be not virtue, it is a great instrument of it, wherein lies a great part of the usefulness and comfort of life. In the right management of this lies a great part of prudence; and about money is the great mistake of men whilst they are either too covetous or too careless of it. If you throw it away idly, you lose your great support and best friend. If you hug it too closely, you lose it and yourself too. To be thought prudent and liberal, provident and good natured, are things worth your endeavour to obtain—which perhaps you will do better by avoiding the occasions of expense than by frugal limiting them when occasion hath made them necessary . . .

[1] He became Dean of Ross in Ireland on 19 January 1663/4 (*Fasti Ecclesiae Hibernicae*, I. Ed. H. Cotton, Dublin, 1851).
[2] *The Gentleman's Magazine*, 1797, I. p. 97.

It was about this time that Locke began to read Descartes. Lady Masham said:[1]

> The first books (as Mr. Locke himself has told me) which gave him a relish of philosophical studies were those of Descartes. He was rejoiced in reading of these because though he very often differed in opinion from this writer, yet he found that what he said was very intelligible; from whence he was encouraged to think that his not having understood others had, possibly, not proceeded altogether from a defect in his understanding.

The chief philosophical works of Descartes then available were his *Discourse on the Method of Rightly Conducting the Reason and Seeking for Truth in the Sciences*, first published in 1637, and the *Meditations on First Philosophy*, published in 1641. Descartes wrote the *Meditations* in Latin, but the *Discourse* in French, 'in the hope', he explained, 'that those who avail themselves of their natural reason alone may be better judges of my opinions than those who give heed only to the writings of the ancients'. A Latin translation of the *Discourse* published in Amsterdam in 1644, was the version which Locke read.

Descartes revolutionised European philosophy; and whatever the defects of his system, his historical importance is second only to that of Aristotle. He introduced the method of systematic doubt by deciding to believe nothing unless he had proof of its truth. Descartes was a mathematician as well as a philosopher, and the proof he proposed to accept was proof of the mathematical kind: rational certainty reached by deductive argument. His criterion was, as he said, to be the 'clearness and distinctness of ideas'.

The first truth which Descartes accepted was the truth of his own existence. Thinking, he argued, entailed the existence of a thinking thing: *cogito ergo sum*. The 'I' which was thus proved to exist was an incorporeal entity: a mind, of which thinking was the distinctive characteristic, not a material body, of which extension, or the occupation of space, was the distinctive characteristic. Descartes's difficulty was to pass from his assurance of the existence of mind to any assurance of the existence of matter. But he had no difficulty in proving, according to his method, the existence of God, who was, like mind, incorporeal.

Descartes distinguished three kinds of ideas: innate ideas, adventitious ideas (or ideas which come from without the mind)

[1] Amsterdam: Remonstrants' MSS. J. 57a.

and factitious ideas (or ideas produced within the mind). He believed in innate ideas only in the sense that reason was innate: men were born with the faculty with which they came to discern rational truths—among others, the truth of God's existence. Descartes had not the same confidence about adventitious ideas. Derived, as they were, from sensory perception, such ideas were blurred and confused. They yielded no clear and distinct idea of the reality of the external world. To demonstrate his point, he chose as an example of a material body a piece of wax. A piece of wax has perceptible qualities: a certain taste, a certain smell, a certain colour; it is hard, cold and of a specific shape and size; if it is struck it makes a sound. Put near fire, the wax ceases to be hard and cold, it loses its shape and acquires a different colour, taste and smell; if it is struck it makes no sound.

Does the same wax [Descartes asked] [1] remain after this change? We must confess that it remains; none would judge otherwise. What then did I know so distinctly in this piece of wax? It could certainly be nothing of all that the senses brought to my notice, since all those things which fall under taste, smell, sight, touch, and hearing, are found to be changed, and yet the same wax remains.

The same wax remains even though nothing remains but a certain extended thing which is flexible and movable. Then again, Descartes asked, what is extension? It is not, he answered, a thing seen, but a concept understood by the mind. Thus our knowledge of the material world is not what our senses show us, but what our minds, or our faculty of understanding, apprehends.

Descartes realised that his theory did not wholly answer the questions of whether the external world existed at all or whether any sensory perceptions could be considered veridical. Here he was thrown back on the intellectual idea of God. God whose existence he had proved by rational argument was by definition good, so it necessarily followed that God would not deceive his creatures. Since God had planted in all men a belief in the reality of the external world, that belief must be true.

Descartes realised also that his rigid distinction between mind and matter raised the problem of how the mind and the body of a man could interact. He solved this problem ingeniously, though not, as

[1] *The Philosophical Works of Descartes.* Trans. E. S. Haldane and F. R. T. Ross (Cambridge, 1931), I, p. 154.

he realised, satisfactorily, by suggesting that the 'pineal gland', which is attached by a stalk to the cerebrum, was the organ through which the mind of a man was in contact with the body.

Locke read Descartes eagerly, but critically. The Cartesian method of systematic doubt he welcomed; but the Cartesian method of rationalistic or deductive reconstruction he rejected, and rejected from the point of view of a Boyleian scientist. All his connections with 'experimental philosophy' had taught Locke to look to inductive methods for knowledge of the universe.

Locke was not the first man to read Descartes from the standpoint of a scientist. Both his appreciation of Descartes and his misgivings had already been felt and expressed by Pierre Gassendi.[1] This philosopher's criticisms of Descartes were printed in a letter to the author added to the second Latin (1642) edition of Descartes's *Meditations*, and further elaborated in Gassendi's own *Disquisitio Metaphysica*, published in Amsterdam in 1644. Both these books Locke read.

Against Descartes Gassendi argued that all knowledge is derived from sensory observation: that 'every idea which exists in the mind originates in the senses'. For this reason, he rejected not only the doctrine of innate ideas, but the whole of Cartesian metaphysics.

> . . . you indeed call material things doubtful; [Gassendi wrote in his published letter to Descartes] [2] but if you cared to confess the truth, you would acknowledge that you are not less certain of the existence of the body which you inhabit, and of all the things that surround you, than of your own existence.

As for Descartes's attempt to show by means of the example of a piece of wax that only the understanding and not the senses can apprehend such mutable material things, Gassendi admitted that the concept of wax or its substratum could be abstracted from its accidents.

> But, [he asked] [3] is it the case that this secures a distinct perception of the substance or nature of the wax? We indeed conceive that besides

[1] Pierre Gassendi (1592–1655), though a Catholic priest, attacked both the Scholastic philosophers and Cartesians from the point of view of a scientific empiricism derived from Epicurus. In addition to the works published in his lifetime there appeared posthumously *Commentarius de vita, moribus et placitis Epicuri* (1659) and *Syntagma philosophiae Epicuri* (1684).

[2] Haldane and Ross, *op. cit.*, II, p. 144.

[3] *Ibid.*, p. 147.

the colour, the figure, the capacity for being liquefied, etc., there is something which is the subject of the accidents and the observed changes of the wax; but as to what that is, or what is its nature, we are ignorant. Nay, it always eludes our apprehension and it is only by conjecture that we think there must be some substratum. Hence I marvel how you can maintain that, after you have finished stripping off those forms, as it were the vestures, of the wax, you perceive perfectly and very clearly what the wax is.

Gassendi also challenged Descartes's view that more could be known about the mind than could be known about the body; science had taught men much about the human body, and Gassendi said he doubted whether Descartes could 'reveal and demonstrate' so much about the mind or incorporeal substance.

Gassendi did not deny that Descartes might have 'many ideas which have not entered into you by way of the senses', but he added: 'it is easy for you to have them because you construct them out of those [ideas] which have so entered. . . .' [1] Gassendi also asked Descartes how, if he were an incorporeal entity, unextended and indivisible, could he be a physical body; and, if he were both, how could the two intermingle that had nothing in common? Even if he, the incorporeal spirit, claimed to be united with the body through the brain, the difficulty would be the same, for if the point at which interaction occurs is a physical point, 'such a point is extended and is certainly not devoid of parts' whereas if 'it is a mathematical point you know that it is given only by the imagination'.[2]

Although Gassendi wrote so cogently against Cartesian metaphysics, he was not opposed to metaphysics altogether. He did not share the extreme view of Hobbes that 'that which is not body is no part of the universe',[3] but he did maintain that sound philosophy must rest on observation, and be tested by scientific methods.

Locke agreed, and when he began a decade later to write philosophy himself, this was the kind of philosophy he wrote. Locke never acknowledged what he owed to Gassendi, but at least he did not deny it as he denied his debt to Hobbes.

In the spring of 1667 Lord Ashley invited Locke to go and live with him in London as his personal physician. The offer was tempting. After the plague and the fire, new life was stirring everywhere

[1] Haldane and Ross, *op. cit.*, II, p. 185.   [2] *Ibid.*, p. 199.
[3] *Leviathan*, IV, § xlvi.

in the capital, and London had much to offer a scientific *virtuoso*. Gresham's College and the new Royal Society in London had come to be more important centres of research and experiment than either university. Willis and Lower had already moved to London, and Boyle was preparing to follow them.   Sydenham was also there.

Locke accepted Ashley's proposal, packed up his belongings in Christ Church, let his rooms to an undergraduate, and set off for Exeter House in the Strand. According to Lady Masham's testimony,[1] from that time forward Locke 'was with my Lord Ashley as a man at home, and lived in the family much esteemed'.

[1] Amsterdam: Remonstrants' MSS. J. 57a.

Chapter Nine

ANTHONY ASHLEY COOPER

LORD ASHLEY was a remarkable man. Born Anthony Ashley Cooper at Wimborne St. Giles, Dorset, in 1621, he was left motherless at the age of seven and fatherless at nine—fatherless, but a baronet and the owner of a large estate. He went up to Exeter College, Oxford, when he was sixteen and left two years later to marry Lord Coventry's daughter, Margaret. He never grew much above five feet tall.

In the Civil War he served for a time in the Royalist Army under Hertford, but in March 1644 he transferred his allegiance to the Parliamentary, or winning, side. He was not yet twenty-two. Dryden, who hated him, thus described:[1]

> A martial hero first with early care
> Blown, like a pigmy, by the winds to war;
> A beardless chief, a rebel ere a man,
> So young his hatred to his prince began.

Sir Anthony went over to the Puritans for the sake, he said, of freedom and the Protestant faith, having come to the conclusion that the King had no intention of preserving either. The Puritans were at first suspicious, but it was not long before they made Sir Anthony commander-in-chief of their troops in Dorset. His religious sympathies, however, were Presbyterian, and on the new-modelling of the army he was relieved of his command. He was put off with the office of high sheriff of Wiltshire. A deputy lieutenant of that county at the time was Alexander Popham.

In his domestic life Sir Anthony experienced some grief. His first wife died, after four miscarriages, in 1646; his second wife, Frances Cecil, sister of the Royalist Earl of Exeter, died seven years later. Then in 1656 the baronet married, at the age of thirty-five,

---

[1] *The Medal*, ll. 26–9.

a third wife, Margaret, daughter of the second Lord Spencer, and in the same year he found himself a seat in the House of Commons; the political career of Anthony Ashley Cooper then began in earnest.

Although Cromwell never liked 'the little man with three names', there was no dramatic conflict between them. But after the Lord Protector's death, Sir Anthony was arrested by Cromwell's successors and was accused of conspiring with other Presbyterians and Royalists to overthrow the republic and recall the King. One of his fellow plotters was said to have been Alexander Popham.

The charge was not ill founded. The rebellion had been set to begin on 1 August 1659, and the King moved secretly to Calais to be ready to enter England if the rising succeeded; but the only notable action took place in Cheshire under George Booth, and he was soon subdued.

According to a letter written by a Royalist agent,[1] Alexander Popham's share in the exploit was inglorious:

> Alexander Popham was . . . chosen one of seven generals to take care of the army in the absence of Haselrig, Walton and Morley, expected two days after, so that his dignity lasted double the time of Bibulus's consulship, and to us appeared twice as ridiculous. Sir A. A. Cooper seems very eager in establishing these people. . . .

However eager he had been in establishing these people, Sir Anthony Ashley Cooper succeeded in covering most of his tracks. At his trial he was found not guilty and acquitted. Going back to politics with his vigour and courage renewed, he was re-elected to the House of Commons in the following January, and was soon one of the leading personalities in Parliament. Behind the scenes he was still in touch with Alexander Popham, and the pair of them urged General Monk to invite the King to return on certain conditions; and although Monk chose, when he sent the invitation, to make it unconditional, Sir Anthony's overtures were not fruitless. Monk recommended him to Charles as a trustworthy friend and a valuable ally, so that immediately on the Restoration he was made a Privy Councillor, and in less than a year he had been raised to the peerage Lord Ashley.

Charles doubted if he was a trustworthy friend, but accepted him

---

[1] Brodrick to Hyde, quoted by Christie, I, 202.

as an ally. The Restoration Parliaments were Anglican, and they forced on the King's first Minister, Clarendon, who was in fact a moderate conservative, that policy of compulsory conformity unjustly known to history as the Clarendon Code. Ashley was the most ardent opponent of the Code, the most eloquent champion of toleration. He opposed the Corporation Bill, the Act of Uniformity, the Five Mile Act and all the other measures which were designed to curb the liberties of Dissenting Protestants. In doing so, he had the private approval of the King. Charles at heart was not an Anglican: in good times he was irreligious, and in bad times a Papist. His own desire was to let everyone believe and worship as they pleased.

Ashley did not go as far as this, but his views on toleration were far closer to the King's than they were to those of the Anglican majority in Parliament. Ashley's 'speciality' was trade. Though a considerable landowner, he was chiefly interested in stock-holding and colonial expansion; he was the part-owner of slave-ships and 'plantations', he was the leading member of the Committee for Trade, and when the province of Carolina was founded in 1663 and put under the control of a board of Lords Proprietors, Ashley seized most of the strings.

Ashley's very zeal for toleration was indeed but an aspect of his interest in trade. It was not simply a case of his desiring toleration of dissenters because of his own Presbyterian views, still less a case of his having achieved a Christ-like forbearance beyond the spiritual range of the average sensual man. Ashley opposed religious persecution because religious persecution divided a nation, drove many of its most industrious citizens to emigrate, and generally impeded commercial development. He saw more clearly than most Englishmen of his time how colonial expansion and international trade could be made to bring enormous fortunes to investors like himself and at the same time increase the wealth and power of the country as a whole. The example of Holland had taught him how trade and toleration could flourish splendidly together. He was the complete progressive capitalist in politics; he might almost have been invented by Marx.

Ashley was never a handsome man. Besides his dwarfish stature, he had a plain face with big ears and monkey's eyes. His critics have made much of his reputed addiction to the pleasures of the brothel. The King is supposed to have called him 'the greatest whoremaster in England';[1] and he was seen as the original of 'Antonio' in Otway's play *Venice Preserved*:[2]

> To lewdness every night the lecher ran,
> Show me all London such another man.

Roger North,[3] in saying that Ashley was 'not behindhand in the modish pleasures of the time', mentions a deformed old gentleman called Sir Paul Neile [4] who was called Ashley's groom 'because he watered his mares (I forebear the vulgar word) in Hyde Park with Rhenish wine and sugar, and not seldom a bait of cheesecakes'. There is possibly some truth in these stories; certainly I see no reason for supposing (with Christie and Airey [5]) that he was chaste; but I believe Ashley's reputation as a voluptuary has been built up by his enemies and critics because they have not been able to find a sufficiently telling case against him as a statesman.

Exeter House was one of the patrician dwellings—in any country but England they would be called 'palaces'—in the Strand. It was on the north, or less fashionable side, and when Locke first went there, it was by no means the grandest house [6] in Westminster, though it was later enlarged to challenge its rivals. In 1667 it was barely large enough for Ashley's establishment, but everything was done to make Locke comfortable. Ashley put a room at his disposal, and had it fitted up with bookshelves and cabinets and all the other equipment a savant might need. Space was also found at Exeter House for scientific experiments, in which Ashley, like King Charles

---

[1] Brown, p. 214. (Ashley is said to have replied 'Of a subject, Sire', but this only makes the story sound the more apocryphal.)

[2] *Vide* John Lord Campbell, *Lives of the Lord Chancellors*, 1857, Vol. IV, p. 234.

[3] *Examen*, 1740, p. 60. (North is not, however, a very reliable witness, and he detested all Whigs.)

[4] Sir Paul Neile (or Neal) was one of the founders of the Royal Society, a wealthy amateur of science who assisted Wren in several of his experiments at Oxford.

[5] Christie gives the following very curious reasons for denying the accusations of immorality: (1) that Ashley's name is not once mentioned in the *Memoirs* of Grammont; (2) that he was 'the affectionate husband of three wives in succession'; (3) that he was 'careful of his estate, which is not commonly the case with men of profligate habits'; (4) that he 'had many intellectual pursuits besides politics'; (5) that 'one of his chief friends and most frequent companions was Locke, a man not only of pre-eminent intellect, but also of austere virtue'. In the D.N.B. Osmund Airey says, 'Shaftesbury's private life was of rare purity for the age'.

[6] It was built by one of the Cecils, William Lord Burleigh; later his son Lord Exeter, and then Alexander Popham's brother Edward lived there.

himself, took a personal interest: Ashley was not only a Fellow (an insignificant fact for a nobleman), but also a councillor of the Royal Society.

One of Locke's notebooks, now in an American private collection,[1] bears witness to the scientific activities which went forward at Exeter House as early as 1667. It contains lists of London chemists from whom scientific glasses and other equipment was ordered in Ashley's name as well as Locke's, and miscellaneous notes give details of the experiments conducted.

Another notebook [2] Locke kept at the time shows that literary interests were not forgotten. The fact that many of the excerpts he copied from the books he was reading relate to the virtues and achievements of great men is an interesting sign of his arrival in the great world.

The year 1667 was a critical one in English history. The war with Holland which had occasioned Locke's diplomatic journey to Cleves with Sir Walter Vane was still on. Unfortunately a great many Englishmen had forgotten it. The plague of 1665 and the fire of 1666 had given Londoners more urgent things to think about. Fighting men, sailors especially, who had done so well in the early stages of the war, had been demoralised by boredom and by delays in receiving their pay.[3] The officers, particularly (it was said) those recruited from among the Frenchified cavalier courtiers, gave no energetic lead. Clarendon had never approved of the war, and Parliament had come out openly in favour of ending it. The King might have been resolute enough, but he was so short of money, so confident that the war would be soon over, that he had his largest fighting ships laid up in the river Medway.

What happened as a result of all this Locke himself described in a letter to Strachey dated June 15: [4]

[1] That of Sydney Edelstein Esq. of New York City. The notebook is bound together in sheep-skin with the Goldsmiths' Almanac for 1667.

[2] B.L. MSS. Locke, F. 14. A small octavo volume of some 200 pages with excerpts from books in English and Latin.

[3] For example, the officers and seamen of the frigates *Harp* and *Mary* petitioned the Admiralty in 1667 saying that there was 'above fifty-two months' pay due to them', that they were 'going naked for want of clothes', and that their wives and children were 'in a starving condition', which, they said, 'together are worse ten thousand times than to die by the hands of an enemy'. (Quoted by Andrew Browning, *English Historical Documents 1660–1714*, London, 1953, p. 831.)

[4] B.L. MSS. Locke, c. 24, f. 245.

The Dutch have burned seven of our ships in Chatham, viz. the Royal James, Royal Oak, London, Unity, St. Matthias, Charles V, and the Royal Charles, which some say they have towed off, others that they have burned. One man of war of theirs was blown up, and three others, they say, are stuck in the sands. The rest of their fleet is fallen down out of the Medway into the Thames. It was neither excess of courage in them, nor want of courage in us that brought this loss upon us, for when the English had powder and shot they fought like themselves, and made the Dutch feel them. But whether it were fortune or fate or anything else, let time and tongues tell you, for I profess I would not believe what every mouth speaks.

Englishmen generally refused, with Locke, to blame the Navy. They blamed the Lord Chancellor instead. Even in Parliament, where the members knew well enough that Clarendon was not responsible for what had gone wrong, and that he had in truth opposed the policy which had brought about the disaster, they fell upon him as a scapegoat. Clarendon held on until August, but then his fall was complete; the King abandoned him to enemies, and after dismissal and impeachment, there was no alternative to exile.

Clarendon's fall was the cue for Ashley's rise. Ashley had always been staunchly nationalist or patriotic. As the spokesman of commercial imperialism, he had always urged a strong line against the Dutch as England's chief mercantile competitors, and he could point to the Dutch invasion of the Medway as proof of the wisdom of his counsel. But Ashley did not choose to appear as Clarendon's open adversary. On the contrary, he had supported the Chancellor on many issues and opposed his impeachment. He was not yet ready to bid for the seals which Clarendon surrendered. He was ready nevertheless to take, in early autumn, one step towards the highest office. He consented then to become, with Buckingham, Arlington, Lauderdale and Clifford, one of that ministry of five which was afterwards known as the Cabal: and even then he was content to follow where others took it in turn to lead.

Ashley's taking office in the Cabal meant that science languished for a while at Exeter House. Locke wrote to Boyle on 12 November 1667,[1] saying:

The place I am at present in, and the remove I am like to make (for I believe I shall once more cross the seas before I settle) have kept me

---

[1] Boyle, V, p. 568.

from attempting any further experiments in chemistry, though I find my fingers still itch to be at it. . . .

With no time for chemistry, Locke had none for gallantry, and perhaps no longer an itch for it. Scribelia wrote plaintively:[1]

> . . . I am come, my Best, from the country, where I have been this fortnight. . . . I have a thousand questions to ask you, but dare not. Are you changed and do you now think indifferently of the affection you have framed in my soul?
> . . . When you come in[to] my thoughts, I groan to death. But all will be well. . . .
> My sister goes this week to Wales for money. Direct yours to me at my —— in Angeirs Street. Burn this letter. Tell no one of this I send you. . . . Farewell.

The world remembers Locke as a great theorist of toleration, but Ashley was a champion of toleration before Locke was, when Locke's views on toleration were indeed quite otherwise. This is not to say that Locke acquired his mature opinions on toleration from Ashley, for by the time he met Ashley Locke's views had come into line with his, but it was Ashley who made Locke give systematic attention to the subject and furthered his evolution as a liberal.

Locke wrote a substantial essay on toleration in 1667; and as no fewer than four drafts[2] of it still exist, there is no doubt that he gave it a great deal of time and care. His renown as a theorist of toleration is based on the *Letters for Toleration* and other political works which he published during the reign of William III; but most of the principles he set forth in those *Letters* were already contained in the manuscript essay of 1667.

Locke argued in that essay that the 'trust, power and authority' of the civil ruler, sovereign or magistrate of any society was vested in him solely for the purpose of securing 'the good, preservation and peace of men in that society'. For if 'men could live peaceably and quietly together' without a common ruler, 'there would be no need at all of magistrates or politics'.

---

[1] B.L. MSS. Locke, c. 8, f. 65.

[2] The earliest draft, inscribed '*Sic cogitavit Atticus*', is in the Henry E. Huntington Library, San Marino, California (Call number: HM 584). Another draft is in the Public Record Office (30/24/47/1: printed in F.B., I, pp. 174–94); a third draft is in a commonplace book now in the possession of Mr. Arthur Houghton, Jnr., of Wye Plantation, Queenstown, Maryland; a fourth (and apparently the last) version is in the Lovelace Collection (B.L. MSS. Locke, c. 28, f. 21).

In order to clarify the problem of toleration Locke divided men's actions and opinions into three kinds. First, there were those actions and opinions which did not concern politics at all. These included speculative opinions and methods of divine worship. Secondly, there were those actions and opinions which were neither good nor bad in themselves, but which impinged upon other people and thus concerned society. Thirdly, there were those actions which were good or bad in themselves—namely, virtues and vices.

Locke argued that only actions and opinions of the *first* kind had 'an absolute and universal right to toleration'. This right derived from the fact that they did not affect society, but were either wholly private or concerned God alone.

Opinions of the second kind Locke illustrated with examples: belief in divorce and polygamy, and belief in freedom to breed children and dispose of estates.

> These opinions and the actions following from them, [he wrote] have a title also to toleration, but only so far as they do not tend to the disturbance of the State or do not cause greater inconvenience than advantage to the community.

But, he added, while it might be permissible for the magistrate to prohibit the *publishing* of any of these opinions if they tended to the disturbance of the public good, no man ought to be forced to renounce his opinion, or assent to a contrary opinion, because such coercion would not alter a man's actual beliefs, but only make him a hypocrite. The magistrate should never prohibit publishing unless he had 'seriously and impartially considered and debated' that such a course was really necessary for 'the peace, safety or security of his people'.

As for the third class of actions, those good or bad in themselves, Locke held that civil rulers had 'nothing to do with the good of men's souls or their concernments in another life'. The magistrate ought not to 'command the practise of any vice', but neither was it his duty to *punish* every vice. God would punish vice and reward virtue. The duty of the magistrate was simply to keep the peace.

Locke attempted to show just how these principles should be applied in the political situation of 1667. Catholics, he argued, should *not* be tolerated, because their opinions were 'absolutely destructive of all governments except the Pope's'. Protestant dissenters, on the other hand, should be tolerated because their beliefs

ANTHONY ASHLEY COOPER, FIRST EARL
OF SHAFTESBURY, 1672
by John Greenhill

JOHN LOCKE, 1689
by Hermann Verelst

were in no way inimical to the safety of the realm; and, what was more, if the dissenters were not tolerated, they would emigrate to other countries, and the loss would be England's.

In May of 1668 Ashley was taken seriously ill, and Locke's duties as his physician came to the forefront. For twelve years Ashley had suffered from a suppurating hydatid cyst of the liver.[1] A discharge from the cyst caused his illness of 1668. Pepys wrote in his *Diary* of 19 June that year: 'My Lord Ashley is like to die, having some imposthume in his breast, that he hath been fain to be cut into his body.' Having consulted Sydenham and other doctors, Locke had a surgeon barber open his patient's abdomen and he drained the abscess through a silver tube. Until early September he gave treatment three times daily. Then Locke consulted his medical friends once more. Should he remove the silver tube? One said yes; three, including Sydenham, thought it would be unwise to take it away while the abscess was still suppurating; and as this was also Locke's opinion, the tube remained. Ashley was wonderfully restored to health as a result of the operation. He wore the silver, then a gold tube for the rest of his life, and although the wits of the time found it a subject for mirth Ashley did not mind. He was well again; and he believed that he owed his life to Locke. According to Ashley's grandson:[2]

> After this cure Mr. Locke grew so much in esteem with my grandfather that as great a man as he had experienced him in physic, he looked upon this but as his least part. He encouraged him to turn his thoughts another way, nor would he suffer him to practise physic except in his own family and as a kindness to some particular friend.

It was Ashley who discovered and helped Locke to discover his own true genius. Before he went to Exeter House, Locke was a minor Oxford scholar, an ex-diplomatist of small experience, an amateur scientist, an unpublished writer and unqualified physician. In Ashley's home he blossomed into a philosopher, an economist and a medical *virtuoso*; and a part of the credit for his doing so must go to the ugly little nobleman who was his patron and host.

[1] This diagnosis has been given by Sir William Osler in *John Locke as a Physician* in *The Lancet*, 20 October, 1900. Locke's notes are in the Public Record Office (30/24/47).
[2] Amsterdam, Remonstrants' MSS. J. 20 (The third Earl of Shaftesbury to Jean le Clerc, 8 February 1705/6).

I

Ashley also employed Locke as one of his political advisers. As his grandson[1] said:

> He put him upon the study of the religious and civil affairs of the nation with whatsoever related to the business of a Minister of State, in which he was so successful that my grandfather began soon to use him as a friend, and consult with him upon occasions of that kind. He was not only with him in his library and closet but in company with the great men of those times, the Duke of Buckingham,[2] Lord Halifax[3] and others, who, being men of wit and learning, were as much taken with him, for together with his serious, respectful and humble character, he had a mixture of pleasantry and becoming boldness of speech. The liberty he could take with these great men was peculiar to such a genius as his.

Locke did not get much material reward for the work he did for Ashley, but, on the other hand, Locke had his own means. An account book[4] in the Lovelace Collection contains a record of the income Locke received from his property in Somerset between 1664 and 1672. During the six months ending on Lady Day, 1669, he noted the following receipts:

Rent due:	Rent			Tax Rep.			Rec'd		
	£	s.	d.	£	s.	d.	£	s.	d.
R. Harol, Beluton	12	5	0	2	16	11	9	8	1
J. Atkins, Old Downe	1	10	0		1	0	1	9	0
T. Summers, Tineing and Parocks	2	12	6	—			2	12	6
T. Summers, Henly Grove	1	7	6	—			1	7	6
T. Summers, Taxes 1/12		4	0	—				4	0
F. Lyance, Buckhill	8	10	0	1	6	9	7	3	3
T. Jones, Nineworthys	1	0	0	—			1	0	0
T. Jones, Taxes 1/9		4	0	—				4	0
J. Anthony, Buckfurlong	2	10	0	—			2	10	0
A. Hopkins, house and common mead	4	18	0	—			4	18	0
J. Flower, Furze		15	0	—					
B. Smith, Humber brook		3	0	—				3	0
B. Smith, Tivening			1	—					

[1] Amsterdam, Remonstrants' MSS. J. 20 (The third Earl of Shaftesbury to Jean le Clerc, 8 February 1705/6).

[2] George Villiers, second Duke of Buckingham (1628–87), the first minister of the Cabal: 'The man was of no religion, but notoriously and professedly lustful, and yet of greater wit and parts, and sounder principles as to the interest of humanity and the common good than most lords of the court' (*Reliquiae Baxterianae*, III, p. 21).

[3] George Savile, first Marquis of Halifax (1633–95), 'The Trimmer' because of his devotion to the expedient, was nevertheless an extremist in the early years of his association with Ashley.

[4] B.L. MSS. Locke, F. 12, f. 22.

Rent due:	Rent £ s. d.			Tax Rep. £ s. d.			Rec'd £ s. d.		
Kent's tenement		2	0	—				2	0
A. Fleury's tenement		2	0	—				2	0
Lokier's tenement			6						
Gardiner's tenement		1	0						
L[1]	40	0	0	—			40	0	0
Christ Church A Squib[2] chamber	5	10	0	—			5	10	0

These figures show that Locke was drawing an income of about £240 a year in addition to his revenues from Christ Church and the profits from his investments in the slave trade and elsewhere.[3] It was no princely income, but it meant that he could afford to be Ashley's 'friend' rather than his employee, though on one occasion later Locke came close to complaining that Shaftesbury had used him meanly.[4]

[1] This £40 from 'L' recurs in 1670, but does not recur in 1671 when William Dawson is named as paying Locke no less than £87 10s. per half-year.

[2] The tenant of Locke's chamber at Christ Church. A subsequent tenant was an undergraduate named Saunders. In 1673 Locke noted: 'Mr. Wall let my chamber to Sir Richard Anderson's sons for £10 per an. to begin at Allhallowstide '73 and to give a month's warning of leaving.' (B.L. MSS. Locke, c. 1, f. 42.)

[3] Between 1671 and 1675 he invested in Richard Thompson's company alone miscellaneous sums on short-term loan totalling £1,016. He put £400 in the raw-silk trade in 1673; he bought £400 stock in the Royal African Company in 1674 and £200 more in 1675. The £100 stock he bought in the Bahama Adventurers in 1675 he sold the following year for £127 10s. In 1676 he lent Lady Windham £600 on mortgage and drew £36 a year interest. Locke might therefore be considered a member of the investing class whose interests his economic writings signally upheld.

[4] Locke to Pembroke, 8 December 1684 (p. 247 below).

Chapter Ten

AT EXETER HOUSE

ON 23 November 1668 Locke was elected a Fellow of the Royal Society. He was then aged thirty-six. His sponsor was Sir Paul Neile, one of the pioneers of the Society, Wren's collaborator in the laboratory and Ashley's friend. Locke was received by a man he knew for the second President of the Royal Society was Joseph Williamson, who had been a poor and undistinguished schoolfellow of Locke's at Westminster and had since become one of the leading administrators in the realm.

The Royal Society, being directly descended from the philosophical club which Wilkins and Goddard had conducted at Oxford (and earlier still in London), had received its charter in 1663, and held meetings every Wednesday or Thursday for scientific experiments, demonstrations and discussions. The annual meeting took place on St. Andrew's Day, though Sir William Petty suggested that St. Thomas's Day would have been more suitable for a society of empiricists, since 'St. Thomas would not believe till he had seen and put his finger into the holes'.[1] Among the first Fellows were most of the old Oxford names: Wilkins, Goddard, Wren, Willis, Lower, Boyle, Hooke, together with the new Savilian professors at that University, respectively Seth Ward of Astronomy and John Wallis of Geometry. Indeed the 'early meetings of the Royal Society were largely taken up with experimental demonstrations by the Oxford Fellows'.[2]

But by 1668 the Society had two hundred members, and its activities were becoming more miscellaneous. The King's being a Fellow had made the Royal Society almost too fashionable. Peers like Ashley and Buckingham and Sandwich, who were genuinely interested in empirical science; amateur savants like Kenelm Digby, Isaac Barrow and John Evelyn; men of letters like Dryden and

[1] Aubrey, p. 272.
[2] Crombie *op cit.*, p. 23.

Aubrey; civil servants like Samuel Pepys and Thomas Povey were the most outstanding, but not the most representative Fellows. Whereas the first President, Lord Brouncker, had been a mathematician, Joseph Williamson was chiefly interested in historical studies, and he encouraged a tendency to eclecticism. Many of the activities of the Society were scientific only in the widest possible sense of that term, and some were not scientific at all.

Locke was appointed to a committee of eleven for 'considering and directing experiments', but he did not give much of his time to it. He preferred to work in a smaller unit than the Royal Society. He founded a little club which met regularly in his room at Exeter House to discuss scientific, theological and philosophical questions. The members included Mapletoft, Sydenham and Tyrrell; and Ashley himself was not the least among them.[1] To judge from the procedure of clubs which Locke formed in later years, one may believe that its meetings were held in the evenings over a bottle of wine and that papers were read in turn by each of the several members and then discussed by the others. It may well be that Ashley wrote several such papers and that some were on philosophical subjects.[2]

Although Ashley wanted him to give his time to other matters besides medicine, Locke did not abandon that subject entirely. He began a book,[3] in which he, with Sydenham, intended to review the whole state of clinical medicine; he accompanied Sydenham on professional visits and helped him collect data on smallpox. One completely new subject claimed him: economics. This subject arose just then because Ashley had been appointed within the Cabal government to the post of Chancellor of the Exchequer.

Locke's most important book on economics, *Some Considerations of the Lowering of Interest and Raising the Value of Money*, was not published until 1692, but the greater part of it was written in 1668.

[1] In an article in *Mind* (LXI, 241, 90: January, 1952) on 'Locke and the First Lord Shaftesbury' (Ashley became Earl of Shaftesbury in 1672) Peter Laslett writes: 'Locke's position in Shaftesbury's household after 1667 was such that much of his intellectual activity must have gone forward in Shaftesbury's company and have been directed towards Shaftesbury himself.'

[2] Peter Laslett (*loc. cit.*) draws attention to philosophical manuscripts among the papers seized from Exeter House by government agents in 1681, and suggests that some of these manuscripts were of Shaftesbury's own composition.

[3] *De Arte Medica. Vide* also K. E. Dewhurst on Locke and Sydenham in *The Practitioner*, Sept., 1955, pp. 314–320, the *Bulletin of the History of Medicine*, XXIX, 5, pp. 393–400; the *Irish Journal of Medical Science*, August, 1956, pp. 365–384.

In the dedication to an unnamed M.P.,[1] which was printed at the beginning of the book, Locke wrote:

> You have put me upon looking out my old papers which have so long lain by and been forgotten. Upon this new survey of them, I find not my thoughts to differ from those I had near twenty years since. They have to me still the appearance of truth.

These 'old papers'[2] run to fifty-eight manuscript pages and contain a plea for a new approach to the problem of interest, put forward on economic as distinct from political grounds.

One of the medieval legacies which the Renaissance world had to overthrow in order to achieve economic progress was the deep-seated belief that usury was wrong. When usury was legalised in England in 1546 the Government had thought it necessary to impose a legal limit of ten per cent, which was reduced progressively until it stood at six per cent in 1651.

By that time there had come to be a clear difference between the money-lender and the investor. Usurers continued to charge, however illegally, excessive rates of interest, while honest public investors —the forerunners of the modern shareholder—suffered as a result of the laws which restricted the percentage. Nevertheless in 1665 Sir Josiah Child published two pamphlets[3] advocating a further reduction of the legal rate of interest to four per cent on the grounds that the low rate of interest enforced by law in Holland was the key to the commercial wealth of that nation.

Locke's manuscript of 1668 was written as a reply to Sir Josiah Child and began thus:

> The first thing to be considered is whether the price of the hire of money can be regulated by law; and to that, I think, generally speaking that 'tis manifest it cannot. For, since it is impossible to make a law that shall hinder a man from giving away his money or estate to whom he pleases, it will be impossible by any contrivance of law, to hinder men . . . to purchase money to be lent to them at what rate soever their occasions shall make necessary for them to have it.

Locke claimed that a reduction in the rate of interest would make borrowing more difficult, encourage perjury and impede trade. He

---

[1] Sir John Somers, M.P.

[2] B.L. MSS. Locke, d. 2 and c. 8.

[3] *Brief Observations concerning Trade and the Interest on Money* and *Discourses upon Trade.*

pointed out that money had its market rate, liable, like anything else, to fluctuate; and he concluded that this market rate, and not any rate fixed by law, should be the rate of interest payable for money. He said:

> Money has a value as it is capable by exchange to procure us the necessaries and conveniences of life, and in this it has the nature of a commodity; only with this difference that it serves us commonly by its exchange, never almost by its consumption.

Locke was easily infected with Ashley's zeal for commercial imperialism, seeing as clearly as his patron saw the possibilities it offered for personal and national enrichment. Their interest was directed chiefly towards North America and the islands of the Caribbean. Raleigh's failure to establish a prosperous British colony in Virginia had discouraged many Englishmen, but Ashley had his eyes on the Puritan colonies of the north-eastern seaboard; their success justified, he believed, hopes of better things in the south. The province of Carolina was the chief centre of his colonial ambitions.

In 1668 Ashley persuaded Locke to become secretary to the Lords Proprietors of Carolina, to assist them both in advertising their province and in drawing up a constitution for it. Advertisement was needed in order to induce settlers to emigrate to Carolina and develop its resources, and a constitution was needed because the King had entrusted the Lords Proprietors with full responsibility for its government.

The advertisements which Locke helped to draft promised liberty of conscience to all settlers, 'they behaving themselves peaceably and quietly and not using this liberty to licentiousness nor the civil injury or outward disturbance of others'.

A copy, in Locke's hand, of *The Fundamental Constitutions for the Government of Carolina* which reposes in the Public Record Office,[1] has long been familiar to students of Locke. The fact of its being in Locke's hand has led many such scholars to conclude that Locke composed it (it has been printed in several editions of Locke's *Works*), whereas that circumstance is in fact evidence only of Locke's secretarial services to the Lords Proprietors.

It is clear from other evidence, however, that Locke *did* have a considerable say in the framing of the *Fundamental Constitutions.*

[1] P.R.O. 30/24/47/3. It is in a vellum-covered notebook of seventy-five leaves dated 21 July 1669.

Notably there is a letter [1] from Sir Peter Colleton, a man well informed in colonial matters, pleading for 'that excellent form of government in the composure of which you had so great a hand' to be put into effect.

The *Fundamental Constitutions* were frankly designed to 'avoid erecting a numerous democracy' and to 'establish the Lords Proprietors equally and without confusion'. The political framework proposed was a manorial system; it provided for a legislative assembly balanced between the common people and the nobility in such a way that the power of the commoners should not outweigh that of their betters. There was to be religious toleration, but belief in God was to be compulsory: 'No man shall be permitted to be a freeman of Carolina, or have any estate or habitation in it, who does not acknowledge a God and that God is publicly to be worshipped.'

Ashley and Locke believed that the prosperity of the colonists and the profits of the Lords Proprietors must coincide. But the colonists who began to settle there in 1669 thought otherwise. The provisions of the *Fundamental Constitutions* never came into effect. The supremacy of the Lords Proprietors was repudiated in Carolina long before the Declaration of Independence and the War of 1775.

Minutes in Locke's hand [2] show that he attended regularly, in his capacity as Secretary, the meetings of the Lords Proprietors of Carolina until June 1675. The Lords Proprietors, who had the power to grant titles of nobility, bestowed on him in April 1671 the rank of landgrave in the aristocracy of Carolina—the title to be his and his heirs for ever. At the same time they gave him four thousand 'baronia', or estates of land, in the colony.[3] As the aristocracy of Carolina never materialised, the title was an insubstantial one, and even the land appears to have yielded no rent.

Sometimes Ashley sought Locke's help and advice in delicate domestic questions as well as in public and intellectual ones. His son and only child, also Anthony Ashley Cooper, was a problem and a disappointment to him. Dryden wrote of the boy as being 'born

---

[1] Written in 1673 (B.L. MSS. Locke, c. 6, f. 215). Sir Peter Colleton was the brother of Sir John Colleton, one of the Lords Proprietors of Carolina. This letter appears to have been written in spring, 1674.

[2] *Ibid.*, c. 30, f. 1.

[3] A notebook Locke kept in 1672 contains a great number of entries on the subject of Carolina. The notebook was in the possession of the late Lady Rosemary Diana de Hosszu of Tilsworth Manor, Bedfordshire.

a shapeless lump, like anarchy',[1] and although his defects were in fact of mind and health rather than of beauty, this did not diminish the dismay of Ashley, who set great store by mental and physical strength.

Ashley's grandson told Jean le Clerc:[2]

> When Mr. Locke first came into the family, my father was a youth of about fifteen or sixteen. Him my grandfather entrusted wholly to Mr. Locke for what remained of his education. He was an only child, and of no firm health, which induced my grandfather, in concern for his family, to think of marrying him as soon as possible. He was too young and inexperienced to choose a wife for himself, and my grandfather too much in business to choose one for him. The affair was nice: for though my grandfather required not a great fortune, he insisted on good blood, good person and constitution, and above all, good education and a character as remote as possible from that of Court- or town-bred lady. All this was thrown upon Mr. Locke, who being already so good a judge of men, my grandfather doubted not of his equal judgement in women.

Whether or not the girl was indeed Locke's choice, it was certainly he who negotiated the terms of the marriage. The chosen bride was Lady Dorothy Manners, the daughter aged twenty of the Earl of Rutland. In August 1669 Locke took his 'pupil' to Belvoir Castle and effected the introductions. Ashley told Locke[3] he was impatient for the nuptials to take place 'both to satisfy my son and avoid all uncertainties in an affair so agreeable to all my wishes.' For this reason the wedding was solemnised forthwith, and young Anthony Ashley Cooper returned to London with a wife.

Meanwhile Locke was neglecting other matters. Scribelia had written to him in April saying:[4]

> My dear A[tticus],
> How hard is it for you to disguise your thoughts, soul and heart to one that knows it so well as I do . . . You love me still in spite of all my folly . . . You have over-acted the indifferent part, but 'twas only to requite a seeming and mistaken letter too too unhappy since it has brought us both to a nearer meeting, I believe, in the next world, since we will not in this. But take this truth as it really is. I did not

---

[1] *Absalom and Achitophel,* line 172.
[2] Amsterdam: Remonstrants' MSS. J. 20.
[3] 6 September 1669 (P.R.O. 30/24/4/176).
[4] 11 April 1669 (B.L. MSS. Locke, c. 8, f. 66).

intend any disturbance to you, and if you were near me I could convince you that for two years I only expressed my dislike to your absence—an impatience very incident to love. I vow this was the sense of it. Now I beg you to let all unkind thoughts pass, and if you are not better engaged, receive to your breast the kind affection of your Scribelia. Banish ill thoughts of her, and consider a woman cannot be always wise . . .

Now I entreat you to have a great care of your life as you regard mine. Take all the peace you can possible in the assurance that I love you tenderly, that I value your life beyond my own and that I am certain I shall see you unless you take a greater care to be rid of me than to keep me. You see, my A[tticus], I do not take either the way of a high passionate humour or an indifferent one. You may freely guess my proceeding is beyond all that ever was in this case, but I owe it to my inclination and my justice to continue,

Yours,
S[cribelia].

It seems very possible that Locke *did* take greater care to be rid of Scribelia than to keep her. At any rate, after this letter there is no evidence of any further relationship between them, unless a letter dated simply 'November 25'[1] was written later; I think it was probably written in 1667 or 1668. It is signed 'Thomas Willson', but is in Scribelia's hand, and reads as follows:

Your former kindness and helps to the preferment which I have, has fixed in me an extraordinary affection to your service . . . This you are to reward with the assurance of your health. 'Tis that only [which] is wished for here, and 'tis that only [which] is begged of by me. Delay it not then, Sir, lest my cousin have some grounds to believe London has wrought that change in you which the severest considerations formerly could not. You know what they were. You know the unhappiness that parted you . . .

Let me know of all things and tell me somewhat of my friend Atticus to whom I wrote two months ago, but I believe it came not to his hands. This, I hope, will bring you a thousand good hearty wishes from, Sir,

Your most obliged Servant
Thomas Willson.

My respects to my honest friend Mr. Thomas of New College. I will after your next tell you my thoughts of your University. May it flourish when I am dead and forgotten. Farewell. Direct yours to my cousin R. as you did long ago, to be left where I am at Angiere Street, Flanders. November the 25th. My true respects to Atticus.

---

[1] B.L. MSS. Locke, c. 8, f 67.

To whatever year this letter belongs, its writer was not far wrong in her conjecture that London had (from her point of view) 'wrought that change' in Locke 'which the severest considerations formerly could not'.

This is not to suggest that Locke had taken to the 'modish pleasures of the town'. By the time he had reached his middle thirties Locke was far too bourgeois, prudent and self-protective. There is a ring of authenticity in the following avowal: [1]

Thus, I think:—it is a man's proper business to seek happiness and avoid misery. Happiness consists in what delights and contents the mind, misery is what disturbs, discomposes or torments it. I will therefore make it my business to seek satisfaction and delight and avoid uneasiness and disquiet and to have as much of the one and as little of the other as may be. But here I must have a care I mistake not, for if I prefer a short pleasure to a lasting one, it is plain I cross my own happiness.

Let me then see wherein consist the most lasting pleasures of this life and that so far as I can observe is in these things:—

1st Health, without which no sensual pleasure can have any relish.

2nd Reputation, for that I find everybody is pleased with and the want of it is a constant torment.

3rd Knowledge, for the little knowledge I have, I find I would not sell at any rate, nor part with for any other pleasure.

4th Doing good. For I find the well-cooked meat I ate today does now no more delight me, nay, I am diseased after a full meal. The perfumes I smelt yesterday now no more affect me with any pleasure. But the good turn I did yesterday, a year, seven years since, continues still to please me as often as I reflect on it.

5th. The expectation of eternal and incomprehensible happiness in another world is that also which carries a constant pleasure with it.

If, then, I will faithfully pursue that happiness I propose to myself, whatever pleasure offers itself to me, I must carefully look that it cross not any of those five great and constant pleasures above mentioned. For example, the fruit I see tempts me with the taste of it that I love, but if I endanger my health, I part with a constant and lasting desire for a very short and transient pleasure, and so foolishly make myself unhappy, and am not true to my own interest. Hunting, plays and other innocent diversions delight me: if I make use of them to refresh myself after study and business, they preserve my health, restore the vigour of my mind, and increase my pleasure; but if I spend all, or the greatest part of my time in them, they hinder my improvement in knowledge

[1] B.L. MSS. Locke, c. 28, ff. 143–4.

and useful arts, they blast my credit, and give me up to the uneasy state of shame, ignorance and contempt, in which I cannot but be very unhappy. Drinking, gaming and vicious delights will do me this mischief, not only by wasting my time, but by a positive efficacy endanger my health, impair my parts, imprint ill habits, lessen my esteem, and leave a constant lasting torment on my conscience.

Therefore all vicious and unlawful pleasures I will always avoid, because such a mastery of my passions will afford me a constant pleasure greater than any such enjoyments, and also deliver me from the certain evil of several kinds, that by indulging myself in a present temptation I shall certainly afterwards suffer. All innocent diversions and delights, as far as they will contribute to my health, and consist with my improvement, condition, and my other more solid pleasures of knowledge and reputation, I will enjoy, but no further, and this I will carefully watch and examine, that I may not be deceived by the flattery of a present pleasure to lose a greater.

Many epithets might be used to describe the ethics set forth in this document: 'Hobbesian' for its hedonism, 'Aristotelian' for its emphasis on moderation, 'pagan', 'utilitarian', 'humanistic'. The one word which does not suggest itself, despite the reference to eternal life, is Christian. This is not only because of the absence of any mention of the Bible, of the ten Commandments, of duty, Church or conscience; it is because the whole argument is built on a utilitarian principle.

As a theorist Locke never wholly forsook this sort of enlightened hedonism, though he left it to later moralists, notably to Bishop Butler, to effect a marriage of enlightened hedonism with Christian ethics. Even so Locke was always and essentially a deeply religious man, a fact which is sometimes not appreciated because he spent so much energy and time attacking orthodox religion. His religion was that of the Latitudinarian wing of the Church of England. His creed was short, but he held to it with the utmost assurance.

The year 1668 was an important one in his spiritual development, for in that year Benjamin Whichcote,[1] the leading Latitudinarian divine of the Cambridge School, was inducted Vicar of St. Lawrence Jewry, in the City of London, and Locke became a member of his congregation.

Latitudinarianism was not a new thing then. It had a history of

[1] Benjamin Whichcote (1609–83) had been Provost of King's College, Cambridge, 1644–60. Among his published works is a volume of *Select Sermons*, edited by the third Earl of Shaftesbury, and printed in London in 1698.

over thirty years and was the product of an even older and wider movement in the Church of England, namely Rational Theology.

'There is nothing so intrinsically rational as religion is', Whichcote said; [1] 'nothing that can so justify itself; nothing that has so pure reason to recommend itself'.

Belief in Reason was not, of course, peculiar to Latitudinarianism. Richard Hooker had taught Rational Theology to the majority of English Churchmen, and there was never a more devoted servant of that principle than Archbishop William Laud. The Latitudinarians differed from Laud and the majority of Anglicans partly in favouring toleration, principally in holding that Reason justified only a very limited number of dogmas.

'Truth lies in a little compass and narrow room', Whichcote said,[2] 'vitals in religion are few.'

Latitudinarianism was originally an Oxford movement, which grew up in the 1630's under the patronage of Lucius Cary, second Viscount Falkland (1610?–43), largely, indeed, under the roof of Falkland's house at Great Tew in Oxfordshire. Its principal Oxford theologians were, besides the young viscount himself, William Chillingworth (1602–44) and John Hales (1584–1656). These men were loyal Anglicans, conservatives and Royalists, and Laud, a man liberal in theological opinion however imperious in ecclesiastical government, protected them. Chillingworth and Hales did not recommend toleration for mere prudential reasons, but they did believe that to strip the Christian doctrine down to its bare essentials would have the effect of broadening the national Church so that all could join.

A more direct and eloquent champion of toleration was a younger theologian of the Great Tew circle, Jeremy Taylor (1613–67), remembered today primarily as a stylist, but celebrated in his own time as a moralist. His *Discourse of the Liberty of Prophesying*, first printed in 1647, probably did as much as any other book to convert Locke to the idea of toleration, although Locke did not read it until nearly twenty years after it was published.

Latitudinarianism was primarily the religion of the minimal creed. Its exponents did not specifically challenge more than one or two Christian dogmas—and those were ones already in some disrepute, but neither did they give specific assent to more than one or two

---

[1] *Moral and Religious Aphorisms*, 1753, No. 457.
[2] *Ibid.*, Nos. 1007–8.

dogmas. They demolished the basis on which most dogmas rested and then remained discreetly silent.

Latitudinarianism being essentially an Anglican movement, was temporarily engulfed by the Commonwealth. Even such a liberal Independent as John Owen was completely orthodox in his Bible Christianity; far from having any leanings towards the minimal creed, Owen was engaged by the Council of State in 1655 to write an official refutation of Socinianism.[1]

'Socinian' would be too strong a word to apply to the early Latitudinarians, though it *was* applied to them, having already a pejorative force. Later Latitudinarians, including Locke after 1688, were more deserving of the name. Socinianism was Latitudinarianism pushed to its logical conclusion; and a particular characteristic of the Latitudinarians was that they did *not* push things to their logical conclusion. They would not have thought of doing anything so immoderate.

The Latitudinarian and the Unitarian had much in common, but their differences were crucial ones. The Latitudinarians were attached to their Church, which, like Hooker, they regarded as a national institution to which all Englishmen could properly belong, not as a brotherhood of saints or as a society of men of identical persuasions. The Church of England allowed considerable variety of 'interpretation' of her creed, and the Latitudinarians believed in taking every advantage of that liberty. Latitudinarians were for the most part content to doubt what the Unitarian expressly denied. The Unitarian had two faults in the eyes of the Latitudinarian: first, he was a sectarian in a country where sectarianism was a bad thing politically; secondly, in his very repudiation of dogma he was dogmatic. The Latitudinarian remembered the message of Hooker: 'Think ye are men, deem it not impossible for you to err'.

Besides Whichcote there were several distinguished Latitudinarian preachers in Restoration London, among others John Tillotson (1630–94) and Edward Fowler (1632–1714), both personal friends of Locke's; Edward Stillingfleet (1635–99), afterwards a renegade to orthodoxy and an enemy of Locke's; and Simon Patrick (1626–1707). After the Glorious Revolution, Tillotson became Archbishop of Canterbury and the others became bishops.

One of the most influential Latitudinarians in London in the

[1] *Vide* H. J. McLachlan *Socinianism in Seventeenth-Century England* (Oxford, 1951), pp. 205 *et seq.*

1660's was a layman, a City friend of Ashley's called Thomas Firmin. Most of the leading Latitudinarians met each other at Firmin's house next to the George Inn in Lombard Street. For while Firmin, a wealthy mercer by trade, was far more openly Socinian than most of the Latitudinarians, and often had refugee Socinians staying under his roof, he remained a Churchman, and his hospitality was always of the liberal kind so acceptable to the clergy. Locke became one of Firmin's many regular guests, and it was probably in the Lombard Street *salon* that Locke first made the acquaintance of Whichcote and the other Latitudinarian divines.

A second centre of Latitudinarianism was the junior university, where the movement was linked with the school of metaphysical philosophy known as Cambridge Platonism. Whichcote himself was of this school. Its other leading exponents were Ralph Cudworth (1617–88), Henry More (1614–87) and John Smith (1618–52).

Gilbert Burnet, a Latitudinarian of Locke's own generation, met the members of the Cambridge school in 1663, and wrote of them as follows: [1]

> They declared against superstition on the one hand and enthusiasm on the other. They loved the constitution of the Church and the liturgy, and could well live under them: but they did not think it unlawful to live under another form. They wished that things might have been carried with more moderation. And they continued to keep a good correspondence with those who had differed from them in opinion, and allowed a great freedom both in philosophy and in divinity. . . .

As much could be said of Latitudinarians generally. They all believed that Christians should unite on the broad common ground of essentials in religion, while agreeing to differ over non-essentials; they all believed that reason could be relied upon to determine what was and what was not essential.

The peculiarity of the Cambridge school was the philosophy with which they augmented the exiguous tenets of their theology. Falkland, Chillingworth and Hales, the Oxford men, had been content with scepticism; the Cambridge Latitudinarians, Puritans by birth and breeding, were not. They could not do without some metaphysical assurance. They resembled in many ways the Platonic

[1] Bishop Burnet's History, Oxford, 1823, I, pp. 323–4. It is interesting to compare a similar account of the Great Tew group in *The Life of Edward, Earl of Clarendon, written by Himself*, Oxford, 1759, I, pp. 37 ff.

Academy over which Marsilio Ficino presided in fifteenth century Florence. Like those Florentines, the Cambridge men were as much Plotinists as Platonists, and they emphasised the mystical as against the practical elements in their Master's teaching. With Plato and Plotinus they combined some part of Descartes, but they rejected much of Descartes's rationalism, which they thought could easily be used in the interests of atheism and materialism. Descartes had divided the universe into the mental and the mechanical; the Cambridge Platonists saw it as one spiritual whole, a physical universe pervaded by the soul of nature, knowable only to minds in harmony with the divine principle, at one with God.

Locke never made the same mistake of looking to philosophy for an emotional substitute for religion.

Chapter Eleven

FIRST PHILOSOPHY

WITHIN the Cabal ministry there was strong rivalry and a personal animosity between the several members, but the Government held together. Buckingham and Ashley, with their leanings towards Dissent, and Arlington and Clifford, with their leanings towards Romanism, were equally in favour of religious toleration; while the anti-Dutch sentiments of Buckingham and Ashley gave them few occasions to differ from Arlington and Clifford, who were pro-French.

There was no corresponding basis for agreement between the Government and Parliament. The majority in Parliament was Anglican, and since the fall of Clarendon it had become more hostile than ever to the idea of toleration. In 1668 the Commons had passed a new Conventicle Bill, and although that measure was obstructed in the Lords, further laws against dissenters were introduced early in 1669.

This last rebuff caused Ashley to despair of securing toleration by Parliamentary means, and he turned his thoughts in the alternative direction. Why, he asked himself, should toleration not be introduced by Charles under royal prerogative?

Ashley consulted Locke, and with Locke's help he drew up a memorial to urge this course upon the King. He did so with some hopes of success, knowing that the King personally and all his chief Ministers were sympathetic.

One cannot help wondering what can have been in Locke's mind. He must have known that Charles would authorise, and Arlington and Clifford support, only a policy of toleration which extended to Catholic recusants as well as to Protestant dissenters; whereas Locke himself had always been opposed to the toleration of recusants. In 1659, in his letter to Henry Stubbe; in 1661, in his answer to Bagshawe; in 1667, in his essay on toleration; in 1688, in his *Epistola de Tolerantia*—in all these documents Locke declared that it would be

K

wrong to grant liberty to Papists. Ashley is remembered as one of the most passionate anti-Catholics in English history. How could either of them have urged toleration by prerogative in 1669?

The fact of the matter is that neither Ashley nor Locke then realised the extent of Charles's Catholic sympathies. Again so far as Ashley was concerned anti-Popery was not a prominent feature of his policy in 1669. He was at that time intensely, almost obsessively, anti-Dutch, and the Dutch, of course, were stalwart Protestants. The Peace of Breda, which had followed the invasion of the Medway in 1667, had been signed on Dutch terms,[1] and Ashley was impatient to get at Dutch throats in another war. He would have welcomed any ally, however Popish, in a struggle against the triumphant competitors of English trade. It may well be that Locke did not agree with him; and even Ashley seems seriously to have hoped it might be possible to persuade the King to agree to the toleration of dissenters without extending the same privilege to recusants; such at any rate was the policy Ashley recommended in the memorial[2] he presented to the King in 1669. In this document Ashley reproduced the central argument of Locke's essay of 1667. Catholics, he said, should not be tolerated because 'the laws have determined the principles of the Romish religion to be inconsistent with the safety of your Majesty's person'; Fifth Monarchists should not be tolerated because they were 'professed opposers of all human government'. Ashley was willing for the offices under the Crown to be limited to Anglicans, but otherwise he pleaded for Protestant dissenters to be given 'liberty to assemble for their own manner of worship, in such places as they can procure, and that the doors of the meeting place do stand open to all while they are at their exercises of prayer and teaching'. Ashley did not forget the economic argument in favour of toleration: the fact that so many Englishmen were emigrating 'to enjoy the liberty of their mistaken consciences' was, he said, a drain on the wealth of the nation.

---

[1] 'In July [1667] peace was signed at Breda. France restored her West Indies conquests in return for Acadia. England kept New York, New Jersey and Delaware; the Dutch retained all West Africa except Cape Coast Castle, besides Pulo Run and Guiana. On the question of saluting the flag we reduced our claim to the Channel alone, while the Navigation Act was amended to allow Holland to re-export the products of Germany and Belgium. This was an ignominious peace . . .' (Keith Feiling, *A History of England*, 1950, p. 548).
[2] This document is printed *in extenso* by Christie, II, Appendix 1.

One of the most influential books written at that period against toleration was *A Discourse of Ecclesiastical Politie*,[1] by Samuel Parker.[2] After reading the book Locke wrote down a few queries on some sheets of paper [3] which have lately come to light. I have thought Locke's notes worth printing here, setting them out in dialogue form with the appropriate quotations from Samuel Parker:

Parker (p. 11): [4] . . . the peace and tranquillity of the Commonwealth, which, though it be the prime and most important end of government, can never be sufficiently secured unless religion be subject to the authority of the supreme power, in that it has the strongest influence upon human affairs . . . For 'tis certain nothing more governs the minds of men than the apprehensions of religion.

Locke: Whether [this] proves anything but that the magistrate's business being only to preserve peace, those wrong opinions are to be restrained that have a tendency to disturb it (and this is by every sober man to be allowed)?

Parker (p. 12): . . . as true piety secures the public weal by taming and civilising the passions of men, and inuring them to a mild, gentle and governable spirit, so superstition and wrong notions of God and worship are the most powerful engines to overturn its settlement. And therefore unless princes have power to bind their subjects to that religion that they apprehend most advantageous to public peace and tranquillity, and restrain those religious mistakes that tend to its subversion, they are no better than statues and images of authority. . . .

Locke: Whether assigning these ill effects that follow to 'wrong notions of God and his worship' he does not suppose the magistrate's power to proceed from being in the right? Whether by 'bind the subject to his religion' he means that whether the magistrate's opinion be right or wrong he has power to force the subject to renounce his own opinions however quiet and peaceable, and declare assent and consent to those of the magistrate? And if so why Christ and the Apostles directed not their discourses and addressed their miracles to the princes and magistrates of the world to persuade them, whereas by

[1] *A Discourse of Ecclesiastical Politie: Wherein The Authority of the Civil Magistrate Over the Consciences of Subjects in Matters of Religion is Asserted; The Mischiefs and Inconveniences of Toleration are represented, And All Pretenses Pleaded in Behalf of Liberty of Conscience are Fully Answered*. (The book appeared anonymously, and although on sale in 1669 bore the date '1670.')
[2] Samuel Parker (1640–88) then chaplain to Archbishop Sheldon subsequently Jacobite Bishop of Oxford.
[3] The document was bought by the Bodleian Library in 1953 (B.L. MSS. Locke, c. 29, ff. 7–9).
[4] The page references are to the first edition of Parker's book.

preaching to and converting the people, they according to this doctrine [lay] under a necessity of being either seditious or martyrs.

Parker (p. 21): For if Conscience be ever able to break down the restraints of government, and all men have licence to follow their own persuasions, the mischief is infinite . . . Insomuch that there was never yet any Commonwealth that gave a real liberty to men's imaginations, that was not suddenly overrun with numberless divisions and subdivisions of sects.

Locke: Whether [the] subdivision of opinions into small sects be of such danger to the government?

Parker (p. 24): Because the Church of Rome, by her unreasonable impositions, has invaded the fundamental liberties of mankind they [the dissenters] presently conclude all restraints upon licentious practices and persuasions about religion under the hated name of Popery.

Locke: What fundamental liberties of mankind were invaded by the Church of Rome that will not be in the same condition under the civil magistrate according to his [Parker's] doctrine, since the power of the Church of Rome was allowed and their decrees enforced by the civil magistrate?

Parker (p. 26): But seeing no man can be subject to contradictory obligations, 'tis by consequence utterly impossible he should be subject to two supreme powers.

Locke: The end of government being public peace 'tis no question the supreme power must have an uncontrollable right to judge and ordain all things that may conduce to it, but yet the question will be whether uniformity established by law be (as is here supposed) a necessary means to it: *i.e.* whether it be at all dangerous to the magistrate that he believing free will some of his subjects shall believe predestination, or whether it be more necessary for his government to make laws for wearing surplices than it is for wearing vests?

Parker (p. 29): . . . the wisdom of Providence . . . so ordered affairs that no man could be born into the world without being subject to some superior; every father being by nature vested with a right to govern his children. And the first governments in the world were established purely upon the natural rights of paternal authority which afterward grew up to a kingly power by the increase of posterity.

Locke: Whether allowing the paternal right of governments (which is asserted not proved) that paternal monarchy descended upon [the] death of the father it descended wholly to the eldest son, or else that the brothers had an equal power over their respective affairs. If the first then monarchy is certainly *jure naturali*, but there can be but one rightful monarch over the whole world, *i.e.*, the right heir of Adam;

if the second, all government, whether monarchical or other, is only from the consent of the people.

Parker (p. 144): Nothing more concerns the interest of the Civil Magistrate than to take care what particular doctrines are taught within his dominions, because some are particularly advantageous to the ends of government, and others as naturally tending to its disturbance.

Locke: Whether it will follow that the magistrate ought to force men by the severity of laws and penalties to be of the same mind with him in the speculative opinions in religion or worship God with the same ceremonies? That the magistrate should restrain seditious doctrines who denies, but because he may, then has he power over all other doctrines to forbid or impose? If he has not your argument is short, if he has, how far is this short of Mr. Hobbes's doctrine?

Parker (p. 153): . . . Fanaticism is both the greatest and the easiest vice that is incident to religion; 'tis a weed that thrives in all soils, and there is the same fanatic spirit that mixes itself with all the religions in the world.

Locke: . . . if it mixes itself with all religions I desire him [i.e. Parker] to examine those that be of the Church of England what spirit it is which sets him so zealously to stir up the magistrate to persecute all those who dissent from him in those opinions and ways of worship the public support whereof is to give him preferment?

In the England of 1669–70 it was the doctrine of Parker, and not that of Locke and Ashley, which won the day. Charles read Ashley's memorial sympathetically, but he was too conscious of the hostility of Parliament to do as Ashley wished. In April 1670 Parliament registered once again its opposition to the idea of toleration by passing a new and even more stringent Conventicle Act to curb the Nonconformists. In May Charles registered his contempt for Parliament by signing the secret treaty of Dover.

On the opposite side of the Strand from Exeter House and close to Charing Cross was a second and more splendid patrician mansion to which Locke had the *entrée*, Northumberland House,[1] one of three dwellings—the others being Syon and Petworth—of the

---

[1] Northumberland House was built *c.* 1605 by Henry Howard, Earl of Northampton, and passed by marriage in 1642 to the Percy family. It originally formed three sides of a quadrangle the fourth side remaining open to the garden and the river. The tenth earl of Northumberland had a splendid new front built by Inigo Jones. The original front was 162 feet in length and the court 81 feet square. The house was demolished by act of Parliament in 1873 to make way for Northumberland Avenue. (*Vide* H. B. Wheatley, *London Past and Present*, 1891, II, pp. 603–5.)

Percys, Earls of Northumberland. The Percys were related to the Coopers, and Elizabeth, wife of the eleventh Earl, was a cousin of Ashley's third wife. Locke also had his own links with Northumberland House. Two of his friends since schooldays, John Mapletoft and Thomas Blomer, had been employed by the tenth Earl of Northumberland, who was said to have conducted himself more like a feudal potentate than a seventeenth century nobleman. Blomer was his chaplain, and Mapletoft the tutor of his son Jocelin.

In October 1668 the tenth Earl died and his title passed to Mapletoft's former pupil, then aged twenty-four. The eleventh Earl maintained his father's enormous establishment, partly for himself, partly for his wife, Elizabeth, youngest daughter of the Earl of Southampton. Mapletoft, no longer a pedagogue, served them as their family physician. Blomer stayed on as the new Earl's chaplain, and Mrs. Blomer was attached to the young Countess's retinue.

Dorothy Blomer, who was a cousin of Locke's, enjoyed a sentimental friendship with him, but she was not the only woman at Northumberland House to do so. As Black Hall was to him in his early years at Oxford, so was Northumberland House to Locke in his first years in London—a 'place where at least two Muses dwell', though once again it is difficult to distinguish any one of those 'Muses' from the others. Besides Dorothy Blomer there was Mrs. Anna Grigg (Mrs. Blomer's sister), Mrs. Margaret Beavis and Mrs. Anne Beavis. It is possible that Mrs. Margaret Beavis and Mrs. Anne Beavis were one and the same person.

A letter [1] Mrs. Grigg wrote to Locke in 1680 mentions her friendship with Locke having lasted twelve years. Locke's friendships with the other women appear also to date from 1668 or 1669. It is probable that both Mrs. Grigg and Mrs. Blomer were sisters of Locke's cousin Elizabeth Stratton. They both addressed him as their 'Dear Brother'. Anne Grigg was the wife of Thomas Grigg, sometime Fellow of Trinity College, Oxford, rector of St. Andrew Undershaft, London, and (after 1667) a Prebendary of St. Paul's.

Mrs. Anne Beavis appears to have been employed as Lady Northumberland's companion; and in a letter [2] she wrote to Locke

[1] *Vide* references to 'my sister Blomer' in Mrs. Grigg's letter to Locke of 13 September 1676 (B.L. MSS. Locke, c. 10, f. 119) and to her sister Betty in a letter dated 5 June 1680 (B.L. MSS. Locke, c. 10, f. 126), and to twelve years' friendship with Locke in her letter to him dated 22 May 1680 (B.L. MSS. Locke, c. 10, f. 124).

[2] 1 August 1678. B.L. MSS. Locke, c. 3, f. 163. (This letter from Mrs. Anne Beavis, the only one known to me extant, is signed 'A. B.')

in 1678 she referred to herself as Locke's 'governess'. She was then travelling in France with Lady Northumberland. So, eight years before, was Mrs. Margaret Beavis (who may or may not have been the same person), to whom, at Blois, Locke addressed the following letter on 24 January 1669/70:[1]

> My dearest Sister,
> You must excuse me if, believing you an extraordinary person, I expect extraordinary things of you. I am sure you have all the qualifications of an excellent friend, and yet I would not have you concerned for the calamities of those I think you have a kindness for. I desire you should be (as you are) very good natured, yet I would forbid you sympathy and a tender sense of others' sorrows. I confess ingeniously I know not how in my own thoughts to reconcile these difficulties, and can hope only to find it done in your actions, and though I cannot tell the way wherein this is to be brought about yet I do not much doubt of it whilst I consider you have a soul large enough to be capable of things that seem to be at very great distance, which other people know not well how to put together.
> I allow therefore my sister to be as civil, as kind, as grateful as she please, but if that near and affectionate relation she owns brings any disquiet or trouble to my sister, I shall not take it very kindly. I have twenty reasons to the same purpose to add to the preachment you received from me just before the sealing of your last letter of the 20th instant, which I forbear to trouble you with here because methinks to a rational creature one should not need to make use of arguments to persuade her to be happy, the first degree whereof is to be rid of trouble and vexation.
> If you will do this you at the same time cure me of all those misfortunes you apprehended might give occasion to my exhortations. I have no cause (I thank God) for melancholy thoughts but what you breed there, and all that I said in that letter was designed to come before the ill news and to break the force of that blow which I feared would fall too heavy on you.

A day or two earlier Locke had drafted a letter [2] in very similar terms to Mrs. Blomer, who was also in France with Lord and Lady Northumberland *en route* for Italy. In this letter Locke urged his friend not to weep over other people's sorrows:

> I that earnestly wish you the enjoyment of perfect happiness, cannot but desire and advise that you should feel nothing at all of others' misfortune and as little as you can of your own.

[1] B.M. Add. MSS. 32,094, f. 222.   [2] P.R.O. 30/24/47.

Locke said he hoped he had convinced her that 'a philosopher of the Royal Society may hold discourse with a female virtuoso without any danger of dulness' and warned her: 'We philosophers are always in earnest and always expect our rules and advices to be followed.'

Mrs. Blomer replied on 24 January:[1]

> My dear Brother:
> . . . I can with great security protest that nature could not have given you a sister that would have been (in her concern and value for you) half what I am, though but an adopted one . . .
> You give me a great deal of advice, which I receive with a sense proportionate to the benefit you designed me in it . . . I confess, with you, that wise persons will be content with their troubles, without hunting abroad for them in the concernments of others; but still there are some things that may very reasonably touch them.

Mrs. Blomer next referred to 'melancholy hints' Locke had given her of his 'retiring out of the bustle of this life', and expressed the hope that the 'late fierce cold' had spared his lungs.

Already Locke had begun to suffer seriously from the disease which was to torment him for the rest of his life, asthma. The smoke and fog of London was such that the air was worse than it is today, especially near the river, where Exeter House was. In winter Locke coughed day and night and found it increasingly difficult to breathe.

Though a sick man himself, he resumed the practice of medicine, albeit only on a part-time basis, and Ashley was content for him to do so, for the patient who first claimed Locke's services was she on whom all Ashley's hopes for his posterity were pinned, his daughter-in-law. In December 1669 Lady Dorothy Cooper, who was pregnant, fell ill, and despite Locke's ministrations she miscarried. But she got well again, and her mother, Lady Rutland, wrote[2] gratefully to Locke saying, 'I am sure I owe much to your care of my dear child'.

The year 1670 brought more illness—and worse—to the same circle. In May the Earl of Northumberland, aged twenty-five, was stricken with a fever on his Italian tour and died before the end of the month at Turin. In August Thomas Grigg, aged thirty-two, was taken ill in London; and although Locke was at his bedside daily for

---

[1] P.R.O. 30/24/47/20 (Mrs. Blomer signed herself as Locke's 'faithful and most affectionate B. D.', thus reversing her initials after Locke's own habit).
[2] 31 January 1669/70 (P.R.O. 30/24/4/185).

two weeks, Grigg also died, leaving, besides his widow Anne, a son, William.

Locke had more success with his other patients. Mr. Beavis, the husband either of Margaret or Anne Beavis (though these may be the names of the same person) was another invalid, but Locke was able in July [1] to send Mapletoft who had gone to Copenhagen as physician to the English Ambassador, Lord Essex, 'the good news of Mr. Beavis's happy recovery'.

Lady Dorothy Cooper was both pregnant and ill once more in August, but this time Locke was able to pull her through without a miscarriage.

'The Lord preserve her,' Lady Rutland wrote [2] to him, 'and reward your compassionate care for her.'

Mrs. Blomer, having by that time returned with Lady Northumberland from their continental tour, wrote [3] in early September to thank Locke for his 'charitable care' of her 'poor little disconsolate sister', Anne Grigg. In the same letter Mrs. Blomer mentioned that Lady Northumberland was sick.

So just then was Locke himself. His lungs hurt him so much that he had to leave London to spend the month of September in Oxford. After he had explained this in a letter to Mrs. Blomer, who had gone down to Petworth, his cousin replied [3] saying that such tidings 'from a man not accustomed to represent things worse than they are, cannot but create such apprehensions in me as must of necessity be very uneasy and lasting'.

In October 1670 Locke visited David Thomas at Salisbury; he was still poorly, and he wrote from that city to Mapletoft [4] describing his symptoms. He said that at Oxford 'I mended apace, and my cough sensibly abated'; but he feared the air of Salisbury would not be so advantageous.

Mapletoft had evidently advised Locke against spending another winter in London and had even gone so far as to arrange for him to winter elsewhere. It is not clear precisely what Mapletoft's arrangements were, but a remark in Mrs. Blomer's letter of 12

---

[1] 10 July 1670 (*European Magazine*, 1788, XIV, p. 321). This is one of thirteen letters printed in the *European Magazine* in 1788 and 1789 from originals in the possession of 'Mr. Mapletoft, an eminent surgeon at Chertsey, who is grandson to Dr. Mapletoft'.

[2] 27 August 1670. (P.R.O. 30/24/4/190.)

[3] 12 September 1670. (*ibid.*, 30/24/47/9.)

[4] *European Magazine* (1788), XIV, p. 401.

September shows that Locke had promised to go to France with the Countess of Northumberland the following spring.[1] Locke thanked Mapletoft for the 'winter quarters' he had provided for him, which quarters, he said, 'I think not only preferable to the solitariness of the grave, but the gaiety of courts or other admired places'. Nevertheless, Locke had other ideas about the future. He proposed to return to Oxford, having already persuaded Ashley that it would be best for him to do so. His intention was to spend the terms at the University and the vacations at Exeter House. He had been fired once more with his old ambition to be a medical don, but he knew he could not do so without the degree of D.M. In November 1670 Ashley tried to have one given him.[2] The Duke of Ormonde, Clarendon's successor as Chancellor of Oxford University, was then preparing to bestow a number of honorary degrees to mark the forthcoming visit to the University of the Prince of Orange, so the moment was opportune.

However, both John Fell, Dean of Christ Church, and Richard Allestrey, Provost of Eton, neither of them a medical man, objected and Locke begged his patron to withdraw his nomination.

Ashley did so in the course of a distinctly indignant letter [3] to the Dean:

> You are well acquainted with the kindness I have great reason to have to Mr. Locke, on whose behalf I prevailed with the Duke of Ormonde for his assistance towards the attaining his doctor's degree at the reception of the Prince of Orange, and I am apt to think the instance of your Chancellor, and the relation he has to me, would not have been denied by the University. But Mr. Locke, understanding the Provost of Eton declared himself and you dissatisfied with it, has importuned me to give him leave to decline it, which, upon conference with my worthy friend the Bishop of Rochester I have done, and returned his grace's letter, though my Lord Bishop of Rochester can tell you I could not but complain to him that your chapter had not been so kind to him in Mr. Locke's affairs as I thought I might justly expect, considering him a member of their House, having done both my life and

[1] 'I doubt there will be a necessity of our going again into France, which I cannot think of with any pleasure. In the meantime prepare yourself against next spring and remember you are to go with us'. In the event Lady Northumberland did not go to France until 1672.

[2] In London Locke was in that same month made Registrar to the Commissioners of Excise, but the position seems to have been a sinecure. (B.L. MSS. Locke, c. 25, f. 12.)

[3] 8 December 1670. (P.R.O. 30/24/47/10.)

family that service I own from him, and I being that quality I am under his Majesty, under which title only I pretend to any favour from them.

All that I request now of you and them is that since he will not allow me to do him this kindness, you will give me leave to bespeak your favour for the next faculty place, and that a more powerful hand may not take it from him. I rely very much on my Lord [Bishop of] Rochester's mediation and your own kindness to me. . . .

Years passed before Locke secured a faculty place at Christ Church and then Ashley's intervention had nothing to do with it; he never received the degree of D.M.

Disappointed as Locke may have been, Ashley was very pleased to have him under his own roof and not at Oxford in the winter of 1670/1, as the time of Lady Dorothy Cooper's delivery approached. On 26 February her child was born. To Ashley's delight it was a boy, a grandson to inherit his title and estate. The boy grew up to be Anthony Ashley Cooper, third Earl of Shaftesbury, moralist and author.

Locke, who attended the confinement, was warmly thanked both by Ashley and by Dorothy Cooper's mother, Lady Rutland, who also exclaimed:[1] 'The Lord's name be blessed and praised for her well-doing, and safely bringing that noble family so hopeful an heir. . . .'

The circumstances of Dorothy Cooper's confinement may well have been in Locke's mind when he came some years later to write some 'midwifery notes'[2] including the following:

If she be with child let her not do as is usual with women of condition mew herself up in her chamber for fear of miscarrying, much less confine herself to her bed. This makes the body and spirits weak, which is one great cause of miscarriage to which the constant fear of miscarriage which this management keeps constantly up in the mind of the breeding woman, upon any slight accident joining itself seldom fails to produce an abortion. For the mind being kept in constant apprehension of miscarriage every least occasion turns that apprehension into a real fright and what that produces in teeming women experience teaches us. Hence we see that amongst the poor and labouring country women not one of ten miscarry in comparison of the aborting to be found amongst people of quality.

[1] 7 March 1670/1. (P.R.O. 30/24/47/11.)
[2] B.L. MSS. Locke, c. 29, ff. 95–8. These notes were published with a commentary by Kenneth Dewhurst in the *Lancet* (4 September 1954).

Locke was called upon to look after Ashley's grandson almost constantly during the first months of the child's life, and when in early summer the father and mother went to stay with the Rutlands at Belvoir[1] and Lady Ashley was visiting Lady Northumberland, the philosopher was left in sole charge of the 'hopeful heir'.

Mrs. Blomer, who gave birth to a child of her own about the same time as Lady Dorothy Cooper, afterwards urged Locke to come to Petworth to see the 'little spark', but he may well have felt by that time that he had seen enough of new-born babies; and besides, he was busy just then with his *Essay Concerning Human Understanding*.

The *Essay* was not written in its final form until the later 1680's, but at least two drafts of it were made in 1671. In the 'Epistle to the Reader' printed at the beginning of the published version, Locke said:

> Were it fit to trouble thee with the history of this *Essay*, I should tell thee that five or six friends, meeting in my chamber and discoursing on a subject very remote from this, found themselves quickly at a stand by the difficulties that arose on every side. After we had awhile puzzled ourselves, without coming any nearer a resolution of those doubts which perplexed us, it came into my thoughts that we took a wrong course; and that before we set ourselves upon enquiries of that nature it was necessary to examine our own abilities, and see what objects our understandings were or were not fitted to deal with. This I proposed to the company, who all readily assented; and thereupon it was agreed that this should be our first enquiry. Some hasty and un-digested thoughts, on a subject I had never before considered, which I set down against our next meeting gave the first entrance into the dis-course; which having been thus begun by chance was continued by entreaty, written by incoherent parcels, and after long intervals of neglect, resumed again, as my humour or occasions permitted; and at last, in a retirement where an attendance on my health gave me leisure, it was brought into that order thou now seest it.

The conversations from which the book sprang took place at Exeter House in the early months of 1671. James Tyrrell was one of the 'five or six friends', and in a manuscript note in his copy of the published *Essay* (now in the British Museum) Tyrrell records that the discourse, on the occasion when Locke 'first raised the issue of

---

[1] Lady Dorothy wrote to Locke from Belvoir on 1 July 1671 'I wish I was at St. Giles . . . and then I should see you.' (P.R.O. 30/24/47/12.)

human understanding' was 'about the principles of morality and revealed religion': Tyrrell also recalls the occasion as being 'in winter 1673', but on this point his memory must have deceived him. The occasion could not have been later than the early months of 1671, because there is clear evidence that Locke was writing a draft of the *Essay* in the summer of that year.

A sentence in one draft reads: [1]

> For having seen water yesterday I shall always know and it will be always an unquestionable true proposition to me that water did exist 10 Jul. [16]71.

The date 1671 appears also on a second draft in Locke's hand. Both these drafts, known to Locke scholars as Draft A [2] and Draft B [3] have been printed, the first, edited by Professor Aaron and Mr. Jocelyn Gibb, in 1936; the second, edited by Dr. Rand, [4] in 1931. Draft A is a first, rough draft, although it is presumably an extension of, and not the original manuscript of the 'hasty and undigested thoughts' Locke had sat down to discuss with his friends. And yet Draft A is something more than a crude version of what appears in the more carefully written Draft B, for it contains some of Locke's first reflections on several topics which are not dealt with in Draft B, but which have an important place in the final version of the *Essay*.

The history of the composition of the *Essay Concerning Human Understanding* has yet to be written, and it is far too complicated a subject to be dealt with in the compass of this biography. I shall give some account of its contents in a later chapter. Suffice it for the present to record that at the time Locke wrote the early drafts he was partly in London, partly at Wimborne St. Giles, partly at Oxford. In September 1671 he went to stay in Somerset with John Strachey.

From Sutton Court Locke wrote on 7 October 1671 [5] to Mapletoft to report on his state of health. If he was still less well than he would have liked to be, he was better than he had been during the

---

[1] Aaron and Gibb, p. 41.

[2] The original manuscript is now in the collection of Mr. Arthur Houghton, Jnr.

[3] The original manuscript is still in the Lovelace Collection (B.L. MSS. Locke, F. 26).

[4] *An essay concerning the understanding, knowledge, opinion and assent.* Edited by Benjamin Rand, Cambridge (Mass.), 1931.

[5] *European Magazine* (1788), XIV, p. 322.

previous year, and he was reluctant to go abroad for a cure as
Mapletoft had recommended.

> I am now making haste back again to London, [he explained] . . .
> then having made you judge of my state of health, desire your advice
> what you think best to be done, wherein you are to deal with the
> same freedom, since nothing will be able to make me leave those friends
> I have in England but the positive direction of some of those friends
> for my going.

That 'positive direction' came within a year.

Chapter Twelve

THE SECRETARY OF PRESENTATIONS

THE year 1672 was, in many ways, Ashley's *annus mirabilis*. It brought the war with Holland he had been striving for; it brought him an earldom; it brought several political changes he had advocated, and when it ended he was at the head of the Government.

At the very outset of the year Ashley's loyalty was sorely tested. On 2 January, as a preliminary to a declaration of war, the King issued an order to stop any payments out of the Exchequer on any securities whatever. Clifford seems to have suggested his doing this. Ashley, the spokesman of finance and commerce, was naturally outraged; but he managed to restrain himself from open opposition. In public, in fact, he spoke in defence of the 'Stop'; privately he urged the King in the strongest terms to repudiate it. He wrote[1] to Charles saying:

> It is contrary to common justice among men, and also to the law and several statutes of the realm . . . It is against your Majesty's constant promises. It must amaze mankind and will ruin thousands, amongst whom are a number of poor widows and orphans . . . It will immediately cause the greatest damp on trade that has been known.

The King was not persuaded by Ashley's reasoning, but he remembered the argument of an earlier communication he had received from the same quarter, namely the memorial of 1669 urging the introduction of toleration by prerogative. Charles told Ashley he would be willing to issue a Declaration of Indulgence provided he could be assured of its legality, and he asked Ashley, with Lauderdale and Clifford, to investigate the constitutional aspects. The task was passed on to Locke, who in turn reported favourably.

---

[1] The lucid marshalling of the points of this memorandum suggests the hand of Locke. (*Vide* Shaftesbury's letter to Locke dated 23 November 1674, printed in Christie, II, pp. 60–4.) The memorandum is published in B. Martyn, *Shaftesbury*, 1836, I, p. 415.

Religious toleration, his report pointed out, was an ecclesiastical matter, and the King, as Head of the Church of England, was supreme in ecclesiastical jurisdiction. There could therefore be no question of the King's invading the constitutional rights of Parliament by issuing a Declaration of Indulgence on royal prerogative.[1]

Charles issued his Declaration on 15 March 1671/2. With it he introduced the sort of toleration he himself wanted and not that limited kind which Ashley and Locke had proposed; he suspended 'all and all manner of penal laws in matters ecclesiastical, against whatever sort of Nonconformists or recusants'.

Two days later the war against the Dutch began, and on 23 April Ashley was raised in the peerage to the rank of Earl of Shaftesbury. But things were not entirely as they seemed.

At Dover in May 1670 Charles had made a secret treaty with the King of France, promising, in return for financial aid, to declare himself as soon as the affairs of his country permitted, a convert to Catholicism. Besides two million livres Charles was to receive, if necessary on the occasion of his conversion, the services of six thousand French troops. In the same agreement there were other clauses: France would join England in a war against Holland, accepting the Duke of York as commander of the allied fleet, and offering the English a liberal war subsidy.

Charles revealed the anti-Dutch clauses of the treaty to Shaftesbury and Buckingham; the more sensational clauses he disclosed only to his brother and other Catholic intimates. The war which Shaftesbury hailed as a patriotic one was welcomed by York as part of the Dover policy of Romanising England.

The King himself had no enthusiasm for the war. He would much rather have postponed it. Peace was cheaper: and he was not altogether sure of victory. The majority of Englishmen were as unenthusiastic as he.

The progress of the war earned it no more popularity. The English fleet under York was surprised in Sole Bay, and the projected military assault on Zeeland frustrated. The success of the French army against the Dutch was hardly more palatable to the English than the failure of their own Navy. The French victories were, indeed, such as to alarm all but the most fervent Francophiles.

[1] P.R.O. 30/24/6B/429 (*vide* also another paper in Locke's hand on the origin of ecclesiastical government: P.R.O. 30/24/6B/430).

Turenne and Condé overran five Dutch provinces, reached Utrecht, and were sufficiently near The Hague itself to precipitate that revolution as a result of which Prince William of Orange was installed as Stadholder.

Uneasy as the situation was, Shaftesbury allowed his friend and counsellor a holiday in the autumn of 1672. Locke went to France with Lady Northumberland and a party which also included Mapletoft as physician, Blomer as chaplain, Mrs. Blomer and Mrs. Beavis.

Lady Northumberland, aged at this time twenty-six, was not only very rich but also very beautiful. Her beauty moreover was of the kind most appreciated at that period, as Lely's portrait shows. To the modern taste her nose may appear too large and her mouth too much the rosebud, but by any standards she would be counted an exceedingly attractive and marriageable widow.

Buckingham suggested that the Duke of York should be commanded to marry her, but nothing came of the idea. It was inevitably rumoured that she went to France in 1672 to protect her person from the immoral designs of the King. Inevitably also women admired her less than men. '*Je n'en fus point du tout éblouie*', Madam de Lafayette remarked to Madame de Sévigné after she had met the Countess.

Locke enjoyed his visit to France in her company. From Paris he wrote in October 1672 [1] to Strachey telling him how he had seen 'the Louvre; the Seine, the Pont Neuf over it; Paris; and what is the perfection and glory of all, the King of France himself.'

His admiration for the country was not unqualified. John Locke in France was very much John Bull abroad:

> . . . I saw vast and magnificent buildings as big almost as others' dominions, preparing only for one man, and yet there be a great many other two-legged creatures, but 'tis not the way of [France] much to consider them. . . .

Of the religious communities he wrote:

> . . . men that had forsaken the world and women that professed retirement and poverty have yet in the ornaments of their buildings and the hatchments of their trinkets all the mighty riches exquisite art could produce of convenience, beauty or curiosity.

[1] Rand, pp. 78/9.

L

He added:

> If the air of the country has given me but half so much health as it
> has vanity, I shall quickly be as strong as I am now conceited. . . . I
> wish you were but here to see how I could cock my hat, strut and
> shake my garniture; talk fast, loud, confidently, and nothing to the
> purpose; slight you and everybody. I protest it is worth your seeing.
> But I wish you would do yourself the kindness to come quickly, for I
> fear my French seasoning . . . may in time decay.

His stay in France proved to be a brief one. In less than a month,
Shaftesbury recalled him to London.

When he reached home, Locke wrote [1] to Mapletoft asking him to
convey

> all manner of thanks . . . to that excellent Lady to whose favour I owe
> my voyage and all the advantages of it. This you are to put into the
> best words you can find, and in this occasion you cannot say too much.
> For if Lioncourt and Chantilly, St. Germains and the Louvre be sights
> which cannot be sufficiently admired, I'm sure there cannot be enough
> said in return for that favour which added a grace even to those fine
> places, and made me value the sight of them more than otherwise I
> should have done.

While Locke was in France, Shaftesbury had realised one of his
political ambitions. He had secured the King's consent for the
establishment of a Council of Trade and Plantations. Government
committees for trade had existed for many years, and since 1670
there had been a second committee for plantations, or colonies;
but Shaftesbury, believing that questions of overseas possessions
were inseparable from questions of trade, and that neither of the
existing committees was organised on the scale it should be, proposed their fusion in a single and more powerful body. The King
agreed to this proposal, appointed a new Council of Trade and
Plantations and made Shaftesbury its President on 27 September.

Locke's precipitate return from France may well have prompted
the suspicion that he was about to become Secretary to the Council
of Trade. His connection with Shaftesbury and his experience with
other colonial bodies might seem to have made him a likely nominee.
But in fact Benjamin Worsley, who had been Shaftesbury's adviser
on colonial affairs for longer than Locke, was appointed Secretary.

---

[1] 19 October 1672 (*European Magazine*, XV, p. 9).

The creation of the Council may have had nothing whatever to do with Shaftesbury's urgent summons to Locke in October.

Other and even more important things were brewing. There was a crisis in the Government, and in November the King offered Shaftesbury the post of Lord High Chancellor of England, the most powerful ministerial office in the realm.

Shaftesbury accepted, though he knew the King had not made the offer for the purpose of bestowing glory. The policy of war with Holland and of toleration at home had brought nothing but trouble in its train, and as that policy was so much Shaftesbury's policy, the King thought it was Shaftesbury's duty to rescue the situation.

Charles had tried to end the war with Holland on honourable terms by offering to his nephew of Orange a treaty which would save the Dutch from complete disaster at the hands of the French in return for paying England a large indemnity and ceding a few seaports. Desperate as his plight was, the new Stadholder rejected these overtures; and England had perforce to remain at war with Holland. The Declaration of Indulgence was even more disliked by the majority of Englishmen than was the war. Although fifteen hundred Nonconformist ministers were given licences to preach under the provisions of the Declaration, many dissenters, who hated Papists even more than Churchmen did, joined the Anglican opposition to a policy which combined liberty for them with liberty for Catholics. The Exchequer Stop had alienated the very commercial classes who ought, on Shaftesbury's reasoning, to be the most eager for war with Holland, and fear of rising French hegemony was everywhere rife. Parliament had not been allowed to sit for nearly two years, and Charles realised he would have soon to summon it because he could not carry on much longer without the money Parliament alone could provide. He realised, too, that the mood of Parliament would be a nasty one. He gave the seals to Shaftesbury in the hope that Shaftesbury would be able to stand between him and Parliamentary hostility, and if Shaftesbury lost his popularity in Parliament, Charles would not, in any case, be sorry.

Locke was given a post of relative obscurity: that of Secretary of Presentations. His responsibility was that of supervising such ecclesiastical matters as came under the Chancellor's control; the salary £300 a year. It is not quite clear whether Locke was disappointed with this place, or whether he was content to serve his master confidentially behind the scenes.

Shaftesbury himself made a great show of splendour and power. He adopted a new grand manner in all things, saying that it was necessary to the prestige of his office to adopt the appropriate 'port and way of living'. He travelled between Exeter House and White-hall with his gentlemen and footmen walking beside his coach—and more than once these attendants included Locke. Shaftesbury tried to lease Northumberland House, and failing to do so had Exeter House enlarged to facilitate more lavish entertainment. He even went so far as to re-introduce the equestrian procession of judges from the Strand to Westminster Hall for the opening of the Term, but the horsemanship of the judges did not match the occasion, and he did not ask them to ride again.

Shaftesbury rejoiced in fine robes, and Roger North says he sat 'on the Bench in an ash-coloured gown, silver-laced and full-ribboned pantaloons displayed, without any black at all in his garb unless it were his hat'.[1] A portrait of Shaftesbury in his robes was painted in 1672 by John Greenhill, who also painted Locke at the same time. Locke praised Greenhill, in a little verse [2] for those 'matchless pieces' which 'are than ourselves less subject to decay'.

Locke's face in Greenhill's portrait is a handsome one. The large dark eyes bespeak romantic languors, while the curve of the mouth suggests a worldly cynicism more characteristic of the epoch than the man. The nose is large, the lips full, the chin dimpled, but the peruke conceals that majesty of brow which so effectively proclaims the scholar in later and more famous portraits.

In a list [3] of 'my Lord Chancellor's family' dated Christmas 1672 John Locke figures as the Secretary of Presentations, and is repre-sented as being entitled with Mr. Bennet, the Secretary for De-fendants, and six other principal officers of Shaftesbury's establish-ment at Exeter House to dine at the table of the steward, Thomas Stringer, and 'to have wine'. He, with the other principal officers, was expected in term time to attend prayers at seven and at eleven o'clock in the morning and at six in the evening. But it would be a mistake to deduce from these instructions that Shaftesbury had turned pious on mounting the Woolsack. The chapel at Exeter

---

[1] *Examen ed. cit.,* p. 60.
[2] The verse was written in a copy of Cowley's poems which Locke gave to Green-hill (B. Martyn, *op. cit.,* II, p. 13).
[3] P.R.O. 30/24/4/236.

House was open to the public, and the devotions he required of his entourage were but another part of the show.

Parliament re-assembled on 5 February 1672/3. After a brief address from the throne in which Charles blandly explained that he had delayed the summons to Parliament so long only in order 'to ease you and the country ' [1] he left it to Shaftesbury to justify his policy to the two Houses.

Shaftesbury then made one of the most celebrated speeches [2] of his whole career. He begged Parliament to give generous support for the war against Holland. He said the Dutch were the only real competitors against the English for 'trade and power at sea'; the only people who stood between England and 'an universal Empire as great as Rome'.

He did not hesitate to make Parliament responsible for the war.

> But you judged aright [he said] that at any rate *delenda est Carthago*: that government was to be brought down; and therefore the King may well say to you ' 'Tis your war'. He took his measures from you, and they were just and right ones, and he expects a suitable assistance in so necessary and expensive an action. . . .

Shaftesbury appealed to the patriotism of the Houses. He said the Dutch believed that the English Parliament was against the war, and he begged the Lords and Commons to prove the Dutch mistaken by 'a hearty conjunction at this time in supplying his Majesty'.

In the same speech Shaftesbury defended the 'Exchequer Stop' as 'a necessary expedient resorted to much against the King's will,' and he gave voice to the incontrovertible truth that the bankers would have nothing to complain of if Parliament agreed to pay them what they wanted. He also defended the Declaration of Indulgence; the King, he said, was 'a true defender of the Church of England', but was 'not convinced that violent ways are the interest of religion or of the Church'.

Locke, it was afterwards said,[3] was engaged by Shaftesbury 'to stand at his elbow' while he made this speech 'with a written copy to prompt him in case of failure in his repetition'. But I am not sure

[1] Christie, II, Appendix V, p. lxiii.
[2] *Ibid.*, pp. lxiii–lxix.
[3] By the third Earl of Shaftesbury (Amsterdam: Remonstrants' MSS. J. 20).

that this was absolutely true. Shaftesbury soon became very ashamed of having made the speech, and the suggestion that he needed someone to prompt him was part of the story that the speech was not of his own composition, but was dictated to him by the King.

Many Members of Parliament were shocked by his words, especially by the quotation from Cato; but Shaftesbury did at least succeed in stirring up some enthusiasm for the war. Where he failed was in his defence of the Declaration of Indulgence. He could not dissuade the House of Commons from drawing up an Address to the King asking for its withdrawal.

In his reply to Parliament, Charles made the point (which was originally Locke's point) that the King's prerogative in matters ecclesiastical, unlike his prerogative in matters civil, was his by right. He offered, however, to compromise. He would continue to tolerate dissenters and recusants, but would abandon his further intention of altering the structure of the Anglican Church to make membership more acceptable to Nonconformists. The Commons replied by denying the right of the King to suspend the law in matters ecclesiastical. Shaftesbury argued that this was a legal question and therefore one to be submitted to the House of Lords as the highest court in the realm. Their Lordships' findings favoured the right of Parliament against the prerogative of the King.

Charles, who had in the meantime tried and failed to extract another subvention from Louis, decided to capitulate. The Commons had made it clear that they would vote a generous supply in return for the withdrawal of the Declaration of Indulgence, and on the principle 'that money mattered more than religion',[1] the King revoked his Declaration just twelve months after he had issued it.

Parliament was still not satisfied. At the end of March it passed a Test Act which compelled every holder of public office, whether civil or military, to take the sacraments according to the Church of England. The measure became law, and both York and Clifford were deprived of office by it. When it was discussed in the House of Lords, members noticed that Shaftesbury had not the same zeal for toleration he had shown in previous debates.

It was soon apparent that he had changed completely. The champion of toleration and of Carthaginian war against Holland had abruptly become the champion of Parliament against prerogative,

[1] Feiling, *op. cit.*, p. 554.

bitterly anti-Popish and anti-French. The fact is that Shaftesbury had found out from Clifford about the secret treaty of Dover.

It was obvious that Shaftesbury's term of office as Lord Chancellor could not last much longer. Charles had appointed him because he was the great antagonist of High Anglicans and of Holland; he did not want him when he became an even greater antagonist of Roman Catholics and of France. The most remarkable thing is that Shaftesbury held on as long as he did.

Despite a revival of Dutch fortunes in the war, England generally became, like Shaftesbury, increasingly Protestant as the months went by. There was a cry for yet more stringent measures against Popery. Six days after an unusually spirited celebration of Guy Fawkes Day throughout the country Shaftesbury was dismissed.

From the time of Shaftesbury's Chancellorship dates the first documentary evidence I have been able to find of Locke's relationship with that delightful antiquarian and historian of human character, John Aubrey. Aubrey was yet another West-countryman, and I have already mentioned the possibility that he and Locke had met as boys; they must certainly have met at the early functions of the Royal Society.

Among the Shaftesbury Papers[1] is a letter Aubrey wrote to Locke on Shrove Tuesday 1672/3 commending a manuscript by Thomas Hobbes, who was Aubrey's great friend. Aubrey is important to this narrative, not only in his own right as a man of letters, but also because of the link he provides between the two philosophers. Aubrey wrote:

> Sir
> I cannot but present to you my thanks for your great humanity and kindness to me, as also for the honour you do me to peruse my scribblings.[2] I was at your lodging twice to have kissed your hand before I came out of town, to have recommended an MS or two (worthy of your perusal) of my old friend Mr. Thomas Hobbes. One is a treatise concerning the law,[3] which I importuned him to undertake about eight years since, and then in order thereto presented him with my Lord Bacon's *Elements of the Law*. All men will give the old gentleman[4]

[1] P.R.O. 30/24/7/493.
[2] Presumably portions of Aubrey's *North Wilts* or his *Natural History of Wiltshire*.
[3] Presumably *De Legibus*.
[4] In 1673 Hobbes was eighty-five.

that right as to acknowledge his great felicity in well defining—especially the common superstruction of their old fashioned axioms, right or wrong, for grand practisers have not the leisure to be analytics. Mr. Hobbes seemed then something doubtful he should not have days enough left to get about such a work. In this treatise he is highly for the King's prerogative. Chief Justice Hale [1] has read it and very much mislikes it; is his enemy and will not license it. Judge Vaughan [2] has perused it and very much commends it, but is afraid to license it for fear of giving displeasure.

'Tis pity fire should consume it, or that it should miscarry, as I have known some excellent things. I never expected to see it printed, and intended to have a copy, which the bookseller will let me have for 50s. and, God willing, will have one on my return. He writes short, and therefore the fitter for your reading, because so full of business. When you go by the Palsgrave Head Tavern, be pleased to call on Mr. W. Crooke [3] at the Green Dragon and remember me to him (by the same token I desired Mr. Hobbes to give his works to Magdalen Hall [4])—and he will show it to you. I have a conceit that if your Lord [5] saw it, he would like it. You may see likewise [Mr. Hobbes's] *History of England from 1640 to 1660* [6] about a quire of paper which the King has read and likes extremely, but tells me there is so much truth in it he dares not license for fear of displeasing the Bishops. The old gentleman is still very strangely vigorous. If you see him (which he would take kindly) pray my service to him.

God grant length of days to our illustrious Lord Chancellor, [7] who seriously deserves a statue for the good he has already begun. I humbly beg your pardon for giving you this trouble and to be assured that I am affectionately, sir,

Your most humble servant
Jo: Aubrey.

In a postscript Aubrey adds: 'About May I hope to kiss your hands.'

---

[1] Sir Matthew Hale was Chief Justice of the King's Bench. Aubrey says he 'was not only just, but wonderfully charitable and open handed, and did not sound a trumpet neither, as the hypocrites do' (*Brief Lives*, ed. Powell, p. 211).

[2] Sir John Vaughan was Chief Justice of Common Pleas. Aubrey tells us he was Hobbes's 'great acquaintance, to whom he made visits three times or more in a week —out of Term in the morning, in Term-time in the afternoon' (*ibid.*, p. 259).

[3] William Crooke kept a bookseller's shop, from which he also published, at the Green Dragon without Temple Bar, 1667–94. Plomer says he was no doubt the son of Andrew Crooke, who published Hobbes's *Leviathan* in 1651, and who also kept a Green Dragon—in St. Paul's Churchyard—until his death in 1674.

[4] Hobbes had been an undergraduate at Magdalen Hall, Oxford.

[5] Shaftesbury.

[6] Published in 1669 as *Behemoth*.   [7] Shaftesbury.

When he wrote this letter Aubrey was in dire financial straits. He had never been well off, and he had no aptitude for earning money. He worked hard, but only at his unremunerative anti-quarian studies; and while he showed some skill in avoiding his creditors, a disastrous betrothal to a litigious woman led to his financial ruin. Aubrey sold his house in 1671, and afterwards his friends implored him for his own sake to seek employment. His letter to Locke might be read as that of a man eager to ingratiate himself with the Lord Chancellor, in the hope of securing a place in the public service. I believe that would be a false interpretation. Aubrey had greeted destitution with positive relief: 'I was in as much affliction as mortal could be, and never quiet till all was gone.'[1] Mr. Anthony Powell, Aubrey's principal biographer, has written: 'The fact was that he was unwilling to take a job; he had plenty to engage him in his own work'.[2] I think it most probable that Aubrey wrote to Locke with the intention of helping his old friend Hobbes, by soliciting the interest of Shaftesbury on his behalf. Locke's reply to Aubrey seems to have perished. This is all the more a pity because it would have thrown some light on Locke's attitude towards Hobbes. Aubrey's letter is the only evidence I have found for supposing that on at least one occasion the two philosophers met.

Although Shaftesbury's removal from the Woolsack caused Locke to lose his place as Secretary of Presentations, he had by then acquired another, and more interesting, post. Benjamin Worsley, a dissenter, had refused in the summer of 1673 to take the Tests, and on 15 October Locke was sworn in as his successor at the Council of Trade and Plantations.

The Council of Trade was a fact-finding, not an executive body, and its secretary was for this reason a more important man than any of the councillors. Locke was an efficient secretary. The work of the Council was (I quote here from Professor Keith[3]) 'conscien-tiously done, meetings were frequent, complaints and memorials from the colonies were sedulously examined, and information on colonial conditions accepted from all with experience, local or English, of the conduct of colonial relations. The instructions to be given to Governors were carefully prepared, and colonial legislation

---

[1] Aubrey, p. xv. [2] *Ibid.*, p. xvi.
[3] A. B. Keith: *Constitutional History of the First British Empire* (Oxford, 1930), p. 60.

scrutinised'.[1] The Council had also to investigate home trade, to consider the improvement of produce and of manufactured goods, the development of fisheries, harbours and navigable rivers, the increase of exports and the elimination of abuses in trade.

So far as domestic trade was concerned, there was little to cause the Council anxiety. England, having none of the internal customs barriers which divided France and Germany, was already the largest trading unit in Europe. London could draw on the resources of the remotest English counties, even of Scotland, for supplies. There was a brisk exchange of goods between all parts of the country, and the volume of trade had not then grown, as it did in the eighteenth century, to such proportions that the transport system could not carry it efficiently.

The Council was chiefly preoccupied with foreign trade. The British Empire had not been founded as an empire, nor, in spite of the phrase 'The Old Colonial System' so dear to some historians, was it systematically conducted. The colonies were expected to contribute towards the economy of England, to supply England with raw materials, to buy English goods, and to abstain from competition with English industries. In return England accepted the responsibility of protecting the colonies by sea and against any European enemy, although the colonists had to raise their own militia for local defence. Various Acts of Trade were passed by Parliament to ensure that colonies fulfilled their share of the bargain. These Acts prescribed that certain 'enumerated' commodities, such as tobacco and sugar should come to England only, and that all goods leaving or entering colonial ports should be carried in English ships.

The investigations of the Council of Trade served to elucidate these principles. One thing in particular they emphasised: that it was in the English interest to concentrate on tropical or sub-tropical colonies such as the southern provinces of North America and the West Indies, which could sell England the goods she needed and buy English exports, and not to develop the more northerly New England colonies, which turned out the same goods as England herself produced. Indeed, the New England colonies were recognised as a menace to the commercial interests of the mother country;

[1] Besides the official documents preserved in the Public Record Office, a number of papers containing information on these questions is in the Lovelace Collection at the Bodleian Library (MSS. Locke, c. 30, c. 36, d. 7, c. 9, etc.).

and the Acts of Trade were extended to forbid, among other things, the export of New England cloth and iron. But although the New England colonies were inhabited by the self-consciously virtuous, laws of this kind were often disobeyed there.

In 1673 there were few Crown colonies: Virginia, Jamaica, Barbados and five smaller West Indian islands only. New Jersey, New York, Maryland and Carolina all belonged to noble proprietors, Hudson's Bay and the Bermudas were under trading companies, and the New England settlements were locally ruled. Elsewhere in the world British trade was monopolised by the other chartered companies: the Muscovy Company, the Africa Company, the Levant Company and the East India Company. Of these companies the last was seen to be the most important for precisely the same reason as were the more southerly American possessions in the colonial sphere: the East Indies took English exports and supplied England with goods she needed. After 1661, when Charles II acquired Bombay as part of his Portuguese wife's dowry, that Indian city was rapidly developed to succeed Surat and Madras as the metropolis of English trade with the East.

While the Council of Trade could not influence the directors of the chartered companies as it could the colonial governors, whose instructions it helped to draft, their activities were closely scrutinised from the point of view of public policy. The Council also confronted the problem of Ireland—a Crown colony in all but name. The English Government was alarmed in 1673 by the competition of Irish wool with English wool, and the Privy Council asked the Council of Trade to consider the question of prohibiting the entry of Irish woollen yarn into England. Shaftesbury, still a member of the Council of Trade for some months after he had been deprived of the seals (his time to go came when he was dismissed from the Privy Council in May 1674) opposed such prohibition as an inadequate solution to the problem.[1]

Locke's interest in the colonies was not purely theoretical and bureaucratic. Towards the end of 1672 Shaftesbury had inaugurated a new company of merchant adventurers to trade with the Bahamas, which the King had ceded to the Lords Proprietors of Carolina two years before. Locke himself became one of these merchant adventurers: the others included John Mapletoft, Thomas Stringer and Henry Aldrich. Locke put up £200 in the first instance, which

[1] Brown, p. 148.

was more than some of the others did. His friend in Barbados, Sir Peter Colleton, wrote to him in May, 1673,[1] to give him the following advice:

> The Bahamas trade will turn to account if you meddle not with planting . . . if other men will plant there (I mean the Bahamas) hinder them not, they improve our province. But I would neither have your nor my Lord Shaftesbury engage in it.

Locke accepted this counsel of prudence and was later able to sell out his stock at a profit. He also received (the only reward he ever received) from Lord Shaftesbury an annuity on favourable terms.[2] But his post as secretary to the Council of Trade and Plantations was less remunerating than it had promised to be. Soon after his appointment his salary was raised on paper from £500 to £800; in reality, not a penny of it ever reached him.

In March 1674/5 Locke was relieved of his duties. The King's new chief Minister, the Earl of Danby, had decided, as 'a measure of economy', to dissolve the Council of Trade and transfer its duties to a committee of the Privy Council afterwards known as the Lords of Trade.

This Danby, who had become by 1675 the most powerful politician in the Court, had been born (in 1632) Thomas Osborne, and risen from the relative obscurity of a Yorkshire baronet as a protégé of Buckingham, whom, in due course, he repaid by helping to overthrow. When, as a result of Clifford's refusal to take the Test, the place of Lord High Treasurer became vacant in June 1673, the King chose Osborne to fill it and made him a baron. Shaftesbury was then Lord High Chancellor. But within five months Shaftesbury had departed, and Osborne wasted no time in sweeping Buckingham and Arlington out of his own path to power; in June 1674 he became Earl of Danby.

Danby had gone into politics with nothing but his wits, but those political wits were matched by no man's except by Shaftesbury's and the King's, and he was Shaftesbury's most formidable rival.

Danby's aim was to keep the King independent alike of Parliament and France. It was a policy which required great ingenuity to put into effect; for whence, if not from Parliament or France, was the

---

[1] 28 May 1673. (P.R.O. 30/24/48/90.)
[2] This annuity was worth £100 a year, but it was not a gift. Locke bought it for £700. The security was a farm at Kingston on Lord Shaftesbury's estate in Dorset.

King to get the money he so badly needed? Danby's method was to
exploit every authorised source of royal taxation, and to economise
on every expenditure. For a time his method worked well.[1]

Shaftesbury was not idle in opposition. He avoided, at first,
too flagrant provocation of the King and Danby, preferring to
concentrate on building up his own party. Close to Exeter House
was a tavern, the Swan, in King Street, Covent Garden; there
Shaftesbury dined regularly with his chosen friends from the House
of Lords, including Halifax, Salisbury and Clare, and their most
important supporters in the Commons, including Nathaniel Carew,
Robert Thomas, Thomas Lee, Elias Harvey and William Sacheverell.
This was the beginning of Shaftesbury's political club, the Green
Ribbon Club, and the nucleus of his party, the Whig or Country
Party.

Some members of the club made tentative moves against Popery
in high places. One of their victims was Pepys,[2] then Secretary of the
Navy and a newcomer to the House of Commons. Sir Robert
Thomas, a supporter of Shaftesbury's in that House, accused Pepys
in February 1673/4 of being a secret Catholic, of having converted his
wife to Popery and of keeping crucifixes and altars in his house.[3] As
Pepys's wife was dead and his house had been destroyed by fire, this
charge was difficult either to prove or refute. When Pepys denied it,
Sir Robert Thomas named Sir John Banks and Lord Shaftesbury as
witnesses. But Shaftesbury, summoned to give evidence, said he
had never seen an altar at Pepys's house, although he had an imperfect recollection of seeing something very like a crucifix.[4] Sir
John Banks said he had never seen either an altar or a crucifix, and

---

[1] 'By skilful manipulation the revenue was increased by well over £100,000.
Despite the collapse of the Government's credit, due to the Stop of the Exchequer,
he reduced the rate of interest on all but small loans immediately required to 8 per
cent. The army and navy left on his hands were paid off in money, not in tickets,
at an expense of about £800,000. Arrears due to the dockyards, in old tickets, to
sick and wounded men, and to the household, were discharged to the amount of
over £300,000.' Andrew Browning, *Thomas Osborne* (Oxford, 1913), p. 21.

[2] Samuel Pepys (1633–1703), the diarist, was educated at St. Paul's School and
Cambridge. He married in 1655 a Huguenot, Elizabeth St. Michel, who died in 1669.
After employment as secretary to Sir Edward Montagu, he was made 'clerk of the
acts of the navy' under the Lord High Admiral, the Duke of York, to whom he was
personally devoted. Pepys was made 'secretary for the affairs of the navy' in June
1673.

[3] Arthur Bryant, *Samuel Pepys: the Years of Peril* (1952), p. 91.

[4] Pepys did in fact possess a print of the Passion, and such pictures were known in
the seventeenth century as 'crucifixes' (*ibid.*, p. 93).

he added that he did not think Pepys was at all inclined to Popery.[1] Pepys was exonerated, and Shaftesbury decided to treat the whole episode as a joke. The time had not yet come for an all-out anti-Popish campaign.

Nor had the King as yet abandoned the hope of placating Shaftesbury. Early in 1675, Charles proposed to create the office of Vicar-General or Minister of Ecclesiastical Affairs, as Shaftesbury had once suggested he should, and he sent Lord Mordaunt to St. Giles to offer the post to Shaftesbury, whom he had not long before ordered to stay away from London. Having advance news of the offer, Shaftesbury wrote [2] to Lord Carlisle:

> ...I hear from all quarters ... that a great office with a strange name is preparing for me, and such like. I am ashamed that I was thought so easy a fool by them that should know me better. But I will assure your Lordship there is no place or condition will invite me to Court during this parliament nor until I see the King thinks frequent new parliaments as much his interest as they are the people's right. ...

Presumably Shaftesbury said much the same to the King himself. At any rate he refused the offer, and the demand for an election and 'frequent new parliaments' was for the next year or two the main plank of the open Whig policy. Shaftesbury urged it in several pamphlets as well as in speeches to the House of Lords.[3] One such pamphlet, entitled *A Letter from a Person of Quality to his Friend in the Country*,[4] was for many years attributed to Locke. P. des Maizeaux printed it in 1720 in his *Collection of Several Pieces of Mr. John Locke* [5] from manuscripts given him by Locke's cousin Peter King. It is more likely that the pamphlet was written by Shaftesbury himself with Locke's help.

More interesting than Locke's share in the exposition of the open Whig policy is the question of his share in the development of the hidden Whig policy after 1675. For Whig policy entered just then on one of its darkest phases. Its prime objective was to get rid of Danby. And such at that time was also the prime objective of French policy. In principle the Whigs were anti-French; but under

[1] Sir John Banks, a wealthy East India merchant, was politically sympathetic to Shaftesbury, but he had profitable business links with the Admiralty through Pepys.
[2] P.R.O. 30/24/5/284.
[3] Especially his attack on standing parliaments and a standing army on 20 November. (Feiling: *A History of the Tory Party*, Oxford, 1924, p. 162.)
[4] The title page bears beside the title only the words: 'Printed in the Year 1675'.
[5] Pp. 57–149.

Danby's ministry they found themselves in a situation where their short-term interests were identical with those of France. French emissaries made secret overtures[1] to Shaftesbury and his chief lieutenants, offering the support of Louis against Danby if the Whigs would moderate their opposition to France and the Duke of York. A bargain was struck. French money was subsequently used to strengthen this alliance with the Whigs, but by that time Shaftesbury was imprisoned in the Tower of London, and the Whig principals in the negotiations were Russell and Sydney.

Secret relations between the French court and the English Opposition began in 1676 and lasted until the spring of 1679, when their object was accomplished and Danby removed from power.

And what, the reader may ask, has all this to do with Locke? Perhaps nothing. But the curious thing is that Locke went to France just before the deal was made and he returned to England immediately its end was achieved. Shaftesbury's grandson, in a letter he wrote[2] in 1704, said:

> ... when my grandfather quitted the Court and began to be in danger from it, Mr. Locke now shared with him in dangers as before in honours and advantages. He entrusted him with his secretest negotiations, and made use of his assistant pen in matters that nearly concerned the State and were fit to be made public to raise that spirit in the nation which was necessary against the prevailing Popish Party.
>
> It was for something of this kind that got air, and out of tenderness to Mr. Locke that my grandfather in the year 1674[3] sent him abroad to travel, an improvement which my grandfather was glad to add to those he had already given him.
>
> His [Mr. Locke's] health served as a very just excuse.

There is, however, very little other evidence to link Locke's name with the Whig activities of 1676–9.

[1] Andrew Browning, *Earl of Danby* (Glasgow, 1951), I, p. 165.
[2] Amsterdam: Remonstrants' MSS. J. 20.
[3] A mistake. Locke went to France in November 1675.

Chapter Thirteen

IN FRANCE

LOCKE did not go directly from Exeter House to France. He returned in the first instance to Oxford and resumed for a time the study of medicine. Having secured at long last the degree of Bachelor of Medicine, he received from the Chancellor of the University on 6 February 1674/5, a faculty to practise as a physician. At the same time he was appointed to one of the two medical studentships at Christ Church.

'Locke', wrote Humphrey Prideaux [1] to his Civil Service friend John Ellis, 'hath wriggled into Ireland's faculty place, and intendeth this Act to proceed Doctor in Physic.'

Locke did not 'proceed Doctor in Physic', and they were surprised at Christ Church in November when, instead of doing so, he packed his bags, let his room in Canterbury quadrangle,[2] and went abroad. Health was, as Shaftesbury's grandson said, the excuse; it may even have been the real reason. Sydenham [3] thought Locke had been working too hard, and urged him to cherish himself as much as he could. He warned him that 'bodies broken with business' lacked the necessary store of 'needful heat'. He advised him to go to bed at eight o'clock every night; to eat only 'meats of easy digestion', and to abstain entirely from wine, taking instead some 'small mild beer'. The one thing he did not recommend was France.

However, there is nothing incompatible with the hypothesis that he went there for his health in Locke's recorded movements in France. He travelled almost at once to Montpellier, a health resort specialising in the treatment of phthisis, the very disease which Locke believed (mistakenly) that he had. He did not travel alone.

'George Walls', wrote Prideaux [4] to Ellis, 'goes to London on

[1] 7 February 1674/5. B.M. Add. MSS. 28,929. f. 13
[2] Locke's tenant was Richard Old, subsequently (1676–92) rector of Radbourne, Warwickshire.
[3] Sydenham to Locke. (P.R.O. 30/24/47/2; undated but probably written in 1675.)
[4] 8 November 1675 (B.M. Add. MSS. 28,929 f. 20).

Monday in order to a journey into France. What is his business there I know not, unless it be to be John Locke's chaplain, whom he accompanieth thither'.

George Walls, who rose in due course to be a canon both of Worcester and St. Paul's, was at that time one of the clerical Students of Christ Church. He was aged thirty.

Before Locke left England inventories were drawn up of his belongings in Oxford and London. George Walls made a list of the things of Locke's he had delivered to David Thomas at New College and of the furniture which remained in Locke's rooms at Christ Church. Trunks, boxes, manuscripts and chemical glasses went to Thomas; tables, chairs and 'a picture' remained at the House. Two items recorded among those left in London have some special interest: a trunk marked with the romantically mysterious initials 'E. P.', and 'my portrait'. This latter was probably the portrait of Locke which was painted in 1672 by John Greenhill and which now belongs to the National Portrait Gallery.[1]

From the time of his departure for France—if not before—Locke wrote a daily journal in vellum-bound almanacs,[2] and he kept up the habit with diminishing regularity until the last years of his life. This record shows that Locke and Walls landed at Calais on Sunday 14 November by the Julian calendar, on *24 November* by the Gregorian calendar. As far as Abbeville, they accompanied the English Ambassador Extraordinary to the French Court, Lord Berkeley of Stratton. They reached Paris on *4 December*, and Locke noted in his journal: 'At the Vil Brisack [3] we were in pension for 20s.[4] a day, but paid beside for fire and candle. . . .'

After only ten days in Paris the two travellers set off for Lyons, going by road as far as Châlons, and then on by river boat, which they liked better. Locke played cards on board to beguile the tedium of the journey, and at the overnight stops he did not fail to notice that 'Monsieur l'Abbé and a woman lay in the same chamber'.

[1] It was sold to the N.P.G. in 1954 by Mr. W. Sanford of Chipley Park.

[2] B.L. MSS. Locke, F. 1–F. 10 and B.M. Add. MSS. 15642. Lough prints a transcript of most of the entries Locke wrote in his journals during his years in France. The omissions are (1) lists of books and of Locke's notes on his reading (separately published by J. Lough in the *Library*, London, December 1953); (2) notes entitled *Atlantis*; (3) weather observations; (4) Biblical notes; (5) medical notes; (6) notes on coins and currencies; and (7) philosophical notes (most of which have been published by Aaron and Gibb or by W. von Leyden).

[3] The Ville de Brisach was a Protestant inn in the rue de Seine (Lough, p. 1).

[4] 20s. 20 sous, or one livre. Locke received about 13 *livres* for a pound sterling.

M

(He recorded this information discreetly in shorthand.[1]) At Lyons Locke was entertained by an amateur naturalist named William Charlton,[2] who became one of his life-long friends and correspondents, but he did not spend long in the place. By *4 January 1676*, Walls and he were in Montpellier. They put up at 'Mr. Puech's[3] house, being told that that part of the town which lay towards the sea was less healthy . . . the south and south-east winds being counted unhealthy, coming off from the sea'.

At the same time Locke and Walls jointly engaged the services of a Mr. Pasty to give them an hour's lesson in French five times a week.[4]

Locke established himself in Montpellier for the next fifteen months, though he did leave the town during the great heats of summer and also to make tours of Provence and Languedoc. In a letter to an unnamed friend,[5] he wrote thus of the hardships which beset travellers in France:

Are they summoned before day to rise? Coarse and stinking lodging makes them forward. Are dirty, heavy boots to be put on? Want of slippers takes away all reluctancy. Is lean, ill-dressed meat to be ate? A good stomach bids it welcome. Are you to be dismounted and thrust into a rascally inn, four or five in a chamber? Ten or eleven leagues on a dull, hobbling jade will make you glad of it.

He complained of inns where 'the whole bill of fare' was 'nothing but a cabbage and a frog that was caught in it and some haws of the last season'; though he admitted there were times when he had found congenial lodgings:

Good mutton and a good supper here, clean sheets of the country and a pretty girl to lay them on . . . Do not wonder that a man of my constitution and gravity mention to you a handsome face amongst his remarks, for I imagine that a traveller, though he carries a cough with him, goes not yet out of his way when he takes notice of strange and extraordinary things.

[1] *19 December 1675.*
[2] Otherwise William Courten (1642–1704). He was something of a mystery-man, but not, apparently, connected with politics.
[3] Lough (p. 16) reports that the Montpellier tax rolls give the name of Jacques Puech, an apothecary, as living in the rue du Puits de Fer.
[4] *Journal, 9 January 1676.*
[5] B.L. MSS. c. 25 f. 19 (Lough, pp. 276–81).

In letters such as these Locke described his adversities in elaborate and mildly humorous detail: in his journal he recorded only bare and mostly dull facts. Locke was not an artist, and he was in many ways a surprisingly unperceptive traveller. He had no gift for describing natural beauty, no sense of history, and his immediate response to splendid architecture was to measure the building and leave it at that. But Locke's philistinism was in no sense an aberration. He wanted to get away from the imagination, away from the vague glamour of medieval things, from reverence for tradition, from mysticism, enthusiasm and *gloire*; away from all private visionary insights and down to the plain, measurable, publicly verifiable facts; and this desire was central to his whole mission as a philosopher and reformer.

From his earliest days in Montpellier, Locke made notes in his journal about the position of the Protestants, who were still numerous in the city—more than eight thousand in a population of thirty thousand.[1] His testimony on the subject is not always reliable. For example, he noted on *31 January 1676* that the Protestants of Uzès were forbidden 'this year' to send a Protestant deputy to the States at Montpellier, whereas it is clear from the records that Protestant deputies had been excluded from a much earlier date.[2] But on *5 February 1676*, a day 'so warm that the sunbeams were rather troublesome than not', Locke wrote in his journal a more accurate account:

> The Protestants have here common justice generally, unless it be against a new convert, whom they will favour. They pay no more taxes than their neighbours, are only incapable of public charges and offices. They have had within these ten years at least 160 churches pulled down. They and the Papist laity live together friendly enough in these parts. They sometimes get and sometimes lose proselytes. There is nothing done against those that come over to the reformed religion, unless they be such as have before turned Papist and relapse: these sometimes they prosecute. The number of Protestants in these latter years neither increases nor decreases much. Those that go over to the Church of Rome are usually drawn away by fair promises that most commonly fail them, or else money if they be poor. The Protestants live not better than the Papists.

This item is attributed to 'Dr. Barbeyrac', and it is the earliest evidence of Locke's having met that great Protestant physician.

[1] Bonno, p. 50.   [2] Lough, p. 27.

Locke saw much of him afterwards, and, very probably, learned more than a little from him about medical science. Locke also made the acquaintance of another Protestant savant of Montpellier, one Pierre Magnol, at that time also a physician, though remembered as a naturalist (the Magnolia is named after him). Magnol was eventually converted to the Roman Church and elected a Professor at Montpellier University, but when Locke was there neither he nor Barbeyrac was eligible for an academic post.

Other new friends Locke made in Montpellier included Pierre Jolly, one of the medical graduates of the University and an enthusiastic astronomer. It was with him that Locke witnessed on *11 June 1676* an eclipse of the sun. Among the philosophers of the place he met Pierre Sylvain Régis, a prominent populariser of Cartesianism; and although, as Locke noted in his journal,[1] the French Government had forbidden the teaching of Cartesian philosophy in the schools and universities, that philosophy could still be debated in private; and being forbidden in the one place, it was probably all the more discussed in the other.

Professor Bonno, in his analysis [2] of Locke's record of his reading during his sojourn at Montpellier, has shown that he possessed or consulted all the best current French books in the fields of science, travel, medicine, religion, education, philosophy, and history (especially the history of Protestantism in France); M. Bonno notes a particular interest in the writings of Pascal. But there is little evidence of Locke's having any taste for literature as such. As M. Bonno says, his reading lists 'n'indiquent qu'une curiosité très discrète chez un voyageur séjournant en France à une époque marquée par l'abondante floraison des chefs-d'oeuvre du classicisme'.[3]

In Montpellier Locke attended several meetings of the States of Languedoc, and at least on one occasion a civic service at the cathedral: [4]

> The States every morning go to Notre Dame to prayers, where mass is sung. All the while the priest who says mass is at the altar saying the office, you cannot hear him a word, and indeed the music is the pleasanter of the two . . . The Cardinal [5] sat uppermost, nearest the altar, and had a velvet quishon,[6] richly laced with broad silver and gold lace; the bishops had none at all. He also had his book and repeated his

---

[1] *22 March 1676.*   [2] Bonno, pp. 49–63.
[3] *Ibid.*, p. 52.   [4] *7 February 1676.*
[5] Pierre de Bonzi.   [6] Cushion.

office apart very genteelly with an unconcerned look, talking every now and then and laughing with the bishops next to him. He keeps a very fine mistress [1] in the town, which some of the very Papists complain of, and has some very fine boys in his train.

Once more Locke was prudent enough to record his morsel of ecclesiastical scandal, which (as a zealous Protestant?) he obviously relished, in shorthand. On Shrove Tuesday there was a carnival at Montpellier, and Locke described 'dancing in the streets in all manner of habits and disguises, to all sorts of music, brass kettles and frying pans not excepted'.[2]

In March he went with a friend, either George Walls or William Charlton (who had joined them in Montpellier), on an excursion to Balaruc, a watering-place of Languedoc which reminded him of Bath in Somerset, except that at Balaruc 'they bathe stark naked and often times men and women together'.[3] Returning to Montpellier, he noted in his journal:

> Clysters are very frequently prescribed in the practice of physic here and the apothecaries' men administer them indifferently to men and women. Only the meaner sort of women about Montpellier are with difficulty brought to take them after this manner.[4]

In the spring Locke went even farther afield. He visited such places as Aix, Avignon and Hyères, and he saw the French fleet at Toulon. He commented briefly on the buildings and the vine-yards, but what struck him most in Provence was the poverty of the country. He recalled [5] that he had seen ' more barren ground than fruitful', and that the people had 'five acres of poverty for one of riches'. He added:

> I remember at Aix in a gardener's house, where we found them eating, their Sunday dinner was nothing but slices of congealed blood fried in oil. . . .

Locke noticed on the road that everyone carried pistols,[6] and even in Montpellier he had to record [7] that 'several murders' had been

---

[1] Lough (p. 30) identifies her as Jeanne de Gévaudan.
[2] *18 February 1676.*   [3] *5 March 1676.*
[4] *17 March 1676.* 'In the medical practice of the seventeenth and eighteenth centuries, the clyster was employed as freely and frequently as the hypodermic syringe today' (Aldous Huxley, *The Devils of Loudun*, 1952, p. 132).
[5] *23 April 1676.*   [6] *26 March 1676.*
[7] *18 March 1676.*

'committed here since I came hither and more attempted, one by a brother on his sister in the house where I lay'.

Clearly life was not dull in Montpellier, but Locke's health was none the better for his being there.

'I am sorry to hear that your cough doth increase upon you', Thomas Stringer wrote to him in April.[1] 'Sir Paul Neile is still of the opinion that to come to England and marry a young woman is the best remedy.'

Whether because of the attempted murder or for some other reason, Locke left his rooms with M. Puech to lodge at the house of a Monsieur Fesquet. Then by the end of July, the town had become so hot that he was obliged to seek a retreat for the next few weeks at a farm near Celleneuve, and when he returned to Montpellier it was to take up fresh lodgings once more—this time with an apothecary named Henri Verchand.

English society was not lacking in Montpellier. One acquaintance Locke made there was with William Wycherley,[2] the dramatist. Another, which ripened into friendship, was with Thomas Herbert, whom he may possibly have already met as an undergraduate at Oxford. This Thomas Herbert had entered Christ Church in 1673 at the age of sixteen. He had been travelling in Italy before he reached Montpellier in 1676, and he had already made some study of law. Later he entered politics, and as eighth Earl of Pembroke became a famous *virtuoso* and collector. At the age of fifty it was said of him that he was 'a good judge in all the several sciences' and 'a great encourager of learning and learned men' and that he was 'plain in his dress; speaks little; of good countenance though very ill shaped; tall, thin, and stoops'.[3] He was not universally admired; Hearne, for example, said of him that [4] he 'is not a man of that deep penetration nor of that profound learning he is taken to be'. Nevertheless he proved a faithful friend to Locke (as Locke testified when he dedicated his *Essay Concerning Human Understanding* to him), in evil times as well as good. But in the autumn of 1676 'evil times' were years ahead, and Thomas Herbert [5] was still a minor.

[1] B.L. MSS. Locke, c. 19, f. 122.
[2] The evidence for this is in a letter from Locke to William Charlton, dated *19 September 1678* (offered for sale by Messrs. Robinson, Pall Mall, London, in 1954).
[3] J. Macky, *Memoirs*, 1733, p. 22.
[4] *Remarks and Collections*, 9 February 1707–8.
[5] Some indication of the nature of Locke's relations with Thomas Herbert is given

The autumn of Locke's first year in Montpellier was short, and early in November he noticed 'as much coughing at church as I ever heard in London';[1] by the beginning of December there was 'hard snow'.[2] However, the weather was already 'very warm'[3] again by mid-January, and in February Locke set off to visit some of the smaller towns of south-west France, including Carcassonne and Castelnaudary. Neither of these last pleased him much, but he was most impressed by Pierre Riquet's Canal de Languedoc, the 'greatest engineering achievement of the reign of Louis XIV'.[4]

At Montpellier bad news awaited Locke. Shaftesbury had been arrested. In 1676 that statesman gave up his house in the Strand and bought another, Thanet House, in Aldersgate Street, thus moving even closer to those City friends whose company the King had told him to quit. When Parliament met in February 1676/7 (for the first time since 1675) he called for an immediate dissolution. He said that parliaments were annual before common law and the current parliament therefore illegal. This assertion so incensed his fellow peers that Shaftesbury and his three supporters—Buckingham, Salisbury and Wharton—were sent to the Tower.

Shaftesbury's imprisonment lasted for over a year, but the conditions were not severe. He was allowed to have his own servant, to

by the following entries under 'Herbert' in a notebook Locke kept at Montpellier (B.L. MSS. Locke F. 15, ff. 28–9).

'At the playhouse 3 July lent him £1–10 value of moneys. Everlasting almanak. Last journal. Lent him in the limonade house 8 July 0–5 . . . [Lent him at Montpellier le voiage d'Espagne.] Lent him 10 June 77 Heptameron rustici, Geog. Chronological tables, Launay's Introduction a la Philosophi. . . . Lent him Aug 6 4 pistols, Borrowed of him 18th 0–10–0, Corneilles peices and the examens upon them. . . . Les beautys de la Perse, 3 pt of Monconys 4 Oct 77, Borrowed of him 21 Oct—£220–0 and given him note for it. pd. Lent him 1 Nov Le Conformation entre les ceremonies etc. Borrowed of him 6 Nov pd 1–10, Lent him 22 Nov—22–0. Lent him 6 Dec—66–0, Lent him 16 Dec—5–10, Borrowed of him 18 Dec—2–10, Borrowed of him Jan 15—3–0, Lent him 15 Jan—1–0—Paid me 15 Jan—7–0, Owes me upon account—60–0. Paid Jan 24—60–0; Lent me 26 Jan—3–0, [His notes on several texts of scripture out of Mr. Altham's book]. Dr. 28 Feb for 80 crowns. Lent him 240, paid by a bill on Mr. Chomoley, Cr. 10 Mar by 1 crown lent me 3–0. Dr. 19 Mar for 4 vol of Essay de Morale—1–12. [Cholmoley at the Golden Ancher over agt St. Dunstans Church Fleet Street.] (All the foregoing entries except those enclosed in square brackets were crossed out, probably after the settlement of the debt or the return of the book.)

[1] *8 November 1676.*   [2] *3 December 1676.*
[3] *16 January 1677.*   [4] Lough, p. 128.

furnish his own table and to correspond with his family and friends. He even took the trouble during his first fortnight in the Tower to write to Locke this letter: [1]

> Sir John Banks, my intimate good friend, is sending his son into France to travel about that country for four or five months. He hath already learned the French tongue but [Sir John] is only willing to let him see the manners of those people. Sir John intends to send him over to Paris about a fortnight hence, in the custody of Sir Richard Dutton, who is going thither, and is very desirous, if you will undertake that charge, to have him recommended to your care. [2]

Sir John Banks was a man of humble birth who had built himself a prodigious fortune as an East India merchant. He had a house at Olantigh, near Canterbury, 'a charming wife and a family of clever children'. [3] The son of whom he wished Locke to take charge was named Caleb.

Sir John himself wrote to Locke [4] asking him if he would travel with his son into Italy. He mentioned Pepys as well as Shaftesbury as having approved of the plan: an interesting conjunction of names after the episode of Pepys's Popish picture. It was one of the secrets of Sir John Banks's success that he could be at the same time friends with Whigs and Tories, and clearly Pepys did not allow his dislike of Shaftesbury to affect his esteem for Locke.

Locke accepted Sir John's proposal and on *26 March* he set out to meet young Banks in Paris. He went first to Toulouse where he found occasion to write one of his usual sarcastic notes about holy relics: [5]

> At the Church of St. Sernin they tell us they have the bodies entire of six of the apostles and the head of a seventh. This is much, considering what need there is of such relics in other places, but yet notwithstanding they promise you seven of the twelve apostles. They are not half so liberal as the Count de ——, who invited the Duke of Vernule to Toulouse and told him he would see there the 100 apostles.

[1] Christie, II, p. 235.
[2] Sir John Banks's was not the first request of its kind Locke received. On 11 July 1676, Samuel Eyre wrote to ask if he would take charge of Mrs. Pierpoynt's fifteen-year-old son in France.
[3] Arthur Bryant, *op. cit.*, p. 53.
[4] 26 February 1676/7 (B.L. MSS. Locke, c. 3, f. 66).
[5] *30 March 1677.*

On his way to Paris Locke was delayed as the result of an accident. He found himself 'feverish' and with

> an extraordinary pain in my head, having between Toulouse and [Agen] had a very cold and untoward passage by water, and a great pole having fell upon my head in the boat. Not knowing which to impute it to, but willing above all to secure my head as much as I could, if that had received any harm, I took a clyster in the afternoon, and the next morning, the pain in my head continuing with great violence, I bleeded, I believe, between eleven and twelve ounces. . . .'[1]

Though suffering from a tertian ague, otherwise malaria, Locke continued his journey as far as Bordeaux; but then he had to spend the next six weeks on a sick-bed.

It was the beginning of June before he reached the capital. Caleb Banks awaited him patiently. Sir John had already assured the philosopher that 'my son is not given to any extravagancy, but I hope you will find him a person of that temper and conversation that you will be pleased with, and in all things submitting to you.'

Locke liked the boy except for the fact, apparent from a draft letter of Locke's to Sir John dated *9 June*[2], that he would not at once hand over the money his father had given him for his tutor. But three days later Locke recorded in his journal: 'Received from Mr. Banks 631 livres 18, the value of fifty pounds sterling which Sir John presented me.'

One of the first things Locke did in Paris was to write[3] to Robert Boyle to 'beg the favour of two or three lines from your hand to recommend me to the acquaintance of anyone of the *virtuosi* you shall think fit here'. He added that Boyle's 'bare name' would open doors 'where otherwise one like me, without port and name, that have little tongue and less knowledge, shall hardly get entrance'.

In his journal Locke recorded: 'I removed to Mr. de Launay's, *June 10*'. Professor Lough has made the interesting suggestion that Locke's host was possibly Gilles de Launay, who is mentioned in a letter of Bayle (dated *24 June 1677*[4]) as teaching in public lectures the philosophy of Gassendi. Launay wrote an *Introduction à la philosophie* and at least three other philosophical works which were in Locke's possession in Paris.[5] Launay was no great thinker in his

---

[1] *14 May 1677.*   [2] B.L. MSS. Locke, c. 24, f. 20.
[3] Boyle, V, p. 569.   [4] *Oeuvres*, La Haye, 1737, I, p. 49.
[5] Lough, p. 150.

own right, and it is Locke's intellectual debt to Gassendi which gives the interest to this possibility of his having lodged in the house of a leading populariser of Gassendian thought.

Another and greater exponent of Gassendi Locke did certainly come to know in Paris: namely François Bernier,[1] author of the *Abrégé de la philosophie de Gassendi*. But Bernier was also an orientalist and, strange to say, all Locke's references to him in his journal deal with Bernier's knowledge of the East; none with Gassendi, or indeed with any philosophical question at all. Bernier, the author of several travel books, stimulated in Locke an interest in the literature of travel which lasted all his life. The two men also shared an interest in medicine, and it is hardly conceivable that they did not discuss philosophy as well, for Bernier had only just published his abridgement of Gassendi at the time of his first interviews with Locke.

In the meantime the education of Caleb Banks was not neglected. Locke took him to see all the interesting sights in and around Paris. Together they visited the Tapisseries des Gobelins, the Académie de Peinture, the Invalides, the Louvre, the Benedictine Abbey of St. Germain, St. Cloud, the Royal Library and the abbey of Ste. Geneviève among other places. That which Locke liked best, to judge from the entries in his journal and his repeated visits, was Versailles. On at least one occasion his pupil and he saw the King there, walking with Madame Montespan. Locke noted that 'the King seemed to be mightily well pleased with his water-works'.[2] Locke's journal suggests that the water-works pleased him mightily as well: he described them more fully than anything else he saw at Versailles.

On *1 July 1677* George Walls left Paris to return to England, and Locke was left alone with his pupil. He soon felt his old desire to quit the city, and proposed to Sir John Banks that his pupil should travel with him. When Sir John suggested that it would be better for his son's education for them to stay where they were,[3] Locke replied saying:[4] 'The great benefit to be found by travel is by constant changing of company; and conversing every day with

---

[1] François Bernier (1620–88) was a doctor of medicine from Montpellier, who had spent thirteen years in the East as physician to Aureng-Zebe and published his *Histoire de la dernière Revolution des Etats du Grand Mogol* in 1671.

[2] Journal: *23 June 1677*.

[3] B.L. MSS. Locke, c. 3, f. 88.

[4] *28 August 1677*. F.B., I, 378.

unknown strangers is to get a becoming confidence and not to be abashed at new faces.'

Travelling about the Continent with Caleb Banks was not the only project Locke had in mind that summer. His friend John Mapletoft was contemplating marriage, a step which would oblige that physician to vacate the post of Professor of Medicine at Gresham's College, London. Locke had hopes of succeeding to the chair, and he told [1] Mapletoft frankly that were he to marry, 'nobody will be readier, as you may guess, to throw an old shoe after you'. When Mapletoft replied saying he was not sure whether to marry or not, Locke wrote [2] to egg him on: 'I'm sure you will be much happier than any forlorn bachelor can be.' In the same letter Locke begged his friend both to remember his interest in the matter and to 'keep the matter as secret and private as you can'.

In October [3] Mapletoft assured Locke that the arrangement for him to succeed to the chair at Gresham College still held good, but that he, Mapletoft, was not, as yet, vacating it; and the following month [4] he announced that the marriage was definitely off.

Meanwhile Locke and Banks were still in Paris. They went several times to the plays at the theatres—unfortunately Locke's journal is not informative as to *which* plays they saw—and once they attended the opera at Fontainebleau: [5]

Here at night we saw *Alceste*, an opera, where the music, both vocal and of instruments, was very good. At the opera the King and Queen sat in chairs with arms. On the right hand of the King sat Madame Montespan, and a little nearer the stage on her right hand, Mademoiselle, the King of England's niece. On the left hand of the Queen sat Monsieur, and of his left hand, advancing towards the stage, Madame, and so forward towards the stage other ladies of the Court, all on tabourets except the King and Queen.

The following night, Locke recorded:

. . . we saw a ball, where the King and Queen and the great persons of the Court danced, and the King himself took pains to clear the room to make place for the dancers. The Queen was very rich in jewels (and there needed her stiffness to support so great a treasure) and so were several of her ladies. The King, Queen, etc. were placed as at the opera. The Duc d'Enghien sat behind the Dauphin on that side.

---

[1] *22 June 1677* (*European Magazine*, XV, p. 10).   [2] *9 August 1677* (ibid., p. 89).
[3] B.L. MSS. Locke, c. 15, f. 209.   [4] *Ibid.*, f. 211.   [5] *Journal, 23 September 1677*.

Locke was not sorry to be lingering in Paris, in spite of his avowed belief that it would be good for his pupil to take to the road, if only because he had made the acquaintance of Henri Justel. Justel was then aged fifty-seven, and although a Protestant, he held the office of Secrétaire du Roi, receiving also from Louis XIV a pension of a thousand livres 'à cause de son commerce avec la plupart des savants hommes de l'Europe'.[1] Justel held a weekly *salon* at his house in Paris, and was able to introduce Locke to the best intellectual society of the city. Justel's guests were by no means all Frenchmen: they had included Pufendorf, Leibniz, Falconieri, Magalotti and several of the most eminent members of the Royal Society. Although no more than thirteen letters from Justel to Locke survive in the Lovelace Collection,[2] each bears witness to the close friendship which existed between them and to the wide range of their common interests. Having decided to remain in Paris, Locke took rooms on the rue de Boucherie, with Moïse Charas,[3] the author of *Pharmacopée Royale*, and his interest in medicine was thus quickened. There is nothing in the papers he preserved which points to political activity, though on one occasion Shaftesbury sent a message [4] from the Tower of London asking Locke to send him maps of Champagne, Luxembourg and Lorraine 'because the war in all probability will come there again'. When Shaftesbury's secretary Stringer [5] wrote to thank Locke for the maps, he explained that his employer's 'chief divertissement' in the Tower was reading 'books, maps and papers', and that he was better in health and fatter 'than ever I saw him', thanks, Stringer thought, to his 'temperance and well ordering of himself' in prison.

In *November 1677* Locke's friend from Montpellier, Thomas Herbert, later Earl of Pembroke, was taken ill in Paris, and Locke was called upon, as a physician, to treat him.[6] Herbert had generalised septicaemia, probably due to gonorrhoea, but his fever

---

[1] Bonno, p. 65.

[2] B.L. MSS. Locke, c. 12. *Vide* also Bonno, pp. 107–16 ('Les Relations épistolaires de Locke avec Justel').

[3] Moïse Charas (*c.* 1618–98) was then demonstrator in Chemistry at the Jardin des Plantes. In 1680 he fled to England as a Protestant refugee, and became apothecary royal to Charles II. Eventually, after being persecuted by the Inquisition in Holland, he was converted to the Roman faith and returned to France, where he was welcomed and honoured by the Académie des Sciences.

[4] Christie, II, p. 248.

[5] *Ibid.*, p. 250.

[6] Locke's Journal (*17–25 November 1677*) contains a full record of the case.

had gone by the end of the month. Then on *2 December* Locke wrote in his journal:

> About six or seven o'clock I was called to my Lady Ambassadress, whom I found crying out in one of her fits.[1]

The Lady Ambassadress thus distressed was Ralph Montagu's wife, the Countess of Northumberland. Her husband, though he lived to become a duke, was then a commoner, and she retained the title she had acquired on her first marriage. Her second marriage was not an altogether happy one. There is evidence that quarrels began in the first two months, and the omniscient Mrs. Jameson says [2] that Lady Northumberland 'pined in the midst of her splendour for calmer and more domestic happiness'.

When Locke was called to see her, however, her trouble seemed rather to be toothache. Believing it to be toothache her French doctors had had two—sound—teeth pulled out, and failed to relieve the pain. Locke diagnosed trigeminal neuralgia, and sent a report to his medical friends in London.[3] His diagnosis is, according to Dr. Kenneth Dewhurst,[4] the first of its kind in medical history, and was a perfectly correct diagnosis. After a little hesitation, Locke ventured to purge 'my lady *ambassadrice* to the extent of seven or eight workings' and although she was pregnant, she responded to the treatment satisfactorily.[5]

Locke's presence in the English Ambassadress's household at this particular time provides the only circumstantial link between his French sojourn and the secret alliance between Louis and the Whigs. It was the critical phase of the whole story, and the English Ambassador in Paris was the key figure. Pressed by Danby to link his family with the anti-French forces in Europe, Charles had consented to the marriage of his niece Princess Mary to Prince William of Orange, and Montagu was sent to Paris to squeeze the French on behalf of the Dutch.[6]

Behind Montagu's mission was a distinct threat of English military intervention on the Dutch side. The French replied by offering Charles as much money as he wished if he would promise to stay neutral.[7] Montagu passed on this offer at the end of December:

[1] Locke's Journal (*16–27 December 1677*) contains detailed notes on her case.
[2] *Beauties of the Court of Charles II*, p. 134.
[3] *European Magazine*, XV, pp. 185–6.   [4] In a forthcoming article on the case.
[5] *Vide Lancet*, 1828–9, II, p. 367.   [6] Browning, *Earl of Danby*, I, p. 255.
[7] Montagu to Charles II. 29 December 1677 (*ibid.*, II, pp. 299–303)

early in January [1] he sent Danby the news that the second Marquis de Ruvigny was coming to London to distribute the money among the leaders of the Opposition if Charles did not take it and do as the French desired. In March,[2] Montagu reported that Ruvigny, then in London and disappointed by Charles's reception, was already working in league with the Whigs. Russell, a cousin of Ruvigny's wife, was later named as the central Whig figure in the drama.

Shaftesbury, imprisoned in the Tower, could not exercise his leadership at this stage; but it is hardly likely that he was ignorant of what was going on. Had Locke been at the time an agent of the Whig intelligence, he was singularly well placed, as Lady Northumberland's physician, to find out not only what was going on, but also what Montagu knew of what was going on. One cannot, on the basis of the evidence, say more.

Turning from the hypothetical to matters of established fact, we turn also from politics to scholarship. Locke made the acquaintance early in 1678 of Nicholas Thoynard, who remained his lifelong friend and his most assiduous correspondent.[3] An Orléanais, three years older than Locke, Thoynard combined an intense interest in the Scriptures with a catholic enthusiasm for experimental science and inventions of every kind. His principal work, *Evangeliorum Harmonia Graeco-Latina*, was then being published in serial form, and Locke, having seen some part of it, described it in his journal as 'very useful'.

Through Thoynard Locke met even more of the leading French savants. They included the Abbé Fromentin and the Abbé Renaudot, scholars; Massiac and Sainte-Colombe, explorers; Godefroy and Gendron, physicians;[4] Hubin and Hautefeuille, inventors. Scientific life in Paris had much to offer the interested foreigner in the 1670's. The inauguration of the *Journal des Savants* in 1665 and the foundation of the Académie des Sciences the following year had initiated a period of intense activity in every department of learning. Thoynard introduced Locke to all the official institutions and to a number of private laboratories.

Caleb Banks, in the meantime, was pursuing other interests, the

---

[1] Browning, *Earl of Danby*, II, p. 325.   [2] *Ibid.*, II, pp. 341–2.
[3] A large volume in the Lovelace Collection (B.L. MSS. Locke, c. 21) is entirely filled with letters from Thoynard to Locke.
Fifty-eight letters from Locke to Thoynard appear in Ollion. Locke wrote either in French or, less often, in Latin. *Vide* also Bonno, pp. 116–29.
[4] Most of Locke's notes in his journal for *1678* are medical ones.

nature of which may be deduced from the following letter he
received from a young woman who was also in Paris (I have left it
in her own delightful spelling):

> I did not think you had ben so ill bred as to denid a lady so small a
> favor sa that was I desier of you bout sin you ar so uncind I am resalf
> to wat of you as soun as my clos is mad wich will not be long forst
> I am suer you ar the worst naterd man in the world suer your corig is
> not so litell as to be dantd by a woman I hop the sit of me would not a
> fritid you mouch bout rather then a disableg you I would a pot on a
> mask I hat myself when I think that ever I should have the lest of
> passion for won that hats me now far well the worst of men.[1]

Whether to escape such reproaches, or because of the natural
eagerness of youth to travel, Caleb Banks wished to get away from
Paris. Locke was willing, but Lady Banks longed for her son's
return, and Sir John, who had originally sent his son to France for
six months only, was slow to authorise a longer absence. At this
point Samuel Pepys intervened, and, according to his biographer,
Sir Arthur Bryant,[2] 'succeeded in persuading' Sir John and Lady
Banks to let their son stay in France and travel south with Locke.

Among the papers the philosopher left in Paris 'in a black trunk'
was his essay *De Intellectu* (one, at least, of the first two drafts) and
his English translation of the *Essais de Morale* of Pierre Nicole.[3]
This last document he presented to the Countess of Shaftesbury.[4]

> It was a bold thing [Locke wrote to her] [5] for one that had but begun
> to learn French to attempt a translation out of it. And it is yet bolder
> to design it as a present to you. Fashion, which takes the liberty to
> authorise whatever it pleases, must be my excuse. And since one is
> allowed by custom to bring vanity with one out of France, and with

---

[1] I can find no clue to the identity of the writer. But the letter got into Locke's
hands, and remained there, for it is marked 'To C. B. 78' in Locke's writing and is
among his papers (B.L. MSS. Locke, c. 23, f. 201).

[2] *Op. cit.*, p. 161.

[3] Pierre Nicole (1625–95) had been expelled from the Sorbonne for Jansenism in
1655 and thereupon retired to Port Royal to meditate and write. He was the friend
of Pascal and Arnauld, and he published his *Essais de Morale* in 1671.

[4] This Lady Shaftesbury was the Earl's third wife. She was born (in January 1627)
Lady Margaret Spencer, sixth daughter of William, Lord Spencer of Wormleighton.
She was also the sister of Henry, first Earl of Sunderland. She married Shaftesbury
at St. Paul's, Covent Garden, on 30 August 1655.

[5] *Discourses translated from Nicole's Essays* by John Locke. Edited by Thomas
Hancock, 1828, p. xxiii.

confidence to present as marks of respect at home, any sort of toys [1]
one hath picked up abroad; I crave leave to make use of my privilege as
a traveller, and to offer your ladyship a new French production in a
dress of my own making.

Of the eleven essays which Nicole published in 1671, Locke
translated three. Two—one on the preservation of peace (which
Voltaire considered a masterpiece unequalled even in ancient
literature) and one on the existence of God—Locke translated fairly
correctly, if not very elegantly. But in the third there is a deliberate
distortion of Nicole's text, astonishing in its audacity.

In the original text, Nicole, having pointed out that the mysteries
of religion were beyond the understanding of even the most learned
men, wrote: [2]

Cependant les auteurs des nouvelles hérésies ont persuadé cent
millions d'hommes qu'il n'y avoit rien en cela qui surpassât la force de
l'esprit des plus simples. C'est même par-là qu'ils les ont attirés d'entre
le peuple. Ceux qui les ont suivis ont trouvé qu'il étoit beau de dis-
cerner eux-mêmes la véritable religion, par la discussion des dogmes, et
ils ont considéré ce droit d'en juger, qu'on leur attribuoit, comme un
avantage considérable que l'Eglise Romaine leur avoit injustement ravi.
On ne doit pas néanmoins chercher ailleurs que dans la foiblesse même
de l'homme, la cause de cette présomption.

This attack on the Protestants is turned in Locke's 'translation' into
the following attack on Rome [3]—unthinkable as having been written
by the loyal Catholic Nicole was:

[1] Nicole's *Essais* were fashionable reading in France. Madame de Sévigné wrote
(to Madame de Grignan on *23 September 1671*): 'Je poursuis cette *Morale* de Nicole,
que je trouve délicieuse; elle ne m'a encore donné aucune leçon contre la pluie, mais
j'en attends, car j'y trouve tout; et la conformité à la volonte de Dieu me pourroit
suffire, si je ne voulois un remède spécifique. Enfin je trouve ce livre admirable'.
[2] *Essais de Morale*, Paris, 1781, I., pp. 37–8.
[3] Among Locke's papers in the Lovelace Collection there is a shorthand note
(B.L. MSS. Locke, c. 28, f. 44), which gives the following justification of his mis-
translation of Nicole: 'When I first set upon it, I strictly followed the original, but
afterwards upon a review, finding as I thought some of the author's arguments might
be rendered with a little more advantage to his cause than in the way he had urged
them, I made bold to follow his design rather than his words, and therefore have
taken the liberty in § 29 and § 31 of the first treatise to dispense a little with the strict
formality of the translator. In § 41 of the 2nd treatise I confess I have gone a little
farther and turned the author's argument directly against himself, which will plainly
appear if you compare those which are the author's words with what I have made
him speak in the translation'.

And yet the supporters of an old usurpation persuade the world that there is nothing in all this which exceeds their power; to which they have, by force, compelled so many hundred millions to submit, and have severely handled multitudes that have dared but to question it. 'Tis by this terror and the threats of Hell to boot, upon the least inquiry, the least wavering in this point, that they have held people in subjection. And the hierarchy of Rome, having found the secret of dominion over men's consciences, and considered it as an advantage too great to be parted with, hath always thundered against those that, asserting their just right, have withdrawn from that slavery and, under the name of heretics, hath treated them as rebels. This monstrous presumption (in those who are really persuaded of such power amongst them) is the product of human weakness, and arises only from this: that man is so far removed from an acquaintance with truth, that he knows not the marks and signs of it.[1]

The philosopher and his pupil took to the road on *9 July*. Like many another traveller in France, he was troubled by bed-bugs, but he discovered a remedy: [2]

Take the leaves of kidney beans (*phaseolorum*) and put them under your pillow or some convenient place about your bed. They will draw the *punaises* to them and keep you from being bit.

On their journey Locke and Banks visited Orleans, Tours, Saumur, Angers, Chinon and the Château de Richelieu, which Locke described as 'the most complete piece of building in France, where in the outside is an exact symmetry, in the inside convenience and beauty, the richest gilding and best statues that are to be seen anywhere'.[3]

They travelled next to La Rochelle, where they learned more about the persecution of Protestants, and to Colbert's newly created naval port of Rochefort, where two of Thoynard's ubiquitous friends 'very civilly conducted us',[4] and where the Governor himself entertained them to dinner. By the middle of September they had reached Bordeaux. One of the several excursions they made from that city was to country 'whence comes the Graves wine',[5] and Locke was horrified by the poverty of the peasants he met there:

[1] *Discourses, ed. cit.*, p. 65.
[2] Journal *16 July 1678.*
[3] *31 August 1678.*
[4] *8 September 1678.*
[5] *15 September 1678.*

Their ordinary food, rye bread and water. Flesh is a thing seldom seasons their pots . . . And yet they say that in . . . several other parts of France the peasants are much more miserable than these. . . .[1]

About this time Locke wrote to Sir John Banks asking if he could take his son on a journey to Italy. Once again Samuel Pepys intervened on behalf of the project, and urged Sir John and Lady Banks to give their consent.[2]

Before they left Bordeaux Locke visited and admired the Carthusian convent,[3] and he took his pupil to worship at the temple at Bègles, which was destined to be demolished, with many other Protestant churches, in 1685.

Having reached Montpellier the travellers lodged with an Irishman named Cheney, and Locke renewed old acquaintances. Then on *30 October* he packed his books, left them with William Charlton to be sent on to Paris the following spring, and took horse with Caleb Banks for Lyons.

At Lyons a disappointment awaited them. They learned that the road across Mount Cenis was already snow-covered and impassable. 'If all the world should go to Rome,' Locke wrote [4] despairingly to Mapletoft, 'I think I should never.'

The journey as far as Lyons was not, however, wasted, for there Locke met and engaged as his servant a young man who was to remain with him for many years to come. By name Sylvanus Brownover, and by birth German, this youth was possessed of exceptional qualities, intellectual, artistic and moral. He began as Locke's valet; it was not long before he was working as his amanuensis too.

Caleb Banks and Brownover accompanied Locke to Paris, where the philosopher resumed his social intercourse with the *virtuosi*, principally with Thoynard. Locke's journal acknowledges Thoynard as the source of such miscellaneous information as the following:

Mr. Thoynard showed me a letter wherein was reported for certain of a man here in France that flies with four wings laid over his shoulders,

---

[1] *15 September 1678.*

[2] Pepys insisted that this consent be given on four conditions: Caleb Banks 'must be careful of his health; must write home at least once a week and never let "my lady, the best of mothers, labour under a dearth of letters"; must rely in all things upon the advice of Mr. Locke; and be back by the spring . . .' (Bryant, *op. cit.*, pp. 161–2).

[3] *24 September 1678.*   [4] *8 November 1678* (*European Magazine*, XV, p. 353).

moving those behind with his feet as those before with his hands, and the motion of the wings is diagonal, the right wing before and the left wing behind supporting and operating at the same time, and thus he hath flown over his neighbours' houses. . . .[1]

The story of the Nuns of Loudun possessed was nothing but a contrivance of Cardinal Richelieu to destroy a man Grandier, he suspected to have writ a book against him, who was condemned for witchcraft in the case and burnt for it. The scene was managed by the Capucins and the nuns played their tricks well, but all was a cheat.[2]

Early in 1679,[3] Locke witnessed a royal review of the French troops and made notes on the splendid military uniforms, then something of a novelty. He also recorded:

The observation of Lent in Paris has come almost to nothing. Meat is openly to be had in the shambles and a dispensation commonly to be had from the Curate without any more ado, and people of sense laugh at it. . . .[4]

Later he noted, in shorthand, the scandals of Père le Clerc 'procurator of the Jesuits in Paris', who was imprisoned for 'too much familiarity with an abbess', and Père Faverolles ('of the same convent') who 'was well whipped and then turned out for keeping a mistress, another man's wife'.[5]

Locke's journal sometimes betrays a surprising credulity:

In Portugal there are usually nine girls born for one boy. They impute it to this: that the men marry not till they are pretty old and wasted with debauchery and the pox, and then they marry the women very young. . . .[6]

In *March 1679* he went to inspect the library of Jacques Auguste de Thou, which was up for sale, and while he was there he

had the honour to see the Prince of Conti, now in his seventeenth year, a very comely young gentleman, but the beauties of his mind far excel those of his body, being for his age very learned. He speaks Italian and German as a native, understands Latin well, and Spanish and Portuguese indifferently, and is, as I am told, going to learn English. A great

---

[1] *30 November 1678*. The entry refers to Besnier of Sablé, a locksmith and one of the greatest impostors in the history of aviation. (C. H. Gibbs-Smith, *A History of Flying*, 1953, pp. 51–2.)

[2] *14 December 1678*. Aldous Huxley, *op. cit.*, gives a full account of this celebrated case.

[3] *5 January 1679*.   [4] *6 January 1679*.   [5] *13 February 1679*.   [6] *14 February 1679*.

lover of justice and honour, very civil and obliging to all, and one
that desires the acquaintance of persons of merit of any kind, and
though I can pretend to none that might recommend me to one of the
first Princes of the Blood of France, yet he did me the honour to ask me
several questions there, and to repeat his commands to me to wait
upon him at his house.[1]

Two days later Locke had, however, to report:

I went this morning with Mr. Thoynard to wait on the Prince of
Conti, but he was hasted away yesterday to St. Germain, the Dauphin
being ill.[2]

During his next few weeks in Paris, Locke made the acquaintance
of Père Cherubin, the celebrated writer on optics, who showed him
his lenses and other apparatus; [3] of the Abbé Jean Picard, the great
astronomer, who taught him the principle of the pendulum; [4] and
of Olaf Römer,[5] the Danish astronomer who was the first to
measure the speed of light.

Then on *2 May* Locke left Paris to return to England. Olaf Römer
as well as Caleb Banks went with him, but Römer was a bad sailor,
and on the day of their embarkation at Calais for the crossing, Locke
wrote to Thoynard 'Aujourdhui je crois il sacrifiera au Neptune du
fond de son coeur ou estomack'.[6] They set sail on *8 May* 'at eleven
o'clock in the Charlotte Yacht—Capt. Sanderson commander'. [7]

Locke had left Paris only just in time to evade one of his most

[1] *13 February* (Lough corrects to *13 March*) *1679*.
[2] *15 February* (Lough corrects to *15 March*), *1679*.
[3] *Ibid*. Père Cherubin was a Capucin, and Locke noted in his journal (*19 March
1679*) 'The Capucins are the strictest and severest order in France. . . . As soon as
they find anyone to have any inclinations any way, as P. Cherubin in optics and
telescopes, to take from him all he has done or may be useful to him in that science,
and employ him in something quite contrary; but he has now a particular lock and
key to his cell which the *gardien's* key opens not, by order of the King.'
[4] *17 March 1679*.
[5] Olaf Römer (1644–1710) was taken to France by Picard to help with his astro-
nomical studies and became tutor in mathematics to the Dauphin. He spent most of
his time in Paris until 1681 when he returned to Copenhagen as Astronomer Royal.
[6] Ollion, p. 23. Professor Ollion, who edited for publication Locke's letters to
Thoynard, wrote: 'Locke sut assurément assez le français pour l'écrire convenable-
ment. . . . La plupart de ses fautes soit d'orthographe, soit de syntaxe, s'expliquent
par sa nationalité . . . on risquerait d'être injuste pour le style français de Locke,
si l'on ne remarquait qu'il emploie d'ordinaire les termes avec beaucoup de propriété;
son vocabulaire est précis et très étendu; les tournures ne sont pas toujours fort aisées,
mais d'une façon un peu traînante parfois—comme en anglais, il arrive toujours
à dire clairement ce qu'il pense . . .' (*op. cit.*, pp. ix–x).
[7] Journal *8 May 1679*.

importunate friends, and his most prolix correspondent, Denis
Grenville. A Cornishman, Grenville achieved his ultimate and only
distinction as James II's Archbishop of York in exile. When he
pursued Locke in France he was a rich, unbeneficed Anglican
clergyman, tormented by religious doubts, and maddeningly
anxious to talk them over.

Grenville wrote at least three letters to Locke in *March 1677*.
In the first [1] he begged Locke to defer his departure from Paris so
that he might accompany him to Italy. He offered to share with
Locke the goods which fortune had bestowed on him, so eager was
he to have Locke act as 'man-midwife' to his thoughts. This proposal was repeated in a second letter.[2] Then, having failed to persuade Locke to travel with him, Grenville wrote a long letter [3]
conveying some of the thoughts with which his mind was so un-
comfortably pregnant. He began with the subject of *recreation*.

Grenville's letter elicited from Locke a long letter, which I shall
summarise very briefly.[4] Locke explained that recreation was a
thing ordained 'to restore the mind or body, tired with labour to its
former strength and vigour'. Thus 'there can be no general rule set
to different persons as to the sort of recreation they should follow.
However, Locke added a few generalisations: (1) the best time for
recreating the mind is when it feels itself weary and flagging; (2) the
best recreation for sedentary persons is bodily exercise; of those of
bustling employment, sedentary recreation; (3) of all bodily
exercises those in the open air are best.

In *January 1678*, when Locke was still at Montpellier, Grenville
wrote to him from Aix,[5] where he was staying with his sister, asking
Locke to be his 'bosom friend'. Three months later [6] Grenville
renewed the attack, sending his 'dear Friend' three further records
of his thoughts. The first paper dealt with *temporal business*, the
author complaining that he had never been able to attend simul-
taneously to his spiritual concerns and his secular business. In the
second paper, on *study*, Grenville confessed that he gave more time
to considering what to study than he gave to any definite subject of
study. The third paper, entitled *Conversation*, revealed the author's
difficulties in dividing his life between solitude and social intercourse.
On each of these subjects Grenville hoped to have Locke's opinion.

---

[1] B.L. MSS. Locke, c. 10, f. 62. [2] *Ibid.*, f. 64. [3] *Ibid.*, f. 66.
[4] This letter is printed *in extenso* in F.B., I, 388–90.
[5] B.L. MSS. Locke, c. 10, f. 70. [6] *Ibid.*, c. 10, f. 74.

In his reply [1] Locke asked: 'Shall I not pass with you for a great empiric if I offer but one remedy for the three maladies you complain of?' He went on to suggest, however, that all three difficulties derived from Grenville's belief that 'a man is obliged strictly and precisely at all times to do that which is absolutely best'. Locke said he did not share this belief, holding that God had left men great latitude except in the rare occasions when there was no alternative to the duty of doing one particular thing:

> I cannot conceive it to be the design of God . . . to clog every action of our lives, even the minutest of them (which will follow if the one thing that is best is always to be done), with infinite consideration before we begin it, and unavoidable perplexity and doubt when it is done.

Learning that Locke was bound for Italy, Grenville wrote him on *21 November 1678* [2] to give voice to his dismay, and he took advantage of the occasion to send yet another of his little essays. Its subject was devotion, and it related Grenville's difficulties in finding a middle way between devotion as an employment of the soul and devotion as external exercises in certain forms, times and postures.

Locke replied [3] with a characteristic appeal to commonsense. He urged Grenville to deal with life's problems one by one: such he said, 'has usually been my way with myself, to which, I think, I owe a great part of my quiet'. He added the following points for Grenville's consideration:

> First, we are not born in heaven, but in this world, where our being is to be preserved with meat, drink and clothing and other necessaries that are not born with us, but must be got with forecast, care and labour, and therefore we cannot be all devotion, all praises and halle-lujahs, and perpetually in vision of things above . . .

On the other hand, Locke reminded him that 'we are not born in this world to stay here for ever so we must remember our Maker and the world to come'. Thirdly, since 'we are born with ignorance of those things that concern the conduct of our lives in this world', it follows that 'enquiry, study and meditation is necessary'. Fourthly, 'we are born members of commonwealths', so that we 'cannot spend

---

[1] *23 March 1678* (B.M. Add. MSS. 4290, ff. 109–114: copy).
[2] B.L. MSS. Locke, c. 10, f. 89.
[3] *6 December 1678* (B.M. Add. MSS. 4290, ff. 115–119: copy).

all our time in retired devotion or study'. Fifthly, we are 'so constituted that any employment of mind, any exercise of body, will weary us to continue longer in that employment', and 'we have a need of recreation to set us going with fresh vigour and activity'.

In the same letter Locke mentioned that he was not going to Italy, after all. This news took Grenville post haste to Paris, but by the time he arrived his correspondent was already on his way to London.

Chapter Fourteen

THE POPISH PLOT

LOCKE went immediately on his arrival in London on 30 April[1] to Thanet House, Shaftesbury's new City home. He found everyone in the highest spirits. Shaftesbury's political fortunes were soaring; Danby was down. Shaftesbury was in the Government; Danby was in the Tower.

Shaftesbury had emerged from the Tower in February 1677/8 none the worse for his twelve months' imprisonment, and in better health than he had been for many years. Moreover he found his various schemes against Danby already bearing fruit. Montagu, tempted by Whig agents, turned against Danby, and became the instrument of his ruin. Montagu betrayed Danby because his old friend had disappointed his hopes of a Secretaryship of State. Himself the intermediary in so many intrigues between the English and the French, Montagu boldly accused Danby of having secret dealings with Louis. Incriminating documents were produced, and Danby, already falling, was impeached by Parliament, relieved by Charles of the white staff of Treasurer, and sent to the Tower of London for several years.

Shaftesbury was well prepared for Danby's fall. He knew that as soon as it happened, he, Shaftesbury, would be face to face with the King himself. That thought did not cause Shaftesbury to falter. He believed he could gain the support of a force not weaker than that which the King could command, and that was the support of public opinion.

Shaftesbury's idea was to rally the people in the name of England and Freedom and the Protestant religion against Popery. Almost providentially in the autumn of 1678 an ace was placed in his hand. A man named Titus Oates came forward with the charge that there was a Popish Plot afoot to kill the King and place his Catholic brother York upon the throne. Titus Oates was an obvious

[1] By the Julian calendar. *Vide* Locke's journal for that date.

scoundrel, with the worst possible reputation, but Shaftesbury decided to believe him. In any case, what made Titus Oates so valuable an ally in the Whiggish cause was not so much the veri-similitude of his testimony as what happened after he had testified: Sir Edmund Bury Godfrey, the magistrate before whom he had made his deposition, was subsequently picked up on Primrose Hill dead and to all appearances murdered. It was not difficult to make the public believe that the magistrate had been murdered by those very Popish agents who were plotting to kill the King.

Fear of further 'Jesuit atrocities' gripped the nation. Miles Prance, a Catholic silversmith, was arrested and confessed under torture to complicity in the plot. Scroggs, the Lord Chief Justice, sentenced no fewer than twenty-one men to death, some of them accused of nothing worse than uttering treasonable words. Catholics were ordered to leave the capital, while 'Oates was maintained at the public expense, and lorded it in London like the saviour of his country'.[1]

Oates was the hero of the hour, but Shaftesbury was the master of the situation. In Parliament he was the leader of the Protestant zealots, the chief prosecutor of the Popish Plot. The King had to bow to his success. After Danby's fall he appointed a coalition government, and in that ministry Shaftesbury returned to office as Lord President of the Council.

Lady Masham in her memoir wrote:[2]

> In the year '79 the Earl of Shaftesbury being made Lord President of the Council, Mr. Locke (as it is said) was sent for home . . .

Precisely what Locke did for Shaftesbury it is impossible, in the absence of any definite evidence, to say. The only reference to Shaftesbury in Locke's discreet journals for this period are references to minor financial transactions. They contain no mention of politics.

It would be interesting to know what Locke thought of the Popish Plot. No one can be astonished that Shaftesbury, a professional politician without pretensions to middle-class morality, should have exploited the lies of Titus Oates. But what of Locke, the philosopher and Christian moralist? Could he justify his attitude? Conceivably he could. For although the Popish Plot as outlined by Titus Oates

---

[1] G. N. Clark, *The Later Stuarts 1660–1714*, Oxford 1947, p. 90.
[2] Amsterdam: Remonstrants' MSS. J. 57a.

was fictitious, there was nevertheless a *real* Popish Plot, namely that initiated at Dover in 1670 between Charles II and Louis XIV, and as that conspiracy could not be revealed, the story of Titus Oates had to be given public credence in order that Parliament might thwart the real plot by acting against the mythical one.

Shaftesbury's activities in 1679 were for the most part above board. He was prosecuting plotters rather than plotting himself. Thus, as a model of respectability, he was able to press the Habeas Corpus Bill through Parliament. After all those months in the Tower, Shaftesbury felt this to be a measure close to his heart, even though it would not, had it been effective in 1677, have saved him personally. In securing its enactment, he did something which even his most hostile critics admit to have been a lasting service to the cause of civil liberty.

In the private meetings of the Council he sponsored more controversial proposals. The Council was asked to consider introducing a legal instrument which would curb the powers of a Catholic King, should one succeed to the throne. The suggestion was put forward by Charles in the hope of reconciling the Whigs to his brother's succession. But Shaftesbury was not to be appeased. The limiting instrument, he protested, would 'substitute democracy for monarchy', and Shaftesbury, like most of his contemporaries, was vigorously opposed to democracy. He had only one answer to the problem of a Catholic succeeding to the throne, and that answer was to forbid any Catholic succession; in effect, to exclude the Duke of York.

Every day the matter became more urgent. The Queen had given Charles no children, and it seemed less and less likely that she ever would. The probability of York remaining the legitimate heir became steadily stronger.

Shaftesbury's policy in this situation was limited in the first place to the demand for the exclusion of the Duke of York. To this extent he had the majority in Parliament behind him. Only later did he advocate the succession, in place of York, of the King's illegitimate son, the Duke of Monmouth.

Charles, who was at no time willing even to consider the enthronement of his bastard, was hardly less adamant against the exclusion of his brother, and his patience with Shaftesbury was wearing thin in the autumn of 1679. He put up with Shaftesbury as President of the Council because he had to put up with Parliament, and he put up with Parliament because he so desperately needed money. But by this time he had made friends with the French again. His alternative source of revenue was once more open to him now that Danby was out of the way. So on 15 October Charles prorogued his second 'Exclusion' Parliament, and on the same day he dismissed the President of the Council. Shaftesbury was never again to return to office.

Much of Locke's time after his return from France was claimed by Shaftesbury, although the philosopher did not spend it all in London. In June he went to Bexwells in Essex [1] to stay for a short time with Shaftesbury's secretary Thomas Stringer and his wife Jane. It was from there that Locke wrote to Thoynard [2] saying he had 'not had time' to go to the Royal Society, without saying what had taken up his time. On the other hand, this letter—and several others Locke wrote to Thoynard that summer—did deal in an unhurried way with a wide range of topics: science, theology, history, cartography, inventions, and so on. Locke even offered Thoynard *une belle fille pour estre votre femme* if only he would come to England,[3] but Thoynard resisted the bait.[4]

In Locke's journal for 12 July there occurs the following entry:

Found at Thanet House the things I had left with Mr. Stringer at Exeter House on 12 November 1675; except my picture which he had removed to his house at Bexwells.

The removal of this picture—the Greenhill portrait—was to lead to a quarrel between Locke and Stringer, but not immediately.

In mid-August the philosopher was preparing for a journey 'into the west' [5] when, 'late at night', he 'received a summons' from Sir John and Lady Banks to go to Caleb Banks, 'who lay sick' at

---

[1] Lady Masham wrote: 'Though he had found some advantage to his health by his travels into France, yet it was not so established but that after his return he was still less able than formerly to continue long in London without retreating now and then to some neighbouring village for a few days or weeks. . . . And thus mostly with my Lord Shaftesbury, and sometimes at Oxford, he passed his time, till my Lord Shaftesbury's departure into Holland in the month of December in the year 1682.' (Amsterdam: Remonstrants' MSS. J. 57a).

[2] 6 June 1679 (Ollion, p. 23. French).

[3] *Ibid.*, p. 26.   [4] *Ibid.*, p. 30.

[5] Shaftesbury was then at St. Giles; but Locke clearly intended a journey further west to Somerset.

Olantigh in Kent.[1] He found the boy suffering from a fever and administered quinine.[2]

The treatment was not immediately effective and Locke asked Sydenham for advice. Sydenham twice wrote [3] to assure him that quinine was the only remedy.

While he was at Olantigh, Locke heard a ghost story, and, having some interest in what is nowadays known as 'psychical research', he wrote it down in his journal: [4]

> Mr. —— Jacob of Merton College in Oxford dying at Dr. Jacob's house in Canterbury, about a fortnight after his death the Doctor, lying in the chamber where he died, was waked by a cold hand that gripped him by the wrist. Looking up he saw the said Mr. Jacob by his bedside in his shirt, it being clear moonshine; from there the spectrum retired and sat him down at a little distance from the bed, where he in a settled posture, fixed his eyes on the Doctor, and the Doctor on him, but doubting whether it might be a dream, he shut his eyes, concluding that if it were a fancy he should see it as well with his eyes shut, but then he saw nothing. Opening them again, he saw him still sitting in the same place and posture, and it was so light of the moonshine that he plainly saw his black whiskers which he had in his lifetime turned up, and to assure himself that he was awake, he looked about the room and saw plainly several things there very plainly all which he found in the same places in the morning, having continued this about ⅛ hour he turned away on the other side and so lay without sleeping till the morning but heard and saw nothing more.
>
> The next night he lay also without sleeping all night, but nothing appeared, but he was heard to walk several times in the house after but was never seen but once by his maid and another woman sitting in the backside on a woodpile, where the maid affirmed she saw him without knowing he had appeared to the doctor. The Doctor also once at —— near Rye, where the said Mr. Jacob was born, felt something pull the clothes of the bed from him, which he held fast, and the same thing has happened to him in other places.

By 5 September Locke was able to record that Caleb Banks was almost well again. But the next day Locke himself was ill.

---

[1] Locke to Grenville 16 September 1679 (B.L. MSS. Locke, c. 24, f. 50).

[2] The progress of Caleb Banks's illness is recorded in detail in Locke's journal, where the patient is referred to as 'C.B.' This presumably explains the curious error made by Fox Bourne in naming Locke's patient 'his sick friend, Mr. Beavis' (F.B., I, 434).

[3] B.L. MSS. Locke, c. 19, f. 167-9.

[4] 26 and 27 August 1679 (B.M. Add. MSS. 15,642, f. 141).

In the morning about 8 or 9 I began to fall into a sweat which, without increasing the clothes I ordinarily had upon my bed or taking anything but a little warm small beer once or twice, continued with great violence and a grievous pain in my head till about 8 or 9 at night.[1]

A fortnight passed before Locke was well again. During his illness he received yet another of Denis Grenville's pressing invitations [2] to participate in a journey northwards. In his reply Locke explained why he was at Sir John Banks's house, and said that until his patient's recovery was complete

I shall not be able to go hence, and after that I must go as far as Somersetshire [to see] about my own business, which required my being there in the first place after my return to England.[3]

A few days later Locke began a letter to Thoynard,[4] in reply to one in which that friend had sent him news of Bernier's marriage and travels in Abyssinia. Locke, no longer urging Thoynard to marry the '*belle fille*' he had found for him, remarked apropos of Bernier:

I wish very earnestly that neither marriage nor death (which are so very nearly the same thing) nor anything hinders the return of them from whom I hope to receive a splendid enlightenment about that little-known country.

In the same letter he suggested:

When you feel the desire to learn the English language, you have only to follow my method and read every day a chapter of the New Testament, and in a month's time you will become a master.

By Monday, 22 September, Locke was able to record that Caleb Banks had 'mended exceedingly' and ten days later the philosopher returned to London. He remained there until Christmas, when he went on to Oxford. His journey 'into the west' was put off until the following February.

In a letter to Thoynard [5] Locke reproached his friend for adopting the manner of *grand seigneur* and describing nothing in his letters but jokes, supper-parties and debauches in Paris. But Locke at the age of

---

[1] Journal 6 September 1679.
[2] Grenville to Locke 3 September 1679 (B.L. MSS. Locke, c. 10, f. 108).
[3] 16 September 1679, *ibid.*, c. 24, f. 50.
[4] Ollion, p. 36 (French).
[5] 29 October 1679, Ollion, p. 42 (French).

forty-seven was not quite so solemn as this protest suggests, if one may judge from a verse entitled *Love and Cats* which he dictated (and possibly composed) in the year 1679. Two versions,[1] one Latin and the other English, survive in the handwriting of his amanuensis, Sylvanus Brownover. The following is the English version:

Amantis Appellatio ad Feles

Ye cats that at midnight spit love at each other
And best know the pangs of a passionate lover

I appeal to your scratches and tattered fur
If the business of love be no more than to purr

You know by experience the hot fit is soon o'er
Puss puss lass not long but turns to cat whore

Men ride many miles
Cats tread many tiles
Both hazard their blood in the fray

But the cats when they fall
From an house or a wall
Keep their feet, mount their tails, and away.

In Oxford at Christmastide, Locke resumed the use of his rooms at Christ Church. Samuel Thomas, Chaplain of Christ Church, who had taken charge of his possessions, and collected the money owing to him, paid Locke £176 4s. 10d., representing the rent for his rooms and his college stipend from Michaelmas 1675 to Christmas 1679.

Locke noted in his journal for 24 January:

The water in my weather glass, which had been left in Mr. Thomas's hands, was at 12 o'clock at 39°. And the weather has been of this mild temper ever since Christmas Day.

On the third day of February Locke left Oxford to make his long-projected trip to the west. Before he did so he bought, for 4s. 6d., copies of Sir Robert Filmer's *Patriarcha* and *Inquest*.[2] This purchase is an interesting one, for *Patriarcha* was the classic statement of seven-

---

[1] B.L. MSS. Locke, c. 32, f. 14.   [2] *Ibid.*, c. 1, f. 111.

teenth-century Toryism, and Locke's principal political work, his *Two Treatises of Government*, was written in reply to it.

During those winter weeks at Oxford, Locke completed a little manuscript book on the growth and culture of vines and olives, the result of observations he had made in France. The book was specially written for Lord Shaftesbury, and Locke sent it to him, with an introductory letter, dated 1 February 1679/80, in which he expressed the hope that Shaftesbury would be interested to see something good for a change 'come out of France'. The manuscript is in the Public Record Office,[1] and has been published in book form.[2]

On the day of his departure from Oxford, Locke made a list of the things he had left 'in Mr. [Nathaniel] Hodge's Chambers under Mr. [George] Walls's care'. They included:

One box marked C. B. No. 2.
Intellectus.[3] Almanack '76, '77, '78, '79[4] and other books. Two adversaria[5] in leather and one other deal box whereof Syl[6] has an account.
One hat-case with my beaver in it,
One cloth suit of last November, with silver buckles on the pockets and stockings,
One velvet coat,
One Bac. Med.'s gown.

In the evening of 4 February Locke's old friend David Thomas welcomed him at Salisbury; it was over four years since they had met. A letter from Joseph Hoskins, a Christ Church man then in London, reached Locke while he was there and brought news from the capital. As David Thomas was a zealous Whig, one can hardly doubt that the two friends discussed its contents. It is one of the very few letters touching on political matters which Locke preserved. In the course of it Hoskins[7] reported that Monmouth was out of favour and would not be restored; that there was a great dispute in London as to whether Sunderland or Lawrence Hyde would become Lord High Treasurer, and that Sydney Godolphin would be one of the Secretaries. Hoskins also mentioned that

---

[1] P.R.O. 30/24/47/35.
[2] *Observations on the Growth and Culture of Vines and Olives.* W. Sandby. 1766.
[3] An early draft of *The Essay of Human Understanding.*
[4] Locke's journals for 1676–9 were written in almanacs he had specially bound.
[5] '*Adversaria Physica*' and '*Adversaria Ethica*'.
[6] Sylvanus Brownover.
[7] 5 February 1679/80 (B.L. MSS. Locke, c. 11, f. 230).

alterations were being made in the Commissioners of the Justices of the Peace, but very secretly. Harris, the publisher of the *Protestant Intelligencer*, had been indicted for selling a book called *The Appeal*.

Hoskins was well informed. Monmouth, who had returned unasked to London from his Dutch exile towards the end of 1679, was in disgrace with his father and had been stripped of his remaining offices. Lawrence Hyde became First Lord of the Treasury, but his rival Sunderland (who had Whiggish inclinations) was also given office, forming with Godolphin the ministry of the 'Chits'. The 'very secret' alterations in the Commissioners of the Justices of the Peace were designed by Charles to increase Tory influence in that quarter, but the changes were not immediately effective. Neither Whigs nor Tories were to score any decisive gains in 1680.

From Salisbury Locke set off in mid-February for Sutton to visit his cousins, the Strattons, and to look into his affairs as a landowner. In Somerset he may have felt far from politics. A letter Shaftesbury wrote him in March might suggest that he, too, was remote from the struggle for power:[1]

> We long to see you here, and hope you have almost ended your travels. Somersetshire, no doubt, will perfect your breeding; after France and Oxford you could not go to a properer place. My wife finds you profit much there, for you have recovered your skill in Cheddar Cheese, and for a demonstration have sent us one of the best we have seen.
>
> I thank you for your care about my grandchild, but having wearied myself with consideration every way, I resolve to have him in my house. I long to speak with you about it.
>
> For news we have little. Only our government here are as truly zealous for the advancement of the Protestant religion, as it is established in the Church of England, that they are sending the Common Prayer Book the second time into Scotland. No doubt but my Lord Lauderdale [2] knows it will agree with their present constitution, but surely he was much mistaken when he administered the Covenant to England. But we shall see how the Tripods and the holy Altar will agree. My Lord of Ormonde is said to be dying.[3] So that you have Irish and Scotch news; and for English you make as much at Bristol as in any part of the kingdom.
>
> Thus recommending you to the Bishop of Bath and Wells (whose

---

[1] 20 March 1679/80, B.L. MSS. Locke, c. 7, f. 72.
[2] Lauderdale was then Secretary for Scotland. He resigned in October 1680.
[3] Ormonde was Lord-Lieutenant of Ireland. He did not die until 1688.

strong beer is the only spiritual thing any Somersetshire gentleman knows) I rest

Your affectionate and assured friend,

Shaftesbury.

The 'grandchild' mentioned in this letter was he who grew up to be the celebrated third Earl of Shaftesbury, author of *Characteristics*. Disappointed with the physical and intellectual powers of his only son, the first Earl had adopted this grandson as his own child, and Locke helped him plan the boy's education.

After Locke's death the third Earl wrote—somewhat boastfully, perhaps, for Locke was by that time a name renowned throughout Europe—of the philosopher's share in the education of himself and of his brothers and sisters:

> I was his more peculiar charge, being, as eldest son, taken by my grandfather and bred under his immediate care, Mr. Locke having the absolute direction of my education, and to whom, next my immediate parents, as I must own the greatest obligation, so I have ever preserved the highest gratitude and duty.[1]

In the same letter the third Earl described Locke as his 'friend and foster-father'.

From Somerset Locke returned to Oxford on 6 April. He stayed there less than two weeks, chiefly in the company of James Tyrrell. Indeed, Tyrrell and he actually collaborated in writing a pamphlet— a reply to a sermon of Edward Stillingfleet's [2] on the 'Mischief of Separation'.[3] Their pamphlet, which was never finished,[4] contained only very conventional arguments in defence of Nonconformity against Stillingfleet's plea for ecclesiastical unity, though it did include one characteristically 'Lockean' passage:

> As to the law of the land, it can never be judged to be a sin not to obey the law of the land commanding to join in communion with the Church of England till it be proved that the civil magistrate has a power to command or determine what church I shall be of . . . It is a part of my liberty as a Christian and as a man to choose of what church or religious society I will be, as most conducing to the salvation of my

---

[1] Amsterdam: Remonstrants' MSS. J. 20.
[2] The same Edward Stillingfleet who, as Bishop of Worcester, later engaged Locke in public controversy over the doctrine of substance in his *Essay Concerning Human Understanding.*   [3] Preached at the Guildhall, London, in May 1680.
[4] The MS. (B.L. MSS. Locke, c. 34) is partly in the hand of Tyrrell, partly in that of Locke, partly in that of another.

o

soul, of which I alone am judge, and over which the magistrate has no power at all. . . .

When Locke left Oxford in mid-April, he went straight to London and to Thanet House. A note of a scientific curiosity in his journal for 18 May—a hailstone of $5\frac{1}{2}$ inches' circumference he had witnessed 'in my Lady Shaftesbury's chamber'—is one clue to his whereabouts. His journal also shows that on 2 June Locke visited Hatfield and dined with James Cecil, third Earl of Salisbury, who was one of Shaftesbury's principal lieutenants in the House of Lords and who had been imprisoned in the Tower with him in 1677.

The sudden illness of the King in May had been the occasion of renewed activity at Thanet House. Monmouth, Russell, Grey and other Whig leaders went regularly to discuss with Shaftesbury the policy to be followed if the King died. It so happened that the King recovered, but in June Shaftesbury made an audacious move in his campaign against the Duke of York. He went to the Court of the King's Bench with a document indicting James as a Papist. Scroggs, after consulting with the King, dismissed the Jury, and the bold stroke failed. But it had some propaganda value.

In London Locke's health worsened, despite the season's being summer. Tyrrell[1] wrote him saying:

D[ear] C[armelin],

. . . You told me in your last that your cough was grown worse, but I suppose it is no constant alarm or else you would not have let your enemy gain strength all this while without labouring to dislodge him.

You do not tell me whether you intend to come immediately to Oxford or to my house or to make some other journey first. But if you intend to see Lysis,[2] you must meet him at Oxford the week after the Act, since I hear he does not intend to stay there above a week or ten days. I believe he had been there now had it not been Act week, and you know he does not love bustle. As for what you write about Syl, I am sorry you were forced to part with him,[3] for I had a good opinion of the lad. As for another boy, I know a good many that want masters, but whether you want them or no I cannot determine until you see them yourself. . . .

[1] 9 July 1680, B.L. MSS. Locke, c. 22, f. 38.
[2] Lysis was Nathaniel Hodges of Christ Church. Two extant letters from Hodges to Locke (*ibid.*, c. 11, f. 211–12) are addressed one to 'Dear Carmelin' the other to 'D. C.' and signed 'Lysis'.
[3] Locke's parting with Sylvanus Brownover proved to be no more than temporary.

News I can send you none, but that the Kings Players [1] are come down and here is a great appearance of a very full Act.[2] There is a doubt whether the Terrae Filii, being clergymen, will dare perform what they have undertook, for the Bishop threatens them much if they undertake it; for it seems he thinks it is not fit they should play the fools before all assemblies alike, but tomorrow will resolve the doubt. . . .

Musidore.

In the same month of July Locke was invited to St. Giles. Shaftesbury had retired to the country to work out yet another of his schemes against the Duke of York, and Monmouth had gone with him. Locke followed them there on 21 July and remained at St. Giles until the end of the month. After Locke had returned to London, Monmouth set out on a splendid progress through the West Country. At Exeter, crowds, reputedly of thousands, greeted the royal bastard with cries of 'God bless the King and the Duke of Monmouth. No Pope. No popery nor pensioners.' [3]

Locke wrote to Shaftesbury from London, 5 August: [4]

. . . your Lordship will pardon me if I take the liberty to trouble you with one piece of news. I was told today by one who had it whispered to him as a very true and serious secret, viz, that my Lord Sunderland was to go Lord Lieutenant of Ireland, the Duke [5] to retire thither, and that the white staff [6] would speedily be sent to your lordship, and that the Duchess of Portsmouth was soliciting it with all her endeavours.

This, though it be so extraordinary that it seems fit to be put amongst huntsmen's stories (and therefore I have desired Mr. Percival [7] to give it to you as you are returning from the chase), yet it is apt to make one reflect upon what is very much believed, that there must be a parliament; and in preparation thereunto there is already great striving amongst those who think themselves most in danger who shall be

---

[1] *L. and T.*, ii, 490, (8 July 1680): 'King's Players began to act in my brother Robert's tennis-court'.

[2] *Ibid.*, ii, 490 (10 July, 1680): 'Music lecture and music speech in the Theatre; 2,000 people at least. All well done and gave good content. Mr. (Edmund) Northen of Christ Church, reader (of the Music speech) and Mr. James Allestrey of Christ Church the year before. But 'tis a shame that the world should be thus guided by folly to follow an English speech and neglect divinity, philosophy, etc. Ancient and solid learning decays, as it appears by the neglect of solid lectures to hear an English one in the Theatre, and music'.

[3] Brown, p. 270.   [4] F.B., I, 416.   [5] The Duke of York.

[6] i.e. the office of Secretary of State, then held by Sunderland.

[7] Mr. Percival was Shaftesbury's banker.

thrown to the dogs. And who can think it other than good court-breeding, that might become a duke or a duchess, to strain courtesy in the case, and each desire to prefer the other as most deserving?

This is agreed, that there is a great ferment working now at court, and 'tis not everybody knows who influences. Mr. Brisbane,[1] who is looked on as none of the most inconsiderable of men in employment, is newly turned out of his judge advocate's place, and nobody knows the hand that hurt him, though it were the Commissioners of the Admiralty that visibly gave him the blow.

The Duke of Ormond, 'tis believed, will certainly be sent for over. 'Tis hard to conceive it shall be to make way for my Lord of Essex [2] though he be a man of known merit, and harder that it should be to succeed to the care of Aldersgate [3] upon occasion. 'Tis certain his son's [4] ravings in his fever plainly showed how full his head was with Tangier, and many conclude that sunk him to his grave. But who knows the secrets of fate? Your lordship has seen many a lusty undertaker go before you. My Lord Latimer,[5] 'tis reported, has his bed-chamber-man's place, as my Lord Lumley that of the Earl of Rochester, whose penitential confessions, I am told, are speedily to be published by Dr. Burnet [6] who was with him till a little before his death.

If what His Majesty is reported to have said to the Lord Mayor yesterday, when he presented the Common Hall petition to him, be true, 'tis probable that Whitehall is as little dissatisfied as the city over-joyed with Bethel's [7] choice, for 'tis the talk that His Majesty said that he hoped he might prove (as several others who had been represented to him as enemies) a very good servant, and particularly named Lawson, as one who served him faithfully and died in his service. . . .

My Lord Russell [8] I found not at home when I went to wait on him today from your lordship. . . .

My Lady Northumberland goes not into France.

[1] John Brisbane, Secretary of the Admiralty, had been known to Locke in Paris.

[2] The Earl of Essex (1631–83), who had held in politics an intermediate position between Whig and Tory, switched in 1680 to full support of Shaftesbury.

[3] Clearly a reference to Shaftesbury whose London home, Thanet House, was in Aldersgate.

[4] The Earl of Ossory, son of the Duke of Ormond, had lately died on a fruitless expedition to save Tangier from the Moors.

[5] Eldest son of the Earl of Danby.

[6] Gilbert Burnet (1643–1715), later the Bishop and historian. He converted the poet Rochester, a model Restoration rake, on his deathbed, and published (in 1680): *Some Passages in the Life and Death of John Wilmot, Earl of Rochester.*

[7] Slingsby Bethel (1617–97) was elected Sheriff of London on 24 June 1680. He was a Whig—Burnet called him 'a known republican in principle'—and he figures as Shimei in Dryden's *Absalom and Achitophel.*

[8] William, Lord Russell (1639–83), Shaftesbury's leading supporter in the House of Commons.

I have not had the opportunity this one day that I have been in town to go and wait on Mr. Anthony.[1] But Mr. Tanner, who was here this morning, assured me he was perfectly well.

I met many of your Lordship's friends today, who have asked me when you will be in town again, with an earnestness as if they wanted you already. . . .

One important item in this letter—the rumour that Sunderland's office was about to be offered to Shaftesbury—was false. Charles had resolved, by this time, to make no further attempt to appease or silence Shaftesbury by such tactics. On the other hand, the King was not as yet ready to let this resolution be known, and had dissimulated his anger at the several successes the Whigs had scored against his policy in the City and elsewhere. It also seems true that the Duchess of Portsmouth was working in Shaftesbury's interest at Court; so much so that some observers conjectured that Shaftesbury must have promised secretly to desert Monmouth and to support the claims to the succession of her son the Duke of Richmond. Shaftesbury's attachment to Monmouth was, in fact, unswerving.

Locke's letter to Shaftesbury might easily be taken for the letter of a moderately well-informed London gentleman writing to a country nobleman completely out of touch with the Court and the capital. Shaftesbury was not at all out of touch; and in that very month of August 1680 Locke was preparing to go to France again on what may well have been a mission connected with Shaftesbury's political campaign. In the event, he did not go. It is not clear why the plan was changed. But in a letter to Thoynard dated 30 August 1680,[2] Locke said:

The hope that I had to see you again in France was the most compelling motive that I had for the journey I had planned, but fortune goes on crossing my plans as she has done since my return to England: so much so that I have not been able to dispose of myself as I should like, but on the contrary, I find myself in places where I would not have thought of choosing to go.

While the reader may doubt that the hope of seeing Thoynard *was* Locke's 'most compelling motive', the rest of the foregoing sentence is easily credible. It was presumably because of what he was doing for Shaftesbury that Locke was unable to dispose of himself as he would otherwise have liked.

---

[1] Shaftesbury's grandson.   [2] Ollion, p. 61 (French).

Shaftesbury returned to London in mid-September and despite ill-health, worked hard on the Exclusion Bill which he intended to push through the next session of Parliament. This Bill was designed simply to exclude the Duke of York (or any other Papist) from the throne. It was not intended at the same time to nominate Monmouth as Charles's successor. Shaftesbury was sensible enough to fight his battles one at a time. Some of his more impetuous allies were anxious to have James tried for treason in connection with the Popish Plot, to exclude him, in short, by hanging him; but Shaftesbury thought it sufficient to have the Duke impeached, and he delegated to Locke the task of ascertaining the legality of Bishops' assistance at criminal trials.[1] The King's reply to these tactics was to try to divert the Whigs' persecution of Catholics from the Duke to *other* Papists. He was determined to defend his brother's rights. When, on 15 November 1680, the Exclusion Bill came before the House of Lords, the Bishops supported Charles and the legitimate succession. The Bill had passed the House of Commons, but the Lords rejected it by 63 votes to 30, the Bishops voting solidly against it. Shaftesbury then thought out another expedient, namely that the King should divorce his sterile Queen and marry a Protestant. Charles was present in the House of Lords when Shaftesbury affirmed his faith that, given a fertile wife, His Majesty would have no difficulty in begetting children; and the general laughter showed that Shaftesbury was not alone in this belief. But Shaftesbury fell ill again, and was unable to press on with his divorce proposal; and when he recovered, he dropped it, realising then that the King would never consent to it.

Locke, in the meantime, had gone to Oxford. Politics followed him there. Towards the end of that month the King decided that the cities of Westminster and London were too Whiggish for Parliament to meet in its usual premises, and accordingly he summoned a meeting in Oxford. Shaftesbury's secretary Stringer at once wrote to Locke asking his help in finding accommodation there. When this letter reached him, Locke was sick himself and had retired to the house of a friend outside Oxford, probably that of James Tyrrell at Oakley. Stringer's request was passed to a friend at Exeter College, Dr. Bury, who, in turn, pointed out in a letter[2] to Locke how difficult it would be to serve Lord Shaftesbury in the matter. The

---

[1] Brown, p. 271.
[2] 2 February 1680/1 (B.L. MSS. Locke, c. 4, f. 214).

King, Dr. Bury explained, would need Christ Church, Corpus Christi and Merton for the Court; and the other colleges were already bespoken by ambassadors and privy counsellors. Dr. Bury added that the Duke of Monmouth would be staying with a neighbour of his, Alderman Wright,[1] and he was afraid he could not find anything better than makeshift accommodation for the Earl of Shaftesbury.

Locke also wrote to several other Oxford friends, and thus helped to find accommodation for Shaftesbury's party both at Balliol and at the house of his friend Dr. Wallis, the mathematician. Shaftesbury sent Locke a message saying:[2]

> I am extremely obliged to you, and so are all the rest of the Lords for the trouble we have put you to. This bearer comes from us all, to take possession of our allotments in Balliol College and to provide us things necessary. He is ordered to address himself in the first place to you. . . .

Sir Paul Neile also wrote to Locke[3] asking him to investigate two chambers he had been offered at Corpus Christi College; and to let him know which was the better, as he, Locke, was 'my only friend at Oxford'.

Sir Paul's letter ended with the words:

> Sir, your ingenious raillery concerning the pot, I shall not endeavour to answer till I have the opportunity to see my Lord and you together, nor shall I say more but seriously to profess that with the trouble I now put upon you I have given you an opportunity infinitely to oblige me to be,
>
> Your humble servant,
> Paul Neile.

If you cannot get sheets conveniently let me know and I will bring a pair in my clothbag for myself and then any ordinary pair will serve for my servant.

Shaftesbury and his friends arrived in Oxford radiant with confidence, and the Protestant townspeople gave them a resounding welcome. The London Whigs wore ribbons in their hats, bearing the motto: 'No Popery. No Slavery.' Shaftesbury himself made

---

[1] Alderman Wright was a leading Whig in Oxford City politics.
[2] 19 February 1680/1 (B.L. MSS. Locke, c. 7, f. 76).
[3] 22 February 1680/1, MS. in the possession of the Earl of Lovelace (Transcript in B.L. MSS. Locke, c. 39, f. 4).

an even more splendid entry into Oxford than Monmouth had made before him. Everyone was ready for a climax. Charles, by this time, had dismissed Sunderland from his office of Secretary of State for supporting exclusion. He had dismissed Essex from the Privy Council. Salisbury had avoided dismissal only by resigning.

At Oxford, however, the King met at first more determined opposition than he had expected, and he offered several compromises to Parliament. He even suggested a plan of regency which would give his brother the royal title but deny him actual power. But the Commons would not meet him. They insisted on absolute exclusion of the Popish Duke something Charles would not have. Locke recovered from his sickness in time to keep a close watch on all that happened during the Oxford Parliament. On 26 March, the sixth day of that parliament, he reported to Stringer [1] that there was 'a general despair that nothing will be done for the protestant settlement and security'. Such fears were justified. Two days later Charles thwarted Shaftesbury's moves against the Duke by dissolving the Parliament abruptly.

On 16 May, after a brief visit to Tyrrell at Oakley, Locke wrote in his journal:

> The three great things that govern mankind are reason, passion and superstition. The first governs a few, the two last share the bulk of mankind and possess them in their turns. But superstition most powerfully produces the greatest mischief.

This pessimistic observation might be read as a sign of the times. For in spite of the King's high-handed behaviour at Oxford (or perhaps because of it) public opinion was beginning to turn against the Whigs. People were coming to believe that the Popish Plot was a fraud, and their zeal for Protestant revenge inevitably abated.

On 20 May Locke left Oxford to join Shaftesbury in London. Writing to Thoynard (who had proposed to visit England) Locke told him, in his cordial flattering way: [2]

> I came to London in the real hope of embracing you here soon; but instead of that I find you resolved to remove yourself yet further away.

Thoynard had decided to go to Orleans instead of London.

---

[1] B. Martyn *op. cit.*, pp. 269–275.
[2] 31 May 1681, Ollion, p. 102 (French).

An entry in Locke's journal for 18 June refers to his own illness of the previous January:

Dr. Sydenham's way of curing a phthisis was strong drink, keeping in bed and a clyster every day.

The way I cured myself was keeping constantly in bed for about a fortnight (a month would have been could I have spared it), eating and drinking as I used to do at other times, and taking about one drachm theniac andrem veter every night.

It was *not* phthisis of which Locke had cured himself. To judge from his record of his symptoms it was still his old disease—asthma exacerbated by anxiety; and in the summer of 1681 he had reason to be anxious.

On 2 July Shaftesbury was arrested. Thanet House was searched. Several of the men who had supplied him with evidence of the Popish Plot having already been proved to be perjurers, Shaftesbury was sent to the Tower on a charge of high treason. His health slumped with his confidence. He became so sick with the ague that the Lieutenant of the Tower had him removed to Sir John Moore's house, which was 'very cool this hot weather'.[1] While Shaftesbury was a prisoner[2] one of his humble supporters, a joiner named Stephen College, was sent to Oxford and accused of high treason. Shaftesbury engaged lawyers to defend him, but the jury found the joiner guilty and he was hanged. College was the first Whig martyr. For a moment Shaftesbury's courage faltered. He offered to emigrate to the New World, and to quit politics for ever. But Charles refused, and Shaftesbury remained in the Tower.

By chance—if it was by chance—Locke appears also to have been contemplating a voyage to the New World. Sir Thomas Lynch[3] invited the philosopher to sail with him to Jamaica. Locke declined. Sir Thomas said he was not surprised that Locke should prefer the tranquillity and conversation of Oxford to the dangers of a journey to the New World.

---

[1] C.S.P. Dom 1680/1, p. 405.

[2] In his absence, Lady Shaftesbury's health improved—if one may judge from the following curious item in Locke's journal dated 1 August 1681: 'Three stone quart jugs—fill them with the urine of a patient as it is made, stay them close, bury them a yard underground and lay a tile over them that the earth fall not close upon them; and so bury them in the earth. This was done to the Countess of Shaftesbury without her knowing of it, and she had not from that time till now any of those violent nephritical pains she was wont to have'.

[3] B.L. MSS. Locke, c. 15, f. 185.

In truth—though as yet Locke did not perhaps fully realise it—
he was in greater danger at Oxford than he would have been at
sea. He was surrounded by enemies and false friends. One such was
the Librarian of Christ Church, the Rev. Humphrey Prideaux, a
particular friend of Locke's friend George Walls.[1] Prideaux had
arrived at Christ Church at the age of twenty in 1668; he stayed on
as lecturer in Hebrew and he wrote a famous biography of Mahomet.
He made it his business from 1679 onwards to keep an eye on Locke
and report on Locke's movements to an Under-Secretary of State
named John Ellis. Prideaux was thus, in effect, an unpaid Government spy. His letters to Ellis have been preserved. In one dated
25 October, 1681,[2] Prideaux wrote: 'The pamphlet entitled *No
Protestant Plot* is with us, and John Locke is said to be the author of
it.'

This pamphlet was the third of three published at Shaftesbury's
expense in 1681. Whether Locke did in fact write it is uncertain.
Shaftesbury's biographer says it was 'drawn up under his [i.e.
Shaftesbury's] direction',[3] but the style is less recognisably Shaftesbury's than is that of the earlier pamphlet *Some Modest Reflections on
the Commitment of the Earl of Shaftesbury*. Locke may well have had
a hand in writing *No Protestant Plot*, even though he was not its sole
author.

James Tyrrell, writing to Locke on 26 June,[4] said: '. . . I hope now
Term is done you will resolve what to do with yourself this summer
and let your friends know it . . .' But Locke preferred to keep his
plans to himself, and he was thought to have gone abroad.

George Walls wrote from Christ Church on 27 October,[5] telling
Locke 'I am now convinced (which some here will not believe) that
you are not in France . . .'

No Protestant Plot seems to have been a remarkably successful
pamphlet, and it helped to create an atmosphere more favourable to
Shaftesbury in time for his judicial examination at the end of
November. The jury was made up of substantial City men, some
of them personal acquaintances of Shaftesbury and all of them of
Whiggish sympathies. Their verdict was *ignoramus*, and Shaftesbury
was released. By this time he had recovered his health and his

---

[1] In his letters to Locke (B.L. MSS. Locke, c. 23) Walls often sent greetings to
Prideaux.

[2] B.M. Add. MSS. 28,929, f. 77.   [3] Brown, p. 287.

[4] B.L. MSS. Locke, c. 22, f. 42.   [5] *Ibid.*, c. 23, f. 42.

confidence; and he was a model of aristocratic calm as he left the Tower to receive the congratulations of his seemingly devoted followers. There were City banquets and dinners in his honour, and a medal was struck bearing his image.

But there also appeared a poem called *Absalom and Achitophel*, by Locke's old schoolfellow John Dryden. Of all the literature occasioned by Shaftesbury's political career, this poem and *The Medal* alone are of enduring literary merit. *Absalom and Achitophel* has given posterity its picture of Shaftesbury:

> A name to all succeeding ages curst:
> For close designs and crooked counsels fit,
> Sagacious, bold and turbulent of wit,
> Restless, unfix'd in principles and place,
> In power unpleased, impatient of disgrace;
> A fiery soul which, working out its way,
> Fretted the pigmy body to decay
> And o'er informed the tenement of clay.
> A daring pilot in extremity;
> Pleased with the danger when the waves went high,
> He sought the storms; but for a calm unfit
> Would steer too nigh the sands to boast his wit.

Dryden's portrait of Shaftesbury is as false in parts as it is cruel. Shaftesbury was never 'unfix'd in principles'. More than once he changed his policy dramatically, but he was not for that reason a turncoat—as, incidentally, Dryden himself was. Shaftesbury changed his policy on those occasions either because the situation changed or because his understanding of the situation changed. To be steadfast in principle in such situations he *had* to change his policy.

The principles in which Shaftesbury was steadfast were those of patriotism, Protestantism and freedom. His patriotism was both nationalist and imperialist, and open to criticism from several standpoints; his Protestantism could not be expected to endear him to Catholics, nor his zeal for civil liberty to commend him to votaries of social discipline and the closed society. But one does not need to share his principles to see that Shaftesbury was true to them.

Even Dryden praised his sagacity; and in Shaftesbury's connection with Locke alone there is ample evidence of true intellectual distinction. He was ruthless but he had undoubted courage. He was indeed, as Dryden said, 'a daring pilot in extremity', and in December 1681 he settled on a policy more extreme than any he had yet pursued. He decided to organise a revolution, to expel the autocratic Charles by force of arms and put Monmouth on the throne in his place.

Chapter Fifteen

SOME TREATISES OF GOVERNMENT

RICHARD JANEWAY,[1] a Whiggish bookseller, of Queen's Head in Paternoster Row, published in 1681 a substantial little volume called *Patriarcha Non Monarcha or The Patriarch Unmonarch'd*. It was a reply to an influential exposition of Tory philosophy and the divine right of kings, *Patriarcha* by Sir Robert Filmer. *Patriarcha Non Monarcha* bore no author's name; on the title-page it was described as being 'by a Lover of Truth and of his Country', and the Preface was signed 'Philalethes'.

The author was in fact James Tyrrell. He began the book with an attack on Filmer's conception of monarchy, which he called

> an absolute Monarchy, *jure divino*, so that no other government can be lawfully exercised, nor the least limitations set to it without sacrilege and diminution of that sovereignty which is derived from no less an original than God himself; and by denying that Princes can ever be obliged by any fundamental or after-contracts or concessions, or by any coronation oaths, to abstain from the Lives, Liberties or Properties [2] of their Subjects, farther than as they themselves shall think it convenient . . .[3]

Against Filmer's extreme royalism, Tyrrell set out to defend the belief

> that Mankind is naturally endowed and born with Freedom from Subjection, and at liberty to choose what form of government it please; and that the Power which any man hath over others was at first bestowed according to the discretion of the multitude.[3]

---

[1] He was arrested for publishing a seditious libel in 1681, but he seems to have been released soon afterwards (F. S. Siebert, *Freedom of the Press in England*, Urbane, Illinois, 1952, pp. 269, 281).

[2] Compare Locke's *Second Treatise* (Chapter IX, s. 123) where he describes how men created political society 'for the mutual preservation of their Lives, Liberties and Estates, which I call by the general name Property'.

[3] *P.N.M.*, p. A2.

Tyrrell was thus upholding a social contract theory of the origin of government against Filmer's belief that the authority of a king over his people, being based on the authority of a father over his children, was instituted by God.

Tyrrell argued, first, that the authority of a father over his children was not absolute, but subject to universal moral laws; secondly, that even if paternal authority *were* absolute, the absolute authority of a king could not be derived from it; because the relationship of a king to his people is not, like that of a father to his children, a natural one.

Tyrrell maintained that a king is as much under the law as are his subjects. He recognised, but did not dwell on the implications of this principle, that subjects have a right to resist a sovereign who defies the law. Indeed, he took care to say:

> Neither would I be thought to encourage princes to stretch their power to the utmost limits, nor yet to stir up subjects to take arms as soon as ever they think themselves injured, since the populace is but too apt, where they are left to be their own judges, to pronounce sentence in their own favour.[1]

Tyrrell was a prudent writer; not only did he embellish his book with an engraving of Charles II, he also took care to speak throughout of the rule of law as that principle of government which was enthroned in the United Kingdom and of the doctrine of absolute sovereignty as something utterly alien. He ended his book with the observation that there *were* countries where the principle of absolute government which Filmer and his followers admired was 'practised in its full splendour', and 'all the hurt I wish those gentlemen is that they were all settled in any of them'.[2]

Tyrrell's argument is often strikingly 'Lockean';[3] but although Locke and Tyrrell often met at the time when Tyrrell was writing *Patriarcha Non Monarcha*, there is no evidence of any collaboration. The fact of the matter, as I believe, was that Locke was writing his *own* answer to Filmer at much the same time as Tyrrell was writing

[1] *P.N.M.*, p. 123.   [2] *Ibid.*, p. 259.

[3] Dr. A. H. Maclean has drawn attention to another treatise on government in which much of Locke's argument was anticipated, namely *Politica Sacra et Civilis* (1660) by George Lawson (*Cambridge Historical Journal*, IX, i, pp. 69–77). A note in one of Locke's commonplace books—' '79 . . . Shaftesbury: Lawson's book of the English Government' (B.L. MSS. Locke, F. 28, p. 40)—suggests that Locke read Lawson in 1679.

his. Locke, that is to say, wrote his *Two Treatises of Government* in or about the year 1681.

Two wrong ideas about Locke's *Government* have gained currency in text-books; the first is that the book was written after 1688 to justify the Glorious Revolution; the second that it was written as a reply to the political philosophy of Thomas Hobbes. Neither view stands up well to scrutiny. The first of the *Two Treatises* is a detailed refutation of Filmer; and the second sets out an alternative political philosophy to Filmer's. This definite connection helps to date Locke's book as one written, like *Patriarcha Non Monarcha*, when the writings of Filmer were at the height of their fashion after the first publication, in 1680, of *Patriarcha*.

When Locke's *Two Treatises of Government* came out in 1689 it carried a Preface to the Reader in which the author explained:

> . . . thou hast here the beginning and end of a discourse concerning government; what fate has otherwise disposed of the papers that should have filled up the middle and were more than all the rest, it is not worth while to tell thee. These which remain I hope are sufficient to establish the throne of our great restorer, King William, and to make good his title in the consent of the people. . . .

The textbook idea that Locke's *Government* was written after 1688 is presumably derived from the second sentence of this paragraph; but it can be sustained only if the first sentence is wholly neglected. For that first sentence plainly hints that the work was written some considerable time before it was sent in 1689 to the printer in London. Assuredly Locke revised the book in 1689 to serve as a '*pièce d'occasion*',[1] but this does not mean that it was originally designed for the purpose which it ultimately served.

Fox Bourne thought it probable that the first of Locke's *Two Treatises* was 'prepared' in 1681 or 1682,[2] the second during his last year in Holland. But the close connection there is between the argument of the two parts of the book suggests that they were 'prepared' at one and the same time: Locke's own words about the reader having 'here the beginning and end *of a discourse* concerning government' cannot be reconciled with the notion of the *Two Treatises* being separate discourses written at different times. This means that the book was originally written, or, in Fox Bourne's

[1] This phrase occurs in J. W. Gough, *Locke's Political Philosophy*, Oxford, 1950, p. 123.
[2] F.B., I, p. 466.

word 'prepared', either *c.* 1681 or *c.* 1689, and there is very little indeed to be said for the later date.[1]

To say that the *Two Treatises of Government* was originally written *c.* 1681 is not to deny that it was a *pièce d'occasion*, but to claim that it was a *pièce* of a different occasion; not something written after the event to 'justify' a revolution, but something written before the event to promote a revolution. To date Locke's book *c.* 1681 is to link it with Shaftesbury's revolutionary movement for a Protestant succession.

Locke did not pretend, as Tyrrell did, that the principle of absolute monarchy was something unEnglish. He wrote of it as a real and present menace; and the 'right of rebellion', implicit in Tyrrell, is explicit and emphasised in Locke. Perhaps the emphasis was added when Locke modified the book for publication in 1689; but some assertion of the right to rebellion must always have been there, for it is central to the argument of the book.

It is extremely interesting to compare and contrast what Locke says in the *Two Treatises of Government* with what Hobbes says in his *Leviathan*; but Locke did not write his book as an answer to the *Leviathan*, as a philosophical book in reply to another philosophical book; he wrote it as an answer to *Patriarcha*, one polemical book in reply to another. At the level of practical politics Hobbes had not then a fraction of the importance of Filmer.[2] Hobbes was a great philosopher, but he was almost as much disliked by the Tories as he was disliked by the Whigs. His teaching was far too severe, pessimistic, Machiavellian to be popular. Filmer struck an altogether different note. Where Hobbes frankly avowed that people were driven by fear and self-interest, Filmer appealed to those nobler emotions by which people preferred to think they were animated; and while Hobbes worked on a scientific analysis of human nature, Filmer's point of reference was the Bible. He was not a rigorous thinker, he was intellectually inferior to Hobbes in almost every way; but he was important because he said what people listened to and believed.

The first of Locke's *Two Treatises* corresponds fairly closely to the argument of *Patriarcha Non Monarcha*. Locke attacked Filmer's

---

[1] On the other hand, there is a great deal to be said for the earlier date. Mr. Peter Laslett (to whom I am much indebted for clarifying this question) has set out the case in detail in his forthcoming edition of the *Two Treatises of Government* to be published by the Cambridge University Press.

[2] *Vide* Peter Laslett's introduction to his edition of *Patriarcha* (Oxford, 1949).

claim that because men were born into subjection to their parents, men were therefore born into political subjection. He said the Scriptures gave no authority for thinking that a father had an absolute authority over his children, and therefore the absolute authority of a Prince could not be deduced from this premiss. Further Locke said, as Tyrrell had said, that Princes were only metaphorically, not literally, the fathers of their people. As for Filmer's appeal to the descent of temporal rulers from Adam, Locke pointed out that since everybody is descended from Adam, no one man's particular title to rule another could be based on his descent from Adam, all knowledge of the eldest line of Adam's posterity having long since been lost.

Locke turned in his *Second Treatise* to the question of the true 'original' of political power. Rejecting the notion that 'all government in the world is the product only of force and violence', he claimed to find the origin of civil society in a form of social contract. He believed it was a fact of history that men had once lived in a condition of primitive anarchy or 'a state of nature' and that they came together and instituted governments for the promotion of their common interests. Having long since abandoned his early quasi-Hobbesian view that men were naturally rapacious, he now emphasised men's natural goodness and rationality. He said that even before the creation of governments or 'civil society' there had been one kind of law—natural law:

> The state of nature has a law of nature to govern it, which obliges everyone: and Reason, which is that law, teaches all mankind, who will but consult it, that being all equal and independent, no one ought to harm another in his life, health, liberty, or possessions. For men being all the workmanship of one omnipotent and infinitely wise Maker, all the servants of one sovereign Master, sent into the world by His order, and about His business, they are His property, whose workmanship they are, made to last during His, not one another's pleasure; and being furnished with like faculties, sharing all in one community of nature, there cannot be supposed any such subordination among us that may authorise us to destroy one another, as if we were made for one another's uses, as the inferior ranks of creatures are for ours.[1]

I have quoted this paragraph partly in order to emphasise a fact which is often neglected in discussions of Locke's politics, namely that his political theory was based, as Filmer's was, on his religious

[1] *Second Treatise*, II, 6.

convictions. It is often said that Locke took an optimistic view of mankind; but he did so only because he believed that men were God's workmanship. He thought a law of nature existed only because God proclaimed it. He believed that men had natural rights, not simply on the traditional Stoic grounds that the very possession of reason entitled men to such rights, but because he believed that God had given men such rights. Nature and Reason were not for Locke, as for so many other theorists, peculiar metaphysical entities with law-giving and privilege-bestowing powers of their own, even though he did sometimes write as if he thought they were; behind Nature and Reason Locke always discerned the person and voice of God.

On the other hand, Locke's version of the social contract lacks the brisk clarity of Hobbes. Hobbes argued that in coming together and appointing a sovereign to rule them, men necessarily surrendered the liberty they enjoyed in the state of nature; they could not, after all, be both ruled and free from rule. Locke held that liberty was one of those natural rights which men brought with them from the state of nature into civil society. He did not think men's liberty had ever been absolute; even in the state of nature it had been limited by the ordinances of natural law. And far from thinking that men surrendered their liberty by creating political societies, Locke believed they had *increased* their liberty by providing a framework of security in which they were less likely to be frustrated in fulfilling their desires than they had been in the more hazardous conditions of primitive anarchy. Even if in a state of nature there had been more *theoretical* liberty, there had been less *actual* liberty.

Locke's views on property are of especial importance. He regarded property as a natural right, the basis of that right being the fact that property was created by a man's own labour. More than once Locke said that 'the chief end' of political society 'is the preservation of property'.[1] Elsewhere he described the chief end of civil society as the provision of a system of justice:

> the end of civil society [is] to avoid and remedy those inconveniences of the state of nature which necessarily follow from every man's being judge in his own case, by setting up a known Authority, to which everyone of that society may appeal upon any injury received or controversy that may arise and which everyone of the society ought to obey. . . .[2]

[1] *Second Treatise*, VII, 85 and IX, 124.   [2] *Ibid.*, VII, 90.

Locke was an early champion of the minimal state, of what was later known—in England at any rate—as 'liberalism'. Some of his contemporaries believed that it was part of a government's duty to save the souls of the citizens. Locke maintained that a government had *no other* duties beyond those for which governments were first instituted, namely the preservation of life, liberty and property; and he was strongly opposed to governments attempting to do anything else.

In one celebrated passage he wrote:

> When any number of men have so consented to make one community or government, they are thereby presently incorporated and make one body politic, wherein the majority have a right to act and conclude the rest.[1]

Locke did not think that this principle necessarily entailed democracy, although it is hardly surprising that many of his followers should have felt that it did. He simply pointed out that the majority of the people in instituting a civil society might choose one of several forms of government; they *might* choose democracy, but equally they might choose an oligarchy or an elective monarchy or an hereditary monarchy. For Locke the important word in the paragraph I have quoted was the word '*consented*'. He believed, and believed passionately, that the consent of the people was the sole basis of a government's authority. The exercise of civil power was, he said, a trust placed in the ruler or rulers by the people. If a ruler violated that trust, and especially if a ruler disobeyed the precepts of natural law which government was created to sustain, the citizens would not only be morally justified in resisting him, it was their moral duty to do so:

> Wherever law ends, tyranny begins, if the law be transgressed to another's harm. And whosoever in authority exceeds the power given him by the law, and makes use of the force he has under his command to compass that upon the subject which the law allows not, ceases . . . to be a magistrate, and acting without authority may be opposed as any other man, who by force invades the right of another.[2]

Thus Locke justified the use of rebellious force against 'unjust and unlawful force'. A sovereign who used unlawful force *himself* created this situation in which it was lawful to resist him.

---

[1] *Second Treatise*, VIII, 95.   [2] *Ibid.*, XVIII, 202.

In his last chapter, entitled *Of the Dissolution of Government*, Locke set forth in the plainest terms those arguments which would have served to justify armed resistance to Charles II in the early 1680's: 'Let us suppose', he suggested, 'the legislative [authority of a particular community]

> placed in the concurrence of three distinct persons: (1) A single hereditary Person, having the constant supreme executive power, and with it the power of convoking and dissolving the other two within certain periods of time, (2) an assembly of hereditary nobility, (3) an assembly of representatives chosen *pro tempore* by the people.[1]

Given this form of government, Locke argued that when the hereditary person or Prince 'sets up his own arbitrary will in place of the laws', then that Prince is in effect changing the legislative.[2] Secondly, when the Prince hinders the assembly from meeting 'in its due time or from acting freely, pursuant to those ends for which it was constituted', then again, the legislative is altered.[3] Thirdly, 'when by the arbitrary power of the Prince the electors or ways of election are altered without the consent and contrary to the . . . interest of the people, there also the legislative is altered'.[4] Fourthly, 'the delivery also of the people into the subjection of a foreign power' constitutes a change of the legislative.[5]

Locke's contention was that the Prince who alters the legislative in such ways as these is *himself* guilty of dissolving the government:

> For laws not being made for themselves, but to be by their execution the bonds of the society, to keep every part of the body politic in its due place and function, when that totally ceases, the *government* visibly *ceases*, and the people become a confused multitude without order or connection. Where there is no longer the administration of justice, for the securing of men's rights, nor any remaining power within the community to direct the force, or provide for the necessities of the public, there certainly is no government left . . .[6]

> In these and the like cases, where the *government is dissolved*, the people are at liberty to provide for themselves, by erecting a new legislative, differing from the other by the change of persons or form or both as they shall find it most for their safety and good. For the *society* can never by the fault of another lose the native and original right it has to preserve itself, which can only be done by a settled legislative, and a fair and impartial execution of the laws made by it.[7]

---

[1] *Second Treatise*, XIX, 213. [2] *Ibid.*, 214. [3] *Ibid.*, 215.
[4] *Ibid.*, 216. [5] *Ibid.*, 217. [6] *Ibid.*, 219. [7] *Ibid.*, 220.

Locke summed up his argument by saying that whenever a ruler tries 'to take away and destroy the property of the people, or to reduce them to slavery', that ruler puts himself 'into a state of war with the people, who are thereupon absolved from any further obedience, and are left to the common refuge, which God hath provided for all men against force and violence'.[1]

That common refuge was, of course, rebellion.

[1] *Second Treatise*, XIX, 222.

Chapter Sixteen

THE PROTESTANT PLOT

LOCKE was by no means wholly occupied with revolutionary politics in the early 1680's, although most of his personal friends were Whigs. There are some among his acquaintances who remain shadowy personalities, mere names that occur in his papers and letters. One such was John Richards, a young married man with a small family. Locke was the godfather of one of his children, and in December 1681 he stood guarantor for Richards when Richards took his family to India, having been appointed to a post there by a London trading company. The journey was ill-fated. Richards died on the way; his wife had a miscarriage and was put ashore in India seriously ill.

Locke was also called upon to help his cousin John Bonville to establish himself as a pewterer. This enterprise was more fortunate. Locke lent Bonville twenty pounds, and ten years later the pewterer was prosperous enough to act from time to time as his banker.

Another and more important name enters Locke's biography at this point—that of Edward Clarke. One of Locke's Somerset cousins, Mary Jepp, had married Clarke in 1675, but Locke seems not to have met him until his visit to Somerset in 1680. Edward Clarke was a prosperous landowner, born in 1651, and a Wadham man. He became one of Locke's closest friends, filling, in effect, the void created by the death of John Strachey in 1674. Locke came to think of Clarke's Somerset home, Chipley Park, as he had previously thought of Sutton Court. Chipley is a Jacobean manor house which still stands (albeit much rebuilt) in its own parkland between Milverton and Wellington. Edward Clarke's descendants still live there. Some of the trees which Locke sent as saplings from the continent still grow there. Portraits of Edward Clarke and his family still grace the drawing room walls, and until the 1920's most of Locke's letters to Clarke were preserved in the house, though only a handful now remains. The portrait of Clarke shows an exceedingly handsome man, with a fair complexion, straight nose, full lips and large brown eyes. The expression is intelligent, cheerful and tolerant, and the clothes are splendid. Altogether it is a portrait which completely satisfies the popular notion of a cavalier. Mary Clarke looks decidedly less striking; her nose is large, her lips small, and only a pair of pretty blue eyes redeems the face from mediocrity. However, there are good reasons for thinking that Mary Clarke was a charming woman, and Locke always gallantly pretended that she was beautiful.

Yet another friend came into Locke's life in the year 1682. Her name was Damaris Cudworth, and she was destined to be closer to Locke than any other human being.

Damaris Cudworth was the daughter of Ralph Cudworth, the Cambridge Platonist. She was born in 1658 and brought up in the Master's Lodge [1] of Christ's College. She was a remarkably well-educated woman, and Locke found much to talk about with her. As the daughter of a philosopher, she was something of a philosopher herself. Moreover, as the daughter of a Cambridge Platonist, she was something of a Cambridge Platonist as well.[2] Locke had to strive hard to convert her to his own more empirical philosophy, and he never brought her all the way over; for the rest of her life she remained her father's daughter [3] as much as Locke's disciple.

Locke and Damaris Cudworth were not, however, mere intellectual friends united by an interest in philosophy. They formed a romantic attachment, they wrote love letters to each other under the names of 'Philander' and 'Philoclea' [4] and they exchanged verses.[5] It is the verses which give one the clearest picture of their relationship. These were probably written some time in 1682 or 1683, after the poets had known each other for at least a year.

The poem by Damaris Cudworth is the shorter, and the better written of the two. I print it *in extenso*:

---

[1] The Old Lodge between the college chapel and Hobson street (F. A. Keynes, *Byeways of Cambridge History*, Cambridge, 1947, p. 119).

[2] Ralph Cudworth's most important philosophical work, *The True Intellectual System of the Universe* had been published only four years before Locke met Damaris Cudworth.

[3] *Vide* J. A. Passmore *Ralph Cudworth* (Cambridge, 1953).

[4] Forty letters from Philoclea to Locke, written between January 1681/2 and April 1688 survive in the Lovelace Collection (B.L. MSS. Locke, c. 17).

[5] *Ibid.*, c. 32, ff. 19–21.

Say wherefore is't that Damon flies
From the weak charms of Clora's eyes?
Weak charms they surely needs must be
Which till this hour he could not see.
Nor is she now more fair than when
Their first acquaintance they began,
When the gay shepherd laughed at love,
Swore it no generous heart could move,
Disease of fools, fond lunacy,
To Clora's face oft would he cry,
On me your friendship but bestow,
Friendship the only good below,
Fair Shepherdess I'll ask no more,
Since to give more exceeds your power.
Damon the mighty gift then gained,
With wit exalted now maintained,
No happy lover's greatest bliss
More than a shadow was to his
Which all refin'd found no alloy
And like to fate, nought could destroy.
Long did the happy youth thus live:
He could not ask nor could thee give
Till wandering the other day
Lo, on the ground the Shepherd lay
Pensive, as unseen Clora thought
Whom heedless steps had hither brought
To hear bewail his misery,
Complain of loss of liberty,
Curse his own stubborn pride and then
With tears and sighs begin again,
Ask pardon of philosophy
For passion's rude apostasy,
Resolve he would no captive be
But set himself by reason free,
He paused on this awhile, but straight
Ah Damon cried, it is too late;
Thou yesterday the will didst lose
Today the power to refuse,
Condemned a sacrifice to be,
Oppose not then thy destiny,
Appease love's God, let Clora know
How much to thee her charms do owe,
Her pity thee cannot deny
Tho' all her powers thou didst defy.

More difficult the conquest is
The nobler sure esteemed it is.
Mistaken Damon, she replied,
Did then herself no longer hide;
Conquests so hardly gained do show
We nothing to the conquered owe
Nor can I challenge any part
In captivating thy rough heart.
Since I am still the same as when
My powers and loves you did disdain.
Just destiny thy love does cause,
Submitting thee to human laws
Who proudly wouldst exempted be
Through ignorance or vanity;
The friendship once I gave retain
But think from me no more to gain
To whom thy passion comes too late
That scorn a conquest given by fate.
With this she left the trembling swain
Half dead with grief at her disdain
Who for his love no cure can find
But breathes his plaints into the wind.
Not daring Clora's eyes to see
Since her unjust severity
Who still insensible remains,
His constant passion still disdains
And laughs at all his grief and pains.

It seems reasonable to believe that this poem tells the history, from Damaris Cudworth's point of view, of her relationship with Locke. Thus it appears that Damaris originally offered Locke her love, but that he had replied with the offer of friendship; later his desire for friendship changed to a desire for love, and it was then her turn to offer only friendship and his turn to protest. Each regarded the other's offer of mere friendship as no better than disdain.

Locke's reply I print in a slightly abridged form:

But this disdain could not yet move
The constancy of Damon's love;
Her hand in his he gently took
And with a kind but dying look,
He thus replied:

.   .   .   .   .

My freedom I to you resign,
The freedom which you know was mine,
A freedom once so great so strong,
'Twas blamed for holding out so long.
I friendship begged and did obtain
And thought myself a happy swain,
But 'twas not ignorance nor pride
Made me ask nothing else beside.
He that asks friendship asks the heart
Unless there be some better part;
And that were only made a toy
To please some idle wanton boy.
I thought by this 'twould well be known
I now no longer was my own:
Yours friendship made me; from that hour
Was I not always in your power?
Friendship first warmed me with desire
And lodged in me a secret fire,
Which either time or some kind blast
Was sure to make flame out at last.
If with kind words you breath'd new heat
And made it soon your Mastery get,
Or a look like lightning came;
That on a sudden raised the flame
It matters not now to enquire—
Your power prevailed and all's on fire

.   .   .   .   .

Your cold disdain bids me no longer live,
Your friendship bids me hope all you can give.
Pray tell me Clora with what art you will
Preserve your friend and yet your lover kill?
Then with a sigh closing what he had said
Upon her bosom drop'd his drooping head.

Whether Locke wished to be Damaris Cudworth's husband as
well as her loving admirer it is difficult to tell. The letters of Damaris
Cudworth provide less illumination than the verses. A letter to
Locke dated 6 January 1681/2 [1] and signed 'Philoclea' may have
been the first she ever sent him. It certainly seems to have been
written in reply to the first letter she had ever received from
him:

[1] B.L. MSS. Locke, c. 17, f. 77.

Sir,

Be it under whatever pretence you please that you have sent me a letter you ought not to fear that it should be ill taken, since nothing can be liable to a misinterpretation that you say, who, as I believe, you would not really deceive, so perhaps should you design it, you might not find it very easy, there being something necessary besides wit to make one succeed in it. You might therefore without any apprehension have written to me all that you pleased. The idea that I have formed of you in my mind, could you have designed ill, would have secured me, and otherwise I am not unwilling to contribute to your diversion in what I have found so agreeable an entertainment. . . .

About five weeks later Damaris Cudworth was writing to Locke as his 'governess'[1]—a rôle he was oddly fond of inviting his women friends to assume—but the word 'love' is used more sparingly in subsequent letters. Nevertheless there are numerous references to the conditions of friendship, to misunderstandings and lovers' quarrels. 'Philoclea' told 'Philander' about her occasional illnesses and more frequent bouts of depression. She also had at times to remind him that she was a woman of feeling. Having, for example, explained in one letter[2] that she has 'no ill opinion of the Platonists (since I have spent most of my life among philosophers of that sect)', she declared in another[3] that she was resolved to become a Stoic. She attributed the heat of her temper to her Welsh blood, claiming descent from Kadwalader.[4] After her decision to become a Stoic, she told Locke that she was reading Seneca and Anthony le Grand on *The Passions*.

Locke's romantic attachment to Damaris Cudworth was not successfully concealed from his friends, and there are several arch references to her in surviving letters from his other women correspondents. But Locke probably had more serious matters to conceal in 1682. For this was the most critical year in Shaftesbury's struggle against the Stuarts.

Whiggish City jurymen had so far saved Shaftesbury from prison and the scaffold; but in 1682 the King contrived to put an end to the Whig control of juries. The election of Sir John Moore as Lord

---

[1] B.L. MSS. Locke, c. 17, f. 79. Philoclea to Locke 16 February 1681/2: 'It being for your honour that your governess should have something in her more than is common to the rest of her sex, I do not much wonder if you should really endeavour to fancy that she has so'.   [2] 9 March 1681/2 (*ibid.*, f. 83).
[3] 6 May 1682 (*ibid.*, f. 91).   [4] 23 March 1681/2 (*ibid.*, f. 85).

Mayor of London had given the King his opening. Moore's sympathies were mildly Tory, and the King suggested to him that he should choose Tory sheriffs, who would in turn choose sympathetic juries. The Mayor was willing, but the law ordained that sheriffs must be elected by the liverymen, not appointed by the mayor. The Whig liverymen nominated Dubois and Papillon as candidates for sheriffs; North and Box were proposed at the King's suggestion in the Tory interest. The Mayor declared North and Box elected; the outgoing Whig sheriffs declared Dubois and Papillon returned. Obviously there had been cheating on one side, if not on both sides. Rightly or wrongly the election of North and Box was upheld. The City was henceforth in the King's grip; and having once got control of the country magistracy, Charles turned next to revoke the powers of the chartered boroughs. The influence of the Duke of York increased at court, and as it did so, the more confident Shaftesbury became of the righteousness of the one remaining way to power: rebellion.

Parliament was silenced; the courts were perverted to the will of the King; dissenters were being persecuted; bribes from the King of France governed foreign policy; a Papist would soon occupy the throne. Was this not, Shaftesbury asked himself, sufficient provocation? Given able leadership, surely the freedom-loving people of England would not hold back?

Shaftesbury believed in his own able leadership. He had a private army of 'ten thousand brisk boys from Wapping'. He was in touch with the Protestants in France and with Argyll in Scotland. His candidate for the throne, the Duke of Monmouth, was as eager for revolution as he. All that was lacking was popular support, but Shaftesbury did not realise how much that support was lacking. He took his popularity in the City of London as evidence of popularity in the nation at large. He was wrong.

The British people had still too clear and painful memories of the revolutionary 1640's. They were no longer impressed by the Popish plots, and they had no particular hatred for the Duke of York. Furthermore, the Tories knew well what Shaftesbury was up to, and all his activities were being watched. So were those of his lieutenants. At Oxford Humphrey Prideaux still kept his eye on Locke. Writing to Ellis on 14 March 1681/2[1] that Tory spy reported:

---

[1] B.M. Add. MSS. 28929.

John Locke lives a very cunning unintelligible life here, being two days in town and three out, and no one knows whither he goes, or when he goes, or when he returns. Certainly there is some Whig intrigue amanaging, but here not a word of politics comes from him, nothing of news or anything else concerning our present affairs, as if he were not at all concerned in them. If anyone asks him what news when he returns from a progress, his answer is 'We know nothing'.

A few days later Prideaux [1] reported:

Where J[ohn] L[ocke] goes I cannot by any means learn, all his voyages being so cunningly contrived; sometimes he will go to some acquaintances of his near the town, and then he will let anybody know where he is; but other times, when I am assured he goes elsewhere, no one knows where he goes, and therefore the other is made use of only for a blind. He hath in his last sally been absent at least ten days, where I cannot learn. Last night he returned; and sometimes he himself goes out and leaves his man behind, who shall then be seen in the quadrangle to make people believe his master is at home, for he will not let one come to his chamber, and therefore it is not certain when he is there or when he is absent. I fancy there are projects afoot.

Locke's journal records several trips made during the first few months of 1682 from Oxford to Oakley (so one may conjecture that the Tyrrells were those 'acquaintances of his near the town'), and journeys to Burford, Abingdon, Reading and elsewhere.

In May 1682 he was contemplating a visit to Bath or to the rival watering-place, Tunbridge Wells. The Clarkes were also thinking of going to Tunbridge Wells, and Locke wrote in a gallant letter [2] to Mary Clarke:

Wit and good nature meeting in a fair young lady as they do in you make the best resemblance of an angel that we know; and he that is blessed with the conversation and friendship of a person so extraordinary enjoys all that remains of paradise in this world.

In her reply [3] Mary Clarke wrote:

This afternoon I was to wait on Mr. Stringer, and I understood by him he desires if you meet him at Reading to persuade you to go with him to Bath. But if he prevails I am undone, for I depend on seeing you in town to advise Mr. Clarke if there be anything needful for him

---

[1] 19 March 1681/2, B.M. Add. MSS., f. 96.
[2] 7 May 1682 (Rand, pp. 84–5).
[3] 23 May 1682, B.L. MSS. Locke, c. 6, f. 177.

to take before he drinks Tunbridge Waters, and the advice of anybody else will give me no satisfaction at all.[1]

When Locke left Oxford on 30 May, he went first to London, leaving his horse, named 'Sorrell', with Tyrrell at Oakley. Once more he stayed at Thanet House, dividing his time between Shaftesbury and Damaris Cudworth. It was August before he reached Tunbridge Wells. There is a hint of jealousy in a letter [2] 'Philoclea' wrote to him while he was on holiday:

> I have much curiosity to know the poetess you speak of, and also who was this year the most celebrated beauty at the Wells.

In another letter [3] she sent Locke that August, Damaris Cudworth wrote:

> As for your second question—whether I think that the lady who wrote to you left her heart at London, or no, when she came from there —if she has wit, as you say she has, I do assure you that she did not.

The reference is clearly to Damaris Cudworth herself; she had but lately left London for Cambridge. The letter continued:

> But though perhaps, for all your compliment, she may not have very much [wit], yet I assure you that those who know her do her the honour to believe that she takes as much care of her heart as many wiser people. However it be, she nevertheless thinks herself much obliged to that friend of hers who would be so careful of it for her; and I dare not be assured that it may not be an occasion of making her more negligent for the future than she has ever been for the time that is past.

In the following autumn and winter 'Philoclea' seems to have been much depressed. On one occasion [4] she said she had abandoned her old belief that 'the happiness of life consisted principally in society and friendship' and that she had elected solitude. She added: 'I now believe that one must care for nobody, have no friends, love only oneself'.

Locke, for his part, was worried rather than depressed. Shaftesbury's revolution was not going according to plan. In the summer

---

[1] In October Mary Clarke gave birth to a daughter Elizabeth, who was later to be a favourite of Locke's.

[2] 29 August 1682, B.L. MSS. Locke, c. 17, f. 101.

[3] *Ibid.*, f. 99.

[4] 28 October 1682 (*ibid.*, f. 107).

Monmouth had been sent on a progress through Cheshire, where, after some skirmishes, he was arrested. When Monmouth was released, Shaftesbury urged him to go back to Cheshire while he, Shaftesbury, mustered his forces in the City and other Whig leaders led a rising in the West. But Monmouth hesitated, and while he hesitated the Government learned of Shaftesbury's plan, and issued a warrant for his arrest. Shaftesbury slipped away from Thanet House and went into hiding.

From Oxford, where Locke had gone in September to keep the Michaelmas term, Humphrey Prideaux reported on 24 October:[1]

> John Locke lives very quietly with us, and not a word ever drops from his mouth that discovers anything of his heart within. Now his master is fled, I suppose we shall have him altogether. He seems to be a man of very good converse, and that we have of him will content; as for all else he keeps it to himself, and therefore troubles not us with it, nor we him.

At his hiding-place in the City Shaftesbury waited for several weeks for his Whig lieutenants to strike their promised blows. They disappointed him. Essex thought the time was not yet ripe. Russell and the Southampton House set (including Ralph Montagu), who wanted the Prince of Orange to succeed to the throne, were unwilling to act on behalf of Monmouth. In November Shaftesbury realised at last that his supporters were not going to rise. He also saw that he could not expect to elude the King's agents much longer. He dressed himself as a Presbyterian minister and, accompanied by his servant Wheelock, disguised as his nephew, he took ship from Harwich for Holland on 28 November 1682. After a short visit to Rotterdam, he went to Amsterdam, where he was welcomed warmly as a refugee with money—something not often seen. His political *entourage* included Robert Ferguson, William Thompson and a wine-dealer named Shepherd, all well known to the English intelligence service.[2]

At the end of the Michaelmas Term, Locke left Oxford to spend the Christmas vacation in London. A letter[3] he received during the vacation from Richard Old of Christ Church shows that he had

---

[1] B.M. Add. MSS. 28,929.
[2] *The Dispatches of Thomas Plott and Thomas Chudleigh*, Ed. F. A. Middlebush. The Hague, 1926, p. 196.
[3] 6 January 1682/3 (B.L. MSS. Locke, c. 16, f. 175).

hoped to occupy Henry Aldrich's [1] former rooms on his return to the House. As Aldrich was a pleasure-loving, hard-drinking, heavy-smoking clergyman, his rooms were probably very comfortable ones. But Richard Old informed Locke that the rooms had been given on the Bishop of Oxford's instructions to another member of the college. Locke would have to put up with other quarters. Meanwhile he was preparing to remove his belongings from Thanet House. He wrote in his journal on 16 January 1682/3:

> Sent my Lord's [i.e. Shaftesbury's] picture to Mrs. Clarke and removed [it] afterwards to Dr. Goodall's, and sent Mrs. Sanders to remove my picture to Mersham.

This Dr. Goodall,[2] an old friend of Sydenham's, lived at the Royal College of Physicians in Warwick Lane where he provided Locke with a *pied à terre* when he left Thanet House. Locke had been asked to spend the Christmas of 1682 with the Stringers at Bexwells, but had declined their invitation—Mrs. Stringer put this down to the presence in London of Damaris Cudworth, and she was probably right. Locke also went several times during the holiday season to Clapham, where Elizabeth Birch was looking after Shaftesbury's grandson, and he paid at least one visit to Lady King's house in Salisbury Court, Fleet Street, where Mary Clarke was staying.

The end of month brought bad news from Amsterdam. Shaftesbury had been taken ill with what was called gout of the stomach, and at noon on *21 January 1683* he died in the arms of his servant Wheelock. His body was sent home to be buried at Wimborne St. Giles.

A memoir of Shaftesbury was printed among Locke's *Posthumous Works* [3] in 1706, but this truncated document contains very little besides a bald narrative of the events of Shaftesbury's life up to 1660, during which time he was not yet known to Locke. A better notion of Locke's appreciation of Shaftesbury can be gained from Lady Masham's recollections of what she had heard Locke say about him: [4]

[1] Henry Aldrich (1647–1715) matriculated at Christ Church, 1662; M.A. 1669; D.D. 1682; Dean of Christ Church, 1689, and Vice-Chancellor, 1692–5.

[2] Charles Goodall (1642–1712) took his M.D. at Cambridge in 1670 after studying medicine at Leyden. He was a Fellow and subsequently President of the Royal College of Physicians.

[3] *The Posthumous Works of Mr. John Locke*, London, printed by W. B. for A. and J. Churchill at the Black Swan in Pater-Noster-Row 1706, pp. 281–310.

[4] Amsterdam: Remonstrants' MSS. J. 57a.

JOHN LOCKE, 1696
by M. Dahl

EDWARD CLARKE, c. 1673
by John Greenhill

This great man, esteemed by all parties in his country to be the ablest and most consummate statesman in it, if not of the age he lived in; who had a compass of thought, soundness of judgement and sharpness of penetration that (in some extraordinary instances of his sagacity [1]) has been fancied almost more than merely human, was no less admirable in the qualities and accomplishments that fit men for society.

He was very communicative in his nature, had conversed with books a good deal, had with men much more; and having been deeply engaged in the public affairs of his time at an age when others are scarce thought fit to begin to meddle with them, he had, whilst young, acquired that experience of things and knowledge of men which few have till they are old, and though this permitted him not the leisure to be any great reader yet being able (as he was) presently to discern the strength of any argument, and where the weight of it turned, having, besides, the advantage of an excellent memory: he always understood more of the books he read from a cursory reading of them than most other men did who dwelt longer upon them.

As he had every qualification of an excellent speaker (in which great endowment he was esteemed to surpass all who were his contemporaries in either House of Parliament), there was in his wit as much vivacity as there was strength and profoundness in his judgement; to which being added a temper naturally gay (unalloyed with melancholy even in age and under his greatest troubles) this happy conjunction gave ever to his most ordinary conversation a very peculiar and agreeable mixture of mirth with instruction, which was still so much the more pleasing, in that as he himself was always easy, he loved that others should be so in his company, being a great enemy to constraint and formality, and having, above all men, the art of living familiarly without lessening anything at all of his dignity. Everything in him was natural, and had a noble air of freedom, expressive of the character of a mind that abhorred slavery, not because he could not be the master, but because he could not suffer such an indignity to human nature. And these qualities (so far as they were capable of it) he inspired into all that were about him. In short, Mr. Locke, so long as he lived, remembered with much delight the time he had spent with my Lord Shaftesbury's conversation, and never spoke of his known abilities with esteem only, but even with admiration.

In a letter to Clarke dated 22 February,[2] Locke explained that he intended ('God willing') to be on his way to Wimborne St. Giles

---

[1] Locke's fragmentary Memoir emphasises Shaftesbury's sagacity: 'And indeed I never knew anyone penetrate so quick into men's breasts, and from a small opening survey that dark cabinet as he would' (*Posthumous Works*, p. 292).

[2] Rand, pp. 90–1.

Q

the next morning. He spoke of some small accident having hindered
his going that same day with David Thomas; in the meantime he
had seen Clarke's wife and little daughter in London, and had 'discourse' with the mother on feeding and other problems of rearing
an infant.

Locke reached St. Giles in time for the funeral. On Monday
26 February he recorded the occasion in his journal briefly thus:

'E[arl] Shaftesbury buried.'

He stayed at St. Giles until 6 April, when he returned, through
Basingstoke, to London.

I have mentioned Locke's interest in John Richards, who set out
for India and died on the way. Locke described the case in a letter he
wrote from London in April 1683 [1] to Damaris Cudworth's brother
Charles, a Fellow of Christ's College, Cambridge, who was then
about to leave for India. Locke asked him to find Richards's widow
in India, and to give her a letter on his behalf. He also referred to
his friendship with Damaris Cudworth:

> . . . in the conversation I have had the happiness to have sometimes
> with your sister here, I have observed her often to speak of you with
> more tenderness and concern than all the rest of the world, which has
> made me conclude it must be something extraordinary in you which
> has raised in her (who is so good a judge) so particular an esteem and
> affection beyond what is due to the bare ties of nature and blood. And
> I cannot but think that your souls are akin as well as your bodies, and
> that yours as well as hers is not of the ordinary alloy.

On 29 May Locke wrote in his journal: 'This day I removed to
Dr. Goodall's.' In mid-June he left for Oxford, visiting Tyrrell at
Oakley on the way; on 18 June he rode to Cirencester, and returned
the next day to Oxford. His journal reveals no more about his
movements until the beginning of September.

Shaftesbury's death did not diminish the wrath of his enemies
and 1683 was a black year for his friends. There was a certain irony
in the reversal of political fortunes. Until 1681 the Whigs had
hounded down 'traitors' and 'conspirators', and on the evidence of
notorious liars, dozens of worthy men, including Lord Stafford and

[1] B.L. MSS. Locke, c. 24, f. 35.

Archbishop Plunket, had been executed for their part in the Popish Plot to kill the King and enthrone his brother James. In 1683, the leading Whigs were indicted, and on the testimony of other notorious liars, several of them lost their lives for their share in a Protestant Plot to kill the King and enthrone his bastard Monmouth.

There occurred in June 1683, an incident comparable to, but very much more sensational than, the mysterious death of Sir Edmund Bury Godfrey on Primrose Hill. Certain Whigs proposed, it was said, to kidnap the King and his brother at Rye House, near Hoddesdon, in Hertfordshire, on their return from the races at Newmarket. As it happened a fire at Newmarket brought the King back to Whitehall earlier than expected, and the plan was frustrated. A few weeks later the secret was sold to the government, and several leading Whigs were arrested.

Already a number of lesser Whigs had suffered the fate of Stephen College. After Rye House, it was the turn of the great. Essex, Russell and Algernon Sydney [1] were arrested. Howard of Escrick, [2] who had shared the leadership of the Whig Party with them (and with Monmouth and Hampden [3]) since Shaftesbury's withdrawal, turned informer. He was about as reliable a witness as Titus Oates, but his lies were needed by the Tories as those of Oates had been needed by the Whigs. Monmouth and Grey [4] escaped to Holland.

At Oxford, where the University officially condemned the

[1] Algernon Sydney (1622–83) fought on the Parliamentary side in the Civil War, and was wounded at Marston Moor. An outspoken regicide, he remained abroad for some time after the restoration of Charles II, living the life of a scholar in Rome. In 1665 he decided he could serve his ideals better by coming out of his retirement and taking part in political activity.

[2] William, third Baron Howard of Escrick (1626?–94), a prominent Anabaptist under the Commonwealth, was reconciled to Charles II by Hyde. He was imprisoned as a Dutch spy in 1674, but released on confession. He sat on the Lords' committee which credited Titus Oates's allegations. He was imprisoned again in 1681, but released the following February.

[3] John Hampden (1653–96) was elected to Parliament in 1679, but spent much of his time in Paris, where he was assumed to be the chief secret agent of the Whig Party. He returned to England in 1682, and at once became one of the Opposition leaders. Arrested after the Rye House Plot, he was imprisoned on a charge of fomenting insurrection. He pleaded guilty and begged for the King's mercy. Charles, content with his humiliation, released him.

[4] Ford, third Baron Grey of Wark (1655–1701) was a Protestant zealot, who was undeterred by his religious convictions from seducing his wife's eighteen-year-old sister, Henrietta Berkeley. For this offence he was tried and found guilty in January 1682/3. He was arrested after the Rye House Plot the following summer, but escaped from the Tower.

doctrine that resistance to the King is lawful, Locke felt the net drawing in around him. The indictment of Algernon Sydney must have caused him particular alarm. It was not that Sydney was close to Locke; on the contrary, Sydney had been ill-regarded at Thanet House, and had only come to power among the Whigs after Shaftesbury had withdrawn and through the creation of the Council of Six [1] to lead the party. Locke's particular concern about Sydney's fate was his concern for a fellow intellectual, a fellow Whig theorist. There was more than one charge against Sydney. Not only was he accused of complicity in the Rye House plot. He was accused of writing seditious and treasonable manuscripts. Among other things he had written a Reply to Sir Robert Filmer's *Patriarcha*.

Locke's fears were well grounded. Humphrey Prideaux was no longer the only spy who was reporting his movements. On 13 July, the following official report was sent from Serjeant Richard Holloway to Secretary Jenkins: [2]

> . . . it is taken notice of in Oxford that from Mr. Locke's chamber in Christ Church, that was a great confidant if not secretary, to the late Earl of Shaftesbury, in a clandestine way several handbaskets of papers are carried to Mr. James Tyrrell's house at Oakely, near Brill, in Buckinghamshire, about seven miles from Oxford, or to Mr. Pawling's, [3] the mercer's, house in Oxford. Though Mr. Tyrrell is [the] son of a very good man, Sir Timothy Tyrrell [Kt.] yet he and Mr. Pawling are reported to be disaffected. It is thought convenient to make a search by a deputy lieutenant at Oakely, but who is Lieutenant or deputy of that county I cannot say, and if you at the same time direct a search by our Lord Lieutenant or one of his deputies at Mr. Pawling's, and that the Bishop of Oxford and Vice-Chancellor then search Mr. Locke's chamber it may conduce to his Majesty's service. I am going to attend the Norfolk circuit next Tuesday and if you have any commands afterwards, you will direct them to the Bishop or the Vice Chancellor.

[1] The 'six' were Essex, Russell, Monmouth, Hampden, Howard and Sydney.
[2] *C.S.P. Dom.* (1683), p. 109.
[3] References to Mr. Pawling also occur in letters from the Bishop of Oxford to Secretary Jenkins reproduced in the *C.S.P. Dom.* (1683). The first dated 25 August reads: 'Unless you remove the High Steward, Alderman Wright and Mr. Pawling and set the city [of Oxford] entirely on a loyal bottom your reformation will signify nothing and all will return in a short time to the old pass.' The second occurs in the letter dated 8 September, urging the full surrender of the charter of the city of Oxford: 'Indeed it was the artifice of Alderman Wright, Mr. Pawling and other incendiaries to persuade the people that if they gave up their charter they should be utterly undone . . .'

Locke paid a short visit to the West country,[1] and then decided to follow the example of Shaftesbury and quit the country. He destroyed a great number of his papers, including (it is said [2]) Shaftesbury's autobiography; and 'many' other papers he sent on 26 August 1683 with a letter to Edward Clarke [3] saying:

> You will know how and how far and in what occasions they are to be made use of better than I. What you dislike you may burn.[4] I have sent amongst them a letter of attorney to Mr. P. P.[5]; if you think that a fit place to lodge money in, pray give it him. . . .

My Lady Shaftesbury has, I suppose, money in one Mr. Prince's or some other hands in Amsterdam. Pray talk with her about it, for that probably may suit both her and my occasions, but mention not me but a friend of yours you will be responsible for, for I would be private at least till you hear from me again.

You remember the word *papers*. This enclosed will guide you to a gentlewoman in whose hand are lodged the writings concerning my annuity. Those I think were best to be sealed up and left with her still. In another paper sealed up you will find a bond of Dr. Thomas's [6] for

[1] Lady Masham wrote: 'The times growing more troublesome to those of my Lord Shaftesbury's principles as to public matters, and especially dangerous for such as had been intimate with him, Mr. Locke with reason apprehended himself not to be very safe in England: for though he knew there was no just matter of accusation against him, yet it was not unlikely, as things then were, but that he might have come to be questioned; and should he on any pretence have been put under confinement, though for no very long time, yet such was the state of his health, that his life must have been thereby much endangered. On this account therefore he thought it most advisable for him to withdraw. And going first into the West of England to some friends he had there, he soon after retired out of England' (Amsterdam: Remonstrants' MSS. J. 57a).

[2] Lord Campbell (*op. cit.*, IV, p. 233) writes: 'We have deeply to regret the loss of (Shaftesbury's) autobiography, which he entrusted to Mr. Locke and which was burnt in the panic occasioned by the execution of Algernon Sydney for having in his possession a speculative treatise upon government. The philosopher has by no means made atonement for his timidity by his *Memoirs Relating to the Life of Anthony First Earl of Shaftesbury*—an extremely jejune and perfunctory performance.' I share Lord Campbell's opinion of the *Memoirs*, but I have not been able to find any proof of his story about the burning of Shaftesbury's autobiography.

[3] Rand, p. 95.

[4] Clarke fell into trouble with the authorities after the Monmouth Rebellion and may have taken advantage of this authority to burn Locke's papers then.

[5] Peter Percival, the banker.

[6] In the Lovelace Collection (B.L. MSS., c. 20, f. 54) there is a declaration in the hand of Edward Clarke dated 24 September 1683 which reads: 'I then received from Mrs. Rabsy-Smithsby one Bond wherein Dr. Thomas stood bound in £100 for the payments of £50 to Mr. John Locke or his assigns; which by Mr. Locke's own order was to be delivered to Dr. Thomas by me'.

fifty pounds, which pray deliver him, with other writings of the like kind, which dispose of as you think fit, though I think they will be best there till you have occasion to make use of them. There is another paper also sealed up, which what it contains I suppose you will guess by the shape of it from what I have formerly told you. You may consider whether you think it best to lie there or no. There is also a purse of gold, about 100 guineas I suppose in value. The ruby ring in it give her, and all the other pieces that are wrapped up in little papers to keep them for me. The onyx ring with a seal cut in it, if you please, accept from me . . . when Syll comes to town for his subsistence or journey pray supply him. I have ordered him to receive money in other places, of which, if you will ask him, he will give you an account.

Locke told Clarke that he had arranged to send him a little red trunk containing his account book, so that Clarke would be able to inform himself in detail about his affairs. Clarke would also be receiving from Mr. Pawling 'my hat and clothes—which I should be glad to receive if they could be sent me'.

Locke's letter continued:

Pray talk with Dr. Thomas about the best way of securing the books and goods in my chamber at Christ Church if there should be any danger. There is a pair of silver candlesticks, too, and a silver standish of mine in Mr. Percivall's hands. When a safe and sure way of returning money to me is found I would have them also turned into money and returned to me. Upon consideration I have thought it best to make a will which you will find amongst the other papers, by which you may be legally entitled to whatsoever I leave. . . .

In a postscript Locke wrote:

All my wearing linen, flannel shirts, waistcoats, stockings, . . . either at Dr. Goodall's or Oxford, I would have sent to me. My old suits and a cloak at London I would have sold . . .

By this time Locke had very wisely ceased to record his movements in his journal, but if anyone had intercepted this letter to Edward Clarke, that person would not only have detected that the writer was leaving England, but that he was leaving for Holland, for the reference to Amsterdam is unmistakable. For this reason one might presume that Locke did not dispatch the letter until the last moment before his embarkation.

I do not know where he embarked; one of the Thames or Medway ports is as likely as Harwich. All his journal shows is that on *Friday 7 September, 1683*, Locke was in Rotterdam.

Chapter Seventeen

AMSTERDAM

LOCKE was pleased with Holland. Of Rotterdam he wrote in his journal on 7 *September* that 'the cleanliness of the town and the convenience for shipping to come into almost every street' was 'very admirable'. But he did not linger in that city; the presence of certain Scots exiles with political views akin to his own detained him not at all. He went on, as most of the English exiles did, to Amsterdam.

Again he liked what he found. One can understand why, for Amsterdam is still in many ways as it was in 1683; and the paintings of Rembrandt and his contemporaries have preserved for us the living detail of the things Locke saw. Much that has now the patina of age was then fairly new; the three central canals—the Heerengracht, the Keizersgracht and the Prinsengracht—had been dug in that same century, and the splendid gabled houses of the *haute bourgeoisie* along the quays were about as old as Locke himself. The wealth of Amsterdam had never been, like that of Venice, ostentatious; even the biggest houses on the canals were not palaces; and if there was a sermon in the stones of Amsterdam, it proclaimed solidity, restraint, independence and thrift—principles wholly congenial to the prophet of liberty, security and property. Locke in Amsterdam was decidedly *chez lui*.

The city burghers were proud and money-minded, and for those very reasons they differed from the more strict and pious Calvinists of other parts of Holland; and success in international trade had come with tolerance. Religious minorities, Catholics not excepted, were allowed to worship as they pleased in Amsterdam so long as they did so discreetly. Several buildings on the Keizersgracht and the Heerengracht concealed behind a façade of domestic architecture an illegal Roman or Dissenting chapel which the city authorities chose not to investigate. Political refugees were accepted as willingly in Amsterdam as religious nonconformists; and although it is true that Locke's exact contemporary Spinoza was driven from the city, his persecutors were his fellow Jews and not the city burghers.

Locke's journal tells the reader little about his doings in his first few weeks in Amsterdam. That his servant Sylvanus Brownover was with him; that he found lodgings first with a man named Wilm;[1] that he received English money from Edward Clarke; that he read the *Voyages* of Struys and other travel books—these facts his record shows, and, among other things, that he was concerned, as one could guess he would be, about the papers Tyrrell had of his in England.[2]

Locke afterwards said [3] he had spent most of his time during that winter in Holland writing his *Essay Concerning Human Understanding*. He was rather lonely at first. He wrote [4] to Clarke saying that which 'most sensibly touches me in my own private affairs is my absence from a man I so perfectly love and esteem.' But his health improved in Holland,[5] possibly because of the cleaner air, and possibly because he felt safe. Writing to invite the Clarkes to visit him in Amsterdam, Locke promised [6] Mary Clarke that if she should 'please to come hither' she should not hear him 'cough once in a whole day'. But Mrs. Clarke was too busy having babies, and could only write him letters. These Locke gratefully acknowledged:[6]

> If your lying-in will, as you say, produce long letters as certainly as I find it does fine children, I advise for my own sake as well as that of your family that Master and you would get to work again as hard as you can drive that you might lie in again as soon as may be.

The weather in Holland was exceptionally cold: 'the hardest winter', Locke called it,[7] 'in the memory of man'. The canals were frozen over with ice more than two feet thick. Though Locke him-

[1] Locke moved from Wilm's house to Reinburg's on *6 November 1683*.

[2] Locke wrote in his journal on *25 October 1683*: 'By what Mr. Tyrrell writes me 3rd instant, I suppose my box of manuscripts which were at Mr. Pawling's are removed to his house, wherein was also Thevenot's *Voyages* in folio. I conclude also my quilt and blankets and two Turkey carpets are there, for he thanks me for the Turkish carpet I sent to his lady, which was packed with them, and writes me word all was done by Dr. Thomas and Mr. Pawling as I directed these things to be done.'

[3] Locke to Clarke *1 January 1685* (Rand, p. 117).

[4] *21 November 1683* (ibid., p. 98).

[5] Lady Masham said that Locke enjoyed in Holland 'better health than he had of a long time done in England or even in the fine air of Montpellier'. (Amsterdam: Remonstrants' MSS. J. 57a.)

[6] [*December 1683*] Rand, p. 101.

[7] Journal: *3 March 1684*.

self flourished, many people, birds and animals died. One of these victims was a lioness, and through her death Locke came to meet the man who was to be his best Dutch friend. His earliest acquaintances in Amsterdam were medical men such as Peter Guenellon,[1] whom he had known in France, and Caspar Sibelius.[2] Guenellon took advantage of the lioness's death to conduct a post-mortem in the presence of various persons interested in such things. One of these spectators was Philip van Limborch, a Professor of Theology at the Remonstrants' seminary on the Keizersgracht. Locke, who had heard of the professor, and was anxious to know about the Remonstrants, introduced himself, and friendship ripened swiftly.[3]

The Remonstrants were the liberal Nonconformists of Holland. Founded by Episcopius, whose great-nephew Limborch was, they derived their name from a remonstrance presented to the States-General in 1610. Committed to the principles of rational theology and the minimal creed, they left questions of faith to the individual's own reading of the Scriptures, and put their emphasis on morality: they were as strictly Puritan in matters of conduct as they were tolerant in matters of belief. Condemned by the Synod of Dort in 1619, they were among the dissenters who built their chapel in the Keizersgracht behind the façade of a private house, and apart from the baroque organ case, added in 1700, the building is still as it was when Locke was there. The Remonstrants were too intellectual a sect to be a very popular one, but their number in Amsterdam included some influential members of the liberal professions.

Philip van Limborch had not, to judge from the portrait which still hangs in the vestry of the Keizersgracht chapel, the appearance of a typical Puritan divine. He is represented as a fat and cheerful man; and far from conveying an immediate impression of austerity and piety, his countenance is rubicund, worldly and humorous;

[1] Peter Guenellon was born in Amsterdam *circa* 1650, matriculated at Leyden in 1667, but graduated in medicine from Padua. He had worked at the Charité in Paris, before returning to Amsterdam to settle in medical practice. He married, in April 1680, Cornelia Maria Veen, nineteen-year-old daughter of Dr. Egbertus Veen.

[2] Caspar Sibelius, then a medical practitioner in Amsterdam, removed soon afterwards to Deventer. In 1692, believing there was no prospect of advancement as a doctor in Holland, he emigrated to the British Isles and changed his name to Sibley.

[3] Limborch recalled many years afterwards: '[Mr. Locke] introduced himself to me, and we afterwards had many conversations about religion, in which he acknowledged that he had long attributed to the Remonstrants doctrines very different from those which they held, and now that he understood what they really were, he was surprised to find how closely they agreed with many of his own opinions' (F.B., II, p. 6).

pudgy hands rest lightly on the ample stomach, and his dark eyebrows are lifted in the comically quizzical manner of the late Sir George Robey. Limborch was born in Amsterdam in 1633 and, belonging to the leading Remonstrant family, he was trained for the ministry of his denomination from early youth. At Gouda, where he had his first congregation, Limborch began editing the works of his great-uncle Episcopius for publication, and in consequence he entered into correspondence with several foreign scholars, including Ralph Cudworth and the other Cambridge Platonists, with whose latitudinarian theology and whose doctrine of tolerance (if not with their mysticism) Limborch was much in sympathy.

He was fifty,[1] a year younger than Locke, when they met in 1684;[2] and he was then at work on his *Theologia Christiana*, a book similar in many respects to Locke's later *Reasonableness of Christianity*. Limborch maintained, as Locke did, that the essential truths of Christianity were simple ones and all acceptable to reason. There was room, he argued, for religious doubt; and society, he thought, could accommodate all shades of dissent, so long as it was cemented by a general acceptance of Christian ethics. Limborch's toleration, like Locke's, stopped short of Roman Catholics.

The large proportion of theological notes among Locke's entries in his journal during the early months of *1684* bears witness to the interests which his new friendship had rekindled. A letter from Tyrrell,[3] which must have reached him some time in *February*, reminded Locke of other studies. Tyrrell spoke of the manuscripts which had come from Mr. Pawling's house into his custody,[4] and mentioned in particular one essay of Locke's on human nature. He said: 'I have read [the papers] over with all the care I could a second time, and like them better than at first.' Between this essay and the writings of Hobbes and Duhamel on human nature, Tyrrell was kind enough to say that he found 'as much difference as between a short epitome and an exact work'. Tyrrell wanted Locke to give more thought to the subject. But Locke had other things to think about.

---

[1] Limborch was twice married: first, in 1660, to Elisabeth van Sorgen, who died in 1663, leaving one daughter; and for the second time in 1674 to Cornelia van der Kerk, a widow, by whom he had two children, Geertruid and Frans.

[2] Most of the letters which subsequently passed between Locke and Limborch have been preserved, principally in the Amsterdam University Library (Remonstrants' MSS.), the Bodleian Library (Locke MSS.) and the British Museum.

[3] B.L. MSS. Locke, c. 22, f. 50.   [4] *Vide* Locke's journal *25 October 1683*.

Spring came, and he welcomed it. He wrote to Mary Clarke: [1]

Now this terrible winter is almost over (for the ice is now going apace) methinks you and I had two very good deliverances: you have been well delivered of a fine girl and I of a scurvy cough, which I think, had I been on your side the water, this fierce long cold weather would have delivered me over to the worms.

After an interval of two years in their correspondence, Nicholas Thoynard wrote to Locke in *May 1684* [2] to apologise for his silence, and to say that he had been through a time of affliction since they were last in touch. Locke replied at once, and henceforth he and Thoynard wrote to each other as fully and freely as of old. Thoynard continued to have difficulties over the publication of his great work on the *Harmonie de Saintes Écritures*, and at one time he proposed to go to Amsterdam and find a printer for it there,[3] only to abandon the idea when he discovered that paper cost more in Holland than it cost in France.[4]

In the middle of *July*, Locke changed his lodgings again, taking rooms with a man named van der Velde.[5] But he did not remain in Amsterdam for the whole of the summer. In mid-August Sylvanus Brownover packed their bags, and master and servant set off together to tour the Dutch republic. They went first to Alkmaar,[6] which Locke called 'very clean' but 'decaying'; then to Hoorn, which was 'not half so clean',[7] and on to Enkhuysen, where Locke had the equivocal pleasure of sleeping where Charles II had slept twenty-three years earlier,[8] but got a poor supper of 'a salad of two old hens ill-dressed and a little melon' shared between five guests. Crossing the Zuyder Zee to Friesland, he visited the little university town of Franeker, where he noticed,[9] with a certain satisfaction, that the architecture of the schools and library was undistinguished although the university had 'produced many learned men', thus proving that 'knowledge depends not on the stateliness of the buildings, etc.' Going on through Leeuwarden, where he saw nothing to excite his interest, he next visited an outlying village

---

[1] *18 March 1684*, Rand, p. 109.

[2] Thoynard to Locke, *24 May 1684* (in French), B.L. MSS. Locke, c. 21, f. 139.

[3] Thoynard to Locke *10 August 1684*, ibid., c. 21, f. 141 (French).

[4] Thoynard to Locke *November 1684*, ibid., Locke, c. 21, f. 142 (French).

[5] Jacob van der Velde kept a bookshop on the Corte Niezel near the Old Church of Amsterdam, but he seems to have had a house on the Keizersgracht.

[6] Journal *15 August 1684*.   [7] Journal *17 August 1684*.

[8] Journal *18 August 1684*.   [9] Journal *19 August 1684*.

on behalf of Damaris Cudworth, who had written to him that summer [1] saying that she hoped she 'was absolutely cured of promising myself any great pleasure in the world', but wanting to know about the Labadists, who had a settlement in Friesland. These people were followers of Jean de la Badie (1610–74), a French Jesuit who had turned Protestant and established a self-supporting communitarian Christian brotherhood. Locke's attitude towards the settlement was profoundly suspicious. Sectarianism he did not mind; but he hated the idea of abolishing private property. In his journal [2] he wrote:

[The Labadists] receive all ages, sexes, and degrees upon approbation after trial. They live all in common and whoever is admitted is to give, with himself, all that he has to the Lord, i.e. to the Church, which is managed by officers appointed by the church. For it is a fundamental miscarriage and as such will deserve cutting off to possess anything in property. Those who are obliged by any reason to go abroad, or for their health should be obliged to live abroad, have [an] allowance made them by the church out of their common stock. Their rule is the word of God and mutual brotherly love one to another. The discipline whereby they prevent or correct offences is, first brotherly reprehension, if that suffices not the next is suspension from the sacrament and also from their common table, if this makes not an amendment, they cut him off from their body. They meet every morning about five of the clock when some discourse is made to them upon some place of Scripture, before and after which they pray. And then they go everyone about their private occupations, for they have amongst them of almost all trades. Nobody is compelled to work by any set rule, but they do it out of an instinct of charity and duty. . . . Their clothes are plain and modest, their mien and behaviour demure, and a little affected, if I mistake not. They are very civil one to another as well as to strangers, carefully saluting one another with their hats as often as they meet.

Locke noticed also that their leader Yvon [3] had 'established a perfect empire over them' and he also felt that the Labadists 'suggest a little of Tartuffe' because 'their discourse carries with it a supposition of more purity in them than ordinary, and as if nobody were on the way to heaven but they'.

[1] 16 June 1684 (B.L. MSS. Locke, c. 17, f. 114).

[2] *22 August 1684.*

[3] Pierre Yvon (1646–1707), who succeeded La Badie as leader of the sect, had been his pupil and was, like him, a Frenchman.

Locke must have described the sect in much the same terms to Damaris Cudworth, for she told him when she wrote him next: [1] 'Notwithstanding the character which you have given of the Labadists, I acknowledge that I like [them] very well.' She had, however, the grace to add that she was 'much more disposed to see Holland than Friesland', and that 'the sight of a place where love and business might be so well reconciled is as much worth my curiosity as that of the Labadists'.

At the end of *August*, Locke went on to Groningen,[2] another university town, and he returned to Leeuwarden in time to witness the state entry of Henry Casimir, Prince of Nassau [3] and governor of the Province. 'The cavalcade and solemnity', Locke ambiguously recorded, 'was suitable to the greatness of the government.' [4]

After another week touring the smaller towns and villages of Friesland, he went south through Groening,[5] where he liked the pretty new church, to Deventer, so as to spend the next ten days in the company of Dr. Sibelius, who had moved there from Amsterdam. Numerous medical notes in Locke's journal for that time point to the nature of their conversations. After this sojourn he went on to Arnhem and Nijmegen. He found the changed aspect of the countryside agreeable; 'the borders of the cornfields', being 'set with rows of oaks two or three or four deep', made it 'look like a country full of woods'.[6] After a journey by boat down the Waal, and a short stay in Utrecht, Locke returned to Amsterdam on *10 October*, having been travelling about for the better part of two months. It was not long before he went away once again: this time to visit Leyden, where he stayed long enough to make several new acquaintances in the medical world, and to hear the son of Gronovius deliver a solemn oration in the university. Locke noted in his journal [7] while he was in Leyden:

The exercise for a Doctor of Physic's degree is examination by the professors in private and answering in the schools for one hour in defence of whatever the candidate has printed in his thesis, any part whereof the opponent has liberty to oppose. The opponents are usually the friends of the respondent, each whereof, before he begins, asks

[1] 25 August 1684 (B.L. MSS. Locke, c. 17, f. 116).

[2] *24 August 1684.*

[3] Locke described the prince as 'about twenty-eight years old, little, and not very handsome, but, as they say, a man of parts, loving and well beloved of his country'.

[4] *29 August 1684.*   [5] Journal, *5 September 1684.*

[6] *Journal, 19 September 1684.*   [7] *31 October 1684.*

leave of the promoter, who is one of the professors the candidate makes choice of. They who are Doctors dispute with their hats on, the others bare. And those I saw dispute, that they might not mistake, had their arguments written down. I suggest their studies tend most to practice, for in disputing no one that I heard urged any argument beyond one or two syllogisms.

But despite his being so favourably impressed with the medical training provided by the Dutch universities, and despite his personal contacts with Dutch physicians, Locke did not pursue his own medical studies at all intensely in Holland. He made the aquaintance of Anthony van Leeuwenhoek, the man who first demonstrated organisms under the microscope; and he collected statistical records of the weather and of deaths in Amsterdam, intending to work out the correlation between variations in the weather and the mortality bills. But on the whole, Locke in his years of exile concentrated on philosophy at the expense of medical science.

One of Locke's letters to Damaris Cudworth went astray, and she wrote [1] him in some pique saying she had been hoping 'before this' to have received 'an answer from you to my last letter' and 'some encouragement to go into Holland'; 'but', she added, 'I find you are not in such a haste to see your governess, whatever you would have her believe'. She added that, if she were to contemplate matrimony, she would have an 'extreme desire to marry a Labadist'. As things turned out, Damaris Cudworth never went to visit Locke in Holland and she did not marry a Labadist.

[1] 8 October 1684 (B.L. MSS. Locke, c. 17, f. 118).

Chapter Eighteen

THOUGHTS CONCERNING EDUCATION

MANY of Locke's letters from Holland to Edward and
Mary Clarke contained recommendations on the upbringing and education of children. Locke wrote to the Clarkes
with the combined authority of physician, friend and pedagogue,
and in the case of their daughter Elizabeth he claimed the rights of a
lover too:

> You know (he told Mary Clarke [1]) or at least ought to believe, that
> when I have a mistress I am very tender of her, and therefore if my
> pretty Miss Betty be ordered otherwise than I think convenient, father
> and mother and all will be sure to hear of it . . . We old bachelors are
> as positive as you married women, and think it sometimes as reasonable
> to have our wills.

He wrote at even greater length about the upbringing of the
Clarkes' son; at such length, indeed, that he was later able to make a
book of what he had written. That book was not published until
1693,[2] but as the letters belong to the period of Locke's Dutch exile,
I propose to interrupt the narrative at this point to give a brief
summary of his 'thoughts concerning education'.

Locke's views on education were, like his views on several other
questions, curiously compounded of the conventional and the
revolutionary. As might be expected, he dealt first with matters of
health. He maintained that 'most children's constitutions are either
spoiled, or at least harmed, by cockering and tenderness'. He
thought children should wear fewer and lighter clothes, that they
should swim often, and that even in winter their feet should be
washed daily in cold water. Indeed, he recommended that a child
should 'have his shoes so thin that they might leak and let in water'.
Girls should wear loose clothes: 'Narrow breasts, short and stinking

[1] *18 March 1684*: Rand, p. 109.
[2] Further editions of *Thoughts Concerning Education* were published in Locke's
lifetime and the considerable enlargement of these later editions shows that Locke's
interest in the subject continued.

breath, ill lungs and crookedness are the natural and almost constant effects of hard bodices and clothes that pinch.' Diet should be plain and simple, only small beer should be drunk, and children should have little or no medicine. He added the singular proposal that children's meals should be irregular, so that their stomachs should not come to expect food at particular times; Locke also forbade fruit as 'a thing totally unwholesome' for children. But he emphasized the importance of regular stools. Costiveness 'being an indisposition I had a particular reason to inquire into',[1] Locke said he had found the best method to be that of going to the stool directly after breakfast.

Generally he favoured the Spartan approach to the training of children. It was wrong, he thought, to indulge a child:

> For if the child must have grapes or sugar-plums when he has a mind to them, rather than make the poor baby cry or be out of humour, why, if he is grown up, must he not be satisfied too, if his desires carry him to wine or women?

Nevertheless Locke spoke strongly against corporal punishment. He also suggested that rewards ought not to be physical pleasures, and urged parents to use the better, and more powerful, incentives of 'esteem and disgrace'. He thought that fear and awe ought to give parents their first hold over children, and that love and friendship should later compel obedience.

Locke found 'the principle of all virtue' in 'the power of denying ourselves the satisfaction of our own desires, when reason does not authorise them' and on these grounds he urged that 'children should be used to submit their desires and go without their longings even from their very cradle'.

He was sufficiently Hobbesian still to admit that children loved liberty and dominion over others; but he advised parents to learn to distinguish between the 'wants of nature and the wants of fancy'. Whatever compliance the wants of nature might require, the wants of fancy should never be satisfied. Clothes, for example, children had to have, 'but if they speak for this stuff or that colour', then they should be denied it. Realising that this might be considered too stern a doctrine, he emphasised that it was offered as an alternative to the rod; it was intended to teach children 'the art of stifling their desires'.

---

[1] In a letter to Clarke, written in *December 1684*, Locke described himself as 'naturally costive' (Rand, p. 116).

JOHN LOCKE, 1698
by Sir Godfrey Kneller

PHILIP VAN LIMBORCH
by Christoffel Lubienecki

Locke thought that curiosity in children should be neither discouraged nor discountenanced. But he pointed out that wisdom was beyond them, and he did not think they should be allowed to learn cunning instead. He believed in letting them have playthings, but any dawdling or laziness in their studies should be checked by setting them to manual labour. He said that particular care should be taken to prevent them from telling lies—something so very common in adult life that children could hardly help picking it up. He recommended that children should be taught to love and reverence the Supreme Being, but he did not dwell, as so many educational theorists do, on the importance of religion.

He suggested that a thorough knowledge of the world and its vices should, by degrees, be acquired by a young gentleman; and he urged fathers to make their sons their friends 'as fast as their age, discretion and good behaviour could allow it'.

He would reserve the greatest severity for the very young. A typical bachelor, Locke did not think parents should tolerate their children's crying. For that, he thought, only served 'to encourage effeminacy'. Pettish crying, particularly, should be treated severely, and 'where a positive command will not do it, blows must'. Courage and fortitude should be developed in the same way. To this end he suggested two methods: the first, keeping the child away from any fright when young; the second, accustoming the child to suffer pain. Despite his objection to the infliction of pain as a *punishment*, Locke thought it good for a child to be knocked about from time to time to harden it.

On the other hand, he suggested that care should be taken to prevent children from being cruel, as he had observed they often were to such creatures as birds and butterflies. He suspected that this was due to bad examples:

> All the entertainment and talk of history is of nothing almost but fighting and killing: and the honour and renown that is bestowed on conquerors (who are for the most part but the great butchers of mankind) further mislead growing youth, who by this means come to think slaughter the laudable business of mankind, and the most heroic of virtues.

Concerning education in the narrower sense, Locke's views were decidedly 'progressive'.[1] He was strongly opposed to what he called

---

[1] Locke even espoused that favourite cause of the crank progressive, spelling reform, although it is not mentioned in his treatise *On Education*. The following

'the ordinary method of education', namely the 'charging of children's memories' with rules and principles. He suggested instead that unconscious habits should be bred in children by practice. Manners were better learned by example than by precept, and the intellectual disciplines should be made interesting and attractive. He thought that Latin could be learned like French—not from the study of grammar books, but through the experience of speaking it.

Believing that examples were more important than rules, Locke urged parents to keep their children away from the society of the lower class of domestic servants, whose ill manners were apt 'horribly to infect children', and whose 'flatteries take off the edge and force of the parent's rebukes'. For similar reasons he urged parents to keep their sons away from schools, and to have them educated at home. In schools, boys inevitably fell into the company of undesirable companions. Locke seemed ready to admit that a boy might have a better classical education at a school, but even so he would recommend a school only to the father who 'thought it worth while to hazard your son's innocence and virtue for a little Latin and Greek'. On the whole, Locke thought education at the hands of a tutor more likely to give a boy 'a genteel carriage, manly thoughts, and a sense of what is worthy and becoming'. For the business of a tutor did not stop short at teaching his pupil Latin and logic:

> To form a young gentleman as he should be, it is fit his governor should himself be well-bred, understand the ways of carriage and measures of civility in all the variety of persons, times and places, and keep his pupil, as much as his age requires, constantly to the observation of them. This is an art not to be taught or learned from books.

As to the particular subjects of study, Locke suggested that children should be taught to dance as soon as they were capable, because it gave them poise and confidence. He believed they could

---

appears in shorthand in his Journal (dated *15 August 1676*): 'Spelling: . . . How little a lover so ever I am of fresh fashions . . . considering that letters are but the lasting marks of sounds, I think we would avoid much confusion and great many needless difficulties if we would always apply as near as we could the same characters to the same pronounciation. [It would] perhaps look a little strange and awkward at first to make a change all at once, as in this paragraph, so much is custom able to confirm us in love and admiration even of inconveniences, though it cannot but be acknowledged that it would be much better if it were reformed, and nobody can deny that it may be done by degrees and must have a beginning. It would prevent a great many mistakes and make languages of which we have so great a need and so constant use much *easier* to be learnt, read and written by all strangers, by the women and illiterate of the same country.'

be cozened into a knowledge of letters, beginning first with reading, then going on to writing and then to drawing. He also proposed, rather oddly at this stage, shorthand. Next he recommended that the pupil should learn French, and afterwards Latin. Opposed to the conventional emphasis on grammar, Locke was equally opposed to the pupil learning by heart 'great parcels' of the Latin authors, and to a boy's being made to compose Latin verses: 'for if he has no genius to poetry, it is the most unreasonable thing in the world to torment a child and waste his time about that which can never succeed'. After Latin, Locke advised the study (in this order) of geography, chronology, arithmetic, geometry and history. As for ethics, he confessed: 'I know not whether the pupil should read *any* discourse of morality but what he finds in the Bible'; but he did think it worth recommending some study of Tully's *De Officiis* and the juristic writings of Pufendorf and Grotius as well as the principles of English law. Tully had the added advantage of providing an excellent model of prose style, especially if read in conjunction with Voiture. Locke did not consider rhetoric and logic suitable subjects for the young. Although he favoured dancing, he was against music and painting; he approved of riding, and regarded wrestling as better than fencing (a skill which led young men into duels). For recreation, he recommended gardening and husbandry, or some other manual craft, and even book-keeping—all of which were *useful* recreations, and therefore very much more desirable than cards or dice.

Locke did not recommend Greek. He admitted that no scholar could do without Greek, but, he explained, 'I am not now considering the education of a professed scholar, but of a gentleman.' And Greek was not, like Latin, indispensable to a gentleman. Locke criticised the upper-class custom of sending young men on the grand tour of continental Europe between the ages of sixteen and twenty-one. At that age young men were too eager, Locke thought, to secure and enjoy their freedom to benefit from travel. He would prefer them to go as boys under sixteen with a tutor or, better still, as men over twenty-one alone.

Above all else, Locke stressed the importance of manners:

Without good breeding his other accomplishments make him pass but for proud, conceited, vain or foolish. Courage in an ill-bred man has the air, and escapes not the opinion of brutality. Learning becomes pedantry; wit, buffoonery; plainness, rusticity; good nature, fawning.

And though he admitted it might sound strange 'in the mouth of a bookish man', Locke added, 'Learning is the least part of good breeding.'

In 1703, towards the end of his life, he wrote another paper on 'reading and study', this time for the mature gentleman.[1] Locke pointed out that the greatest part of a gentleman's 'business and usefulness in the world is by the influence of what he says or writes to others', so that he needed to read not only to increase his knowledge, but to enable him to communicate that knowledge to others. Yet a gentleman need not have an universal knowledge: he should rather concentrate on 'moral and political knowledge', on those studies 'which treat of virtues and vices, of civil society and the arts of government, and will take in also law and history'.

Locke emphasised that learning was not simply the accumulation of knowledge; it was also a matter of knowing how to judge and discriminate between good and bad arguments.

> When a man by use hath got this faculty of observing and judging of the reasoning and coherence of what he reads, and how it proves what it pretends to teach; he is then and not till then in the right way of improving his understanding, and enlarging his knowledge by reading.

After right reading came right speaking, the essentials of which Locke described as perspicuity and sound reasoning:

> Perspicuity consists in the using of proper terms for the ideas or thoughts which he would have pass from his own mind into that of another man.

As for ethics, Locke said once more that he would advise a gentleman to read no book other than the New Testament, except perhaps Tully's *De Officiis*. On political theory, he recommended Pufendorf's *De Jure Naturali et Gentium* ('the best book of that kind'), the first book of Hooker's *Ecclesiastical Polity*, Algernon Sydney's *Discourses Concerning Government* (which, he said, 'I have never read'), Peter Paxton's *Civil Polity*, Pufendorf's *De Officio Hominis et Civis*, and, very coyly, '*Two Treatises of Government* printed in 1690'— this last being Locke's own. Having next named various well-known books on geography and travel and history, Locke said:

> To fit a gentleman for the conduct of himself, whether as a private man, or as interested in the government of his country, nothing can be

[1] *Several Pieces*, pp. 231–45.

more necessary than the knowledge of men; which, though it be to be had chiefly from experience, and, next to that, from a judicious reading of history, yet there are books that of purpose treat of human nature, which help to give an insight into it. Such are those treating of the passions, and how they are moved, whereof Aristotle in his second book of *Rhetoric* hath admirably discoursed, and that in a little compass. . . . La Bruyère's *Characters* are also an admirable piece of painting. . . . Satirical writings also, such as Juvenal and Persius and above all Horace. Though they paint the deformities of man, yet thereby they teach us to know them.

Locke did not forget another use of reading, 'which is for diversion and delight':

> Such are poetical writings, especially dramatic, if they be free from prophaneness, obscenity and what corrupts good manners; for such pitch should not be handled.
> Of all the books of fiction I know none that equals Cervantes's *History of Don Quixote* in usefulness, pleasantry and a constant decorum.
> And indeed [Locke adds] no writings can be pleasant which have not nature at the bottom and are not drawn after her copy.

In this last apophthegm Locke summed up the principle which dominated eighteenth century aesthetics; it was a principle which the eighteenth century learned primarily from him.

Chapter Nineteen

DR. VAN DER LINDEN

IN November 1684 John Fell, the Dean of Christ Church, received a letter [1] from the Court to say that 'being given to understand that one Mr. Locke, who belonged to the late Earl of Shaftesbury, and has upon several occasions behaved himself very factiously and undutifully to the government' was still a Student of the House, the King wished to have him removed from that place.

Lady Masham reported [2] twenty years later that Dr. Fell received 'this harsh command with trouble'; and that having discussed the matter with James Tyrrell he 'was so well satisfied of Mr. Locke's innocence that instead of obeying the order . . . he summoned him to return home by the 1st of January following . . . to answer for himself'.

The Dean was probably *not* 'satisfied with Mr. Locke's innocence', but he was a just man, and would certainly have wished to give Locke a fair hearing. At any rate he replied [3] to the Court saying, of Locke, that

> . . . I have for diverse years had an eye upon him, but so close has his guard been on himself, that after several strict inquiries I may confidently affirm there is not anyone in the college, however familiar with him, who has heard him speak a word either against or so much as concerning the government; and although very frequently both in public and in private, discourses have been purposely introduced to the disparagement of his master, the Earl of Shaftesbury, his party and designs, he could never be provoked to take any notice or discover in word or look the least concern; so that I believe there is not in the world such a master of taciturnity and passion.

> He has here a physician's place, which frees him from the exercises of the college, and the obligations which others have to residence in it,

[1] Sunderland to Fell: 3 November 1684 (P.R.O. 30/24/47/22).
[2] Amsterdam: Remonstrants' MSS. J. 57a.
[3] Fell to Sunderland: 8 November 1684 (P.R.O. 30/24/47/22).

and he is now abroad upon want of health; but notwithstanding that, I have summoned him to return home, which is done with this prospect, that if he comes not back he will be liable to expulsion for contumacy; if he does he will be answerable to your Lordship for what he shall be found to have done amiss; it being probable that though he may have been made thus cautious here, where he knew himself to be suspected, he has laid himself more open in London, where a general liberty of speaking was used, and where the execrable designs against his Majesty and his government were managed and pursued. . . .

The Dean's proposal to give Locke a chance to defend himself proved not acceptable at Whitehall,[1] and a few days later he was duly expelled from the college [2] by the King's express command.

Was Locke unjustly used, or was there some truth in the charges? He himself denied them all unequivocally. He did so, for example, in a letter to Lord Pembroke, dated 8 December 1684 [3] in which he appealed to his noble friend to take notice of 'an unfortunate and exposed innocence'. Locke asked Lord Pembroke whether he, in the many years he had known him, 'ever observed anything in me of the kind I am charged with'. He urged Pembroke to ask the Dean of Christ Church 'whether my carriage in the College for so long a time carried with it the least mark of undutiful [sic] against the government'.

Next Locke mentioned Shaftesbury. He said 'chance and not my own seeking . . . threw me into his acquaintance and family'. Admitting that Shaftesbury had treated him with 'great civility and kindness' Locke added:

> Yet some of my friends, when they considered how small an advancement of my fortune I had made in so long an attendance have thought I had no great reason to brag of the effects of that kindness. I say not this to complain of my dead master, it would be in no way very decent in me. But in this extremity I cannot but complain of it as a hard case: that having reaped so little advantage from my service to him whilst living I should suffer so much on that account now he is dead.

Locke said he had never been of any clubs or cabals. He had made little acquaintance and kept little company in a house where so much came; and now, in Holland, when he had hoped to find

---

[1] Sunderland to Fell: 11 November 1684 (P.R.O. 30/24/47/22).
[2] Fell to Sunderland: 16 November 1684 (*ibid.*).
[3] Christ Church, Oxford: MS. collections. The letter was written from Amsterdam, but Locke explained that he had arranged to pass the winter in Utrecht.

repose, 'I am suspected to [have] writ divers scandalous seditious
libels'. In fact, apart from some verses, he said: 'I here solemnly
protest in the presence of God, that I am not the author, not only of
any libel, but not of any pamphlet or treatise whatsoever in
print. . . .'

Locke went on to deny the second charge against him: that he
was keeping company in Amsterdam with disaffected Englishmen.
He wrote: 'Those who are particularly named for my companions,
I assure your Lordship with the truth I would speak my last breath I
never saw out of England, nor in so long a time before I left it.'

As for the question why he had chosen Holland and not France
'for a change of air', Locke said he found it suited his health better:
'Besides wine also sensibly hurts my lungs and water since my last
sickness gives me the colique, and there is but little beer in France,
none in the southern parts'. These considerations had made his
choice necessary.

Locke explained he had been spending his time in Holland writing
out his thoughts *De Intellectu*, and in a postscript he asked if he might
send Lord Pembroke a part of the manuscript.

Several points in this letter call for comment.

(1) Locke's appeal to Dr. Fell 'whether my carriage in the college'
had ever seemed 'undutiful' was shrewdly addressed: but there were
others besides the Dean in Christ Church. One who had long
considered Locke's 'carriage in the college' highly suspicious—
Prideaux—reported to John Ellis on 12 November 1684 [1] a rumour
that Locke was lodging together in Amsterdam with Thomas Dare
of Taunton, one of the most notorious of the 'disaffected Englishmen' there. Prideaux also recalled from his own memory an
episode which had happened in Christ Church hall when Robert
West was arrested after the Rye House plot. Locke, Prideaux said,
had been 'very solicitous to know of us at the table who this West
was, at which one made an unlucky reply that he was the very same
person whom he [Locke] had treated at his chamber and caressed at
so great a rate when [Stephen] College was tried here at Oxford,
which put the gentleman into a profound silence and the next thing
we heard of him was that he was fled'.

Elsewhere in Oxford Anthony Wood noted [2] that when Locke left
Christ Church he had taken away with him several letters and

---

[1] B.M. Add. MSS. 28,929, f. 110.
[2] *L. and T.*, III, p. 117.

writings that would have 'spoken truth', but that he was 'never searched—which if he had been Popishly affected it would have been done'. Wood added: 'This Locke is supposed to be the author of "The Hue and Cry after the Earl of Essex his Blood", the same Earl of Essex who cut his throat in the Tower'.

So whatever Dr. Fell's testimony, Locke's reputation in Oxford was not altogether what he wanted Lord Pembroke to believe.

(2) Locke's comment on Shaftesbury is significantly at odds with what he said at other and better times about his former patron. Here, and here, so far as I can ascertain, alone, did Locke even hint that Shaftesbury had treated him parsimoniously.

(3) The story that the beer of Holland had drawn him to that country is so singular as to be positively comical.

(4) Locke's statement that he had never even seen the 'disaffected Englishmen' with whom he was said to be keeping company in Holland could not be more unequivocal. It was, however, false.

Among the men 'particularly named' as his companions was Thomas Dare. In Locke's own journal there is evidence that he met Dare soon after he, Locke, arrived in Amsterdam, and that he continued to see him at regular intervals until Dare left the country. For one thing Locke received his money from England through Dare—though he sometimes also received it through Isaac Hayes, another known English revolutionist. Locke's journal records financial dealings with Thomas Dare on *10, 29 and 30 December, 1683; 21 and 23 March, 4, 7, 8, and 11 April, 7 and 27 July, 1 August, 1, 11, 14, 20 October, 3, 17, 30 November, 1684;* [1] *3 January, 19 February, 7 and 16 April, 18, 25 and 30 May, 1 June, 1685.*

Thomas Dare as a goldsmith and former alderman of Taunton was a close political friend of Shaftesbury in Shaftesbury's lifetime, and one of the first of his followers to seek refuge in Amsterdam. He specialised in maintaining links between the fugitives in Holland and their friends at home. He served Monmouth—who reached Amsterdam towards the end of *1683*—as his political secretary, and he was comptroller to the committee by which the Monmouth Rebellion was organised. Apart from Monmouth himself, no 'disaffected person' in Amsterdam was more important politically or more notorious.

Although Locke had dealings with Thomas Dare, I do not wish to suggest that he did all that he was accused of doing. For one thing,

---

[1] All dates up to this point are prior to Locke's letter to Lord Pembroke.

he did not write the pamphlet he was said to have written about Lord Essex's death. In a letter [1] to Clarke, Locke protested: 'I am so far from writing any [libels] that I take care not to read anything that looks that way'.

The true author of the *Hue and Cry* pamphlet about Lord Essex's death was Robert Ferguson, a Scots revolutionist and professional pamphleteer then in Amsterdam, and acting as Monmouth's chaplain. I have no grounds for thinking that Locke himself had written any 'treatise or pamphlet in print'; but I fancy he went too far in saying that he had not even *read* the so-called libels, for there is among his papers now in the Bodleian Library a manuscript about the death of the Earl of Essex (not in Locke's hand) which argues, as does the *Hue and Cry* pamphlet, that the reported suicide was really a case of murder.

Furthermore, I do not doubt that Locke spoke truth when he said he spent most of his time during the winter of 1684–5 in Utrecht; but I am far from sharing Fox Bourne's belief that Locke went to Utrecht to get away from the society in Amsterdam of the other English refugees 'with whose political designs', says Fox Bourne,[2] 'he had little or no sympathy'. Fox Bourne knew little about the English refugees in Holland. He did not realise that Utrecht was a centre of revolutionary conspiracy as important as Amsterdam itself.

There are no references to Thomas Dare in Locke's journal after the summer of 1685 for the good reason that Thomas Dare was dead.[3] That was the summer of Monmouth's abortive rebellion in the West of England and of Argyle's invasion of Scotland. Dare sailed with the Duke as paymaster to his little army; he was put ashore on 10 June to raise support in Somerset, but a few days later he insulted Andrew Fletcher, one of Monmouth's few aristocratic lieutenants, and Fletcher shot him dead. It was not long before the whole rebel army was wiped out, Monmouth executed, and his supporters punished harshly. Two of his officers, Ford Lord Grey of Wark and Nathaniel Wade, bought their pardon by turning in-

---

[1] *1 January 1685* (Rand, p. 117).   [2] F.B., II, p. 17

[3] After Dare's death, Locke received a letter dated *July 24* [*1685*] from the widow, Ellen Dare, explaining that she could not yet pay him the money he had asked for. But she promised that as soon as possible 'your money shall be paid, for there is nothing more a trouble to me than not being able to pay'. She said Mr. Le Bon had undertaken to try to dispose of a bill her husband had drawn just before he left. (MSS. Locke, c. 7, f. 190.)

former. Their depositions gave rise to the belief that Locke had contributed money to the Monmouth rebellion. Not that Locke's biographers have accepted this story. Fox Bourne dismissed it as 'preposterous', but Fox Bourne knew only the testimony of Grey, and misunderstood it, as others have done.

Wade's confession (of which the manuscript is preserved at the British Museum [1]) is more interesting than Grey's. Wade recalled how he had met Shaftesbury in London when that nobleman was raising a revolutionary army. After Shaftesbury's death he, Wade, had tried to carry on the work, but he was discovered, and fled to Amsterdam. There he was advised by Thomas Dare to go elsewhere, and so went on to Switzerland, where he remained until April, 1684, when news of a revolutionary conspiracy going forward under Argyle's leadership in Utrecht brought him back to Holland. Mrs. Smith, the widow of a rich Englishman with whom Argyle lodged in Utrecht, offered to contribute handsomely towards the cost of the projected invasion of England or Scotland, and the winter of 1684/5 passed in preparations.

'All this while,' Wade [2] said, 'the Duke of Monmouth and his party know nothing of this affair.' Then 'at length the Duke of Monmouth and my Lord Argyle had an interview at Mr. Dare's in Amsterdam, where they immediately agreed and resolved to act in conjunction.'

Argyle, too poor to sustain any further delays, put to sea precipitately with an equipage 'which cost about £9,000. £1,000 was given by Mr. Lock and the rest I suppose by Madame Smith. . . .' [3]

Wade said that Monmouth had prepared his little fleet with more care than Argyle had done, though Monmouth had had to pawn 'all he had in the world' to get the money he needed through Mr. Daniel le Blon.[4] 'This equipage of the Duke of Monmouth cost over £5,500; as I remember £400 was given by Mr. Lock £100 by William Rumbold, £500 by Sir Patience Ward, and the rest was the Duke's own.' [5]

Lord Grey's testimony confirms that of Wade on the money question. He also said that Argyle had received, among other

[1] B.M., Harleian MSS. 6845, ff. 264 *et seq.*

[2] *Ibid.*, f. 270.

[3] *Ibid.*, f. 270 verso.

[4] There are several references to this name in Locke's papers. The 'Mr. Le Bon' mentioned in Ellen Dare's letter of *July 24, 1685* is doubtless the same man.

[5] B.M., Harleian MSS. 6845, f. 272.

donations, 'near a £1,000 from Mr. Locke',[1] and that Monmouth had received contributions from 'Mrs. Smith, Mr. Lock, Monsieur Oylinbrooke, Monsieur de Blund,[2] Mr. Bernardiston, and one or two others whose names I do not remember.'[3]

The reader will notice that neither Wade nor Grey named Mr. *John* Locke; in fact I believe they were both referring to another man. The clue here is a deposition made by Ezekiel Everest on January 19 1683/4 [4] informing the British government how Argyle with several Scotsmen 'and one Smith and his wife with Lock a tobacconist of London had come to Cleves and then returned to Holland. Smith and his wife and Lock with some part of the company went to Utrecht, where they are now'. Later, Everest mentioned the presence of Sir Patience Ward in Utrecht.[5]

Lock the tobacconist thus connected with Argyle, the Smiths, Sir Patience Ward and Scotsmen is clearly not Locke the philosopher. The Mr. Lock (or Locke, the spelling varies) who is mentioned by Wade and Grey is connected with Argyle, the Smiths, Sir Patience Ward and Scotsmen; and for this reason I believe that their Mr. Lock is the tobacconist of London and not the subject of this biography.

I should not have expected the philosopher to give money to the rebel funds: he was not a giving man. But I can readily imagine his taking part in the deliberations which led to the rebellion: although, again, I should have expected his voice to be that of prudence and caution; and since the will of the hot-heads prevailed, Locke may well have 'expected nothing of Monmouth's undertaking', as Le Clerc [6] said he did; though this remark was part of the story that Locke had never anything to do with the rebels.

His journal proves Locke's links with Dare and Hayes and Le Blon; Wade's deposition mentions other names which are connected with Locke's. One is that of John Freke,[7] named as a member of Shaftesbury's inner political circle; another is that of Sir Walter Yonge,[8] who was expected by Monmouth to rise in arms with him in Devon, but failed to do so. Both Freke and Yonge went from England to visit Locke in Holland when the excitements of the rebellion had abated: and both were his friends for many years.

However, Locke never altered his testimony that he had kept aloof

---

[1] Ford Grey, *The Secret History of the Rye House Plot etc.*, 1754, p. 112.
[2] Daniel de Blon again? [3] Grey, *op. cit.*, p. 118.
[4] C.S.P. Dom., 1683-4, p. 223.
[5] *Ibid.*, p. 227. [6] *Éloge*, p. xlv.
[7] B.M., Harleian MSS. 6845, f. 282. [8] *Ibid.*, f. 264.

from plotters and passed the winter of *1684–5* at Utrecht writing his *Essay Concerning Human Understanding*. Doubtless he did write much of the *Essay* then. On *May 3 1685* [1] when he heard from Clarke that Pembroke would like to see the manuscript, Locke explained that it had 'grown to at least three quires of paper' and that 'such a bulk is not of easy despatch'. Yet even the *Essay* provides a link between Locke and the rebels: for in a list of things recorded in the journal for *30 November 1684* as being 'chez Mr. Dare' is 'Fol: *de Intellectu*'. [2]

At all events the English government sought the extradition of Locke, together with other alleged conspirators in Holland. His name was eighty-fourth and last on the list presented by King James's agent to the States General.[3]

In England Clarke himself was arrested on 8 June, charged with being in correspondence with traitors in Holland. In petitioning Judge Jeffreys for his release, Clarke protested that his father had been a sufferer in 'the late rebellious times', and he swore that he himself had done nothing to incur the King's displeasure. After bonds had been given, Clarke was fortunate enough to be released.

The warrant for Locke's arrest, however, remained effective, and he decided to go underground. He had difficulty in finding someone to hide him, but in the end Dr. Guenellon's father-in-law, Dr. Veen,[4] agreed to do so. Limborch afterwards recalled: [5]

> By Dr. Veen's direction I offered [Mr. Locke] his house as a place of concealment in which he could stay without anyone's knowledge. I took him there; often visited him in his solitude and conversed with him for many hours at a time. All his friends' letters were by his desire sent to me to be forwarded to him, so that his honourable hiding-place might not be discovered. He entrusted to me his will and other valuables and gave me in writing the names of his nearest relatives, in order that I might communicate with them if anything happened to him. . . . Though Mr. Locke enjoyed in Dr. Veen's house all the services that friendship and good nature could render, the confinement was painful to him, the access of only two or three friends being allowed to him. Solitude wearied him and he longed to breathe a freer air.

[1] Rand, p. 136.
[2] Another item in the list is 'Copy 1 2 8°'.
[3] *Éloge*, p. xlv.
[4] Egbertus Veen (1629–1709) a medical practitioner whose house was on the corner of the Keizersgracht and the Westmarkt in Amsterdam.
[5] Limborch to Lady Masham, *2 March 1705* (F.B., II, pp. 22–5).

While he was in hiding Locke had a letter from Damaris Cud-worth to tell him she was married.[1] It is difficult to imagine the feelings with which Locke received this news that his 'Philoclea' had finally chosen another; but he cannot have been entirely sur-prised, for the word 'marriage' had occurred in several of the letters[2] she had written him during the previous twelve months. Her bridegroom was a widower, Sir Francis Masham, a baronet of North-Country origins, who had established some powerful connec-tions by marriage. His first wife, the daughter of Sir William Scott, had died, leaving him with eight sons and one daughter. His country seat was Oates, near High Laver, in Essex. Of both the house and the family I shall have more to tell in later chapters.

Other interesting news reached Locke from England in August 1685. It came in a letter[3] from Lord Pembroke written on the 20th of that month:

> Sir,
>
> I have often written to you with great satisfaction in hopes of an answer. You will easily therefore conclude with how much more I write now, since it will be the occasion of enjoying your company here in England.
>
> I need not tell you I have omitted no opportunity of contradicting all false reports to the King, and (as in so good a cause none can but succeed) I have so satisfied the King that he has assured me he will never believe any ill reports of you. He bid me write to you to come over; I told him I would then bring you to kiss his hand, and he was fully satisfied I should.
>
> Pray for my sake let me see you before this summer be over. I believe you will not mistrust me; I am sure none can the King's word. Your having so many friends, lest you should mistake who I am, I must subscribe myself,
>
> Your friend
Pembroke.

Locke did not hesitate to reject this advice. Far, indeed, from returning to England, he went into even closer concealment. He left Amsterdam for Cleves. On 28 September[4] he wrote from that city to Limborch saying:

---

[1] 14 August 1685 (B.L. MSS. Locke, c. 17, f. 126).
[2] *Ibid.*, c. 17, f. 128.
[3] *Ibid.*, c. 11, f. 193.
[4] Amsterdam: Remonstrants' MSS. Ba. 255b (Latin).

I think I shall stay here a long time for my health's sake. The pleasantness of the place, and my love of quiet, if not of idleness, as wel as my dislike of the trouble of travelling, keep me here.

He signed the letter 'Lamy' and he asked Limborch to write to him under that name, care of Mr. Meyer, secretary to the Elector of Brandenburg. In Cleves, Locke found time to read a number of theological works, including one of Limborch's own in manuscript, which he praised[1] for its rationality and impartiality, and another called *Sentiments de Quelques Théologiens de Hollande sur l'Histoire Critique du Vieux Testament*, which he liked less. This latter was an attack on Catholic theology from the point of view of liberal Protestant theology, but its liberalism was so very extreme that it seemed to some readers to eliminate theology altogether. Limborch told Locke[2] he thought the book should never have been published. Limborch had reason to feel as strongly as he did because the author was a Remonstrant, a newly elected professor on his own staff at the seminary at Amsterdam, by name Jean le Clerc.[3] Locke was already acquainted with Le Clerc, and was later to know him well, to regard him, indeed, as a better theologian than Limborch. But in that autumn of 1685 Locke was almost as critical as Limborch was of Le Clerc's extreme persuasions. Even so, Locke confessed to being in a dilemma on the subject of the verbal inspiration of the Scriptures:[4]

If everything in the holy Scriptures is to be indiscriminately accepted by us as divinely inspired, a great opportunity will be given to philosophers for doubting our faith and sincerity. If on the other hand, any part is regarded as of merely human composition, what becomes of the divine authority of the Scriptures, without which the Christian religion falls to the ground?

Despite his intention to remain at Cleves for 'a long time', Locke returned after a few weeks to Amsterdam and his old hiding-place

[1] *6 October 1685*, Amsterdam: Remonstrants' MSS. Ba. 255d (Latin).

[2] *1 October 1685*, B.L. MSS. Locke, c. 14, f. 1 (Latin).

[3] Jean le Clerc or Clericus (1657–1736) was born at Geneva, and studied under Mestrezat at Grenoble. Taking Protestant orders, he became minister to the Walloon and Savoyard congregations in London in 1682, but soon moved to Holland and joined the Remonstrants. Already a prodigy of learning, he became Professor successively of Hebrew, Belles-Lettres, and Church History at the Seminary in Amsterdam. His published works are numerous. His brother was Daniel le Clerc (1652–1728), a famous Swiss physician.

[4] Amsterdam: Remonstrants' MSS. Ba. 255d (Latin).

at Dr. Veen's house. Limborch, who had disliked the idea of Locke's leaving Holland in the first place (and described the man who had offered him refuge in Cleves as a 'vain braggart' [1]), was pleased to welcome him back. Locke began to move about the streets of the city again, though he prudently assumed the name of a Dutch physician, 'Dr. van der Linden'.

In Amsterdam just then Jean le Clerc was collecting material for his new periodical *La Bibliothèque Universelle*, which he proposed to run on lines similar to the *Nouvelles de la République de Lettres* which Pierre Bayle had started two years previously in Rotterdam. He enrolled Locke as a contributor, and in the second number of his periodical he printed Locke's *Method of Indexing a Commonplace Book*.[2] Le Clerc could thus claim the distinction of being the first editor to publish Locke's prose—at any rate, his signed prose.

In the meantime Locke had received a truly indignant letter [3] from James Tyrrell, who had been upset, first, by Locke's demand for the repayment of a small debt, and secondly, by Locke's request that he should hand over to Edward Clarke some papers in his custody:

> I could not [Tyrrell wrote] but call to mind that I heard you say that you liked not to leave your papers and writings in London, because of fire and other accidents; and yet you could send for all that you had left with me to be consigned to a hand that had no place else at that time to keep them in. Whether they have been since removed to any safer place I never enquired, since it is none of my business, but if that

[1] Limborch to Lady Masham: *2 March 1705* (F.B., II, p. 25).

[2] Locke's method consists of a series of lines separated into groups of five beside each letter of the alphabet, as follows in the case of the letter 'B'.

	a	3
	e	16
B	i	2
	o	8
	u	4

Over each of the five lines is written a vowel; and any word can therefore be indexed according to its initial letter and its first vowel by writing the number of the page on the appropriate line. In the example given, the word 'Bath' would appear on page 3, the word 'bread' on page 16, the word 'British' on page 2, and so forth.

[3] 20 January 1685/6 (B.L. MSS. Locke, c. 22, f. 52).

gentleman's papers had been seized (as they were long since like to have been) I know not in what condition you might have been like-wise. . . . It vexed me a little to see another hand, perhaps not long known, so much preferred before mine.

Tyrrell's reproaches were intensified:

So likewise [it vexed me] that last summer you could forbid my writing to you until you gave me notice of your return from your tour, and then could continue six months silent without even letting me know whether you were dead or alive; which troubled me very much, being then alarmed with so many false reports concerning you, not fit to be committed to this paper.

Tyrrell's distress at being ousted from Locke's confidence by a newer friend is easy to understand; but his protests were not likely to —and did not—restore him to his lost position.

In *May 1686* Locke was emboldened to emerge from hiding. A list of conspirators whose extradition had been authorised by the Dutch States General was officially proclaimed, and (thanks, per-haps, to Pembroke's intervention) Locke's name was not on it. He dropped the pseudonym of 'Dr. van der Linden'; but he con-tinued to move circumspectly and to correspond with certain friends in England as 'Dr. Lynne'.

The summer was enlivened for him by the society of Sir Walter Yonge,[1] a Devonshire baronet and one of Shaftesbury's old lieutenants in the House of Commons, who was travelling about the Dutch and Belgian Netherlands with his sister Isabella Duke, his brother-in-law Richard Duke, and widowed sister-in-law Elizabeth Yonge. Sir Walter and another well-known Whig, who was also with his party, by name John Freke,[2] sent an invitation[3] to Locke to join them all in Rotterdam in June. Among other things, Sir Walter wanted Locke's help and advice in buying books. A few years before, the baronet had built a new

---

[1] Sir Walter Yonge, of Colyton, Devon, was baptized on 8 September 1653, matriculated at Exeter College, Oxford, in 1670, and succeeded his father as Baronet in the same year. From 1679 until 1681 he was M.P. for Honiton. His first wife died in 1679 and he did not remarry until 1691.

[2] John Freke was a lawyer. The son of John Freke of Strickland, Dorset, he had entered Wadham College, Oxford, in April 1669, aged seventeen. He was called to the Bar from the Middle Temple in 1676.

[3] *8 June 1686* (B.L. MSS. Locke, c. 23, f. 144).

S

house at Escott, near Tallaton, Devon, and he was eager to have a good library there, although, as he admitted, he already had more good books than he could ever hope to read.[1]

From Rotterdam Locke went with his English friends to Utrecht, but he returned to Amsterdam towards the end of July when Sir Walter's party went on to Belgium. Sir Walter's sister, Isabella Duke, writing to Locke from Spa [2] to thank him for a letter he had written her, declared: 'There never was so much good nature, so much wit, so much friendship, and so much flattery put together in one letter before'. A few weeks later Isabella Duke wrote to Locke to say that she might be able to spend the next winter with him at Utrecht.

Prompted perhaps by his hope of spending the winter in Utrecht with Isabella Duke, Locke took rooms in that city with a painter named Gulick,[3] from whose house he wrote at the beginning of October [4] to Limborch saying: 'I have at last reached a place where I feel at rest'. Locke implied in this letter that he had left Amsterdam because he could not find lodgings in that perennially overcrowded city, but Damaris Masham imputed the move to the presence in Utrecht of an attractive woman. She wrote [5] to Locke saying:

> For the preference you pretend to give me over your Dutch mistress, you must pardon me if, not being willing to question the truth of what you say, I believe notwithstanding what you tell me of her merit. . . . A mistress is the most dangerous thing in the world to a friend, and therefore she must pardon me if I cannot be very much hers.

Damaris Masham mentioned the possibility of the Dutch lady making Locke marry her; for she could not imagine his remaining long unattached 'in a country where agreeable women are but scarce'. In another playful letter written from Cambridge two days later,[6] 'Philoclea' expressed doubt as to her ability of persuading Locke of her regard, as she put it, in 'my own absence and your mistress's presence'.

[1] *17 June 1687* (B.L. MSS. Locke, c. 23, f. 155).

[2] *29 July 1686* (*ibid.*, c. 8, f. 2).

[3] Jacob van Gulick (or Gillig) was born at Utrecht *circa* 1636, the son of Michiel Gulick. He married, first, in 1661, Hester Willerts; secondly, in 1681, Elisabeth Glover. He rented a house 'op het St. Pieterskerkhof' in January 1686 (*Oud-Holland*, XIII, pp. 37–9).

[4] *2 October 1686*, Amsterdam: Remonstrants' MSS. Ba. 255i (Latin).

[5] 7 October 1686, B.L. MSS. Locke, c. 17, f. 136.

[6] 9 October 1686, *ibid.*, c. 17, f. 138.

This reference to 'a Dutch mistress' may mean that Damaris Masham had got hold of a confused version of the plans of Isabella Duke. As things turned out Mrs. Duke did not go to Utrecht that winter after all.

In September [1] Locke sent Clarke the third book of his *Essay Concerning Human Understanding* asking him to show it to Lord Pembroke, but not to mention it to James Tyrrell, or 'Mr. Oakley' as that friend was called in their letters. Clarke did as he was bidden, but he had to report in December [2] that 'Mr. Oakley' had 'heard your treatise' was in Lord Pembroke's hands; though he, Clarke, hoped he had put Tyrrell off the trail by saying that he believed Locke had sent Lord Pembroke only an 'abstract' of his thoughts on the subject.[3]

In Utrecht Locke was still busily writing the fourth book of his *Essay*, but he had also written during 1686 another work which, though short, was destined to be, in its way, hardly less influential than the *Essay* itself. This other was a *Letter on Toleration*, originally addressed to Philip van Limborch, and published in Latin—the language in which Locke wrote it—at Gouda in 1689. In this *Letter* he attacked the idea that Christianity could be promoted or defended by force. Christ Himself, Locke said, was the Prince of Peace; and He had used always persuasion, never coercion. Indeed, Locke said, it was impossible to save men's souls by persecuting, tormenting and destroying them. Once again he thought it necessary 'to distinguish exactly the business of civil government from that of religion'. The business of the civil government was to secure men's lives, liberty, health and possessions. The salvation of souls was the business of religion; the civil authority had nothing to do with it. Locke held that the ecclesiastical authority ought to have no physical power behind it other than the sanction of excommunication.

He condemned the intolerance of so many Christians and declared that anyone who was 'sincerely solicitous' for the Kingdom of God ought to apply himself to 'rooting out' such immoralities as

---

[1] Clarke to Locke 16 October 1686 (B.L. MSS. Locke, c. 6, f. 20).

[2] 4 December 1686 (Rand, p. 174).

[3] Tyrrell, however, learned the truth from David Thomas ('Adrian') and wrote to Locke on 26 December 1686 (B.L. MSS. Locke, c. 22, f. 54) saying he was glad that Locke's papers were in 'so good a hand'.

'adultery, fornication, uncleanness, lasciviousness, idolatry and such like things' rather than the 'extirpation of sects'.

A *Preface to the Reader*, printed in the English edition of the *Letter* contains a sentence which is commonly attributed to Locke, one which was in fact quoted by Lord King as an epigraph to his *Life* of Locke:

> Absolute Liberty, just and true Liberty, equal and impartial Liberty is the thing we stand in need of.

These words were not Locke's. The Preface was supplied by the translator William Popple, an avowed Socinian. Locke did *not* believe in Absolute Liberty. He did not believe in liberty for atheists because he thought that covenants and oaths, which were the bonds of human society, could have no hold on an atheist; and he did not believe in liberty for Roman Catholics, because he regarded Catholics as the agents of a foreign power and a potential menace to the realm.

A man who believed in something much more like Absolute Liberty than Locke ever did arrived in Holland in 1686. His name was William Penn. Having been expelled from Christ Church twenty-two years earlier than Locke, Penn was more of a radical but less of a Whig. In fact he was not a Whig at all. He was a Quaker, with a certain sympathy for Catholics; and he was a personal friend of James II. The intolerance which Penn, as a Quaker, had suffered had been Anglican, not Catholic intolerance. It was the Anglicans who had expelled him from Christ Church; and when the Anglicans had put him in the Tower in 1668 for publishing an unlicensed theological pamphlet, it was the Catholic Duke of York who secured his release. When the Duke of York became James II he set free no fewer than 1,200 Quakers from prison during the first year of his reign. Nor was the situation any different in the colonies. Quakers were persecuted in all the Calvinist and Anglican American provinces, but they enjoyed complete liberty of conscience in Lord Baltimore's Catholic colony of Maryland. Penn could see no reason whatever for denying the same freedom to Catholics.

Penn was altogether a singular man: he was at once a pacifist and a swordsman, a mystic and a shrewd administrator, a preacher and a courtier, a reformer and an overlord, an ascetic and a *gourmet*. Receiving from the English King a large province in North America in lieu of a Crown debt to his father, he had found himself the proprietor of a colony—of Pennsylvania—and thus in the position, unique in Quaker history, of being able to create a model society or Christian Utopia. He crossed the Atlantic in 1682, and his first Frame of Government for Pennsylvania bore the date of that year. He gave a copy of it to Locke in Holland in 1686.

The Quakerly constitution which Penn had drafted was not a democratic one. Civil liberties were assured, and there was to be an elected assembly, but the greatest power was vested in a second chamber or upper house. When Penn offered this Frame of Government to the people of Pennsylvania they did not like it. They wanted a constitution at least as democratic as that of the neighbouring province of New Jersey.

'For the love of God and me and the poor country,' Penn said [1] to his people, 'be not so governmentish, so noisy and open in your dissatisfactions.'

Locke, when he examined Penn's Frame of Government, did not object to its being undemocratic, but he had other faults to find. He copied into his journal excerpts from the proposed laws of Pennsylvania together with comments of his own. The following [2] are the most interesting:

§ And if any person shall abuse or deride any other for his different persuasion and practice in matters of religion, such shall be looked on as a disturber of the peace and punished accordingly.

[J. L.]: Matter of perpetual prosecution and animosity.

§Whosoever shall speak loosely and prophanely of Almighty God, Christ Jesus, the Holy Spirit and the Scriptures of truth shall pay 5s. or 5 days imprisonment.

[J. L.]: Q. What is loosely or prophanely?

§ Adultery to be punished with 12 months imprisonment in the house of correction and longer if the chief magistrate think meet.

[J. L.]: Arbitrary power.

§ Incest: forfeiture of half the estate.

[J. L.]: To whom?

The foregoing notes refer to the *laws* of Pennsylvania. The following notes refer to the political structure:

[1] Robert Proud, *History of Pennsylvania*, Philadelphia, 1798, II, p. 297.
[2] *Journal, November 1686.*

§ The freemen to meet in one place to choose their provincial council of seventy-two.

[J. L.]: Inconvenient.

[They] shall choose [the] seventy-two of most note for their wisdom, virtue and ability.

[J. L.]: What if they are not such?

§ Two-thirds of the provincial council to be a quorum in matters of moment and one-third in matters of lesser moment.

[J. L.]: Query the precise boundary between matters of moment and matters of lesser moment?

§ That the governor and provincial council shall take care of the peace and safety of the province.

[J. L.]: Otherwise than by the execution of the laws? If not, this paragraph is superfluous.

§ Punish malversation in the Treasury.

[J. L.]: Arbitrarily?

§ Erect and order all public schools.

[J. L.]: The surest check upon liberty of conscience, suppressing all displeasing opinions in the bud. . . .

§ The Governor and Council to create what courts of justice and officers they think fit.

[J. L.]: Dangerous.

Locke's final comment on Penn's constitution was devastating:

But the whole is so far from a frame of government that it scarce contains a part of the materials.

At the end of November Locke received an unexpected blow. He was told he must leave Utrecht. Since June he had supposed himself free from danger so long as he remained on Dutch soil, but some enemy must have reported him to the Utrecht authorities as an 'undesirable alien'.

He wrote to Limborch on *12 December 1686*:[1]

The expulsion of which you have heard I do not understand, nor do I wish it talked about, although perhaps I shall have to come to you again. I confess that a removal from this place will be somewhat inconvenient to me on account of my luggage. I require books, for which it is not easy to find a place of storage. If I can get no other quarters, I hope you will forgive me if I send them to you, and ask you to stow them away in some garret or other in your house, until I find a more

---

[1] Amsterdam: Remonstrants' MSS. Ba. 255l (Latin).

convenient place. My only regret is that I give trouble to my friends. This rest does not affect me.

He also asked Limborch to look out lodgings for him in Amsterdam, to which city a day or two later he returned. Lodgings were not to be had, and Locke had once more to accept the private hospitality of his Remonstrant friends.

He 'found reason',[1] though he did not say what reason, that winter to alter his will; and explained in a letter [2] to Edward Clarke:

> My uncle [Peter Locke] left issue only by two daughters. William Stratton's wife, one of them, is thereby one of the co-heirs of that little estate at Belluton, etc. My intention is, if he [William Stratton] acquit himself well in looking after my affairs, in acknowledgment of his pains and kindness to settle the whole estate on his son by my cousin, during the son's life and his sister's, reserving a reasonable rent to my heirs. For the other daughter of my uncle has left a son too [Peter King, to whom] I have very little obligation.
>
> This is my intention if my cousin Stratton so look after my affairs in his hands [and] his negligence occasion me not either loss or trouble. But if I find he manages it so ill that I make little or nothing of it, I shall think of disposing of it in some other way.

On the last day of the year 1686 the last book of Locke's *Essay Concerning Human Understanding* was finished. The author sent the manuscript to Clarke with a letter [3] saying:

> You have here at length the fourth and last book of my scattered thoughts concerning the *Understanding*, and I see now more than ever that I have reason to call them scattered, since never having looked them over all together till since this last part was done, I find the ill effects of writing in patches and at distant times as this whole Essay has been. For there are so many repetitions in it, and so many things still misplaced, that though I venture it confused as it is, to your friendship, yet I cannot think these papers in a condition to be showed anyone else till by another review I have reduced them into yet better order.

[1] Locke to Clarke, *14 December 1686* (Rand, p. 175).
[2] *26/8 January 1687* (*ibid.*, p. 184).
[3] *31 December 1686* (*ibid.*, p. 177).

Chapter Twenty

THE ESSAY CONCERNING HUMAN UNDERSTANDING

IN the Epistle to the Reader, printed at the beginning of the published version of his *Essay Concerning Human Understanding*, Locke says that in an age of such 'master builders' as Boyle and Sydenham and Huygenius and 'the incomparable Mr. Newton' it is, for him, 'ambition enough to be employed as an under-labourer in clearing the ground a little and removing some of the rubbish that lies in the way to knowledge'. Despite this modest explanation of his purpose, Locke is generally, and, I think, rightly, believed to have done much more. He has indeed been called the founder of modern empiricism. In a sense perhaps he was. And yet his empiricism was of a peculiar kind, for he also entertained several notions which are all characteristic of rationalism—of 'rationalism', that is, which is by definition antithetical to empiricism.[1]

The earliest draft of the *Essay* ('Draft A') begins with an unequivocal assertion of empiricism: 'I imagine that all knowledge is founded on and ultimately derives itself from sense, or something analogous to it, which may be called sensation.' A similar pronouncement is made in the second Book of the final version.[2] But Locke's rationalism must not be underestimated. He maintains, for example, as the Thomists do, that the existence of God can be established by rational proofs;[3] and his doctrine of substance,[4] equivocal as it is, is still more scholastic than empirical; and he never

[1] Rationalism in this sense is a theory which maintains that it is possible to have knowledge of synthetic truths, including existential propositions, *a priori*; empiricism maintains that synthetic truths can only be established on the basis of sensory observation and introspection.

[2] 'Our observation, employed either about external sensible objects, or about the internal operations of our minds, perceived and reflected on by ourselves, is that which supplies our understanding with all the materials of thinking.' *Essay*, II, i., 2 (In *Draft B*, where the opening resembles that of the *Essay*, Locke does not reach this point until § 17).

[3] *Essay*, IV, x.   [4] *Ibid.*, II, xxiii.

moves an inch from the belief that the principles of morality are as demonstrable as those of geometry.[1]

These examples are by no means the whole of the story. There were two main intellectual currents which governed the development of Locke's mind. One was the unformulated *ad hoc* empiricism of Newton and Boyle and the other Royal Society *virtuosi*. The other was the systematic rationalism of Descartes.[2] The two currents met in Locke as they had met in Gassendi, though in Locke the empirical stream was the stronger one, and his historic mission was to formulate the unformulated empiricism of the *virtuosi* in a manner which was significantly new.

Yet the influence of Descartes is obvious in the very way Locke sets about his task. He says he proposes 'to enquire into the original, certainty, and extent of human knowledge'.[3] He thinks that some sort of epistemological credential can be provided for knowledge by tracing it back to its origins in sensing. 'Originals' are thus linked to 'certainty' and 'extent'; and this preoccupation with 'certainty' and 'extent' is very characteristic of the Cartesian mind. Indeed, there is something alien to empiricism in Locke's whole aim of determining *in advance* the limits of human knowledge.

A recurrent word—perhaps the most important word—in the *Essay* is a Cartesian one: 'idea'. Locke's use of the word is curious. He does not merely say that we have ideas in our minds when we think; he says we have ideas in our minds when we see, hear, smile, taste, or feel. The core of his epistemology is the notion that the objects of perception are not *things*, but ideas which are derived in

---

[1] *Essay*, IV, iii, 18. This assertion is anticipated by an entry in Locke's journal (B.L. MSS. Locke, F 5) dated 26 July 1681: 'There are two sorts of knowledge in the world: general and particular founded upon two different principles, i.e. true ideas and matters of fact or history. All genuine knowledge is founded only upon true ideas, and so far as we have these, we are capable of demonstration of [demonstrable] certain knowledge, for he that has a true idea of a circle or a triangle is capable of knowing any demonstration. . . . The first and great step therefore to knowledge is to get the mind furnished with these true ideas which the mind being capable of having of moral things as well as figure, I cannot but think morality as well as mathematics capable of demonstration if men would employ their understanding to think about it and not give themselves up to the lazy traditional way of talking one after another.'

[2] *Vide* in this connection 'The Influence of Descartes on John Locke: A Bibliographical Study', by C. S. Ware (Mrs. C. S. Johnson), in *Revue Internationale de Philosophie*, Paris, April 1956, pp. 1–21.

[3] *Essay*, Intro. 2.

part from things in the external world but which also depend to some extent in our own minds for their existence. Locke defines an 'idea' as the 'object of the understanding',[1] whether it is a notion, an entity, or an illusion; perception being for him a 'species of understanding'.

Looking as he does to 'originals' for the credential of 'certainty', Locke next asks: How do ideas come to be in our minds?

His *Essay* in its final form begins with a refutation of the doctrine that certain principles are innate.[2] He suggests that certain principles have been thought to be innate only because men cannot remember when they first learned them. Locke's belief is that we are born in total ignorance, and that even our theoretical ideas of identity, quantity and substance are derived from experience.

Locke says a child gets its idea of black and white, of sweet and bitter *before* and not after it gets an idea of impossibility or identity: 'The senses at first let in particular ideas, and furnish the yet empty cabinet. . . .'[3] Afterwards the mind abstracts these theoretical ideas, and so 'comes to be furnished with ideas and language, the materials about which to exercise its discursive faculty'.[3] In the child's development, 'the use of reason becomes daily more visible as these materials that give it employment increase'.[3]

Locke has thus to defend the belief that everything which he calls an idea is derived from sensation, though he admits that idea may also be produced by what he calls reflection—'remembering, considering, reasoning, etc.'[4] He says that ideas are of two kinds: simple and complex. Simple ideas are those which the mind receives passively. Complex ideas are produced by the exercise of the mind's own powers.[5]

It is in his chapters on 'simple ideas'[6] that Locke sets out the main lines of his theory of perception. Asked what it is that they see, smell, hear, taste or touch when they look, smell, listen, taste or touch, most people would answer 'things', though they might add, 'but sometimes illusions, chimeras, mirages, which are not real things'. They would probably agree that there are two elements in perception: the observer and the object. Locke differs from this plain view in two respects: first, he says that what we perceive is

---

[1] *Essay*, Introduction, § 8.
[2] *Ibid.*, I, i–iii.
[3] *Ibid.*, I, i, 15.
[4] *Ibid.*, II, i.
[5] *Ibid.*, II, xii.
[6] *Ibid.*, II, ii–xii.

always an idea, as distinct from a thing; secondly, that there are not two but three elements in perception: the observer, the idea and the object the idea represents.

The reasoning which leads Locke to this conclusion is not difficult to appreciate; it is an argument which is heard by every under-graduate who reads philosophy. We look at a penny. We are asked to describe it: it is circular in shape and some sort of brown in colour and of modest dimensions. But do we really see just this? We look again and what we see is elliptical, not circular; in some lights it is golden, in others black; close to the eye, it is large, sur-veyed from across the room, it is tiny. The actual penny, we admit, cannot be *both* circular and elliptical, *both* golden all over and black all over. So we may be led to agree that there must be something which is one and something which is the other, something which changes and something which does not, the 'penny' we see and the real penny, or, in Locke's own words, the 'idea' in the mind of the observer and the material 'body' itself.

Or take the case of an illusion. 'Is this', Macbeth asked, 'a dagger which I see before me?' It is not, as we all know, a *real* dagger. But it is not nothing. It is, Locke would say, an 'idea', but one which is wholly *mind*-dependent and so distinct from an idea representing a material object or body.

Locke argues that material objects or bodies possess certain qualities which are 'utterly inseparable from the body in what state soever it be'.[1] These qualities, which Locke calls *primary* qualities, are impenetrability, extension, figure, mobility and number. They are 'primary' because a material object must always retain them, however much it is altered in other ways. There are also *secondary* [2] qualities, such as colour, taste and sound. Secondary qualities vary with the percipient. In fact Locke says more than this. He says that secondary qualities depend for their existence on the mind of a percipient.

A flower is not coloured to a blind man's eye, and a violin makes no music to a deaf man's ear. This, according to Locke, is because colour and sound are secondary qualities, which are 'only powers' [3] of producing various ideas in the minds of people equipped with the

[1] *Essay*, II, viii, 9.

[2] *Ibid.* Boyle in his book *The Origin of Formes and Qualities* published at Oxford in 1666, distinguished the qualities of matter as primary and secondary, as indeed did several other seventeenth century writers before Locke.

[3] *Essay*, II, viii, 23.

appropriate senses. But even for the blind and the deaf flowers and violins have extension, impenetrability, figure, mobility and number, for such qualities are in no way dependent on an observer. The secondary qualities may change whenever observers change; primary qualities can change only if they change (or are changed) in themselves.

Locke's theory of perception has attracted more notice than the rest of his *Essay*, possibly because, as a theory, it is both easily defended and easily refuted. It is easily defended in the twentieth century on the basis of what is said by many physicists about the structure of the universe and by many physiologists about the mechanism of perception. The penny we give a child looks brown, feels warm, and tastes sharp if the child is imprudent enough to place it on his tongue. The penny we give to the scientist is described as a congeries of electrons and protons. Seeing, feeling, tasting pennies is no mystery to him. He tells us that certain light-waves strike the retina of the observer's eye, while waves of the other kinds strike nerve terminals of the other sorts; and these processes produce those modifications of the neurological system which we call 'seeing', 'feeling' or 'tasting' a penny. Neither the electrons nor the protons, neither the waves outside nor the modifications inside the system, are, however, brown or warm or astringent. Hence the reluctance of the scientist to say that the 'real' penny is brown or warm or astringent. But he has no corresponding reluctance to say that the 'real' penny has shape, size, impenetrability or position in space, for these are the sort of qualities with which physicists as such deal.

Nor is the distinction between primary and secondary qualities acceptable only to physicists: the plain man might be willing to agree if he tried to imagine an object divested one by one of its qualities; he could imagine it divested in turn of smell and taste and the other secondary qualities, but he could not imagine it divested of impenetrability or shape or size or position in space. For a body divested of such qualities would cease to be a body: a body without primary qualities would not exist at all.

Thus the case for the Lockean epistemology can still be made. Unfortunately, such arguments owe, as Locke's own arguments owed, much of their plausibility to confusion. The modern physicists who lend their suffrage to the Lockean theory of primary and secondary qualities are deceived about the significance of their own discoveries. In describing perceptual experience in terms of electrons and light-waves and so on they are explaining *how* it happens that we see things. They are not correcting our account of *what* it is we see. Because tables and chairs are analysed by physics as congeries of electrons and protons it does not follow that the tables and chairs we see are any less *real* than the electrons and the protons.

Electrons are perhaps in a sense more 'fundamental' than tables and chairs; but this does not mean that electrons are real and tables and chairs unreal. Primary qualities might also be said to be more fundamental than secondary qualities; but again it does not follow from this that primary qualities are actual properties of bodies, and secondary qualities merely mind-dependent ideas. As Berkeley demonstrated, whatever arguments there are for regarding secondary qualities as mind-dependent ideas apply equally to primary qualities. If secondary qualities cannot exist unperceived, what reason have we for thinking that primary qualities can?

If we are aware in our perceptual experience only of ideas which represent objects, and never of the objects themselves, there can be no means of knowing what, if anything, is represented by these ideas. The human predicament, according to Locke's account of it, is like that of a man permanently imprisoned in a sort of diving bell, receiving some signals from without and some from within his apparatus, but having no means of knowing which, if any, of these signals come from outside; or of testing their authenticity when he thinks they do come from outside. He cannot therefore have any definite knowledge whatever of the external world.

Locke, it must in fairness be said, sees this last difficulty himself, and he admits he does not know how to answer it.

After his attempt in the second Book to investigate what he calls the 'instruments or materials of our knowledge', Locke does not pass immediately to the question of what knowledge is. Such, he says, was his original intention, but 'on a nearer approach' he has come to see it is necessary first to consider the 'nature, use and signification of language'.[1] This is the subject of his third Book. His treatment of the subject is neither fully developed nor wholly consistent. First, it suffers from its dependence on the muddled and equivocal doctrine of ideas. Secondly, it involves the highly

[1] *Essay*, II, xxxiii, 19.

dubious notion that language exists *solely* for the purpose of communication.

Locke calls words 'external sensible signs' by which the 'invisible ideas' which our 'thoughts are made up of' may be 'made known to others'.[1]

Here he is suggesting that words are needed for talking but not for thinking. Surely he is wrong. Thinking itself consists often, though certainly not always, of words. Very many of our thoughts are 'made up' of words. The 'invisible ideas' of which Locke says they are made up are a fiction. Thoughts, being as often as not already in words, need no interpretation for the purposes of communication: they have only to be spoken aloud or written down.

But even if Locke begins his third Book with a mistake, he goes on to make many excellent points, and to anticipate much of modern analytic philosophy. A considerable part, and not the least valuable part, of this Book is directed against the scholastic theory that general words stand for 'real essences'. Locke argues that such words stand for what he likes to call 'sorts', by which he means that man, for example, is a sort and 'man' a sortal word. Only particular words or proper names have real essences. General words or common names have merely *nominal* essences, and are applicable to things only so far as things possess the attributes which men have arbitrarily chosen to indicate by those particular words:

> . . . men making abstract ideas, and settling them in their minds with proper names annexed to them, do thereby enable themselves to consider things, and discourse of them, as it were, in bundles, for the easier and readier improvement and communication of their knowledge, which would advance but slowly were their thoughts and words confined only to particulars.[2]

He argues that the words

> 'essential' and 'not essential' relate only to our abstract ideas, and the names annexed to them; which amounts to no more than this: that whatever particular thing has not in it those qualities which any general term stands for, cannot be ranked under that species, nor be called by that name, since that abstract idea is the very essence of that species.
>
> Thus, if the idea of body with some people [i.e. Cartesians] be bare extension or space, then solidity is not essential to body. If others make the idea to which they give the name *body* to be solidity and extension,

---

[1] *Essay*, III, ii, 1.   [2] *Ibid.*, III, iii, 20.

then solidity is essential to body. That therefore, and that alone, is considered as essential which makes a part of the complex idea the name of a sort stands for, without which no particular thing can be reckoned of that sort, nor be entitled to that name.[1]

Locke says 'a definition is nothing else but the showing the meaning of one word by several other not synonymous terms'.[2] On this basis he declares that 'simple ideas are not capable of any definition'.[3] What he means is that the meaning of a word like 'pineapple' can be taught only by showing the pupil an example of, or a picture of, a pineapple. This process is nowadays known as 'ostensive' definition, but Locke would not have considered that 'ostensive' definition was, properly speaking, definition at all.

The words of which we *can* learn the meaning from other words, are, Locke says, those which represent complex ideas or mixed modes. Precisely because complex ideas consist of several simple ones, the words which represent them can be defined by means of words (already known) signifying simple ideas. Complex ideas are, in a sense, 'collections' of ideas:

> In such collections of ideas, passing under one name, definition—or the teaching the signification of one word by several others—has place, and may make us understand the names of things which never came within the reach of our senses, and frame ideas suitable to those in other men's minds when they use those names, provided that none of the terms of the definition stand for any such simple ideas, which he to whom the explication is made has never yet had in his thought.[4]

This is why it is possible to learn the meaning of words like 'incest' and 'adultery' without witnessing actual instances of incest and adultery. Such complex ideas are 'made by the mind',[5] but 'they are not made at random and jumbled together without any reason at all'; [6] they serve 'by short sounds to signify with ease and dispatch general conceptions'.[6]

The meaning of all words is established by convention, and convention in the use of words like 'incest' and 'adultery' is unequivocal. In the case of many other words the meaning established by convention is by no means so precise. As examples of this large class of *vague* words Locke mentions 'duty' and 'honour'.

[1] *Essay*, III, vi, 4–5.   [2] *Ibid.*, III, iv, 6.
[3] *Ibid.*, III, iv, 4.   [4] *Ibid.*, III, iv, 12.
[5] *Ibid.*, III, v, 6.   [6] *Ibid.*, III, v, 7.

He says that one of the consequences of the doctrine of *real essences* is that philosophers are led to take up words like 'duty' and 'honour' with a view to seeking their true meaning. Many such philosophers claim even to have *found* their true meaning. Locke shows the endeavour to be futile and the achievement illusory. There is, in such cases, no real meaning to find: and the 'real meaning' which each of these philosophers purports to have found is nothing other than his own conception of what the word should mean. Such philosophers offer their own stipulative definition as the true definition, whereas, in fact, no stipulative definition is ever true or false; only lexicographical definitions which report the conventional use and usage of words can be true or false. A lexicographical definition can be no more precise than conventional use. And the conventional use of many words is often fluid and unsteady. Ambiguous words abound in every language.[1]

As Locke points out, 'the very nature of words makes it almost unavoidable for many of them to be doubtful and uncertain in their significations'; [2] and he shows how important it is for people to recognise the imperfections of language. He also draws attention to 'the several *wilful* faults and neglects which men are guilty of in this way of communication'.[3]

Deliberate misuse and distortion of language is usually done in the interests of persuasion, and it is done in several ways. Among those Locke mentions are the following: (1) Men coin new words which have no clear or determinate ideas annexed to them; or they take words to which conventional usage has already affixed distinct meanings, and they employ them without finding out what that meaning is; (2) Men use words *inconstantly*. Locke says, 'It is hard to find a discourse written on any subject, especially of controversy, wherein one shall not observe, if he read with attention, the same words . . . used sometimes for one collection of simple ideas and sometimes for another . . .'.[4] (3) Philosophers more than other men cultivate *affected obscurity* 'by either applying old words to new and unusual significations, or introducing new and ambiguous terms without defining either; or else putting them so together as may confound their ordinary meaning'.[5] This last habit, Locke observes, has passed 'hitherto under the laudable and esteemed names of *subtlety*

---

[1] This point is lucidly developed by Richard Robinson, *Definition* (Oxford, 1949).
[2] *Essay*, III, ix, 1.   [3] *Ibid.*, III, x, 1.
[4] *Ibid.*, III, x, 5.   [5] *Ibid.*, III, x, 6.

and *acuteness'*,[1] whereas in truth it destroys the instruments of knowledge and communication.

On this point Locke rises to eloquence:

> He that hath names without ideas, wants meaning in his words, and speaks only empty sounds. He that hath complex ideas without names for them, wants liberty and dispatch in his expressions and is necessitated to use periphrases. He that uses his words loosely and unsteadily will either be not minded or not understood. He that applies his names to ideas different from their common use, wants propriety in his language and speaks gibberish. And he that hath the ideas of substances disagreeing with the real existence of things, so far wants the materials of true knowledge in his understanding and hath instead thereof chimeras.[2]

Unfortunately Locke himself is guilty of the very abuses of language against which he writes so forcefully. In his 'new way with ideas' he 'applies the name' of 'idea' in a way which is 'different' from 'common use' and he thereby lays himself open to his own charge of 'speaking gibberish'. What is more he uses the word 'idea', the key word of his *Essay*, 'unsteadily and inconstantly'. Professor Gilbert Ryle has distinguished not less than five different uses to which Locke puts 'this Pandora's box of a word'.[3]

Indeed, Locke's attachment to the 'new way of ideas' is responsible for one of the greatest weaknesses of his theory of language. By insisting that general words must stand for abstract ideas, Locke blinds himself to the fact, which elsewhere he comes very close to seeing, that general words do not 'stand for' anything at all. To know the meaning of a general word is to know how to use it. To ask what a general word 'stands for' in the way that one might reasonably ask what a proper name stands for, is to open the door to all manner of confusion and perplexity.

Yet although Locke does not, and thinking in his terminology of ideas, probably could not see this, he does say at the end of his discussion of 'real and nominal essences' that many controversies which are supposed to be about reality are in fact purely verbal. He shows that often when men think they are at variance on a matter of principle they are only at variance in their use of a word; and that often when men think they are in agreement with one another they

---

[1] *Essay*, III, x, 8.   [2] *Ibid.*, III, x. 31.
[3] *John Locke: Tercentenary Addresses* (Oxford, 1933), p. 17.

T

are not using the same words in the same way, and are therefore in fact at variance. Locke even goes so far as to say that *most* of the disputes in the world are merely verbal, and there again he proclaims himself a forerunner not only of analysis but of logical positivism, too.

The last Book of the *Essay* is the most difficult of the four: the most confused and confusing, the most incomplete and tantalising, and yet in many ways the most important. Locke begins by saying that knowledge is 'nothing but the perception of the connection of and agreement, or disagreement and repugnancy of any of our ideas'.[1] This agreement (or disagreement), he suggests, may be of four kinds: (1) identity or diversity, (2) relation, (3) co-existence, (4) real existence. Our knowledge is sometimes *intuitive*, as when the mind perceives the agreement or disagreement between ideas immediately without the intervention of any other ideas, and sometimes *demonstrative*, as when it is reached through the medium of other ideas. Whatever falls short of intuitive or demonstrative certainty is not knowledge, but only *faith* or *opinion*.[2] There is also a third degree of knowledge, less certain than the first two, but which goes beyond mere probability, and this is sensitive knowledge, or knowledge of what is actually present before our senses at any given time.

This distinction between intuitive, demonstrative and sensitive knowledge comes straight from Descartes. The view that *knowledge* begins with intuitive relations between ideas is Locke's version of Cartesian intuition of relations between simple natures. He adds the thesis that abstract ideas are derived from ideas of sense to give an empiricist flavour to this particular *réchauffé*, but it falls short of a consistently empirical analysis.

Locke claims that we have intuitive knowledge of our own existence: 'we perceive it so plainly . . . that it neither needs nor is capable of any proof'.[3] David Hume, who more or less adopted the Lockean doctrine of ideas, disputed this on the grounds that he had no perceptual experience which conveyed to him the idea of a self:

> For my part, when I enter most intimately into what I call *myself*, I always stumble on some particular perception or other, of heat or cold,

---

[1] *Essay*, IV, i, 1–2.   [2] *Ibid.*, IV, ii, 14.   [3] *Ibid.*, IV, ix, 3.

light or shade, love or hatred, pain or pleasure. I never can catch myself at any time without a perception, and never can observe anything but the perception.[1]

Critics generally have taken Hume's side on this matter, but my own view is that Hume's account of the self is no more accurate than Locke's;[2] what Hume does show is that commonsense certainty of one's own existence cannot be reconciled with the Lockean doctrine of ideas. But this only proves, I think, that the doctrine of ideas is wrong.

Locke's emphasis in the fourth Book is on human ignorance. Our knowledge, he says, 'is not only limited to the paucity and imperfections of the ideas we have, and which we employ about it. . . .'[3] It is something still more circumscribed.

Our knowledge of identity and diversity in ideas extends only as far as our ideas themselves; our knowledge of their co-existence extends but a little way because knowledge of any necessary connection between primary and secondary qualities is, according to Locke, unattainable. As for our knowledge of the relations between abstract ideas, Locke confesses he does not know how far it extends.

With the area of certainty thus diminished, Locke does not deny us the possibility of an assurance which falls short of knowledge. His doctrine of substance is an example of one sort of assurance. He maintains that substance is somehow present in all things or bodies, although we do not see or feel it. What we see and feel are the primary and secondary qualities of things. Substance is what stands under or props up those qualities. The word '*substance*' is a transliteration of the Latin *substantia*, itself derived from *sub*, 'under', and *stare*, 'stand'. Locke says he believes in its existence because he thinks that the qualities and properties we discern must belong to or inhere in *something*, even though we do not discern that 'something'. That it is a mysterious 'something' Locke freely admits:

> . . . it seems probable to me, that the simple ideas we receive from sensation and reflection are the boundaries of our thoughts; beyond which the mind, whatever efforts it would make, is not able to advance one jot, nor can it make any discoveries, when it would pry into the nature and hidden causes of those ideas.[4]

---

[1] *A Treatise of Human Nature*, Book One, IV, § 6.
[2] For some criticisms of Hume's theory of the self *vide* C. A. Mace in the *Proceedings of the Aristotelian Society* (Supplementary Volume), London, 1939.
[3] *Essay*, IV, iii, 6. [4] *Ibid.*, II, xxiii, 29.

Berkeley accused Locke of 'bantering with substance', but critics in Locke's own time brought an even more serious charge against him. They accused him of undermining religion. The scholastic doctrine of substance was important to Christian theologians because it enabled them to give a rational explanation of the otherwise baffling dogmas of the Eucharist, the Incarnation and the Trinity. It was for this reason that Dr. Stillingfleet, Bishop of Worcester, said that Locke, having 'almost discarded substance out of the reasonable part of the world', had thereby promoted atheism. Locke denied that he had done anything of the kind, and in his published *Letters to the Bishop of Worcester* he repeated what he had said in the *Essay* to the effect that men's rational minds *cannot conceive* how ideas 'should exist alone nor in one another', and so 'suppose them existing in and supported by some common subject'. Locke's point was that one *had* to believe in substance, even though he could find no proof of its existence.

Dr. Stillingfleet had grounds for his alarm, and his criticism was a valid one. For the sort of case Locke made in defence of the doctrine of substance was essentially an irrational one, and, as Professor O'Connor has said,[1] could only prepare the way for elimination of that doctrine from philosophy.

Locke did not himself, however, eliminate the doctrine of substance from philosophy because Locke himself was not only a philosopher. He was also a theologian. However limited his creed, however extreme his latitudinarianism, he was still a Christian. He did not think anyone should accept on faith anything '*inconsistent* with the clear and self-evident dictates of reason',[2] but he was willing to accept on faith certain propositions which neither reason nor empirical investigation could yield.

In that section of the *Essay* where he explains the difference between faith and reason, Locke defines *reason* as 'the discovery of the certainty or probability' of truths derived from 'sensation or reflection', and *faith* as 'assent to any proposition . . . upon the credit of the proposer as coming from God' by means of revelation, which must be hearkened to in matters where reason can afford no knowledge.[3] As an example of a proposition based on faith he gives the proposition that the dead shall rise. Experience affords no evidence of its truth, but it can be assented to because it is not contrary to

---

[1] D. J. O'Connor, *John Locke*, Harmondsworth, 1952, p. 73.
[2] *Essay*, IV, xviii, 10.   [3] *Ibid.*, 2.

reason and because it has the authority of the Gospels. On the other hand, the proposition that the body of Christ is in more than one place at the same time—a proposition implicit in the Catholic doctrine of transubstantiation—is contrary to reason, and cannot therefore be accepted, even as a truth of revelation.

The fourth edition of the *Essay* contains an additional chapter entitled 'Of Enthusiasm', in which Locke attacks the Protestant extremists who claim to have private illuminations from God. These illuminations Locke refuses to dignify with the name of 'revelations'; he calls them 'the ungrounded fancies of a man's own brain'.[1] He notices that no proofs are ever offered of the supposedly divine illuminations, instead 'confidence of being right is made an argument of truth'. He writes sharply:

> But it is not the strength of our private persuasion within ourselves that can warrant it to be a light or motion from heaven: nothing can do that but the written Word of God without us, or that standard of reason which is common to us with all men.[2]

By the 'Word of God' Locke means, of course, the Bible; but he reads the Bible critically. Anything which is inconsistent with reason he rejects as being some sort of mistake; the rest he accepts on faith. In addition to the kinds of knowledge and assurance I have already mentioned, Locke adumbrates, even though he does not fully clarify, another kind of assurance: scientific probability.

Professor Ryle,[3] in his well-known tercentenary paper, points out that Locke came 'within an inch of saying that . . . propositions which express "scientifical knowledge" are hypothetical. *They do not directly describe real existences.* They say what properties *would* follow, if something had certain other properties, and not that anything has them.'

Ryle explains the importance of this discovery. It revealed that mathematics did not, as the Cartesians believed, describe the real world: and that many philosophical statements which had been supposed to be 'entological' merely said 'what *would follow* about an ordinary object *if* it were of such and such a character'.

Ryle also shows how Locke moved from the realisation that there can be no knowing synthetic *a priori* truths which are also existential, to consider the basis of scientific laws, which are not merely lists of particular observations, but are general propositions holding good of

[1] *Essay*, IV, xix, 3.   [2] *Ibid.*, IV, xix, 16.   [3] Ryle, *op. cit.*, p. 32.

unobserved as well as observed instances of the particular type of phenomenon under examination. Locke asks how it is that we classify things in nature into sorts, for he sees that the general propositions of science will all be of the form that every object of a certain sort has certain properties: a creature is classified as a lion or a metal as gold, for example, because it is seen to possess certain qualities and is similar to other objects which have the same or very similar qualities. Thus the definitions we give of natural kinds do no more than list the properties we find to be concomitant. Just how many properties ought to be treated as necessarily concomitant we cannot know. 'But', Ryle continues:

> in Book IV especially he puts his finger on the real nerve of the difficulty, which is, of course, the nerve of the whole problem of induction. . . . The general propositions of the physical and other inductive sciences rest on the evidence of regularly observed concomitances of properties; and these concomitances are not self-evident or necessary. So the conclusions of these sciences can never reach the certainty of mathematics, and in Locke's rigorous use of the term science, they cannot constitute scientific knowledge. They cannot rise higher than probability.[1]

Ryle makes a wholly twentieth-century case for the greatness of Locke. He takes seriously Locke's claim to be an under-labourer removing some of the rubbish that lies in the way of knowledge, and suggests that Locke achieved it by teaching the whole educated world

> . . . that there are differences in kind, and roughly what those differences are, between mathematics, philosophy, natural science, theology, inspiration, history and commonsense acquaintanceship with the world around us. In a word, his achievement is that he gave us not a theory of knowledge but a theory of sciences. . . . He taught us to distinguish between the types of our inquiries, and thus made us begin to understand the questions that we ask.[2]

Professor Kemp Smith, a philosopher of a different generation and a very different standpoint from Ryle's, also sees Locke's chief merit not in the answers he gave, but in the questions he was the first to raise: 'the questions which he sets us asking are the problems which, as we have to recognise, still retain their central position' [3] in philosophy.

[1] Ryle, *op. cit.*, pp. 35–6.   [2] *Ibid.*, p. 38.
[3] Norman Kemp Smith: *John Locke* (Manchester, 1933), p. 30.

The *Essay Concerning Human Understanding* is a very English book, both in its merits and its faults. Its tone is at once moral and pragmatic, its style is homely rather than elegant, its idioms are often commercial. The pursuit of Truth, Locke said, 'is a duty we owe to God . . . and a duty also we owe our own selves'; [1] utility, for him, was at one with piety. He described Truth as the 'proper riches and furniture of the mind', and has indeed been mocked for doing so; [2] but he did not claim to have added to that 'stock'; he tried to show the conditions, or some of the conditions, under which the mind could acquire its proper riches and furniture. In this at any rate he abundantly succeeded.

[1] King, I, p. 187.
[2] Notably by T. S. Gregory in *The Listener* (11 November, 1954).

Chapter Twenty-one

ROTTERDAM

AT the beginning of the year *1687* a friend of William Penn's in Rotterdam, a Quaker named Benjamin Furly, invited Locke to join his household as a paying guest. Locke accepted; and he lived with Furly for the next two years. This Furly was an Englishman, the son of a former Mayor of Colchester, in which town he had been born in 1636.[1] Converted (with his father) to the Quaker faith in 1655, Benjamin Furly had emigrated to Holland as a young man and become a merchant. With the usual Quaker flair for business, he had prospered quickly, and while he was still in his twenties he bought a fine large house by the Haringvliet at Rotterdam, and a few years later he moved to an even more splendid one in the Scheepmakers Haven at the corner of the Bierstraat. When Locke went to live with him in February *1687*, Furly had two houses, the one in the Scheepmakers Haven, which he used chiefly for business, and yet another one in the Wijnstraat. Furly married his first wife, Dorothy Grainge, some time before *1665*, but his first child, Benjohan, was not born until *1681*. Four other children followed in quick succession.

Furly in his early years had been a Quaker extremist, and something of a burden to his leader, George Fox. Among other things, Furly insisted on wearing his hat during prayers at Friends' Meetings, for two very curious reasons: one, that since Friends taught equality between man and man (and thus refused to doff the hat to magistrates), they should apply the same principle to the relation between man and God; the other, that there was no difference 'betwixt the man and woman outward'.[2] Fox was furious about this.

'Oh that thou shouldst lift up thy heel against the righteous!' he exclaimed [3] to Furly, choosing an odd metaphor to describe some-

[1] William I. Hull, *Benjamin Furly and Quakerism in Rotterdam* (Swarthmore, U.S.A., 1941).
[2] London: Friends House Library, Crosse MSS., f. 22-5.
[3] Swarthmore (U.S.A.) MSS., VII, f. 107.

one's failure to lift his hat, but making it quite clear that he thought Furly a 'very dangerous spirit' [1] in the Society of Friends. Furly gave way to Fox, and even went so far as to publish a *Recantation on the Hat Question*. With maturity Furly lost his extreme convictions, and finally, by an ironical twist of events, he was more or less dismissed by the Quakers in Holland for having 'uncovered his head in courtship' [2] to a rich widow. This last breach of Quaker etiquette happened when Furly was an elderly man, but already at the age of fifty, when Locke went to live with him, he was much more broad-minded and liberal than most seventeenth-century Quakers.

When the province of Pennsylvania was established Penn sent Furly a copy of his *Frame of Government* and *Laws of Pennsylvania*. Furly's comments on these papers have been preserved by the Historical Society of Pennsylvania,[3] and it is interesting to compare them with the criticisms of Penn's scheme which appear in Locke's journal. Locke wrote his criticisms in *November 1686*; Furly's were written in *1682*, written therefore in time to influence Penn, and according to one of Penn's biographers,[4] the provisions for the protection of aliens inserted in the Act of Settlement at Philadelphia were 'the fruit of Furly's suggestion'. Unlike Locke, Furly was critical of Penn's departure from democratic principles, and he urged Penn to give his assembly the right 'to make and abolish all laws'. He also suggested a means of ending slavery, and he proposed a form of income tax to pay for free schools, hospitals and almshouses. Clearly, therefore, Furly—who had once been a close friend of that left-wing republican Algernon Sydney—must be counted among the early theorists of the Welfare State. In contrast to his views, Locke's seem all the more strikingly right wing and *bourgeois*.

A vivid description of Furly in later age was published by the German book-collector Zacharias Conrad Uffenbach,[5] who visited Rotterdam in 1710; he found 'an old, tall, slender, earnest, man' wearing only a thin, threadbare coat, despite the November weather, but looking thoroughly patriarchal. Uffenbach was impressed by Furly's library [6] of over four thousand volumes, including many

---

[1] Swarthmore (U.S.A.) MSS., I, f. 330. [2] Hull, *op. cit.*, p. 157.
[3] *Vide* also Julius F. Sachse, *Benjamin Furly* (Philadelphia, 1895), pp. 23–32.
[4] *Ibid.*, p. 23. [5] *Merkwürdige Reisen* (Ulm, 1723).
[6] After Furly's death in March 1714 his library was sold by auction. It fetched £7,638 19s. A catalogue was printed by Fritsch and Bohm (Rotterdam, 1714).

rare books, especially *suspectae fidei*; but he was disappointed by Furly's reluctance to talk about bibliographical matters. He complained that Furly refused to discuss any subject but the persecution of religious minorities by Catholic and Protestant governments alike. The only book he was allowed to examine was the original manuscript of the *Liber Sententiarum Inquisitionis Tholosanae*.[1] Uffenbach also recorded his amazement that a mere merchant, especially one of humble birth, should be as learned as Furly was in Latin, Hebrew and other languages.

Furly's sons and daughters were all very young when Locke arrived at Rotterdam; and, being fond of children, the philosopher soon made friends with them, especially with the youngest boy, Arent, whom he called 'Toetie'. When he grew up Arent Furly went to England to work, at Locke's suggestion, for the Earl of Peterborough, and to become a friend of the third Lord Shaftesbury. The elder boys, Benjohan [2] and John, known to Locke as 'Broer Benny' and 'Broer Jan', eventually followed their father into business in Holland. The daughters were called Joanna and Rachel.

Locke was happy in Furly's house; but his social life in Rotterdam was not confined to the home. He formed yet another club. He had only just set one up in Amsterdam [3] on the lines of that which

---

[1] More about this manuscript below.

[2] Benjohan's daughter Dorothy married Thomas Forster of Walthamstow, Essex. Their great-grandson, Thomas Ignatius Forster, published in 1830 some of the letters Benjamin Furly had received from Locke, Sydney and the third Earl of Shaftesbury. In his preface to this book, Forster explained that the letters had come into his hands on the death of his father in 1825, 'together with a large collection of the manuscript correspondence and other works of some celebrated writers who flourished in the seventeenth and eighteenth centuries'. He added: 'Perhaps the most curious object in the whole parcel of papers to which I allude is a MS. copy of Mr. Locke's *Essay Concerning Human Understanding*, written in a very neat hand, in a small 12mo book, but much crossed out and altered, and full of corrections in the author's own handwriting. There is a date 1685 to this book; but it is written in a much blacker ink than the rest of the work, and is evidently inserted at a subsequent period, at a mere guess; for I have good reason to believe the MS. in question to be the original copy of the work, just as Mr. Locke first wrote it, and even before he ever seriously thought of sending it to the press' (*Original Letters*, pp. iii–v). This MS. of the *Essay* is now in the Pierpont Morgan Library, U.S.A.

[3] Jean le Clerc wrote: 'En 1687 il voulut que M. de Limborch et moi et quelques autres de nos amis fissions des conférences, pour lesquelles on s'assembleroit tour à tour, une fois la semaine, tantôt chez les uns et tantôt chez les autres, et où l'on proposeroit quelque question, sur laquelle chacun diroit son avis dans l'Assemblee suivante. J'ai encore les Loix, qu'il souhaitoit qu'on observât, ecrites de sa main en Latin. Mais nos conférences furent interompues par son absence, parce qu'il alla à Rotterdam. . . .' (*Éloge*, p. li).

had met in Exeter House in Shaftesbury's lifetime; but the club in Rotterdam—which was called The Lantern—proved an even greater success. Furly, in spite of his high seriousness and his Quakerism, was fond of his pipe and his wine; and he introduced into The Lantern a convivial spirit which was alien to the Remonstrants of Amsterdam, but which Locke himself could still appreciate.

He told Limborch in a letter dated *14 February 1687*:[1] 'In Amsterdam I gave little thought to politics, here I cannot pay much attention to literary matters.'

A friend, he explained, had been claiming much of his time since he had been in Rotterdam. Although Locke's journal, in which the entries become increasingly irregular, slapdash and exiguous[2] in the year *1687*, affords no clue, other papers indicate that his visitor was John Freke, the Whig lawyer.

Locke wrote to Limborch on *8 March*[3] to apologise once more for having neglected his correspondence:

> Business of another kind prevented me, and though that immediate business is completed by the departure for England of the person with whom I was engaged, and I have now leisure enough for writing letters, I cannot get back into my old ways.

Only the day before, Locke had sent to Edward Clarke ('or in his absence J. Bonville') by 'Mr. Mol' the fourth and last book of his *Essay Concerning Human Understanding*.[4] His great philosophical masterpiece was now complete and the author could turn his mind to other matters.

Although there is little to be learned from Locke's own journal,[5] a small account book[6] kept by Sylvanus Brownover gives some idea of where he and his master went in the year *1687*. It records the cost of a dinner at Leyden on *21 April*; a porter at Delft on *23 July*; a chaise at Amsterdam on *28 July*; a journey to Haarlem and Leyden

---

[1] Amsterdam: Remonstrants' MSS. Ba. 255n (Latin).

[2] The first entry of a personal nature in Locke's journal for *1687* is one dated *8 February*: 'Paid Syl. a quarter's wages due Christmas last: Fl. 11; Item, given him to buy a hat: Fl. 4; Item, to buy breeches: Fl. 9.14. In all this quarter: Fl. 34.14.'

[3] Amsterdam: Remonstrants' MSS. Ba. 255o (Latin).

[4] 'I. 4. de Intellectu Humano'.

[5] Locke's journal for this period is, strange to say, full of entries on the subject of perfumes and gloves. Under the date *9 July* there is an entry of some 18,000 words in Brownover's handwriting and in Spanish with the heading 'Una Regeta para adouar Guanter siu ageite'.

[6] B.L. MSS. Locke, F. 34.

on *14 August*, to Rotterdam on *15 August*, to The Hague and back again on *26 September*; a dinner at The Hague on *13 October*, a porter at Delft on *14 October*; two nights' lodging at The Hague on *24 October*; journeys to Delft and Leyden on *15 November* and to Amsterdam on *16 November*. It was presumably on these visits to The Hague that Locke was presented to and made the acquaintance of Prince William.

Events in England were, in the meantime, gathering momentum. In April James II had issued his Declaration of Indulgence, which assured liberty of public worship to all denominations including Catholics and abolished the Anglican tests for admission to public offices.

James Tyrrell wrote to Locke on 6 May 1687:[1]

> Your discourse about the liberty of conscience would not do amiss now, to dispose people's minds to pass it into law whenever the Parliament sits. The thing [the Declaration of Indulgence] gives so general a satisfaction, that more are displeased at the manner of doing it than at the thing itself. So that I find few but the High Church [of England] men highly displeased.

Tyrrell's favourable account of the Declaration of Indulgence *may* have been designed for security's sake in case the letter should fall into official hands, but it is quite possible that Tyrrell's approval was authentic, that he took the same view of the Declaration of Indulgence as William Penn, with whom he was in close touch at the time.

Locke thought differently. Locke regarded the Declaration of Indulgence as a stratagem designed to foist a Popish rule on England, and time was to show that he was not far wrong.

James was rich enough to rule without the aid of Parliament. He built up a sizeable army, and Catholics were conspicuous among the officers he commissioned. He appointed a Catholic, Sir Edward Hales, Governor of the Tower, and the Catholic Earl of Tyrconnel Lord-Deputy in Ireland. As a Naval man, James had a special interest in his fleet, and he appointed a Catholic, Sir Roger Strickland, to command it. His closest Minister, the Earl of Sunderland, was converted to Rome; a Papal Nuncio was received, and a move was made to restore the Catholic hierarchy. Protestants were denied the right to carry arms.

---

[1] B.L. MSS. Locke, c. 22, f. 56.

Locke's most influential friend at The Hague was an English nobleman in exile there, Viscount Mordaunt. Born in 1658, Charles Mordaunt had matriculated at Christ Church in 1674, and left soon afterwards to begin an adventurous career at sea. His ship was impounded in 1680, not, as might have been supposed, for piracy, but because he had failed to pay his crew's wages. Shore-bound, young Mordaunt had taken to politics. He joined Shaftesbury's party, but only in time to witness its decline; and though closely connected with Essex, Russell and Sydney, he was spared their fate in 1683. He remained in England long enough to make an anti-Popish speech in the House of Lords during the reign of James II, and then fled to Holland. He went straight to Prince William and urged him 'to undertake the business of England', and (according to Burnet) he was the first English nobleman to do so.[1] Although William thought him too 'romantical',[2] Mordaunt came to have great influence at The Hague, and Locke, as Mordaunt's friend, owed much to that influence. Burnet himself Locke seems not to have known at all well. Indeed, according to Burnet's principal biographers,[3] Burnet held 'rigorously aloof' from such Whigs as Locke. Burnet, a personal friend of Argyll, though not a man of Argyll's political views, had left England after the Monmouth Rising, fearing to be found guilty by association. After travelling about the Continent he had settled in The Hague in the autumn of 1686; he was still anti-Whig, and wrote to a fellow Scotsman:[4]

> Here I fancy I may stay for some time. I have nothing to do neither with the Scots at Rotterdam nor with the English that are believed to be in Amsterdam, for as I have seen none of them, so am I resolved that my soul shall never enter into their secrets ... and I am further than ever from all things that lead to the drawing the sword against those in whose hands God has put it.

However, when William Penn, on a visit to The Hague in 1687, urged Burnet to return to England and make his peace with James II, Burnet refused. His views had moved to the Left; and, what was more, he had fallen in love with a Dutch heiress. It may be true

[1] *Bishop Burnet's History*, Oxford, 1823, III, p. 261.
[2] *A Supplement to Bishop Burnet's History* (Ed. H. Foxcroft), Oxford, 1902, p. xx.
[3] T. E. S. Clarke and H. C. Foxcroft, *Life of Gilbert Burnet*, 1907, p. 228
[4] To James Fall on *26 September 1686* (B.L. Add. MSS. D.23, f. 1).

that Burnet still 'held aloof' from Locke, but he corresponded, if only on theological matters, with both Limborch and Le Clerc.[1]

One of James's most unpopular and foolish moves in England was against the universities. His first action was against Cambridge. John Freke, in a letter [2] to Locke, mentioned this news and said it:

> makes all the Heads and Fellows of Houses there (and at Oxford, too) tremble; but I suppose had you continued a member of Christ Church you would not have been afraid, and therefore I desire to know what you would give to be restored to, and whether I shall use my interest to get you your place again. Mr. Cl[arke] is with me while I write you this and is very angry that I ask you the question.

Locke was angry, too; and his sharp reply to Freke elicited a placating letter: [3]

> Tell my friend who is so fond of a retirement amongst a few books and friends that I am sorry I express myself so ill that he did not understand me when I offered him my interest to restore him to his ancient seat. I thought when I had told him how much that place was altered and expected daily to be more and more altered for the worse, he would never have desired to see it again, and I believe when he reads it again he will see that I intended only to [be] droll on the subject.

Locke engaged in a more tranquil correspondence that summer with a friend from his years in France, William Charleton, alias William Courten, who had gone to live in the Middle Temple with a collection of scientific and other curiosities which was fast becoming famous.[4] Locke contributed many items to that collection, and Charleton in turn sent similar things to Locke in Holland.[5]

---

[1] *Vide* B.L. Eng. Theol., c. 23; and Burnet letters in the Remonstrants' MSS. in Amsterdam.

[2] B.L. MSS. Locke, c. 8, f. 167.   [3] 3 June 1687 (*ibid.*, f. 169).

[4] John Evelyn, who went to inspect it in company with the Countess of Sunderland, recorded in his *Diary* on 16 December 1686 that Charleton 'showed us such a collection as I have never seen in all my travels abroad, either of private gentlemen or of princes. It consisted of miniatures, drawings, shells, insects, medals, natural things, animals (of which divers—I think a hundred—were kept in glasses of spirits of wine), minerals, precious stones, vessels, curiosities in amber, crystals, agate, etc.; all being very perfect and rare in their kind especially his books of birds, fish, flowers, and shells, drawn and miniatured to the life'. The collection passed on Charleton's death to Sir Hans Sloane, and from him to the British Museum.

[5] In the Lovelace Collection (B.L. MSS. Locke, c. 5) there are twenty-nine letters written by Charleton to Locke between *February 1678* and July 1688.

In a letter to Charleton dated *12 August 1687*[1] Locke wrote:

... I have already spoken to a friend of mine to get you any rarities that he can light on in the East India fleet, which is now here every day expected. I the last week put into the hands of Mr. Smith, a bookseller living at the Prince's Arms[2] in Paul's Churchyard, twenty-six draughts of the inhabitants of several remote parts of the world, especially the East Indies. ... For the excellency of the drawing I will not answer, they being done by my boy,[3] who hath faithfully enough represented the originals they were copied from, so that one may see the habits and complexion of the people, which was the main end they were designed for, and therefore you must excuse them if they be not excellent pieces of painting.

I also put into the hands of the said Mr. Smith a little box filled with the seeds and husks of Foeniculum Sinense: the husks have a fine aromatical taste, and are used by the Muscovites to be mixed with their tea, as I have been told; which is not, I imagine, the most sottish thing they are guilty of. If you think the seeds will grow and you find to spare, I would be glad if you would send two or three of them, in my name, to Jacob Bobert, the gardener at the physic garden in Oxford, who may endeavour to raise plants from them. He is a very honest fellow, and will not be unwilling to furnish you with any curiosities of that kind ...

Writing to Charleton a fortnight later,[4] Locke said:

I herewith send you a letter and a little manuscript for my Lord Pembroke, which I beg the favour of you to deliver to his own hands if he be in town, and to send me what answer his Lordship shall please to honour me with. If his lordship be at Wilton, I beg the favour of you to send the whole packet away by the next post to Dr. David Thomas, at Salisbury, with the letter here enclosed to him.

Charleton replied to Locke on 28 August:[5]

I have received both yours of the *12th* and *26th instant* and according to your order, my Lord not being in town, I have sent the letters and manuscript into the country. Mr. Smith the bookseller is not yet

---

[1] B.M. Sloane MSS. 3962 f. 297.

[2] Samuel Smith. Once an apprentice of Moses Pitt, he was now bookseller to the Royal Society. A dealer in foreign books, and, according to Dunton, a good linguist, he was in partnership at Prince's Arms in St. Paul's Churchyard with Benjamin Walford. In his second letter to Charleton printed above Locke refers to Mr. Smith as a bookseller at the Feathers in St. Paul's Churchyard.

[3] Sylvanus Brownover.

[4] *26 August 1687* B.M. Sloane MSS. 3962 f. 295.   [5] B.L. Locke MSS., c. 5, f. 72.

arrived; when he comes I shall enquire of him for the favours you designed me, and send Mr. Bobert some seeds of the Foeniculum Sinense. He was recommended to me not long since by a very good friend, and I gave him a sight of the collection of plants I made at Montpellier and of the fine exotic ones you were pleased to send me, several of which he had never seen before . . .

The 'little manuscript' Locke wanted Charleton to deliver to Pembroke was an epitome of the *Essay Concerning Human Understanding*. Another copy of this epitome seems to have gone to James Tyrrell, for Tyrrell, in a letter to Locke dated 29 August,[1] mentioned 'papers' he had lately received from him. In the same letter Tyrrell said he was sorry that Locke did not feel able to finish his manuscript on the *Law of Nature*.

The history of this last document is discussed by Dr. von Leyden in the introduction to his edition of Locke's *Essays on the Law of Nature*. The probable reason why Locke did not wish in 1687 to print or even to complete his early essays on the Law of Nature is that he had so far departed from his old ideas on the subject that he regarded his early manuscripts as being beyond useful revision.

Another piece of information contained in Tyrrell's letter of 29 August was that his wife had died and that he proposed bringing their little son to Holland to put him under a tutor at Utrecht. Locke, probably anxious not to have too much of Tyrrell, discouraged this last proposal.

At the beginning of *September* Locke fell ill. Among other things, this prevented his attending the auction in Utrecht that month of the library of J. H. Ribbius.[2] Furly went alone, and bought on Locke's behalf books to the value of Fl. 128.7., though his own purchases came to only Fl. 20.12. These figures [3] suggest that Locke was not short of money at the time.

While he was ill, Locke received from Limborch [4] a presentation copy of *De Veritate Religionis Christianae*, which the Remonstrant had written against a learned Jew named Orobio.[5] The learned Jew

[1] B.L. Locke MSS., c. 22, f. 59.

[2] Johannes Hermanus Ribbius (1616–56) had been a well-known Calvinist clergyman, minister in turn of Haaften, Buren and Arnhem, and author of *Christelijcke Troost* (1647).

[3] *Vide* Furly's letters to Locke dated *13 September* and *20 September 1687* (B.L. MSS. Locke, c. 9, ff. 16–21).

[4] Amsterdam: Remonstrants' MSS. Ba. 255s (Latin).

[5] Isaac Orobio de Castio (1620–87), author of 'Cutamen Philosophicum Propugnator Veritatis Divinae ac Naturalis'.

died in the week the book was published, but without having read it, so Limborch could not be thought to have killed him.[1] Locke reviewed the book for Le Clerc.

He did not get well as quickly as he hoped, and early in October he wrote[2] to ask Limborch if Dr. Venn would send him some bottles of laudanum.

'Whenever I think myself quite better,' Locke reported[3] a fortnight later, 'I have another relapse.'

He was still confined to his chamber in mid-December, and then got up before he was fully recovered.[4] His motive for doing so was connected with the publication of the epitome of his *Essay Concerning Human Understanding*.

This epitome, a copy of which Locke had sent to Charleton for Lord Pembroke, was translated into French during the author's illness by Jean le Clerc, who had arranged to publish it in his periodical, the *Bibliothèque Universelle*. Locke wanted to have an epistle dedicatory to the Earl of Pembroke printed with it, but Lord Pembroke demurred:[5]

> Such thoughts need no epistle to recommend them. I do not say so to excuse my name to it, for I shall always be as desirous (by my name) to testify the satisfaction I have in anything you are pleased to write, as I am and ever will be (by my person) ready to vindicate anything you do. But pray do not let the hopes of seeing this [epitome] in print defer the satisfaction of seeing the whole at large, which I hope you will send me as soon as possibly you can. A chain is not to be commended for its strength by taking it asunder. I shall not therefore pretend to

---

[1] Locke told Limborch: 'I lament that Orobio was so soon taken from us, not because you have thus lost the glory of a triumph, for I know that if truth prevail you are indifferent to the reputation of a victory. Yet had he lived, it would have been gratifying to have drawn from him some acknowledgement of the force of your reasonings.' Amsterdam: Remonstrants' MSS. Ba. 255v (Latin) *30 November 1687*.

[2] *6 October 1687*. Amsterdam: Remonstrants' MSS. Ba. 255t (Latin).

[3] *Ibid.*, 255u (Latin).

[4] Writing to Clarke some time in January *1688* (Rand, p. 234), Locke said that his sickness had been 'uneasy, troublesome and long more than it was dangerous'. He explained: 'It began with a looseness which it was a good while before I could master, and when with much ado it was stopped, my stomach was so gone that I could scarce eat anything, and when I got some small matter down it was such a load to me that I wished it out again. When by very slow degrees I was got pretty well of those symptoms, a violent catarrh took me and held me not a little while in great disorder, which with ill weather that hindered my going abroad brought back some part of my former maladies. . . .'

[5] 25 November 1687. B.L. MSS. Locke, c. 11, f. 195.

U

commend this, since I can't do it without repeating the whole. But I will spare no pains where I may approve myself

Your friend and servant

Pembroke.

The epitome accordingly appeared in the eighth number of the *Bibliothèque Universelle*[1] without any dedication and bearing the following title:

"Extrait d'un livre Anglais qui n'est pas encore publié, intitulé Essai Philosophique concernant l'Entendement, où l'on montre quelle est l'étendue de nos connoissances certaines, et la manière dont nous y parvenons. Communiqué par Monsieur Locke."

Locke forwarded a copy of Pembroke's letter to Clarke, telling his friend:[2]

You will perceive by the enclosed that my Lord Pembroke is so well satisfied with the design of my *Essay Concerning Human Understanding* by the abridgements of some parts of it that I have sent him that he desires to see the whole discourse at large. I must therefore beg . . . you to send him that copy that you have, and this enclosed letter, together by a safe hand on the first opportunity. It would ill become me to refuse him this request were he still but what he was formerly, my old friend Mr. Herbert, much less will his present quality and the obligations I have to him permit me to neglect this opportunity of expressing my respects.

Discouraged by Lord Pembroke from publishing an epistle dedicatory to the epitome in the *Bibliothèque Universelle*, Locke nevertheless put one at the beginning of a reprint he had made for private circulation. It was partly because of the importance he attached to this reprint that Locke got up from his sick bed in order to go to Amsterdam and see it through the press. Locke conjectured —with good reason—that a wide distribution of the epitome would stimulate a demand for the publication of the *Essay* as a whole; and as the book was a very long one, some such assurance of public demand was important. His printing of the epistle dedicatory to Lord Pembroke was designed to further the same object: it was virtually a certificate of noble interest. Locke also hoped to receive from readers of the epitome comments and criticisms which might help him to improve or correct faults in the *Essay* before publishing

---

[1] pp. 49–142. [2] *30 December 1687* (Rand, p. 231).

it in full. Such criticisms were expressly solicited in a note [1] at the end of the epitome in the *Bibliothèque Universelle*, but this note was omitted from the reprint, where the epistle dedicatory splendidly assured Lord Pembroke that after *he* had judged his work it would be of small importance to the author what opinions others formed.

Apart from these points there is very little difference between the two printings. The reprint has a different title; it is called not an '*extrait*' but (more correctly) an '*abrégé*' ('*Abrégé d'un Ouvrage intitulé Essai philosophique touchant L'Entendement*'), and Locke's name appears at the end of the epistle, instead of the title-page; but the body of the text is identical, the same type having been used for both with only the running headlines and page-numbers altered.

Before he went to Amsterdam to see the printers, Locke wrote to Dr. Guenellon asking him to find him lodgings in that city, but that physician [2] replied saying that he would insist on entertaining Locke in his own house. Locke accepted his hospitality, but in the austere society of the Amsterdam Remonstrants that Christmas, he missed the gaiety of Furly's household and the Lantern Club. Writing to his Quaker host on Boxing Day, Locke [3] spoke wistfully of

> a cask of mum, a hogshead of cyder, and without doubt even now and then a bottle of wine or a zopy [4] among, for a more effectual remedy against phlegmatic humours and rainy weather; this I suspect, in my absence will make brave work, and heresy will rise up apace in the Lantern when so watered. . . .

Christmas delayed the printers' work on the epitome. Locke, vexed, wrote to Furly [5] complaining of having

> to wait here the leisure of drunken workmen, who have so great a reverence for the holy days that they could not till today quit the cabarets, the places of their devotion, and betake themselves to their profane callings. . . . It costs, as I have already told you, not a little pains and patience to be at any rate an author. . . .

---

[1] 'Encore que l'Auteur n'ait pas une grande envie de voir son Ouvrage imprimé, et qu'il croie qu'on doive avoir plus de respect pour le public que de lui offrir d'abord ce que l'on croit être veritable, avant que de savoir si les autres l'agréeront, ou le jugeront utile; néanmoins il n'est pas si réservé, qu'on ne puisse espérer qu'il se disposera à donner au public son traité entier, lorsque la manière dont cet Abrégé aura été reçu, lui donnera occasion de croire qu'il ne publiera pas mal à propos son Ouvrage' (*Bibliothèque Universelle*, vol. VIII, p. 141).

[2] *13 December 1687* (B.L. MSS. Locke, c. 11, f. 3).

[3] *Original letters*, p. 8.   [4] A pigtail cigar.   [5] *19 January 1688*, ibid., p. 25.

In the same letter Locke made an elliptical reference to rumours of revolutionary activity:

I hear people everywhere grumble, as if they suspected this approaching summer would be full of bustle; but do you mind your collections, as I am resolved to busy my thoughts about finishing my essay *De Intellectu* et *sinere res ire ut volunt*, which by many years' practice I find to be the best politics.

A week later he wrote to Furly saying:[1]

As to the news you send me, I know nothing can be done, after such a reprimand and such misdemeanours, but to put in Marc Coleman's petition. If you think I have not discretion enough to govern myself, I desire discretion may be put into me. I find it not at all talked of here. I have set your friends in England a gaping for the ducks, as well as mine for the sheep, therefore you were best look to it: but not half so much as a certain writer from Rotterdam has set several a gaping about a pardon, for 'tis not he alone whom you mention in a former letter, but here are others too that are at a loss and inquisitive about it, to whom it would be acceptable to receive some further and more particular notice. Pray, therefore if you know anything more concerning that matter, send me word in your next . . .

I suppose tomorrow there will be one sheet printed of my works, and there being but four in all, I hope, now their hands are in, they will go on roundly and not make me wait much longer.

A letter [2] from Edward Clarke brought this news:

My wife and I together with your little Mistress [3] arrived here about four days since, and on Wednesday last I waited on your honourable friend my Lord Pembroke, and with my own hand delivered your four books *De Intellectu* (all sealed up in clean paper) to him, having first carefully taken out all that was particularly written to me at the beginning or ending of any of them. My Lord received them with all imaginable kindness, as also your letter, which I delivered with them, and was very solicitous for your return into England this spring.

---

[1] *26 January 1688, Original Letters*, pp. 33–6.

[2] 27 January 1687/8, B.L. MSS. Locke, c. 6, f. 42.

[3] Apropos of this 'Mistress' Mary Clarke wrote to Locke on 16 February, 'though she is of a very good nature, and very apprehensive for her age, and seems to look mightily concerned when you tell her of a fault, and like a little saint, but next time it is forgotten then without we have had a little of the lady birch's help' (B.L. MSS. Locke, c. 6, f. 182). On *9 March 1688* Locke wrote to urge her not to use the rod (Rand, p. 253).

Locke had not learned this when he wrote to Clarke on *6 February*:[1]

> I suppose ere this comes to your hand you will have delivered the papers to my Lord Pembroke, else I should have desired you the same time to have with my service told him that I hear today or tomorrow the last sheet of the epitome of my *Essay* will be printed, and then I shall have nothing to do but to get it bound as soon as it is dry, and send it him by the first opportunity I can get. For notwithstanding he is pleased to do me the favour to read the whole, and so will see many things in the discourse at large better explained, which could not but be obscure in the extract; yet the abridgement itself will be of some use, since in that he will see my whole design reduced into a better order than when that copy was written.

At the same time Locke mentioned that 'Uncle Adrian' (David Thomas) and 'Mr. Oakley' (James Tyrrell) 'have promised I shall see them both this spring'.

In a letter to Furly dated *20 February*,[2] Locke asked his friend if he could 'find anyone going for England that will carry a little book of philosophy, but of four sheets, and yet has nothing in it of any affairs'.

The remark about the 'little book' (the *abrégé*) having 'nothing in it of any affairs' is interesting. What affairs, one would like to know, were on Locke's mind at that time? Clearly the preparation of the four-sheet reprint was not a sufficient task to keep him engaged for eight or nine weeks in Amsterdam. Part of the explanation may be Locke had become an extremely busy literary journalist. No longer was he merely contributing to the *Bibliothèque Universelle*: he wrote nearly everything which was published there between *July 1687* and *February, 1688*.[3] This meant that he was reviewing most of the outstanding new books in French, Latin, Italian and English. Among several dozen such books were the *Sentimens* of Erasmus, Thomas Stanley's *History of Philosophy*, William Cave's *Apostolici*, and Gregorio Leti's *Ritratti Historici*. The French text of the reviews was presumably a translation of Locke's original English.

I have knowledge of only one other task Locke undertook—a small one which also involved dealings with printers—and that was

---

[1] Rand, p. 243–4.   [2] *Original Letters*, p. 17.

[3] Mr. Laslett has established this fact on the basis of Locke's mark in his own copy of the *Bibliothèque Universelle*, indicating his work in Volumes VI–VIII as follows: VI, pp. 1–127, 229–236, 277–311; VII, pp. 1–49, 85–320; VIII, pp. 1–261.

the supervision of the impression of a little writing-book. In his *Some Thoughts Concerning Education*, Locke says [1] that the best way to teach a child to write is 'to get a plate graved with the characters of such a hand as you like best'; and at the same time to have 'several sheets of good writing-paper' printed with red ink for the child to go over with black ink. Such a writing-book Locke himself had made in Amsterdam that winter on behalf of Benjamin Furly for the use of Furly's youngest child. He informed Furly in his letter of *2 February 1688*: [2]

> . . . I have found a graver which I think will do our business and he tells me of a book-keeper in town who writes better than that writing-master I was with, whom we may get to write a copy as we will and then he will grave after it. The whole charge, as far as I can learn, will be about five ducatoons. . . .

Furly agreed [3] to this proposal and specified that 'I would have them printed upon the best thick writing paper and 500 of them in the palest yellow.'

Dr. Forster, in the first edition of his *Original Letters*,[4] reproduces a plate [5] from the writing-book designed by Locke and engraved by John de Broen.

Whatever Locke's other affairs in Amsterdam, he had need of Furly's help in money matters. Locke wrote: [6]

> Bank money is here at $4\frac{7}{8}$. If you can have so much for it there, draw on Dr. Peter Guenellon for Fl. 15,000 in bank and make your bill or bills payable at as short view as you please. . . .

In his reply,[7] Furly said he could not draw Fl. 15,000 in bank, but that he had Fl. 1,500 from an Italian named Francesco Gallacini. Locke seems not to have understood this arrangement, and Furly wrote [8] to him again, saying:

---

[1] § 160.   [2] *Original Letters*, pp. 37–8.
[3] *21 February 1688* (B.L. MSS. Locke, c. 9, f. 22).
[4] The edition of 1830. This plate does *not* appear in the edition of 1847.
[5] In his letter to Furly of *20 February 1688* (*Original Letters*, p. 15) Locke wrote: '. . . there is nothing that now stays me here [in Amsterdam] but the weather and graving of the plate which, do what I could, I could not get the graver to begin upon till today. I press it with all my might, that I may get it done with all speed, so that I may have some copies of it printed whilst I am here. . . .'
[6] *20 February 1688*, *Original Letters*, p. 15.
[7] *21 February 1688* (B.L. MSS. Locke, c. 9, f. 22).
[8] *26 February 1688* (ibid., f. 29).

Thine of the 25th confirms that doctors are not well skilled in matters of exchange, or else, after I had advised that I had the money and desired the payment of the bill, you would not have written of drawing it again, for once having the money in my hands, I am not so easy as to return it again and put myself to the trouble and hazard of seeking another bill.

The reference to 'doctors' being 'not well skilled in matters of exchange' is mildly amusing in the light of Locke's later renown as an economist. Locke took no offence at the remark, however, and his letters to Furly were full of praise for that merchant's skill as a theologian: 'But you love,' he said [1] admiringly, and with the aid of a characteristic analogy,

to put people beside their principles, which is usually but little better than to remove a child that has becack himself out of the place where notwithstanding that, he sat quietly, whereby you make it be taken notice of that he is besh—.

Another subject which recurs in Locke's letters from Amsterdam is sheep. In a letter [2] to Edward Clarke, Locke told his friend at the end of *December* that he had bought some sheep to send him, but could not find room for them on the boats leaving Rotterdam, and was thus left with a flock on his hands: 'I am like,' he said, 'to turn farmer'. He asked [3] Furly's help in finding freight-room for the animals, but it was not until *6 February* [4] that he was able to inform Clarke that 'our sheep' had 'set sail'.

Clarke received from Locke at about the same time as he received the sheep several copies of the reprint of the *abrégé*. He informed the author, on 2 March, [5] that he had given one to Lord Pembroke, 'who told me he had read over the greatest part of your treatise at large on the subject and that he was much pleased therewith'. Locke had already heard from Clarke that Lord Pembroke was a victim of James's new policy of Romanising the government of the country. [6]

---

[1] *Original Letters*, p. 27.
[2] *30 December 1687* (Rand, pp. 230–2).   [3] *Original Letters*, p. 23.
[4] Rand, p. 243.
[5] B.L. MSS. Locke, c. 6, f. 45.
[6] Clarke to Locke 21 February 1687–8 (*ibid.*, f. 43): Lord Pembroke was 'very lately discharged from those honourable commands which he held over his own county to make room for some other more complying with that which is called his Majesty's present interest'.

Locke sent another copy of the *abrégé* to Robert Boyle, to whom at the same time he wrote saying [1]

> . . . this enclosed paper newly falling into my hands, fresh from the press, and carrying with it the air of something more intelligible and sincere than is usually found in this sort of writings, I could not satisfy the desire I always have to render you any service I can imagine may be acceptable to you, without sending it you as speedily as I could, especially since I can add this farther concerning it: that I am told by a knowing man, and an acquaintance of the publisher, that he has reason to think that the whole work, whereof these aphorisms are but the skeleton, if it were published, would far exceed all that is yet extant on this subject.

Clarke also gave Boyle one of his copies of the *abrégé*; and reported that Boyle, though sick, 'would (as soon as possible) read over *your* abridgement'.[2]

By *4 March* [3] Locke was able to tell Furly he had almost finished with the printers in Amsterdam—'good Christians, orthodox believers' and liars as he called them:

> And 'tis no small joy that I am got so far out of their hands that I can now say with some confidence that I hope to be with you on Saturday next. As an evidence thereof I send you by today's *Veer Scuyt* two boxes and a bundle of books . . .

Two days later Locke wrote in his journal: 'Returned to Rotterdam'; he had written nothing at all in it during *January* and *February*.

While Locke was in Amsterdam, Furly had been busy with one of his antiquarian manuscripts, the *Liber Sententiarum Inquisitionis Tholosanae*,[4] an official Catholic record of the activities of the holy office at Toulouse in the thirteenth and fourteenth centuries. Furly was not, like Locke, a zealous anti-Papist, but his love of liberty and hatred of persecution made him take a particular interest in this document. As it was one of the very few Catholic records of the

---

[1] This letter is printed in Boyle, V, pp. 570–1, with a manifestly incorrect date, viz. '10 October 1687'. Locke had already, in 1687, reminded Boyle of his existence by sending him, through Tyrrell, some comments on Thomas Burnet's *New Theory of the Faith*. This paper, which argues that Thomas Burnet's hypothesis is not consistent with 'philosophy, Scripture or itself' is printed in Boyle's *Works* (Vol. V, p. 620) together with a letter from Tyrrell dated 25 May 1687.

[2] 2 March 1687/8 (B.L. MSS. Locke, c. 6, f. 46). My italics.

[3] *Original Letters*, pp. 41–2.

[4] Locke wrote to Furly from Amsterdam on *19 January 1688* saying: 'I envy your employment in that musty manuscript', but begging him 'to leave for a while your processes, condemnations, prisons and executions'.

Inquisition to fall into Protestant hands, Furly realised that it might be used as a powerful polemical weapon against the kind of religious persecution which it recorded, and he suggested to Locke that it ought to be published. Locke passed on the suggestion to Limborch [1] and Le Clerc. Eventually Limborch used the manuscript [2] as the chief source for his own *Historia Inquisitionis*, but used it in a manner of which Furly could not wholly approve.

Although Locke's religious and political beliefs were, and remained, very different from Furly's, he was influenced by Furly, just as at Amsterdam he had been influenced by the Remonstrants. There is something distinctly Quakerish about a religious movement Locke thought of setting up sometime during the year *1688*. This 'Society of Pacific Christians' seems never to have come into being, but Locke preserved the set of basic principles which he drafted.[3] The society was to be open to all who received the truth revealed in the Scriptures and 'obey the light which enlightens every man'. No one was to be judged by 'outward observances'; and the society would acknowledge the duty of mutual toleration among Christians. Christ was to be the sole Master recognised, and public exhortation would be directed only to 'instruct and encourage one another in the duties of a good life'. It was to be a society with few and plain rules to govern the procedure of its assemblies, and anything which needed regulation was to be settled by the assembly itself or by its elders.

This document shows, among others things, how far Locke was from the traditions of the Church of England, despite his lifelong membership of that communion.

As soon as he got back to Rotterdam, Locke wrote one of his heavily playful letters [4] to Mary Clarke urging her to visit him in Holland, and threatening, if she did not, to believe that 'you are willing I should languish away my life here under the sway of a Dutch

---

[1] Locke to Limborch, *14 March 1688*: 'When you see what the manuscript contains, I think you will agree that it ought to see the light. For it contains authentic records of things done in that barbaric age which have either been forgotten or purposely misrepresented' (Amsterdam: Remonstrants' MSS. Ba 256: Latin).

[2] After Furly's death, the *Liber Sententiarum* passed to his son John, and then to his grandson, Thomas Furly, who sold it to Thomas Secker, Bishop of Oxford, for £80 in 1755. Secker presented it to the British Museum (B.M. Add. MSS. 4697). It is still in magnificent condition.

[3] B.L. MSS. Locke, c. 27, f. 79a.   [4] *9 March 1688* (Rand, pp. 252–4).

mistress'. To Edward Clarke he wrote [1] on a more serious matter. 'I was surprised,' he said, 'that W. P. had procured your cousin a pardon'.

'W. P.' was William Penn; the 'cousin' was Locke himself, and the pardon was one from James II which Locke did not want.[2] Locke was informed that it was James Tyrrell who had asked Penn to intervene with the King on his behalf.

'Mr. Oakley's imprudent meddling in the case upon his own head', Locke protested,[3] 'has yet made [it] more difficult. . . .'

A few days later [4] he told Clarke that it was necessary, and 'for fresh reasons', that Tyrrell should 'unsay' to Penn what he had said and 'own to him that it was without the order or privity of the person concerned'. Locke explained that although he did not want the pardon, neither did he wish to appear to be 'slighting' William Penn.

Locke's hopes, twice postponed, of seeing David Thomas were fulfilled that spring. 'Adrian' reached Rotterdam on *29 March*, and a few days later the two friends set off together to visit, among other places, Leyden, Utrecht and Amsterdam.[5] Before Thomas left for home, Locke asked him to make inquiries in England to see if his *Essay Concerning Human Understanding* might be published there in full. Almost as soon as he reached London, David Thomas wrote [6] to report a conversation with a brother of Awnsham Churchill, the bookseller, who (he said) 'told me that for good books of which they may venture to print 1,000 or 1,120 copies, they give sometimes £20, sometimes £30'. In another letter [7] Thomas told Locke that he had seen Awnsham Churchill himself, who 'says they do not give a value for a copy of a book to be printed, but it is first read by some [one] whom they trust, but that he will print a book at his own charges and the author shall have half the clear profit'.

Thomas also mentioned that Lord Pembroke 'longs to discourse with you about your book' and also that 'he longs to see you'.[8]

[1] *11 March 1688* (Rand., p. 256).

[2] Locke 'would not accept [the pardon] as not owning that he needed it' (Lady Masham: Remonstrants' MSS. J. 57a).

[3] *16 May 1688* (Rand, p. 268).   [4] *21 May 1688* (*ibid.*, p. 270).

[5] Locke's journal and Brownover's notebook (B.L. MSS. Locke, F. 34) jointly yield this information.

[6] 25 April 1688, B.L. MSS. Locke, c. 20, f. 60.

[7] 10 May 1688, *ibid.*, f. 62.   [8] 25 April 1688, *ibid.*, f. 60.

Locke was already confidently looking forward to seeing his *Essay* printed in full, and had even got to the point of deciding to have an engraving of his own likeness printed as a frontispiece. For this last purpose he asked Clarke to recover the Greenhill portrait which the Stringers had in their custody at Bexwells. This request led to difficulties. Clarke had to tell[1] Locke that Stringer was 'resolved not to part with the portrait'. Stringer claimed that the picture was his property as Locke's gift, and that, in any case, it was not suitable for engraving.

Locke was indignant. He drafted a letter[2] to Stringer protesting that:

> If you believe yourself when you say I gave you my picture, I beseech you to consider what you think of yourself when you deny it me upon this occasion. Sure I am you will never persuade anybody else that you think *bona fide* I gave it you whilst you dare not trust it again in my hands.

As for Stringer's doubt about the suitability of the portrait for reproduction, Locke said:

> I hope I may be allowed to be of an age enough to know if I would have print of myself what kind will please me best.

Stringer replied[3] complaining of the hard words and reproaches contained in Locke's letter, and saying:

> . . . you may be well assured I should not have detained [the picture] any more than I did any other of your things . . . if I had not been thoroughly satisfied that you did really and *bona fide* give it me, and that in justice and right it was mine. And therefore your claiming to have it again is a manifest injury, which (as it is demanded) I have no reason to comply with.

Locke's comment, when he wrote next[4] to Clarke, was:

> The truth is [that Stringer] deals with me after a way I could scarce have believed under any other assurance but that of his own hand. He tells me his wife has it under my hand that I gave it to him. I am afraid he strains the matter too far, for having never purposed but to have that picture in my chamber at Oxford when I came to settle there, I am sure I could never give it away in a letter to anyone.

[1] 16 March 1687/8 (B.L. MSS. Locke, c. 6, f. 47).
[2] *Ibid.*, c. 24, f. 261.
[3] 30 April 1688 (P.R.O. 30/24/47).   [4] *16 May 1688* (Rand, p. 267).

The publication of the French epitome in the *Bibliothèque Universelle* and the circulation of the reprint brought the author several letters in praise of his *Essay*. One came from Damaris Masham,[1] who apologised for her inexpert knowledge of philosophy—her sight, she said, was too weak and she had been discouraged from reading books on that subject—but who ventured to challenge Locke's criticism of the doctrine of innate ideas. She suggested that the difference between Locke and those who believed in innate ideas was not 'really so great as it seems', because those other philosophers had never maintained that there was a definite number of ideas inborn, but only that there was 'an active sagacity in the soul'. In thus championing the cause of innate ideas, Damaris Masham was very much a Cudworth.

Another female reader, also a baronet's lady, wrote to Locke praising his epitome but at the same time reporting some criticisms; this was Lady Guise,[2] then living at Utrecht. In his reply Locke wrote: [3]

I see by your Ladyship's letter there are men touchy enough to be put into a heat by my little treatise which I think has none in it. If they are so concerned for truth and religion as becomes sober men, they will answer the end of its publication and show me the mistakes in it. But if they are of those religious men, who when they can show no faults in his book, can look into the heart of the author and there see flaws in the religion of him that wrote it, though there be no thing concerning religion in it, only because it is not suited to the systems they were taught, I leave them to bethink themselves whether they are his disciples whose command it was 'Judge not'. Such gossiping talkers who supply the want of knowledge with a show of zeal, and who if censure and tattle were reason and argument, would certainly be very infallible, I leave to their own good humour and charity, it having seldom been observed that any are forward to suspect or question others' religion, but those who want such a mask to cover some defect in their own. I have so sincerely proposed truth to myself in all I have written, and do so much prefer it to my own opinion that I shall think myself obliged to anyone who will show me where I have missed it.

[1] 7 April 1688 (B.L. MSS. Locke, c. 17, f. 154).

[2] Elizabeth Lady Guise was then a widow. The daughter of John Grabham-Howe of Compton-in-the-Hole, Gloucestershire, she had married (*c.* 1678) Sir John Guise, the second baronet, who died in 1685, aged thirty-one. Her two letters to Locke from Utrecht were dated *17 April* and *10 May 1688* (*ibid.*, c. 11, ff. 129–30).

[3] *21 June 1688, ibid.*, c. 24, f. 51.

Other letters of appreciation came from Thoynard,[1] whose only criticism was of the title (such a capital work, he thought, ought not to be called an 'essay'); and from Dr. Guenellon,[2] who told Locke that he heard the epitome much talked about and admired.

In April, when David Thomas was still with Locke in Holland, Sylvanus Brownover had asked leave to visit his home in Germany.[3] Locke[4] confided to Clarke that although he had promised to re-engage Brownover, he was in fact looking for another servant to replace him. He had thought of doing this before, but once again Locke was to change his mind and take his servant back.

He also said in the same letter to Clarke:

> I know not what stars govern my friends at this time. Mr. Oakley quarrels with me and thinks himself injured, because I do not employ him, and without any communication with me will he do though to my cost. [*sic*] But what is beyond all is Mr. Stringer's answer to that letter you delivered him from me, wherein I allowed his friendship leisure of second thoughts to recollect itself, if ever he had any; and gave him leave to turn the harsh things he said of me in his letter to you into jest if he pleased. But in his answer he has taken pains to second it with such an overflow of gall and spite as required no less than two whole large sheets of paper to wrap it up in. . . .

Locke may have found some reassurance in David Thomas's next letter[5] which brought fresh news:

> I have received an answer from Musidore [i.e. James Tyrrell] who says W. P. told him it was *Joshua Lock*[6] not J. L., and that with this Musidore thought I was satisfied and that he will go to W. P. and make the apology I wrote (I use his own words) if I think it necessary and if it will do you any service.

But Locke did not forgive Tyrrell easily. He complained to Clarke[7] that:

> Mr. Oakley . . . loves to be a man of business. At any rate it would choke him if his tongue might not go, whether with rhyme or reason

---

[1] *15 August 1688*, B.L. MSS. Locke, c. 21, f. 161 (French).

[2] *25 March* and *10 April 1688*, *ibid.*, c. 11, ff. 5–8 (French).

[3] 'Syl went on his journey', Locke wrote in his journal on *17 April*. Brownover wrote to him from Frankfurt on *28 April* (*ibid.*, c. 4, f. 176).

[4] *21 May 1688* (Rand, p. 269).

[5] 10 May 1688: B.L. MSS. Locke, c. 20, f. 62.

[6] Possibly Lock the 'London tobacconist'.

[7] *22 June 1688* (Rand, p. 277).

it matters not. The very mention of his holding his peace is like a cork that makes perfect bottle beer of it, and yet it must sputter. He tells me . . . he has been talking of it to my . . . F [noble Friend?].[1] If he, when he sees you, takes any notice of it to you, you must tell him that Mr. Oakley meddles in business wherein he has neither commission nor knowledge, and loves to be talking he knows not what.

In London that June there happened something which altered the whole political situation of England. The Queen gave birth to a son. Fifteen years of her married life with James II had been barren save for two children who died in infancy; and no one now believed that the Queen would bear another child. This assurance was, indeed, the chief consolation of his Catholic Majesty's Protestant subjects. The heir presumptive was Mary of Orange; and it was assumed that the death of James would instantly bring that Protestant Princess to her father's throne.

The birth of a son to Mary of Modena on 21 June 1688 destroyed this assurance, and introduced the prospect of a Roman Catholic succession. Many Protestant Englishmen simply refused to believe that the birth was genuine, preferring to credit the story that the baby had been put into the royal bed in a warming-pan. Some leading Protestants took practical steps: they approached Prince William of Orange and begged him to come to England with an army and deliver the nation from Popery.

William, however, had learned the lesson of Monmouth's ill-starred rising. He would not act without favourable chances of success and unless he had a firm invitation from a representative body of English statesmen. In *July 1688* that invitation came; it was delivered to The Hague by Arthur Herbert, lately Vice-Admiral of England and a kinsman of the Earl of Pembroke.

These surreptitious doings portended the coming triumph of Lockean political philosophy. When Locke and Shaftesbury had first worked out that philosophy public opinion in England had been against them. Englishmen had then a residual belief in the divine right of kings, and they had still vivid and painful memories of the rebellion against Charles I. If Locke had published his political theory in 1683, it could only have been denounced, like the writings of Algernon Sydney, as a gospel of treason. But in the altered situation which followed the birth of James II's son, the public was ready for new ideas.

[1] Lord Pembroke?

The question of the hour was whether it would be morally wrong to get rid of a monarch who was both a tyrant himself and in a position to perpetuate tyranny. Though Locke had published nothing, his thoughts on the subject were clear. Far from thinking it morally wrong to remove a monarch who had become a tyrant, Locke maintained that it was a duty for citizens to do so. A ruler's authority was a trust; and if he failed in that trust, morality required his replacement by another.

William of Orange was a man who loved power and who cherished his own rights as ruler; but an argument like Locke's, which could woo Englishmen away from their loyalty to James II, would have been music to his ears in 1688.

After David Thomas, Edward Clarke went from England at long last to visit Locke in Holland. He took his wife and daughter Betty with him. They arrived at the end of *July*,[1] and went home at the beginning of September. They seem to have divided their time between Rotterdam and Amsterdam. On his way back Clarke called at Wilton to discuss Locke's *Essay* with Lord Pembroke, who had communicated some criticisms of the manuscript to the author. Clarke wrote[2] to Locke after his interview explaining that Lord Pembroke had intended 'in no sort any objection either to the notions in your book or to the reasons made use of to support them, but purely relating to those repetitions and other small errors therein'. Clarke added that Lord Pembroke 'desires you proceed in your design of publishing it' to oblige not only him but 'all the considering and learned part of mankind'.

In a letter[3] to Clarke, written as soon as he had news of their arrival in England, Locke reported:

> The Doctor[4] and his lady, whom I saw today were glad to hear of your safe arrival at home, and their young gallant Peter desires to have his service to Miss Betty; and yesterday her other gallant Paul, who presented her with Amsterdam, asked for her. How she will do between these two young apostles I know not, unless she will rob Peter to

[1] Locke told Limborch about the arrival of a friend from England in a letter dated *30 July 1688* (Amsterdam: Remonstrants' MSS. Ba. 256e, Latin).
[2] *16 September 1688* (B.L. MSS. Locke, c. 6, f. 52).
[3] *19 October 1688* (Rand, p. 283).
[4] Dr. Guenellon.

pay Paul, for they both pretend vigorously to her; and I cannot blame them, for I love her mightily myself.

Clarke was safely at home, but not sound. As soon as he got to Chipley, he had to take to his bed with the ague; and he apologised [1] to Locke that he had not strength 'to thank my good friend Benjamin [Furly] as I ought' for 'his great kindness to me while I was in Holland'. Locke advised [2] Clarke to take Sydenham's favourite remedy for the ague: Peruvian bark.

The plans which were going forward in Holland for the liberation of England from Popery by William of Orange were by this time an open secret. On 20 October,[3] Locke's old admirer Isabella Duke—she with whom he had once hoped to winter in Utrecht—wrote to him from Otterton, Devon, saying how disappointed she was that he had not returned to England with Mr. Clarke:

> . . . instead of embracing the best of friends and being happy in the enjoyment of your most agreeable, excellent conversation, I am entertained with nothing but rumours of wars and the daily alarms of an expected invasion both from the Dutch and French so that 'tis to be feared we may suffer all the extremities of a winter war. 'Tis full three weeks since we were told the Dutch were on our coast and would be landed before the newsletters could reach our remote country. As yet we hear nothing of their being come, but we are told that we owe our quiet only to the winds that have been cross to their designs—but you know best who live amongst them. 'Tis too late to wish you had given me some hints of this storm. . . .

Locke's journal records a journey on *8 October* to Leyden, but he went back to Rotterdam on *30 October*. In his letter to Clarke of *19 October* [4] he said, apropos of some romantic suggestion of Mrs. Clarke's:

> I am so far from any advances towards love, or mistress or courtship, when the sun is on t'other side of the line, that I think on nothing but the chimney corner, which I think not to be left for a beauty or fortune, wherein a man otherwise disposed might hope to find a paradise.

The chimney corner was not to be left, Locke might have added, for a revolutionary enterprise either. On Thursday *11 November*,

---

[1] 30 September 1688 (B.L. MSS. Locke, c. 6, f. 53).
[2] *19 October 1688* (Rand, p. 281).
[3] B.L. MSS. Locke, c. 8, f. 30. [4] Rand, p. 283.

following a false start made on *29 October*, William's fleet of 400 ships left Holland for England. Admiral Herbert was in command; Lord Mordaunt and Gilbert Burnet and other English supporters accompanied the Prince. Locke remained where he was. Jean le Clerc, observing this, wrote afterwards in an all-too-famous phrase that Locke was '*plutôt timide que courageux*'.[1] Le Clerc might have read more carefully the letter [2] the third Lord Shaftesbury wrote him mentioning the 'dangers' Locke had been through in the past. It was no disgrace for an invalidish man of fifty-six who had experienced some hazards in the early days of the Protestant revolution to leave its fulfilment to others.

The flag of the ship which carried Prince William to England bore the motto *Pro Religione et Libertate*. Religion, very properly, came first. William was invited to England as the enemy of Popery, and not as the protector of religious dissent. Benjamin Furly, however, took the slogan seriously enough to go to The Hague and suggest to the Prince that he might be better able to offer freedom to England if liberty were given first to anti-Calvinist dissenters in Holland. Locke mentioned this interview in a letter [3] to Limborch:

> Our friend Furly had an audience of the Prince before his departure and solicited his intervention to put an end to the persecution attempted in this province at a time particularly unseasonable. He urged the business so warmly that the Prince was pleased to write a letter to the bailiff of Kenmerland, who, by the authority of the synod, had ordered Foecke Floris, minister of a church of Mennonites, to quit the country within eight days on pain of imprisonment. The history of this Foecke Floris you can learn more correctly from others than from us; he was not personally known to our friend Furly until this incident occurred. Believing the common interest of Christians to be involved in the case of this man, our friend took it up and pursued it with the utmost zeal. Had he not been importunate, nothing would have been done. Let us hope that the letter from the Prince will restrain the intemperate passion of the persecutors. . . .

In the Channel the wind proved almost miraculously favourable to William's enterprise, and he landed at Brixham on a day which was, according to the Julian Calendar, the anniversary of another

---

[1] '[M. Locke] n'etoit d'ailleurs aucunement brouillon et plutôt timide que courageux' (*Éloge*, p. xlvi).
[2] Amsterdam: Remonstrants' MSS. J. 20.
[3] *24 November 1688*, ibid Ba. 256f (Latin).

X

red-letter day in the history of English resistance to Popery, 5 November. A considerable army disembarked from the Dutch ships; and the people of the West of England, more Protestant than ever after Jeffreys's Bloody Assize, rallied to the Prince's flag. Plymouth, the vital arsenal, was his. Mordaunt went ahead and raised Dorset and Wiltshire; risings elsewhere followed, and as the Protestant soldiers made their slow progression along the muddy English roads to London they met scarcely any opposition. Tories joined Whigs in welcoming the invasion. When the King's officers, including Churchill, deserted him, he opened negotiations with William, then lost hope, and bolted.

Locke's old friend, Dr. Goodall, of the College of Physicians, wrote to him on 27 December: [1]

> I know you can be no stranger to the wonderful success which God Almighty hath given to the Prince of Orange in his late undertaking to deliver our miserable and distressed kingdoms from Popery and slavery, which mercy we in England esteem no less than the Israelites' deliverance from Egypt by the hand of Moses. . . . I presume you have heard that the King went privately from Whitehall some few days before the Prince came to St. James's with a design for France, but was stopped by some fishermen, and then returned again to Whitehall on the Sunday in the evening, but on the Tuesday (being the day the Prince came to London) he retired to Rochester, and is said to have left the kingdom last Sunday.

Dr. Goodall then gave Locke the text of the Order passed by the peers of the realm and supported by a National Convention of commoners, inviting William to administer the Kingdom. He continued:

> I hope that this will encourage you to return to London as soon as you can settle your affairs in Holland. If you please to come to my house you shall freely command what conveniences that shall afford, which I hope may not be unacceptable to you. . . . If your affairs will not permit you to return speedily, I hope you will not defer your return longer than the time when the Princess comes to England.

Locke *was* encouraged to return to London, and he accepted Dr. Goodall's offer of hospitality. The Princess Mary herself offered him a passage in her convoy. The departure of the Orange revolu-

---

[1] B.L. MSS. Locke, c. 10, f. 23.

tionaries had left Locke among the ladies; and Venus appears to
have risen, as usual, with Mars. In January[1] Locke begged Clarke:

> Do not laugh at me when I talk of a match at this time of day, for
> I can tell you that one of the ladies at this court came not long since to
> this town on purpose to see and be acquainted with me. I am not like
> to be a courtier: where are any of your young spruce blades that have
> such compliments? I have since returned her her visit and we are very
> well pleased one with another.

To Limborch Locke wrote[2] rather more solemnly:

> An English nobleman who went hither with the Prince has asked me
> to take care of his wife on her passage with the Princess from The
> Hague, and I could not do less than accept the office.

The nobleman was Mordaunt, but taking care of his Viscountess
was no mere matter of duty for Locke. He found her extremely
attractive. Lady Mordaunt was named Carey, daughter of Sir
Alexander Fraser, physician to Charles II, and had herself been a
maid of honour to Queen Catherine. She was very pretty, as a
surviving portrait shows: the face is oval, the figure graceful, the
hands have long, tapering fingers; if the full mouth and heavy-
lidded eyes bespeak a certain sensuousness there is also good humour
in the expression.

Several of her letters to Locke are in the Lovelace Collection.
The handwriting is childish and the spelling, even by seventeenth-
century standards, is appalling. Lady Mordaunt's letters are as
recognisably those of an ill-read woman as are Lady Masham's letters
those of a well-read woman. It is difficult to make any sense of
parts of them, but there can be no doubt about their general tone.
They are flirtatious letters. In one of them the writer declares that
'In lovers' language disordered words have more eloquence'.[3] Then
on *31 January 1689*[4] Lady Mordaunt wrote of 'the impressions
received from Mr. Locke' that 'will grow and thrive, having taken
deep root in a soil that is not sandy, though in a woman's heart'.
She added: 'I fear if my Lord sees that expression, he will revoke his
promise'. She begged Locke to give her husband 'leave in his turn
to be jealous, since you were, because I did not write to you'. She

---

[1] *28 January 1689* (Rand, pp. 287–8).
[2] *5 February 1689* (Amsterdam: Remonstrants' MSS. Ba. 256h: Latin).
[3] In modernising I have also corrected Lady Mordaunt's spelling.
[4] B.L. MSS. Locke, c. 16, f. 101.

assured him: 'If you heard his complaints upon that subject you would forgive me, and triumph over a husband, a common thing in your case.' Lady Mordaunt mentioned that she had been 'very ill this fortnight', and would not undertake her journey 'till Monday or Tuesday next'. Her letter also contained some random remarks on politics. Writing of kings, she observed: 'Ours went out like a farthing candle, and has given us by this convention an occasion not of amending the government, but of melting it down and making all new'. This led her 'to wish you were there to give them a right scheme of government, having been infected by that great Man, Lord "tesbury" '.[1]

Lady Mordaunt's remarks are a credit to her political sagacity. There was, indeed, a lack of wise leadership in London. Members of the national convention were by this time quarrelling in a most acrimonious fashion. The Tories wanted a Regency; the Whigs wanted the throne declared vacant. When the Whigs had their way on this point, the Tories proposed that the Princess Mary should succeed her father as Queen regnant. The Whigs insisted on Prince William ruling as king. William told the politicians that if his wife were made sole monarch he would 'go back to Holland and meddle no more in your affairs',[2] and Princess Mary wrote from Holland deploring the efforts to use her name in competition with her husband's.[3] The result was the compromise of William and Mary's joint reign.

Quarrels in the national convention were not limited to such important issues: petty matters were debated just as hotly. Reports of their meetings reached Locke, who wrote to Clarke on *8 February*:[4]

I ... have seen the Prince's letter[5] to the Convention, which carries weight and wisdom in it. But men very much wonder here to hear of committees of privileges, of grievances, etc., as if this were a formal parliament, and were not something of another nature, and had

[1] The reference here is clearly to the first Lord Shaftesbury. A later remark, 'He did not know his grandson's worth so well as my daughter now', is presumably a reference to Shaftesbury's grandson, Lord Ashley, who had been in Holland.

[2] G. J. Renier, *William of Orange*, 1932, p. 127.

[3] Hester W. Chapman, *Mary II*, 1953, p. 156.

[4] Rand, pp. 288-9.

[5] When the Convention met on 22 January they received a letter from the Prince telling them that it rested with them to lay the foundations for the security of the religion, laws and liberties of the people.

not business to do of greater moment and consequence sufficiently pointed out to them by the Prince's letter. People are astonished here to see them meddle with any small matters, and when the settlement of the nation on the sure grounds of peace and security is put into their hands, which can no way so well be done as by restoring our ancient government—the best possible that ever was, if taken and put together all of a piece in its original constitution. If this has not been invaded, men have done very ill to complain; and if it has, men must certainly be so wise by feeling as to know where the frame has been put out of order, or if amiss; and for that now they have an opportunity offered to find remedies, and set up a constitution that may be lasting, for the security of civil rights and the liberty and property of all the subjects of the nation. These are thoughts worthy such a convention as this, which, if (as men suspect here) they think of themselves as a parliament, and put themselves into the slow methods of proceeding usual therein, and think of mending some faults piecemeal, or anything less than the great frame of the government, they will let slip an opportunity which cannot even from things within last long. But if they consider foreign affairs, I wonder any of them can sleep till they see the nation settled in a regular way of acting and putting itself in a posture of defence and support of the common interest of Europe. The spring comes on apace, and if we be, France will not be idle. And if France should prevail with the Emperor for an accommodation (which is more than feared), I beseech you to consider how much time you have to lose in England. I mention not Ireland, because it is in everybody's eye.

In the same letter Locke reproached Clarke because

I do not perceive that you stood to be chosen anywhere, which, when I see you, I shall quarrel with you for not a little: make not the like omission the next election.

He did not tell Clarke that he was soon coming home, but he told Limborch as soon as he received the invitation from Princess Mary.

You will I am sure [Locke then wrote [1] to Limborch] understand the great advantage it would be for me to cross the channel in such good company, crowded as the sea now is with warships and pirates.

Eleven days later Locke wrote [2] again to Limborch:

It was my earnest wish, most excellent friend, before I left this country, to have had an opportunity of visiting my friends at Amsterdam, and especially you. Yet everything has proved adverse, as if on

---

[1] *5 February 1689*, Amsterdam: Remonstrants' MSS. Ba. 256h (Latin).
[2] *16 February 1689, ibid.*, Ba. 256i (Latin).

purpose to thwart me. First the frost, and then my haste; since which the rain has prevented my journey. Last Saturday, going to the Hague that I might prevail on a noble lady [1] to accompany me to Amsterdam, where she had designed to go, a very violent shower overtook me on the road to Delft, and pursued me all the way to the Hague. Thus I arrived wet through, and instead of coming on to you the same evening, I was not only discouraged by the lady from making the journey, on account of the danger to my health, but positively forbidden. . . .

At the coast I found everything prepared for departure, and everyone impatient to set sail; it was generally believed that the Princess's fleet would leave with the first favourable wind. I, indeed, began my intended journey to you, trusting not so much to the wind as to the religion of the Princess, which I scarcely thought would allow her to begin the voyage on the Sabbath, even though an east wind should invite her. But now they wait only for a wind to suit the navigation; then they will at once go on board the ships. I returned yesterday evening, and how long I shall be delayed here I do not know. What I do know is that there is nothing more irksome than to be fatigued with leisure and yet not have time for a purpose one specially desires to accomplish.

Many things have inclined me to seize the present opportunity of sailing homewards: the expectation of my friends; my private affairs, now so long neglected; the frequent piracies and the opportunity of a safe conveyance afforded me by the friendship of the noble lady whom I am accompanying. Yet I trust you will believe that I have found in Holland another homeland; I might almost say other relations. . . .

As for you, best of men, most amiable and esteemed, when I think of your learning, your talents, charm, candour and gentleness, I realise I have found in your friendship alone (not to speak of the others) what must always make me feel grateful for the years I have passed among you. . . .

All Locke's Dutch friends said how sorry they were at his departure, and Le Clerc [2] also asked him to continue to send him contributions from England for his *Bibliothèque Universelle*.

On *15 February* Furly consigned Locke's belongings to a ship, the *William* (master: Pieter Stoop), which was sailing for London. These belongings consisted of sixteen boxes [3] and a small barrel.

---

[1] Lady Mordaunt.   [2] B.L. MSS. Locke, c. 13, f. 29, 12 February 1689 (French).
[3] An entry in Locke's journal dated *February 1689* shows that thirteen of these boxes (nine 'double boxes' and four 'rough deal boxes') contained books; one was a 'little deal box with old linen and woollen in it'; another was a 'little casque with iron furnace in it'.

They were addressed, not to Dr. Goodall, with whom Locke was going to stay in London,[1] but to Awnsham Churchill, the Whiggish bookseller, who had spent some weeks in Holland the previous summer [2] and who had been known to Locke even earlier.[3]

On Sunday *20 February 1689* [4] Locke accompanied Lady Mordaunt to Brill to go aboard the *Isabella*. Sabbatarian inhibitions were forgotten, and the anchor was weighed at three o'clock in the afternoon.[5] It was not long before the low Dutch coast was hidden in the winter mists. Locke was never to see Holland again.

[1] Sir Walter Yonge wrote to Locke at Rotterdam on 17 February 1688/9 to tell him that Lord Pembroke hoped to see him in England (B.L. MSS. Locke, c. 23, f. 162).

[2] In his letter dated 7 July 1688, Thomas wrote to Locke saying: 'I shall send my young man with Mr. Churchill, the bookseller, who will be in Holland about a fortnight hence' (*ibid.*, c. 20, f. 64).

[3] On the back of a letter he received from Clarke dated *26 March 1687* Locke wrote: 'Pay A. Churchill for my hat' (Rand, p. 200).

[4] Two days before Locke had received a bill of exchange for £40 from Benjamin Furly on William Penn. Inevitably as a friend of James II, Penn had been embarrassed by the Orange Revolution. He was more than once accused of disloyalty before the Privy Council, and went into partial retirement. His governorship of Pennsylvania was forfeited until 1694, when he was fully and finally vindicated of treasonable activities.

[5] Furly wrote to Locke on *22 February 1689*: 'I doubt not, hearing that you put to sea about 3 o'clock, but you arrived safely last night at Harwich. If so, I hope thou wilt stay and repose thyself awhile at Colchester, where I am sure thou wilt be most heartily welcome. . . . All in the Lantern salute thee, and do regret thy absence' (*ibid.*, c. 9, f. 32).

Chapter Twenty-two

LONDON

THE *Isabella* reached England on 12 February. The next day William and Mary announced their joint acceptance of the English throne. Locke, who had gone straight from the ship to Dr. Goodall's house in Warwick Lane, was presently offered the post of British Ambassador to Frederick III, Elector of Brandenburg. The invitation came through Mordaunt,[1] to whom Locke replied:[2]

> I cannot but in the highest degree be sensible of the great honour his Majesty has done me in those gracious intentions towards me which I have understood from your Lordship, and it is the most touching displeasure I have ever received from that weak and broken constitution of my health which has so long threatened my life that it now affords me not a body suitable to my mind in so desirable occasion of serving his Majesty. . . .
>
> My Lord, the post that is mentioned to me is, if I mistake not, one of the busiest and most important in all Europe, and therefore would require not only a man of common sense and good intentions, but one whom experience in the methods of such business has filled with skill and dexterity to deal with, not only the reasons of able men, but the more dangerous artifices of cunning men that in such stations must be expected and mastered.

Locke said that it would be better that he should be 'laid by to be forgotten for ever' than that he should 'ambitiously and forwardly' undertake something his 'weak lungs' would prevent his doing properly. Besides, he said, a successful diplomatist had to be able to manage the bottle in drawing out men's thoughts; and the 'warm drinking' of the Germans was beyond him. He thought the King should send someone who could 'drink his share' rather than 'the soberest man' in England.

---

[1] Mordaunt was made a Privy Councillor on 14 February, a gentleman of the bed chamber on 1 March, and first Lord of the Treasury on 8 April.

[2] 21 February 1688/9: B.L. MSS. Locke, c. 24, f. 198.

William was disappointed by Locke's refusal. Failing Cleves, he offered him Vienna or, according to Lady Masham, another capital. But Locke stood firm; he said he would take no diplomatic post, though he was very willing to serve the King at home. The post he eventually accepted was a very modest one, that of a Commissioner of Appeals. Lady Masham described this as 'a place honourable enough for any gentleman' and 'though of no greater value than £200 *per annum*', it suited Locke because it required 'but little attendance'.[1]

The Crown already owed Locke money, for he had never been paid for his services as secretary to the Council of Trade and Plantations under Charles II. He drafted a petition to William III for payment of this debt, and although Lady Masham said Locke withdrew it, 'declining in a time when the government had so great occasion for money to press his claims',[1] there is documentary evidence to show that Locke *did* press it.[2]

Another petition [3] he drafted at this time was for the restitution

[1] Amsterdam: Remonstrants' MSS. J. 57a.

[2] *Vide* C. S. P. Dom: 10 February 1689/90: 'Proceedings upon the petition of John Locke, stating that Charles II conferred on him the office of the Secretary of the Council of Trade and Plantations. Prays for payment of the arrears of his salary of £600 *per annum*. Referred to the Treasury.' Drafts of Locke's petitions for the same debt dated 1693 and 1695 are in the Lovelace Collection (B.L. MSS. Locke, c. 25, ff. 47–9).

[3] One of two drafts in the Lovelace Collection reads as follows (*ibid.*, f. 42):

'To the King's Most Excellent Majesty
'The Humble Petition of John Locke
'Sheweth—That your Petitioner, being Student of Christ Church College in Oxford was in the year 1684, by a letter sent by the Earl of Sunderland, the principal Secretary of State, to the Dean and Chapter of the said College, ordered to be turned out. Dr. Fell, the Bishop of Oxford, and Dean of then said College, finding it against the rules of common justice, as well as the ordinary method of the college, to turn out anyone without [a] hearing, or so much as being accused of any fact which might forfeit his place, especially one who had lived inoffensively in the college so many years, did by a *Moneo* affixed according to the ordinary way of proceeding to the screen in the college hall of the said college, summon your Petitioner, who was then in Holland, to appear at the Christmas following, which was about two months after, to answer anything [that] should be alleged against him; but this regular proceeding not suiting the designs upon the University, another letter was sent the week following, with positive orders to turn your Petitioner out immediately, which was accordingly done.

'Your Petitioner therefore humbly prays that your Majesty, being Visitor of the said College, and having power by your immediate command to rectify what you find amiss there, would out of your great justice and goodness, be graciously pleased to direct the Dean and Chapter of the said College to restore your Petitioner to his Student's place, together with all things belonging unto it, which he formerly enjoyed in the said College.'

of his Studentship at Christ Church. This petition he did withdraw. He is said to have wanted the place restored to him only 'as an acknowledgement that he had been wronged';[1] and apparently this would have been granted him, but finding it would dispossess another, he abandoned the suit.

In mid-March[2] Locke wrote to Limborch to assure him that 'a change of country has not been able to change my disposition towards you'. He explained that he would have written earlier had not social duties since his return, the supervision of his scattered property, and certain labours in the public service, taken up all his time. He added some news of political developments:

> Burnet is appointed Bishop of Salisbury. In Parliament the subject of toleration is now discussed under two forms, 'comprehension' and 'indulgence'. By the first it is proposed to enlarge the bounds of the church, so that by the abolition of some ceremonies, many may be induced to conform. By the other is designed the toleration of those who are either unwilling or unable to unite with the Church of England, even on the proposed conditions—how liberal or rigid these will be I do not know. I suspect, however, that the episcopal clergy are not very favourable to these proposals or to others that are in the air. Whether in this attitude they consult the public interest or their own I will not decide . . .

The King himself had urged both 'comprehension' and 'indulgence', the latter to include the opening of all civil offices to Protestant Dissenters. But William's pleas were vitiated in part by his past policy. When in 1687 James II (and Penn) had tried to secure his approval of the abolition of the Test Act, William had maintained that the Test Act was a bulwark of the Protestant faith. Now, when William himself wished to have the Test Act abolished, his own old argument was used effectively against him in Parliament by Whigs as well as Tories.[3]

---

[1] Lady Masham: Amsterdam: Remonstrants' MSS. J. 57a.

[2] 12 March 1688/9, *ibid.*, Ba. 256j (Latin).

[3] 'The Revolution was a Whig victory; but it was a victory won with the assistance of the Tories and the church. Hence the settlement effected by it was necessarily somewhat of a compromise. Subject to the provisions of the Toleration Act, the Tories secured for the Church of England the retention of its privileged position; as at the Savoy conference, they successfully resisted all attempts at a relaxation of doctrines or formularies which would have permitted Protestant nonconformists to become its members; and in 1700 they secured the insertion of a clause in the Act of Settlement which made it obligatory on the King to join in communion with it. The Whigs secured what was far more important—a Parliamentary settlement of the

William was not an Anglican. He was a Calvinist with certain leanings towards the Presbyterian Dissenters; and the minority in Parliament which thought as he did consisted largely of Whig extremists, even though one 'comprehension' scheme was put forward by the Tory Nottingham. The majority was entirely opposed to 'comprehension'.

Locke's asthma began to worsen almost as soon as he arrived in London. In a letter to his 'Dear Sister', Mrs. Anne Grigg, dated 16 March, he said, 'I find I want still two things very dear to me, that is you and my health'.[1] He described his symptoms—intermittent coughing—in a letter to Dr. Veen.[2]

However, on 18 March the philosopher left Dr. Goodall's house in Warwick Lane and took lodgings with Mrs. Rabsy Smithsby in Dorset Court, Channel Row (now Cannon Row), Westminster. He agreed to pay her £5 10s. a quarter for his lodgings, including board.[3] Brownover crossed from Holland to join him there in May.[4] Mrs. Smithsby seems to have been known to Locke for many years and Edward Clarke had taken rooms with her after the death in 1686 of Lady King, at whose house in Fleet Street he, Clarke, had maintained his London quarters. An inventory[5] in Locke's hand shows that some of his belongings had been sent to Mrs. Smithsby's house—presumably from Lady King's—in 1686. Another set of Locke's boxes had been left in Oxford in the custody

---

succession to the throne, and, consequently, the final rejection of the idea that the King's title depended upon a divine right superior to the law of the land. This victory permanently secured both the superiority of the Parliament in the constitution and the supremacy of the law, because, in the new situation created by the Revolution, the Tories found it to their interest to maintain these Whig ideals' (W. S. Holdsworth, *A History of English Law*, VI, p. 195).

[1] 'The want of your company disturbs me constantly, my cough by intervals. Longleat: Bath Collection (H.M.C. Calendar, II, p. 175).

[2] *8 March 1689* (Leyden: Bibliotheck der Universiteit).

[3] Journal, 26 June 1689. Among other disbursements recorded in Locke's journal for 1689 are: 'A pair of shoes, 4s. 6d . . . lace for my waistcoat, £1. . . . Three iron stands £1 13s. . . . Samuel Clarke, my tailor, £7 15s. . . . Mr. Fox for the newsletter for a quarter of a year now ending £1 . . . a pair of boots, 14s. 6d. . . . Oysters I had from Colchester, 14s.'

[4] Brownover presented Locke with a bill for Fl. 71-9-4 (approx. £6 8s.), being the cost of his out of pocket expenses in Holland from *20 February* until *3 May*—a modest bill, despite the fact that Brownover did not stint himself: bottles of mum, brandy, sack and beer, inn-bills, fares, and laundry-bills are all included (B.L. MSS. Locke, F. 34).

[5] B.L. MSS. Locke, c. 25, f. 38.

of a Mrs. Pont[1] in June 1683, when he was preparing to leave the country. This lot included nine boxes marked 'J. L.', one marked 'C. B.', and two presses marked 'E. P. No. 12–13'.[2] If this Mrs. Pont was the wife of Richard Pont, the Oxford vintner,[3] she had died some sixteen months before Locke's return to England.

A third part of Locke's belongings was that which was forwarded by Benjamin Furly from Rotterdam, and addressed to Awnsham Churchill, the newly appointed King's Bookseller. It is not clear why Churchill, of all people, should have been chosen as the receiving agent for Locke's freight, but there was a good reason why Locke wished to see Churchill as soon as he reached London. The *Essay Concerning Human Understanding* was ready for the press, and Locke had hopes that Churchill would publish it.

Of Locke's life in London after his return from Holland Lady Masham wrote:[4]

> He continued for more than two years after the Revolution much in London enjoying no doubt all the pleasure there that anyone can find who, after having been long in a manner banished from his country, unexpectedly returning to it, sees himself more generally esteemed and respected than ever before. If Mr. Locke had any dissatisfaction in this time it could be only, I suppose, from the ill success now and then of our public affairs, for his private circumstances were as happy I believe as he wished them, and all people of worth had that value for him that I think I may say he might have had what friends he pleased.

Limborch, delighted to hear of Gilbert Burnet's elevation to the See of Salisbury, described him in a letter to Locke[5] as a man whose

[1] On Locke's list of these belongings is written: 'Goods to be delivered to Mrs. El. Pont, in Oxford, by Nic Cally June 4 1683.' The word 'El' was afterwards crossed out (B.L. MSS. Locke, c. 25, f. 35).

[2] Once more the mysterious initials 'E. P.' (indeed twice more, if one likes to include 'Mrs. El. Pont').

[3] 'Richard Pont, vintner and citizen of Oxon, descended from the Ponts of Moreton near to Wallingford in Berks died . . . and was buried in St. Mary's Church, about the middle of the body, without arms on his hearse . . . widow of the said Pont, daughter of . . . Andrews, one of the serjeants of Oxon, died Wednesday, 2 November 1687, and was buried (without arms) by her husband, in fine linen contrary to the Act, and in a rich coffin provided by her only daughter . . . Elizabeth, a vain fop of 18 years of age. This Elizabeth, who was the only surviving daughter of the said Richard Pont, and a rich heiress, was married the day before her mother died to [Nicholas] Stanley M.A. Fellow of All Souls College . . .' (*L. and T.*, III, p. 243: November 1687).

[4] Amsterdam: Remonstrants' MSS. J. 57a.

[5] *Ibid.*, III, D. 16, f. 194 (Latin).

views were at one with theirs on the subject of toleration. In reply Locke[1] sent Limborch more news from London:

Yesterday[2] the inauguration, or, as they call it, the Coronation of the King and Queen was celebrated with great pomp amid the acclamations[3] of a multitude of people, and at the same time I suppose they were proclaimed King and Queen of Scotland, as the Scottish throne had been decreed theirs some days before. Burnet, as Bishop of Salisbury, took part in yesterday's proceedings. He preached before the King and Queen, and everyone was delighted with his sermon. I have no doubt it will be printed, and if so, I shall remember to send you a copy. I saw Burnet this morning and told him you intended to send him a letter of congratulation as soon as you knew he was actually a bishop. Whether as you persuade yourself, he will show the same spirit at Salisbury as he did at Amsterdam some people begin to doubt.[4] I must tell you one story about him. When he paid his first visit to the King after his consecration, his Majesty observed that Burnet's hat was very much larger than usual, and asked the object of so wide a brim. The Bishop replied that that was the shape suitable to his dignity. 'I hope', the King replied, 'that hat will not turn your head.'[5]

In the same letter Locke wrote:

I find you are all anxious to know what public office I mean to ask for. I can tell you in a word—none.[6] On the score of my health I have declined an appointment which I should certainly have been glad to accept if I were younger and stronger than I am. I want nothing now but rest. It would never do for a man who is falling to pieces, and fit only to close his account with life, to rush into a great and new

[1] 12 April 1689, Amsterdam: Remonstrants' MSS. Ba. 256 k (Latin).

[2] This suggests that the letter should have been dated 13 April.

[3] William detested the pomp but enjoyed the acclamations. He called the 'comedy' of the coronation 'die zotte, oude Paepsche ceremoniën' (N. Japikse *Prins Willem III*, Den Haag, 1933, Vol. II, p. 277).

[4] Whatever else might be said about him, Burnet remained loyal to the principle of toleration, and 'his practice in his diocese was still more emphatically so. . . . He did his best by careful examination to secure a learned and competent clergy, and stood out against admitting unqualified nominees to livings: waged war against pluralities; established a Divinity School at Salisbury. He was tolerant both to nonjurors and to presbyterians to a degree which roused the anger of all extreme men' (Osmund Airy, *D.N.B.*).

[5] The fact was that the King had come to dislike Burnet intensely. He gave him Salisbury because he recognised his debt to him, and because Burnet still enjoyed the support and friendship of the Queen. William called Burnet 'een rechte Tartuffe' (Clarke and Foxcroft, *op. cit.*, p. 266).

[6] His post as Commissioner of Appeals, being only a part-time one, was evidently not to be regarded as a public office.

undertaking. . . . Yet though I decline to take any public work, I find myself so occupied with public affairs and the concerns of my friends that I am hardly able to touch a book now. I hope I shall be able one day to return to my old and agreeable ease in the world of letters.

In the meantime Locke was able to use his new influence in the highest quarters on behalf of his friends. He told Clarke[1] of a 'project' he had to have him made auditor to the Queen at a yearly salary of £100 *plus* perquisites. At the same time he mentioned his fears of a French invasion—as a result of the Revolution, England was at war with France again—and he reported rumours of a 'great fleet' being ready to sail from Brest with 'fourteen or fifteen thousand land soldiers' for 'a descent somewhere on our King's dominions'.[2] But what about the 'world of letters'?

As things turned out, Awnsham Churchill did not publish the first edition of Locke's *Essay*. Instead Churchill took another manuscript from Locke to publish anonymously—the *Two Treatises of Civil Government*, a work especially suited to a Whiggish bookseller's list. So anxious, however, was Locke to conceal his authorship of the *Two Treatises of Government* that he preserved none of the letters and other papers relating to its publication.

The bookseller to whom Locke leased the rights of his *Essay Concerning Human Understanding* was Thomas Bassett, best known as a specialist in law books, and then a newcomer to the trade. The agreement[3] Locke made with Bassett and signed on 24 May 1689, is sufficiently interesting to merit its partial reproduction here:

Whereas the said John Locke hath composed and written a Book or Treatise in English entitled *An Essay Concerning Human Understanding* the said John Locke doth grant and agree to and with the said Thomas Bassett that he the said Thomas Bassett shall have the same to print and publish on the terms and in the manner and form following. That

---

[1] 13 April 1689 (Rand, pp. 290–1).

[2] The French fleet did not appear in the Channel until June 1690, when it was warded off by the Dutch. The English fleet was under the command of Arthur Herbert, the same Admiral who had brought William to England and who had been raised to the peerage as Earl of Torrington. 'Most men were in fear that the French would invade', Torrington said. 'But I was always of another opinion, for I always said that, whilst we had a fleet in being they would not dare to make an attempt.' Torrington accordingly kept his ships out of the firing line. He could not persuade the government of his wisdom, and was disgraced.

[3] B.L. MSS. Locke 61.

is to say the same shall be printed on as good paper and in a volume of the size and character of the *History of the Council of Trent* printed in the year 1676, and the printing thereof shall be begun immediately and continued after at the rate of at least four sheets a week until the whole book be printed.

. . . the said Thomas Bassett doth promise to pay to the said John Locke, his executors, administrators or assigns, the sum of ten shillings a sheet for every sheet the said book shall contain, counting, for a sheet so much as is contained in a sheet of Milton's *History of England* in octavo, within seven days after the printing thereof shall be finished, and shall also within seven days after the said book shall be printed, deliver to the said John Locke or his assigns, twenty-five of the said books in sheets, and shall also let the said John Locke have as many more of the said books at the rate of one halfpenny a sheet as he the said John Locke shall desire, within twelve months after the publishing of the same, not exceeding the number of five and twenty more, all which money paid for any of the said five and twenty books, the said Thomas Bassett shall repay to the said John Locke whenever he shall reprint the said treatise.

And the said John Locke doth promise to the said Thomas Bassett to deliver to him on demand from time to time so much of the said book or treatise as shall make two sheets to be printed as above said, upon the said Thomas Bassett's delivery of a copy in print to the said John Locke of what he then last received from him. And in case any controversy shall arise concerning any matter contained in or relating to these articles the said John Locke [and] Thomas Bassett have hereby constituted John Freke of the Middle Temple, Esq., umpire or any one whom he shall in his absence under his hand nominate to be umpire. . . .

The agreement was witnessed by John Freke and Edward Clarke, and in a supplementary note Thomas Bassett stated that the whole book contained fifty-eight sheets; so that Locke was entitled to receive the sum of £29.

On 6 June[1] Locke sent Limborch a fairly sanguine account of the political situation in England:

You have no doubt heard already that Toleration is at length established here by an Act of Parliament—not perhaps to the extent which you . . . would desire; but it is something to have achieved so much. With such a beginning, I trust that those foundations of peace and liberty are laid, on which the Church of Christ was originally established.

[1] Amsterdam: Remonstrants' MSS. Ba. 256l (Latin).

None, except the Roman Catholics,[1] are absolutely forbidden the exercise of their worship, if they are but willing to take the oath of allegiance [2] and renounce Transubstantiation and some other dogmas of the Church of Rome. As to the oath, a dispensation is allowed to Quakers; nor would that confession of faith which you will see in the Act have been imposed upon them (and it is an ill example) but for the officious interference of some of their own body, whose imprudence many others of eminence [3] among them deeply regret.

In short, if 'comprehension' had failed, a large measure of 'indulgence' had been established. Locke told Limborch he had arranged to send a copy of the Toleration Act to Jean le Clerc, who could read English and would translate it for Limborch, who could not. At the same time he thanked Limborch, in his odd sly way, for 'certain tracts on toleration' he had sent him. These 'certain tracts' were writings of Locke himself. Copies of the letter on toleration which Locke had written to Limborch in 1686 had been printed at Gouda. It made a slim volume of ninety-six pages in duodecimo and bore the title: EPISTOLA DE TOLERANTIA *ad Clarissimum Virum T.A.R.P.T.O.L.A. scripta à P.A.P.O.J.L.A.* These initials, according to Jean le Clerc,[4] stand for '*Theologiae apud Remonstrantes Professorem, Tyrannidis Osorem Limburgium Amstelodamensem*' and '*Pacis Amico, Persecutionis Osore, Johanne Lockio Anglo*'.[5]

Once again the author's identity was concealed long after there had ceased to be any need for it. In his passion for secrecy, Locke was sometimes positively mendacious. I will give one example. In his letter to Limborch of 6 June 1689 [6] he said, 'I learn that some Englishman is now engaged in translating one of the tracts'.[7] This

---

[1] Not only Roman Catholics. All those who impugned the Trinity were expressly excepted. Hence, perhaps, Locke's vigorous repudiation of the name of 'Unitarian' or 'Socinian'.

[2] A number of bishops and clergy did in fact refuse to take the oath of allegiance. It included Archbishop Sancroft, four other bishops and four hundred lesser clergy who formed the party of Non-Jurors. One of them was Locke's unfortunate friend Denis Grenville, who ended up as James's Archbishop of York in exile.

[3] Their number may have included Benjamin Furly, who paid a prolonged visit to England during 1689.

[4] *Éloge, avertissement.*

[5] 'Professor of Theology among the Remonstrants, Hater of Tyranny, Limborch, of Amsterdam' and 'A Friend of Peace, Hater of Persecution, John Locke, Englishman'.

[6] Amsterdam: Remonstrants' MSS. Ba. 256 l (Latin).

[7] Limborch sent copies of the *Epistola de Tolerantia* to Locke with a letter dated *16 May 1689* (III, D. 16, f. 203: Latin).

is an obvious reference to the translation of the *Epistola de Tolerantia* then being made by William Popple,[1] the Unitarian merchant and author. Yet Locke wrote in a codicil to his will dated 15 September 1704 [2] of his *Epistola de Tolerantia* having been 'translated into English without my privity'.

Limborch thought Locke's reticence about his pamphlet foolish, and tried to sting him into admitting publicly that he had written it. He informed [3] Locke of the rumours which were abroad in Holland about the author's identity: some people thought Gilbert Burnet had written it, others that the Remonstrants were responsible, though Limborch added politely: 'I know no Remonstrant so learned or so excellent a Latin stylist'. But still Locke did not respond as Limborch hoped.

Among the friends Locke saw regularly after his return to London were the two peers, the Earl of Pembroke and Viscount Mordaunt, the latter being soon raised by William III to the Earldom of Monmouth.[4] According to Lady Masham,[5] Locke spent 'one day every week' with Lord Pembroke 'undisturbed by such as could not bear a part in the best entertainment of rational minds—free discourse concerning useful truths'. At this intellectual *salon* of Lord Pembroke's Locke made a renewed acquaintance with a number of his most distinguished contemporaries. The pleasures of Lord Monmouth's house were simpler. For one thing, the Monmouths lived at Parson's Green, then separated from London by some miles of open country. It was when, in Lady Masham's words, the town air 'made war' on Locke's lungs, that he was most keenly grateful for the refuge afforded by 'Lord Monmouth and his Lady (who both of them always expressed much esteem and friendship for Mr. Locke)'. The house at Parson's Green was 'advantaged with a delightful garden', the beauties of which were celebrated by more than one writer of the time. In its twenty acres there were flowers and lawns and cypress shades, gazebos, fountains, statues, and one of the finest fruit-gardens in Europe. The pity was that Locke

---

1 William Popple, a nephew of the poet Marvell, was an English merchant who had lived in Bordeaux. He was the author of *A Rational Catechism* (1687) and other Unitarian works.

2 B.L. MSS Locke, b.5/14.

3 *15 June 1689* (*ibid.*, c. 14, f. 24: Latin).

4 The Dukedom of that name was erased by the attainder of the royal bastard.

5 Amsterdam: Remonstrants' MSS. J. 57a.

needed to leave London most at the least interesting season of the garden's year.

Lord Monmouth himself was torn from his arcadian retreat in the summer of 1689 to go on another military mission: his King dispatched him to the North of England to inspect his forces there. Lord Monmouth was not favourably impressed by what he saw. In a letter he wrote to Locke from Newcastle on 9 June,[1] he said:

> I must begin with a description of my Lord Delamere's army;[2] it wanted nothing to be a complete regiment but clothes, boots, arms, horses, men and officers: there never was anything so scandalous as that the King should have paid near £9,000 already to that rout of fellows, that have been more disorderly than any, never having all the while but one captain with them. He hath still those same champions with him that saved the nation, in the same or worse equipages [than] they were in the west, mounted upon just such horses, [they] attended the Protestant peer out of town.
>
> Good God, what is the love of money! *O Roma venalis esses*, etc., and so is everything else. Who has got £10,000 by the late-made peer? We take it for granted he gave no more; he offered but fifteen for fifteen years together. Some of our lords take their rest, others their pleasure: my Lords Devonshire [3] and Lumley [4] stay here; Mr. Wharton [5] goes for Scotland. I go to-morrow to Berwick to examine some regiments, and come back the next day to Newcastle, a pleasant journey; at least no reproach shall lie at my door; for I can brag that

<hr/>

[1] B.L. MSS. Locke, c. 16, f. 105.

[2] Henry Booth (1652–1694) second Baron Delamere had raised an army in Cheshire to support Prince William in November 1688. An early Whig, he had been arrested in 1683 on a charge of complicity in the Rye House Plot, and twice imprisoned by James II, but on each occasion his peers had acquitted him. His support of the Prince earned him the Earldom of Warrington and a place second only to Lord Monmouth in William's Treasury. However, his extreme Puritanism soon alienated him from Lord Monmouth, and Burnet records that 'though both most violent Whigs, [they] became great enemies' (*Bishop Burnet's History*, ed. cit., IV, p. 7).

[3] William Cavendish (1640–1707), third Earl (later first Duke) of Devonshire, had supported Shaftesbury's party in its earliest days, but withdrawn from the society of Russell and the militant Whigs in 1683. He felled an officer who called him an exclusionist at James's Court, and was thereafter disgraced. On the Prince's landing he raised an army in Derby and Nottingham to support him.

[4] Richard Lumley, first Baron Lumley (later first Earl of Scarborough), was of Catholic birth and education. A favourite of Charles II, he had helped to capture the Duke of Monmouth for James II. He was converted to Protestantism in 1687, and in 1688 he seized Newcastle for William.

[5] Thomas Wharton (1648–1715), subsequently first Marquis of Wharton, had been a moderate Whig in the House of Commons. He wrote the famous revolutionary song 'Lilli Burlero', and joined the Prince at Exeter in November 1688.

pleasure, when I am engaged in business, never made me go an hour out of my way. Direct your letters to Carlisle.

Lord Pembroke, too, had occasion to leave London on the King's business in the summer of 1689. He was appointed Ambassador Extraordinary to the Netherlands.[1] Locke mentioned this in a letter [2] to Limborch, saying that Lord Pembroke wished to 'make your acquaintance' while he was at The Hague. Locke described Lord Pembroke as 'a great scholar, devoted to all useful arts, and the friend of all learned and honourable men'. In a postscript Locke mentioned that he had himself been on the point of accompanying the new Ambassador, but that imperative business had detained him in London.

Lord Pembroke wrote to Locke from Holland in August [3] asking him to write as often as he could: 'of the number of your letters I shall never be satisfied'. Lord Pembroke averred that people whose 'friendship with one another is occasioned by delight in the same sensual pleasures' could not 'take the satisfaction as they may whose very souls are fitted to unite'; and he hoped that neither distance of time nor of place 'will be able to disunite you from your friend and servant, Pembroke'.

Several members of Locke's Remonstrant circle paid their respects to the new Ambassador at The Hague. Limborch recounted [4] his impressions—which were very favourable—to Locke; and Le Clerc, having given Lord Pembroke a copy of his book on Jansenism, wrote [5] to ask Locke to find out if the Ambassador had liked it.

The imperative business which prevented Locke's going to Holland with Lord Pembroke may well have had to do with the publication of the *Essay Concerning Human Understanding* and the *Two Treatises of Government*. Secretive as he was about his political book, Locke wanted the maximum publicity for his philosophical one, and he still intended to have the Greenhill portrait engraved to serve as a frontispiece. He informed Mrs. Stringer in July [6] that he had healed his breach with her husband, and politely asked her to let him have the picture to reproduce. She complied promptly and

[1] B.M. Add. MSS. 34340, f. 49.
[2] 7 June 1689 (Amsterdam: Remonstrants' MSS. Ba. 256m: Latin).
[3] *12 August 1689* (B.L. MSS. Locke, c. 11, f. 198).
[4] *30 September 1689* (ibid., c. 14, f. 32: Latin).
[5] *7 November 1689* (ibid., c. 13, f. 37: French).
[6] 23 July 1689 (ibid., c. 24, f. 259).

the picture was sent on its way to the engraver. After Locke had thanked her, she replied [1] saying she was glad it had arrived in time 'to give you the satisfaction of a copy to put before your book', which, she said, she was told was 'above my head'. She added: 'I hope you cannot doubt but the picture is at your own disposal, both for time and place'.

'Disposal' was the significant word. Edward Clarke, paying a visit just then to the Stringers at Ivychurch, reported [2] to Locke that although they were 'willing it should remain in your hands till the plate be finished', they still claimed that the portrait was theirs.

Locke maintained with the same conviction that the portrait was his, and by early September [3] Mrs. Stringer was writing to tell him that she was 'very sorry to find by your last letter, as well as your slow return [of the picture] that you are so coldly disposed to a pure, firm and lasting friendship'.

Finally the Greenhill portrait appeared in neither issue of the first edition of the *Essay*, and the portrait which was used as a frontis-piece to the two issues [4] of the second edition published in 1694, was engraved from one drawn *ad vivum* by Sylvanus (or 'Sylvester', as he sometimes spelt his name after he came to England) Brownover.

The original picture, which is oval in shape, and which has been preserved in the lid of a silver box, was made in 1685, and although Locke's face looks very much older than it does in the Greenhill picture, it has nevertheless retained its fulness, and something of its cavalier quality: it is quite unlike the cadaverous and sickly scholar of the famous late portraits by Kneller. It is the face of a man of affairs, commanding rather than sensitive, and distinctly present-minded; almost, one might have said, a politician's face. Indeed, in his own devious and unobtrusive way, Locke *was* a politician, advising and prompting behind the scenes the men who took the stage itself.

One of these men was the new Solicitor-General in William's

---

[1] 29 July 1689 (B.L. MSS. Locke, c. 19, f. 101).

[2] 30 July 1689 (Rand, pp. 294–5).

[3] 5 September 1689 (B.L. MSS. Locke, c. 19, f. 107).

[4] Wing (L. 2740) records only one issue (that bearing the imprint of the Churchills) but there was another entitled *An Essay concerning Humane Understanding. In four books. Written by John Locke Gent. The Second Edition with large additions.* London, Printed for Thomas Dring at the Harrow, over against the Inner Temple Gate in Fleet Street, and Samuel Manship, at the Ship in Cornhill, near the Royal Exchange, MDCXCIV (Copy in B.L.).

Government, John Somers.[1] Somers had not been unknown to Shaftesbury, but he had made his name at the trial of the seven bishops in June 1688,[2] where, as junior defending counsel, his brilliant advocacy was thought to have won the case. A member for Worcester in the Convention Parliament, he presided over the committee which framed, and he probably had the greatest share in writing, the Declaration of Rights which William and Mary had to accept as part of the bargain which gave them the throne. This circumstance lends an added interest to Somers's connection with Locke; but as the Declaration of Rights was complete by 12 February, when Locke landed in England, Somers could not have been in personal touch with him at the time he was at work on that document, although conversations with Locke probably influenced his contribution to the framing of the Bill of Rights [3] which was enacted some months later.

On a visit to his constituency in September Somers [4] sought Locke's advice on the management of his political activities. He wrote:

> The country generally speaking is extremely well disposed in rela-
> tion to the Government, but some few clergymen who have not taken
> the oaths and some that have (and a very little party of such as pay them
> blind obedience) use incredible diligence—by misconstructions of
> everything, false stories and spreading of libels—to infect the people.
> I wish heartily the friends of the government were encouraged to use
> the same diligence in suppressing such doings. . . . Your former
> favours make me bold to presume upon you, and your judgement is

[1] Born in 1651 to a Worcestershire family of smaller gentry, Somers matriculated at Trinity College, Oxford, in 1667 and was called to the Bar at the Middle Temple in 1676. Besides his political and legal work, he also had philosophical and literary interests. Though an ugly man, he possessed a remarkably beautiful voice.

[2] After James II issued his second Declaration of Indulgence in May 1688, Sancroft and six other bishops drew up a petition requesting the King to withdraw the Declaration. For printing and publishing this petition, the seven bishops were arrested and sent to the Tower on the charge of issuing a seditious libel. The jury found them not guilty.

[3] The Bill of Rights was not a Bill of 'the Rights of Man', but of the Rights of Parliament. It removed the King's power to suspend Parliament. It made illegal the raising of a standing army without the consent of Parliament. It denied the King the right to levy taxes without the consent of Parliament. It declared that the election of members of Parliament ought to be free. It upheld the freedom of speech in Parliament against the interference of any court; and it affirmed that Parliament ought to meet frequently.

[4] 25 September 1689 (B.L. MSS. Locke, c. 18, f. 151).

such that I can depend on your instructions as the rules for my behaviour.

Whether it was due to Locke's counsel or his own native genius, Somers rose quickly in the hierarchy of Whig politics and it was not long before he became his party's leading statesman.

In the later months of 1689 Locke had no fewer than three books in the press, and, what is more, these three books were the most important he ever wrote: the *Essay Concerning Human Understanding*,[1] the *Two Treatises of Government*,[2] and *A Letter Concerning Toleration*,[3] William Popple's translation of the *Epistola de Tolerantia*. A licence to print the *Two Treatises on Government* was granted to Awnsham Churchill by the censor James Fraser on 23 August, and printing seems to have begun soon afterwards. The story of the publication of this manuscript is a complicated one. As Locke himself explains in the preface, the book consists of two fragments of a larger work, the central and longest part of which had been lost. Having decided to print it as two treatises in one volume, Locke made certain alterations to the text, notably of the second part,[4] to bring a book, which had originally been written when Shaftesbury was planning to overthrow Charles II, into line with the new political situation following the revolution settlement of 1689. Whatever the original title of the work, it was entered by Awnsham Churchill in the Stationers' Register in Michaelmas Term under that with which it was issued.

Awnsham Churchill also published the *Letter Concerning Tolera-*

[1] *An Essay Concerning Humane Understanding. In Four Books.* London: Printed for Tho. Basset, and sold by Edw. Mory at the Sign of the Three Bibles in St. Paul's Churchyard. MDCXC.

Another issue of this first edition was printed bearing the words Printed by Eliz. Holt, for Thomas Basset, at the George in Fleet Street, near St. Dunstan's Church. MDCXC.

[2] *Two Treatises of Government. In the former, the false Principles, and Foundation of Sir Thomas Filmer, And his Followers Are Detected and Overthrown, The latter is an Essay Concerning The True Original, Extent and End of Civil Government.* London, Printed for Awnsham Churchill, at the Black Swan in Ave-Mary-Lane, by Amen Corner, 1690.

[3] *A Letter Concerning Toleration.* London, Printed for Awnsham Churchill at the Black Swan at Amen Corner.

[4] *Vide Transactions of the Cambridge Bibliographical Society*, Vol. I, Part IV, pp. 341–7 and Vol. II, Part I, pp. 63–87.

tion,[1] which was licensed by the censor on 3 October 1689. First editions of the *Essay Concerning Human Understanding* were on sale in December and of the *Two Treatises of Government* as early as October, 1689, though both were dated '1690', for booksellers then, like magazine publishers today, post-dated their books so that they might look new longer.

Locke posted copies of the one book he acknowledged, the *Essay*, to several friends. Edward Clarke, however, was in London at the time of publication—'I am at the tavern with your husband', Locke wrote to Mary Clarke on 12 December [2] 'and other blades of his gang as debauched as he'—so that he probably received his copy by hand.

James Tyrrell, quick as ever to take offence, found Locke's letter offering him the book disagreeably 'cold and short'.[3] At the same time Tyrrell complained in general terms about Locke's putting him 'from the first rank of friends' into 'the second or third' of his 'ordinary acquaintance'. He added:

> however I give you thanks for the only grateful part of your letter— the kind offer of one of your books *De Intellectu*, which, having already a great value for, from only the rough draft still in my hands, I have therefore so much the greater desire to read it now it is increased with so many new notions. It came down to Oxford last week and many copies are sold of it, and I hear it well approved of by those who have begun the reading of it. For my part, I have read no more than the epistle and part of the preface; and for the rest wait this much desired favour.

In a postscript he wrote:

> Here is lately come down from London a very solid and rational treatise called *Of Government*, in which Sir R. Filmer's principles are

[1] In Popple's (anonymous) Preface to this anonymous pamphlet, it was explained that the Latin version had already been well received on the continent; and argued that no people stood 'in more need of something further both said and done' in the matter of religious toleration than the English:

'We have need of more generous remedies than what have yet been made use of in our distemper. It is neither Declarations of Indulgence nor Acts of Comprehension, such as have yet been practised or projected amongst us, that can do the work. The first will but palliate, the second increase our evil. Absolute liberty, just and true liberty, equal and impartial liberty is the thing that we stand in need of'.

Vide also the Advertisement of *A Letter Concerning Toleration*, London 1800 ('The present Address to the Reader was prefixed by the translator, Mr. Popple'), and Christophersen, p. 15.

[2] Rand, p. 296. Locke wrote in his journal on 3 December: "Sent for 12 of my books to Mrs. Holt by Graves."

[3] 20 December 1689, B.L. MSS. Locke, c. 22, f. 71.

very well confuted, and since Dr. Parr [1] writes me word that some people do me the favour to make me the author of it, I pray ask your friend Mr. Churchill, who presents it, who is the author of it, if it be not a secret, and let me know it if you do me the favour to write to me since I find he speaks of the author of *Patriarcha Non Monarcha* [2] with more respect than he deserves.

Tyrrell had other news for the philosopher. One of Locke's Dutch friends, Dr. Matthew Slade (or Sladus), had immigrated into England early in the year, hoping to improve his fortune as a physician; in the first few months he had not done so, and having borrowed money from Locke to pay his inn bills, he had been put in touch with Tyrrell. After a short stay at Oakley, Dr. Slade set out on 20 December for London, where he intended to spend the Christmas holiday, but hardly had he entered the coach than he had an epileptic fit and died. [3]

Locke transmitted the news on 27 December [4] to Limborch, who had but lately written [5] to Locke to complain, as Tyrrell complained, of neglect. There was in fact no lack of warmth in Locke's attitude to Limborch: his busy London life simply left him no time to answer the long letters which reached him so frequently from Amsterdam.

Parliament became increasingly quarrelsome that winter; and although, despite the war with France, there was general tranquillity in England, civil war was brewing in Scotland, and the supporters of James II were still entrenched in Ireland. William III, impatient with the politicians, dissolved the House of Commons in February. At the general election which followed several of Locke's friends were candidates: Edward Clarke stood at Taunton, Sir William Yonge at Honiton, Sir John Somers [6] at Worcester, and Shaftesbury's grand-

---

[1] Richard Parr (1617–91), Fellow and Chaplain of Exeter College, Oxford, D.D., was the biographer of Tyrrell's uncle, Archbishop Ussher.

[2] James Tyrrell himself.

[3] Four letters from Slade to Locke are in the Lovelace Collection (B.L. MSS. Locke, c. 18, ff. 112–17). Anthony Wood was interested in Dr. Slade and wrote to Tyrrell to ask if that physician was the son or grandson of Dr. Matthew Slade, rector of the gymnasium at Amsterdam, about whom he, Wood, wanted information for his *Athenae Oxoniensis*. Tyrrell forwarded Wood's letter to Locke. In his journal on 3 April 1690 Locke wrote: 'Delivered to Mr. Pawling Dr. Slade's pedigree and five mourning rings directed to Mr. Tyrrell.'

[4] Amsterdam: Remonstrants' MSS. Ba. 256q (Latin).

[5] *27 December 1689* (B.L. MSS. Locke, c. 14, f. 38: Latin).

[6] He had been knighted in October 1689.

son Lord Ashley at Poole. Clarke was stricken with rheumatism during the campaign at Taunton, and his wife said [1] that 'there have been all the foul practices imaginable in the management' of the election; but it was thought that 'Portman and Clarke will carry it if there is not tricks played by the first mentioned'. Clarke and his partner *did* carry it; so elsewhere did Somers, Ashley and Yonge. But generally the election was a Tory victory over the Whigs. When Somers, who had been returned unopposed at Worcester, wrote [2] to ask Locke if he should go back to Westminster for the opening of Parliament or remain on circuit, Locke urged him to put his political duties first, and come forthwith to London.

Locke was not pleased with the result of the election. William III was. In the days when he was aspiring to the English throne, when he had put freedom and the Protestant faith above all things, and hoisted a rebel's colours, William's closest ties were with the Whigs. But now that he was a well-established ruler, he was not less interested in the rights of kings than in the rights of man. The Tory Party, with its historic attachment to those royal rights, had come to have the greater appeal for him; and the Tory leaders had already proved themselves, in his eyes, better skilled than their Whig opponents in the science of administration.

Between William and the leading English politicians there was not, in any case, much affection, or unqualified respect. The politicians sickened the King by their selfish clamour for positions and rewards no less than by their constant bickering over issues which seemed to him intolerably trivial. William wanted a united Britain as part of a united Protestant Front against France; and his Whiggish and moderate ministers had disappointed him. They had even resisted his proposal to lead his own army against the forces of James II in Ireland. The leading English politicians had on their side some cogent reasons for disliking the King, who showed a tactless preference for Dutchmen, not only as companions of the alcove, but as political counsellors, and, still worse, as the principal beneficiaries of his material generosity. Nor was the boorish, proud, jealous and secretive side of William's personality such as to endear him to his ministers. His policy of distributing places between the Whigs and Tories had pleased neither party. Each desired a monopoly of power.

[1] 3 March 1689/90 (B.L. MSS. Locke, c. 6, f. 83).
[2] 5 March 1689/90 (*ibid.*, c. 18, f. 153).

After the resignation of Halifax [1] and the general election, the King gave way to the demand for a one-party administration. He chose a Tory government. Its leader, not immediately, but soon afterwards, was Thomas Osborne, Marquis of Carmarthen. This nobleman was none other than he who, as Earl of Danby, had been Shaftesbury's great rival in the time of Charles II. After his long imprisonment in the Tower of London, Danby had recovered the leadership of the Protestant Tories during the reign of James II, and for carrying that Party over to William at the Revolution he claimed—and received—very high rewards, the marquisate being one of them.

In some respects Carmarthen still resembled Shaftesbury. He was not a popular man, but his Toryism was free from any taint of Jacobitism, he was adaptable and empirical, and he was prodigiously clever at the political game. He was, above all things, a superb organiser. His self-confidence matched his abilities. He installed himself in St. James's Palace and played the part of the King's first minister with splendid *panache*; and he held his position for the next three years. His power during that time was unrivalled, even though, as Professor Browning says,[2] he was never able 'to dominate William III as he had dominated Charles II'.

At the time of Carmarthen's return to power, the story got abroad that Locke had been made Secretary-at-War. The post of Secretary-at-War, unlike that of Secretary of War (a later innovation), was a Civil Service, not a ministerial one, and Locke might well have held it. But the rumour was false. The Secretary-at-War was, and remained, William Blathwayt, secretary also to the Lords of Trade, and a Tory. Blathwayt's predecessor at the War Office was an Irishman named Matthew Locke, and confusion of his name with that of the philosopher was possibly the origin of the rumour.[3]

John Locke was not well enough at the time to have welcomed a new appointment. At Dorset Court he had taken to his bed. And although Mary Clarke attributed his illness to his 'debauches',[4] it was really, as Locke knew, the London fog which had reduced him. His cough was worse than it had ever been before.

[1] This essentially moderate statesman resigned on 8 February 1689/90.
[2] Andrew Browning, *The Earl of Danby*, I, p. 475.
[3] Wood recorded the rumour in his diary on 3 March 1689/90 (*Life and Times*, III, p. 327).
[4] 23 March 1689/90 (B.L. MSS. Locke, c. 6, f. 185).

In April 1690 Locke's first literary adversary appeared in print. An Oxford scholar and clergyman named Jonas Proast,[1] who had been expelled for no disreputable reason from the chaplain's place at All Souls, came out with a pamphlet entitled *The Argument of the 'Letter Concerning Toleration' Briefly Considered and Answered*.[2]

Proast was willing to admit that Locke's[3] policy of toleration might 'tend to the advancement of trade and commerce', which, he shrewdly noted, 'some seem to place above all other considerations'. He said that all he wished to dispute was whether 'the True Religion would be in any way the gainer by it'.

He went on to examine Locke's case in detail. How far was it true, he asked, that belief was (as Locke claimed) 'to be wrought in men by reason and argument, not by outward compulsion'? Proast agreed that rational argument would lead men to the True Religion, but he did not agree that men, left alone, would in fact exercise their reason. Although force could not be used *instead of* argument to effect the same end, it could, Proast claimed, be used to make men *consider* arguments which they might otherwise not consider at all. Therefore, Proast concluded, it was false to say, as Locke had said, that 'all outward force is useless for the promoting True Religion'.

While Locke stressed the reasonableness of man, Proast thought that men arrived at their religious beliefs by processes other than rational deliberation: 'The impressions of education, the reverence and admiration of persons, and the like incompetent motives determine far greater numbers than reason'.

Proast agreed with Locke that *excessive* force should not be used, but he held that *moderate* force, rightly employed, could bring men to a due consideration of spiritual things. As for Locke's contention that the civil ruler or magistrate has 'no right' to use force, Proast questioned the whole theory of society from which this proposition

---

[1] Jonas Proast, a Colchester man of German descent, matriculated at Oxford at Queen's in 1659. He incorporated at Cambridge in 1670, but returned to Oxford some years later as Chaplain first of Queen's, then of All Souls, from which college he was expelled in 1688 by the new Warden (Leopold Finch) 'for contempt' (*L. and T.*, III, p. 263). He was not restored until 1692.

[2] Another Reply to Locke was written by Thomas Long, of Exeter College, Oxford, with the title *The 'Letter for Toleration' Deciphered and the Absurdity and Impiety of an Absolute Toleration Demonstrated* (*Ath. Oxon.*, IV, p. 488). It was published about the same time as Proast's, but, although it is by no means a contemptible document, Locke did not trouble to answer it.

[3] Proast's pamphlet, which was anonymous, referred to Locke as 'our Author' or 'the Author' [of the *Letter Concerning Toleration*].

derived. Whereas Locke held that civil societies existed for the protection of the person and of material interests, Proast preferred to
give priority to man's eternal and spiritual interests; and he rejected
Locke's view that the salvation of souls was no part of the civil
magistrates' business. Proast held that it was the civil magistrates'
duty, first, to oblige the spiritual pastors to perform their duties;
secondly, to oblige their congregations to pay them reverence and
due submission; and, thirdly, to lay 'such penalties upon those who
refuse to embrace their doctrine . . . as may make them *bethink*
themselves and put it out of the power of any foolish humour or
unreasonable prejudice to alienate them from the truth'.

Proast's pamphlet was exceptionally well written, and as its argument was manifestly one which Locke could not afford to ignore,
he bestirred himself at once to write an answer to it.

In that same spring of 1690 Limborch made Locke extremely
angry by giving away the secret of the *Epistola de Tolerantia*. He
told it, in strict confidence, to Dr. Guenellon and Dr. Veen. Limborch explained [1] that Guenellon had asked him directly whether
Locke had written it, and Limborch had not felt he could lie about
it, especially to a man who might afterwards find out the truth and
then be 'very angry with me for deceiving him about a person who
was also a very dear friend of his'. Limborch questioned whether
Locke was wise to go on concealing his authorship of the pamphlet
when the publication of his name 'would attract many new readers
and also lend authority to the pamphlet'.

In his reply [2] Locke wrote:

> I have received your last letter and I am astonished at your account
> of what has passed between you and Dr. Guenellon. I must confess it
> amazes me that these inquisitive men should have found it so easy to
> fish out of you a secret that I had hoped was perfectly safe in your
> keeping. Rumours are abroad about this pamphlet which, having
> troubled me not at all when its authorship was unknown, now threaten
> to ruin me . . .

> All I can say is that if you had confided such a secret to me, I should
> never have divulged it to any friend or acquaintance or any other
> human being on any condition. You do not know what trouble you
> have brought on me. . . .

It must, indeed, have been difficult for Limborch to imagine what

---

[1] *25 April 1690* (B.L. MSS. Locke, c. 14, f. 44: Latin).
[2] *22 April 1690* (*ibid.*, c. 24, f. 155: Latin).

'trouble' he had brought on Locke. But Dr. Guenellon had clearly no intention of keeping the matter secret. In a letter [1] he wrote to Locke, some days before Limborch had written, the doctor said he had heard from Mr. D'Aranda that the *Epistola* was Locke's and that everyone in England knew it, so he, Guenellon, intended to make it known in Holland as well.

After receiving Locke's reproaches, Limborch sent another and fuller explanation [2] of the circumstances in which he had given the secret away, and once more suggested that the revelation could not be a matter of profound importance. Guenellon also wrote again [3] to apologise for vexing Locke, and he too insisted that no harm could come of the truth's being known.

Restored to better health by the better weather, Locke sought at the end of spring the refreshment of cleaner air. He spent some time with the Monmouths at Parson's Green, and then went on to Oates in Essex. No one had been more pleased to welcome him home to England than Damaris Masham, the closest of his women friends. Now a married woman and a mother, his 'Philoclea' was as ready as ever to embrace her beloved philosopher; indeed, as the mistress of a small country house, she was now able to receive him as she could not have done in the past.

Locke left London fully convinced that he had phthisis, but a letter he had from Dr. William Cole [4] in June suggested that this diagnosis was false. Dr. Cole wrote: [5]

... From the accurate account you are pleased to give of your symptoms, and the progress of them, I am much inclined to believe your apprehensions of your condition in relation to your present distemper, are but the same which the most of thinking men (physicians not excepted) have of themselves when indisposed; viz. they make too close reflection on their own diseases, either magnifying them, or not so distinctly perceiving them, through their immediate and great

---

[1] *18 April 1690* (B.L. MSS. Locke, c. 11, f. 32: French).

[2] *12 May 1690* (*ibid.*, c. 14, f. 46: Latin).

[3] *20 June 1690* (*ibid.*, c. 11, f. 34: French).

[4] William Cole (1635–1716), M.D. Oxon (1666), practised at Worcester until 1692, when he moved to London and became a fashionable physician. Though known to Sydenham, he was not of Sydenham's school. He expounded his own 'mechanical' theories of medicine in several successful books, written for the greater part in Latin, and especially admired on the Continent.

[5] 11 June 1690, B.L. MSS. Locke, c. 6, f. 201.

concern which generally makes men form dreadful ideas of things, as the eye does an object brought too near to it. Not but that all phthisis, though ever so recent carry danger, and what at first is but slight catarrh (as they call it) may in a little time, especially if neglected, give the lungs such an atony (if not perhaps in time exulcerate them) as must be fatal. But I hope what you take for a purulent discharge may be only a pituita better ripened than ordinary, and thence may be a sign your cough is taking leave of you. . . .

This letter, coupled with other evidence scattered about Locke's papers, makes it reasonable to conclude that what was wrong with him was still his old trouble, asthma, and not tuberculosis. At Oates, moreover, where he stayed as the guest of Lady Masham until September, Locke seemed to get quite well again.

Some Oxford criticisms of his *Essay* reached the author at Oates through James Tyrrell. In a somewhat ill-tempered reply,[1] which Locke wrote but may not have sent, he said: 'I see you and your friends are so far from understanding me yet rightly that I shall give you the trouble of a few lines to make my meaning clearer, if possible, than it is'.

Tyrrell having raised again his favourite topic of *lex naturae*, Locke protested that he had affirmed (in Book I, section III, paragraph 13 of his *Essay*) 'in as direct words as can ordinarily be made use of to express one's thoughts that there is a Law of Nature knowable by the light of nature'. To Tyrrell's doubts as to whether the existence of divine law could be demonstrated, Locke replied:

Will nothing then pass with you in religion or morality but what you can demonstrate? If you are of so nice a stomach, I am afraid, if I should now examine how much of your religion or morality you could demonstrate, how much you would have left: not but that I think that demonstration in those matters may be carried a great deal farther than it is. . . . But I know not how you would still have me, besides my purpose and against all rules of method, run out into a discourse of the divine law, show how and when it was promulgated to mankind, demonstrate its enforcement by rewards and punishments in another life, and in a place where I had nothing to do with all this, and in a case where some men's bare supposition of such a law, whether true or false, served my turn. . . . I did not design here to treat of the grounds of true morality, which is necessary to true and perfect happiness;

---

[1] 4 August 1690 (B.L. MSS. Locke, c. 24, f. 277).

it had been impertinent if I had so designed: my business was only to show whence men had moral ideas, and what they were. . . .'

In the autumn Locke had planned to go to Somerset, first to join Lady Monmouth at Bath and afterwards to go on to Chipley. But he wrote to inform Clarke on 1 September [1] that 'the ill weather we have had here', the 'entreaties of Sir Francis and my Lady' and 'my cough' had together made him decide to stay at Oates longer than he had originally intended. There were protests. Mrs. Isabella Duke,[2] on holiday in Tunbridge Wells, said that Lady Masham ought not to engross Locke wholly to herself, and Martha Lockhart wrote [3] to him from Kensington Palace protesting, 'I begin really to believe Mr. Locke has forgotten the way to London'.[4]

Martha Lockhart was a woman of the bedchamber to Queen Mary, albeit somewhat disgruntled in that office because she was underpaid. She was also a friend of the Monmouths, and told Locke in her letter of 1 September that Lord Monmouth 'thinks you have forgot him'. At the same time Mrs. Lockhart reported that despite the 'ill tidings' from Scotland,[5] she had never seen the Queen 'merrier nor more seemingly unconcerned in her life'; and that a letter had just arrived from the King in Ireland 'to tell us Limerick holds out, though there was a considerable attack made on the walls'.[6]

When he left Oates, Locke returned at once to his lodgings in London, and it is some measure of his intimacy with Lady Masham that he should complain of 'neglect' because she had failed to write to him for two weeks after his departure. On 30 September he drafted the following letter [7] to her:

Is it possible, Madam, that I, having very little satisfaction in the place I am but what I have from your letters, should yet be in danger to want them out of your neglect of me, and so must I owe it to your

[1] Rand, pp. 299–301.

[2] Mrs. Duke to Locke, 28 August 1690 (B.L. MSS. Locke c. 8, f. 45).

[3] 1 September 1690 (*ibid.*, c. 15, f. 3). This is the first of fifty letters from Martha Lockhart to Locke in the Lovelace Collection.

[4] In another letter (*ibid.*, f. 7) Martha Lockhart wrote: 'My Cousin Cutts could scarce make more enquiries after her lover than she does after you. I dare not let her know you do not return it' (16 September 1690).

[5] The Scots Lowlands had accepted the Orange Revolution as eagerly as England, but Jacobite sentiment was strong in the Highlands, and civil war had broken out in Scotland.

[6] Despite his victory in the Battle of the Boyne on 1 July, William failed to take Limerick, and on 30 August he lifted his siege of that city and returned to London.

[7] B.L. MSS. Locke, c. 24, ff. 189–92.

quarrel with Mrs. Lockhart [1] that I yesterday received the honour of one from you rather than your friendship to me. When I consider you, I know anger is not the general temper of your mind, and when I reflect on myself, methinks that unfriendly passion ought not to have anything to do with what comes from you to me and yet I know not how it so falls out that that is the only advocate I had lately with you, and prevailed on you to write to me at a time when all the interest I had in your calmer thoughts should not, it seems, have procured one word from you.

Pardon me if I complain a little on this occasion which so nearly concerns me, especially since the same true and long established friendship which has made me so tender and sensible in this part, bids me assure you that for all this complaint, it makes me no less sensible of the great obligation I have to you for your writing so often. . . . I am so much a flatterer of myself that I can find several excuses for you if you should sometimes forbear to write but I leave it to you to consider whether you can find in your heart to let any excuses stay those necessary effects of your friendship, and I think it enough that you know that I have such an esteem and respect for you that I cannot but be always much more happy for hearing from you, though the same esteem and respect will hinder me from being angry or quarrelling with you when I do not.

Locke reproached Lady Masham lightly but frankly for losing her temper with Martha Lockhart, and described his efforts to reconcile the two women:

I know not whether I have done well or not, but this I am sure: had I not interested myself for you as for a sister or a daughter or something nearer than those relations, I had never mentioned to you at first I am not ignorant how touchy those things are to meddle with, and 'tis with the same sincerity and freedom which I think you expect from me, I tell you that if you were my daughter I should say 'My dear child, they who are least faulty have advantage enough to make the greater allowance to others, and what boots it so to maintain one's innocence as to lose or disoblige a friend?'

Locke mentioned that his cough was 'a little increased', but he said that thanks to 'the retreat and security' he had lately enjoyed in Essex he could regard his symptoms with less 'apprehension and aversion'. He promised to return to Oates as soon as his business allowed him, and without waiting for ill health to drive him thither.

[1] I cannot discover the precise occasion or issue of Lady Masham's quarrel with Martha Lockhart.

Among the distinguished contemporaries Locke had met at Lord Pembroke's *salon*[1] on his return to England was Isaac Newton. The great physicist was ten years younger than Locke, but his genius had blossomed earlier in life; before he was twenty-five Newton had formulated the principle of gravitation and adumbrated his theory of colours. Elected Lucasian Professor of Mathematics at the age of twenty-seven, he had by that time already invented the reflecting telescope. His great *Principia* was not, however, completed until he was forty-four.

Newton's politics were Whiggish, at any rate strongly anti-Jacobite; and after taking an active part in resisting James II's encroachments on the privileges of his University, he represented Cambridge in the Convention Parliament; it was indeed his political record rather than his scientific attainments which had induced his friends at the University to nominate him.[2] He remained a Member of the House of Commons for only eleven months; and it was his presence in London on parliamentary business which enabled him to attend Lord Pembroke's *salon*.

In the Lovelace Collection[3] there is a manuscript (in Brownover's hand) of Newton's demonstration that the planets move in ellipses, endorsed, in Locke's hand, 'Mr. Newton, March 1689'. The manuscript was printed by Lord King in his biography of Locke, and Newton's biographer, Brewster, having read it there, noted that Newton's propositions were set out 'in a more popular manner than in the *Principia*'.[4] Brewster added: 'There can be no doubt that even in their present modified form, they were beyond the capacity of Mr. Locke'.[5]

Perhaps they were. But whether Locke understood this theory or not, he expressed publicly the utmost respect for the 'incomparable Mr. Newton', as he called him in the preface to the *Essay Concerning Human Understanding*.

---

[1] David Brewster: *Memoirs of the Life, Writings and Discoveries of Sir Isaac Newton* (Edinburgh, 1855), Vol. II, p. 115.

[2] *Ibid.*, p. 112.

[3] B.L. MSS. Locke, c. 31, f. 101. [4] Brewster, *op. cit.*, I, pp. 339–40.

[5] *Ibid.* Brewster also says Locke could not understand the *Principia* 'for want of geometrical knowledge' and he quotes in support of this the authority of Desaguliers (*Course of Experimental Philosophy*, I, p. 8) for the report that Locke asked Huyghens if all the mathematical propositions in Newton's *Principia* were true. 'When [Locke] was assured that he might depend upon their certainty, he took them for granted, and carefully examined the reasonings and corollaries deduced from them' (*op. cit.*, I, p. 339).

z

Isaac Newton was a strange man. If Locke was, as he is so often said to have been, a Puritan, Newton was doubly so—it is said that when Professor Vigani 'told a loose story about a nun', Newton 'broke off all acquaintance with him'.[1] Whereas Locke took such good care of his health, Newton took no care of himself at all: he ate little and irregularly; he seldom went to bed until the small hours of the morning; he went about 'with shoes down at heels, stockings untied ... and his head scarcely combed';[2] he took no recreation, neither riding, walking, bowling, nor any other exercise, 'thinking all hours lost that were not spent in his studies'.[3] Nevertheless, Newton proved himself a most efficient administrator when he left Cambridge for London.

As a friend he was sometimes extemely trying, but Locke, who recognised his genius and shared many of his interests and opinions, was patient, affectionate and loyal. The interests the two men shared were not confined to philosophy, science and politics, but included also theology. Indeed, what remains of their correspondence suggests that religion was the chief subject they discussed. Newton might perhaps have said that science and religion were inseparable; he believed that the 'most beautiful system of sun, planets and comets could only proceed from the counsel and dominion of an intelligent Being',[3] and so regarded science as nothing other than the study of God's workmanship; and the more he learned about the universe the stronger Newton's faith became.

The earliest extant letter he wrote to Locke is dated 28 September 1690;[4] in it Newton referred to 'authors' he had been consulting, and 'papers' he proposed sending to Locke. Both 'authors' and 'papers' were theological ones. Newton added:

> ... I could not forbear sending this letter along to you to let you know how extremely glad I was to hear from you. For though your letter brought me the first news of your having been so dangerously ill, yet by the undertaking of a journey into Holland, I hope you are well recovered. . . .

This 'journey into Holland' was one Locke was often talking about making, but which, when it came to the point, he never made.

[1] Brewster, *op. cit.*, II, p. 93.
[2] Humphrey Newton to Conduitt: 17 January 1727/8 (University Library, Cambridge).
[3] Quoted by W. Dampier, *Shorter History of Science*, 1944, p. 76.
[4] B.L. MSS. Locke, c. 16, f. 37.

On 14 November[1] Newton sent Locke the 'papers'[2] he had promised him in September. Evidently Locke had suggested to Newton that he should allow him to forward these papers—which concerned certain questions of Biblical interpretation—to Jean le Clerc for publication in the *Bibliothèque Universelle*. In his covering letter Newton wrote:

I send you now by the carrier Martin the papers I promised. I fear I have not only made you stay too long for them, but also made them too long by an addition. For upon the receipt of your letter, reviewing what I had by me concerning the text of I John 5, 7,[3] and examining authors a little further about it, I met with something new concerning that other of I Timothy 3, 16,[4] which I thought would be as acceptable to inquisitive men, and might be set down in a little room; but by searching further into authors to find out the bottom of it, it is swelled to the bigness you see. I fear the length of what I say on both texts may occasion you too much trouble, and therefore if at present you get only what concerns the first done into French, that of the other may stay till we see what success the first will have. I have no entire copy besides that I send you, and therefore would not have it lost, because I may perhaps after it has gone abroad long enough in French put it forth in English. What charge you are about it (for I am sure you will be put to some) you must let me know; for the trouble alone is enough for you.

Pray present my most humble service and thanks to my Lord and Lady Monmouth for their so kind remembrance of me for their favour is such that I can never sufficiently acknowledge it.

The 'design' of Lord and Lady Monmouth was to have Newton made Comptroller of the Mint. For Newton was a poor man. His chair at Cambridge carried a very inadequate stipend, and he needed another source of income. The Monmouths' efforts may have deserved his gratitude, but they did not succeed in getting him the post at the Mint until several years had passed.

[1] B.L. MSS. Locke, c. 16 f. 138.

[2] These papers are not in the Lovelace Collection. There is, however, a short list of references to Ezra and Nehemiah (*ibid.*, f. 139).

[3] 'And it is the Spirit that beareth witness, because the Spirit is truth, For there are three that bear record in heaven, the Father, the Word, and the Holy Ghost: and these three are one' (A.V.).

[4] 'And without controversy great is the mystery of godliness: God who was manifest in the flesh, justified in the Spirit, seen of angels, preached unto the Gentiles, believed on in the world, received up with glory' (A.V.).

Newton's letter reached Locke at Oates. Locke went there in mid-October, and was there again when he wrote to Limborch on 7 November [1] to acknowledge the news of the death of the Mrs. Veen, who, with her husband, had sheltered him in Amsterdam in 1685 ('I can never forget the many kindnesses I received from them both'). He was at Oates again on 22 December [2] when he sent Edward Clarke an invitation from Lady Masham to spend Christmas with them there. In this last letter, Locke also wrote:

> Pray if you come hither do the favour to bring me a pair of drawers of swan skin, which I have writ to your neighbour Clarke [3] to make for me. If you wear them down on your own, they will do you no harm this cold weather.

Locke's many intellectual interests, and the new preoccupations of an established author, left him with little time for medical studies, but he continued from time to time to advise his friends about their ailments. Mrs. Elizabeth Yonge, for example, asked his advice in treating a swollen cheek. She described her symptoms by letter [4] and proposed coming to London from Devon to consult him in person; but she was put off. Locke's other women friends were already being crowded out of his life by Lady Masham.

Edward Clarke was unable to spend Christmas in the Masham household and Locke was forced to go to London immediately afterwards. But on 17 January Locke hurried back to Oates, where he was joined a few days later by Newton, who, after his visit, wrote [5] to Locke to 'thank both you and my Lady Massam (*sic*) for your civilities at Oates and for not thinking that I made a long stay there'. Newton said he hoped they would meet again 'in due time, and then I shall be glad to have your judgement upon some of my mystical fancies'.

---

[1] Amsterdam: Remonstrants' MSS. Ba. 256s (Latin). Locke began by saying: 'I have today received your letter of 23 October, in which you reproach me for my silence, not without reason although I am innocent. I answered your very kind letter as soon as I received it, and at great length, for our clergy afford me much to write about. . . . But my letter, I now learn, is at the bottom of the sea. The mail boat was almost captured by the French, and all the letters—mine among them—were thrown overboard to prevent their falling in the hands of the enemy'.

[2] Rand, pp. 302–3.

[3] Samuel Clarke, Locke's tailor in London.

[4] B.L. MSS. Locke, c. 23, ff. 137–9. ·

[5] 7 February 1690/1 (*ibid.*, c. 16, f. 140).

Locke wrote [1] to Furly about this time saying that he was bearing the winter 'pretty well' in Essex, but that when he went to London he 'was almost dead in a fortnight'. This being true, or at any rate Locke's true belief, there was only one sensible thing for him to do about it: to leave London and find a permanent country home. Such is precisely what he did. He went to live at Oakes.

[1] 3 February 1690/1 (*Original Letters*, p. 48).

Chapter Twenty-three

OATES

LADY MASHAM wrote,[1] long afterwards, that it was Locke's poor health which forced him 'to think of a further remove' from London 'and of quitting it for the entire winter at least'.

He had during the years '89, '90 and part of '91 by some considerably long visits, with which he had obliged Sir Francis and me, made trial of the air of this place (which is something above twenty miles from London) and he thought that none would be so suitable to him. His company could not but be very desirable to us, and he had all the assurances we could give him of being always welcome here. But to make him easy in living with us, it was necessary he should do so upon his own terms, which Sir Francis at last consenting to, Mr. Locke then believed himself at home with us; and resolved (if it pleased God) here to end his days, which he did.

Locke's 'terms' were that he should pay a pound a week for his (and his servant's) keep, and a shilling a week for his horse.

He wrote from Oates to Limborch:[2]

I have already told you that I was acquainted with the daughter of Dr. Cudworth, and about her remarkable qualities. She is the wife of a baronet who represents the county (Essex) in the present parliament. They have received me as a guest in their house, and given me a refuge that is very kindly to my health.

The lady herself is well read in theological and philosophical questions, and of such an original mind that very few men could equal her in the abundance of her knowledge and her ability to use it. Her judgement is excellent, and I do not know many people who can bring such clarity of thought to the study of the most difficult subjects. She has also a capacity for searching through and solving problems beyond the range not only of most women but of most men. A weakness of vision now debars her from the reading to which she once applied

[1] Amsterdam: Remonstrants' MSS. J. 57a.
[2] 13 March 1690/1, *ibid.*, Ba. 256t (Latin).

herself with so much assiduity, but this defect is more than redeemed by the keenness of her intellect.

Oates was a small Tudor manor house in the parish of High Laver, a little north of Epping Forest and midway between the small towns of Harlow and Chipping Ongar. It was built in red Essex brick in a rough Gothic style, battlemented in some parts, gabled in others; when Locke went there it had still a moat around it and at least one lake. Oates was levelled to the ground in 1802,[1] but by that time it had been altered to please an eighteenth-century taste, with a park around the house, a handsome drive and lodges at the gates. The park has since become a water-meadow, the drive and the lodges have disappeared, the lakes have become muddy ponds, and only a few trees and relics of outbuildings survive to bear witness to its history.

Locke occupied two rooms on the first floor of the house, a study next to the entrance hall and a sleeping room adjoining.[2] When a French secretary was engaged to work for Locke at Oates, yet another room had to be given over to him. In Mr. Laslett's words: '[Locke's] presence, though it added a European notoriety to the place, and was a modest source of income, was also a little inconvenient, for it left so little room for other guests'.[3]

Locke filled his rooms with his own furniture, and it was not long before his belongings had spilled over into other parts of the house.[4] Besides his chairs and tables, his writing cabinet and his scientific instruments, he accumulated nearly five thousand books. Although he was once described as 'the gentleman now within the moated castle', his rooms looked out on to a lawn and garden, in which he liked to sit in fine weather to read. He enjoyed gardening too; in some respects he was more the master of the house than the baronet himself.

Sir Francis Masham sat for a portrait by Kneller, and this, together with what was written about him at the time, gives us an

---

[1] *Monthly Repository*, Vol. I, p. 176.

[2] Locke mentioned in a letter to Hans Sloane dated 15 March 1703/4 that his windows looked south and east (B.M. Sloane 4039, f. 259).

[3] Peter Laslett, *History Today*, August 1953, pp. 535–43.

[4] On 7 May 1697 Lady Masham signed an 'inventory of what in the new room up two pairs of stairs is Mr. Locke's'. Locke endorsed: 'Of things belonging to me in the room over my study at Oates.' (B.L. MSS. Locke, c. 25, f. 62). Other inventories in the Lovelace Collection give a complete list of everything in the house which Locke owned.

idea of what he was like. He was not a stupid man, but he was a commonplace one. The face in Kneller's portrait has a certain frankness and firmness: the features are those of a landed gentleman used to authority and good living, but they do not suggest fine feeling or cultivation of the mind. One can well believe that Sir Francis was something of a bore; but he was clearly quite an affable one; and it looks as though Locke and he each found it easy enough to accept the other, without being bothered by, or even perhaps much noticing the other's presence.

The household at Oates was not small. There were the sons of Sir Francis Masham's first marriage to his half-French wife—and because of their presence French was a language much spoken in the house—his only daughter, Esther Masham, and his only child by his second wife, Francis (or Frank) Cudworth Masham. These last two children were Locke's favourites: he called them 'Totty' and 'Dab' (or 'Laudabridis') respectively. Lady Masham's mother, Mrs. Ralph Cudworth, also lived in the house during her widowhood,[1] and Sir Francis Masham's mother lived nearby at Matching Hall. Ten servants looked after the family at Oates, and Locke brought with him Sylvanus Brownover, who combined the duties of valet and amanuensis.

No sooner was Locke's removal to Oates accomplished than he was beset with fresh worries about his properties in Somerset. Clarke wrote [2] to warn him that coal-mining at New Tynings would jeopardise his land there; then Locke's cousin, William Stratton, who had acted as his agent in Pensford since the death of Peter Locke, decided to retire from Sutton to Bristol.

Locke told Clarke: [3] 'I am at a loss where to find one to look after my concerns at Pensford if my cousin Stratton give it up.'

A few months later Clarke [4] was able to assure Locke that William Stratton would continue, despite his move to Bristol, 'to take the same care of your concerns as formerly'; and he also held out hope of reasonable compensation being paid for the damage done to Locke's property by the coal-workings.

Letters from Holland brought Locke news of Le Clerc's marriage [5]

---

[1] She was buried at High Laver Church, where a memorial tablet may be seen.
[2] 7 March 1690/1 (Rand, pp. 303–6).   [3] 16 March 1690/1 (*ibid*, p. 312).
[4] 8 July 1691. B.L. MSS. Locke, c. 6, f. 61.
[5] Le Clerc to Locke *11 April 1691* (*ibid.*, c. 13, f. 46: French).

and of the death of Furly's wife. In sending his condolences to Furly Locke said: [1]

> Our friends and relations are but borrowed advantages, lent us during pleasure and must be given back whenever called for. We receive them upon these terms and why should we repine? Or, if we do, what profits it us?

Locke urged Furly not to retire, as he had proposed, from business:

> want of health, want of spirit, want of useful thought, is the state of those who abandon themselves to griefs whereof business is the best, the safest and the quickest cure. . . . Keep in your employment. Increase it, and be as busy in it as you can—now more than ever.

Having spent three weeks in May in London, Locke returned to Oates in time to enjoy the summer in his new home. On 12 June he drafted a high-spirited letter [2] to the Countess of Monmouth.

> I little expected two Ladies should confer notes about me, to find out whether I were not bestowing myself upon a third. 'Twas an honour which, if ever I had been capable of, I thought myself now past. But since your Ladyship, who knows so well the irresistible power of your sex, concludes that neither philosophy, the artificial, nor age, the natural fence against it is sufficiently armed, 'tis better to pass for a Jesuit or anything rather than own myself capable of nothing but flat insensibility when your Ladyship thinks me worth the looking after. . . .

Locke expressed his pleasure at Lady Monmouth's having done him 'the honour to use the names of "jealousy" and "friend"'.

> Had I any talent that way I should certainly make a lampoon upon those ravenous widows, if it were but for the sake of four or five handsome young ladies I was at table with yesterday, who suffer in this common calamity. But at my age it is enough to be in love without poetry.

In the same month Isaac Newton sent Locke a more than usually interesting letter.[3] He began by saying: 'If the scheme you have laid of managing the Controller's place of the M[int] will not give you the trouble of too large a letter, you will oblige me by it'; and he

[1] *Original Letters* (Second Edition), pp. 50–1.
[2] 'To C. M.' (B.L. MSS. Locke, c. 24, f. 195).
[3] 30 June 1691, *ibid.*, c. 16, f. 142.

thanked Locke for 'being so mindful of me and ready to assist me with your interest'. He also expressed his appreciation of Locke's and Lady Masham's having looked into 'my book'—this being, apparently, a book on a Biblical subject.

In the same letter Newton recalled an experiment he had once made 'with the hazard of my eyes' in connection with the theory of colours:

The manner was this. I looked a very little while upon the sun in a looking glass with my right eye and then turned my eyes into a dark corner of my chamber and winked to observe the impression made and the circles of colours which encompassed it and how they decayed by degrees and at last vanished. This I repeated a second and a third time. At the third time, when the phantasm of light and colours about it were almost vanished, intending my fancy upon them to see their last appearance, I found to my amazement that they began to return and little by little to become as lively and vivid as when I had newly looked upon the sun. But when I ceased to intend my fancy upon them they vanished again. After this I found that as often as I went into the dark and intended my mind upon them, as when a man looks earnestly to see anything which is difficult to be seen, I could make the phantasm return without looking any more upon the sun. And the oftener I made it return the more easily I could make it return again. And at length by repeating this without looking any more upon the sun, I made such an impression upon my eye that if I looked upon the clouds or on a book or any bright object, I saw upon it a round bright spot of light like the sun. And which is still stranger, though I looked upon the sun with my right eye only and not with my left, yet my fancy began to make the impression upon my left eye as well as upon my right, for if I shut my right eye and looked upon a book or the clouds with my left eye I could see the spectrum of the sun almost as plain as with my right eye, if I did but intend my fancy a little while upon it. For at first if I shut my right eye, and looked with my left, the spectrum of the sun did not appear till I intended my fancy upon it, but by repeating this appeared every time more easily. And now in a few hours' time, I had brought my eye to such a pass that I could look upon no bright object with either eye, but I saw the sun before me, so that I durst neither write nor read, but to recover the use of my eyes, shut myself up in my chamber made dark for three days together and used all means to divert my imagination from the sun. For if I thought upon him I presently saw his picture, though I was in the dark. But by keeping in the dark and employing my mind about other things, I began in three or four days to have some use of my eyes again, and by forbearing a few days longer to look upon bright objects, recovered them pretty well, though not so well but that for some months after, the spectrum of the sun began to return as often as I began to meditate upon the phenomenon, even though I lay in bed at midnight with my curtains drawn.

Locke was always interested to hear of experiments of this kind, even though it is doubtful whether he fully appreciated the significance of Newton's work in the field of optics.[1]

Three days Locke spent in London were described by Lord Pembroke [2] as too brief a visit. Pembroke said there was no pleasure for him in correspondence with Locke when they might meet, and he assured the philosopher that nothing would end his dissatisfaction but seeing him in person.

Whether in response to this plea or under the pressure of other demands, Locke spent the greater part of the next three months away from Oates, not only in London, but also, in August, at Daunsey. When he returned to Essex in the autumn Clarke's son went to join him there.[3] Clarke had put Locke's system of education into practice in training this son, and as it had not worked out very well, he thought it would be a good idea for Locke to see the boy and find out what was wrong with him. Clarke did not seem to think, or at any rate did not suggest, that there might be something wrong with the theory.

One way and another Locke was kept very busy for the rest of the year; he explained to Limborch [4] that 'so many occupations, not of my seeking, have so engrossed my hours that I have not even

---

[1] 'Newton showed that white light is made up of light of various colours, differently refracted by passing through the prism, the most refracted being violet and the least red. On these results he solved the problem of the rainbow, and explained the colours which disturbed the vision through the then known refracting telescopes . . . (and) he invented a reflecting telescope.

'He examined the colours of thin plates, well known in bubbles and other films. By pressing a glass prism on to a lens of known curvature, the colours were formed into circles which he could measure, since called "Newton's rings". Using light of one colour only, the rings became alternately light and dark; it was then clear that the colours with white light were due to the abstraction of one colour after another in turn' (Sir William Dampier, *op. cit.*, p. 73).

[2] 30 June 1691 (B.L. MSS. Locke, c. 11, f. 200).

[3] On 15 September 1691 Clarke wrote to Lady Masham to arrange for his son to go to Oates 'to give Mr. Locke an opportunity of observing what improvements the child hath made under his tutor' (Rand, p. 315). *Vide* also Houghton Library, Harvard, U.S.A., MS. *46M–98.

[4] 14 November 1691, Amsterdam: Remonstrants' MSS. Ba. 256v (Latin).

had time to pay attention to certain pressing affairs of my own'. It was not a case, he added, of his being devoted to the public service, but rather, he said, 'I have been in a sort of maze in which every day brought fresh business which led in turn to further business which I could neither foresee nor avoid.'

Even so, Locke found time (on 29 November) to draft a letter [1] to Lady Forfar.[2]

> My Lord Forfar has been pleased more than once to tell me I must write to your Ladyship; a good commission had I but wit and gallantry enough. Mrs. Lockhart assures 'twill be acceptable to your Ladyship, and you know she makes me believe what she pleases. 'Tis certain I have obeyed, and your Ladyship has the trouble of it. But I beseech you, be not revenged on me; I had no malice mixed with my deference, though perhaps I might admit it was not without some secret satisfaction in having once had opportunity to tell the finest lady in Scotland the veneration I have for her under the shelter of so good an excuse as she herself must allow.
>
> I am extremely sorry to hear of your Ladyship's sickness, but apprehend it the less as being only the concomitant of a great belly, and I make no doubt but that having now done penance for beginning so late, you will every day increase in ease and strength. Whilst you are breeding you have the power to change the worth and relish of things, and may without the censure of a depraved palate prefer crabs and blackberries to apricots and peaches, and 'tis no ill manners to offer such tash to your Ladyship if you have but cast a look towards them.

Locke also found time to prepare a special edition of *Aesop's Fables* designed to help children learn Latin. His proposal was to print each Latin word above the equivalent English word, and he sent a specimen sheet to Clarke,[3] asking him 'to let Awnsham Churchill have it as soon as you can'. He explained that Churchill intended to offer it to the Stationers Company at their next court, and, if they did not accept it, to publish it himself; Locke hoped

---

[1] B.L. MSS. Locke, c. 24, f. 37.

[2] Robina Lady Forfar was the wife of Archibald Douglas, first Earl of Forfar. She was the daughter of Sir William Lockhart, Ambassador to France, and through her mother (née Robina Sewster) a relative of Oliver Cromwell. At the age of seventeen, in August 1679, she married Lord Forfar. She was a friend and attendant of Queen Mary. Her husband, who had been 'zealous for the Revolution' was a Scottish Privy Councillor to both William III and to Queen Anne. He was one of the commissioners for the Privy Seal, 1689/90, and for the Treasury, 1705/6.

[3] 3 November 1691 (Rand, pp. 317–18).

Churchill *would* do it himself 'because I would have it printed in a fair character and on good paper'.[1]

After spending some November days in London Locke went back to Oates at the beginning of December much reduced in health. He found Clarke's son still there, and wrote [2] promptly to the father imploring him to take the boy away. Locke did not disclose his reason for this, and it is difficult to guess. He admitted 'the child has behaved himself very well', and he asked Clarke to think of some excuse for removing the boy quickly, because Lady Masham would not want him to go and his mother would not expect him to come home so soon.

Clarke did as he was bidden and a few days later [3] Locke wrote to him again on the subject of his son:

> . . . I cannot own that he has made all the proficiency I could have wished, or you might justly have expected. Mr. Passebon himself is of the same mind. Where the fault is, I cannot certainly say. Mr. Passebon lays it wholly on the child's negligence and obstinacy and unconquerable aversion to him. He professes his great pains about him, and endeavours to be advantageous to him, and I believe he speaks truth. But withal he adds that it is not reasonable that you should be any longer at the charge to keep about your son a man that is not like to do him good, and who despairs to answer the expense by a suitable success. Though when he quits this employment he has nothing to subsist till he can find another, yet he cannot consent you should be deceived in your expectation concerning your son, but advises you either to get an Englishman that speaks French who possibly may have more authority with him, or else put him to your French maid's brother to school, where emulation might excite his industry.

A little later [4] Locke was able to recommend to Clarke another French tutor, a Monsieur Soveraigne:

> . . . and if he will undertake the conduct of him, you know I like that way much better than a public school . . . whether he go to Soveraigne or anybody else, I would be glad we might preserve as much of our method of education as could be, and at least not perplex him with

---

[1] The Churchills did publish this book themselves.
[2] 3 December 1691 (Rand, pp. 319–20).
[3] 7 December 1691 (*ibid.*, pp. 321–2).
[4] 27 December 1691 (*ibid.*, p. 327).

grammar, much less with themes, declamation, and making of verses, but only reading and translating prose authors. . . .

Clarke may not have been flattered to see Locke's method of education thus referred to as 'our' method.

In December 1691 a book by Locke entitled *Some Considerations of the Consequences of the Lowering of Interest, and Raising the Value of Money*[1] was brought out in London by the Churchills. It was Locke's first published essay in the field of economics, but he was not, however, a newcomer to the subject. I have mentioned a paper he wrote as early as 1672 against the proposals of Sir Josiah Child for lowering the rate of interest by law. After the Revolution Settlement the issue became topical again; many London merchants wanted cheap money and some of them reproduced Child's old arguments in its favour. Locke was thus prompted to look out his old essay[2] and prepare it for publication.[3] His friend John Somers—the unnamed M.P. to whom it was dedicated—encouraged him to do so.

In this book Locke repeated his original argument that the rate of interest cannot be regulated by law and that money must be left to find its own price in the market, but he also added some new thoughts on an even more pressing economic problem of the day, that of the 'clipped' currency, and it was in connection with this that Locke advocated vigorous government action.

English coins had traditionally been made of gold or silver, but so made that it was not difficult for people to clip thin strips of metal from the edge. As early as 1663 milled coins, which could not so easily be clipped, were introduced, and it was intended that they

---

[1] *Some Considerations of the Consequences of the Lowering of Interest and Raising the Value of Money. In a Letter to a Member of Parliament.* Printed for Awnsham and John Churchill, at the Black-Swan in Pater-Noster-Row, 1692.

[2] In the epistle dedicatory, Locke wrote: 'These notions concerning *coinage* having for the main, as you know, been put into writing above twelve months since, as those other concerning *interest*, a great deal above so many years, I put them now again into your hands with a liberty (since you will have it so) to communicate them farther as you please. If upon a review you continue your favourable opinion of them, and nothing less than publishing will satisfy you, I must desire you to remember that you must be answerable to the world for the style, which is such as a man writes carelessly to his friend, when he seeks truth, not ornament; and studies only to be in the right, and to be understood . . .'

[3] Sir Josiah Child's treatise was republished in 1690 with the title *A New Discourse of Trade*, together with a second part written in 1690, entitled *Of Raising Our Coin*. Sir Dudley North's *Discourses on Trade* was published in 1691.

should supersede the old hammered ones, but all the milled money was sent abroad or melted down, and hammered coins, more often clipped than not, remained the common currency at home. Foreigners very reasonably refused to accept clipped coins at their face value, and as clipped half-crowns, for example, would seldom fetch more than eighteen pence abroad, British trade in export markets was being seriously embarrassed.

Manifestly something would have to be done. A popular proposal was that the clipped coin should be called in and new money of raised nominal value issued to replace it. Locke opposed this solution. The 'raising of the value of money', he said, could only mean 'making a less quantity of it exchange for any other thing than would have been taken for it before'. Locke objected to any scheme which entailed giving currency a greater nominal value than the actual value of the metal. He demanded—and demanded with a sense of urgency which seemed to some misplaced—a general re-coinage according to the old standard and fineness.

He sent a copy of the *Considerations* from Oates [1] to Clarke, who, in writing [2] to thank Locke for the gift, said that he had distributed further copies of the *Considerations* to such effect

that [there] is already a doubt whether the Bill for Lowering the interest of money will ever be read a second time or not, and all that have read the *Considerations* are clearly of opinion the arguments therein are abundantly sufficient to destroy that Bill and all future attempts of the like kind.

Clarke added that there had been 'particular enquiries to know the author'; and Locke, characteristically, wrote back [3] post haste to beg Clarke not to divulge his knowledge. In the same letter he remarked somewhat bitterly: 'I am very glad to hear anything will do any good to any man in any matter in this age'.

Lady Masham wrote [4] after Locke's death:

I am . . . sure that what loss our nation suffered by the slowness with which men were made sensible of what must be the remedy to our disease in the debasing and clipping of our coin might, had he been

---

[1] 11 December 1691 (Rand, pp. 323–4). On the copy he sent Clarke Locke corrected a number of 'great faults' made by the printer, and he asked Clarke to pass them on to Churchill.
[2] 15 December 1691 (*ibid.*, pp. 324–5).
[3] 18 December 1691 (*ibid.*, pp. 325–7).
[4] Amsterdam: Remonstrants' MSS. J. 57a.

hearkened to, have had a much earlier cure, for from the first year of his return into England (when nobody else appeared sensible of this matter) he was very much troubled concerning it; and in talking on the subject of our public affairs, has often said to me that we had one evil which nobody complained of that was more surely ominous than many others wherewith we were easily frightened, and that if that unminded leak in our vessel were not timely looked after, we should infallibly sink, though all the rest were ever so safe. And when at my lodgings in London, the company there finding him often afflicted about a matter which nobody else took any notice of, railed him upon this uneasiness as being a visionary trouble he has more than once replied [that] we might laugh at it, but it would not be long before we should want money to send our servants to market with for bread and meat, which was so true five or six years after that there was not a family in England which did not find this a difficulty.

Locke received two visitors at Oates that Christmas, both of them able to discuss his new book with him: Lord Ashley, as a member of the House of Commons, and Benjamin Furly, who had learned his economics through long experience as a merchant.

Furly had once expressed to Locke the opinion that 'if your Parliaments would never trouble their heads about two things— that is religion and trade—we should grow both religious and rich'.[1] But in time Furly came round to the view that Parliament ought sometimes to intervene in matters of trade. Furly told [2] Locke that, when he first went to Amsterdam in 1655, 'we could not go any- where to receive money without gold scales', because all payments were made in gold. On another occasion [3] he explained:

> . . . the French have long since eased us of that trouble by raising the price of gold in their quarters. In the years 1676 and 1677 we received little else but ducatoons for the corn we sold, now we cannot get a ducatoon for our bills of exchange. They [are] draining us of all our fine silver money and leaving us nothing but our base coin. So that I am now convinced of a necessity of raising the value of a pound of silver and gold, if we intend to keep any in our country or to get any back . . . I hope the Parliament will look into this affair and take some effectual course for stopping it.

Furly may have been converted to Locke's views about coinage and interest, but the reading public was by no means immediately

[1] *21 November 1690* (B.L. MSS. Locke, c. 9, f. 49).
[2] *12 January 1691* (ibid., f. 54).
[3] *25 October 1691* (ibid., f. 83).

persuaded by Locke's[1] writings. His theory of interest was decisively rejected in January 1691/2, when a Bill was passed by the Commons fixing interest at 5 per cent.

Clarke reported the passing of that Bill in a letter to Locke dated 23 January:[2]

> Several attempts were had . . . to have thrown it out, wherein all imaginable reasons were used to that end. In which debate I was not a little pleased to hear the arguments used that are contained in the *Considerations*. . . . But I am satisfied that if an angel from heaven had managed the debate, the votes would have been the same as now. For it is not reason, but a supposed benefit to the borrower that has passed the Bill, and I believe it is that will carry it through the House of Lords . . .

One of the private tasks which had occupied Locke's time during the year 1691 was that of putting into some sort of order a manuscript by Boyle on 'the history of the air'. He told Boyle, candidly, when he returned his papers to him[3] that they were 'not in a condition to be sent to the printer'. He had, he said, done what he could with them, but there were several 'defects and omissions' he could not supply. Locke had been particularly anxious to help his friend because Boyle was very ill. Then, at the end of December, Boyle died.

Boyle carried to the grave the hope that he had at last found out how to multiply gold by combining a certain form of red earth with mercury. He sent the formula separately to Locke, whom he made one of the executors of his will, and to Newton, imposing on each of them an oath of secrecy. Locke, of course, kept the secret. Newton, who had no patience with alchemy, realised that Boyle's recipe was worthless, and felt himself under no obligation to remain silent about it. He wrote to Locke on 26 January 1691/2:[4]

> I understood Mr. Boyle communicated his process about the red earth to you as well as to me, and before his death procured some of the earth for his friends.

---

[1] Several pamphleteers attacked Locke's arguments. *Vide* Nicholas Barbon, *A Discourse concerning Coining the New Money Lighter In Answer to Mr. Locke's Considerations about raising the Value of Money* (1696); Sir Richard Temple, *Some Short Remarks upon Mr. Lock's Book* (1696); *A Review of the Universal Remedy for all Diseases incident to Coin. In a letter to Mr. Locke* (1696); *Some Considerations about the Raising of Coin. In a second letter to Mr. Locke* (1696). (*Vide* also Christophersen, pp. 24–26.)

[2] Rand, pp. 330–1.

[3] Locke to Boyle 21 October 1691 (Boyle, V, p. 571).

[4] B.L. MSS. Locke, c. 16, f. 146.

A A

Asked how he knew all this, Newton replied to Locke: [1]

> Mr. Pawling told me you had writ for some of Mr. Boyle's red earth, and by that I knew you had the receipt.

But Newton did not immediately tell Locke what he thought of Boyle's receipt. He had other things on his mind at the time. He was fretting over the failure of his powerful friends to find him a civil service post, and in his letter of 26 January, he confided to Locke:

> Being convinced that Mr. Montague [2] upon an old grudge which I thought had been worn out, is false with me, I have done with him, and intend to stay still unless my Lord Monmouth be still my friend. I have now no fair prospect of seeing you unless you will be so kind as to repay that visit I made you the last year. . . .

Newton, being a man very easily offended, was probably unfair to Montague. If Montague failed, as Monmouth had failed, to find him a place, it was not necessarily for want of trying, even though, as Newton's biographer justly says, their failure to 'obtain an appointment for the author of the *Principia* will hardly be believed in any country but our own'.[3]

In February, Newton wrote [4] to Locke saying:

> I am very glad my Lord Monmouth is still my friend, but intend not to give his Lordship and you any further trouble. My inclinations are to sit still. I am to beg his Lordship's pardon for pressing into his company the last time I saw him. I had not done it, but that Mr. Pawling pressed me into the room.

Newton had changed his mind about another matter, also. His manuscript on the Scriptures had been forwarded to Le Clerc for translation and publication in French, but now he wrote:

> Let me entreat you to stop their translation and impression so soon as you can for I design to suppress them. If your friend has been at any pains and charge, I will repay it and gratify him.

[1] 16 February 1691/2, B.L. MSS. Locke, c. 16, f. 148.

[2] Charles Montague (b. 1661) was a grandson of the first Earl of Manchester. Educated at Westminster and Trinity College, Cambridge, he had helped Newton to found the Philosophical Society at Cambridge in 1685. He sat with Newton in the Convention Parliament, and there discovered a talent for politics greater than that for scholarship; he soon became a Privy Councillor, Chancellor of the Exchequer and one of William's most important ministers.

[3] Brewster, *op. cit.*, Vol. II, p. 118.

[4] 16 February 1691/2, B.L. MSS. Locke, c. 16, f. 148.

Locke did as he was asked, though Newton's decision was a disappointment for Le Clerc.[1]

Clarke's son was at Oates again in February, and Locke sent the father a report [2] on his progress:

> I am satisfied about your son that he wants not parts, so that if he has not made all the progress we could have desired I lay it wholly upon want of application . . .

For the future Locke still thought a French tutor would be best for the boy 'that he may not lose the French tongue'; and yet Locke so far departed from his doctrine of education as to add:

> . . . or else perhaps I might advise you to [send him to] Westminster, or some other very severe school, where if he were whipped soundly whilst you are looking out another fit tutor for him, he would perhaps be the more pliant and willing to learn at home afterwards.

Locke was much put out that spring by a proposal from Wimborne St. Giles to revise the arrangement whereby he was paid £100 a year on the security of Kingston Farm. He [3] asked Clarke to investigate the matter, and although Clarke [4] was able afterwards to assure him that as long as Ashley lived, Locke 'was safe in his promise', the philosopher was not comforted. He maintained that even if the first Lord Shaftesbury

> had given me this annuity (which has not been a thing unusual for great men to those who have been faithful to them) it would be a shame it should not be paid me; but when it was paid for with all I had got in attending on him for ten or a dozen of the best years of my life, it will be very hard measure to have the trouble which I designed to avoid, instead of the full annuity I purchased.[5]

He begged Clarke to talk to Lord Ashley about the matter, and he sent a letter [6] for him to give to Ashley if he thought it prudent to do so. The letter read thus:

> Among the things that I have loved best in this world, the two that I always preferred to the rest were my Lord your Grandfather and quiet. He was pleased to be so favourable to me, that he himself was

---

[1] Le Clerc to Locke *11 April 1692* (B.L. MSS. Locke, c. 13, f. 54).
[2] 26 February 1691/2 (Rand, pp. 335-7).
[3] 29 February 1691-2 (*ibid.*, p. 338).
[4] 3 March 1691/2 (*ibid.*, pp. 339-40).
[5] Locke to Clarke 11 March 1691/2 (*ibid.*, pp. 342-3).
[6] *Ibid.*, pp. 343-4.

pleased to contrive both for me, and to that purpose when he retired from business into the country, told me that I should be in the country with him; and that he would find out somewhere thereabouts an annuity for me, knowing that I had little money by me. But either meeting with none, or none that he liked, he after some time told me, he would do it himself. This pleased me extremely, knowing myself safe in his Lordship's hands, and so referring the whole matter to him, both for price and security, I paid £800 and Kingston Farm was settled for it. Which, not examining whether it was of a suitable value to such a charge, I took rather as a declaration of my Lord's intention than a security of my annuity. . . . But your Lordship is not ignorant that it has been under deliberation, and advice has been given that instead of receiving an annuity I should be made a farmer. I wish my Lord your Grandfather had been by to have heard it. If his intention to me that I should during my life receive the full hundred pounds yearly without trouble has not been yet crossed, I know how much I owe it to your Lordship, whose justice and the assurance you gave me by Mr. Clarke concerning it I take for so good security. That could your Lordship be but as sure to outlive me, as I should be to rest satisfied with your word, I would desire no other. But your Lordship knows what will become of me if I should have the misfortune to fall into the hands of him that is next. I beg the favour of you, therefore, to complete the kindness and put me out of these dangers.

Clarke's representations were unavailing. A few weeks later Locke reported [1] that Lady Shaftesbury 'talks of building a house on Kingston Farm, and deducting the taxes out of my annuity'. He sent Clarke a letter for Lady Shaftesbury; he did not know whether in his indignation he had 'made it a little too warm', but he asked Clarke to deliver it if he approved of the contents.

Angry as Locke was with the Countess of Shaftesbury, he was still on the best possible terms with the Countess of Monmouth who wrote to him in April [2] begging him to leave his 'learned lady'. She blamed his absence from Parson's Green for her own distracted state of mind: 'What I have lost in losing you [is] my reason'. But she added: 'One of those afternoons you have been so liberal of to Lady Masham would dissipate the mist'. The Countess refused to believe that Locke really liked the seclusion of Essex. 'Pretend no more the bleating of the sheep is music in your ears . . . you and your Lady are Virgil's shepherds, fitter for the State than [the]

[1] Locke to Clarke, 16 May 1692 (Rand, p. 348).
[2] 2 April 1692 (B.L. MSS. Locke, c. 16, f. 103).

country'. She threatened that if Locke did not come and bring her to herself she would take a house in Paris against the next winter.

Changing her approach a little, Lady Monmouth expressed her regret on hearing that Locke was growing fat, 'because', as she put it, 'we ladies do not love the loss of shape':

> When the sun comes and fires go, I hope you will come and recover yours here—I mean at Parson's Green. I fear I shall want all your philosophy to comfort me after my [. . . .] and that I shall have more than the public at stake. But I assure Mr. Locke that nobody can make me any amends for their absence but such a friend as I think you are to your humble servant,
>
> C. Monmouth.

Locke's friend in Queen Mary's household, Martha Lockhart, wrote [1] to him in March 1691:

> to let you know that to the great amazement of all people this day Major Wildman [2] is turned out. I was with him yesterday almost all day. He had not the least suspicion of it; nor today at seven o'clock at night, though 'twas all over the house at noon. I met him at Lady Monmouth's in the evening; he then would not believe there was anything in it, but the minute he left us we had the certainty of it.

Having spent a week [3] in London during April, Locke left Oates again in May. Newton wrote [4] to him on the third day of that month saying:

> Now the churlish weather is almost over I was thinking within a post or two to put you in mind of my desire to see you here, where you shall be as welcome as I can make you. I am glad you have prevented me, because I hope now to see you the sooner. You may lodge conveniently either at the Rose Tavern or Queen's Arms.

---

[1] B.L. MSS. Locke, c. 15, f. 13.

[2] John Wildman (1621–93) one-time friend of Algernon Sydney, and most left-wing of Whig politicians, had landed with William at Brixham. He was appointed Postmaster-General in April 1689. He was summarily dismissed from his office for attempting to discredit the King's Tory adherents by means of fictitious letters which he pretended to have intercepted. However, he had been made an Alderman of London, and he was knighted with other aldermen at the Guildhall on 29 October 1692, a few months after his disgrace. He died the following June.

[3] 22–30 April 1692. Locke stayed as usual 'at Pawlings' (*vide* Journal). There seems to have been some amalgamation of Pawling's household with Mrs. Smithsby's.

[4] B.L. MSS. Locke, c. 16, f. 149.

Locke set off for Cambridge on 10 May. The visit was not a purely social one. He told Clarke [1] that he had been drawn to the place 'by business that was very necessary to be dispatched', though he did not say what that business was. He spent only two days in Cambridge, despite his being 'very much importuned' [1] to stay longer; and no sooner was he back at Oates than he was forced to arrange another trip to London.

> But whip me [he wrote to Clarke [2]] if I can think what I shall do in a crowd or a smoke. I find my head as little suited to [the] one as my lungs to the other. And I am so morose-given or moped by a country retirement that all the world appears a bedlam to me.

From Holland, Locke heard about this time that Limborch's long-awaited *Historia Inquisitionis*, the book largely based on Furly's copy of the *Liber Sententiarum Inquisitionis Tholosanae*, was about to be published. 'For my part I am waiting impatiently for it,' Locke [3] assured Limborch, 'and I know it will be of great benefit to the whole civilised world.'

Limborch then [4] asked Locke if he thought the Archbishop of Canterbury [5] would accept the dedication of the book. Locke undertook to find out, and he was able to tell Limborch in a letter dated 30 June: [6]

> I called on the Archbishop today. When he heard your name, he mentioned that you had sent him a copy of your Reply to the learned Jew, and he excused himself for his failure to acknowledge that book on the grounds that his poor health, his bad sight and other circumstances prevented his reading it. However he praised both the book and the author very warmly.

After he had shown the Archbishop the draft of Limborch's dedication, Locke [7] was able to tell the author that Dr. Tillotson

[1] In a letter dated 13 May 1692 (Rand, pp. 346–7). [2] 16 May 1692, *ibid.*, p. 348.
[3] Amsterdam: Remonstrants' MSS. Ba. 257b (Latin).
[4] *27 June 1692*, B.L. MSS. Locke, c. 14, f. 65 (Latin).
[5] John Tillotson (1630–94) was educated at Clare Hall, Cambridge, where he became a Fellow in 1651. A nonconformist, he was not ordained until after the Restoration. In 1663 he became Chaplain of Lincoln's Inn, chaplain to Charles II, prebend of Canterbury, and (in 1672) Dean of Canterbury. His zeal for protestantism alienated the Stuarts, but he kept his deanery, and was appointed by the chapter at Canterbury to exercise archiepiscopal jurisdiction on the suspension of Sancroft. William III thereafter bestowed the primacy on him.
[6] Amsterdam: Remonstrants' MSS. Ba. 257c (Latin).
[7] Locke to Limborch 2 August 1692, *ibid.*, 257d (Latin).

'objected to nothing in it, save your having said so much about him
—but that he let pass. In proportion to the Archbishop's renown and
his worth is his modesty'.

By the year 1692 Locke was well established as an author, and
while his fame had not as yet reached its peak, his name was
already familiar to every educated Englishman, and references to his
Essay Concerning Human Understanding were beginning to appear in
the published works of other writers. One such reference which
gave Locke particular pleasure occurred in the foreword to a book
called *Dioptrica Nova* by William Molyneux[1] of Dublin, then a
complete stranger to Locke. This author wrote:

> To none do we owe for a greater advancement in this part of
> philosophy [*viz* logic] than to the incomparable Mr. Locke, who, in his
> *Essay Concerning Human Understanding*, has rectified more received
> mistakes, and delivered more profound truths, established on ex-
> perience and observation, for the direction of man's mind in the
> prosecution of *knowledge* . . . than are to be met with in all the volumes
> of the Ancients.

Locke was so pleased that he wrote[2] to Molyneux to thank him
for the 'extraordinary compliment', and confessed, 'If my trifle could
possibly be an occasion of vanity to me, you have done most to make
it so'.

At the same time Locke mentioned that his friend Dr. Sibelius
of Deventer (who was soon to change his name to Sibley) was
coming to Dublin 'with a design to settle there', and he asked
Molyneux to help him in any way he could: 'I shall take it as a
favour done to me.' Locke also asked his correspondent if he were
any relation to a Molyneux he had had the honour of knowing at
Leyden.

---

[1] Molyneux was born in Ireland on 17 April 1656, and educated at T.C.D. He
studied law at the Middle Temple, but, having an ample fortune, he did not practise
at the Bar. He became instead an amateur of philosophy and science, with a special
interest in optics and astronomy. He founded the Philosophical Society of Dublin
under the guidance of Sir William Petty in 1683. A year later the Duke of Ormonde
appointed him surveyor-general of works and buildings to the Irish government.
He was a Protestant, and during the troubled years of the Glorious Revolution he
sheltered from the Irish Catholics in England. He had not long returned to Dublin
when Locke wrote to him in the summer of 1692.

[2] 16 July 1692 S.F.L., p. 1.

In his reply [1] Molyneux told Locke once more of his admiration for the *Essay* and urged Locke to write 'a *Treatise of Morals* drawn up according to the hints you frequently give in your *Essay* of their being demonstrable according to the mathematical method'.

Then Molyneux moved on to very thin ice. He mentioned how, in 1690, he had asked in London for any other books by the author of the *Essay Concerning Human Understanding*:

> I was recommended by some to *Two Discourses Concerning Government* and a little *Treatise Concerning Toleration*. There is neither of them carries your name, and I will not venture to ask whether they are yours or not, this only, I think, no name need be ashamed of either.

Molyneux promised his service to Dr. Sibelius and said that the Molyneux Locke had known in Leyden was his brother Thomas; he himself had been there in 1685, but had not met Locke.

Though Locke must by this time have realised that his authorship of the *Two Treatises* and the *Letters Concerning Toleration* was an open secret, he made no comment on Molyneux's reference to the matter when he came to reply.[2] However, he addressed Molyneux in terms of unusual cordiality:

> There are beauties of the mind as well as of the body that take and prevail at first sight; and, wherever I have met with this, I have readily surrendered myself, and have never yet been deceived in my expectation.

As for Molyneux's suggestion that he should write a Treatise of Morals, Locke admitted that whilst he

> was considering that subject, I thought I saw that morality might be demonstratively made out; yet whether I am able to make it out is another question.

He promised to employ 'some thoughts in that way', but—much to the regret of many other readers as well as Molyneux—he never wrote the projected treatise.

Another manuscript which Locke was busily writing in the summer of 1692 was his *Third Letter for Toleration*. He did not mention this to Molyneux, but he did to Newton. Having sent the physicist one of his chapters (there were no less than ten chapters in this third *Letter*), Locke begged him: 'if you have so much leisure,

---

[1] 27 August 1692 (Pforzheimer MS. 63; *S.F.L.*, pp. 3–6).
[2] 20 September 1692 (*S.F.L.*, pp. 7–10).

to read, correct, censure and send it back by the same hand [i.e. Martin the carrier] this week, else I fear the press will stay'.[1]

At the same time Locke sent Newton a part of Boyle's receipt for increasing gold, reminding him that Boyle had left 'to Dr. Dickson, Dr. Cox and me the inspection of his papers'.

Newton replied on 2 August[2] returning Locke's manuscript on toleration, and at the same time warning Locke against wasting his time with Boyle's receipt. He said it was obvious that Boyle had had the receipt for sixteen or twenty years and yet 'in all this time I cannot find that he has either tried it himself or got it tried with success by anybody else'. He (Newton) knew of a company of chemists who had tried and failed. Boyle, he said, had always kept a part of his receipt from him, so he had made no trial himself. Newton was curious enough to ask Locke if he might have the missing part of the receipt, even though he did not intend to try it. He added:

> In dissuading you from too hasty a trial of this receipt, I have fore-borne to say anything against multiplication [of gold] in general, because you seem persuaded of it, though there is one argument against it which I could never find an answer to, and which, if you will let me have your opinion about it, I will send you in my next.

I have not traced Locke's reply to this letter, but Newton seems to have succeeded in curing him of his faith in Boyle's alchemy. On the other hand, Locke did not fail to publish Boyle's *History of the Air* which had been left to him in a fragmentary form. The first edition of this work, edited and largely re-written by Locke, appeared in 1692. Sending a copy of it to Molyneux, Locke said:[3] 'though left by him very imperfect, yet I think the very design of it will please you'.

The philosopher paid several visits to London that summer. On one such journey he was assailed by a highwayman in Epping Forest, but managed to escape.[4] While he was in London he found time to inaugurate yet another of his clubs. This was called the Dry Club, and the secretary was William Popple, the Unitarian merchant

---

[1] 6 July 1692, Cambridge University Library. Portsmouth Collection.
[2] B.L. MSS. Locke, c. 16, f. 151.
[3] 26 December 1692 (*S.F.L.*, p. 21).
[4] Clarke mentioned his pleasure at hearing Locke 'escaped the highwayman in the forest' in a letter dated 31 August (Rand, p. 350).

who had translated Locke's first *Epistola de Tolerantia*. The rules [1] show that the Dry Club was run on much the same lines as the old Exeter House club and The Lantern, except that there was a special emphasis on religious toleration. Belief in freedom of religious worship and opinion was in fact the basis of membership.[2]

Lord and Lady Monmouth tried to persuade Locke to take the waters at Bath with them at the end of that summer, but Locke, who was then in London, decided not to go. 'I own,' Lord Monmouth wrote to him on 10 September,[3] 'I condemn your ingratitude to these waters that have done greater miracles than ever this season.'

Monmouth offered, if Locke would agree to go, to send his coach to Reading to fetch him 'that you may come the ill part of the way at ease'. He added: 'The weather is very good and our houses were less shook, as we hear, than those about town'.

This last reference was to an earthquake which had happened on 8 September, and which had excited Locke's scientific curiosity.[4] He had described it in his letter to Molyneux on 20 September [5] and asked him if it had reached Dublin.

> If it did I would be glad to know what was the exact time it was felt, if anybody observed it. By the Queen's pendulum at Kensington, which the shake stopped from going, it was 2 p.m. At Whitehall, where I observed it, it was by my watch 2.5 p.m., which, supposing the Queen's pendulum went exact, and adding the equation of that day, it will fall near the time marked by my watch, or a little later. If there could be found people that in the whole extent of it did, by well adjusted clocks exactly observe the time, one might see whether it were all one shock, or proceeded gradually from one place to another.

[1] A copy in Popple's hand is in the Lovelace Collection (B.L. MSS. Locke, c. 25, f. 56).

[2] Popple told Locke in a letter dated 12 November 1692 about four new members: Mr. Hedworth, Mr. Stevens, Dr. Foot and Mr. White (*ibid.*, c. 17, f. 201). Furly, having seen the Dry Club's rules, criticised the one which bound every member to speak on every issue (*vide* Furly to Locke. 17 November 1692. *Ibid.*, c. 9, f. 98).

[3] *Ibid.*, c. 16, f. 109.

[4] On 15 September 1692, Locke noted in his journal: 'V.B. That the earthquake which was September 8th and was then observed by my watch to be about 5 minutes past 2 in the afternoon was by the Queen's pendulum which the shake of the earthquake made stand still just at 2 of the clock and by Mr. Tompion's less than a minute before 2, which agrees well enough with my watch. For adding to the pendulums the equation of 8 September which is six minutes the time of day will fall about five minutes past 2 p.m.'

[5] *S.F.L.*, pp. 10–11.

Lord Monmouth, after failing to lure Locke to Bath, wrote to him in October [1] inviting him to Parson's Green for 'three or four months this winter'. A month later Monmouth wrote [2] again saying:

I am told that so many of your friends have sent you word how desirous they are you should come to town, that I am resolved I will not be of the number, concluding that your health obliges you to stay in the country. I am afraid of mentioning Parson's Green to you, for I find you would be importuned (if so near) to come often to town, and our innocent air would be accused of the ill effects of London smoke. If your acquaintances would make you visits and expect no return, I would do all in my power to tempt you to a Lady [who] would take all possible care of you. She has prepared you a room, [which] I assure you is very warm, and if you take the resolution which she thinks you almost obliged to by your promise, you must send me word of it, for as [she is] your physician, you must refuse none of her prescriptions. And she will not allow you to come up but in a glass coach —this is no compliment—and you can gain no admittance except my coach bring you, which I can send without the least inconvenience . . . but after all, I desire you not to venture coming towards us if it may be prejudicial to your health. . . .

Eight days of the November fogs in London did their worst to Locke, and towards the end of the month he hurried back to Oates. But he had been in London long enough to advertise Limborch's book on the Holy Office among his influential friends. He reported to Limborch [3] on his visits to Archbishop Tillotson, who said he had read the book with particular pleasure, and to Bishop Burnet and the Earl of Pembroke, who had both spoken appreciatively of it. Furthermore, he said:

I have brought your book here with me, that by your kindness Lady Masham and I may this winter enjoy Attic evenings, which could only be enhanced by the presence of the author, and the Attic salt which he always brings with him. I returned hither on Saturday. Today we began to read your work, with what pleasing expectation you may easily judge, but be assured that our gratitude to you was not less than our own delight.

[1] 10 October 1692, B.L. MSS. Locke, c. 16, f. 111.
[2] 19 November 1692 (*ibid.*, f. 113).
[3] 28 November 1692 (Amsterdam: Remonstrants' MSS. Ba. 257f, Latin).

Locke's words conjure up an affecting scene of high-minded domesticity. But there were issues over which he and his Philoclea did not see eye to eye. One was the case of John Norris.[1] Norris was a Platonist of sorts, and he had dedicated two of his published works to Lady Masham. Locke did not like Norris; but he did at least try to. Indeed, he approached Lord Pembroke on Norris's behalf, and persuaded that nobleman to give Norris one of the livings in his possession: the rectory of Bemerton near Salisbury; and to that one-time benefice of the poet George Herbert, Norris was duly inducted in the summer of 1692. In reply to a letter of thanks from Norris, Locke wrote to him on 6 June [2] saying that he had been pleased to help 'a person whom I very much esteem and whose learning and parts I, with a Lady, thought deserved a better station in the world'.

But the fact remained that Norris had attacked Locke's views in print, and Locke found it increasingly difficult to conceal his contempt for him. Norris's criticisms of the *Essay* were published in 1690 as an appendix to his *Christian Blessedness*,[3] a book which achieved a fair measure of success. The Athenian Society subsequently issued Le Clerc's rejoinder to Norris's criticisms of Locke, and in the second edition of his *Christian Blessedness*, published in 1692, Norris added to his appendix against Locke *A Brief Consideration of the Remarks made upon the Foregoing Reflections by the Gentlemen of the Athenian Society*; and in his *Essay Towards the Theory of the Ideal or Intelligible World*, published in 1701 and 1704, Norris renewed his attack on Locke in even greater detail.

Norris was a disciple of Malebranche, and held with that philosopher that God was the only real cause of all events. Although Norris did not accept the traditional view of innate ideas, he maintained against Locke that the so-called innate ideas were to be correctly understood as ideas implanted by God. He also advanced against Locke's empiricism the Malebranche doctrine that the objects of sensory perception are in fact immaterial, the same doctrine which was later elaborated to such remarkable effect by Berkeley.

Norris always wrote respectfully to Locke. 'I am', he declared in

[1] Born in 1657 the son of a Wiltshire clergyman, Norris was educated at Winchester and Exeter College, Oxford. He was elected to All Souls in 1680. His first living was at Newton St. Lee, Somerset, which he accepted on his marriage in 1689.

[2] B.L. MSS. Locke, c. 24, f. 204.

[3] The appendix was entitled *Cursory Reflections upon a book call'd 'An Essay Concerning Human Understanding', written by John Norris, M.A., in a letter to a Friend.*

1690, 'perhaps as great an admirer of him as his most sworn followers', and in 1692 (the year in which Locke got him the living of Bemerton) Norris wrote: 'I honour both his person and admire his book, which, bating only some few things, I think is one of the most exquisite pieces of speculation that is extant'.

Mutual cordiality diminished towards the end of 1692, when Norris opened a letter he had undertaken to take from Lady Masham to Locke. Pawling found out what Norris had done, and reported[1] it to Locke, saying that such men 'are not for human society'. After Locke had written[2] to reproach him Norris protested[3] that Locke should not 'look upon yourself as affronted by me before you know what I have to say for myself'. Locke replied[4] stiffly, and Norris,[5] having persuaded Mrs. Lockhart that his motives were innocent, sent Locke a letter ending with the words: 'If this will satisfy you, well and good, but if not, I have no more to say'. As no further correspondence between Locke and Norris survives in the Lovelace Collection, the suspicion remains that Locke was *not* satisfied.

Lady Masham, on the other hand, continued to correspond with Norris, albeit as one who consistently upheld Locke's philosophical views against his, and she even went so far as to publish a small tract in defence of Locke against Norris, *A Discourse of the Love of God*, which appeared anonymously in 1696.[6]

Locke himself wrote no fewer than three papers against Norris, but forbore to publish them, though he never quarrelled with Molyneux's remark that Norris was an 'obscure enthusiastic man'.[7]

In the autumn of 1692 Locke lent £300 to Martha Lockhart on the security of her diamonds.[8] Soon afterwards he discovered that the jewels were worth far more than £300, and such was his probity that he gave some of them back to her. When Clarke

---

[1] B.L. MSS. Locke, c. 6, f. 210.

[2] I have not traced this letter.

[3] 10 November 1692 (*ibid.*, c. 16, f. 165).

[4] 5 December 1692 (*ibid.*, c. 24, f. 205).

[5] 27 February 1692/3 (*ibid.*, c. 16, f. 167).

[6] Lady Masham wrote another defence of Locke against Norris: *Occasional Thoughts in Reference to a Godly and Virtuous Life*, but this was not published until 1705, after Locke's death.

[7] Molyneux to Locke, 16 March 1696/7 (*S.F.L.*, p. 189). Locke wrote to Molyneux on 22 February 1696/7 (*S.F.L.*, p. 182) saying '[Lady Masham] has, 'tis true, but weak eyes, which Mr. Norris, for reasons he knows best, was resolved to make blind ones'.

[8] *Journal*, 27 September 1692.

criticised his doing so, Locke told [1] him that he did not want to be 'clogged with more than was necessary for sufficient security'; and he said he was also willing for Mrs. Lockhart to have the use, at Christmas and other festive times, of the jewels that he retained.

At the end of October another of Locke's female friends, his little 'wife' Betty Clarke, went to stay at Oates.

> It was kind of you to send my wife to me [Locke wrote [2] to her mother] though I know not how it may prove if she be not very constant. For little master is so mightily in love with her that he professes openly he will get her from me if he can.

'Little Master' was Francis Cudworth Masham, then aged six. A few months before he had written [3] to Locke himself saying: 'I love you mightily'. Manifestly he was a warm-hearted child, even if he was a rival.

But however much Locke enjoyed such youthful company at Oates, he would have preferred to be in London. He confessed to Clarke [4] that 'one of the inconveniences I suffer from my ill lungs is that they usually drive me out of town when most of my friends and those whom I would wish to be near, are in it'.

A few days before he had written [5] to Clarke saying:

> I beg that you would send for Mr. Awnsham Churchill (to whom I have written four or five times, to desire him to send me the sheets which have printed since I came to town, but cannot receive a word from him) and tell him I would by no means have him publish it till I have perused all the remaining sheets. . . .

'It' in this case was Locke's *Third Letter for Toleration*,[6] which he had written in reply to the criticisms of Jonas Proast. Locke's opening paragraph,[7] addressed to his critic, was distinctly aggressive.

> Sir: The business which your *Letter Concerning Toleration* found me engaged in has taken up so much of the time my health would allow me ever since that I doubt whether I should now at all have troubled you or the world with an answer had not some of my friends, suffici-

---

[1] 28 October 1692 (B.M. Add. MSS. 4290).
[2] 28 October 1692 (Rand, pp. 356–7).　　　　[3] B.L. MSS. Locke, c. 16, f. 8.
[4] 11 November 1692 (B.M. Add. MSS. 4290).　　[5] 2 November 1692 (*ibid*).
[6] *A Third Letter for Toleration to the Author of the Third Letter Concerning Toleration*. London. Printed for Awnsham and John Churchill at the Black Swan in Paternoster Row, 1692. The letter, which is signed 'Philanthropus', is dated 20 June 1692.
[7] *Op. cit.*, p. 1.

ently satisfied of the weakness of your arguments with repeated instances, persuaded me it might be of use to Truth in a point of so great moment to clear it from those fallacies which might perhaps puzzle some unwary readers, and therefore prevailed on me to show the wrong grounds and mistaken reasonings you make use of to support your new way of *persecution*. Pardon me, Sir, that I use that name, which you are so much offended at: for if punishment be punishment, though it come short of the discipline of fire and faggot, 'tis as certain that punishment for religion is truly persecution though it be only such punishment as you in your clemency think fit to call '*moderate and convenient penalties*'. But however you please to call them, I doubt not but to let you see that if you will be true to your own principles and stand to what you have said you must carry your '*some degrees of force*' (as you phrase it) to all these degrees which in words you declare against.

Despite his contemptuous treatment there of his critic, Locke was forced in the *Third Letter* to acknowledge a more sceptical attitude towards religion as such than he had previously admitted. Proast's point was that it was the duty of the civil magistrate to uphold the true religion even by force. Locke replied by saying that the true religion was unknowable. He (like his critic) believed in the religion of the Church of England. But he did not *know* that religion was true. Religion rested on faith, not knowledge. The true was that which was known, not simply believed. Belief, however strong, could be false. Hence, since the nature of the true religion was in principle unknowable, Proast's policy amounted to the view that the civil magistrate was obliged to enforce the religion which was thought to be true.

Locke discussed two alternative and conflicting recommendations implicit in Proast's teaching. The first, that the civil magistrates of different nations had the duty of upholding by force what *they* thought the true religion: Presbyterianism in Scotland, Protestantism in Sweden, Catholicism in France, and so forth; the second, that the civil magistrates of different nations had the duty of upholding by force what *Jonas Proast* thought the true religion, namely that of the English Establishment. The first alternative implied that it was a duty to uphold false religions by force (since all the conflicting religions of the world could not be true); the second that it was the duty of foreign potentates to enforce in their own countries the doctrines of the English Church, a suggestion so absurd that Locke did not dwell upon it.

Locke's *Third Letter* contained many excellent points, but it did more to demolish Proast's position than to defend his own from Proast's criticisms. Moreover, compared to the earlier letters it was prolix and diffuse, and thus lost much of its polemical strength. The first edition ran to no fewer than 350 pages. It would probably have been better if it had been a quarter of its length. But the author was not displeased with it, and he had copies sent to Clarke, Ashley, Newton, Somers, Popple, Le Clerc, Wright, Freke and Firmin. It took Proast twelve years to publish a rejoinder; one might well believe that it took him twelve years to read it.

As Christmas drew near Locke wrote [1] to Clarke inviting him to spend the holiday at Oates, but adding the discouraging information that the house was very full.

> I long to talk with you, and mightily desire you should have a little refreshment in the air. But I fear I shall make you an ill compliment to invite you to a bedfellow, and such an one as I am. If you can dispense with that, pray come.

The Act for the Regulation of Printing, which had been passed under Charles II in 1662, came up for renewal by Parliament towards the end of 1692. Locke took a lively interest in the discussions it provoked. This was the Act which enabled the State to control the Press, and although it had been in abeyance from 1679 to 1685 (hence, as Mr. David Ogg [2] has said, 'the great volume of pamphlet literature inspired by the Popish Plot and the Exclusion controversy') it was in many ways more severe than the old 'Star Chamber' Act. In 1692 there was vigorous opposition to its renewal; but that opposition was almost wholly directed, not against the principle of censorship which that Act embodied, but against the monopoly which it conferred on the Company of Stationers. The people who wanted reform or repeal were those, mostly independent book-sellers and printers, who objected to the privileges of the Stationers. It is interesting to notice that this was also Locke's objection to the Act. For he too opposed renewal in the first place, as he explained in a letter to Clarke,[3] as a 'book-buyer'. He did not mention censorship. He simply pointed out the fact that by putting a monopoly 'into the hands of ignorant and lazy Stationers', Parliament had made

---

[1] 23 December 1692 (Rand, pp. 365–6).
[2] *England in the Reigns of James II and William III* (Oxford, 1955), p. 512.
[3] 2 January 1692/3 (Rand, p. 366).

the importing of good editions of classical texts 'excessively dear to scholars', while at the same time the Company of Stationers prevented the printing of good new editions of classical texts in England. However, by the time Clarke received Locke's protest the Act had already been renewed for two more years.

Locke was busy at the time preparing two books of his own for the press: the first edition of his *Some Thoughts Concerning Education* and the second edition of his *Essay Concerning Human Understanding*.[1] William Molyneux had responded [2] to Locke's invitation to send him comments and criticisms of the first edition of the *Essay*; and Locke, in acknowledging [3] Molyneux's remarks admitted that he had been wrong on several points; notably he said he was far from satisfied with what he had written on the freedom of the will:

> I do not wonder to find you think my discourse about *Liberty* a little too fine spun. I had so much that thought of it myself, that I said the same thing of it to some of my friends before it was printed, and told them, that upon that account I judged it best to leave it out, but they persuaded me to the contrary. . . . I own freely to you the weakness of my understanding, that though it be unquestionable that there is omnipotence and omniscience in God our Maker, and I cannot have a clearer perception of anything than that I am free; yet I cannot make freedom in man consistent with omnipotence and omniscience in God, though I am as fully persuaded of both as of any truths I most firmly assent to. And therefore I have long since given off the consideration of that question, resolving all into this short conclusion: that if it be possible for God to make a free agent, then man is free, though I see not the way of it.

In the same letter Locke confessed to Molyneux that 'some parts of' the third book of the *Essay*, 'concerning words' had, 'though the thoughts were easy and clear enough', yet cost him 'more pains to express than all the rest' of the *Essay*.

Two visits to London, one of eleven days in February, the other of five weeks in March and April, had the usual bad effect on Locke's lungs.

'I paid so dear', he informed Clarke [4] when he got back to Oates

---

1 Thomas Bassett wrote to Locke on 28 February 1692/3 offering to publish a new edition of the *Essay* with the alterations and additions Locke had made (B.L. MSS. Locke, c. 3, f. 160).

2 22 December 1692 (*S.F.L.*, p. 13).

3 20 January 1692/3 (*S.F.L.*, pp. 22–31).   4 4 May 1693 (Rand, pp. 373–5).

in May '... and have so hardly mastered the ill effects of it that
I cannot yet think of returning.'

He had already refused an invitation to go to Scotland with
James Johnstone,[1] and now he had also to apologise to John St. John,
who had asked him to go to Battersea, where his son was ill, and
give advice about treatment. In reply to Locke's apology, St. John
wrote:[2]

> I was extremely sorry your health was so impaired by your last
> being in town, and cannot but wish that instead of taking a longer
> journey you would have tried Battersea, where you should have found
> a hearty welcome though worse company. It is now very sweet with
> woodbines and bean blossoms, the natural perfumes of the season.

Yet, for all his protestations, Locke *did* go to London that month
and he did not return to Oates until 2 July.

Molyneux's criticisms of the treatment of the free will problem in
the *Essay* continued to exercise Locke's mind, and the outcome was
the enlarged chapter on *Power*,[3] which he wrote for the second
edition. He sent a summary[4] of it to Molyneux, saying he had
'got into a new view of things which, if I mistake not, will satisfy
you and give you a clearer account of human freedom than hitherto
I have done. . . .' In another letter[5] Locke informed his Irish
friend:

> My *Essay* is now very near ready for another edition, and upon
> review of my alterations, concerning what determines the Will, in
> my cool thoughts I am apt to think them to be right, as far as my
> thoughts can reach in so nice a point; and, in short, is this:—*Liberty* is a
> power to act or not act, accordingly as the mind directs. A power to
> direct the operative faculties to motion or rest in particular instances is
> that which we call *the will*. That which in the train of our voluntary
> actions determines the will to any change of operation is some present
> uneasiness, which is, or at least is always accompanied with that of
> desire. *Desire* is always moved by evil to fly it. . . . But though this
> general desire of happiness operates constantly and invariably in us,

[1] James Johnstone, a nephew of Gilbert Burnet and Ambassador to Prussia from
1690 to 1692, afterwards Secretary of State for Scotland, invited Locke to accompany
him to Scotland in a letter dated 14 March 1692/3 (B.L. MSS. Locke, c. 12, f. 25).
[2] *Ibid.*, c. 18, f. 61: 9 May 1693.
[3] *Essay*, Second Edition (1694), Book II, Chapter XXI (p. 124–52).
[4] 15 July 1693, S.F.L., p. 47.
[5] 23 August 1693, S.F.L., p. 61.

yet the satisfaction of any particular desire can be suspended from determining the will to any subservient action. . . .

Molyneux, having in the meantime, received [1] a copy of the first edition of Locke's *Some Thoughts on Education*, was able to tell him what he thought of it:

> . . . in general, I think you propose nothing in your book but what is very reasonable and very practicable, except only in one particular, which seems to bear hard on the tender spirits of children and the natural affections of parents: 'tis pages 117, 118 where you advise 'that a child should never be suffer'd to have what he *craves*, or so much as *speaks for*, much less if he *cries for it*'. . . . This I can never agree to.[2]

For the rest, Molyneux assured Locke he could subscribe to everything that was recommended. 'And', he added, 'I am not a little pleased when I consider that my own management of my only little one has hitherto been agreeable in the main to your rules, save only in what relates to his hardy breeding'. Molyneux explained that the boy, having come from a 'tender and sickly mother', was not very strong.

In his reply [3] Locke assured Molyneux that the objection he had raised to one rule in his method of education only 'confirms to me that you are the good natured man I took you for, and I do not at all wonder that the affection of a kind father should startle at it at first reading' the book. He suggested that Molyneux had taken his method to be more severe than it was. He entirely agreed that children should be allowed 'full liberty of diversion':

> But being allowed that, as one of their natural wants, they should not yet be permitted to let loose their desires in importunities for what they fancy. . . . Children should, by constant use, learn to be very modest in owning their desires and careful not to ask anything of their parents but what they have reason to think their parents will approve of.

As for Molyneux's son being 'not very strong', Locke insisted that 'to make him strong you must use him hardly as I have directed', but he advised Molyneux to do so 'by very insensible degrees'.

Molyneux was satisfied with Locke's reply to his objections to the severity of the educational method, and he wrote [4] to say he found

---

[1] On 9 August 1693.
[2] 12 August 1693 (Pforzheimer MS. 70; S.F.L., pp. 49–56).
[3] 23 August 1693 (S.F.L., pp. 56–63).
[4] Molyneux to Locke. 16 September 1693 (*ibid.*, pp. 64–5).

Locke's new scheme 'of man's liberty' very just, but he warned Locke that he would soon press him again to write a treatise on ethics.

Isaac Newton had some sort of nervous breakdown in 1693, following an illness the year before. He told Samuel Pepys on 13 September[1] that he was 'extremely troubled at the embroilment' he was in and that he had 'neither ate nor slept well this twelve-month, nor have my former consistency of mind'. To these words Newton appended the following neurotic pronouncement:

> I am now sensible that I must withdraw from your acquaintance and see neither you nor the rest of my friends any more, if I may but leave them quietly.

Three days later Newton wrote an even more curious letter[2] to Locke.

> Sir—Being of the opinion that you endeavoured to embroil me with women and by other means, I was so much affected with it as that when one told me you were sickly and would not live, I answered 'twere better if you were dead. I desire you to forgive me this uncharitableness. For I am now satisfied that what you have done is just and I beg your pardon for my having hard thoughts of you for it, and for representing that you struck at the root of morality in a principle you laid down in your book of ideas, and designed to pursue in another book, and that I took you for a Hobbist.[3] I beg your pardon also for saying or thinking that there was a design to sell me an office, or to embroil me.
>
> I am your most humble & unfortunate servant
>
> Is. Newton.

Realising that Newton must be ill and deranged, Locke drafted a kindly and understanding reply:[4]

---

[1] Newton to Pepys. Brewster, *op. cit.*, ii, p. 142.

[2] 16 September 1693 (B.L. MSS. Locke, c. 16, f. 153). The letter was written from the Bull Inn, Shoreditch.

[3] The ethical (and even the political) doctrines of Thomas Hobbes were still fashionable in some quarters. Dr. Bentley (quoted in Monk's *Life of Bentley*, p. 31) said: 'The taverns and coffee houses, nay, Westminster Hall, and the very Churches, were full [of it]'. He alleged that 'not one English infidel in a hundred was other than a Hobbist'.

[4] B.L. MSS. Locke, c. 24, f. 203.

I have been ever since I first knew you so entirely and sincerely your friend and thought you so much mine that I could not have believed what you tell me of yourself had I had it from anybody else. And though I cannot but be mightily troubled that you should have had so many wrong and unjust thoughts of me, that next to the return of good offices such as from a sincere goodwill I have ever done you, I receive your acknowledgement of the contrary as the kindest thing you could have done me, since it gives me hopes I have not lost a friend I so much valued.

After what your letter expresses I shall not need to say anything to justify myself to you: I shall always think your own reflection on my carriage both to you and all mankind will sufficiently do that. Instead of that, give me leave to assure you that I am more ready to forgive you than you can be to desire it; and I do it so freely and fully that I wish for nothing more than the opportunity to convince you that I truly love and esteem you, and that I have still the same good will for you as if nothing of this had happened.

To confirm this to you more fully I should be glad to meet you anywhere, and the rather because the conclusion of your letter makes me apprehend it would not be wholly useless to you. But whether you think it fit or not I leave wholly to you. I shall always be ready to serve you to my utmost in any way you shall like, and shall only need your commands or permission to do it.

My book is going to the press for a second edition, and though I can answer for the design with which I wrote it, yet since you have so opportunely given me notice of what you have said of it, I should take it as a favour if you would point out to me the places that gave occasion to that censure, [so] that by explaining myself better I may avoid being mistaken by others, or unawares doing the least prejudice to truth or virtue. I am sure you are so much a friend to them both that were you near to me I could expect this from you. But I cannot doubt but you would do a great deal more than this for my sake, who, after all, have all the concern of a friend for you, wish you extremely well, and am without complaint.

Happily, Newton collected himself very quickly after this incident, and by mid-October [1] he was writing to Locke to apologise for what he had previously said.

The last winter by sleeping too often by my fire I got an ill habit of sleeping, and a distemper which this summer has been epidemical put me further out of order, so that when I wrote you I had not slept an hour a night for a fortnight together, and for five nights together not a

[1] 15 October 1693, B.L. MSS. Locke, c. 16, f. 154.

wink. I remember I wrote to you, but what I said of your book I remember not. If you please to send me a transcript of that passage, I will give you an account of it, if I can.

Henceforth, the friendship of Locke and Newton continued unmarred by discord until Locke's death.

Among the visitors to Oates that autumn was a friend from Locke's Rotterdam days, Count van Helmont.[1] After his departure Locke followed him to London and stayed there, despite the wintry weather, until 19 December. In London, he told Limborch,[2] 'I have been occupied by new and unexpected visits and engagements following one another in an endless succession.'

Locke added—to excuse himself perhaps from sending Limborch detailed news of the reception of the *Historia Inquisitionis* in England —'After so long a rustication my recent return to London has brought me as yet into the society of only a few of the *literati*.'

As late as the following January,[3] Locke had again to confess to Limborch that he had not yet finished reading his own copy of the *Historia Inquisitionis*. Possibly he was bored by it. Certainly a letter [4] he wrote to Clarke just after Christmas shows that once he had got back to Oates, he was not particularly pressed for time.

You have all the news and I all the leisure, which is very ill-suited for correspondence, when you have not time to write and I nothing to say, unless it be to trouble you with my affairs. Give me leave, there-fore, to mind you here again of the hundred pounds due to me now at Christmas from my Lord Ashley, and the increase of my security. These things I desire you to speak to him of in the manner we agreed and get effected if you can. . . .

[1] Count van Helmont wrote to Locke in his own English on 2 October 1693 (B.L. MSS. Locke, c. 11, f. 184): 'I give you many thanks for your kind lines of the 23 past and for your directions, which I should have followed sooner if a little indisposition had not detained me, which being abated I find myself able to undertake a journey. In order to it I have taken place at the Pewter Pot to come forth on Saturday next about eight in the morning, hoping to be with you that night, where I shall be very glad to meet The Lady and company in good health. . . . According to your directions I will stay at the Crown at Harlow'.
The letter is signed 'Your loving Friend, F. M. v. Helmont'—a Quakerish manner-ism the Count had probably learned from Furly.
[2] 10 November 1693 (Amsterdam: Remonstrants' MSS. Ba. 257 i).
[3] 13 January 1693/4 (*ibid.*, Ba. 257j).
[4] 27 December 1693 (Rand, pp. 382-3).

Inevitably as a result of the publication of his books and pamphlets, Locke received a number of letters [1] from readers who were strangers to him. Some of these letters were friendly, others were hostile; not all of either kind were signed. One pseudonymous correspondent went so far as to send the philosopher a treatise he had written on a subject Locke had dealt with in print.[2] A fragment of Locke's reply [3] to this correspondent survives:

> ... I know not whether you will think fit to discover yourself to anybody, much less to me, who am, as I am told, a stranger to you. 'Tis what 'tis not for me to desire, and had your treatise fallen into my hands in print, I should not so much as have asked after the author, being obliged to him for the benefit I reaped from the pains he had taken to instruct me. I should not have thought it suitable to the gratitude I owed him, nor to the rules of good manners, to desire to know more of him than he thought fit to discover of himself. But since you are pleased to desire my opinion I cannot but wish I might have the opportunity of discoursing with you several things in your treatise.

This letter shows that Locke, so reticent himself, was also willing to respect the reticence of others.

[1] Some of these letters are preserved in the Lovelace Collection (B.L. MSS. Locke, c. 23).

[2] The precise subject is not stated, but it seems to have been a religious one.

[3] 3 December 1693, *ibid.*, c. 24, f. 17.

Chapter Twenty-four

PUBLIC CONTROVERSIES

SIXTEEN NINETY-THREE had been a bad year for William III. The French had almost completely destroyed the Smyrna Fleet off Cape St. Vincent; an expedition against Brest had been repulsed, and William's armies had been defeated at Neerwinden. Inevitably the King blamed his ministers, and as those ministers were Tories, he had perforce to turn once more to the alternative party. As early as March, the appointment of John Somers as Lord Keeper had heralded a Whig revival.[1] Then in November William took the seals of Secretary of State from Nottingham, and offered them to Shrewsbury. At first Shrewsbury declined them, but when other Whigs [2] were appointed to office, he changed his mind and accepted. Carmarthen held on for a time as Lord President of the Council; he was in fact raised in the peerage to be Duke of Leeds, but that elevation was only a prelude to his fall.

On 25 March 1693/4, Lord Monmouth wrote [3] to Locke:

Shall we pretend more that nothing shall surprize us, and have you heard of our late Whiggish promotion without admiration? . . . Whether to congratulate with your friend or to see the silly looks of the enemy, I suppose you will give us one week in town. There is a little philosophical apartment quite finished in the garden [at Parson's Green] that expects you, and if you will let me know when you will come, it will not be the least inconvenience to me to send my coach twenty miles out of town to meet you and may make your journey more easy.

Monmouth himself did not share in the 'Whiggish promotion'. He had antagonised the King by supporting in the House of Lords

[1] Andrew Browning, *Danby*, I, p. 506.
[2] The new Whig ministers included Pembroke (Lord Privy Seal); Russell (First Lord of the Admiralty) and Montague (Chancellor of the Exchequer).
[3] B.L. MSS. Locke, c. 16, f. 115.

both a motion for an enquiry into the conduct of the war and also a bill to establish triennial parliaments. Far from being promoted, Monmouth was indeed suspended from his post as Gentleman of the Bedchamber; his regiment of foot was given to his brother Henry, and he was no longer summoned to the meetings of the Privy Council.

Locke was not well and Sir William Honeywood wrote [1] to ask if it were true that he wished to give up his place in the Commission of Appeals. Locke did not. Poorly as he felt, he did not wish to surrender his public responsibilities. The return of the Whigs to power and above all the appointment of his friend John Somers as Lord Keeper had quickened his interest in public affairs, especially those concerned with finance and economics. Thus, when the spring renewed his health, Locke hurried to London to be in the thick of things once more.

The warmer weather brought no similar relief to David Thomas, who had been ailing all winter at Salisbury, and who in April died.

Locke wrote a letter [2] of condolence to the son, William Thomas. He told him how 'extremely troubled' he was at the doctor's death; he recalled their 'uninterrupted friendship' of 'many years'; he said how 'sorry' he was for Mrs. Thomas. But by far the greater part of Locke's letter was taken up with a record of money David Thomas owed him and of books his late friend had borrowed and not returned. Even in this time of genuine grief, the philosopher's first thought seems to have been for his material possessions.

In 1694 the Bank of England was founded, largely as a result of the efforts of William Paterson, a Scotsman and a close friend of the new Chancellor of the Exchequer, Montague. The Bank was designed to lend money to the Government at eight per cent interest in return for the privilege of dealing in bullion, bills of exchange and notes. The public was invited to invest £1,200,000. Locke was one of the first to see the value of the scheme and to support it. He wrote to Clarke on 30 June: [3]

> . . . Tuesday last I went to see our friend J. F.[4] Upon discourse with him he told me he had subscribed £300, which made me subscribe £500, and so that matter stands. Last night the subscriptions amounted to £1,100,000 and tonight I suppose they are all full.

---

[1] B.L. MSS. Locke, c. 11, f. 221.   [2] 16 April 1694 (*ibid.*, c. 24, f. 275).
[3] B.M. Add. MSS. 4290 f. 69.   [4] John Freke.

After a few summer days in London Locke set off to pay a few visits to some of his more exalted friends in the country. In a letter to Clarke dated 6 August,[1] he wrote:

> I know not what you and your man John Barber think of us travellers. But if you continue to doubt of what I told you, you may go to Mr. Controller's at Winchington in Buckinghamshire, and there have it verified to him [2] that we ate there ripe Newington peaches the beginning of July which they there had perfect ripe and good in June, we gathering . . . the last that was left. At my Lord Ferrers' [3] we ate the ripe oranges and at the Earl of Chesterfield's [4] the ripe grapes, where also you may see oranges planted and thriving in the ground. . . . These two last houses are in Derbyshire, and if [John] will take into his walk my Lord Montague's at Boughton in Northamptonshire he will there find such a garden as he never yet saw in England.

At the same time Locke expressed his bewilderment at Clarke's refusal to be one of the directors of the new Bank of England, and rebuked him for neglecting such a splendid opportunity.

When Locke sent Molyneux a copy of the second edition of his *Essay*, he apologised [5] for his 'long silence' and explained that it was due to 'the slowness of the press'. This delay in the appearance of the second edition may perhaps be attributed to the fact that the bookseller Bassett, who had published the first edition, had retired from business, and transferred Locke's manuscripts to another bookseller, Samuel Manship.[6]

[1] Rand, pp. 396–7.

[2] John Barber had expressed his hopes that 'nobody should have earlier or better fruit of all kinds than his masters in these parts'. (Clarke to Locke from Chipley, 28 July 1694; B.L. MSS. Locke, c. 6, f. 87.)

[3] Robert Shirley, Lord Ferrers (1650–1717), cup-bearer at the coronation of James II, and a Tory, but a supporter of William in 1688. His houses were Chartley Castle, Staffordshire, and Staunton Harold, County Leicester. Macky in his *Characters* describes him as 'a very honest man: a lover of his country: a great improver of gardening and parking, a keen sportsman; never yet in business but is very capable; a tall fair man'.

[4] Philip Stanhope, second Earl of Chesterfield (1633–1713), was an important supporter of William III at the time of the Revolution, but refusing to take oaths, he debarred himself from office. His houses were at Shelford, Notts; Elvaston, Co. Derby, and in Bloomsbury. He was the patron of Dryden, whose wife had been his mistress. [5] 26 May 1694 (*S.F.L.*, p. 76).

[6] Samuel Manship told Locke of Bassett's retirement from business in a letter dated 10 March 1693/4 (B.L. MSS. Locke, c. 15, f. 204):

'I have sent you what papers that are printed this week and shall continue sending

In thanking Locke for his gift, Molyneux wrote: [1]

My most honoured Friend, for so you have . . . allowed me to call you [2] —and 'tis a title wherein I boast more than in maces and parliament robes—by this you may find I have received the Second Edition of your *Essay*, which I prize as an inestimable treasure of knowledge. 'Tis but a week since it came to me; and I have yet only looked over those parts which are newly added, particularly that of liberty, the alterations wherein I take to be most judiciously made. . . . In time I shall give you my farther thoughts of the other parts of your book.[3] . . . But at present I can only pour out my thanks to you for the favourable character under which you have transmitted me to posterity.

Another friend who wrote to congratulate Locke on the changes and additions he had made to the new edition of his *Essay* was James Tyrrell,[4] who was especially pleased with what Locke had added on 'that great question wherein the freedom of our wills consists'. Tyrrell said: 'You have as well avoided the errors of Mr. Hobbes and the old Fatalists who deny all freedom of the will as also of such who supposed we might will and do everything we pleased'.[5]

---

until it is finished. Mr. Bassett has disposed of the Copy to me and one more. We shall take care to satisfy you as if he had it himself, he having left your agreement with us. . . .'

Manship published two issues of the second edition of the *Essay*: one in collaboration with the Churchills, one in collaboration with Thomas Dring.

[1] 28 July 1694, Pforzheimer MS. 74; *S.F.L.*, pp. 84–5.

[2] In the second edition of his *Essay* (pp. 67–8) Locke referred to Molyneux as a 'thinking Gent. whom, though I have never had the happiness to see, I am proud to call my Friend'.

[3] Molyneux did not do so until 15 January 1694/5 (Pforzheimer MS. 78), when he sent Locke 20 '*errata*', chiefly literal or typographical. He did not mark these corrections in the copy Locke had sent him (now in the Pforzheimer Library).

[4] 18 October 1694 (B.L. MSS. Locke, c. 22, f. 128). Locke had the additions and alterations he had made for the second edition printed on separate slips of paper for distribution (gratis) to owners of copies of the first edition. Tyrrell pasted his set in his copy of the first edition, which is now in the British Museum. Evelyn told Pepys in July 1694: 'Our friend Dr. Locke, I am told, has made an addition to his excellent *Essay* which may be had without purchasing the whole book.' Pepys replied: 'Dr. Locke has set a useful example to other reprinters. I hope it will be followed in books of value.' Needless to say so unprofitable a device was *not* generally adopted.

[5] Tyrrell was unfair to Hobbes. In the *Leviathan* (Chap. XXI) Hobbes argued that the problem of the freedom of the will is a bogus problem based on linguistic confusion. The antithesis of freedom and necessity was false, because freedom and necessity correctly understood were perfectly consistent. Locke followed Hobbes in saying in the *Essay* (Book II, xxi) that the 'question whether a man's will be free or no is altogether improper'. Locke called it a long-agitated but unreasonable problem, which was precisely what Hobbes had already suggested.

After his tour of the grand country houses, Locke seems to have become rather more critical of the company which Oates afforded. Not unnaturally, perhaps, he may have grown a little tired of Lady Masham. But there were others besides Lady Masham at Oates. Among them Sir Francis Masham's daughter, Esther, who was by this time aged nineteen.

Esther Masham preserved some of the letters she received from Locke,[1] the earliest being one written on 23 July 1694. Esther Masham had been spending that summer with Sir Robert and Lady Bernard in Huntingdonshire. She recalled that: 'In raillery Mr. Locke used to call me his Laudabridis and I called him my John. Having heard a rich widow had been visiting Oates, I pretended to be jealous of her.'

Locke's answer was as follows: [2]

> The greatest good the widow is ever like to do me is the having procured me a letter from my Laudabridis and giving me the opportunity to let you know you possess the conquest you have made by a power that will hold it against any widow coming with her hundred thousands. . . . For though I shall not fail you, yet I shall suffer for want of you, and the more faithful I am, the less can I bear the want of your company. . . . If jealousy be allowable in either it will be more excusable in my age and experience than in your gaiety. . . . I suspect my daughter[a] more than you, but not your way. But she has so little ill in her that I cannot take amiss anything she does or designs. Remember me very kindly to her if she be with you still. . . . Everybody here is well and want you—Bully[b] and all. . . .

The letter is signed 'Joannes'.

[a] My cousin Frances Compton, then married to William St. John. She used to call Mr. Locke 'Father'.

[b] Bully was a dog of mine.

[1] Esther Masham copied twelve letters Locke had written her into a notebook of 335 pages, into which she also copied another 131 letters from relations and friends. On her death the notebook passed into the hands of her nephew, the second and last Lord Masham. When this nephew sold Oates in 1773 this notebook, with other books and papers, passed with the house into the Palmer family. Miss Palmer, of Holme Park near Reading, showed the notebook to Fox Bourne, who reproduced several of Locke's letters to Esther Masham. The notebook was sold by a Manchester bookseller to the Newberry Library, Chicago, in 1939. For a description of the notebook see Cranston, *Newberry Library Bulletin*, July, 1950, where Locke's letters to Esther Masham are printed *in extenso*.

[2] 23 July 1694 (Newberry) I reproduce this letter from Esther Masham's transcript: the footnotes indicated by alphabetical letters are hers.

Esther Masham wrote to Locke again on 7 August,[1] saying:

Your letter has as much appeased my jealousy as you can desire it to do. If I can but satisfy you now in my turn that you have no reason to have the same suspicion of me as I had of you, the business will be set pretty right between us. Hitherto what I have seen I assure you has appeared very insipid to me, and yet I am told 'tis the very cream of the country, but I believe 'tis you have given me this distaste of everything I see, for I have yet found nothing so pleasant as being in the garden digging with my John. If you think my absence too long, 'tis not my fault. My wishes have carried me to you several times, but unless I had the good luck to find Fortunatus's hat, I find wishing alone will not do it.

I run as much risk in being from you as you do in being from me. Therefore for my sake take care of yourself, for if you should die for want of me, what must I do for want of you. For both our sakes, therefore, let's take care of ourselves and believe your Laudabridis is faithfully yours.

Your daughter desired me last week to present her humble duty to you, and everybody here presents their service.

In his reply the philosopher said:[2]

. . . Let my Laudabridis . . . be as merry as she can every day and know that I partake in it. . . . Pray when you return bring a little summer with you if you intend to do anything in the garden with your John. For we have had nothing but winter weather since you left, and I write this by the fireside whither the blustering wind and rain, like December, has driven me. I hope for a new Spring when you come back. . . .

During the summer of 1694 the former Oxford merchant who had become Locke's landlord in London, Robert Pawling, moved from Dorset Court to a house near the Inns of Court.

After much toil and labour I thank God my whole family with our goods and chattels are safely arrived in Little Lincolns Inn Fields, over against the Plough Inn [Pawling [3] wrote to Locke]. I had little or no time to assist, but my wife and daughters managed it so well that I think we received no damage in any of our goods, and in a day or two more will have placed everything in our new habitation, which we are

[1] B.L. MSS. Locke, c. 16, f. 3.
[2] 20 August 1694 (Newberry).
[3] 26 July 1694 (B.L. MSS., c. 16, f. 220).

all well pleased with, for the conveniences within doors and its situation, it being in good air and near my business. The chamber we design
for you hath the same furniture the other had, and I think will be
altogether as convenient. If you shall like it, you shall be as welcome
as you were in Dorset Court. . . .

Much as Locke was preoccupied with other matters in 1694, he
did not forget his general scientific interests. He was not allowed to
do so. The new secretary of the Royal Society, a fashionable
physician of Irish birth named Hans Sloane,[1] was busily reanimating
that almost moribund institution; and Locke was one of the eminent
Fellows whose interest Sloane sought to rekindle by energetic
letter-writing.

It was very kindly done of you [Locke wrote to Sloane in
September],[2] to send me some news of the commonwealth of letters
into a place where I seldom meet anything beyond the observation of a
scabby sheep or a lame horse.

Lady Masham would not, one imagines, have been pleased if she
had seen these words. In any case, Locke was still making occasional
visits to London; and five days after he had written to Sloane he
went[3] to stay in the rooms Robert Pawling had prepared for him
at Little Lincolns Inn Fields.

While he was there Locke wrote a curiously urgent letter to Sir
Edward Harley[4] dated 25 September 1694:[5]

Sir—Though I cannot doubt but you are assured there is nobody
more your servant than I, yet I cannot but think a letter from me,
especially of the kind this will be, will somehow surprize you. For it
is no less than to desire you to lay by all that country business which

---

[1] Hans Sloane (1660–1753) physician, naturalist, and *protégé* of Sydenham, became
Secretary of the Royal Society in 1693. He held that office until 1712. His bequests to
the British Museum include a number of Locke manuscripts.

[2] 14 September 1694 (B.M. Add. MSS. 4052).

[3] He thus missed the opportunity of travelling by Lord Monmouth's coach. On
the same day, 19 September, Monmouth wrote to Locke offering his coach, albeit
hesitantly, for as he said: 'I am too well-bred to desire (even) a philosopher to leave
a place which a Lady makes agreeable' (B.L. MSS. Locke, c. 16, f. 117).

[4] Sir Edward Harley (1624–1700), was one of the most respected as well as one of
the oldest Whig leaders in the Commons. He was also a staunch champion of
religious toleration, and the author of *A Scriptural and Rational Account of the Christian
Religion*. This latter, which had much in common with *The Reasonableness of
Christianity* may have had some connection with Locke's urgent message. The book
was published in 1695.

[5] Longleat: Marquis of Bath's Collection (F.B., II, p. 310 n.).

you had reserved to the little time is now between this and the parliament, and to come up to town immediately. So bold a presumption as this, without farther explaining myself, will possibly appear very odd to you, and I myself think it so extravagant that I should not venture to send it you were I not satisfied I should be able to justify myself to you for having done it when you come to town. . . .

The purpose behind this letter I have been unable to discover, but it was obviously political.

At the beginning of October[1] Locke wrote from London to Esther Masham at Oates saying:

I take it amiss of my Stars that they should order me to be out of the way when my Laudabridis, whom I had so long languished for, returned. . . . You may believe then that I shall make all the haste I can to even our long account of absence, and compare thoughts and wishes and sighs, and having quitted that score, begin a new one of mirth and laughing and kind words one to another, with now and then a song amongst . . .

When Locke returned a week later to Oates, he had to turn aside from laughter and song to finish reading Limborch's *Historia Inquisitionis*. By 26 October[2] he had reached the last page and was able to write the complimentary letter which Limborch had been patiently awaiting for so many months. Locke assured the author that his book was

written just as history should be. . . . Everything is established and supported by authorities and documents, so that even those who are greatly interested to refute the work, dare not make the attempt. You have dragged into open day from their hiding places such works of darkness and secret deeds of detestable cruelty, that if there remain among those of the Roman Church, or rather among the satellites of Antichrist, any traces of humanity, they will be at length ashamed of that horrid and execrable tribunal, where every principle of right truth and justice are set at nought. . . .

In the same letter, Locke wrote:

The second edition of my *Essay on the Human Understanding* has gone off quicker than I could have apprehended, nor has that heterodox testament yet raised up anywhere an opponent. . . .

[1] 2 October 1694 (Newberry).
[2] Amsterdam: Remonstrants' MSS. Ba. 257k (Latin).

Rash words? Time was indeed to prove them such, but for the first few months scarcely a discordant note was heard amid the chorus of praise. Even from Oxford, where Locke had learned to look first for enmity, there came signs instead of admiration, interest and approval. A don at Jesus College, by name John Wynne, wrote[1] to Locke asking if he might make an abridgement of the *Essay Concerning Human Understanding* for the use of undergraduates; he suggested to him that the general reading of such a students' version would prove the futility of the old systems of philosophy as taught at Oxford and make way for the new.

Locke was delighted. He drafted a reply[2] thanking Wynne for 'so much civility' and his 'kind thoughts' and to tell him something about the writing of the *Essay*.

> It having been begun by chance and continued with no other design but a free enquiry into that subject, it would have been great vanity in me to publish it with hopes that what had been written for the diversion of my idle hours should be made the serious business of studious men who knew how to employ their time. Those who had leisure to throw away on speculations a little out of the road I guessed might perhaps look into it. If by the credit and recommendation of those who, like you, have entertained it with a favourable opinion, it be read further and got into the hands of men of letters and study, it is more than I could expect for a treatise written in a plain and popular style, which, having in it nothing of the air of learning nor so much as the language of the schools, was little suited to the use or relish of those who, as teachers or learners, applied themselves to the mysteries of Scholastic knowledge. But you, I see, are got above Fashion and Prejudice. And you must give me leave to have no ordinary thoughts of a man, who by these two great opposers of all new efforts at improvement, will not suffer yourself to be hindered from contriving how to make the way to real knowledge more open and easy to those beginners who have set their faces that way. I should be very glad [if] anything in my book could be useful to that purpose.

Locke agreed with Wynne that his 'larger explications' could be looked on as incidental, and that the repetitions might be omitted. While he did not feel that he himself, with his 'little health and less leisure', could make the kind of abridgement Wynne desired, he was fully persuaded that another man might usefully make one:

[1] 31 January 1694/5 (B.L. MSS. Locke, c. 23, f. 111).
[2] 8 February 1694/5 (*ibid.*, c. 24, f. 287).

You, I see, are as much master of my notions as I am myself, and better able to put them together to the purpose you intend. I say not this to decline giving any assistance if you, in civility, should think I can afford you any. The abstract which was published in French in the Bibliothèque Universelle in 1688 will neither in its size n[or] design answer the end you propose, but if the rough draft of it, which I think I have in English somewhere amongst my papers, be of any use to you, you may command it, or whatever service I can do you in any kind.

In thanking Locke for his encouragement, Wynne revealed[1] that he had already made an abstract of the *Essay* for his own use; his design was to enlarge this without altering the author's method or style. He believed that the circulation of the abridgement among undergraduates would not only discredit scholasticism but would also promote the sales of the complete edition of the *Essay*.

Wynne was clearly a man after Locke's own heart, and Locke always defended Wynne's abridgement when others (such as Molyneux) criticised it; Locke also repaid Wynne's interest by furthering his promotion in the Church.[2]

The abridgement was completed within a few months, though its publication was deliberately delayed for a reason Wynne explained to Locke:[3]

> ... Mr. Churchill did me the favour to see me when he was here last week, to whose care (since you were pleased to remit it to me) I have committed the printing of the *Abridgement*. He gave me to understand that he intended speedily another impression of your *Essay*, which he desired might come abroad before the *Abridgement*. I thought it reasonable to leave the timing of it to him, that he might order it so as not to hinder the sale of the *Essay*.

Queen Mary II died in London on 28 December 1694, and Martha Lockhart, as one of her ladies, was able to send Locke an eye-witness account of her death:[4]

---

[1] 26 February 1694/5 (B.L. MSS. Locke, c. 23, f. 113).

[2] On Locke's recommendation Wynne was made chaplain to the Lord Privy Seal (Lord Pembroke) in 1696, and subsequently chaplain to the British Embassy in Holland.

[3] 25 June 1695 (*ibid.*, f. 119).

[4] 5 January 1695, *ibid.*, c. 15, f. 41. This account differs somewhat from that given in Hester W. Chapman, *op. cit.*, pp. 250–4.

... the poor Queen's smallpox was, I verily believe, of the worst sort that could be ... I could heartily have wished that Dr. Radcliffe had not made that fatal mistake of calling it the measles. From Monday night till Tuesday night, that from saying there was no danger it came to the sad discovery of black spots appearing in her face when the same Doctor Radcliffe did assure us she would be all over mortified by morning so that by this mistake some thirty hours was lost which, though the case seemed desperate, there was so much strength that I can't tell if the course [which] was afterwards taken had been tried in time what effects it might have produced.

The King's grief in this occasion seems proportioned to his loss, which the greatest [a] man could make, and he has as deep a sense of it as can be imagined. ...

A greater grief to Locke—whose links were closer to William than to Mary—was the death, only a few weeks earlier, of the Archbishop of Canterbury, John Tillotson. Tillotson, a follower of Whichcote, the Cambridge Platonist, was a staunch Latitudinarian, and what Locke called an 'able and candid investigator of truth'. With such a man as head of the Church of England, Locke could feel reasonably confident of the Anglican propriety of his own beliefs. Tillotson, moreover, was a personal friend; and Locke may not have been guilty of undue exaggeration when he wrote after Tillotson's death to Limborch saying:[1]

There is now scarcely anybody I can consult about doubtful points of divinity. I have, indeed, been robbed, to my great injury and sorrow, of a friend who was both candid and sincere and to whom I was endeared by the intercourse of many years.

Locke never felt quite the same regard for Tillotson's Low Church successor, Thomas Tenison, although he knew him, and had more than one occasion to correspond with him.

In the first months of William's sole reign Parliament discussed once more the Act for the Regulation for Printing. This time Locke took care to send Clarke his arguments against renewal before, and not after, the debates. And this time Locke mentioned something more than the injustice of the monopoly to the book-buyer. He raised, among other points, the issue of freedom. In a memorandum [2] he sent to Clarke he said:

[1] 11 December 1694 (Amsterdam: Remonstrants' MSS. Ba. 257 l).
[2] B.L. MSS. Locke, b. 4, f. 75.

I know not why a man should not have liberty to print whatever he would speak; and to be answerable for the one just as he is for the other, if he transgresses the law in either. But gagging a man for fear he should talk heresy or sedition, has no other ground than such as will make gyves necessary for fear a man should use violence if his hands were free, and must at last end in the imprisonment of all who you will suspect may be guilty of treason or misdemeanour.

As for the clause in the Act which gave the agents of the Government 'power to search all houses and seize upon all books which they but think fit to suspect', Locke said he could 'not imagine' how the 'gentry, let alone the peers of England came thus to prostitute their houses to the visitation and inspection of anybody, much less a messenger upon pretence of searching for books'. He called such a law a 'mark of slavery'.

But the principle of liberty was not the only nor even the primary reason Locke gave for advocating the repeal of the Act. His first considerations were of expediency. He argued that the monopoly vested in the Company of Stationers was uneconomic and contrary to the public interest; that the terms of prohibition under the Act were impossibly vague; and that in any case there were already sufficient safeguards under common law against abuses of the Press.

Both Edward Clarke and John Freke were members of a small committee appointed by the House of Commons in February 1694/5 to prepare new legislation, and so through Clarke, Locke's arguments against the Act reached the House of Commons. His arguments prevailed and the Commons voted for repeal; on the other hand the Lords voted for renewal. The Commons then submitted to the Lords a paper[1] giving eighteen reasons against renewal. In preparing that paper the Commons 'followed Locke's reasoning if not his exact words by emphasising the commercial constraints contained in the Act'.[2] Thirteen of the eighteen arguments were practical; only one questioned the principle of censorship. Once more the Lockean argument won the day, and the Act for the Regulation of Printing was finally abolished. The freedom of the Press thus came to England all but incidentally to the elimination of a commercial monopoly.

Unlike Milton, who called for liberty in the name of liberty, Locke was content to ask for liberty in the name of trade; and unlike Milton, he achieved his end.

---

[1] House of Lords' Journals, XV, pp. 545–6.   [2] Siebert, *op. cit.*, p. 261.

In a letter he sent to Molyneux on 8 March 1695,[1] Locke explained
that the cold weather had kept him 'so close a prisoner within doors'
that he had not been out of the house more than once in the past
three months—and 'that only a mile in a coach'. Locke was fretting
a little in his enforced confinement, and he said he thought
'nobody ought to live only to eat and drink, and count the days he
spends idly. The small remainder of a crazy life I shall, as much as
my health will permit, apply to the search of truth. . . .'

Apropos of this Locke mentioned the recent paper he had written
on Malebranche's *Seeing All Things in God*. He had, he believed,
'laid open the vanity, and inconsistency and unintelligibleness of
that way of explaining human understanding'.[2]

Molyneux having suggested [3] that he should allow a friend of his
in Dublin to translate the *Essay* into Latin, Locke was now pleased
to consent: 'My bookseller', he said, 'has been for some time seeking for a translator'. Molyneux's friend, whose name was Richard
Burridge, was duly engaged by the Churchills and his translation
of the *Essay* appeared in 1701.[4]

In his next letter [5] to Molyneux Locke assured his correspondent,
whom he had never met, that he longed for his society:

> Meditating by oneself is like digging in the mine; it often perhaps
> brings up maiden earth . . . but whether it contain any metal in it is
> never so well tried as in conversation with a knowing judicious friend,

[1] S.F.L., pp. 96–103.

[2] Locke's paper, which was prompted by the writings of Norris, was published
as *An Examination of Père Malebranche's Opinion of Seeing All Things in God*, in 1706.
The heart of Locke's argument against Malebranche is contained in the following
excerpt from § 30: Malebranche 'pretends to explain to us how we come to perceive
anything, and that is, by having the ideas of them present in our minds—for the soul
cannot perceive things at a distance or remote from it, and those ideas are present to
the mind only because God, in whom they are, is present to the mind. This, so far,
hangs together and is of a piece; but when, after this, I am told that their presence in
my mind is not enough to make them be seen, but God must do something further to
discover them to me, I am as much in the dark as I was at first, and all this talk of
their presence in my mind explains nothing of the way wherein I perceive them, nor
ever will, till he also makes me understand what God does more than make them
present to my mind when he discovers them to me. . . .'

[3] Molyneux to Locke, 15 January 1694/5 (S.F.L., p. 94).

[4] *De Intellectu Humano. In quatuor libris. Authore Johanne Lockio Armigero. Editio
quarta aucta & emendata & nunc primum Latine reddita.* Londini. Impressis Aunsham &
Johan. Churchil. This translation together with the French version prepared by
Pierre Coste, established the fame of the *Essay* in Continental Europe.

[5] 26 April 1695 (S.F.L., pp. 107–12).

who carries about him the true touch-stone, which is love of truth in a clear-thinking head.

Locke was not only fretting, he was beginning to sense the failing of his powers. He told Edward Clarke:[1]

> ... I lately found a copy of my will sealed up and writ on in a place where I looked not for it. This made me bethink myself how it came there. After some recollection I fancy that I remember that last summer, having some thoughts to alter something in it when I was in town, I had it from you. ... Pray set me right in this matter in your next. For I find my memory is in many things too short to be relied on.

Clarke replied:[2]

> In answer to what you wrote touching your will, I can only inform you that about twelve months since you asked me for it, which I then delivered to you, as I understood your intentions then were to make some alteration in it, but I have never heard you say anything of it since. ...

The 'search of truth' in which Locke had described himself as being engaged was not confined to philosophical inquiries; he was also working on a religious treatise. This last was published in 1695 with the title *The Reasonableness of Christianity*,[3] and published, one need hardly add, anonymously.

Locke argued in the course of this book that Christianity was the faith delivered by Scripture and that Scripture was 'a collection of writings designed by God for the instruction of the illiterate bulk of mankind in the way of salvation, and therefore generally and in necessary points to be understood in the plain direct meaning of the words or phrases'.

Locke repudiated the doctrine of original sin. He said that Christ came into the world to bring the gift of immortality to the righteous and to supplement the 'law of works' with the 'law of faith'. The 'law of works' Locke defined as 'the law of nature, knowable by reason'; it had been adapted by Moses for the special needs of the Jews, but it was manifest to everyone by the clear light of reason.

---

[1] 26 April 1695 (Rand, p. 412).   [2] B.L. MSS. Locke, c. 6, f. 109.

[3] *The Reasonableness of Christianity, as delivered in the Scriptures*, London: printed for Awnsham and John Churchill at the Black Swan in Pater-Noster-Row, 1695.

By the 'law of faith' Locke meant belief in the goodness of God and the messiahship of Christ.

In thus asserting the rationality of the Gospels, Locke attacked such documents as the Athanasian Creed, and other 'tri-theistic' accretions to the 'simple teaching' of Christ himself, whose mission, Locke claimed, had been to reveal the law of God 'by giving its full and clear sense, free from the corrupting and loosening glosses of the scribes and Pharisees'.

The general character and tone of Locke's argument was plainly Unitarian or Socinian; but he persisted in saying that it was not. He remained, as he had always been, an Anglican; and although the Orange Revolution had considerably strengthened the latitudinarian wing of the Church of England, assent (if only lip-service) to the doctrine of the Trinity was still compulsory by law. *The Reasonableness of Christianity* is a Unitarian or Socinian book in everything but name, and it is, in a way, odd that Locke, who was so scrupulous about the proper usage of words, should have failed to admit it. He did not want the bad name of Unitarian or Socinian, and so he managed to persuade himself that he was not a Unitarian or Socinian.

What Locke refused to see, others did their best to point out to him. *The Reasonableness of Christianity* caused a considerable stir, as, indeed, the author realised it would. After Limborch[1] had told him how his own writings were being attacked by Lutherans and Papists alike, Locke assured[2] that friend that he esteemed him all the more for the rough treatment his work had received. The 'sincere and uncorrupt champion of truth', Locke said, was invariably attacked. Then, as if to illustrate the truth of this remark, Locke told Limborch about the attacks on his own *Reasonableness of Christianity*. 'These things', Locke added, 'are whispered in your ear, for I wish it to be known only to you that I have published anything on this subject'.

The most formidable critic of *The Reasonableness of Christianity*, and Locke's most vigorous opponent in public controversy for the rest of his life, was John Edwards, a Cambridge man whose Calvinistic extremism had proved so intolerable to his colleagues at St. John's that he had been forced to resign his Fellowship of that society. After some years as a beneficed clergyman, Edwards had

[1] 26 April 1695 (*S.F.L.*, p. 365: Latin).
[2] 10 May 1695 (Amsterdam: Remonstrants' MSS. Ba. 257 m: Latin).

retired to a Cambridgeshire village, where he devoted all his time and energies to controversial pamphleteering.[1]

Edwards's first attack on Locke was delivered in print a few months after the appearance of *The Reasonableness of Christianity* and in the course of a book called *The Several Causes and Occasions of Atheism*. This book, which was dedicated to the Archbishop of Canterbury, was directed against a number of quasi-Unitarian theologians from the point of view of Low Church orthodoxy. Locke was attacked for saying that 'nothing is required to be believed by any Christian man but this, that Jesus is the Messiah'. Edwards pointed to the fact that the Scriptures ordained that Christians 'must be *taught* as well as baptized in the faith of the Holy Trinity; Father, Son and Holy Ghost'. Hence, Edwards argued, if Christians must be *taught* this doctrine, 'it is certain they must *believe* it'.

Edwards was by no means a tactful controversialist; and having complained, with some justification, about the poor literary quality of *The Reasonableness of Christianity* he added provocatively:

> Some may attribute this flatness to the ill cause [the author] manages; but for my part, I question whether we have the right author. I cannot persuade myself but that there is an error of the person: at least I will charitably presume so, because I have so good an opinion of the gentleman who wrote of *Human Understanding* and *Education*.

These last words were less than wholly sincere, for within a year or two Edwards was to come out with a most virulent attack on Locke's treatise of *Education*. But Edwards's provocative tactics succeeded—not, of course, in making Locke admit he wrote *The Reasonableness of Christianity*, but in making him write and publish a reply to *The Several Causes and Occasions of Atheism*.

Locke called his reply, which was in print before the end of 1695, *A Vindication of the Reasonableness of Christianity etc. From Mr. Edwards's Reflections*.[2] In the course of this pamphlet, Locke described 'the buzz and flutter and noise which was made' when *The Reasonableness of Christianity* appeared and 'the reports which were raised' as being enough to 'have persuaded the world that it subverted all morality and was designed against the Christian religion'. He declared that such criticisms had 'at first amazed' him but

---

[1] John Edwards (1637–1716) published over forty works between 1690 and his death. He returned to Cambridge in 1697 and received the degree of D.D. in 1699.

[2] Published by Awnsham and John Churchill.

he was certain that 'if there was anything in my book against what anyone called religion it was not against the religion contained in the Gospel'.

Locke pointed out that Edwards's case was built on two propositions: the first, that all Socinians were atheists; the second, that the author of *The Reasonableness of Christianity* was a Socinian. Locke disputed, but quickly passed over the first of these propositions, and concentrated on denying the second. His pamphlet would surely have been a better one if he had concentrated on the first proposition, where Edwards was manifestly wrong. Locke's refutation of the second proposition was not well argued, and the very fact that he fell easily into Edwards's polemical style suggests that he must have been guiltily aware that a part at least of Edwards's case was true. This impression is confirmed by the shifty argument of the following paragraph:

> I know not but it may be true that the Antitrinitarians and Racovians [1] understand [certain texts] as I do: but 'tis more than I know that they do so. I took not my sense of those texts from those writers, but from the Scripture itself, giving light to its own meaning, but one place compared with another. What in this way appears to me its true meaning I shall not decline because I am told it is understood by the Racovians, whom I never yet read; nor embrace the contrary, though the *generality of Divines* I converse with should declare for it.

It was not true that Locke had never read the Racovians. His notebooks contain excerpts in his own hand from their writings,[2] and even if it were true it would be no answer to Edwards to say so. Edwards's argument was that Locke's views were identical with those of the Socinians. Locke repudiated the word, but he did not point to any substantial theological point on which his views were at variance with those of the Socinians. He left Edwards with an easy opening for another attack, and in due time Edwards seized it.[3]

---

[1] I.e. the Socinians.

[2] *Vide* also H. J. McLachlan, *op. cit.*, p. 327.

[3] Edwards's rejoinder was not published until 1696 but in the meantime an anonymous writer entered the controversy to support Locke against Edwards with a pamphlet entitled *The Exceptions of Mr. Edwards in his* 'Causes of Atheism' *against* 'The Reasonableness of Christianity as Delivered in the Scriptures' *examin'd and found Unreasonable, Unscriptural and Injurious*, London, 1695 (no printer or publisher named).

At the end of May the weather was fine enough for Locke to venture on a visit to London. In advising Edward Clarke of his coming, he [1] said: 'I have something which I would gladly propose and have debated in the College'.

The 'College' was yet another of Locke's clubs; not this time a social club, but a political one; it was the medium through which Locke influenced Parliament. The members included Edward Clarke, John Freke and Sir Walter Yonge; and from the early months of *1695* onwards Locke formed the habit of addressing certain letters which he sent to Clarke on political questions to the College as a whole.

Very probably the question Locke hoped to discuss with these friends that summer was the reform of the currency, a national problem which was becoming progressively more serious, and which had begun to touch the philosopher's own pocket. He confided to Clarke: [2]

> I shall I think in the beginning of July have some money [3] paid me in, and perhaps some sooner. Pray tell me whether I cannot refuse clipped money, for I take it not to be the lawful coin of England, and know not why I should receive half the value I lent instead of the whole.

Clarke replied: [4]

> I think you may lawfully refuse all clipped or other money that is diminished in the weight more than by reasonable wearing, or otherwise you may in a very short time be forced to receive a quarter part of what you lent instead of the whole.

Locke was to do a lot more thinking and writing about the clipped money question in the next few months. The reason was as follows. While the King was on the Continent leading his troops in the war against France (and he led them in August to victory at

---

[1] 17 May 1695. B.M. Add. MSS. 4290, f. 74.

[2] 25 May 1695. *Ibid.*, f. 75.

[3] The money referred to may have been the £600 which Locke had lent the late David Thomas; and which was repaid that summer. There were complaints from Mrs. Thomas that Locke had demanded too much interest; namely 5% instead of 4%. But a letter from John Bonville to Clarke (Rand, p. 421) throws other light on the matter. He writes: '. . . That 5% was agreed it appears by the writings. Had they continued it seven or eight years as the Doctor proposed, there would have been but 4½% expected. But they pay it in so soon and without six months' notice as was agreed, it was reasonable that the interest should be paid according to the writings'.

[4] 28 May 1695. B.L. MSS. Locke, c. 6, f. 113.

Namur) his duties at home were delegated to a Council of seven Lords Justices. The first among them was John Somers, the Lord Keeper, another was Lord Pembroke. The most urgent problem they had to deal with was clipped money. Knowing Locke had 'thoughts' on the subject, Somers persuaded his colleagues to call him into consultation. But Locke was not the only or even the first man the Lords Justices invited to address them.

The first was William Lowndes,[1] who had been a Treasury official for sixteen years, and had lately been appointed Secretary of the Treasury by Montague, the Chancellor of the Exchequer. Lowndes proposed to solve the problem by reducing the silver content of the coin.

Locke, on the other hand, advised the Council to undertake recoinage at full value.

On 21 September [2] Somers wrote to Locke at Robert Pawling's house asking if he might have 'one minute's talk' with him the following morning before ten o'clock. Lowndes had produced a rejoinder to Locke's plan, and Somers wanted Locke's comments on it.[3] Locke was again invited to appear before the Lords Justices and to defend his project in person.[4]

A little later Lowndes published his views in a book called *A Report Containing an Essay for the Amendment of the Silver Coins.* Somers wrote to Locke about it: [5]

> You will easily see by the book, which was put in my hand last night, and by the title of a report, which it bears as well as by the advertisement at the end of it, that you were in the right when you said the alteration of the standard was the thing aimed at.
>
> The challenge at the end, if you will allow me to say so, is in some sort directed to you. The proposition which you and I discoursed upon yesterday is endeavoured to be represented as impracticable. The passing of money by weight is said to be ridiculous, at least in little payments. The sudden fall of guineas will be an utter ruin to very great

---

[1] William Lowndes (1652–1724) began his lifelong career in the Treasury in 1679. His report was published in September 1695, and in November of that year he entered the Commons as M.P. for Seaford.

[2] B.L. MSS. Locke, c. 18, f. 156.

[3] On 24 September (*ibid.*, f. 158) Somers wrote again telling Locke he had an abstract of Lowndes's paper he wished to discuss with him.

[4] According to the Calendar of State Papers (Domestic: July–December 1695) the Lords Justices, having heard the views of Lowndes, desired to know the opinion of the others, including Locke, at their meeting on 27 September.

[5] B.L. MSS. Locke, c. 18, f. 159.

numbers. There is no encouragement proposed to invite people to bring the clipped money into the Mint, so that will be melted down to be transported, which will be a certain profit at least till by a law money can be exported. And whilst this doing, nothing [will be] left to carry on commerce, for no one will bring out his guineas to part with them for 20/- when he paid 30/- for them so lately.

These, as I remember, were the objections made use of, and I doubt not you will without great difficulty help us with some expedients for them. I believe it an easier task than to remove (what I see is so fixed) the project of alteration of the standard.

Faced with this challenge, Locke set to work and quickly produced in reply to Lowndes a substantial pamphlet entitled *Further Considerations Concerning the Raising the Value of Money*.[1] In this pamphlet Locke wrote:

> . . . The only way to bring treasure into England is the well-ordering of trade. The only way to bring silver and gold to the mint, for the increase of our stock of money and treasure which shall stay here, is an overbalance of our whole trade. All other ways to increase our money and riches are but projects that will fail us. . . .

Lowndes's latest proposal was to restore clipped money to its real value by issuing one-ounce silver coins, worth five shillings as silver, but bearing the nominal value of six shillings and threepence; and he also proposed that the whole currency should be depreciated by one fifth. His argument was based on the fact that an ounce of silver was worth six and threepence on the market because 'bullion had risen'. Locke in his reply argued that Lowndes's premise was false. An ounce of silver was not, he said, 'worth' six and threepence. An ounce of silver was worth an ounce of silver, whether it was coined or not. Locke wrote:

> One pound of the same goodness will never exchange for a pound and a quarter of the same goodness. And so it is in silver. An ounce of silver will always be of an equal value to an ounce of silver. Nor can it ever rise or fall in respect of itself. An ounce of standard silver can never be worth an ounce and a quarter of standard silver; nor one ounce of uncoined silver exchange for an ounce and a quarter of coined silver. The stamp cannot so much debase its value.

[1] *Further Considerations Concerning Raising the Value of Money, wherein Mr. Lowndes's Arguments for it in his late Report concerning* 'An Essay In the Amendment of the Silver Coins' *are particularly Examined*. London. Printed for A. and J. Churchill at the Black Swan in Paternoster-Row, 1695.

Locke's pamphlet was submitted to the Lords Justices,[1] and at their suggestion published within a matter of days. But in writing to offer to Molyneux a copy, Locke[2] begged him to respect its anonymity: 'You may be sure I do not own it to be mine till you see my name to it'.

Historians have generally held that Locke was right on the money question and Lowndes mistaken, though Mr. C. R. Fay has argued[3] that the only thing wrong with Lowndes's proposals was that they were ahead of their time. At all events the Government took Locke's advice, and despite some setbacks in the House of Lords, his policy won the day.

Re-coinage at the old standard caused some real hardships. Mr. Feavearyear[4] has shown that mismanagement made the process very slow—extending over three years; and that the defective money was taken at various rates much under the nominal value. The new coin was paid out only to people owed money by the Government, which meant that people who were too poor to pay taxes or subscribe to Government loans could get rid of their bad coins only through intermediaries who charged commission. Mr. Fay[5] says that most of the mistakes committed in the process had been foreseen by Lowndes; and that the authorities—who included Isaac Newton of the Mint—had later to adopt expedients which Lowndes had originally proposed.

However, with the aid of a loan of more than a million pounds from the Bank of England (on the security of the Window Tax), re-coinage was eventually accomplished, and history has rightly given Locke a great share of the credit. Lady Masham[6] spoke of his work on the money question as a service to his country for which alone he deserved 'a public monument to immortalise the memory thereof'.

Locke's renown as a man of letters was no less on the Continent than it was at home. In 1695 a Frenchman sent him a translation he had made of *Some Thoughts Concerning Education*. It was not a

---

[1] Locke also explained his views on re-coinage in a letter he wrote on 28 February 1696/7 to Thomas Tenison, Tillotson's successor as Archbishop of Canterbury (Lambeth Palace MSS., Vol. CMXXX; No. 18, and F.B., II, p. 339).
[2] 20 November, 1695 (*S.F.L.*, p. 128).
[3] *Cambridge Historical Journal* (1932), IV, 2, pp. 143–55.
[4] A. E. Feavearyear, *The Pound Sterling* (Oxford, 1931), pp. 127–32.
[5] *Ibid.*, p. 147.　　　[6] Amsterdam: Remonstrants' MSS. J. 57 a.

perfect rendering,[1] but Locke was pleased with it. The translator was a French Protestant aged 27, named Pierre Coste, who had lived in Holland since the revocation of the Edict of Nantes and who was a friend of Dr. Guenellon's. When Locke sent him a copy of the revised edition of his *Education*, Coste[2] wrote most appreciatively of the changes made, and before long Locke had invited him over to England to swell the throng at Oates.

After the death of his cousin William Stratton, Locke wrote on 14 September 1695[3] to Cornelius Lyde at Stanton Wick, Somerset, asking him to take over the management of his property in that county. Locke said he knew no one else he could ask. Moreover, as he said, 'The little estate I have there is a great part of it in your own parish and almost all of it under your eye'.

Lyde agreed, and sought only one favour in return. He asked Locke[4] on behalf of Mary Dolman whether he could do anything for her son, who was a weak lad, but had inclinations to learning. Locke's reply[5] was not a sympathetic one, even though Mary Dolman was a cousin of his, the daughter of his aunt Anne Bonville.[6] He wrote:

> I am, and hope I always shall be, ready to assist according to my power my poor relations, but I do not understand my cousin Mary Dolman's request; if it be that I should breed her son to learning, I desire to be excused. When she speaks out plainly what she desires of me I shall then know what to say . . .

Nine months later Locke relented to the extent of instructing Cornelius Lyde to give Mary Dolman a pound.[7]

Another letter from Locke to Lyde[8] written eight years after these events may be quoted here to illustrate Locke in the rôle of landlord. He sent Lyde a list of rents owing to him, and at the same time said:

---

[1] The *Nouvelle Biographie Générale* describes Coste's translation as '*fidèle mais peu élégante*'.
[2] *13 September 1695*, B.L. MSS. Locke, c. 7, f. 141 (French).
[3] P.M.L. Locke MSS.
[4] 8 April 1696: B.L. MSS. Locke, c. 15, f. 137.
[5] 24 April 1696: P.M.L. Locke MSS.
[6] *Vide* Locke to Lyde, 15 January 1696/7 (*ibid.*).
[7] 15 January 1696/7 (*ibid.*).
[8] 28 June 1703 (*ibid.*).

. . . I have also sent you a warrant for distraining on Mary Cooke if she has not paid you before it comes to your hands. I believe Pensford is not without a bailiff in it. He perhaps will be the fittest to execute it. You must tell my cousin King when you think fittest to direct it to that it may be done accordingly. Eight years is too long to let a rent run up in arrear, upon promise from time to time of payment, which is never done. I am resolved to stay no longer. . . .

Chapter Twenty-five

A COMMISSIONER FOR TRADE

LOCKE spent more time than he liked to spend at that season of the year in London between September and November 1695. Once back at Oates he was disinclined to move, especially for the London meetings of the Court of Appeals. He told Clarke on 2 December:[1] 'I had rather lose two places than one life'.

The possibility of a second place, as yet a secret, was much on Locke's mind just then, and it was because of it that he had remained in London during the previous two months.[2] It had to do with colonies and trade.

The colonial situation had been unsatisfactory—unsatisfactory, that is, from the English point of view—since the Glorious Revolution. Under James II colonial administration had worked well, but under William III the need for propitiating revolutionary governments in the plantations had produced 'an intolerable confusion in management',[3] with constant infringements of the Acts of Trade and an enormous growth of piracy, in which more than a few English captains and English ships participated. The existing Committee for Trade proved itself incapable of dealing with these problems. As a sub-committee of the Privy Council, generally known as the Lords of Trade, it had come into being when Danby abolished Shaftesbury's Council of Trade. It was later altered to a committee of the whole Council and its effective secretary since 1679 had been William Blathwayt,[4] an exceptionally able if also an exceptionally ambitious public servant; but Blathwayt was at the

---

[1] Rand, p. 427.

[2] Locke's journal shows that he was in London from 2 to 28 September, and from 21 October until 18 November.

[3] A. T. S. Goodrick, *Edward Randolph* (Boston, 1909), VI, p. 54.

[4] William Blathwayt (1649–1717) had bought the post of Secretary-at-War from Matthew Locke in 1683, and after serving James II in that capacity until the Orange Revolution, he then adroitly transferred his services to the Prince. He represented Bath in the House of Commons from 1693 to 1707, and built himself a fine country seat Dyrham Park, Glos., from the profits that came his way as a civil servant.

same time William's Secretary-at-War, and his overseas duties in this latter capacity precluded his giving the Committee for Trade the attention it needed. The Lords of Trade themselves were likewise too busy, when they were not too lazy, to attend the meetings. As early as 1692 Lord Mulgrave had advised William to reform the Committee for Trade, choosing 'such as are likely to attend to it, and that it should meet two evenings in a week on fixed days, and not according to the leisure or the humour of a President of the Council'.[1] In 1693 the City of London merchants, despairing of seeing anything done by the Lords of Trade, considered creating their own Board of Trade. Then in 1695 Edward Randolph, William's remarkably gifted, industrious and honest Surveyor-General of Customs in North America, reported after a comprehensive tour of all those territories that the whole system of colonial administration was disintegrating, and that reform was imperative.

Randolph's link with the Government was through Blathwayt, and Blathwayt was not at all surprised at Randolph's report. He had his own ideas about methods of reform, and he had little doubt, as the King's principal adviser on colonial matters, that his proposals would be listened to.

But there were other ideas in the air in 1695. In several quarters men suspected that William was anxious to promote Dutch trade at the expense of the English,[2] and certain Whigs proposed the creation of a Board of Trade *by Parliament* with wide powers to control commerce, appoint convoys, further plantation trade and provide for the poor. On the other hand Somers, the first Minister, sponsored a scheme for a royally-chosen Board, and Mr. Laslett[3] has suggested that Locke himself was the originator of it.[4]

Although the former proposal was well supported it was really a very revolutionary one, for a Board chosen by Parliament would entail considerable inroads into royal prerogative. William was at first

---

[1] Quoted by Gertrude Ann Jacobsen, *William Blathwayt* (New Haven, 1932), p. 147.

[2] A. B. Keith, *Constitutional History of the First British Empire* (Oxford, 1930), p. 273.

[3] 'John Locke as Founder of the Board of Trade', *The Listener*, 18 December 1954.

[4] Several well-known publicists had already put forward schemes for a new Board of Trade. (*Vide* Charles M. Andrews, *Colonial Period of American History*, New Haven, 1938, IV, pp. 281–288.) One of them was a correspondent of Locke's named John Cary, whose *Essay on the State of England in Relation to Trade and Taxes*, Locke called 'the best discourse I have ever read on the subject' (2 May 1696: B.M. Add. MSS. 5540, f. 70).

outraged, then forced to see that reform of the Lords of Trade was inevitable: either he would have to initiate reform himself, or Parliament would take up the Whig idea. By the time he consented to appoint a new Board of Trade, Parliament had done as he feared.

Lord Monmouth, who had been restored to royal favour and was now one of William's Gentlemen of the Bedchamber, wrote to Locke on 12 December 1695 [1] saying:

> I was some days ago extremely pleased when the King was brought to so reasonable a resolution as to determine upon a Council of Trade, where some great men were to assist, but where others with salaries of £1000 a year were to be fixed as the constant labourers. Mr. Locke being to be of this number made me have a better opinion of the thing and comforted me for our last disappointment upon your subject; but according to our accustomed wisdom and prudence when all things had been a good while adjusted, the patent ready for the seal, and some very able and honest men provided for your companions, it was impossible to get the King to sign it; but delaying it from day to day, the Parliament this day fell upon it, and are going to form such a commission to be nominated by themselves. . . . At last the Secretary informs the House at the latter end of the Debate and much consultation that the King had just formed such a commission. . . . What the event will be, I know not, but for the little I am able, I shall endeavour that Mr. Locke may be the choice of the House as well as the King's. . . .

Somers himself wrote to Locke on 17 December [2] to tell him of 'the King's resolution to name you one of the Commissioners for Trade and Plantations' and to ask if Locke would agree.

One might have supposed that Locke would not agree. He was an ill man; he knew enough of what would be expected of a Commissioner of Trade to realise that the appointment would be no sinecure. As it was, Locke went straight to London and gave his consent.

The King had made up his mind, but Parliament, which had not come to a decision even on the coinage issue, had yet to discard the alternative and rival proposal. The Commons debated the issue on 2 January 1695/6, and in the same evening William Popple wrote to Locke, who had by then returned to Oates feeling very unwell after his interview with Somers, the following letter: [3]

> I must discharge my promise of writing to you, though I know it will be done more particularly by other hands than I possibly can.

[1] B.L. MSS. Locke, c. 16, f. 119.   [2] *Ibid.*, c. 18, f. 161.   [3] *Ibid.*, c. 17, f. 219.

D D

But when I tell you what I know, if it be comparatively impertinent, you must blame yourself, and not me, for the trouble of
reading it. . . . This morning the Party that have promoted the
design of a Committee of Trade in the House, being offended at the
postponing of that business, shuffled off the coinage without doing
anything remarkable in it and brought on the subject of the Committee
which had before been appointed. The whole day was spent in
Debates. And in the end without resolving anything about the powers
that this intended Committee should have, but agreeing that the nature
of it should be perfectly different from that intended by the King
(which was mentioned and opined, not by the Court but themselves)
this being only for speculations, as they said, about the improvement of
Trade in time of Peace; this for the effectual security of it in time of
war. After much more of this nature than I can tell, and without agreement upon the number of Commissioners, at seven o'clock at night,
the question was put, whether the Parliament or the King should
name them, and carried for the Parliament by one single voice: on
that side being 175 and on the other side 174. . . . This about the Committee I have, now late, from one that was present at the Debate.
And this is all I can say. . . .

On the same day Edward Clarke [1] informed Locke more briefly
about the Debate and of the House's resolution by a majority of one
vote 'that Commissioners of Trade be appointed by Act of Parliament'. Clarke also told Locke he had the express order of the
Lords of the Treasury to call him to London to attend to his duties as
a Commissioner of Appeals. Clarke explained that 'the whole
management of the revenue is struck at in these appeals'. Sir
William Honeywood also wrote [2] in the same vein.

Locke was too ill to go. Naturally he wondered whether he had
been wise to agree to take on new responsibilities when he found it so
difficult to discharge his existing ones. His doubts increased during
the next three months. Telling Molyneux, in a letter of 30 March,[3]
how he had been 'very ill this winter, not without some apprehensions
of my life', Locke also said:

> The business of our money has so near brought us to ruin that, till
> the Plot broke out, it was everybody's talk, everybody's uneasiness.
> And because I had played the fool to print about it, there was scarce a
> post wherein somebody or other did not give me fresh trouble about

[1] B.L. MSS. Locke, c. 6, f. 99.
[2] 4 January 1695/6 (*ibid.*, c. 11, f. 223).
[3] *S.F.L.*, p. 141.

it. But now Parliament has reduced guineas to two and twenty shillings a piece after the 10th instant, and prohibited the receipt of clipped money after the 4th of May next. The Bill has passed both Houses, and, I believe, will speedily receive the Royal Assent. Though I can never bethink any pains or time of mine, in the service of my country, as far as I may be of any use; yet I must own to you this, and the like subjects, are not those which I now relish, or that do with most pleasure employ my thoughts; and therefore [I] shall not be sorry if I escape a very honourable employment, with a thousand pounds a year salary annexed to it, to which the King was pleased to nominate me some time since. May I have but quiet and leisure, and a competency of health to perfect some thoughts my mind is sometimes upon, I should desire no more for myself in this world, if one thing were added to it, viz. you in my neighbourhood. . . .

The 'Plot' Locke mentioned was one to assassinate the King as a preliminary to a Jacobite invasion. William discovered and frustrated it and communicated the whole story to Parliament on 24 February. Parliament rallied to his side and gave him emergency authority to sustain the realm and punish the conspirators. The most important conspirator arrested was Sir John Fenwick, who tried to extricate himself by informing against other and even more important men. He alleged first that Shrewsbury and then that Godolphin were privy to the plot. Locke's foolish friend Monmouth contrived to have access to Fenwick and urged him to make the same charge against three of his (Monmouth's) personal enemies: Marlborough, Russell and Salisbury. Fenwick's wife betrayed Monmouth, who was duly accused before his peers of concocting incriminating documents, found guilty and sent to the Tower.

William was able to exploit the popularity the Plot brought him to thwart the scheme to appoint a Board of Trade under Parliamentary control. He was still willing that there should be a new Board of Trade, but he insisted that its members should receive their commissions from him. Parliament let him have his way, and before the King set off for Flanders and the Front in May, all was arranged.

Both Blathwayt and Locke were chosen Commissioners of Trade. The others were the Earl of Tankerville,[1] the Earl of

---

[1] Ford Grey (?–1701) the same who had landed with Monmouth in 1685, then turned informer. In 1688 he had deserted James, and thrown in his lot with William. In May 1695 he became a Privy Councillor, and a month later he was created Earl of Tankerville.

Bridgewater,[1] Sir Philip Meadows,[2] John Pollexfen,[3] Abraham Hill [4] and John Methuen.[5] To the disappointment of those who had advocated a Board controlled by merchants, there was only one merchant among the Commissioners, and he—Pollexfen—was more of an economist than a business man.

Bridgewater was chosen president, and the full title of the Board was 'His Majesty's Commissioners for promoting the Trade of this Kingdom and for inspecting and improving the Plantations in America and elsewhere'.[6] The Commissioners were instructed to investigate 'the state and condition of the general trade of England and also of the several particular trades into all foreign parts'. They had further 'to consider of some proper methods for setting on work and employing the poor of the kingdom and making them useful to the public, and thereby easing the nation of that burden'. They were charged with full responsibilities for the colonies (then still known as 'plantations'), 'as well with regard to the administration of the government and justice in those places as in relation to the commerce thereof'.

The Board was asked [7]

> to furnish replies for addresses from the Houses asking for information on colonial defence, on Indian affairs, and on the administration of justice—a vital matter to British merchants doing a large colonial trade. Again violations of the laws of trade, the extension of the use of paper money, or piracy, evoked demands from Parliament, while a keen interest was taken in efforts to grow naval stores, rice, silk, indigo, and other raw material needed for British manufacturers. . . . The Board was also responsible for drafting legislation on its pet topics; thus during its years of activity it yearly sought to have bills carried to resume the colonial charters, it aimed at protection for pine trees suitable

[1] John Egerton (1646–1701), third Earl of Bridgewater, was a statesman of high character and one for whom the King had particular respect. He rose to be First Lord of the Admiralty.

[2] Sir Philip Meadows (1626–1718) had been a prominent diplomatist and was appointed Commissioner for Public Accounts in 1692.

[3] John Pollexfen, economist and merchant, had been a member of the Committee for Trade and Plantations in 1675. In his *Discourse of Trade Coin and Paper Credit* (1697) he put forward a 'labour theory of value', together with a case for free trade.

[4] Abraham Hill (1635–1721), economist, scientist and a member of the Council of the Royal Society, had been comptroller to the See of Canterbury under Tillotson.

[5] John Methuen (1650?–1706) diplomatist, lawyer, M.P. and former ambassador to Portugal.

[6] Manuscripts of the House of Lords (1695–7), pp. 416–19.

[7] Keith, *op. cit.*, pp. 267–8.

for masts, at preferential treatment of naval stores, at encouragement of pig-iron production and discouragement of paper money.

The document setting up the Board of Trade was sealed on 15 May 1696, although, as Locke did not fail to remind the secretary, the salaries of Commissioners were to be paid as from 25 March.[1] The Board did not actually hold its first meeting until 25 June.

Until well into June Locke was confined to his room at Oates. On 19 May Sir William Trumbull,[2] Secretary of State, wrote to him saying:

> . . . I am now to call on you in behalf of the public, whose service requires your help, and consequently your attendance in town. The Council of Trade, whereof you are most worthily appointed a member, must go on with effect, or the greatest inconveniences and mischiefs will follow. I hope your health will permit you to come and make some stay here, and what reluctancy soever you may have to appear among us, I know your love to your country, and your great zeal for our common interests will overcome it, so that I will trouble you no further till I can have the happiness of seeing you here. . . .

Locke had to tell Trumbull in his reply [3] that he was not well enough to come to London; and he sent a similar message to Sir William Honeywood, who had summoned him to a meeting of the Commissioners of Appeals. In his letter [4] to Honeywood, Locke said:

> . . . Had the Spring this year brought with it so much sun and warmth as it used to do, I had according to my resolution waited upon you in town before this time. But the ill effects which my lungs as well as other things have felt from this late cold and winter weather have put off my journey longer than I expected.

However, as soon as Locke was fit enough to travel he went and settled in London until the middle of November. His responsibilities as a Commissioner for Trade imposed a completely new way of life upon him. The salary of a thousand pounds a year was, by the standards of the day, a very handsome one, but the duties were correspondingly arduous. The Board of Trade met not less than three times a week, and its meetings often continued late into the evening. The Commissioners were also obliged to do a considerable amount of preparatory work between the sessions.

---

[1] B.L. MSS. Locke, c. 17, f. 229.   [2] *Ibid.*, c. 22, f. 24.
[3] 22 May 1696 (*ibid.*, c. 24, f. 56).   [4] 22 May 1696 (*ibid.*, f. 55).

It is clear that Locke dominated the first meeting and continued to dominate the Board while his membership of it lasted. His most powerful rival was Blathwayt. This man, who was close to the King, might have expected the more easily to keep the upper hand in a royalty-chosen Board; but Blathwayt started out with a disadvantage: as Secretary-at-War he had to go to Flanders with William, and was thus unable to attend the earliest meetings of the Board in London. Blathwayt went off feeling certain that John Povey his former deputy as secretary to the Lords of Trade would be appointed secretary of the new Commissioners; having a *protégé* in that position would clearly be a great source of strength to him. But Locke forestalled the manoeuvre. One of Blathwayt's friends, Robert Henley, wrote to him on 3 July[1] saying:

> . . . I doubt not but you have had an account of the meeting of the Council of Trade at Whitehall, and though, it may be, the majority of those lords and others named in the committee were for Mr. Povey and Mr. Tollet to be secretaries, yet that was obviated by my Lord Keeper [Somers] who very early disclosed to the Board that one Mr. Popple was nominated thereto by his Majesty, and so there was no room to propose any other; and accordingly, I hear Mr. Popple at this last meeting did officiate as secretary. . . .

This Mr. Popple was Locke's good friend William Popple, the Unitarian merchant who had translated the *Epistola de Tolerantia* and who had since become the secretary of the Dry Club. Locke's one time manservant and secretary, Sylvanus Brownover,[2] who had married and wished to better himself, was taken on as one of Popple's clerks.

Another thing Robert Henley mentioned in his letter to Blathwayt was that he 'had been solicited by him who is a philosopher and by his friends to give them a scheme, and if not that, to communicate my thoughts and observations about trade'. The 'philosopher' could only be one man, and the wording of the sentence points again to the fact, which the documents of the Board of Trade make abundantly clear, that Locke was the leading Commissioner in nearly everything which was undertaken. Even so, in a private letter[3] to Molyneux, written after that friend had congratulated him on his appointment, Locke said:

---

[1] B.M. Add. MSS. 9729, ff. 140–1.
[2] Thomas Kiplin had succeeded Brownover as Locke's manservant.
[3] 2 July 1696 (completed 4 August 1696) (S.F.L., p. 152).

Your congratulations to me I take as you meant kindly and seriously, and it may be it is what another would rejoice in, but if you will give me leave to whisper truth without vanity in the ear of a friend, 'tis a preferment which I shall get nothing by, and I know not whether my country will, though that I shall aim at with all my endeavours.

Riches may be instrumental to so many good purposes that it is, I think, vanity rather than religion or philosophy to pretend to condemn them. But yet they may be purchased too dear. My age and health demand a retreat from bustle and business, and the pursuit of some enquiries I have in my thoughts makes it more desirable than any of those rewards which public employments tempt people with. . . .

Later in the year[1] Locke wrote again to Molyneux asking for information about linen manufacture in Ireland, as this was one of the chief subjects discussed at meetings of the Board for Trade during the summer and autumn of 1696. Molyneux in his reply[2] assured Locke that Ireland was ideally suited for growing flax and hemp, and he thought the Irish could get rich by the linen trade, but he added rather bitterly:

England, most certainly, will never let us thrive by the woollen trade; this is their darling mistress, and they are jealous of any rival. But I see not that we interfere with them in the least by the linen trade.

Molyneux had put his finger on the nub of the question; the English were interested in promoting linen manufacture in Ireland not for the good of the Irish, but as a means to suppress any competition in the woollen market. Of the various schemes discussed at the Board for Trade, the Minutes show that 'that brought in by Mr. Locke was pitched upon'.

A manuscript of these proposals[3] bears the signatures of five Commissioners for Trade including Locke. Its argument is briefly this:

1. The woollen manufacture of Ireland cannot be carried on and continued to be improved there at the rate it hath been of late years without very ill consequences to [England].

2. To hinder, therefore, the growth of woollen manufacture in

[1] 12 September 1696 (*S.F.L.*, pp. 159–61). In the same letter Locke said that his portrait was being painted—evidently for Molyneux.
[2] 26 September 1696 (*ibid.*, pp. 162–8).
[3] B.M. Harleian MSS. 1324. *Vide* also B.L. MSS. Locke, c. 30, ff. 65–75.

Ireland . . . the exportation of all sorts of woollen manufactures out of Ireland should be restrained and penalized.

3. To prevent illegal trade a 'sufficient duty' should be placed on 'all the utensils employed in the making of woollen manufactures' imported into Ireland.

4. But because we can by no means think it advisable that men should be all on a sudden stopped in their way of livelihood till other ways of employment be opened to them . . . we humbly propose that the linen manufacture be set on foot and so encouraged in Ireland as may make it the general trade of that country.

Detailed proposals followed, but although the general argument was accepted by the government, and linen manufacture established as the 'general trade' of Ireland, the actual plan which was followed was not Locke's, but one drawn up by Louis Crommelin.

His position as Commissioner brought Locke a heavier postbag than ever before.[1] Friends, acquaintances and strangers sent him suggestions, petitions and advice; even his enemies wrote to him. Humphrey Prideaux, who as librarian of Christ Church had spied on Locke in his Oxford days, and who had since become Archdeacon of Suffolk, wrote to him as a friend in August 1696[2] about shipwrecks on the coast of East Anglia. Believing the subject 'very pertinent' to Locke's business as a Commissioner for Trade, Prideaux said:

. . . I have known that buoys have industriously been removed to cause wrecks, that wicked people from land have given false signs to decoy ships in distress into places of greatest danger, that they have stripped persons alive and thrown them into the sea for the sake of what they had. . . .

[1] For example, there was the Rev. J. Jackman (chaplain to Lord Leigh of Stoneleigh) who wrote to Locke as 'one of the greatest improvers of the understanding in this age', but questioned the theory of free-will as expounded in the *Essay* (20 June 1696, B.L. MSS. Locke, c. 12, f. 11). Guenellon wrote to tell Locke that the many admirers of *The Reasonableness of Christianity* in Holland included Mr. Hudde, the Burgomaster of Amsterdam (*ibid.*, c. 11, f. 72: French). There were also people who wrote to claim kinship with Locke. Edmund Rumney wrote from Wrington, Locke's birthplace, saying he was his cousin (*ibid.*, c. 18, f. 39). William Warren of Charlton Marshall, Dorset, wrote saying that his father and Locke's were first cousins, and recalling a visit with Locke's brother Thomas to Bristol (*ibid.*, c. 23, f. 63).
[2] 5 August 1696 (*ibid.*, c. 18, f. 8).

This barbarity and rapine was worse off the coasts of England, Prideaux believed, than anywhere else in the world. He said he had seen

> the bodies of those that were cast up after the storm lay[ing] along the shore in great numbers till eaten up by dogs and ravens and other devouring creatures, because no one would be at the charge to bury them, nor so much as to dig a grave for them in the place where the carcasses lay.

If the Archdeacon of Suffolk was no longer Locke's enemy, that fighting parson, John Edwards, was more hostile than ever. In 1696 he published his second attack on *The Reasonableness of Christianity* in a book he called *Socinianism Unmasked*. Edwards wrote sarcastically of those people who spoke 'as if Christianity has never been known before the compiling' of *The Reasonableness of Christianity*, a book which, in his opinion, 'misrepresented maim'd and abused' the Christian faith, and tended to 'Irreligion and Atheism'. As for its author, Edwards said:

> I charge him not with any such thing as a formal designing of this (No, I will not entertain such a thought) but I only take notice how serviceable his papers and opinions are to this purpose.[1]

Edwards protested vigorously against the anonymity the author of the *Reasonableness of Christianity* preserved; and he appealed to him to come into the open.

> Appear no more in masquerade: away with this mummery and show yourself what you are. You have let the world see (and so far we are beholding to you) that '*Socinian*' is a reproachful title, that any one may gather from your being so backward to own it. You would never have taken so much pains to shift off this character if it were not a very scandalous one. Throw off your vizor then, and speak out like a man.[2]

Molyneux read Edwards's book and mentioned the fact to Locke: 'so much unmannerly passion and *Billingsgate* language I have not seen any man use'.[3] Molyneux was tactful enough to say that he did not know who had written *The Reasonableness of Christianity* and would not 'presume to enquire' if Locke were the author. Locke coyly answered:[4]

---

[1] *Op. cit.*, p. 69.
[2] *Ibid.*, p. 111.
[3] 6 June 1696 (*S.F.L.*, p. 150).
[4] 2 July 1696 (*ibid.*, p. 157).

What you say of *The Reasonableness of Christianity* gives me occasion to ask your thoughts of that treatise, and also how it passes amongst you there [in Ireland], for here, at its first coming out it was received with no indifferency, some speaking of it with great commendation, but most censuring it as a very bad book. What you say of Mr. Edwards is so visible that I find all the world of your mind.

A more formidable critic than Mr. Edwards challenged Locke in the same year: his one-time friend Edward Stillingfleet, Bishop of Worcester. It was in *A Discourse in Vindication of the Trinity*, published in 1696, that Stillingfleet named Locke as a Socinian, doing so on the basis not of the anonymous *Reasonableness of Christianity* but of Locke's acknowledged *Essay Concerning Human Understanding*.

Although the philosophy expounded in the *Essay* did not eliminate the concept of substance entirely, it did, as I have explained in an earlier chapter, demolish the traditional scholastic concept of substance. Stillingfleet had a good case. He said Locke's theory entailed Socianism because the traditional concept of substance or something like it was a necessary philosophical basis for the justification of the doctrine of the Trinity. Stillingfleet's accusation was that a man who made belief in the Trinity impossible was, if not a Socinian, a servant of Socinianism.

Locke mentioned the accusation in a letter [1] to Molyneux:

My Book crept into the world about six or seven years ago, without any opposition, and has since passed among some for useful and, the least favourable, for innocent. But as it seems to me, it is agreed by some men that it should no longer do so. Something, I know not what, is at last spied out in it that is like to be troublesome; and therefore it must be an ill book, and be treated accordingly.

Locke was beginning to experience some of that unpleasantness which almost invariably follows hard on the heels of worldly success.

The work of the Board of Trade took up nearly all Locke's time in London. He described [2] himself to Esther Masham as 'a man of trade' concerned with 'coal, fuller's earth, lamp black and hob nails', and when he wanted to write to Limborch he confessed [3] he could

---

[1] 22 February 1696/7 (*S.F.L.*, p. 176).

[2] 1 September 1696 (Newberry).

[3] 3 September 1696 (Amsterdam: Remonstrants' MSS. Ba. 257 n: Latin). During *1698* Locke wrote several letters to Limborch in French.

hardly remember the Latin in which to do so. He very much doubted whether he was using his time as he ought:

> What have I to do with the bustle of public affairs while sinking under the burdens of age and infirmity? I should rather seek retirement, and that quiet, most suitable to my years and my literary occupations.

He was relieved to be able to return to Oates in mid-November and he wrote from there to Clarke saying: [1]

> I got hither, I thank God, very well, and [am free] already of one of my maladies that tormented me constantly every night [in London]. The cramp has spared me all but the first night since I came home . . . yet my lungs do not recover so fast. My cough continues to shake me cruelly, though I find my lungs move better than they did in town and I am not so much oppressed with short breathing as I was there.

His next letter [2] to Clarke struck a still more melancholy note: 'I am just made like that good Doctor of Divinity who professed that the more he knew of this world the less he liked it.'

Locke was not at all well that Christmas. Then immediately after Christmas the Board of Trade started work again, and he was summoned to its meetings. The thought of returning to the smoke of London and the hard work of a commissioner was too much for him. At the beginning of January he decided there was no alternative to his resigning; and on the 7th of that month he drafted the following letter [3] to Somers:

> Some of my brethren, I understand, think my stay in the country long, and desire me to return to bear my part, and to help to dispatch the multitude of business that the present circumstances of trade and the plantations fill their hands with. I cannot but say they are in the right; and I cannot but think, at the same time, that I am [also] in the right to stay in the country, where all my care is little enough to preserve those small remains of health, which a settled and incurable indisposition would quickly make an end of anywhere else.
>
> There remains, therefore, nothing else to be done, but that I should cease to fill up any longer a place that requires a more constant attendance than my strength will allow; and to that purpose, I prevail with your Lordship to move his Majesty that he would be pleased to ease

[1] Undated (Rand, pp. 491–2).
[2] 27 November 1696 (*ibid.*, pp. 494–5).
[3] B.L. MSS. Locke, c. 24, f. 226.

me of the employment that he has been so graciously pleased to honour me with. . . .

Locke said he had looked upon his appointment as an 'honour' and the post as 'one of the most considerable in England', but the fact remained that his health was 'inconsistent with the business'.

Somers wrote [1] back beseeching Locke to change his mind. He urged him to stay at Oates until his health was restored, but not to resign his commission: 'I must say you are much in the wrong, in my opinion, to entertain a thought of it'.

Locke allowed himself to be persuaded; and not only because Somers addressed him in his usual beguiling, mellifluous way, but also because Somers's wishes were almost commands. This man, who had owed so much in his early parliamentary career to Locke's advice, had risen to be to all intents and purposes prime minister.

In writing to withdraw his resignation, Locke [2] explained to Somers:

Untoward health, which complies no more with good manners than with other obligations, must be my excuse to your Lordship for this last, as well as it was a great cause of my first request to you in this affair. If my ill lungs would permit me now presently, as becomes me, to come to town and wait the opportunity of discoursing [with] your Lordship, I should not have so much reason as I have to desire to quit this employment.

Locke took advantage of his enforced idleness at Oates to answer the criticisms of Edward Stillingfleet. This reply, which was entitled *A Letter to the Bishop of Worcester* [3] and dated 7 January 1696/7, was published in early spring. Addressing a bishop, Locke adopted a very much more respectful tone than that which he employed in controversy with Edwards and Proast, and although the style of his *Letter* betrays its hurried composition, Locke made his points effectively. He noticed that the crux of the Bishop's argument was that the Lockean system 'almost discarded substance out of the reasonable part of the world'. Locke admitted he had said

[1] 25 January 1696/7 (B.L. MSS. Locke, c. 18, f. 163).

[2] 1 February 1696/7 (*ibid.*, c. 24, f. 227).

[3] *A Letter to the Right Reverend Edward Ld. Bishop of Worcester Concerning some Passages Relating to Mr. Locke's Essay of Human Understanding in a late discourse of his Lordships in Vindication of the Trinity*, by John Locke, Gent. London. Printed by H. Clark for A. and J. Churchill at the Black Swan in Pater-Noster-Row; and Edw. Castle next Scotland-yard by Whitehall. 1697.

that men have but an 'obscure and relative idea' of what substance is, but he had not said that substance *itself* was obscure and relative. Nor had he 'anywhere said that we could not be convinced by reason of any truth but where all the ideas concerned in that conviction were clear and distinct'. He said:

> knowledge or certainty, in my opinion, lies in the perception of the agreement or disagreement of ideas such as they are, and not always in having perfectly clear and distinct ideas.

Stillingfleet wrote an *Answer to Mr. Locke's Letter*, which was published in May of the same year. This, again, was none the better for having been written in haste. The Bishop had a sound case to make, but he did not make it well. He was not content to show how the elimination of substance was a logical conclusion of Locke's system, and the elimination of the dogma of the Trinity a necessary consequence of eliminating substance. He chose instead unwisely to associate Locke with avowed Socinians,[1] to be rude to Locke and even to distort Locke's argument by misquotation. He made one good point on Locke's confused use of the term 'idea':

> When new terms are made use of by ill men to promote scepticism and infidelity and to overthrow the mysteries of our faith, we have then reason to enquire into them and examine the foundation and tendency of them. . . .
>
> The world has been strangely amused with 'ideas' of late; and we have been told that strange things might be done by the help of 'ideas'; and yet these 'ideas', at last, come to be only common notions of things, which we must make use of in our reasoning. You say in that chapter about the existence of God you thought it most proper to express yourself in the most usual and familiar way, by common words and expressions. I would you had done so quite through your book; for then you had never given that occasion to the enemies of our faith to take up your new way of 'ideas' as an effectual battery, as they

---

[1] The most prominent of these was John Toland (1670–1722). Said to be the illegitimate son of an Irish Catholic priest, Toland had been educated in Scotland and at Leyden, where he met Jean le Clerc, and through him both Locke and Molyneux. His *Christianity Not Mysterious* was more openly Socinian than anything Locke wrote, and caused a great storm on its publication in 1696; it was indeed burned by the common hangman in Dublin. Locke found Toland's friendship a serious embarrassment, especially after Stillingfleet had coupled their names as fellow Socinians. Both Locke and Molyneux were indignant at the persecution of Toland (who was at one time reduced to real penury) but Toland's indiscretion made it difficult for Molyneux, and still more difficult for Locke to help him. (*Vide* the references to 'Mr. T——' in correspondence between Locke and Molyneux in *S.F.L.*, pp. 215 ff.)

imagined, against the mysteries of the Christian faith. But you might
have enjoyed the satisfaction of your ideas long enough before I had
taken notice of them unless I had found them employed about doing
mischief.[1]

Dr. Stillingfleet made very few other points as pertinent as
this.

In his *Reply to the Bishop of Worcester's Answer to his Letter*,[2]
published a few months later, Locke exploited the irrelevant issues
Stillingfleet had introduced to gain the advantage of the argument.
He made even more this time of the distinction between faith, on
which religion rested, and knowledge, which alone could be certain.

> Faith stands by itself, and upon grounds of its own, nor can be
> removed from them and placed on grounds of knowledge. Their
> grounds are so far from being the same or having anything in common,
> but when it is brought to certainty faith is destroyed; it is knowledge
> then and faith no longer. With what assurance soever of believing I
> assent to any article of faith, so that I steadfastly venture my all upon
> it, it is still but believing. Bring it to certainty, and it ceases to be faith.
> 'I believe that Jesus Christ was crucified, dead and buried, rose again
> the third day from the dead, and ascended into heaven.' Let now such
> methods of knowledge or certainty be started as to leave men's more
> doubtful than before; let the grounds of knowledge be resolved into
> what every one pleases, it touches not my faith; the foundation of that
> stands as sure as before, and cannot be at all shaken by it. . . . Whether
> then I am or am not mistaken in the placing certainty in the perception
> of the agreement or disagreement of ideas; whether this account of
> knowledge be true or false, enlarges or straitens the bounds of it more
> than it should, faith stands still upon its own basis, which is not at all
> altered by it; and every article of that has just the same unmoved
> foundation and the very same credibility that it had before.

Stillingfleet wrote an *Answer to Mr. Locke's Second Letter*, but it
was a feeble one. He might have shown that Locke's distinction
between faith and knowledge implied not the rationality of Christianity but an absolute fideism; as it was, the Bishop took another
and less effective line. He refused to accept Locke's distinctions

---

[1] Stillingfleet, *op. cit.*, p. 93.

[2] *Mr. Locke's Reply to the Right Reverend the Lord Bishop of Worcester's Answer to
his Letter Concerning Some Passages Relating to Mr. Locke's Essay of Human Understanding in a Late Discourse of his Lordship's in Vindication of the Trinity*. London:
Printed by H. Clark for A. and J. Churchill at the Black Swan in Pater-Noster-
Row; and E. Castle, next Scotland-yard by Whitehall, 1697.

between faith and knowledge, and insisted that the 'certainty of faith' is stronger than the 'certainty of knowledge'.

Locke's *Reply to the Bishop of Worcester's Answer to his Second Letter* [1] showed signs of impatience, but he had no difficulty in showing that Stillingfleet's argument was vitiated by misuse of language. He apologised with heavy irony, for wishing that 'your lordship, in the run of your learned notions, should be shackled with the ordinary and strict rules of language'; and managed thus to turn the tables against his adversary.

Stillingfleet had failed to sustain his case. He might have recovered the initiative in an answer to Locke's second *Reply*, but he died too soon to write it. Most people, including some with no partiality for Locke (for example, Gilbert Burnet [2]) considered that the Bishop had been worsted.[3]

Locke's protest against the misuse of language by controversial writers was repeated in a memorandum [4] he wrote to John Freke, otherwise the 'Bachelor' and host to the 'College'.[5] Locke wrote:

> You will I think agree with me that there is nothing wherein men more mistake themselves and mislead others than in writing and reading of books whether the writers mislead the readers or *vice versa* I will not examine: so it is they both seem willing to deceive and be deceived. How else could it be that where the one pretends to see reason and to instruct, he should give himself up to a play or abuse of words, which if they can be put so together as to direct something into the fancy of the reader and make now and then the appearance of a repartee or a sharp saying, the business is thought done—'tis a discourse well written, though sense and truth be wholly neglected in it. Again if readers were not willing to cosin themselves, how could they,

---

[1] *Mr. Locke's Reply to the Right Reverend the Lord Bishop of Worcester's Answer to his Second Letter: wherein, besides other incident Matters, what his Lordship has said concerning certainty of Reason, Certainty by Ideas, Certainty of Faith, the Resurrection of the same Body, the Immateriality of the Soul, the Inconsistency of Mr. Locke's Notions with the Articles of the Christian Faith and their Tendency to Scepticism is Examin'd.* London. Printed by H. C. for A. and J. Churchill, etc. 1699.

[2] Gilbert Burnet to Jean le Clerc. (Undated. Amsterdam : Remonstrants' MSS.)

[3] But the Bishop had his champions, too. A pamphlet called *A Free But Modest Answer on the late Controversial Writings of the Lord Bishop of Worcester and Mr. Locke* etc. by F. B., M.A. of Cambridge, was entirely on Stillingfleet's side.

[4] B.L. MSS. Locke, c. 24, f. 46.

[5] John Freke lived at the Licking Post in Red Lion Street, next to the Hen and Chickens, where The College held its sessions. A letter from Freke to Clarke dated 14 September 1701 (Rand, p. 41) mentions a Cheddar cheese, and asks 'if it be intended for the use of the College'.

where they pretend to seek truth and information, content themselves with the jugglery of words and something they know not what that looks like a sprinkling of wit or satire, in all which they find not the least improvement of their knowledge or reason. Those whose aim is to divert and make men laugh—let them write plays and romances, and there sport themselves with words and false images of things as much as they please. But a professor to teach or maintain truth should . . . speak plain and clear and be afraid of a fallacy or equivocation, however prettily it might look and be fit to cheat the reader, who on his side should be an author who pretends instruction abominate all such arts and him that uses them as much as he would a common cheat who endeavours to put off brass money for standard silver . . .

Although Locke spent some part of his rest cure at Oates writing his reply to Stillingfleet, his time was much taken up with other correspondence. He told[1] Molyneux how he had received that winter 'crowds of letters' which were 'indispensably to be answered because they were from people whom either I knew not or cared not for, or was not willing to make bold with'.

There were also letters from people he did care for, among them Jean le Clerc, who was running short of money in Holland and was considering emigrating to England;[2] from Pierre Coste,[3] who was in much the same position; from Elizabeth Berkeley,[4] who wrote at length on miscellaneous spiritual questions; and from Mary Clarke, who was worried as usual about her health.

There was one correspondent whom Locke did 'make bold' to ignore; and this, paradoxically, was his only peer among philosophers then living: Leibniz.[5] Leibniz approached Locke cir-

---

[1] 22 February 1696/7 (*S.F.L.*, pp. 174–5).

[2] Paul d'Aranda sent Locke a graphic account of Le Clerc's miseries in a letter dated *6 February 1697* (B.L. MSS. Locke c. 3, f. 39). He said that Le Clerc had a wife and six children and no income and that being tolerant and Arminian he was excluded from charities. D'Aranda suggested that Locke and Popple and Sir Francis Masham might each contribute a guinea to a fund for Le Clerc's relief. Locke thought some more permanent solution should be found, and he wrote to Molyneux asking if a place could be given Le Clerc in the Irish church. Molyneux said one might be if Le Clerc would take Anglican orders. Le Clerc, however, preferred to remain in Amsterdam.

[3] Coste asked Locke to find him a post as a tutor in England (*ibid.*, c. 7, f. 144: French).

[4] *Ibid.*, c. 3, ff. 203–38. Elizabeth Berkeley was subsequently the wife of Gilbert Burnet.

[5] Gottfried Wilhelm Leibniz (1646–1716) had already established a reputation on the continent as a mathematician and metaphysician. He was regarded with distinct

cuitously. He read the French epitome of Locke's *Essay* and parts, if not all, of the original edition, though his knowledge of English seems to have been less than wholly adequate; and he wrote in or before 1696 a short paper which he called *Réflexions sur l'Essai de l'Entendement Humain de Monsieur Locke.* This paper was communicated through Sir Thomas Burnet of Kemney[1] and a certain Mr. Cunningham[2] to Locke. Sir Thomas assured Locke, in a letter dated 24 March 1696/7[3] 'it is not possible to express in a letter the great character Monsieur Leibniz has of you'. When Locke read Leibniz's paper he was not able to return the compliment. He could not understand it, and rashly decided there was nothing to it. He sent a transcript[4] of the greater part of it to Molyneux saying:

> I must confess to you that Mr. L——'s great name had raised in me an expectation which the sight of his paper did not answer. . . . From whence I only draw this conclusion that even great parts will not master any subject without great thinking and even the largest minds have but narrow swallows.[5]

In a later letter[6] to Molyneux, Locke said of Leibniz's objections: 'This sort of fiddling makes me hardly avoid thinking that he is not that very great man as has been talked of him'.

When Leibniz was informed that Locke had not understood his criticisms of the *Essay* he re-wrote them in a second paper entitled *Echantillon de Réflexions sur le Ier et IIième livres de l'Essai de l'Entendement Humain de M. Locke.* Locke took no notice of this paper. He never entered into direct correspondence with Leibniz, and it was only after Locke's death that Leibniz opened a correspondence with Lady Masham.

Of very much more concern to Locke than the metaphysical perplexities of Leibniz in the spring of 1697 was the illness of Mary

suspicion by English savants because he was believed (falsely) to have appropriated Newton's discoveries.

[1] Not to be confused with Thomas Burnet, the author of *Remarks upon an Essay Concerning Human Understanding.*

[2] Locke said of Cunningham: 'I think him an extraordinary man of parts and learning' (*S.F.L.*, p. 193).

[3] B.L. MSS. Locke, c. 4, f. 197.

[4] This is printed as an appendix to Locke's letter to Molyneux of 10 April 1697 in *S.F.L.* (pp. 196–205).

[5] 10 April 1697 (*ibid.*, pp. 192–6). How characteristic of Locke to refer to Leibniz as 'Mr. L——'.

[6] 3 May 1697 (*ibid.*, pp. 206–211).

E E

Clarke, especially as that lady persisted in regarding Locke as her physician, and would consult no other. Her illness was dropsical and Locke prescribed a spare diet, warming medicines, garlic, exercise and an early bed,[1] but he warned Edward Clarke that his wife's life should not be 'ventured on directions at this distance'[2] and urged them to consult a local doctor. Mrs. Clarke resisted this last suggestion, but somehow, by following Locke's treatment, she managed to get well again by the following September.[3]

Despite all his duties as Commissioner for Trade and as Commissioner for Appeals, despite all the demands of his correspondents, Locke actually found time in those early months of 1697 to write philosophy. He told Molyneux in his letter of April 10:[4]

> I have lately got a little leisure to think of some additions to my book,[5] against the next edition, and within these few days have fallen upon a subject that I know not how far it will lead me. I have written several pages on it, but the matter, the further I go, opens the more upon me, and I cannot yet get sight of any end of it. The title of the chapter will be 'Of the Conduct of the Understanding', which, if I shall pursue, as far as I imagine it will reach, and as it deserves, will, I conclude, make the largest chapter of my *Essay*.

Locke never completed this manuscript on *The Conduct of the Understanding*, and the fourth edition of the *Essay* appeared without it. It was, however, printed two years after his death as the first item in a Collection of his *Posthumous Works*, the editor[6] of which explained that the manuscript consisted of fragmentary notes, the author 'intending if he had lived to have reduced them' into order and 'to have made a complete treatise'. Despite the occurrence of the word 'Understanding' in the titles both of the *Essay* and the *Conduct* their subjects were different. The *Conduct* is largely about what is sometimes called 'clear thinking'. Locke's argument was that a man's actions are governed by his understanding, and not by the will, so that it was 'of the highest concernment that great care should be taken of the understanding, to conduct it right in the search of knowledge and in the judgements it makes'.

---

[1] 8 March 1696/7 (Rand, pp. 504–8).
[2] 8 March 1696/7 (*ibid.*, pp. 503–4).
[3] *Vide* Locke to Clarke, 2 September 1697 (*ibid*, pp. 520–2).
[4] S.F.L., p. 194.
[5] I.e. his *Essay Concerning Human Understanding*.   [6] Probably Peter King.

He pointed out how the understanding could be misled: by reliance on habit and tradition, by prejudice, by putting passion in the place of reason, by partiality for certain opinions, and by an imperfect view of the facts. His reflections on this last point are particularly interesting. He emphasised the danger of the habit of conversing 'but with one sort of men' and of reading 'but one sort of books'. Men who did so, Locke said: [1]

> canton out to themselves a little Goshen in the intellectual world, where light shines, and, as they conclude, day blesses them; but the rest of that vast *expansum* they give up to night and darkness; and so avoid coming near it. They have a pretty traffic with known correspondents in some little creek: within that they confine themselves and are dexterous managers enough of the wares and products of that corner ... but will not venture out into the great ocean of knowledge, to survey the riches that nature hath stored other parts with, no less genuine, no less solid, no less useful than what has fallen to their lot in the admired plenty and sufficiency of their own little spot, which to them contains whatever is good in the universe.

These words tell us a great deal. They show that Locke did not enter and remain in public life from any desire to be a 'universal man'. He was a polymath, it is true, but in an age when it was still possible and indeed desirable for a man to be a polymath. He was very much more than that even before he added to his activities those of a full-time civil servant. But the range of his activities should not be mistaken for evidence of restlessness, boredom or wayward curiosity. Nor again was his public service prompted by a sense of social responsibility alone, though that was certainly there. It was prompted also by a sense of responsibility to himself and his calling. Locke believed that a life of action was a necessary part of the life of reason and that a man could not discover truth by sitting still and thinking, but only by personal experience of life.

At a meeting of the Board of Trade on 15 January 1696/7 it was resolved 'in view of the pressure of business' to distribute the work as follows: 'the business of Virginia and Maryland to Sir Philip Meadows; that of Barbados, Jamaica and the Leeward Islands to Mr. Blathwayt, or in his absence to Mr. Locke; that of Proprietory and Charter colonies and of Bermuda to Mr. Pollexfen; that of New England, Newfoundland to Mr. Hill'.

[1] *Posthumous Works*, pp. 9–10.

In spite of this arrangement Locke was soon running 'the business' of other colonies as well as those assigned to him. He had been quick to see the merits of Edward Randolph, and in Blathwayt's absence, he made the surveyor-general of American customs his own friend.[1] Notwithstanding a notoriously unlikeable personality, Randolph possessed moral qualities more akin to those of Locke than of Blathwayt, and the two men were well suited to work together. Locke's signature is one of five on the memorandum addressed by the Commissioners for Trade on 7 September 1696 [2] to the Lords Justices urging the appointment of an Attorney-General in each American colony and naming Randolph as the referee of every candidate. For Governorships Locke put forward nominees in competition with those sponsored by Blathwayt. And it was Locke's candidates who were chosen.

One of his successes was in having Blathwayt's friend Benjamin Fletcher replaced as Governor of New York in 1697 by the Earl of Bellomont,[3] a leading Irish Whig. Lord Bellomont was in London that year after a term of duty as Governor of New England, and—evidently at Locke's suggestion—he was now appointed to be Governor of Massachusetts and New Hampshire as well as of New York in order to promote the joint defence of those colonies against the French and the Red Indians.

When Locke was at Oates in May 1697 Lord Bellomont wrote [4] to him from London saying:

> . . . I have I confess some interest in wishing you here, because I go uphill in all the steps I make towards my departure for America, and your influence on our great men would, I am confident, dispose them to use more dispatch in sending me away and also send me in a better capacity of serving the King and the countries whereof I am to go than I find I am like to be sent. . . .

Lord Bellomont was a man of enterprise and probity as well as a Whig—hence Locke's appreciation of him. But one of his projects proved singularly ill-fated, and more so for his Whiggish friends in

---

[1] Only upon the return of Tory power in 1700 did Randolph seek reconciliation with Blathwayt. 'I have no other freind [*sic*] but God and you to stand by me', he wrote to Blathwayt on 23 November 1700 (Goodrick, *op. cit.*, VII, p. 641).

[2] *Ibid.*, VII, pp. 493–5.

[3] Richard Coote (1636–1701) first Earl of Bellomont (*cr.* 1689) had been appointed Governor of New England in 1695 with the special mission of suppressing piracy.

[4] B.L. MSS. Locke, c. 7, f. 128.

London than for Lord Bellomont himself. A specialist in the suppression of piracy, Lord Bellomont proposed to a number of Whig leaders in London that they should fit out Captain William Kidd with an armed vessel to put down pirates in the Western Atlantic. The King refused to supply Kidd with a man-of-war, but Lord Bellomont persuaded the Duke of Shrewsbury, Lord Somers, and others to support the Captain as shareholders, and no less than £6,000 was handed over from the English Exchequer to finance the *Adventure Galley*. When Lord Bellomont reached America a shock awaited him: he learned that Captain Kidd had turned pirate himself.

Locke in the meantime had devised a method for dealing with piracy on a larger scale. His papers contain notes [1] written in the summer of 1697 outlining a proposal that 'all the Christian princes and states now assembled by their Ministers in Holland'—for negotiations leading to the Peace of Ryswick were then going on at The Hague—should offer a general amnesty to any of their subjects engaged in piracy, provided that 'within six months after the publication thereof they bring the ship into some of the ports in that country in Europe to which it belonged' and thence 'repair to the several dominions of which they are subjects there to receive their pardons'. Further, Locke proposed that 'whoever shall not come in within the time limited . . . shall by the joint force of all the said princes and their allies be prosecuted to the utmost parts of the world'.

It is not clear what Locke's fellow Commissioners thought of this idea; but it was certainly not taken up at The Hague and piracy continued to be one of the main problems with which the Board of Trade had to contend.

Another question in which Locke took a keen interest was that of Virginia. Although 'the business of Virginia' had been allocated in January to Philip Meadows, Locke soon made it his own responsibility. His chief adviser on the question seems to have been James Blair, the Bishop of London's commissary in Virginia and President of William and Mary College in that province.

Among the colonial papers in the Lovelace Collection is a document [2] of considerable length on the problems of Virginia together with recommendations for reform. The paper is partly in Locke's

---

[1] B.L. MSS. Locke, c. 30, f. 62 (dated '1697').
[2] *Ibid.*, e. 9 (the paper runs to 68 pages of manuscript or approximately 10,000 words).

hand, partly in that of an amanuensis. The information it contains resembles that of the report presented by Henry Hartwell, James Blair and Edward Chilton to William Popple in October 1697,[1] and points to a clear liaison between these three witnesses and Locke in the preparation of their report.

Both documents drew attention to the contrast between the natural riches of Virginia, its vast potentialities, and the state of affairs which in fact prevailed. Virginia was the 'poorest, miserablest and worst country in America'. The failure to settle the people in towns was named as the root cause of economic distress, and the compulsory resettlement of the people by royal prerogative was recommended. Maladministration was rife in the province—not least in the person of the Governor. Tobacco was almost the only product of Virginia, and quantities of it were used there instead of money. Although it was contrary to the interest of the people, the Governor encouraged the use of tobacco as currency because he could make more profit himself. The Governor was indeed alleged to be a virtual dictator, in spite of the existence of what was supposed to be a free representative council. The administration of justice was said to be unsatisfactory because no one was certain whether the laws of England or the locally-made laws of Virginia were superior in cases where the two laws were at variance.

On the basis of this report the Board of Trade resolved to ask the King to appoint a new Governor of Virginia. Once again Locke had a candidate in the field: the then Governor of Maryland, Francis Nicholson, who had apparently been recommended to him by Edward Randolph.

Francis Nicholson had written to Locke from Annapolis, Maryland, as early as 30 March 1697 [2] saying:

> I hope you will be pleased to excuse this presumption, but I should be very much wanting in my duty if I did not own how much I am obliged to your Honour for being my friend, and having a good opinion of me, which Edward Randolph Esq. writ me an account of. Though I have not the happiness of being personally acquainted with the most ingenious and learned author of *Human Understanding*, yet if he is pleased to continue his favourable opinion of me, I shall endeavour (God willing) not to do anything which may give you occasion to withdraw your Honour's protection of me.

[1] C.S.P. *America and West Indies 1696–7*, § 1,396. *Vide* also C.S.P. *America and West Indies 1697–1698*, § 767.   [2] B.L. MSS. Locke, c. 16, f. 157.

The Reverend Mr. James Blair, President of the Royal College of William and Mary in Virginia, is desired by us as the Trustees of the said college to go for England in order to solicit some affairs of the said college. This is designed (God willing) by him. And if your Honour pleases he will give you a full account of all the Virginia affairs, especially concerning the College. And to enrich the Library of it we are humble intercessors for all your Honour's Works. . . .

In 1698 [1] Francis Nicholson was duly appointed Governor of Virginia, thus displacing Blathwayt's friend Edmund Andros. That the appointment was due to Locke's efforts is clear from the following letter [2] written to him by James Blair, after the latter's return to Virginia:

The tranquillity we begin to enjoy in this country by the happy change of our Governor and government is so great that I who have the happiness to know by whose means those blessings were procured have all the reason in the world to take all occasions of expressing my gratitude for them, and to pray to God to reward those noble public souls that bestow so many of their thoughts in contriving the relief of the oppressed and the happiness of mankind. Dear Sir, think not that I speak this from any other principle or design I have, but only from a sense how much this whole country in general and myself in particular are beholding to you for the thoughts you were pleased to bestow on our late unhappy circumstances and the methods you contrived to relieve us. You are to look for your reward from a better hand. Only give me leave to say that I think no sort of good works are preferable to those that have such an universal good influence on whole countries to make all the people happy.

This country is so barren of action that it affords nothing to satisfy your curiosity. Our new Governor Col. Nicholson is very heartily welcomed to this place. Sir Edmund Andros is gone home mighty angry not only for the loss of such a good government, but for being succeeded by such a person, whom of all others, he had the least kindness for. I doubt not if he or his great friend [3] at your Board can get him to be put into any post wherein he can reach this country, we shall feel the effects of his resentment and revenge to the utmost of his power. . . .

Francis Nicholson himself wrote to Locke on 26 May 1698 [4] saying:

---

[1] His commission was dispatched on 23 August 1698 (C.S.P. *America and West Indies*, 1697–8, § 766).   [2] 8 February 1698/9, B.L. MSS. Locke, c. 4, f. 10.
[3] Blathwayt.   [4] B.L. MSS. Locke, c. 16, f. 159.

Gratitude obliges me to pay you the best of my acknowledgement for your having been pleased not only to speak favourably of me, but to recommend me to some of his most sacred Majesty's great ministers of state, which the reverend Mr. Blair gives me an account of.

Writing again some months later,[1] Governor Nicholson said:

> ... The Rev. Mr. President Blair has acquainted me how very zealous you were in using your great interest for my being so very advantageously removed hither. And I shall endeavour (God willing) so to behave myself in my station here that you may never have cause to be concerned that you were so very instrumental in accomplishing that affair. ...

The principal domestic issue before the Board of Trade during the sessions of 1697 was that of unemployment and pauperism. Each Commissioner was invited to submit a scheme for solving the problem. Locke's scheme [2] was rejected by the Board; but it is a remarkable document, and it throws a great deal of light on the workings of the writer's mind.

At the outset he briskly diagnosed the causes of poverty and unemployment. They were, he said, neither 'scarcity of provisions or want of employment', but 'the relaxation of discipline and the corruption of manners, virtue and industry being as constant companions on the one side as vice and idleness on the other'. From this he deduced that the first step 'towards setting the poor on work ought to be a restraint of their debauchery by a strict execution of the laws against it, more particularly by the suppression of superfluous brandy shops and unnecessary alehouses'.

As the 'suppression of begging drones' by execution of existing laws might not be effective, Locke recommended a new law: 'that all men sound of limb and mind, above fourteen and under fifty, begging in maritime counties outside their own parish without a pass' should be arrested and sent 'to the next seaport town, there kept at hard labour till some of His Majesty's ships, coming in or near there, give an opportunity of putting them on board, where they shall serve three years, under strict discipline at soldier's pay ...' Locke also proposed that men 'above fifty or maimed' likewise caught begging without a pass shall be sent 'to the next House of

---

[1] 4 February 1698/9 (B.L. MSS. Locke, c. 16, f. 161).

[2] P.R.O. Board of Trade Papers. There is an early draft in the Lovelace Collection (*ibid.*, c. 30 f. 94).

Correction there to be kept at hard labour for three years', and that 'whoever shall counterfeit a pass shall lose his ears for the first time that he is found guilty thereof, and the second time he shall be transported to the plantations'. For females, however, Locke favoured lighter punishments; girls over fourteen should go to the House of Correction for three months, while those under fourteen should, like boys, be 'soundly whipped'.

Methods were suggested for 'taking away the pretence' that there was no work for the idle to do. First, guardians should have power to put the idle to work with private employers for less than the usual rate of pay, under threat of empressment. Secondly, pauper schools should be set up in every parish to enable both mothers and children to work productively. As an economical diet for the pauper children, Locke suggested that they should have their 'bellyful of bread daily . . . and to this may be also added, without any trouble, in cold weather, if it be thought needful, a little warm water-gruel; for the same fire that warms the room may be made use of to boil a pot of it'. By this means, 'computing all the earnings of a child from three to fourteen years of age, the nourishment and teaching of such a child during that whole time will cost the parish nothing', instead of the £50 or £60 such pauper children cost their parishes under existing poor law schemes.

Locke did not fail to add:

> Another advantage also of bringing children thus to a working school is that by this means they may be obliged to come constantly to church every Sunday . . . whereby they may be brought into some sense of religion . . .

This appalling document, which appeared to Locke's Victorian Quaker biographer Fox Bourne as evidence of an 'excellent philanthropy'[1] did not commend itself to his contemporaries,[2] and

---

[1] F.B., II, p. 391.

[2] After the rejection of his scheme, Locke informed Clarke on 25 February 1697/8. (Rand, p. 533):
'. . . I wrote some time since to Mr. Popple to give you a copy of my project about the better relief and employment of the poor, since our Board thought not fit to make use of it, that now the House [of Commons] was up on that consideration, that you might make use of it, [if] it should suggest to you anything that you might think useful in the case. It is a matter that requires every Englishman's best thoughts, for there is not any one thing that I know upon the right regulation whereof the prosperity of his country more depends. And whilst I have any breath left, I shall always be an Englishman. . . .'

it was not until the Poor Law Reforms of 1834 that anything like it was enacted by Parliament: the 'excellent philanthropy' Locke recommended was precisely that which Dickens so passionately castigated.

It is only fair to add at this point the testimony of Lady Masham on the subject of Locke's methods of charity: [1]

> He was naturally compassionate and exceedingly charitable to those in want. But his charity was always directed to encourage working, laborious, industrious people, and not to relieve idle beggars, to whom he never gave anything, or would suffer his friends to do so before him, saying such people as these were 'robbers of the poor': and asking those that went for to relieve them whether they knew none that they were sure were in want and deserved help? If so, how could they satisfy themselves to give anything they could spare to such as they knew not to be in need, but who probably deserved to be so? One article of his enquiry when any objects of charity were recommended to him used to be whether they were people that duly attended the public worship of God in any congregation whatever? And if they did not, but were such as spent their time on Sundays lazily at home, or worse employed in an alehouse, they were sure to be more sparingly relieved than others in the same circumstances. People who had been industrious, but were through age or infirmity passed labour, he was very bountiful to, and he used to blame that sparingness with which such were ordinarily relieved, as if it sufficed only that they should be kept from starving or extreme misery whereas they had, he said, a right to live comfortably in the world. Waste of anything he could not bear to see. . . . Nor would he (if he could help it) let anything be destroyed which could serve for the nourishment, maintenance, or allowable pleasure of any creature, though but the birds of the air. He yet thought very blameable that fondness for birds, dogs or other such creatures which makes some people feed them with such meat as their poor neighbours want and would be glad of.

In August 1697 Locke received an affectionate letter [2] signed 'Peterborough'. The writer was the former Earl of Monmouth, who had lately succeeded an uncle to the more ancient earldom of Peterborough. The House of Lords had taken a surprisingly lenient view of his behaviour in the Fenwick case, and he had been liberated from the Tower after only three months' imprisonment. Now, as

---

[1] Amsterdam: Remonstrants' MSS. J. 57 a.
[2] B.L. MSS. Locke, c. 16, f. 121.

Earl of Peterborough, he might well have been expected to settle down to a more tranquil and conventional life. He would probably have done so had his uncle's title been accompanied by his uncle's fortune; but it was not. Peterborough, who had always been a spendthrift, was by this time poorer than ever, and his insecurity led him into further and more complicated quarrels. It is the measure of his personal charm that his quarrels were almost always ended in reconciliation and that his enemies were often afterwards among his best friends.

It would not be difficult to understand if Peterborough's friendship had been a source of embarrassment to Locke in 1697. As it was, Locke, like other scholars who profited from Peterborough's generosity, contrived to overlook that nobleman's defects. Locke readily answered Peterborough's inquiries with an account of his recent doings, and Peterborough wrote to him again, at the beginning of September,[1] saying:

> I hope in four or five days after you have received this to see you in London, for I take it for granted the Essex Lady is not to attract while the sun has so much influence.

Peterborough was right. Locke's summers were now dedicated to London and the Board of Trade; his winters only to Oates and Lady Masham. In a letter to Esther Masham (dated 24 August[2]), Locke told his 'dear Dab' that as he could not have her company without winter, the thought of being with her 'goes a great way towards reconciling me to my old and great enemy'.

So it is probable that Locke went some time that autumn to Parson's Green. At all events, Lady Peterborough asked his advice on the education of her son, Lord Mordaunt, and a draft[3] of Locke's reply is still extant. He wrote:

> . . . I have always thought that to direct a young gentleman's studies right, it is absolutely necessary to know what course of life—either by the distinction of his quality or fortune or by the choice and determination of his parents—he is designed to. . . . My Lord Mordaunt's birth, without any more ado, tells everyone what he is to be in the world and directs us to consider what may conduct to make him an accomplished and great man in his country. But your Ladyship's enquiry being now barely in reference to the choice and conduct of his

[1] 4 September 1697 (B.L. MSS. Locke, f. 123).
[2] Newberry.   [3] B.L. MSS. Locke, c. 24, f. 196.

studies 'twill be beside the present business to meddle with anything but books and learning. . . .

History is esteemed one of the most necessary studies for a gentleman, and is itself one of the most entertaining and most easy. And so it is; and therefore should be begun with.

Locke recommended that Lord Mordaunt should read Livy, accompanying the study of history with that of geography and of morality. 'I mean not', he explained, 'the ethics of the schools', but Tully, Pufendorf, Aristotle and 'above all The New Testament', wherein, Locke said, 'a man may learn how to live which is the business of ethics, and not how to define and distinguish and dispute about the names of virtues and vice'.[1] He added:

True politics I look on as a part of moral philosophy, which is nothing but the art of conducting men right in society, and support-ing a community amongst its neighbours. Wherein Aristotle may be best to begin with, and then afterwards if he pleases he may descend to more modern writers of government, either as to the foundations and forms of politic societies, or the art of ruling them.

Locke was still in London in mid-October when Esther Masham wrote to complain of his absence from Oates and to confess or to pretend a jealousy of the beautiful Duchess of Grafton,[2] whom Locke had found time to visit. He replied [3] to Esther saying:

Beauty and honour are two tempting things, but a heart, dear Dab, that you are possessed of is proof against all of that kind. If therefore you have any more jealousy, but just so much as shows your concern for me, you are unjust to yourself and your Joannes, too. The wishes I made to be with you remain the same I brought to town with me, and if you can but defend me against your own fears, I promise to defend you against all the Duchesses and Beauties in Christendom.

I believe you as innocent as the country can produce, and I think I may presume I shall hold out longer against the false fashions than the ill air of the town: for my heart, I am sure, is better than my lungs, so

[1] These words, directed against the traditional scholastic philosophy, also set Locke apart from the present-day philosophers who are in many respects the inheritors of his empiricism but who maintain that ethics 'is the logical study of the language of morals' (R. M. Hare, *The Language of Morals*, Oxford, 1952, p. v).

[2] The first Duchess of Grafton (only child of the first Earl of Arlington) was then a widow of thirty years of age (her husband having been mortally wounded in the siege of Cork). She was celebrated for her grace and virtue, and her picture is among the 'Beauties' at Hampton Court.

[3] 13 October 1697 (Newberry).

that your part is safe. I do not much rejoice in the *'plump'* you make
such a show of in your letter. If you were so much concerned as you
talk of, you would pine away a little in my absence. . . .

Writing that same month [1] to Limborch, Locke said that since the
beginning of his controversy with the Bishop of Worcester ('who
is indeed the aggressor') the academic clergy had become 'mar-
vellously excited' against the *Essay Concerning Human Understanding*,
and what had hitherto been approved was 'at length discovered by
the pious care of these doctors to abound in errors (or at least to
contain a hiding place for such errors) and the very grounds of
scepticism'.

Locke's *Essay* was attacked in print [2] by, among others, James
Lowde in *A Discourse Concerning the Nature of Man*; by John Milner
in *An Account of Mr. Locke's Religion, Out of his Own Writings*; by
John Sergeant, a Popish priest, in his *Solid Philosophy*; by Thomas
Burnet in his *Remarks upon an Essay Concerning Human Understanding*;
by Thomas Becconsall, a Fellow of Brasenose College, in *The
Grounds and Foundation of Natural Religion*; and at some length by
Henry Lee, Rector of Tichmarsh, in *Anti-Scepticism; or Notes upon
each Chapter of Mr. Locke's Essay Concerning Human Understanding*.[3]

The complaint of all these writers was that Locke's philosophy was
inimical to religion. He answered only two of them: Lowde, very
briefly in the second edition of his *Essay*,[4] and Burnet in an appendix
to his second pamphlet against Stillingfleet.[5] Not one of these
attacks distressed Locke nearly as much as that which was delivered
on *The Reasonableness of Christianity* and *Some Thoughts Concerning
Education* by his old enemy John Edwards. Edwards's *Brief Vindication of the Fundamental Articles of the Christian Faith* was published in
London in 1697 and dedicated 'to Both Universities' in the following
terms:

A late Writer [6] hath taken the confidence to make very disrespectful,
indecent, rude and scurrilous reflections upon you, and hath with that
scorn and insolence, which are peculiar to him, and cannot be supposed

[1] 29 October 1697. Amsterdam: Remonstrants' MSS. Ba. 257 p and q (French and
Latin).
[2] *vide* Christophersen, pp. 29–57.
[3] For an account of the attacks of Norris and Whitby *vide* p. 364 above and p. 442
below.
[4] London, 1694. The Epistle to the Reader.
[5] London, 1697. Appendix, pp. 1–7. [6] Locke.

to be in any other man, censured your studies and ways and methods of learning, which are at this day owned and practised by you.

After naming Popes Paul II and Sixtus IV as past enemies of the universities, Edwards wrote:

> Mr. Hobbes is a modern instance, who was wont to decry the university studies and learning because he had espoused a set of notions which were destructive not only to academic but all religious principles. But a later instance we have in one Mr. Locke, who though he infinitely comes short of the fore-named person in parts and good letters, yet hath taken the courage to tread in his old friend's steps, and publicly to proclaim his dislike of university men and to remonstrate against the methods they take in bringing up of youth. . . . Nor is he pleased with our old Christianity, but hath offered a new scheme to the world, the same (the very same in words, as well as to the thing) with what Mr. Hobbes propounded as the perfect and complete model of faith viz: To believe in Christ is nothing else than to believe that Jesus is the Christ: and no other faith, besides this article, is required to eternal life (*De Cive* cap. 18). . . . This is the doctrine which is revived and furbished up in the pretended *Reasonableness* of *Christianity*: and you see whence it is borrowed. When that Writer was framing a New Christianity, he took Hobbes's *Leviathan* for the *New Testament*, and the Philosopher of Malmesbury for our Saviour and the Apostles. . . .

In the text of his book Edwards called Locke 'a lewd declaimer', a 'raving tutor and reformer', a 'profligate scribe', 'perfidious scribbler', 'a university hater' and 'hater of women'. He also declared that in the 'art of scolding' he questioned 'whether any of the sisterhood at Billingsgate' could outstrip Locke.

Edwards took a positively Freudian view of some aspects of Locke's educational theory: [1]

> I might here harmlessly divert the reader with [Mr. Locke's] Scotch-hoppers and Dibstones, with his documents about milk-pottage and water-gruel and his teaching children to evacuate dextrously, which latter succeeds only when the Party is present, it being promoted by his Vespasian looks. He hath spent some time, he saith, in the study of physic, and especially of the guts, which he very feelingly and concernedly discourses of as if they were that part of the body which he most minds. . . .

[1] Edwards, *op. cit.*, p. 17.

Later Edwards exclaimed:[1]

> We see the physic has worked, as all the filth and excrements of [Mr. Locke's] papers show. Dirt and ordure and dunghills are the frequent embellishments of his style.

Even worse things were in Edwards's original manuscript, but withdrawn under pressure. He had even gone so far as to call Locke the 'governor of the seraglio at Oates'. This particular libel, though never printed, was nevertheless communicated to Locke in an anonymous letter addressed to his bookseller John Churchill.[2] What upset Locke more than anything else was that Edwards's book had been given an *imprimatur* by the Vice-Chancellor of Cambridge University (Henry James), the Master of Trinity (John Covel), the Master of Emmanuel (John Balderston) and the Regius Professor of Divinity (John Beaumont). It seemed to Locke outrageous that such academic dignitaries should expressly sanction so scurrilous a book, and the affront was all the more painful because he had supposed that Dr. Covel, the Master of Trinity, was his friend. From London Locke wrote to Covel on 29 September 1697[3] saying:

> I am told the booksellers in Cambridge have made bolder than they should with the book you will herewith receive, by pasting a paper over the Author's Epistle to the Bookseller. 'Tis pity so excellent a treatise as this should lose the authority and recommendation your name gives to it. I therefore send you one with all its ornaments displayed, as our shops here afford them. And you will do well to keep it safe, that posterity may know, as well as this present age, who lent his helping hand to usher into the world so cleanly a piece of divinity and such a just model of managing of controversy in religion, to be a pattern for the youth in his own college, and the rest of the university to imitate. This is all at present, till I have fitter opportunity to talk with you about what the dull stationer here made bold to strike out notwithstanding the warrant of your *Imprimatur*. 'Tis not that I pretend to be interested in the controversy wherein Mr. Edwards is a party, but hearing he had named me in the title of his book, I thought myself concerned to read it. And having perused it, I think it will not misbecome our old acquaintance to do you this right. I lay all those titles you have thought me worthy of at your feet, and am, [etc.].

---

[1] Edwards, *op. cit.*, p. 21.
[2] B.L. MSS. Locke, c. 23, f. 200.
[3] B.M. Add. MSS. 22,910, f. 463.

On 4 October,[1] Covel wrote to explain what he called the 'plain truth of the matter':

> The Author was of my own year, and I knew him formerly better it seems than I know him now. He meeting me one day told me that he had a new book for the press, which Mr. Professor and the Vice-Chancellor had perused and they had given their *Imprimatur* to it, and he asked my leave to add my name also. I told him if it was what they had read and approved of, I should not deny him that (which, indeed, I then thought a) small favour. You tell me that you have read over the book, which I solemnly protest is more than ever I yet did, and till it was printed I assure you I never so much as saw it or knew the least syllable of its contents, much less of your name. . . .

The Master sent his deepest apologies to his 'old friend (for I will yet lay claim to your friendship)' and confessed himself 'extremely guilty of too much credulity'. But Locke was not content to let the matter rest. He wrote next to protest to the Archbishop of Canterbury, John Tenison, from whom he received at Christmastide the following letter: [2]

> Dr. James the Vice-Chancellor of Cambridge came to me together with the Bishop of Ely in order to the giving you satisfaction about the *Imprimatur*: but upon inquiry I found you had been gone about a fortnight into the country.
>
> Dr. James assured me that before he gave the *Imprimatur* he had ordered the blotting out of divers passages, and particularly that about Oates-Hall: that Mr. Edwards had written to him that he had smoothed many things; and that he himself perused the book with the less care because the Doctor had acquainted him with the approbation of Dr. Beaumont, though his hand was not then to the *Imprimatur*. . . .
>
> Whitehall (they say) was never mentioned, nor the horrid word you told me of: but there was mention of the seraglio at Oates, which gave great offence and was ordered to be struck out. This is the sum of what was said by Dr. James. God give you health.

Locke drafted a reply [3] to the Archbishop in a tone of marked asperity:

> . . . By what Dr. James says, I find he gave his *imprimatur* to the book upon confidence that Mr. Edwards had obeyed his order of blotting out diverse passages in it, and was satisfied with Mr. Edwards writing

---

[1] B.L. MSS. Locke, c. 7, f. 161.
[2] 21 December 1697 (*ibid.*, c. 19, f. 185).
[3] 15 January 1697/8 (*ibid.*, c. 24, f. 270).

him word *that he had smoothed many things.* How Mr. Edwards had smoothed it would have been very evident to the world if the book-sellers who printed his book in London (for the printer in Cambridge would not defile his press with it) had not smoothed it over again and blotted out many things, so much care had the booksellers of the reputa-tion of their presses and shops that they would not give it their *im-primatur* till those passages which the modesty of these tradesmen could not bear were blotted out and till they saw it was done, not trusting to Mr. E[dwar]ds's smoothing.

But Dr. James says that *Mr. Ed[ward]s was forbidden to print the imprimatur at London, though he did it, displeasing thereby the Licencers, and the Chancellor himself, the Duke of Somerset.*

Supposing this [is] all so, as he says, I appeal to your Grace and my Lord Bishop of Ely whether this story of Dr. James, told to your Grace, can be satisfaction to me or anybody. The book is gone and goes abroad into the world with those Reverend licencers' names to the *Imprimatur.* The Vice-Chancellor, the Professor of Divinity and other eminent Doctors of Divinity and Heads of Houses in the University of Cambridge are published by Mr. Edwards as approvers of his book. 'Tis alleged that they and others are displeased with him for it. But the world sees not any mark of the least displeasure. . . .

It was a long time before Locke's anger was abated.

During the winter of 1697/8 Locke was able to spend less time than ever at Oates. He left London at the beginning of December feeling very sick,[1] and though his spirits were quickly restored in the country air he remained an ailing man. Writing to Molyneux in mid-January,[2] he confessed that even in his 'wonted refuge' his lungs were still weak. Dressing and undressing was 'a labour that I am fain to rest after to recover my breath'; reading itself was a 'burden to me'; and, he said, he had not been 'once out of the house since I came last hither'.

Two weeks after he had written in this way to Molyneux, when he was, in fact, feeling even worse, Locke received a summons to wait upon the King at Kensington. Kensington, assuredly, was not

---

[1] From Oates Locke wrote on 6 December 1697 to Clarke saying that he had found 'the benefit of the air here' in a very short time; it had 'in a great measure taken off that horrible oppression which I had . . . upon my lungs in town'. His nights passed 'without that panting for breath which so often tormented me in town' (Rand, p. 525).

[2] 10 January 1697/8 (*S.F.L.*, pp. 253–261).

F F

London; William had gone to live there partly to keep away from the smoke of Whitehall which he, being as asthmatic as Locke, hated as Locke did. But Kensington was twenty-five miles from Oates, the cold was arctic, and the roads were covered with snow. However, Locke was not a man to disobey a royal command. He climbed into the coach that had been sent to fetch him, and went.

What was the purpose of this urgent summons? Locke himself was very secretive about it. When Lady Masham asked him, all he would say was 'that the King had a desire to talk to him about his own health, as believing there was much similitude in their cases'.[1] Lady Masham was too shrewd to believe this: the King, she thought, had 'too great a regard for Mr. Locke's health to expose it to such a journey without some important reason for so doing'.[1] She was not deceived. The King had offered Locke a post.

As much, and more, may be learned from a letter Locke wrote to Somers as soon as he had got back to Oates. The draft[2] reads as follows:

> Sunday, in the evening, after waiting on the King [at Kensington], I was to wait upon your Lordship, it being, as I understood him, his Majesty's pleasure that I should do so before I returned hither. My misfortune in missing your Lordship then I hoped to repair by an early diligence the next morning, but the night that came between destroyed that purpose and me almost with it. For when I was laid in my bed, my breath failed me. This obliged me to sit upright in my bed, where I continued in this posture a good part of the night with hopes that my shortness of breath would abate and my lungs grow so good-natured as to let me lie down to get a little sleep, whereof I had great need. But my breath constantly failing me as often as I laid [my head] upon my pillow, at three I got up and so sat by the fire till morning. My case being brought to this extremity, there was no room for any other thought but to get out of town immediately. For after the two precedent nights without any rest I concluded [that] the agonies I laboured under so long in the second of those would hardly fail to be (?) death the third if I stayed in town. As bad weather therefore as it was, I was forced early on Monday morning to seek a passage, and by good luck found an empty Cambridge coach just setting out which brought me hither.

> His Majesty was so favourable to me as to propose the employment your Lordship mentioned. But the true knowledge of my own weak

---

[1] Amsterdam: Remonstrants' MSS. J. 57a.
[2] B.L. MSS. Locke, c. 24, f. 228.

state of health made me beg his Majesty to think of some fitter person, and one more able to serve him in that important post—to which I added my want of experience for such a business. That your Lordship may not think this an expression barely of modesty, I crave leave to explain it to your Lordship, though therein I discover my weakness. My temper, always shy of a crowd and strangers, has made my acquaintances few and my conversation too narrow and particular to get the skill of dealing with men in their various humours, and drawing out their secrets. Whether this was a fault or no in a man that designed no bustle in the world I know not. This I am sure: it will let your Lordship see I am too much a novice in the world for the employment proposed. . . .

The King was graciously pleased to order me to go into the country to take care of my health. These four or five days have given me a proof to what a low state my lungs are now brought, and how little they can bear the least shock. . . .

My Lord, I should not trouble you with an account of the prevailing decays of an old pair of lungs were it not my duty to take care his Majesty should be disappointed, [*sic*] and therefore that he lay any [*sic*] expectation on that which, to my great misfortune every way, I find would certainly fail him. . . .

I do not only fear, but am sure, my broken health will never permit me to accept the great honour his Majesty meant me.

Precisely what employment William offered Locke this letter does not show. Manifestly it was a diplomatic post, and probably it was that of Embassy Secretary in Paris, the very position which was to be held sixty-seven years later by David Hume. The British diplomatic mission to France was of vastly greater importance, however, in 1698 than it was in 1765. The Peace of Ryswick had only just been ratified, and diplomatic relations were being opened for the first time between the Orange monarchy in London and the King of France. So much importance did William attach to the mission that he chose his closest friend William Bentinck, Earl of Portland, to go to Paris as Ambassador. The urgency of the mission owed much to the fact that Charles II of Spain was near the point of death, and William foresaw the danger to peace and security which the uncertainty of the Spanish succession entailed. As between the conflicting claims of the Austrian candidate, the Archduke Charles, and the French candidate, Philip of Anjou, William aspired to reach a compromise while Charles II of Spain still lived. Further, to strengthen his bargaining hand and as a precaution against failure, he proposed to maintain the armed strength of England and the Netherlands at a war-like level, and to perpetuate his past alliances. It was obvious to William that the assimilation of the enormous domains of Spain either by France or by Austria would destroy the whole European balance of power. He looked to partition as the only tolerable solution, and what persuasion could not accomplish, force, he believed, would have to ensure. But what was obvious to William was not obvious to English politicians or to England generally. The English had had enough of war and slumped into one of their occasional moods of isolationism. Parliament had decided to disarm. Hence it was all the more imperative for diplomatic methods to succeed. In January 1697/8 William's mind was almost wholly preoccupied with his embassy to France, and coupled with Locke's own account of their interview, this seems to preclude any other conjecture as to the subject they discussed.

Locke's trip to Kensington left him very ill indeed and he did not make the recovery he hoped for. Lady Masham testified that 'we never thought him so well again as he was before'.[1] Perhaps the most remarkable thing is that Locke was able to return at all to his work at the Board of Trade; for he did so when summer came. He told Clarke in mid-March[2] that he could barely go into the open air, 'for I have not breath enough yet to walk'; he could just manage 'to crawl to a seat we have in the terrace walk where I can at my ease lazily enjoy the sun and breathe the fresh air'. He had not the heart to carry on with his writings. He confessed to Molyneux:[3]

> For I am in doubt whether it be fit for me to trouble the press with any new matter; or, if I did, I look on my life as so near worn out that it would be folly to hope to finish anything of moment in the small remainder of it.

Locke asked his Irish friend to become his literary executor, and told him there were other matters 'I would be glad to talk with you about before I die'. The surprising, ironical thing was that Locke lived longer than Molyneux. However, the same language of doleful resignation recurs in a letter Locke wrote from Oates on

[1] Amsterdam: Remonstrants' MSS. J. 57a.
[2] 19 March 1697/8 (Rand, pp. 534–5).
[3] 6 April 1698 (S.F.L., p. 266).

28 April[1] to Furly. After mentioning two days in London which had almost killed him, Locke said:

> I have been here ever since, and in the chimney corner, and write this by the fireside, for we have yet no warmth from the sun, though the days are almost at their full length, and it was but yesterday morning that it snowed very hard for near two hours together. . . . I am little furnished with news, and want it less. I have lived long enough to see that a man's endeavours are ill laid out upon anything but himself, and his expectations very uncertain when placed upon what others pretend or promise to do.

The next day Locke wrote [2] to Esther Masham complaining of the continued cold and begging her to 'come and comfort your poor solitary *berger*'. Cold Locke may have been, but he was not solitary. He did not even lack young female society, for his young 'wife', Elizabeth Clarke, now nearly sixteen, was with him. She, admittedly, was not quite herself; Lady Masham, as well as Locke, noticed how 'reserved' she was; and Locke reported the fact to her father.[3] Clarke was not surprised. He already had his own suspicions; he believed Betty was in love, and that she was carrying on a clandestine correspondence with a young admirer. Locke was charged to watch her; but when Locke wrote next to Clarke he had to report: 'My Lady [Masham] and I have as strict an eye as possible over that affair, but there is yet not the least appearance of a letter going or coming'.[4] However, a fortnight later Locke informed [5] his friend that when his daughter had opened and read Clarke's last letter to her 'the blood came suddenly to her face and she was in great disorder'; and he suggested that if Clarke could recall what he had written to her he might 'possibly from thence have some further light into the matter you suspect'.

Possibly (the suggestion is Benjamin Rand's [6]) the other party to this suspected love affair was the son of Thomas Stringer. Betty had been staying at Ivychurch in 1697, and subsequently Mrs. Stringer proposed that their son might marry her; but Thomas Stringer stopped the match.

---

[1] *Original Letters* (Second Edition), p. 64.
[2] 29 April 1698 (Newberry).
[3] 7 May 1698 (B.M. Add. MSS. 4290 f. 87).
[4] 13 May 1698 (Rand, p. 537).
[5] 30 May 1698 (Chipley Park Collection: Rand, pp. 540–1).
[6] *Op. cit.*, p. 59.

If Locke found his little 'wife' a disappointing companion that spring, he could still not reasonably complain of solitude. For he now enjoyed besides the usual company at Oates that of Pierre Coste, who had been taken on by Sir Francis Masham as tutor [1] to his youngest son, Frank, but whose services were also available to and made use of by Locke. Pierre Coste remained at Oates for over seven years until after Locke's death, acting sometimes as the philosopher's secretary, sometimes as a general intellectual *aide*. A few weeks after Locke's death Coste wrote a letter to the *Nouvelles de la République des Lettres* [2] in which he gave a brief memorial sketch of the philosopher. He paid tribute to Locke's 'love of truth', his 'great knowledge of the world and the business of it', his liberality in giving counsel, his orderly way of life, his gift for conversing with men of all conditions and capacities, his skill as a courtier and his devotion to the Scriptures. He also recalled Locke's capacity for relaxation: 'When an occasion naturally offered he gave himself up to the charms of a free and cheerful conversation; he remembered a great many agreeable stories, which he always brought in properly and generally made them yet more delightful by his natural and agreeable way of telling them'. Coste's one criticism of Locke on this occasion was that he was 'naturally somewhat choleric'.[3] This criticism must surely have been just, as even Lady Masham admitted it: 'The passion he was naturally most prone to was anger'.[4]

On 8 June 1698 a young man named Peter King was called to the Bar at the Middle Temple. He was a grandson of Peter Locke, the philosopher's uncle, and the son of Jerome King an Exeter drysalter and grocer. Peter King had published in 1691, when he was twenty-two, a book on the primitive Church which interested his cousin at

[1] Locke told Molyneux in his letter of 10 January 1697/8 (*S.F.L.*, p. 256): 'Mr. Coste is now in the house with me here, and is tutor to my Lady Masham's son. I need not, I think now, answer your questions about his skill in mathematics and natural history; I think it is not much. But he is an ingenious man, and we like him very well for our purpose. . . .'   [2] *February, 1705* (pp. 154 ff.).

[3] Later and elsewhere Pierre Coste seems to have found other things to complain of. An anonymous writer in the *Several Pieces* (p. iii) alleges that Coste 'in several writings and in his common conversation throughout France, Holland and England has aspersed and blackened the memory of Mr. Locke in those very respects wherein he was his panegyrist before'.

[4] Amsterdam: Remonstrants' MSS. J. 57a. She added: 'But his great good sense and good breeding so far subdued this that it was rarely troublesome.'

Oates. After he had read it Locke encouraged the author to give up the trade into which he was to follow his father, and go to the University of Leyden. Peter King spent three years there before he returned to London to read for the Bar.

Locke proposed to his young cousin that he should follow a combined career of politics and law, and although King is said to have been indolent by nature, his career was a remarkable success, for he rose in time to be Lord High Chancellor of England. The philosopher, who was increasingly conscious that death was drawing near and that he was not only childless but without nephews or nieces, began to look on this cousin as his next of kin. He made Peter King his heir, and treated him almost as an adopted son. He wrote many letters to give him the benefit of his wisdom and experience, and in return he expected, and received, many small services from King. After the young man had been called to the Bar, Locke sent [1] him some advice on how to conduct himself in court. He urged him to make his first speech there on 'some easy plain matter that you are perfectly master of', so 'that you may not be out in what you have to say nor be liable to stumble'.

One of the friends Locke met again in London that summer was Isaac Newton,[2] who had been made Warden of the Mint soon after Locke had been made a Commissioner for Trade. Newton was called in to advise the Board of Trade on coinage for the American colonies. An acquaintance with Christopher Wren was also renewed in the course of Locke's public duties and the Abbé du Bos,[3] arrived in England with an introduction from Nicholas Thoynard.[4] But the most memorable event of the summer for Locke was the appearance in London, at long last, of William Molyneux with whom he had corresponded on such intimate terms but never previously met. The two friends spent five weeks together, chiefly in London but partly at Oates. The satisfaction was as much Molyneux's as Locke's. The Irishman spoke afterwards of this visit as 'the happiest scene of my whole life'.[5]

[1] 27 June 1698 (B.L. MSS. Locke, c. 40, f. 11).

[2] In his Journal Locke wrote on 19 July 1698: 'Mr. Newton told me that there had been coined in all the mints since the calling in of the clipped money 6,500,000 or thereabouts in [silver]'.

[3] A number of letters from the Abbé du Bos, preserved in the Lovelace Collection has been printed by G. Bonno, *Revue de Littérature Comparée* (1950, pp. 481–520).

[4] 'Enfin, Monsieur, j'ay eu le bonheur de voir votre excellent ami Mr. du Bos,' Locke wrote to Thoynard on 14 July 1698 (Ollion p. 130).

[5] S.F.L., p. 272.

Even in the joyous society of this particular friend Locke did not forget his enemies; at any rate he did not forget John Edwards. Though Dr. Covel, the Master of Trinity, had apologised handsomely in private for putting his name to Edwards's book, Locke was now determined to have a public apology. He wrote to the Master on 26 July [1] saying:

> . . . The Discourse you . . . made me about the *Imprimatur* so fully satisfied me that I was not mistaken in your friendship that I shall not be unwilling you should put into my hands the means of vindicating you to the world in that matter. I therefore desire you that you would now send me the letter that you offered to write to me, that I might publish concerning that affair. For though your name stands printed equally amongst the others, yet I shall be glad to have it in my power to clear you in that point and to show the world that they ought not to involve you in the same opinion with the others which that memorable transaction, when examined and looked into, will be found to deserve.

The Master did as he was bidden. He gave Locke permission [2] to publish a letter [3] stating that if he, Covel, 'had been in the least conscious of your unhandsome usage in that piece [by Edwards] I could not have so much injured myself or you, or so far violated the common bonds of friendship between us as to have approved of it'.

After this Locke forgave the Master completely, and a few months later he was writing [4] to say how much he was 'longing' to see him at Oates.

While Molyneux was in London, both he and Locke sat for their portraits by Sir Godfrey Kneller, [5] each intending to present his own to the other so that both might enjoy in the absence of the original the companionship of the likeness. Neither picture was complete when Molyneux left for Dublin in September, but Locke parted with his friend, as he afterwards recalled, [6] 'with all the hope and promises to myself of seeing him again and enjoying him longer the next Spring'.

Locke's hope was rudely shattered. Less than a month after he had returned to Dublin, William Molyneux died. He was only forty-

[1] B.M. Add. MSS. 22,910, f. 477.
[2] B.L. MSS. Locke, c. 7, ff. 170-1.　　　　　　　　[3] *Ibid.*, f. 163.
[4] 12 March 1698/9 (B.M. Add. MSS. 22,910, f. 479).
[5] *Journal.* 21 September 1698.
[6] Locke to Richard Burridge. 27 October 1698 (*S.F.L.*, p. 275).

two. A truly stricken Locke wrote to Molyneux's brother Thomas:[1]

> Death has with a violent hand ... snatched from you a dear brother. ... I bear too great a share in the loss, and am too sensibly touched with it myself ... to do anything but mingle my tears with yours. I have lost in your brother, not only an ingenious and learned acquaintance that all the world esteemed, but an intimate and sincere friend whom I truly loved and by whom I was truly loved. And what a loss that is, those only can be sensible who know how valuable and how scarce a true friend is and how far to be preferred to all other sorts of treasure.

Before the death of Molyneux, Locke had seriously considered paying another visit to France and possibly to Holland also. Limborch was delighted at this prospect of a reunion with his old friend,[2] but Locke had to disappoint him. 'My journey to France', he wrote to inform him at the beginning of October,[3] 'is likely to come to nothing'. It did come to nothing. Locke spent the winter as usual at Oates.

His valet Kiplin left his service in November, and Locke sought King's help in finding another. (Kiplin's successor, who joined Locke the following January, was a young man named James Dorington.) Relying more and more on King's aid in matters small and large, Locke felt constrained to advise his cousin how he ought to conduct his life. He reminded him[4] of the importance of being 'a man of order in business'—'give me leave to tell you that the sooner and the more you are so, the more will it be for your ease and the saving [of] your time'. When a few weeks later King bought Locke some knitted gloves, Locke did not hesitate to complain[5] that they were gloves 'with half fingers', albeit adding good humouredly enough: 'in revenge, if you ever desire me to buy socks for you, I shall be sure to take care that they shall not cover your toes'.

Locke's correspondents in the early months of *1699* included two controversial authors, one of whom was his critic, the other his

[1] 27 October 1698 (*S.F.L.*, p. 290).
[2] Limborch to Locke. 12 September 1698 (Amsterdam: Remonstrants' MSS. III, D. 16, f. 207, Latin).
[3] 4 October 1698 (*ibid.*, Ba. 528g, French).
[4] 5 December 1698 (B.L. MSS. Locke, c. 40, f. 23).
[5] 16 January 1698/9 (*ibid.*, f. 28).

champion. The critic was Daniel Whitby, a clergyman who took exception to Locke's views on the resurrection. Having received a letter from Dr. Whitby,[1] Locke dictated a reply [2] deploring public controversy, and also denying that the views Whitby had attributed to him were his. Whitby took Locke's reply for a sign that Locke had nothing to say against his objections, and when, a few years later, he brought out his *Paraphrase and Commentary on the New Testament*,[3] he treated Locke as a defeated adversary. Locke thereupon drafted for Whitby the following sharp rebuke: [4]

> . . . By what you published in the preface to the Corinthians in your first edition I find that what you took my indisposition of health and aversion to controversy made me say in answer to yours of the 11th of January 1698/9 as an yielding of the cause. If I trouble you again on this occasion it is to undeceive you in this point, but still with my former design of avoiding controversy in print if you will permit me. As to your opinion of the same bodies being raised [on the resurrection of the dead] I have nothing to say. You may if you please establish it with what arguments you have without concerning me in it. . . .

Whitby's reply [5] was worthy of Stillingfleet himself. He said that having re-read his preface, he found that

> I had neither named you nor your book nor referred to any page of it, but only expressed in your good English what the Socinians had in substance said before in Latin, they being perfectly of your opinion and using the same arguments for it. . . .

A very different writer was Samuel Bolde, who came out in print in Locke's defence. Bolde was a latitudinarian divine who had already suffered for his convictions; at any rate he had been expelled from the living of Shapwick, Dorset, because of them, though he seems to have been securely established as Rector of Steeple in the same county from 1682 until his death. Bolde's most important pamphlet in support of Locke, entitled *Some Considerations on the Principal Objections and Arguments which have been Publish'd against Mr. Locke's Essay of the Human Understanding*, was issued by the Churchills at the beginning of May 1699.

---

[1] 11 January 1698/9 (B.L. MSS. Locke, c. 23, f. 94).
[2] 17 January 1698/9 (*ibid.*, c. 24, f. 283).
[3] Whitby's books were published by the Churchills.
[4] 17 September 1702 (*ibid.*, c. 24, f. 285).
[5] 28 October 1702 (*ibid.*, c. 23, f. 97).

Locke wrote a letter[1] to Bolde to thank him for what he had done:

> Your reasonings are so strong and just, and your friendship to me so visible, that everything must be welcome to me that comes from your pen, let it be of what kind soever.

In the same letter he said:

> how a rational man that should enquire and know for himself, can content himself with a faith or a religion taken upon trust, or with such a servile submission of his understanding as to admit all and nothing else but what fashion makes passable among men, is to me astonishing ... I read the word of God without prepossession or bias, and come to it with a resolution to take my sense from it, and not with a design to bring it to the sense of my system.[2]

In spite of having gone down to Oates the previous October with a bad cough, and in spite of that winter's having been (according to Evelyn[3]) the wettest for fifty years, Locke found himself better in health than he had been for some time.

It was the turn of the Clarke family to be ill. Mary Clarke had a recurrence of her old dropsical trouble, her husband caught an infection of the chest or lungs, and their son had some nervous affliction. Locke advised Mrs. Clarke to avoid 'all things that may make a chill mixture in your blood and fill your veins with watery humours';[4] he advised Edward Clarke to come to Oates and get well.[5] In recommending the son to see a physician[5] Locke was quick to pooh-pooh the idea that young Clarke's 'melancholia', as it was called in the language of the time, was due to anything but an organic cause: and even when the father said he had found out a plausible psychological explanation, Locke maintained that if not 'wholly founded in his body' he still thought it was 'in part'.[6] Though he is often called a psychological philosopher, Locke was clearly not a psychologically-minded physician. He was even capable of expressing surprise that this one of all Clarke's children

---

[1] *The Museum*, 1746, ii, p. 205.
[2] Another friendly pamphleteer was Mrs. Catherine Cockburn, who published, in 1702, an anonymous *Defence of the Essay of Human Understanding*.
[3] *Diary*, 25 June 1699.
[4] 12 April 1699 (Rand, p. 544).
[5] 28 April 1699 (*ibid.*, pp. 544–5).
[6] 3 May 1699 (*ibid.*, p. 547).

should suffer from 'despondency' when 'all the rest have vigorous and active minds'.[1]

In the summer Locke went once more to London to attend to his duties at the Board of Trade. The letters he wrote at the time show that his spirits remained good. He told Esther Masham[2] of a happy visit he had paid to another of his 'daughters', Frances St. John; he thanked Esther for the care she was taking of his 'brew house and drink';[3] and a few days later he recommended 'a soop brandy' for Lady Masham to make her 'better natured'.[4] He related in a bright letter to Mary Clarke dated 19 August[5] how

> A gentleman came to visit me at ten o'clock in the morning and his visit lasted till past ten at night. You may guess by this that the town is grown so thin of company that those few that are left in it live and visit after the same manner as if they were in the country.

He did not name his visitor. It may have been P. des Maizeaux, of whose proposed emigration to England Le Clerc had informed Locke in June:[6] or it may equally have been Locke's old schoolfellow Robert South, who, for all his High Church Tory sentiments, wrote to Locke more than once that year[7] to express his admiration for Locke's writings and to pay his respects.

Ever since its inception the Board of Trade had been interested in the Company of Scotland Trading to Africa and the Indies, and in that Company's project of colonising Darien, an isthmus some miles south of Panama. Interested, but not, however, sympathetic. For the Scots were not then thought of as fellow British subjects, but as foreign competitors with English trade. The theorist of the Darien scheme was William Paterson, one of the original promoters of the Bank of England, and the Scottish people supported it with

---

[1] 3 May 1699 (Rand, p. 547).

[2] 21 July 1699 (Newberry).

[3] In a footnote to his transcript of this letter Esther Masham wrote: 'Mr. Locke drank nothing but water. What he calls his Brewhouse was the stone in the form of a great morter of so spungy a stone that water being put in used to run through it in a very short time and strained the water from any dirt that might be in it'. This was evidently one of the stones Locke had had sent him from the Canary Islands.

[4] 27 July 1699 (Newberry).

[5] Rand, pp. 549–50.

[6] *18 June 1699* (B.L. MSS. Locke, c. 13, f. 129, French).

[7] On 18 June 1699 and 6 December 1699 (*ibid.*, c. 18, ff. 171–4).

liberality out of all proportion to the wealth of their country. When the Scotland Company was formed in 1695 many English merchants were willing to help its activities against the English African and East India Companies' monopoly, but intense Parliamentary pressure by those monopolists bullied the English shareholders out of the Company; and it was left to the Board of Trade to devise ways of killing what had become a purely Scots' enterprise.

Locke's papers [1] show that he took care to inform himself very fully about the Darien scheme from the earliest days. The information he collected may have been even better than that available at Edinburgh, for the reports indicate the hazards as well as the potentialities of colonising Darien. He learned that while the climate and the general geographical characteristics of the place were bad, the isthmus had the great advantage of being on the main highway of the Spanish gold and silver traffic. But in that very advantage the Board of Trade detected an argument for suppressing the scheme. For to set up a colony on the Spanish trade route would be an affront to a friendly power, and a breach of the Treaty of Madrid.

On 20 May 1697 [2] the Lords Justices sent the Board of Trade a letter asking the (rhetorical?) questions whether the Scots' designs on Darien 'may be to the injury of the Spaniards or prejudicial to the Trade of this Kingdom?' On 10 August 1697 [3] the Board replied answering 'yes' to both these questions.

This solicitude for the welfare of the Spaniards [4] may have struck the Scots as a choice example of English humbug; but the desire to avoid provoking war with Spain was genuine. Spain had been England's war-time ally, and her King was visibly dying. An affront just then might easily drive him into the arms of France.

The English Government declared the scheme illegal, and ordered its colonial governors to give it neither aid nor recognition; but these measures proved to be unnecessary.

A letter [5] from a man named Sheils written aboard the Scots

[1] *Vide* especially B.L. MSS. Locke, c. 30, ff. 40, 125–8.

[2] *Ibid.*, c. 30, f. 47.

[3] *Ibid.*, f. 49. The letter was signed by Bridgewater, Tankerville, Pollexfen, Locke and Hill.

[4] Two supposed authorities, Dampier and Lionel Wafer, told the Board that Darien lay outside Spanish territory. Some Commissioners seem to have been impressed by this evidence, but Locke was not, and neither was the absentee Blathwayt (Jacobsen *op. cit.*, pp. 326–7).

[5] B.L. MSS. Locke, c. 30, f. 112. (This is a copy, not the original letter.)

vessel the *Rising Sun* on Christmas Day 1699 brought Locke news that the enterprise was failing disastrously. The colonists had been stricken with fever on the voyage out, their supplies proved inadequate, and several of their ships had been wrecked.

On 16 January 1699/1700[1] the Board was once more asked—this time by the House of Lords—whether the Darien scheme was inconsistent with the Peace Treaty with Spain, destructive to English trade or prejudicial to English colonies; and once again the Board of Trade replied that the scheme was all those things.[2]

In the end political action was not needed to destroy the Darien scheme. Providence had done the job effectively enough. The colony had to be evacuated, and the Scots company lost all its ships.

From New York Lord Bellomont wrote a private letter[3] to Locke in May 1699, explaining the difficulties of a situation where he had 'the misfortune to succeed' a Governor 'who has not only left everything in disorder by a corrupt management, but also did it with premeditation and design'. Lord Bellomont complained of lack of funds to pay his troops and of trained lawyers to work the judicial system, and he asked Locke to intercede with the Lord Chancellor (Lord Somers) for aid.

By all accounts Lord Bellomont was an excellent Governor. There had been no war with the French or Red Indians, and he was able to concentrate his energies on suppressing pirates. He had some remarkable successes, although he protested to Locke in a lugubrious letter,[4] written from Boston the following autumn:

> Pirates do so increase in these plantations that they will destroy the trade of England, especially that to the E. Indies, if a speedy remedy be

[1] Locke wrote to Edward Clarke on 18 January 1699/1700 saying: 'When I read what I find in the *Enquiry into the causes of the miscarriages of the Scots colony at Darien* p. 16 and p. 41 at the bottom and compare it with what was said to me before I came out of town I cannot but have reason to think that the Order sent from the House of Lords to our Board on Tuesday the 16th instant had in the movers and promoters of it some regard to me in particular. I desire therefore to know by whom it was moved. I desire you also to have your eye upon that business and watch it and also acquaint the gent. in the corner with my apprehensions, which are not groundless, and desire his care in the case. . . .'
(Henry E. Huntingdon Library, California, Call Number HM 7096.)
[2] 18 January 1699/1700 (B.L. MSS. Locke, c. 30, f. 117).
[3] 12 May 1699 (*ibid.*, c. 7, f. 134).
[4] 7 September 1699 (*ibid.*, f. 136).

not taken to suppress 'em. We have had two or three new Pirate ships on these coasts lately. They rob our trading ships of the stoutest and likeliest of their men and of all their provisions ... and then they declare themselves bound for Madagascar and the Red Sea.

He explained that nothing but men-of-war could capture the pirates, but, he added, 'The Lords of the Admiralty are pleased not to allow us a single ship'.

In a postscript to his letter, Lord Bellomont mentioned his personal grievances:

> I labour more than all the Governors that are in America to serve England, and yet I suffer extremely, my allowance being so short for the government of New York that it will not half maintain me, and I am sent a begging to this province [i.e. Massachusetts] for a salary, where they are the most parsimonious people on earth.

Some weeks before he wrote this letter to Locke, Lord Bellomont had captured that most impudent of pirates, Captain Kidd. He did so by a simple stratagem. Kidd had written to Lord Bellomont saying there was no legal case against him. Lord Bellomont thereupon invited Kidd to come to Boston and prove his argument; and as soon as he had him there he imprisoned him. Then when Lord Bellomont learned that there was indeed no crime of piracy according to New England law, he sent Captain Kidd under arrest to London for trial by English law. The frigate which conveyed him reached England at the beginning of April 1700.

Lord Bellomont may then have felt he had done his duty as a good colonial governor; but he had done no service to his fellow Whigs in London. The arrival of Captain Kidd and his arrest by the Marshal of the Admiralty created a great public stir; but apart from Kidd himself, who was duly hanged on a trumped-up charge of murder, the man who suffered most was the head of the Government, Somers.

Opposition to Somers had been gathering strength in Parliament for some time past: he was believed to have advised the King to make the unpopular Partition Treaties, to be in favour of increasing the army, and to be against the Bill for the resumption of the grants of forfeited Irish estates. The case of Captain Kidd gave Somers's enemies the opportunity they were looking for. Not only had the Lord Chancellor with other Whigs sponsored Kidd's enterprise, he had actually affixed the great seal to Kidd's commission. On

10 April a motion was put forward in the House of Commons for an address to the King begging him to exclude Somers from his Councils and presence. The motion was defeated, but by so small a majority that William thought it best for Somers to retire. The Lord Chancellor agreed, though he hoped that his doing so would not be taken as an admission of guilt.

Somers's departure from the Woolsack was the cue for Locke's retirement from the Board of Trade. While he had drawn his pay with scrupulous regularity,[1] he had been absent from many meetings of the Board during the winter of 1699/1700, and bad weather kept him in 'the chimney corner' until the end of April. The fall of Somers presaged a rise of Blathwayt's friends and thus of Blathwayt's power in the Board of Trade. Locke was too old and too ill to play a losing game. He went to London in May, with the single intention, as he revealed in a letter to Thoynard:[2] that of resigning from the Board of Trade.

This time no one urged him to change his mind. Locke was said[3] to have forestalled any such persuasion by surrendering his commission to the King 'without saying anything to anyone' beforehand. William received it, the story goes, 'unwillingly', but seeing Locke was adamant, released the philosopher from this 'the last public business he undertook'.[3]

---

[1] On 4 December 1699 Locke told King he had 'a thousand pounds lying dead by me', and soliciting advice as to how best he might invest it. (B.L. MSS. Locke, c. 40, f. 50.) On 23 February 1699/1700 he told King of another five or six hundred pounds he would 'be glad to have well placed out'. (*Ibid.*, f. 66.)

[2] 21 May 1700 (Ollion, p. 139).

[3] Lady Masham to Jean le Clerc (Amsterdam: Remonstrants' MSS. J. 57a).

Chapter Twenty-six

LAST YEARS

Whidth—HEN Limborch heard that Locke had retired from the Board of Trade, he wrote[1] to commend his decision to spend the remainder of his life 'in rest, study and religious meditations'.

The first few weeks of his retirement Locke devoted primarily to rest. It was a change for him to be able to pass a whole summer in the country, and he spent his time in the open air. He wrote[2] to Clarke, who was taking the waters at Tunbridge Wells, urging him to do likewise. 'I know nothing so likely to produce quiet sleep as riding about gently in the air for many hours every day. . . . I am on horseback every day.'

This holiday lasted until the end of August. Then Locke was forced to stop riding because of a 'swelling' which appeared on his back. It was not a boil, he said;[3] in fact he did not know what it was, but it marked the beginning of a disagreeable sickness. Early in October Locke told Clarke:[4]

> The swelling I mentioned to you in my back I could not get to break there, and it is gone from thence, but the humour that is in it I think is fallen into my leg, where it has caused me very sharp pains, and is broke in two or three places. I spend most of my time in bed, and have ate nothing for some days but water-gruel. . . .

A day or two later Peter King wrote[5] to ask if Locke would be coming to London to welcome King William on his Majesty's return from Holland. Locke replied saying that he had received his cousin's letter in bed and 'in bed I now write you this answer'. He added:[6]

[1] *20 July 1700* (Amsterdam: Remonstrants' MSS. III, D. 16, f. 189: Latin).
[2] 23 August 1700 (B.M. Add. MSS. 4290, f. 90).
[3] To Clarke: 2 September 1700 (Rand, p. 562).
[4] 3 October 1700 (B.M. Add. MS. 4290, f. 96).
[5] 5 October 1700 (B.L. MSS. Locke, c. 12, f. 108).
[6] 14 October 1700 (*ibid.*, c. 40, f. 77).

Not that I am confined to my bed by any great increase of my old distemper—that, I thank God, the spending [of] this summer in the country has made as tolerable to me as I could expect. Age I know will not mend ill lungs, and therefore my old disease of my breast must go on as it does its old train. But there is a new malady has lately befallen me and has obliged me for some time past to spend most of my time in my bed. A humour has fallen down and made me a sore leg. Being up, I find, increases the pain and spreading of it, against which I take sanctuary in my bed as one of the best remedies I can use. When I shall be able to return to my former liberty of living I cannot tell, much less when I shall be able to take a journey.

Locke ended his letter by asking his cousin to come to Oates. King went and Locke was grateful for the visit. They talked about a subject very close to the philosopher's heart—money: and after their deliberations King invested yet another £2,000 of his cousin's capital in a good security.[1]

On 5 November, Locke was able to report (to Clarke [2]) that his leg was now 'so well that it confines me no longer to the lazy lying much in bed'; the only trouble, he found, was that 'I breathe much worse now than when my leg was ill'. However, he was determined to look on the bright side of things: [3]

. . . I think I ought to be content that I am at all amongst the living. It is not spleen that suggests this thought, but the news I heard this post that my old friend Mr. [Nathaniel] Hodges is dead. He, Dr. [David] Thomas and I were intimate in our younger days at the university. They two are gone, and who would have thought that I, much the weakest and most unlikely of the three, should have outlived them?

The tedium of 'lying much in bed' had been relieved for Locke by scientific books and papers sent him by the Secretary of the Royal Society. In writing [4] to thank Hans Sloane, he said: '. . . give me leave to own to you that I am ashamed to be so much enriched by you in philosophical knowledge without furnishing anything to your collections.'

All he could offer Sloane was a register of the weather he had kept for the past ten years. Sloane [5] was pleased to accept this offer and

---

[1] *Vide* Locke's Journal 17 December 1700: 'My Cousin King did on November 19 lend to Sir Richard Gipps £2000 of my money upon a mortgage'.
[2] B.M. Add. MSS. 4290, f. 100.
[3] *Ibid.*, f. 103.
[4] 27 December 1700 (B.M. Sloane MSS. 4038, f. 113).
[5] 2 January 1700/1 (B.L. MSS. Locke, c. 18, f. 122).

the register was published soon afterwards in the *Transactions* of the Royal Society.

At the General Election of January 1700/1 Peter King was returned to Parliament for Beer Alston. He did not wish to let politics interfere with his career at the Bar, and he so far misunderstood his cousin as to seek his approval for such a *modus vivendi*. Locke was shocked. He wrote several stern letters to remind King of his parliamentary duties. In one, dated 27 January,[1] he urged him not to think of going on circuit, but to stay in London for the next meeting of the House of Commons. In another, written three days later,[2] Locke said that King's presence in London was absolutely necessary in all respects, 'whether I consider the public or your own private concerns'. He did not expect his cousin to speak in the House as yet, but he did wish him there to 'communicate' his 'light or apprehension' to some 'honest member' who was an experienced speaker.

There were good reasons for Locke's insistence just then on the importance of parliamentary duties. The election of January 1700/1 had given the Tories the upper hand in the House of Commons, and the international situation was critical. The King of Spain had died the previous November, leaving, in a will, his entire dominions to Philip of Anjou. Louis XIV, who naturally preferred that his grandson should have the whole rather than a part of the Spanish kingdom, accepted the will as binding and repudiated the partition treaties he had made with William.

Many Englishmen told themselves that there was no cause in this for alarm, and that so long as the crowns of France and Spain remained separate all would be well. William did not think so, and neither did Locke; they both saw in this new situation a threat not merely of war, but of something much worse, the enslavement of Europe by France.

The new Parliament, which went into session on 6 February, found much to talk about besides defence. Locke could not understand what was the matter with the politicians. To Edward Clarke, who had kept his seat despite the general Whig defeat, Locke protested[3] that there was no subject 'at present fit to take up your

[1] B.L. MSS. Locke, c. 40, f. 98.
[2] 31 January 1700/1 (*ibid.*, f. 100).
[3] 14 February 1700/1 (B.M. Add. MSS. 4290, f. 106).

time and thought' except providing 'a security for us and the rest of Europe'. In a message to Peter King dated 27 February,[1] Locke wrote:

> I am glad to hear it said that the House seems in a good disposition and resolved to support England against France, but wonder at myself for saying I am glad, it being prodigious for anyone to think it could ever be otherwise. And yet I find some here wonder that whilst the King of France makes such a mighty collection of forces in Flanders just over against us, we hear not of raising any land soldiers on this side [of] the water.

A few days later Locke sent another impassioned letter[2] to Peter King to ask how he could 'think of being a week together absent from your trust in Parliament' until he saw the kingdom 'in a posture of defence against the ruin that threatens it'. At the same time he wrote:

> The reason why I pressed you to stay in town was to give the world a testimony how much you preferred the public to your private interest and how true you were to any trust you undertook. This is no small character nor of small advantage to a man coming into the world. Besides I thought it no good husbandry for a man to get a fee or two and lose Westminster Hall. For I assure you Westminster Hall is at stake, and I wonder how any of the House can sleep till he sees England in a better state of defence. . . .

Locke assured his young cousin very earnestly that the advice he gave him was nothing other than the advice he would give his own son.[3] He said that war was inevitable[4] and he warned his cousin as a Member of Parliament not to be deceived about the intentions of Louis XIV:[5]

> The good King of France desires only that you would take his word and let him be quiet till he has got the West Indies into his hands and his grandson well established in Spain, and then you may be sure you shall be as safe as he will let you be in your religion, property and trade, to all which who can be such an infidel as not to believe him a great friend?

Visitors at Easter included the third Lord Shaftesbury and Peter King, and the following month brought young Francis Limborch,

[1] B.L. MSS. Locke, c. 40, f. 114.   [2] 3 March 1700/1 (*ibid.*, f. 116).
[3] 20 March 1700/1 (*ibid.*, f. 122).   [4] 28 March 1701 (*ibid.*, f. 126).
[5] 5 April 1701 (*ibid.*, f. 128).

who had been sent to enter business in England. The boy's 'arrival is very welcome to us all', Locke [1] assured the father, 'and all the more welcome to me because your placing him in my care is another proof of your confidence in me'.

In June, having engaged another valet—a young man named William Shaw—in place of James Dorington, Locke ventured on a trip to London. He took Francis Limborch with him; indeed, it was probably in order to introduce that young man to the London business world that Locke made the journey at all. James Tyrrell wished to see Locke in London to discuss his literary activities,[2] but this object would have had no attraction for Locke, especially as Tyrrell was still excusing himself from paying that 'small sum I owe you'. Elizabeth Clarke took Locke's appearance in London as a sign that he was 'master of so much more health than you are used to be'; [3] and she was able to report that her father's health also was better than it had been 'for this two years last past'.[4]

Locke did not linger in the capital. His legs were still swollen, and his lungs cried out for the country air. Once back at Oates, he was called upon to exercise his medical skill among the local cottagers—a sick man tending the sick, but very willing to help when he could.[5]

Francis Cudworth Masham informed his sister Esther on 7 November [6] that 'Mr. Locke's legs do not pain him now that he has got a screen for them'; but the wintry weather which came a week later brought about a relapse. 'My illness,' Locke wrote to Limborch, 'makes me so weak that it is very difficult for me to write at all.' [7] He said the same thing to Clarke six weeks later,[8] when, on top of everything else, he had 'a very great cold which very much indisposes me for everything, even writing itself'.

[1] 21 May 1701. Amsterdam: Remonstrants' MSS. Ba. 528m.

[2] *Vide* Tyrrell to Locke. 30 May 1701 (B.L. MSS. Locke, c. 22, f. 141).

[3] 5 July 1701 (*ibid.*, c. 6, f. 157).

[4] 6 September 1701 (*ibid.*, f. 159).

[5] Concerning one of his cases Locke wrote to Sloane on 22 August 1701 (B.M. Add. MSS. 4052): 'I have a patient here sick of the fever of this season. It seems not to be violent but I am told it is a sort that is not easily got off. I desire to know of you whether the fevers in town are, and what method you find most successful in them'. Sloane replied on 23 August 1701 (B.L. MSS. Locke, c. 18, f. 124) informing Locke that there were two kinds of fever then raging in London. He named as a cure one of Locke's favoured remedies: Peruvian bark.

[6] Newberry.

[7] 13 November 1701 (Amsterdam: Remonstrants' MSS. Ba. 258p).

[8] 28 December 1701 (Rand, p. 583).

Even so, Locke was not too ill to read the public prints and news-letters, and his interest in politics was still keen. The King had but lately returned from Holland, after sealing an anti-French alliance with the Dutch and the Austrians; William had also come to an understanding with Robert Harley, the new Tory Speaker of the House of Commons which assured him of Tory support for a militant foreign policy; and he had at last named Marlborough his deputy and successor as commander-in-chief of British arms. After reading William's speech to Parliament in January, Locke told his cousin [1] that the people could not 'do less than with joined hearts and hands return [his Majesty] addresses of thanks for his taking such care of them'. William received his ovation, and then, choosing his moment more opportunely than anyone would have thought him likely to, he died.

Locke in the meantime had gone deaf. This began with 'a violent pain' in one of his ears.[2] The pain passed, but his hearing was seriously impaired. Dr. Alexander Geekie suggested that Locke's legs and ear were affected by the same disorder;[3] he advised applying nothing to the ear, but some months later he sent Locke an ear-trumpet.[4]

Just at the time when Locke went deaf, Peter King became interested in a young woman in London, and he asked his cousin at Oates if he thought he should marry her. Unfortunately, King explained, the girl had some physical defect. Locke advised[5] against marriage 'if the defect be to any considerable degree', but he warned Peter King to be tactful:

> For whatever reason a man may have to refuse a woman that is offered him, it must never be known that it was anything in her person. Such a discovery makes a mortal quarrel.

It turned out that the girl had Locke's own affliction, deafness, though not 'exceedingly' so. Peter King promised[6] to talk the matter over at Oates before making up his mind, and in the end he decided not to marry her.

---

[1] 3 January 1701/2 (B.L. MSS. Locke, c. 40, f. 191).
[2] *Vide* Locke to King 8 January 1701/2. (*Ibid.*, f. 193.)
[3] 10 March and 13 March 1701/2 (*ibid.*, c. 9, ff. 220–22). In the former letter Geekie sent Locke an account of the *post mortem* on William III, which he had attended.
[4] 9 October 1702 (*ibid.*, c. 9, f. 234).
[5] 1 March 1701/2 (*ibid.*, c. 40, f. 208).
[6] *Ibid.*, c. 12, f. 178.

In April Locke heard that Limborch was ill, with apoplexy, and he wrote [1] to advise blood-letting: 'Whatever threatens your health I always ascribe to that fulness of blood to which you are naturally disposed.' Locke's own health improved in May, and he was so excited by the declaration of war against France and Spain, that he decided to go to London. His resolution was to be there on Monday, 18 May, 'and that early in the day'.[2]

The trip was a disappointment. Locke went, but he found he had over-estimated his powers, and after one night at Little Lincoln's Inn Fields he had to go back to the country,[3] where he could not help feeling rather bored. He complained [4] to Peter King that there was 'not much conversation' at Oates, and he hinted plainly that 'your company for some time (a thing you have never done yet) will be very acceptable'. Locke was disappointed that summer of a visit from Benjamin Furly, although he did have the company of Furly's son Arent. In October [5] Locke confessed to Furly that he was not only deaf but much in need of intellectual stimulation:

I think myself upon the brink of another world, and being ready to leave those shufflings which have generally too broad a mixture of folly and corruption, should not despair with you to find matters more suited to the thoughts of rational creatures to entertain us. Do not think now I am grown either a stoic or a mystic. I can laugh as heartily as ever, and be in pain for the public as much as you. I am not grown into a sullenness that puts off humanity—no, nor mirth neither. Come and try. . . .

In the absence of conversation, Locke was spending more and more time in those religious meditations to which Limborch had expected him to devote the years of his retirement. In particular he was studying the Epistles of St. Paul, stung, perhaps, to such endeavours by John Edwards's remark that the author of *The Reasonableness of Christianity* seemed to know only the Gospels and

[1] 20 April 1702 (Amsterdam: Remonstrants' MSS. Ba. 258q: Latin).

[2] Locke to King, 13 May 1702 (B.L. MSS. Locke, c. 40, f. 216).

[3] 'I am old and infirm,' he told King, 'and . . . my ill health permitted me to stay in town but one night' (19 June 1702: *ibid.*, f. 222).

[4] 17 August 1702 and 4 September 1702 (*ibid.*, ff. 232–35).

[5] 12 October 1702 (*Original Letters*, Second Edition, p. 134). This same letter contains an interesting reference to Pierre Bayle: 'Pray give my service particularly to Monsieur Bayle when he comes in your way. However I value his opinion in the front rank of those who have got my book [presumably the *Essay Concerning Human Understanding*] yet he will not do me the favour to let me know what he thinks of it, one way or other'.

the Acts of the Apostles. Locke's method of studying the Epistles of St. Paul was to copy out the text in full in one column of a two-column page, and to write a paraphrase and notes in the other. He made these abridgements and commentaries for his own instruction, but he was persuaded to prepare them for publication, persuaded possibly by Lady Masham, who had to some extent participated in the studies. In a preface he wrote for the published version,[1] Locke explained how he had gone about it. For long he could not understand the 'doctrinal and discursive parts' of the Epistles; but in time he came to realise that there might be many causes of their obscurity. They were, after all, letters; and in letters a man left out many things he would include if he were writing for the general public. The several letters of St. Paul, moreover, were addressed to different sorts of people; they were written by a man who had but an imperfect command of Greek, and who was not, in any case, a systematic thinker. These circumstances alone might make for much confusion, and the perversions of St. Paul's meaning by opinionated and biased commentators made that confusion the worse confounded. Locke admitted that St. Paul had 'light from heaven' when he wrote, but he would concede no more divine inspiration than this, and he did not think that the writings of St. Paul should be in any way exempt from rational criticism.

Locke claimed no authority whatever for his own paraphrases:

> As far as they carry light and conviction to any other man's understanding, so far I hope my labour may be of use to him. Beyond the evidence it carries with it I advise him not to follow mine or any other

---

[1] The abridgements were published posthumously in the following order:

1. *A Paraphrase and Notes on the Epistle of St. Paul to the Galatians*, London, Printed for Awnsham and John Churchill, at the Black Swan in Pater-noster-row, 1705.

2. *A Paraphrase and Notes on the First Epistle of St. Paul to the Corinthians*, London, Printed for Awnsham and John Churchill, at the Black Swan in Pater-noster-row, 1706.

3 *A Paraphrase and Notes on the Second Epistle of St. Paul to the Corinthians*, London. Printed for Awnsham and John Churchill, at the Black Swan in Pater-noster-row, 1706.

4. *A Paraphrase and Notes on the Epistle to St. Paul to the Romans*, London, Printed for Awnsham and John Churchill at the Black Swan in Pater-noster-row, 1707.

5. *A Paraphrase and Notes on the Epistle of St. Paul to the Ephesians*, London, Printed for Awnsham and John Churchill at the Black Swan in Pater-noster-row, 1707.

6. *A Paraphrase and Notes on the Epistles of St. Paul to the Galatians, I & II Corinthians, Romans, Ephesians. To which is Prefix'd an Essay for the Understanding of St. Paul's Epistles, by consulting St. Paul Himself.* London, Printed by J. H. for Awnsham and John Churchill at the Black Swan in Pater-noster-row, 1707.

man's interpretation. We are all men: liable to errors and infected with them. . . .

He added that he would not have published the papers at all if some very sober, judicious Christians, divines of the Church of England, had not professed that the papers had enabled them to understand the epistles 'much better than they did before'.

The accession of Queen Anne, which had revived the fortunes of the Tories generally, had also improved the prospects of Lord Peterborough, who, though far too capricious and unpredictable to be reckoned a member of any party, depended, since he had antagonised the Whigs, on the good graces of their rivals.

In Queen Anne's reign Lord Peterborough was destined to become a 'great man', but not immediately, and not in politics. War gave him, as it has given many another 'difficult' and courageous man, his opportunity. He was offered the command of a joint Anglo-Dutch fleet which was to be sent to attack the Spanish in the West Indies, and told he would have to embark in November or December of that year. He accepted gladly.

Locke, who seems to have betrayed no feelings at the time of the quarrel between Peterborough and Somers, was delighted at the news. He only wished that he were well enough to travel to London to bid farewell to his old friend. There was, he told Peter King,[1]

> nothing I have borne so uneasily from the decays of my age, my troublesome ear, my breathless lungs, and my being unable to stir, as the being stopped in paying my respects in person upon his going upon such an expedition.

Informed that Locke was not fit to travel to London, Lord Peterborough decided to go to Oates and take his leave of the philosopher there; and Lady Peterborough proposed to accompany her husband. Locke was overjoyed at the idea. He wrote, on 15 November,[2] to Peter King:

> I desire you to return my most humble thanks to my Lord Peterborough for the extraordinary favour he designs me. And I am utterly ashamed it should cost him so much trouble. But the joy I am in with the hopes I have of kissing his hands before he leaves England makes me overlook everything else and think of nothing but the happiness of

[1] 4 November 1702 (B.L. MSS. Locke, c. 40, f. 237).   [2] *Ibid.*, f. 244.

seeing him on Friday next. I shall not fail, God willing, to be at the Crown at Epping by eleven of the clock at farthest. And I wish his Lordship's affairs would permit him to set out so early as to be there by that time, the days being now short, and the ways dirty, and I would not have him benighted. Pray therefore, if you can, prevail with him to be there by eleven. I will be sure to be there before that time. The Crown is the best Inn in Epping and there I will attend his Lordship on Friday next. . . .

Next day Locke wrote to his cousin again: [1]

One thing I had forgot in the haste I wrote [in] to mention, but the wet which has fallen since has put me in mind of, and that is to put his Lordship in mind to enquire at the Green Man, just at the entrance of Epping Forest, whether the Epping coach continues still to come over the Forest, or else because of the sloughs caused by the wet, that coach has left the forest way and now goes by Chigwell and Abridge, which is a gravelly way hard at bottom. My Lord may be informed at the Green Man which at present of these two is the best way. This I desire you to let him know.

In spite of these cautionary messages, Peterborough went 'several miles out of the way'.[2] But the visit was a success, and Locke remembered it with great pleasure and gratitude, not least because Lady Peterborough was also there.

One outcome of the visit was that Peterborough engaged Benjamin Furly's son Arent as his secretary; Furly himself was reluctant for the boy to go on a hazardous expedition, but both Locke and the third Lord Shaftesbury [3] favoured his going, and the appointment was made. Another nominee of Locke's, a destitute bookbinder named Banbury (introduced by Lady Calverley [4]) was also engaged. On Boxing Day Peterborough wrote to Locke: [5]

The lady that made you a visit with me would not let me write till I could tell you all was gone afore, and that the first easterly wind we follow. I wish we were as sure of success as we are of your good wishes, and I assure you Sir, I have some pretence to them from the very sincere respect and inclination I have ever had for you. Our Vigo [6] success

---

[1] 16 November 1702 (B.L. MSS. Locke, c. 40, f. 245).
[2] Locke to King 23 November 1702 (*ibid.*, f. 247).
[3] Shaftesbury to Furly: November 1702: P.R.O. 30/24/20/65.
[4] Lady Calverley to Locke: 28 November 1702 (B.L. MSS. Locke c. 5, f. 7).
[5] *Ibid.*, c. 16, f. 125.
[6] Admiral Sir George Rooke, who had led an unsuccessful expedition to Cadiz in July, destroyed the Spanish treasure fleet in Vigo Bay in October.

has a little abated our vigour, a fault too often committed by the English, and we seem not so willing as the Dutch to raise new recruits for the next campaign. I confess (after the schoolboy fashion) I am for giving the enemy the rising blow when they are down, and I hope to convince you in the West Indies, that if Providence gives us successes, we will not sleep upon them. Sir, if I make a prosperous voyage, and live to come back again, I shall not have a greater pleasure than to meet you where we parted last.

Sir,

Your most affectionate Friend and Servant,

Peterboro.

As events turned out, they did *not* follow the 'first easterly wind'. A month later, Peterborough [1] informed his friend at Oates:

Had I not, with Dr. Locke, left off wondering at anything long ago, I might with surprize write this letter and you receive it with amazement, when I let you know our American expedition is fallen as a mushroom rises in a night. . . .

The Dutch had withdrawn their offer of support for the expedition and Peterborough refused to go with a small English fleet alone. He was delayed in England for over two years.

In February 1702/3 Dr. John Hudson,[2] Bodley's Librarian at Oxford, asked Locke if he would be willing to give copies of his works to the Bodleian Library. He explained that the booksellers were committed by their agreements to supply a copy of every book they published, but they had not done so for many years. Locke consented; he instructed the Churchills to send Dr. Hudson a copy each of the *Essay*, of *Some Thoughts concerning Education* and of his pamphlets about interest and money. In writing [3] to thank him, Dr. Hudson said that he would not presume to inquire if these were *all* the books Locke intended for the Bodleian. He would have been foolish to have so presumed. Even in the catalogue of his own library at Oates,[4] Locke classified neither the *Two Treatises on Government* nor the *Letters Concerning Toleration* (as he did his other books) under 'Locke'. But he did not deny Dr. Hudson what Dr.

[1] 27 January 1702/3 (B.L. MSS. Locke, c. 16, f. 127).
[2] 6 February 1702/3 (*ibid.*, c. 11, f. 232).   [3] 20 April 1703 (*ibid.*, f. 234).
[4] *Ibid.*, F. 16, F. 17, E. 3. Another catalogue is still in the possession of Lord Lovelace.

Hudson so plainly expected. Locke waited till his death was close
at hand and then in a codicil[1] to his will he bequeathed to the
Bodleian Library copies of 'all the books whereof I am the author
which have been published without my name'.[2]

The unexpected recovery of his hearing[3] put Locke in a more
cheerful humour during the year *1703*, and for the first time in
many months he was able fully to enjoy the society of those friends
who went in increasing numbers to visit him at Oates. Samuel
Bolde as well as Peter King was there in January; James Tyrrell and
Anthony Collins went a few weeks later.

This Anthony Collins was a clever Etonian of twenty-seven who
was a passionate admirer of Locke's religious and philosophical
writings and who had literary ambitions of his own. If Collins's
admiration was somewhat uncritical, Locke did not find it for that
reason any less acceptable. At the age of seventy, he was more than
ever eager for his views to have the assent of the young, especially
of young writers. He took to Anthony Collins at once. He told[4]
Peter King afterwards that he looked upon his new friend 'in all
respects as a very valuable acquaintance', and added: 'A generation
of such young men to come upon the stage as the old drop off would
give new life to the age'.

This was putting it mildly. To Anthony Collins himself Locke
wrote letters which bespoke something much warmer than admiration. He described the 'confirmation' of Collins's friendship as 'the
greatest favour I can receive';[5] in another letter[6] he begged Collins
to correspond without formality and on equal terms; and a few days
later he asked:[7] 'Why do you make yourself so necessary to me?

---

[1] The codicil is dated 15 September 1704 (B.L. MSS. Locke, b. 5, No. 14).

[2] Locke's list was as follows:

  1. *Epistola de Tolerantia* published in Holland 'and afterwards translated into
English without my privity'.

  2. *A Second Letter concerning Toleration.*

  3. *A Third letter for Toleration.*

  4. *Two Treatises of Government*, 'Whereof Mr. Churchill has published several
editions but all very incorrect'.

  5. *The Reasonableness of Christianity.*

  6 *A Vindication of the Reasonableness of Christianity.*

  7. *A second vindication of the Reasonableness of Christianity.*

[3] *Vide* Tyrrell to Locke, 15 February 1702/3 (B.L. MSS. Locke, c. 22, f. 153).

[4] 7 May 1703 (*ibid.*, c. 40, f. 275).

[5] 3 June 1703 (Pforzheimer MS. 42; *Several Pieces*, pp. 254–5).

[6] 18 June 1703 (*ibid.*, MS. 43; *Several Pieces*, pp. 255–7, but incomplete).

[7] 24 June 1703 (*ibid.*, MS. 44; *Several Pieces*, pp. 257–9).

I thought myself pretty loose from the world, but I begin to feel you fasten me to it again'.

Collins, whose wife died soon after his first meeting with Locke,[1] was very willing to accept the consolations of philosophy and friendship, and he wrote to Locke as Locke hoped he would.

After receiving one affectionate and self-deprecatory letter [2] from him, the philosopher [3] thanked Collins for saying 'a great many kind things' and assured him, 'I believe all you say'.

> Think that I am as much pleased with your company as much obliged by your conversation as you are by mine, and you set me at rest, and I am the most satisfied man in the world. You complain of a great many defects [in yourself] and that complaint is the highest recommendation I could desire to make me love and esteem you and desire your friendship. And if I were now setting out in the world, I should think it my great happiness to have such a companion as you, who had a true relish of truth . . . and, if I mistake not you have as much of it as I ever met with in anybody. What then is wanting to make you equal the best; a friend for anyone to be proud of . . . ?

During the summer of 1703 a second young woman was suggested as a possible bride for Peter King. This time it was Locke who put the idea to King: for the candidate was none other than the philosopher's own 'wife', Betty Clarke. Locke told [4] his cousin: 'I have neither concern nor inclination one way or the other', and he asked him to communicate his decision through Mr. Freke. Two days later, Locke wrote [5] to King:

> By the last post I acquainted you that Mrs. C—— had desired me to let you understand that if you were at liberty and had any inclination, you should be very kindly received. Since that Mr. C—— beginning the discourse with me ended in expressions of a very high esteem of you.[6]

---

[1] *Vide* Tyrrell to Locke, 6 May 1703 (B.L. MSS. Locke, c. 22, f. 157). Collins's children seem to have found refuge at Parson's Green (*vide* Locke to King, 1 November 1703: *ibid.*, c. 40, f. 309).

[2] 21 October 1703 (*ibid.*, c. 7, f. 3).

[3] 29 October 1703 (Pforzheimer MS. 48; *Several Pieces*, pp. 271-5).

[4] 1 June 1703 (B.L. MSS. Locke, c. 40, f. 283).

[5] 3 June 1703 (*ibid.*, f. 285).

[6] Edward Clarke wrote to Locke on 8 June 1703 (*ibid.*, c. 6, f. 146) thanking him for the hopes he had given 'of your assistance for reviving the affair in relation to Mr. King, and I do assure you there shall be nothing wanting on our parts to bring it to a happy conclusion, which is, and ever was, heartily desired by yours etc'.

King did not accept this proposal. He was to marry in the following year, but a bride of his own finding.

Among the friends who saw the manuscript of Locke's paraphrases of the Epistles of St. Paul was Isaac Newton. Disappointed
of a hope of 'going to Cambridge this summer and calling at Oates
on my way', Newton sent Locke his comments on the manuscript
in a letter.[1] His chief criticism was of Locke's interpretation of St.
Paul as holding that 'the unbelieving husband is sanctified or made a
Christian in his wife'. Newton suggested that St. Paul's words
would be more correctly interpreted as follows:

> 'For the unbelieving husband is sanctified or cleansed by the believing
> wife, so that it is lawful to keep him company, and the unbelieving wife
> is sanctified by the husband, else were the children of such parents to be
> separated from you and avoided as unclean; but now by nursing and
> educating them in your families, you allow that they are holy.'

Later in the year Locke sent Peter King to Newton's London
home with a message which evidently had something to do with the
paraphrases of St. Paul.[2] He told his cousin he would find the great
savant 'a very extraordinary man'.[3]

Locke also sought King's aid in having a gold tumbler made as a
present for Lady Peterborough. He was willing to pay about fifty
pounds for it. Within a very short time it had been made by the
goldsmith James Seamer and delivered.

Peter King reported to Locke on 11 November: [4]

> I have presented your letter and gold tumbler to the Countess of
> Peterborough, with whom I had a great deal of discourse. She received
> your present with great expressions of respect and kindness for you, and
> says that she will come down to Oates and see you there in a little time.
> She told me that she should always keep with the greatest care any mark
> of Mr. Locke's favour, but that without this kind remembrance, she
> should never have forgot a gentleman who deserved so well of every-
> one, and particularly of her. She told me long stories of her bringing
> you over from Holland, and your obliging her with a ramble in an
> open calesh for 150 miles, and at last told me that for your sake she
> should study to do me any kindness that lay in her power.

---

[1] 15 May 1703 (B.L. MSS. Locke, c. 16, f. 155).
[2] 1 November 1703 (*ibid.*, c. 40, f. 308).
[3] 8 November 1703 (*ibid.*, f. 310).   [4] *Ibid.*, c. 12, f. 212.

Two days later King wrote: [1]

I gave you an account by my last of the discourse I had with my Lady Peterborough; since which I have met my Lord, who, in his jocular way, thinks that he has reason to suspect an intimacy between you and his Lady, if he were not sure that you follow the rules of true philosophy.

Within a week Peter King was able to inform his cousin that he had been to Isaac Newton's. He explained that there were other people present, so that Newton 'could not freely discourse of your papers', but he 'whispered me that he had read them half over'.

That same November Awnsham Churchill [2] sent Locke two books in which the philosopher was particularly interested. One was the special edition of *Aesop's Fables* [3] which Locke himself had devised to teach Latin to English children or English to foreigners by having the Latin and English texts printed on alternate lines, with the corresponding words in the two languages one above the other. In a preface, the anonymous editor (Locke), explained the purpose of the book, and argued that the experience of 'women and children learning the French tongue' proved 'that it is not an impossible thing to learn a language without first beginning with the rules of grammar'.

The other work Locke received was the Churchills' *Collection of Voyages* [4] in four fat folio volumes. This was an anthology of chronicles of travel, of the kind Locke had collected and read with interest over many years. He may even have suggested the idea of such a book to Awnsham Churchill; he helped Churchill to find contributions for it, but he did not, as some historians have suggested, edit the book or write the introductory essay. Awnsham Churchill regarded the book—a bold publishing venture—as very much his own. [5]

[1] B.L. MSS. Locke, c. 12, f. 214.

[2] Awnsham Churchill to Locke, 17 November 1703 (*ibid.*, c. 5, f. 202) 'I send herewith an *Aesop Interlineary* . . .'

[3] *Aesop's Fables in English & Latin, Interlineary, For The Benefit of those who Not having a Master, would learn Either of these Tongues.* With sculptures, London, Printed for A. and J. Churchill at the Black Swan in Pater-noster-row. 1703.

[4] Awnsham Churchill to Locke, 25 November 1703 (B.L. MSS. Locke, c. 5, f. 204): 'I sent Saturday per Lenham [the carrier] in a box a Collection of Voyages which I pray you to accept of . . .'

[5] Awnsham Churchill to Locke 17 November 1703 (*ibid.*, c. 5, f. 202): 'I am very busy just now publishing my Collection of Voyages'.

A catastrophic storm hit England late in November 1703. In London alone (according to James Tyrrell [1]) it brought down 'the roofs of a great many houses, and killed nearly twenty persons'. In the country the effects were almost as bad. 'Everyone that one sees', Locke said,[2] 'brings some new story of mischief'.

But not all the news he received was bad. Edward Clarke, who had been far from well for several years past, was able to tell Locke at the beginning of December [3] that 'by following your good advice my health is in a great measure restored to me'.

Locke replied [4] saying:

> At a time when one could hear nothing on all hands but sad stories, it was no small satisfaction to me to receive from you the good news of the recovery of your health. It is what I have long heartily wished and desired. And it was a charitable kindness to give me an assurance of a thing you know would be so pleasing to me to divert my thoughts a little from the sad objects it had everywhere else. I shall not so far indulge my own melancholy or furnish matter to yours by troubling you with reflections which the ravage made by this storm at sea and land does suggest. I rather choose to congratulate to you the happy escape of your wife, children and the rest of your family from the danger the hurricane threatened.

A few days later Locke enjoyed an even greater satisfaction. Lord and Lady Peterborough paid him another visit at Oates. It was only a short one. They stayed, as Locke later explained to King,[5] 'not much above an hour' leaving before noon, because the Earl had to 'be in town the next day'. But Locke was very grateful for 'the extraordinary honour'.

Some three weeks later, having in the meantime spent Christmas at Oates, Peter King had occasion to seek Locke's advice. He wrote to his cousin saying: [6]

> When I was at Oates I did but hint to you a certain matter, which I will now explain more at large. Mrs. H——n is to be married to an Herefordshire gentleman and a friend of yours had a proposal of the like kind made to him of the daughter of Mr. Seys, a Glamorganshire gentleman, the son of Serjeant Seys.

---

[1] 27 November 1703 (B.L. MSS. Locke, c. 22, f. 163).
[2] 29 November 1703 (*ibid.*, c. 40, f. 316).
[3] 2 December 1703 (*ibid.*, c. 6, f. 147).
[4] 6 December 1703 (Rand, pp. 593–4).
[5] 15 December 1703 (B.L. MSS. Locke, c, 40, f. 324).
[6] *Ibid.*, c. 12, f. 224.

The 'friend of yours' was, of course, Peter King himself. He explained that the daughter was near eighteen years old, 'an agreeable woman, thiftily and carefully bred', lived in London with a rich maiden aunt who would 'principally consider her', and offered a dowry of £4,000: 'the like sum is expected from your friend'. King thought that by waiting the friend might meet with a greater fortune, but doubted if he would find a woman and family circumstances that would better please him. However, he was determined not to act without Locke's consent.

Locke replied thus:[1]

> The gentleman you mention knows the relations, likes the lady, and is pleased with the family circumstances; so that to all this there can be nothing said by one who is wholly a stranger to every particular of it. The only question that remains is about the aunt, and the management of that depends upon the knowledge of her character; whether she be to be pressed to any positive promise or be left to herself without saying a word cannot be said but by one who is well acquainted with her, and can make some judgement from thence what is to be expected. The best advice I can give the gentleman upon the whole matter is that he get some friend to debate and transact for him. . . . One thing I think will be of great consequence, viz. to sound the young lady's mind and see whether she will be content to set out privately and in a meaner way at first. If she comes with an expectation of coach and equipage and show at first, it will have one of these ill consequences: that either she will be discontented to find herself disappointed, which is a dangerous beginning, or else our friend may be engaged in too great a way of expense before he sees where he is. . . .

Peter King was encouraged by these words to go ahead, and within a few weeks he announced his betrothal to Anne, the only daughter of Richard Seys of Boverton Court, Glamorgan.

Ever since the accession of Queen Anne, Tory extremists had been thirsting for Whiggish blood. Many things had changed for the better since she had come to the throne, especially under Marlborough in battle. But an illiberal spirit was abroad in the country. The Tories were particularly eager to suppress 'Occasional Conformity', a practice by which people who attended Dissenting chapels as a general rule took the sacraments of the Church of

[1] 10 January 1703/4 (B.L. MSS. Locke, c. 40, f. 332).

England once a year or so in order to qualify for the privileges conferred on communicants by the Test Acts. Many churchmen naturally objected to the patent insincerity and hypocrisy of this practice, but Whigs like Locke defended it because they thought it diminished the injustice of the Test Acts. Locke probably discussed 'Occasional Conformity' with Lord Peterborough when the Peterboroughs visited him in December 1703, for Peterborough, though no longer a Whig, vigorously resisted the Bill against Occasional Conformity in the House of Lords and helped to defeat it.

Other and less defensible measures were put forward in Parliament by certain Tories, including one Bill of which Clarke sent news to Locke in January,[1] 'to restrain the liberty of the press'. Besides such general attacks on Whiggish principles there were personal attacks on Locke. Proast, who had been silent for twelve years, renewed his assault on the *Letters for Toleration* with yet another pamphlet;[2] and at Oxford a resolution was moved at a meeting of Heads of colleges to suppress the *Essay Concerning Human Understanding*. Locke took it all very calmly, attributing such manifestations of intolerance to defects of human reason.

'To be rational', he told Collins,[3] 'is so glorious a thing that two-legged creatures generally content themselves with the title.'

An account of the proposed suppression of his *Essay* at Oxford University reached Locke from the Recorder of that city, a staunch Whig named William Wright.[4] His letter,[5] which was addressed to Tyrrell, read as follows:

> Since my return to this place I have enquired into the proceedings of the Heads of Houses concerning Mr. Locke's books, and am informed that at a meeting towards the end of November last they agreed to prohibit all scholars to read any of these books, or the books of Mr. [Le] Clerc, and ordered a programma to be prepared for that purpose

---

[1] 13 January 1703/4 (B.L. MSS. Locke, c. 6, f. 150).
[2] Locke began, but did not finish, a reply to this pamphlet.
[3] 24 January 1703/4 (Pforzheimer MS. 50; *Several Pieces*, p. 278, but incomplete).
[4] William Wright, junior (b. 1659), was the son of Alderman William Wright of Oxford. He matriculated at Trinity College, Oxford, in 1674, was called to the bar from the Inner Temple in 1682 and became Recorder of Oxford in 1688. Wood (in *L. and T.*, iii, p. 489) alleges that on 23 September 1695 Recorder Wright led a party of drunken men 'of the fanatical or factious sort' through Oxford after 8 p.m. breaking windows, abusing people, hooting and making disturbances at the doors of civic dignitaries.
[5] 19 February 1703/4 (B.L. MSS. Locke, c. 23, f. 109).

against their next meeting, and adjourned to another day. At the day of their adjournment Dr. Edwards [1] was present, and advised them not to publish the programma, but rather to let all the Heads of Houses admonish the tutors not to read to their pupils or to suffer their pupils to read any of those books. So the matter fell, and no notice has been taken of it since. If any minutes were taken by the Registrar of the proceedings of either of these meetings, I hope I may be able to send them to you in a short time. The Doctor who procured the issuing out of the programma has been as likely to promote it as another, but he expects preferment from a noble friend of that great man. . . .

Wright's letter to Tyrrell had been forwarded to Locke by Anthony Collins, and it was to him that Locke addressed his reply: [2]

. . . The gentleman that wrote you the letter which you sent me is an extraordinary man, and the fittest in the world to go on with that enquiry. Pray let him at any rate get the precise time, the persons present, and the minutes of the registrar taken of their proceedings; and this without notice, or seeming concerned to hear them, as much as may be. And I would beg you not to talk of this matter till we have got the whole matter of fact, which will be a pleasant story, and of good use. . . .

Next Tyrrell himself wrote [3] to Locke saying that William Wright's report was not entirely correct. It was true, he said, that the suppression of Locke's *Essay* had been recommended by one of the Heads of colleges ('whose name I cannot yet learn') but the affair had

ended only in a secret agreement among some of them that the tutors (they recommended) should be advised neither to read your *Essay* nor Le Clerc's *Physics* nor *Logic* to their pupils, since those works had much discouraged the noble art of disputation (or hog-shearing as we call it). Though even as to this, though I have discussed with some tutors in New College and University, yet I do not hear there are any such instructions given in those colleges, though their Heads are high [4] enough in their way; but granting that the thing be true, I hope you will not impute the indiscreet zeal of a few men to the whole University. . . .

---

[1] Jonathan Edwards (1649–1712), Principal of Jesus College (1686–1712).
[2] 24 February 1703/4 (Pforzheimer MS. 51; *Several Pieces*, pp. 285–7).
[3] 28 February 1703/4 (B.L. MSS. Locke, c. 22, f. 165).
[4] Of the High Church party.

In response to Locke's request (through Collins) for more information, William Wright had to report [1] that he had failed to elicit 'a more particular account of those proceedings'. He continued:

> The Registrar disowns what he knows or ever heard of the design. Others say that at the first meeting only a verbal order was given to prepare an instrument for the purpose you have heard. I perceived all of them are ashamed of the matter and think it no credit to them to own there was ever any such intention. . . .

Tyrrell was able to send [2] Locke rather fuller details:

> . . . in the beginning of November last there was a meeting of the Heads of Houses then in town; it was there proposed by Dr. Mill [3] and seconded by Dr. Maunder [4] that there was a great decay of logical exercises in the University which could not be attributed to anything so much as the new philosophy which was too much read, in particular your book and Le Clerc's; philosophy against which it was proposed that a programma should [be] published, forbidding all tutors to read them with their pupils. This was like at first to have passed till it was opposed by some others there present, and particularly by Dr. Dunster,[5] who not only vindicated your book, but said that he thought the making the programma would do more harm than good, first by making so much noise abroad as if the University were about to forbid the reading of all philosophy since that of Aristotle; next, that he thought that instead of the end proposed, it would make young men more desirous to buy and read those books when they were once forbid than they were before. Then at another meeting their resolution upon the whole was that upon Dr. Edwards's [6] proposal they agreed that instead of a programma, all heads of houses should give the tutors instructions not to read those books to their pupils and to prevent them doing it by themselves as much as lay in their power: and yet I do not find after all that any such thing has been put into execution in those colleges in which I have my acquaintance as particularly in University, Magdalen, New College and Jesus, all which have heads that are sufficiently for the High Church Party; so that I believe they, finding it like to have little effect, they have thought fit to let it drop. . . .

---

[1] To Collins. 3 March 1703/4 (B.L. MSS. Locke, c. 23, f. 110).
[2] April 1704 (*ibid.*, c. 22, f. 167).
[3] John Mill (1645–1707), Principal of St. Edmund Hall (1685–1707).
[4] Roger Mander or Maunder (1649–1704), Master of Balliol (1685–1704).
[5] Thomas Dunster (1657–1719), Warden of Wadham (1689–1719).
[6] Jonathan Edwards.

Locke had not felt persecuted by the moves against his work in Oxford, nor did he feel any intense relief when they came to nothing. He merely commented drily that the 'worthy Heads' of colleges were 'not yet grown up to perfect infallibility'.[1] He had become more Stoical in his old age, and he was consciously preparing himself for death. Inviting Peter King to Oates towards the end of February, he said:[2] 'This may be the last time I see you'. He explained that he spoke this 'not from despondency of mind, but from what I feel in my body'. To Anthony Collins, who was at Waltham looking after his estate there, Locke wrote:[3]

> 'Tis with regret I consider you so long in Essex without enjoying you any part of the time. Essex methinks (pardon the extravagancy— extraordinary passions and cases excuse it), when you are to go into it, should all be Oates, and your journey be no whither but thither.

Locke had already[4] asked Collins to undertake a small commission for him in London: to buy a set of the plays of Molière and have it well bound. This was to be yet another present for Lady Peterborough, and when it was ready, Locke[5] asked Collins, in the absence on circuit of Peter King, to deliver the present to her. Collins did so, and afterwards assured Locke it had been a pleasure to serve him. Indeed he wished to thank Locke for the opportunity of going there. Locke answered:[6]

> Excuse me, I entreat you if, for decency's sake I stop a little short of [believing] that, and let it satisfy you that I believe . . . you spare no pains for your friends and that you take a pleasure in doing me kindness.

In mid-March[7] Locke sent Hans Sloane the register of weather he had kept at Oates, the observations having been made, he explained, 'partly from the windows of my study, which are east and south'. He added:

> I have often thought that if such a register as this or one that were better contrived . . . were kept in every county in England, and so

---

[1] *Several Pieces*, p. 295.   [2] 26 February 1703/4 (B.L. MSS. Locke, c. 40, f. 361).
[3] 7 February 1703/4 (*Several Pieces*, p. 281).
[4] 24 January 1703/4 (Pforzheimer MS. 50; *Several Pieces*, pp. 278–280).
[5] 6 March 1703/4 (*Several Pieces*, pp. 291–3).
[6] 13 March 1703/4 (*ibid.*, pp. 293–4).
[7] 15 March 1703/4 (B.M. Sloane MSS. 4039, ff. 259–70). This copy is in the hand of an amanuensis with corrections and notes in Locke's own hand. The original MS. is still owned by Lord Lovelace.

constantly published, many things relating to the air, winds, health, fruitfulness, etc. might by a sagacious man be collected from them, and several rules and observations concerning the extent of winds and rains, etc. be in time established to the great advantage of mankind. . . .

At just this time Collins sent [1] Locke a summary of Norris's new book *An Essay Towards the Theory of the Ideal or Intelligible World.* Locke's comment [2] was:

Men of Mr. Norris's way seem to me to decree rather than to argue. They, against all evidence of sense and reason, decree brutes to be machines, only because their hypothesis requires it; and then with a like authority suppose, as you rightly observe, what they should prove, *viz.* that whatsoever thinks is immaterial.

In April Locke confessed both to King [3] and to Clarke [4] that he had reason to expect his life to end soon. He said, too, that the 'fine weather' of the spring had been 'so far from relieving me that I have been far the worse for it'. Even a visit from the Bishop of Gloucester [5] failed to revive his spirits, for that genial prelate arrived 'in no very good state of health', and Locke found that 'two groaning people' made 'but an uncomfortable consort'.[6]

However, a visit from Anthony Collins proved to be a tonic. 'Everyone here', Locke assured [6] his young friend, 'finds himself obliged by your late good company.'

As for myself, if you had not convinced me by a sensible experiment, I could not have believed I could have had so many happy days together. I shall always pray that yours may be multiplied. Could I in the least contribute anything thereunto, I should think myself happy in this poor decaying state of my health; which though it affords me little in this world to enjoy, yet I find the charms of your company make me not feel the want of strength or breath or anything else.

With summer coming Locke hit upon the idea of having a little carriage [7]—something like a lady's hunting chaise—specially made

[1] 15 March 1703/4 (B.L. MSS. Locke, c. 7, f. 26).
[2] 21 March 1703/4 (*Several Pieces*, p. 298).
[3] 21 April 1704 (B.L. MSS. Locke, c. 40, f. 363).
[4] 28 April 1704 (Rand, p. 599).
[5] Edward Fowler (1632–1714) a Whig bishop and a moderate latitudinarian.
[6] Locke to Collins. 19 May 1704 (Pforzheimer MS. 53; *Several Pieces*, pp. 306–8).
[7] Locke to Collins 25 May 1704 (Pforzheimer MS. 54; *Several Pieces*, pp. 309–10 but incomplete).

for him so that he could drive in the open air. But by the first of June [1] he was writing thus to Peter King:

Pray be sure to order your matters so as to spend all the next week with me. As far as I can impartially guess, it will be the last week I am ever like to have with you. For if I mistake not very much, I have very little time left in this world. This comfortable and to me usually restorative season of the year has no effect upon me for the better; on the contrary, my shortness of breath and uneasiness every day increases; my stomach, without any visible cause, sensibly decays, so that all appearances concur to warn me that the dissolution of this cottage is not far off. Refuse not therefore to help me to pass some of the last hours of my life as easily as may be in the conversation of one who is not only the nearest but the dearest to me of any man in the world. . . .

Death was not, in fact, quite so near; and some three weeks later [2] Locke wrote to Collins:

I now every moment wish the chaise done; not out of any impatience I am in for the machine, but for the man; the man, I say, that is to come in it; a man that has not his fellow; and, to all that, loves me.

Having heard from Collins about an attack [3] on his *Essay* which had been made by William Sherlock [4] in a new book called *A Discourse Concerning the Happiness of Good Men*, Locke protested that the arguments of Dr. Sherlock were

too subtle for me and my dull sight cannot perceive their connections. I am not envious, and therefore shall not be troubled if others find themselves instructed with so extraordinary and sublime a way of reasoning. I am content with my own mediocrity.

Collins took the chaise [5] to Oates in July, and Locke was well enough to drive out in it as soon as it came. But Collins was only one among several visitors to Oates that summer. Another was John

---

[1] B.L. MSS. Locke, c. 40, f. 386.

[2] 23 June 1704 (Pforzheimer MS. 58; *Several Pieces*, pp. 319–320, but incomplete).

[3] Dr. Robert South also mentioned this attack in a letter to Locke and urged him to reply to it (18 July 1704: B.L. MSS. Locke, c. 18, f. 175).

[4] William Sherlock (1641 ?–1707) was a powerful non-juror who changed his mind in 1690 and received as a reward the Deanery of St. Paul's in 1691. He was a celebrated preacher and a controversialist who specialised in baiting Socinians. He was later Bishop of London.

[5] Collins also took some chocolate, caps and flannel shirts from Mrs. Rabsy-Smithsby (*vide* her letter to Locke of 17 August 1704, *ibid.*, f. 147).

Shute, aged twenty-four, a lawyer whom Collins might well have regarded as a rival.[1] Locke's interest in Shute prompted the poet Watts to write:

> Shute is the darling of his years,
> Young Shute his better likeness bears;
> All but his wrinkles and his hairs
> Are copied in his son.

Shute was one of Locke's liberal disciples, the author of several pamphlets in favour of toleration and freedom. He had made Locke's acquaintance by sending him copies of these works and acknowledging Locke as his 'master'. Locke responded cordially, but Shute was certainly not his 'son' or even 'the darling of his years'.[2]

Another young man who visited Locke at Oates that summer was his old pupil, Anthony, third Earl of Shaftesbury. This nobleman was not, like his grandfather, a politician by temperament. He had been pressed—by Locke among others—to enter the Commons while still a minor, and he had been a loyal supporter of Somers in both Houses in turn. But Shaftesbury was too independent in his views to be a good party man, and too nervous to be an effective public speaker. When, on the accession of Anne, Tory influence robbed him of his vice-admiralty of Dorset, he was not entirely sorry. He was by that time a sick man. He had asthma, as Locke had, but more seriously than Locke had it; and he had always combined his parliamentary duties with long hours of study and literary work. Locke said of him that 'the sword was too sharp for the scabbard',[3] and (probably on Locke's advice) Shaftesbury went in 1703 to recruit his health in Holland. He lodged for about a year with Benjamin Furly, and had only lately returned from Rotterdam when he went to visit Locke.

Shaftesbury was then aged thirty-four. The only writings of his that had been published by that time were his introduction to Whichcote's *Sermons* and an early edition of *Inquiry After Virtue*, which had been printed without his permission by his protégé John Toland. Although the introduction to Whichcote expounds a

---

[1] In fact Collins and Shute became good friends for the rest of their lives.

[2] Shute, however, did very nicely for himself. He found another and richer friend than Locke; inherited a large fortune, and at the age of forty-two was created Viscount Barrington of Ardglass in the Irish peerage.

[3] Thomas Fowler, *Shaftesbury and Hutcheson* (1882), p. 15.

guarded and acceptable form of Latitudinarian theology, the un-official edition of the *Inquiry*, which Shaftesbury wrote when he was twenty, shows that he was already at that age a Socinian. His Socinianism developed later into a form of Neo-Platonism; and his extreme sensibility led him to react sharply against Locke's robust and philistine empiricism.[1] The third Lord Shaftesbury won great renown as an early champion of aestheticism, as a Man of Feeling in the Age of Reason; but it was not as a distinguished moralist and writer that he visited Locke in 1704. He went as a former pupil, a defeated politician and an invalid.

Awnsham Churchill, who had also been abroad, was yet another visitor, and in August Collins proposed that Sir Godfrey Kneller should go to Oates and paint a second portrait of Locke. The philosopher consented. He told [2] Collins:

> I have long since surrendered myself to you. . . . Judge then whether I am willing my shadow should be in possession of one with whom my heart is, and to whom all that I am, had I anything besides my heart worth the presenting, doth belong. Sir Godfrey, I doubt not, will make it very like. If it were possible for his pencil to make a speaking picture, it should tell you every day how much I love and esteem you, and how pleased I am to be so much as in effigy near a person with whom I should be glad to spend an age to come.

Sir Godfrey went, and while he was at Oates he painted besides Locke's portrait, portraits of Sir Francis Masham [3] and Lady Masham.[4]

[1] Shaftesbury's most vigorous attack on Locke's ethics and metaphysics comes in the eighth of his *Several Letters written by a Noble Lord to a Young Man at the University* (1716). There Shaftesbury says that much as he honours Locke for his political, economic, educational and religious writings, nevertheless ' 'Twas Mr. Locke that struck at all fundamentals, threw all order and virtue out of the world . . ' (*vide* also Fowler, *op. cit.*, pp. 44–6).

[2] 16 August 1704 (*Several Pieces*, pp. 323–4).

[3] This portrait is now in the possession of H. D. Shields, Esq., of Culford, Bury St. Edmunds.

[4] In a letter dated 11 September 1704 (*Several Pieces*, pp. 324–6) Locke asked Collins how he liked the portrait of Lady Masham. He also said: '. . . . pray get Sir Godfrey to write upon it, on the back side "Lady Masham 1704", and on the back side of mine "John Locke 1704". This he did on Mr. Molyneux's, and mine, the last he drew: and this is necessary to be done, or else the pictures of private persons are lost in two or three generations. . . ." On 26 September 1704 (B.L. MSS. Locke, c. 7, f. 59) Collins replied, '. . . I have now my Lady's picture in a frame hung up in my chamber. When you desire to have it, it shall be sent you down with all imaginable care. . . .' The present whereabouts of this portrait is unknown to me.

During the year 1704 Locke made various preparations for his death: 'few people', Lady Masham said;[1] 'do so sensibly see death approaching them as he did', although 'no one could observe the least alteration in his humour, always cheerful, civil, conversible to the last day'. In April he wrote his last will,[2] disposing of his property and specifying the manner in which he wished to be buried. He left £3,000 in trust for Francis Cudworth Masham, minor bequests amounting to some £1,500, and the residue to his cousin Peter King. Half his books he left (with £10 and his 'plate, clock and Molyneux's picture') to Francis Cudworth Masham; most, but not all of the other books he left, with his manuscripts, to Peter King. The minor bequests were as follows:[3] Dr. Veen, £5; Dr. Guenellon, £20; Mrs. Guenellon, £10; Peter Guenellon, £5; Ben Furly, £5; P. Stratton, £50; Edward Clarke, £200; Elizabeth Clarke, £200 and her mother's picture; William Grigg,[4] £200 and his Grotius; John Bonville, £200; Sir Francis Masham, £10 and furniture; Lady Masham, £10 and a ruby ring, a diamond ring and some books; Esther Masham, £10; Mary Doleman, £6 p.a.; Poor of the parishes of High Laver, Publow and St. Thomas, Pensford, £2 each; for apprenticing poor children of Pensford, £10 p.a. during his executors' lifetime; Lady Masham for the poor of High Laver £10 p.a. for 10 years; Anthony Collins, £10 and books and maps; Awnsham Churchill, £10; chief maidservant, £2; menial servants, £1 each; William Shaw,[5] £5 and his wearing apparel; clothing for four poor men, £20.

In a codicil dated 15 September 1704[6] Locke named the books that were to go to Bodley's Library; he left Sir Godfrey Kneller's picture of Lady Masham to her son Francis, another £10 to Mrs. Mary Clarke, another £100 to John Freke (with £10 'to buy himself a ring'), another £100 also to Anthony Collins, whom, at about the same time,[7] he asked to become a trustee for Francis

---

[1] To Richard Laughton 8 November 1704 (F.B., II, p. 556).

[2] 11 April 1704 (B.L. MSS. Locke, b. 5, No. 14).

[3] B.L. MSS. Locke, b. 5, No. 14 and see also lists drawn up by Locke and extracted from the will by Peter King, *ibid.*, c. 25, ff. 71 and 77 respectively.

[4] William Grigg was the son of Mrs. Anne Grigg and the late Thomas Grigg. He became a pensioner at Jesus College, Cambridge, in 1684 from St. Paul's School. He was a Fellow of his College from 1696 until 1713, when he was elected Master of Clare, holding that office, with several church benefices, until his death in 1726.

[5] Locke's valet.   [6] B.L. MSS. Locke, b. 5, No. 14.

[7] On 23 August 1704 Locke wrote a letter 'For Anthony Collins Esq To be deliver'd to him after my decease', putting what he designed for Masham 'into your

Cudworth Masham. In the same codicil Locke bequeathed £10 each to James Johnstoun of Twickenham and Robert Pawling and £5 to his cousin Ann Hazel. Locke's own accounts show that his estate was worth something approaching £20,000 at the time of his death.[1]

On 4 August [2] Locke began what he realised would probably be his last letter to Philip van Limborch. Limborch having sent him an account [3] of conflicts among the Dutch Protestants and a renewed assurance of his affection, Locke said:

> Why should I harass you in the midst of your learned pursuits and such literary intercourse as is worthy of a mind like yours, with a sick man's complaints and laboured words—words which show too plainly how their author gasps for breath? Yet it delights me to find that your affection follows your old friend even to the grave. . . . Farewell, dear friend; may happiness attend you.

In September there was rejoicing at Oates. Peter King married the daughter of Richard Seys, and Locke organised a festive dinner in honour of the bride and groom. On 16 September, his cousin's wedding day, Locke wrote [4] to him saying:

> I am just rose from dinner where the bride and bridegroom's health was heartily drunk again and again with wishes that this day may be the beginning of a very happy life to them both. We hope we have hit the time right, if not it is your fault, who have misled us.
>
> I desire you to bring me down twenty guineas, the wooden standish at Mr. Pawling's and the *Turkish Travels* of your Exeter man. I know you will not forget. But there are other things of more importance on this occasion which you must not forget nor omit; viz.
>
> 4 dried neats' tongues.
>
> 12 partridges that are fresh and will bear the carriage and keep a day

---

hands and management' (*Several Pieces*, p. 328, where however Masham's name is not printed). This letter suggests, as was not the case, that Collins was to be sole trustee. Peter King and Awnsham Churchill were also made responsible for the money (Pforzheimer MS. 60).

[1] A list of 'debts and stock belonging to me' dated 29 September 1704 (B.L. MSS. Locke, B.1, f. 283) shows a total of £12,037. In addition to this Locke owned real property of no inconsiderable value, over five thousand books, scientific instruments, jewellery, furniture and other personal belongings as well as his copyrights.

[2] Amsterdam Remonstrants' MSS. Ba. 258 t (Latin).

[3] *21 June 1704* (B.L. MSS. Locke, c. 14, f. 157, Latin).

[4] *Ibid.*, c. 40, f. 402.

after they are here, for 'tis to no purpose to bring down stinking things of good name that will stink and must be thrown away after all the trouble one has been at about them, as I was lately served. Therefore if you cannot light upon partridges that are very fresh bring but six.

4 pheasants. The same I said of the partridges I say of the pheasants:—the full number if fresh; else only half.

4 turkey poults ready larded if they be not out of season.

4 fresh aburn rabbits if they are to be got.

Plovers of woodcocks or snipes or whatever else is good to be got at the poulterers except ordinary tame fowl.

12 Chichester male lobsters if they can be got alive; if not 6 dead ones that are sweet.

2 large crabs that are fresh.

Crawfish and prawns if they are to be got.

A double barrel of the best right Colchester oysters if they are fresh come in.

Not knowing whether you have anybody better to get these things for you I have by this post written to Mr. Gray [1] to find you out as soon as he receives my letter to offer you his service to get such things as you shall direct him. . . .

Locke named the sweetmeats and fruits he wished King to bring, but told him that if there were anything his wife loved, he was to be sure that there was provision made of that and plentifully.

Locke also mentioned King's father-in-law.

Mr. Seys's intention of a visit to me I take as I ought for a very great honour. If he comes, you may assure him he will be extremely welcome to Sir Francis and my Lady, but must be content to receive from me an old bachelor a plain country entertainment. In particular, you must prepare him, if he comes, for a poor lodging, for you know how much this house is in want of rooms to receive and lodge persons of condition. . . .

The next day Locke wrote [2] again to Peter King, because, as he said, he could not forbear once more to 'wish you and my cousin your wife joy'. He reminded King to give his (Locke's) wedding present of toilet furniture to his bride before they left London for Oates, where, he said, they would be eight at table if the bride's father came, otherwise seven.

The bride's father did go, and the party was a great success. Locke had reason to rejoice. He had no relation closer than Peter King to

---

[1] John Gray had been a cook in the Shaftesbury household.
[2] 17 September 1704 (B.L. MSS. Locke, c. 40, f. 404).

perpetuate his line, and his feelings towards the marriage were akin to those of a father towards the marriage of an only son. He was not to know that Peter King would found a noble dynasty, that his descendants would be barons and later earls; nor would this have seemed of the first importance to Locke; what mattered to him was the prospect of *some* descendants, the promise of birth and life now that he was so close to death.

Locke presided at the wedding feast as host. On either side sat the bride and groom. Farther down the table were Sir Francis Masham, who could on this occasion be content to be a guest in his own house, Richard Seys, Esther Masham, Frank Masham and Lady Masham, the hostess. Besides the lavish food there was wine; [1] and Locke could allow himself for once to be less abstemious than usual. There were speeches and laughter, and the seventy-two-year-old philosopher talked and laughed as much as the others did. He said he had only one regret, and that was that Anthony Collins was not there.[2] But nothing could dampen Locke's spirits that day: and if anyone at all felt an undertone of melancholy, it was Damaris Lady Masham. She, who had known Locke and loved him for over twenty years, who had cherished him for the better part of thirteen years, realised that this was probably the last festivity her 'Philander' would ever enjoy.

The end was indeed at hand. After the bride and groom had returned to London, Locke was still able to write one or two more light-hearted letters [3] to Peter King about his lodgings, about presents, and even about a coronation souvenir he wanted Newton to have cast for him at the Mint; but on 25 October [4] he felt the end so near that he completed a solemn farewell message to his cousin:

> That you will faithfully execute all that you find in my Will I cannot doubt, my dear Cousin. Nor can I less depend upon your following my directions and complying with my desires in things not fit to be put into so solemn and public a writing.

---

[1] Some of it being perhaps that sent to Oates by another cousin, Samuel Locke, a London merchant.

[2] On 1 October 1704 (*Several Pieces*, p. 326), Locke wrote to Collins: 'To complete the satisfaction I have lately had here, there has been nothing wanting but your company. The coming of his father-in-law, joined with the straitness of the lodging in this house, hindered me from having my cousin King and you together, and so cut off one part of the enjoyment which you know is very valuable to me'.

[3] B.L. MSS. Locke, c. 40, ff. 406–11.

[4] *Ibid.*, f. 412. (This letter was begun on 4 October.)

You will find amongst my papers several subjects proposed to my thoughts, which are very little more than extempory views laid down in sudden and imperfect draughts, which, though intended to be revised and further looked into afterwards, yet by the intervention of business or preferable enquiries happen to be thrust aside and so lay neglected and sometimes quite forgotten. . . .

1st. My discourse of *Seeing all things in God* which though upon examination it appears to me and I think I have shown to be a very groundless opinion, and thereupon have been pressed by some friends . . . to make it public, yet I could never consent to print it, both because I am no friend to controversy and also because it is an opinion that spreads not and is like to die of itself or at least to do no great harm. I therefore think it best that it should not be published; but yet I do not absolutely forbid it. . . .

2nd. You are not a stranger to a little discourse I wrote about *Miracles*, on occasion of Mr. Fleetwood's book on that subject. . . . If, upon serious consideration you and some other of my judicious friends think it may be of use to the Christian religion and not unseasonable at this time, and fit for the public . . . you may do with it as you think good.

3rd. *The Conduct of the Understanding* I have always thought ever since it first came into my mind to be a subject very well worth consideration. . . . What I have done in it is very far from a just treatise. . . . But those particulars that have occurred to me and I have set down being as I guess sufficient to make men see some faults in the conduct of their understandings, and suspect there may be others, you may also do with as you think fit. For they may perhaps serve to excite others to enquire further into it, and treat of it more fully than I have done. But the heads and chapters must be reduced into order.[1]

4th. In some papers inscribed *Physica* you will see the entrance upon some thoughts that deserve to be revised and further considered. . . . Whether you think it fittest for the fire or a corner of your study I must leave to you. I am sure the present temper of this age will not bear it and whether you shall ever live to see the time fit to communicate it, you must judge:

[1] The papers mentioned in these three paragraphs were published in *Posthumous Works of Mr. John Locke*: viz. I. Of the Conduct of the Understanding. II. An Examination of P. Malebranche's Opinion of Seeing all things in God. III. A Discourse of Miracles. IV. Part of a Fourth Letter for Toleration. V. Memoirs relating to the Life of Anthony, first Earl of Shaftesbury. To which is added, VI. His New Method of a Common Place Book, written originally in French, and now translated into English. London, Printed by W. B. for A. and J. Churchill at the Black Swan in Pater-Noster-Row. 1706. In an Advertisement to the Reader (written presumably by Peter King) the unfinished nature of the contents is explained.

5th. Those who have seen what I have done upon some of *St. Paul's Epistles* are all very desirous it should be printed, persuading themselves it will be of great use to religion in giving the true sense of those Epistles. . . .

I know not whether you will find any other papers of mine worth the keeping. I am sure there are none that look towards printing.

Locke then asked King to deliver 'three sheets of memoirs' to a 'person you will easily guess', a sealed packet and a brass ruler to Isaac Newton, and his hone to Edward Clarke. He also instructed his cousin not to allow any of the money which would come to him as trustee for Francis Cudworth Masham to be lent to Sir Francis Masham:

> Remember it is my earnest request to you to take care of Sir Francis's youngest son Francis Cudworth Masham in all his concerns as if he were your brother. He has never failed to pay me all the respect and do me all the good offices he was capable of performing with all manner of cheerfulness and delight in it so that I cannot acknowledge it too much. . . .
>
> I wish you all manner of prosperity in this world and the everlasting happiness of the world to come. That I loved you I think you are convinced. God send us a happy meeting in the resurrection of the Just. Adieu.

On Thursday 26 October Pierre Coste went into Locke's bedroom and found the philosopher on his knees and 'unable to rise again without assistance'. [1] Coste could not help noticing that the swelling of Locke's legs had much increased, and that his strength was ebbing away.

The next morning Lady Masham [2] sought Locke in his study and not finding him there, passed into his bedroom. Locke told her he was not well enough to dress. He said he had exhausted himself the day before, and that he did not expect to leave his bed again. He refused food, and in the afternoon he seemed worse.

'About five o'clock in the evening', Coste recalled, 'he fell into a sweat accompanied with an extreme weakness that made us fear for his life'. Presently Locke said: 'My work here is almost at an end,

---

[1] *Several Pieces*, p. xxi.

[2] For her account of Locke's last hours see Le Clerc's *Éloge*; Esther Masham's letter to Mr. Smith (B.M. Add. MSS. 4311, f. 143; F.B. II, pp. 558–60).

and thank God for it. I may perhaps die tonight; but I cannot live above three or four days. Remember me in your evening prayers'.

The family decided to hold their prayers in Locke's bedroom.[1] After this consolation Locke felt strong enough to take a little nourishment. He asked for some mum, and in spoonfuls from Lady Masham's hand he drank the health of those around him.

Lady Masham then sat alone with him until midnight. Locke reminded her about his instructions concerning the disposal of his body; and he said to her: 'I have lived long enough, and I thank God I have enjoyed a happy life; but after all this life is nothing but vanity'.

Lady Masham wished to sit all night at his bedside, but he would not let her. He did not sleep, but on the following morning— Saturday 28 October—he decided to rise from his bed. Servants carried him to an armchair in his study. He took some small beer, and then decided to dress.

Thus reclining, he must have looked much as he appears in the portrait Kneller had painted only a few weeks before: a thin, melancholy, immensely distinguished old man, his brow tall, his hair white but plentiful, his nose large and patrician, his lips still full, and the heavy-lidded eyes looking larger and more eloquent than ever above the shrunken cheeks.

Lady Masham, who afterwards so oddly described him [2] as '*un second père*', sat at his side once more, talking or reading from the Psalms. At three o'clock in the afternoon he became restless. He moved to another seat. Then he lifted his hands to his face, closed his eyes, and died.

Locke's instructions for the disposal of his body were these: [3]

My will is to be buried as privately as with decency may be, particularly my will is to be buried in a plain wooden coffin not covered with cloth or any otherwise adorned: that cost will be better laid out in covering the poor. . . .

[1] *Several Pieces*, p. xxi.
[2] In a letter to Philip van Limborch, 26 December, 1704 (Amsterdam: Remonstrants' MSS: French).
[3] B.L. MSS. Locke, b. 5, No. 14.

He was buried, in the manner he desired, in the churchyard of High Laver, in a tomb hard against the south wall of the church. The incumbent, Samuel Lowe, whose sermons had sometimes moved the philosopher to mirth, read the order for the burial of the dead beside his grave.[1] Afterwards the mourners retired to Oates to drink canary wine. In due time an epitaph composed by Locke himself was carved by Edward Buckingham on a marble tablet to go above the grave. This tablet was moved some years ago to the interior of the church, and there, with sufficient light and Latin, the visitor may read:

Siste Viator
Hic juxta situs est JOHANNES LOCKE. Si
qualis fuerit rogas, mediocritate sua
contentum se vixisse respondet. Literis
innutritus eo usque tantum profecit, ut
veritati unice litaret. Hoc ex scriptis
illius disce; quae quod de eo reliquum
est majori fide tibi exhibebunt, quam
epitaphii suspecta elogia. Virtutes si quas
habuit, minores sane quam sibi
laudi duceret tibi in exemplum proponeret; vitia
una sepeliantur. Morum exemplum si
quaeras in Evangelio habes: vitiorum
utinam nusquam: mortalitatis certe (quod
    prosit) hic et ubique.

[1] 'Expenses about Mr. Locke's funeral' compiled by Peter King (B.L. MSS. Locke, c. 25, f. 75) were as follows:

	£	s.	d.
Charges of two horses at Oates	1	15	0
Paid Mrs. Graves for attending him in his sickness	2	3	0
Paid the undertaker	33	0	0
Paid the coachman to drink		2	6
Paid Martin the clerk for making the grave		10	0
Paid Mr. Loe the Minister		10	0
Paid Raymond for going to London and the woman who watched by Mr. Locke and stretched him out		17	6
Paid Mr. Rous for proving his Will	4	15	0
Paid Mr. Collins for cloth for mourning	4	19	6
Paid Mr. Warle the tailor	8	3	6
Paid for canary for his funeral	2	1	6
Paid two men for bearing him		2	0

I I

Natum Anno Dom. 1632 Aug. 29°
Mortuum Anno Dom. 1704 Oct. 28°
Memorat haec tabula brevi et ipse interitura.[1]

John Locke was a great man; indeed so great a man that his biographer cannot grasp the measure of that greatness. His biographer
is perforce too close to him. Only an historian of European thought
with a panoramic vision, could judge his stature. But this at least one
can say here: Locke did not merely enlarge men's knowledge, he
changed their ways of thinking.

[1] 'Stay traveller.

'Near this place lies John Locke. If you wonder what kind of man he was, the
answer is that he was one contented with his modest lot. A scholar by training, he
devoted his studies wholly to the pursuit of truth. Such you may learn from his
writings, which will also tell you whatever else there is to be said about him more
faithfully than the dubious eulogies of an epitaph. His virtues, if he had any, were too
slight to serve either to his own credit or as an example to you. Let his vices be
interred with him. An example of virtue, you have already in the Gospels; an
example of vice is something one could wish did not exist; an example of mortality
(and may you learn from it) you have assuredly here and everywhere. That he was
born on August 29, 1632, and died on October 28, 1704, this tablet, which itself will
quickly perish, is a record.'

INDEX

N.B. *Dates:* Throughout this book dates printed in Roman type follow the Julian (Old Style) calendar; those in italic type the Gregorian (New Style) calendar.

EUROPEAN POLITICAL THOUGHT

Traditions and Endurance

An Arno Press Collection

Althusius, Johannes. **Politica Methodice Digesta of Johannes Althusius (Althaus).** 1932

Bagge, Dominique. **Les Idées Politiques en France sous la Restauration.** 1952

Baudrillart, Henri. **Publicistes Modernes.** 1863

Bayle, Francis. **Les Idées Politiques de Joseph de Maistre** and Peter Richard Rohden. **Joseph de Maistre als Politischer Theoretiker.** 1945/1929. 2 vols. in 1

Beer, M[ax]. **A History of British Socialism.** 1929. 2 vols. in 1

Bluntschli, J[ohann] C[aspar]. **Geschichte des Allgemeinen Statsrechts und der Politik.** 1864

Bodin, Jean. **The Six Bookes of a Commonweale.** 1962

Bouglé, C[élestin Charles Alfred]. **La Sociologie de Proudhon.** 1911

Bouglé, C[élestin Charles Alfred]. **L'Oeuvre d'Henri de Saint-Simon** and Friedrich Muckle. **Saint-Simon und die Ökonomische Geschichtstheorie.** 1925/1906. 2 vols. in 1

Burckhardt, Jacob. **Weltgeschichtliche Betrachtungen.** 1929

Chaix-Ruy, Jules. **La Formation de la Pensée Philosophique de G.-B. Vico.** 1943

Chinard, Gilbert. **Jefferson et les Idéologues.** 1925

Constant, Benjamin. **Cours de Politique Constitutionnelle.** 1872. 2 vols.

Cortés, Juan Donoso. **Ensayo sobre el Catolicismo, el Liberalismo y el Socialismo** and Edmund Schramm. **Donoso Cortés.** 1851/1935. 2 vols. in 1

Cotta, Sergio. **Montesquieu e la Scienza della Società.** 1953

Cottu, [Charles]. **De l'Administration de la Justice Criminelle en Angleterre, et de l'Esprit du Gouvernement Anglais.** 1822

Cranston, Maurice. **John Locke.** 1957

Dempf, Alois. **Christliche Staatsphilosophie in Spanien.** 1937

Deslandres, Maurice. **Histoire Constitutionelle de la France de 1789 à 1870.** 1932/1937. 3 vols.

Dolléans, Édouard. **Histoire du Mouvement Ouvrier.** 1948/1953. 3 vols. in 2

Flint, Robert. **Vico.** 1901

Gadave, René. **Un Théoricien Anglais du Droit Public au XVIIe Siècle.** 1907

Gewirth, Alan. **Marsilius of Padua.** 1956. 2 vols. in 1

Guizot, François Pierre Guillaume. **Essais sur l'Histoire de France.** 1865

Hillebrand, Karl. **Zeiten, Völker und Menschen.** 1886. 7 vols. in 4

Hubert, René. **Histoire de la Pédagogie.** 1949

Huit, C. **La Vie et les Oeuvres de Ballanche.** 1904

Jannet, Claudio. **Les États-Unis Contemporains ou les Moeurs, les Institutions et les Idées depuis la Guerre de la Sécession.** 1876

Jefferson, Thomas. **Mélanges Politiques et Philosophiques Extraits des Mémoires et de la Correspondance de Thomas Jefferson.** 1833. 2 vols. in 1

Lanson, G[ustave]. **Bossuet.** 1894

Lehmann, William C. **John Millar of Glasgow, 1735-1801.** 1960

Leroy, André-Louis. **David Hume.** 1953

De Lolme, J.L. **The Constitution of England** *and* Jean-Pierre Machelon. **Les Idées Politiques de J.L. de Lolme, 1741-1806.** 1807/1969. 2 vols. in 1

Luccioni, Jean. **La Pensée Politique de Platon.** 1958

MacCunn, John. **Six Radical Thinkers.** 1907

McIlwain, Charles Howard. **The High Court of Parliament.** 1910

Mayer, J.P. **Alexis de Tocqueville.** 1972

Mayer, J.P., ed. **Fundamental Studies on Jean Bodin.** 1979

Mayer, J.P., ed. **The Impact of the 18th Brumaire.** 1979

Mayer, J.P. **Max Weber and German Politics.** 1956

Mayer, J.P. **Political Thought in France.** 1943

Mommsen, Theodor. **Abriss des Römischen Staatsrechts.** 1907

Morley, John. **Edmund Burke.** 1867

Moulinié, Henri. **De Bonald.** 1916

Péllissier, Georges. **Les Écrivains Politiques en France avant la Révolution.** 1884

Perthes, Clemens Theodor. **Das Deutsche Staatsleben vor der Revolution.** 1845

Ranke, Leopold von. **Über die Epochen der Neuren Geschichte** *and* **Das Politische Gespräch und Andere Schriften zur Wissenschaftslehre.** 1917/1925. 2 vols. in 1

Rémond, Gabriel. **Royer-Collard.** 1933

Rémusat, Charles de. **L'Angleterre au XVIIIe Siècle.** 1865. 2 vols. in 1

Reybaud, Louis. **Études sur les Réformateurs ou Socialistes Modernes.** 1864. 2 vols. in 1

Robin, Léon. **Aristote.** 1944

Rommen, Heinrich. **Die Staatslehre des Franz Suarez S.J.** 1926

Rommen, Heinrich A. **The Natural Law.** 1947

Saresberiensis, Ioannis. **Episcopi Carnotensis Policratici.** 1909.
2 vols. in 1

Schemann, Ludwig. **Gobineau** and **Alexis de Tocqueville.** 1913/1911.
3 vols. in 2

Sée, Henri. **Les Idées Politiques en France au XVIIe Siècle.** 1923

Sée, Henri. **Les Idées Politiques en France au XVIIIe Siècle.** 1920

Sidney, Algernon. **Discourses Concerning Government.** 1698

Sieyès, Emmanuel. **Qu'est-ce que le Tiers État?** and C.A. Sainte-Beuve.
Sieyès. 1888/1885. 2 vols. in 1

Sorel, Georges. **Les Illusions de Progrès.** 1911

Staël, Madame la Baronne de. **Considérations sur les Principaux
Événemens de la Révolution Françoise.** 1818. 3 vols. in 2

Tocqueville, Alexis de. **Journeys to England and Ireland.** 1958

Toreltsch, Ernst. **Augustin, die Christliche Antike und das Mittelalter.**
1915

Vinet, A. **Moralistes des Seizième et Dix-Septième Siècles.** 1904

Vorländer, Franz. **Geschichte der Philosophischen Moral, Rechts- und
Staats-Lehre der Engländer und Franzosen.** 1855

Waitz, Georg. **Grundzüge der Politik.** 1862

Wilamowitz-Moellendorff, Ulrich von and B. Niese. **Staat und
Gesellschaft der Griechen und Römer.** 1923